Beta Sigma Phi
Home Sweet Home Cooking
Company's Coming

W9-BYO-998

Beta Sigma Phi

Home Sweet Home Cooking

Company's Coming

Home Sweet Home

EDITORIAL STAFF

Managing Editor	Mary Jane Blount
Executive Editor	Debbie Seigenthaler
Project Managers	Georgia Brazil, Mary Cummings Maribel S. Wood
Editors	Christie Carlucci, Jane Hinshaw Linda Jones, Debbie Van Mol Mary Wilson
Associate Editors	Judy Jackson, Carolyn King Jim Simpson
Typographers	Pam Newsome Sara Anglin, Jessie Anglin
Award Selection Judges	Bill Ross Mary Jane Blount Charlene Sproles
Test Kitchen	Charlene Sproles

Cover Photograph: Borden, Inc.; Page 1: California Beef Council;
Page 2: Courtesy of the Hershey Foods Corporation

© Favorite Recipes® Press, A Division of Heritage House, Inc. MCMLXLIII
P.O. Box 305141, Nashville, Tennessee 37230

ISBN: 0-87197-377-4
Library of Congress Number: 93-71693

All rights reserved. No part of this book may be reproduced in any form or
by any means without prior written permission of the Publisher excepting
brief quotes in connection with reviews written specifically for inclusion in
a magazine or newspaper.

Manufactured in the United States of America
First Printing 1993

Recipes for photographs are on pages 212–213.

Contents

*Asterisk beside contributor name indicates submission of similar recipe.

 **Beta Sigma Phi**

Linda Rostenberg

Dear Beta Sigma Phis:

Question: What are the two most dreaded words in the English language to a busy woman? **Answer:** "Company's coming!"

That sentence can create an instant panic attack in the coolest corporate executive—unless you have our new Beta Sigma Phi cookbook, *Home Sweet Home Cooking: Company's Coming*. Instantly, sorority sisters provide you with a ton of great ideas that can turn your panic into pure professionalism!

A beautiful home-cooked meal is a great gift to family, friends, business connections, you name it. This year's cookbook has attracted more recipes than ever before (we've created two books this year—check out the companion book *Home Sweet Home Cooking: Family Favorites*). As usual, we've awarded prizes in various food categories, and these top winners are specially marked by a diamond symbol ❖ in the book.

We've got such a wonderful collection of cooking and craft ideas for you—probably the best ever. That seems only appropriate, since this is our silver anniversary year of cookbook collections with our friends at Favorite Recipes® Press.

We hope you'll enjoy this book and its sister—they make great (and reasonably priced) gifts, and who knows? You may get a good old-fashioned home-cooked meal out of the deal!

Yours in Beta Sigma Phi,

Linda Rostenberg

Linda Rostenberg
Beta Sigma Phi International
Executive Council

Prime-Time Menus

Throughout the week, we are often too strapped for time to think about meal planning. We grab a casserole from the freezer, throw together a salad, and call it dinner. But every once in a while there comes a time to pull out all the stops, and our Prime-Time Menus are designed for just such occasions. Maybe you're celebrating a raise or promotion or having the boss over for dinner! Maybe it's a big anniversary or birthday, or perhaps you've just decide to create a memorable evening for yourself and friends. Whatever the reason, this is the time to forget about the constraints of diets and go all out with a meal that speaks for itself and announces, "this night is different—this night is special." Enjoy!

Home Sweet Home

Holiday Feast

Cornish Hens à l'Orange
Rice Pilaf
Green Bean Bundles
Fruit Medley

This is one of my family's favorite holiday dinners, but it is elegant to serve at special occasions any time of the year. I served it to my sorority sisters at Ending Day last year and asked each guest to bring a place setting of her formal china to set the table. We had a good time discussing everyone's taste in china.

Lois Black, Beta Rho
Leesville, South Carolina

CORNISH HENS À L'ORANGE

8 Cornish hens	*1/2 cup water*
1/4 cup each garlic powder, salt and pepper	*1 cup butter or margarine*
8 peeled whole medium onions	*1 12-ounce jar orange marmalade*
	2 tablespoons soy sauce

Rinse hens inside and out; rub with garlic powder, salt and pepper. Place onions in cavities. Chill for 24 hours or longer. Preheat oven to 350 degrees. Place hens in large roasting pan with space between; add water to pan. Heat remaining ingredients in saucepan until very warm. Brush over hens. Roast for 1¹/2 hours or until cooked through, brushing frequently with sauce; cover legs with foil if necessary to prevent overbrowning. Serve hot or at room temperature. Yield: 8 servings.

RICE PILAF

2 cups uncooked rice	*4 cups beef broth*
2/3 cup chopped green bell pepper	*1 4-ounce jar chopped pimentos, drained*
1 cup chopped green onions	*1/2 cup slivered almonds*
1/4 cup olive oil	*1 teaspoon salt*
2 tablespoons Worcestershire sauce	*1/4 teaspoon cayenne pepper*

Preheat oven to 350 degrees. Combine all ingredients in bowl; mix well. Spoon into greased 2-quart baking dish. Bake, covered, for 45 minutes. Toss lightly before serving. Yield: 8 servings.

GREEN BEAN BUNDLES

3 20-ounce cans whole green beans	*1 tablespoon sesame oil*
1 10-ounce can French onion soup	*8 thin red bell pepper rings*

Drain beans and arrange in shallow 2-quart glass dish. Bring soup to a boil in saucepan; remove from heat. Stir in sesame oil. Pour over beans. Marinate in refrigerator for 12 hours to overnight. Cook pepper rings in water in saucepan until tender; drain. Microwave beans on High for 10 minutes or until heated through. Arrange in bundles on serving plates; top each with pepper ring. Yield: 8 servings.

FRUIT MEDLEY

1 16-ounce package pitted prunes	*1 21-ounce can cherry pie filling*
1 6-ounce package dried apricots	*1¹/2 cups water*
1 13-ounce can pineapple chunks, drained	*1/4 cup dry sherry*
	1/2 cup slivered almonds

Preheat oven to 350 degrees. Combine all ingredients in large bowl; mix well. Spoon into deep 9-inch glass baking dish. Bake, covered, for 1¹/2 hours. Serve warm or at room temperature. Do not use metal baking pan as it will cause fruit to discolor. Yield: 8 servings.

Holiday Bridge Luncheon

Chicken Loaf with Mushroom Gravy
Peas and Onions Amandine
Cranberry Waldorf Salad
Hot Rolls
Butter
Sherbet

See index for similar recipes.

I have prepared this for bridge luncheons, holiday luncheons, sorority suppers and Mothers' Club luncheons. It is easy to prepare in advance and the recipes can easily be increased. Garnish each plate with a celery curl and an orange twist and the chicken loaf with a sprig of parsley for a festive touch.

Jenelle Harris, Preceptor Alpha Phi
Altus, Oklahoma

CHICKEN LOAF WITH MUSHROOM GRAVY

1 4-pound chicken	1 tablespoon (or more)
1 10-ounce can cream	chopped onion
of mushroom soup	3 cups milk and/or broth
2 cups fresh bread	4 eggs, beaten
crumbs	1¹/2 cups broth
1 cup cooked rice	All-purpose flour
1¹/2 teaspoons salt	Milk
¹/3 cup chopped	2 hard-cooked eggs,
pimento	chopped

Rinse chicken well. Cook in water to cover in large saucepan until tender; drain. Chop chicken into bite-sized pieces, discarding skin and bones. Preheat oven to 350 degrees. Reserve ¹/2 cup soup. Combine remaining soup with chicken, bread crumbs, rice, salt, pimento, onion, milk and eggs in bowl, mixing well. Spoon into greased 9-by-13-inch baking dish. Bake for 1 hour or until set. Combine 1¹/2 cups broth with reserved soup in saucepan; mix well. Cook until heated through. Blend enough flour and milk in bowl to thicken gravy to desired consistency. Stir into soup mixture. Cook until thickened, stirring constantly. Stir in hard-cooked eggs. Heat to serving temperature. Cut chicken loaf into squares to serve. Serve chicken loaf with mushroom gravy. Yield: 8 servings.

PEAS AND ONIONS AMANDINE

1 cup diagonally-sliced	1 8-ounce can whole
celery	onions or 1 bunch
Salt to taste	sliced green onions
¹/2 cup slivered	1 10-ounce package
blanched almonds	frozen green peas,
¹/2 cup melted butter or	cooked
margarine	Pepper to taste

Cook celery in salted water in saucepan until tender-crisp; drain. Brown almonds lightly in butter in skillet. Add onions, peas, celery, salt and pepper. Cook until heated through. Yield: 8 servings.

CRANBERRY WALDORF SALAD

1 3-ounce package	¹/2 cup chopped celery
strawberry gelatin	¹/4 cup chopped pecans
1 cup boiling water	Mayonnaise
1 cup cranberry sauce	Grated orange rind or
¹/2 cup chopped apples	chopped pecans

Dissolve gelatin in boiling water in bowl. Add cranberry sauce, apples, celery and ¹/4 cup pecans; mix well. Spoon into mold or square dish. Chill until set. Unmold onto serving plate or cut into servings. Top servings with dollop of mayonnaise and garnish with sprinkle of grated orange rind or additional chopped pecans. Yield: 8 servings.

Day-After-Christmas Birthday Dinner

Swiss Chicken Casserole
Cottage Potatoes
Steamed Broccoli and Cauliflower
Tossed Salad
Dressing
Birthday Cake

See index for similar recipes.

This was the menu at the 80th birthday celebration of our new son-in-law's mother on the day after Christmas in Naperville, Illinois. We were with our daughter's new family for the first time that holiday season. We spent five days with them and grew very close as a family. It was one of our best Christmases and one that I will always remember.

Mary Jo Kundrat, Eta
Marion, Ohio

SWISS CHICKEN CASSEROLE

6 chicken breast filets	¹/4 cup milk
6 4-by-4-inch slices	2 cups herb-seasoned
Swiss cheese	stuffing mix
1 10-ounce can cream	¹/4 cup melted butter or
of chicken soup	margarine

Preheat oven to 350 degrees. Rinse chicken and pat dry; arrange in 8-by-12-inch baking dish. Top with cheese slices. Combine soup and milk in bowl; mix well. Spread over chicken. Sprinkle with stuffing mix; drizzle butter over top. Bake, covered, for 50 minutes. Yield: 6 servings.

COTTAGE POTATOES

15 medium potatoes,	1 teaspoon salt
peeled, chopped	1 cup milk
1 large onion, minced	¹/2 cup melted margarine
8 ounces American	
cheese, chopped	

Preheat oven to 350 degrees. Combine potatoes, onion, cheese and salt in medium bowl; mix well. Spoon into large baking dish. Pour mixture of milk and margarine over top. Bake for 1 hour. Yield: 6 to 12 servings.

❖ Christmas Dinner for Ten

Slow-Cooker Ham with Cherry Sauce
Sweet Potato Casserole
Make-Ahead Mashed Potatoes
Barbecued Green Beans
Waldorf Apple Salad
Never-Fail Dinner Rolls — Date Cake

See index for similar recipes.

This dinner allows the cook time to enjoy the holiday, too, as everything can be prepared in advance. And with 10 diners, surely some will help with the cleanup!

Helen Schoenrock, Laureate Pi
Fairbury, Nebraska

SLOW-COOKER HAM WITH CHERRY SAUCE

1 4- to 5-pound ready-to-eat cured ham	1/4 cup sugar
Liquid smoke	1/4 teaspoon ground cloves
1 21-ounce can cherry pie filling	

Sprinkle ham with liquid smoke; wrap in foil. Place in slow cooker. Cook on Low for 6 to 12 hours or until done to taste. Combine cherry pie filling, sugar and cloves in saucepan; mix well. Cook just until sugar melts. Serve cherry sauce from chafing dish with ham. Yield: 10 servings.

SWEET POTATO CASSEROLE

6 sweet potatoes, cooked, cut into halves	2 tablespoons melted margarine
1/2 cup packed light brown sugar	3 tablespoons orange juice
Cinnamon and salt to taste	6 to 8 ounces marshmallows
3 tablespoons chopped nuts	

Place sweet potatoes in 2-quart glass dish. Sprinkle with brown sugar, cinnamon, salt and nuts; drizzle with margarine and orange juice. Microwave on Medium for 8 to 9 minutes or until heated through. Top with marshmallows. Microwave on Medium for 4 minutes. Yield: 10 servings.

MAKE-AHEAD MASHED POTATOES

9 large potatoes, peeled	2 teaspoons onion salt
6 ounces cream cheese	1 teaspoon salt
1 cup sour cream	1/4 teaspoon pepper
2 tablespoons butter or margarine	Butter or margarine

Cook potatoes in water to cover in saucepan until tender; drain. Mash in bowl until smooth. Add next 6 ingredients; beat until smooth. Cool to room temperature. Store in refrigerator for up to 2 weeks. Preheat oven to 350 degrees. Spoon desired amount of potatoes into baking dish; dot with butter. Bake for 30 minutes or until heated through.
Yield: 10 to 12 servings.

BARBECUED GREEN BEANS

4 to 6 slices bacon, chopped	1/4 cup packed light brown sugar
1/4 cup chopped onion	2 16-ounce cans green beans, drained
1/4 cup catsup	
1/4 cup barbecue sauce	

Preheat oven to 350 degrees. Fry bacon in skillet until crisp; remove with slotted spoon. Stir in onion, catsup, barbecue sauce and brown sugar. Add beans and bacon; mix gently. Spoon into baking dish. Bake for 30 minutes. Yield: 10 servings.

WALDORF APPLE SALAD

1/2 cup sugar	3 red apples, chopped
2 tablespoons all-purpose flour	1 cup miniature marshmallows
1 cup water	1/2 cup chopped celery
2 tablespoons vinegar	1/2 cup chopped nuts
1 tablespoon butter or margarine	1/2 cup crushed pineapple (optional)
1 teaspoon vanilla extract	1/4 head lettuce, chopped (optional)

Combine first 6 ingredients in saucepan for dressing; mix well. Bring to a boil and cook until thickened, stirring constantly. Cool to room temperature. Combine apples, marshmallows, celery, nuts, pineapple and lettuce in salad bowl. Add dressing; mix lightly. Yield: 10 servings.

DATE CAKE

2 teaspoons baking soda	2 cups sifted all-purpose flour
1 cup boiling water	1/2 cup chopped nuts
1 cup chopped dates	Whipped topping or whipped cream
1 cup sugar	Red or green maraschino cherries
1 teaspoon vanilla extract	
1/4 teaspoon black walnut extract	
1 cup mayonnaise-type salad dressing	

Preheat oven to 350 degrees. Dissolve baking soda in boiling water. Pour over dates in bowl. Stir in sugar, flavorings and salad dressing. Add flour gradually, mixing well after each addition. Stir in nuts. Spoon into greased and floured 9-by-13-inch cake pan. Bake for 35 minutes. Top each serving with whipped topping or whipped cream and cherry.
Yield: 10 to 12 servings.

Let It Snow Holiday Party

Cheese Ball — Crackers
Brunswick Stew
Cucumber and Onion Salad
Noodle Pudding
Egg Twist and Multigrain Breads
Dessert Buffet
Wassail — Eggnog

See index for similar recipes.

Let It Snow was the theme of our Physical Medicine Services party for 40 department members, which was held at my 1928 English cottage. There was "snow" sprinkled on the sidewalk, snowflakes pressed and sponged on windows, a roaring fire, lots of lighted candles, red and white tablecloths and holiday attire. The special event was a Dessert Contest. The most original entry was a yule log decorated with a miniature holiday scene; the most attractive was a sinful chocolate-mint swirl pie decorated with mint leaves and raspberries; most festive was a white cake topped with white "snowflakes." After dinner, we played Christmas Trivia. Each guest took home an icicle from the Victorian tree.

Katie Gundersen Watson, Preceptor Beta Kappa
Monrovia, California

BRUNSWICK STEW

1 pound beef brisket or rump roast	2¹/2 quarts boiling water
1 teaspoon paprika	2 cups fresh lima beans
Salt to taste	2 cups fresh or canned corn
4¹/2 pounds cut-up chicken	3 medium tomatoes, cut into quarters
4 ounces bacon, chopped	3 potatoes, chopped
1 medium onion, chopped	

Cut beef into 2-inch cubes. Sprinkle with paprika and salt; let stand for 30 minutes. Rinse chicken and pat dry. Fry bacon in large saucepan. Add onion. Cook, covered, for several minutes; drain. Add beef, chicken and water. Bring to a boil; reduce heat. Simmer, covered, for 2 hours. Add lima beans, corn, tomatoes and potatoes; mix well. Simmer for 1 hour or until ingredients are tender. Yield: 15 servings.

CUCUMBER AND ONION SALAD

3 (or more) cucumbers, peeled	1 teaspoon cider vinegar
1 large onion	1¹/2 teaspoons sugar
¹/2 cup sour cream	³/4 teaspoon salt
	Pepper to taste

Cut cucumbers into thin slices; cut onion into thin strips. Combine in serving dish. Combine sour cream, vinegar, sugar, salt and pepper in bowl; mix well. Add to cucumber mixture; mix gently. Chill until serving time. Yield: 15 servings.

NOODLE PUDDING

8 ounces uncooked medium egg noodles	Salt to taste
4 eggs	6 tablespoons vegetable oil
2 tablespoons sugar	1¹/2 cups golden seedless raisins
2 tablespoons lemon juice	2 16-ounce cans crushed pineapple
2 teaspoons vanilla extract	

Preheat oven to 400 degrees. Cook noodles using package directions; drain. Beat eggs with next 4 ingredients in large mixer bowl. Add noodles and oil; mix gently. Fold in raisins and pineapple. Spoon into greased 3-quart baking dish. Bake for 40 minutes or until set and golden brown. Serve warm or chilled as side dish or dessert. Yield: 15 servings.

Easy Supper Party

Grilled Chicken Breasts
Baked Potatoes — Steamed Broccoli
Fruit Salad — Easy Rolls
Sherbet — Coffee — Tea

See index for similar recipes.

This simple meal can easily be adjusted to suit the number of guests and gives the hostess time to visit and enjoy the party.

Bernice C. Nordin
Edna, Texas

❖ Swedish Christmas Dinner

Meat and Cheese Tray
Swedish Christmas Ham
Swedish Meatballs
Brown Potatoes — Green Beans
Swedish Slaw
Swedish Rye Bread
Rice Pudding
Swedish Drommars
Swedish Kakor
Glögg

See index for similar recipes.

I prepare the family Christmas dinner each year and I try to make it interesting as well as fun. For two years, we had a traditional English dinner and last year we had this Swedish menu. The meat and cheese tray is our appetizer version of the Swedish smorgasbord; headcheese, liver paté and Havarti cheese are traditionally included. We had so much fun researching the project that we have decided to do a different country every year. We learned that Christmas and Midsummer's Eve are the most important holidays in Sweden. The Christmas season begins with St. Lucia Day on December 13 and ends on January 13. It begins with The Festival of Light on St. Lucia Day to celebrate the return of more hours of daylight to the dark Swedish winters. The role of St. Lucia is played by a girl in each household. She rises early in the morning and dresses in a white dress and a crown of evergreens topped by seven lighted candles. She serves her family coffee and special Lucia buns in bed. Straw toys and decorations and lighted candles are important elements in the holiday celebration. The straw goat stands ready to butt any disobedient child during the season. Swedish children believe that elves called Juul Nisse help them with many holiday tasks; they thank the elves by leaving food on the table for them at night.

Tami J. Walker, Alpha Rho
Havana, Illinois

SWEDISH CHRISTMAS HAM

1 5- to 7-pound lightly smoked, fully cooked ham	1/4 to 1/3 cup fine dry bread crumbs
1 egg	1 cup whipping cream
1 tablespoon hot mustard pepper	1/4 cup hot mustard
Black pepper to taste	1 teaspoon chopped chives

Preheat oven to 325 degrees. Trim fat from ham; place on rack in shallow roasting pan. Beat egg in small mixer bowl for 5 minutes or until thick. Fold in mustard pepper. Brush over ham; sprinkle with black pepper and bread crumbs. Bake for 1 1/2 to 2 1/4 hours or to 140 degrees on meat thermometer. Beat whipping cream until soft peaks form. Fold in mustard and chives. Serve with ham.
Yield: 10 to 12 servings.

SWEDISH MEATBALLS

8 ounces ground beef	2 tablespoons finely chopped onion
8 ounces ground pork	
1/2 cup dry bread crumbs	1/2 teaspoon Worcestershire sauce
1/4 cup milk	
1 egg	1 teaspoon salt

Combine ground beef, ground pork, bread crumbs, milk, egg, onion, Worcestershire sauce and salt in large bowl; mix well. Shape into twenty 1 1/2-inch meatballs. Cook in nonstick skillet over medium heat for 20 minutes or until brown on all sides.
Yield: 20 meatballs.

SWEDISH RYE BREAD

1 envelope dry yeast	2 1/2 cups medium rye flour, stirred
1/4 cup warm water	
1/2 cup packed light brown sugar	3 tablespoons caraway seed
1/4 cup molasses	3 1/2 to 4 cups sifted all-purpose flour
2 tablespoons shortening	
1 tablespoon salt	Melted butter or margarine
1 1/2 cups hot water	

Dissolve yeast in 1/4 cup warm water. Mix brown sugar, molasses, shortening and salt in bowl. Stir in 1 1/2 cups hot water. Add rye flour; mix well. Add yeast mixture and caraway seed; mix well. Add enough all-purpose flour to make a soft dough, mixing well. Let rest, covered, in warm place for 10 minutes. Knead on floured surface for 10 minutes or until smooth and elastic. Place in greased bowl, turning to coat surface. Let rise for 2 hours or until doubled in bulk. Shape into 2 round loaves; place on greased baking sheet. Let rise, covered, for 2 hours. Preheat oven to 375 degrees. Bake bread for 30 minutes. Brush tops with butter. Cool on wire rack.
Yield: 2 loaves.

RICE PUDDING

3/4 cup uncooked long grain rice, cooked	*1 teaspoon almond extract*
5 cups milk	*6 egg whites*
6 eggs, beaten	*1/2 cup sugar*
3/4 cup sugar	*1 15-ounce jar lingonberries or cranberries*
2 teaspoons vanilla extract	

Preheat oven to 350 degrees. Combine rice, milk, eggs, 3/4 cup sugar and flavorings in large bowl. Stir in hot rice. Spoon into 9-by-13-inch baking dish. Bake for 20 minutes; reduce oven temperature to 300 degrees. Bake for 1 hour longer; increase oven temperature to 350 degrees. Beat egg whites in mixer bowl until soft peaks form. Add 1/2 cup sugar gradually, beating constantly until stiff peaks form. Spread over pudding. Bake for 10 to 15 minutes or until golden brown. Serve warm or cool with lingonberries. Yield: 12 to 15 servings.

SWEDISH DROMMARS

1 cup butter or margarine, softened	*1/2 teaspoon each cream of tartar and baking soda*
1/2 cup sugar	
2 cups all-purpose flour	

Preheat oven to 375 degrees. Cream butter in mixer bowl until light. Add sugar, beating until fluffy. Add mixture of dry ingredients; mix well. Shape into 3/4-inch balls; place on ungreased cookie sheet. Press indentation in each center. Bake for 7 to 9 minutes or until light brown. Cool on cookie sheet for several minutes; remove to wire rack to cool completely. Yield: 7 to 8 dozen.

SWEDISH KAKOR

1 cup butter or margarine, softened	*1 cup ground almonds*
1 cup sugar	*2 eggs, beaten*
	3 cups all-purpose flour

Preheat oven to 350 degrees. Cream butter and sugar in mixer bowl until light and fluffy. Add remaining ingredients; mix well. Roll on floured surface and cut into desired shapes. Place on cookie sheet. Bake until golden brown. Cool on cookie sheet for several minutes; cool completely on wire rack. Yield: 6 dozen.

GLÖGG

Sweet vermouth, Port, Apple Amber and orange juice	*2 cinnamon sticks*
	1/2 teaspoon each whole allspice and whole cloves
2 tablespoons light brown sugar	*Nutmeg to taste*

Combine equal parts wines, Apple Amber and orange juice with remaining ingredients in saucepan. Heat to serving temperature. Yield: variable.

Progressive Dinner

Appetizers — Amaretto Slush
Turkey — Dressing
Potatoes au Gratin — Broccoli Casserole
Tossed Salad — Hot Rolls —Pecan Pie
Cherry Pie — Coffee — Tea — Wine

See index for similar recipes.

Our Chapter livened up late January and celebrated several birthdays and anniversaries with a traditional menu Progressive Dinner. We went to a different home for each course, with a final stop for desserts, games and socializing.

Jeanne Sagovac, Xi Zeta Nu
Troy, Illinois

AMARETTO SLUSH

1 12-ounce can frozen lemonade concentrate	*12 ounces water*
	10 ounces Amaretto
1 12-ounce can frozen limeade concentrate	*Lemon-lime soda, chilled*

Combine first 4 ingredients in freezer container; mix well. Freeze for 2 days. Scoop slush into glasses, filling half full. Fill with soda. Yield: 12 servings.

DRESSING

1 cup chicken stock	*1 cup chopped onion*
2 chicken bouillon cubes	*1 cup chopped celery*
	1/2 cup margarine
1/2 cup raisins (optional)	*1 cup chopped peeled apple*
1 pound pork sausage	*2 eggs, beaten*
1 16-ounce (or more) loaf French bread, crumbled, dried	*1/4 teaspoon pepper*
	Milk (optional)

Bring chicken stock to a boil in saucepan; remove from heat. Add bouillon cubes, stirring to dissolve. Add raisins; let stand to plump. Brown sausage in skillet, stirring until crumbly; drain. Combine with bread in large bowl. Sauté onion and celery in margarine in same skillet for several minutes. Add to sausage mixture with apple, eggs, pepper, raisins and stock; toss lightly to mix well. Add a small amount of milk if necessary for desired consistency. Spoon into turkey cavity and bake using instructions for turkey. May spoon remaining dressing into baking dish and bake, covered, in moderate oven for 30 minutes; bake, uncovered, for 15 minutes longer. Yield: 12 servings.

Holiday Victorian Tea Party

Cucumber Sandwiches — Deviled Puffs
Victorian Shortcakes — Cream Wafers
Swedish Tea Ring
Assorted Teas

See index for similar recipes.

I planned this menu as a refreshment/program idea that "Woman Cannot Live on Tea Alone." A tea party is a great way to slow down the pace during the holidays by inviting good friends to share sweets, savories, a selection of teas and herbal teas and lots of "happy talk." You can serve the refreshments on pretty china and use cloth napkins for a touch of elegance. The treats can be prepared in advance and the table cleaned up quickly.

B.J. McKenzie, Xi Gamma Xi
Beverly, West Virginia

CUCUMBER SANDWICHES

12 slices white bread	2 large cucumbers,
8 ounces cream cheese,	peeled, thinly sliced
softened	

Trim crusts from bread. Spread bread gently with cream cheese; cut into quarters. Place 1 slice of cucumber on each small sandwich. Place on doily-lined serving plate. May chill, covered, until serving time. Yield: 48 sandwiches.

DEVILED PUFFS

1/2 cup butter or	3 4-ounce cans deviled
margarine	ham
1 cup water	1/3 cup sour cream
1 cup all-purpose flour	3/4 teaspoon each onion
4 eggs	salt and pepper
1 tablespoon horseradish	

Preheat oven to 400 degrees. Bring butter and water to a rolling boil in saucepan. Stir in flour. Cook over low heat for 1 minute or until mixture forms ball, stirring constantly; remove from heat. Beat in eggs all at once, beating until mixture is smooth and glossy. Drop by slightly rounded teaspoonfuls onto ungreased baking sheet. Bake for 25 minutes or until puffed and golden brown. Remove to wire rack away from drafts to cool. Combine remaining ingredients

in bowl; mix well. Cut off tops of puffs; remove any filaments of soft dough. Fill with ham mixture. Yield: 6 dozen.

VICTORIAN SHORTCAKES

1 1/2 cups all-purpose	1/2 cup milk
flour	2 egg whites
2 teaspoons baking	2 tablespoons
powder	confectioners' sugar
1/2 teaspoon salt	2 baskets fresh
1/4 cup margarine,	strawberries, sliced
softened	2 cups sweetened
1/2 cup sugar	whipped cream
2 teaspoons vanilla	
extract	

Preheat oven to 350 degrees. Sift flour, baking powder and salt together. Cream margarine, sugar and vanilla in medium mixer bowl until light and fluffy. Add dry ingredients and milk; mix well at low speed. Beat egg whites in small mixer bowl until stiff peaks form. Fold into batter. Spoon into 12 greased muffin cups. Bake for 15 to 20 minutes or until centers spring back when lightly touched. Place on serving plates. Sift confectioners' sugar over shortcakes. Top with strawberries and whipped cream. Yield: 12 servings.

CREAM WAFERS

1 cup butter, softened	3/4 cup confectioners'
1/3 cup whipping cream	sugar
2 cups all-purpose flour	1 teaspoon vanilla
Sugar	extract
1/4 cup butter or	
margarine, softened	

Combine 1 cup butter, whipping cream and flour in mixer bowl; mix well. Chill, covered, in refrigerator. Preheat oven to 375 degrees. Roll 1/3 of the dough at a time 1/8 inch thick on floured cloth, reserving remaining dough in refrigerator until ready to use. Cut into 1 1/2-inch circles. Coat both sides with sugar on waxed paper; place on ungreased baking sheet. Prick each circle 4 times with fork. Bake for 7 to 9 minutes or until set but not brown. Cool on wire rack. Cream 1/4 cup butter, confectioners' sugar and vanilla in mixer bowl until light and fluffy, adding a few drops of water if needed for desired consistency. Spread filling over half the cookies; top with remaining cookies. May tint filling as desired with food coloring. Yield: 5 dozen.

Donna Chiarello, Xi Kappa Beta, Follansbee, West Virginia, suggests rolling cookie dough on surface sprinkled with confectioners' sugar rather than flour.

SWEDISH TEA RING

1 envelope dry yeast
1/4 cup 105- to 115-
  degree water
1 egg
1 tablespoon sugar
2 1/2 cups baking mix
2 tablespoons
  margarine, softened
1/3 cup packed light
  brown sugar

1/3 cup raisins
2 teaspoons cinnamon
1 cup confectioners'
  sugar
2 teaspoons (or less)
  warm water
1/2 teaspoon vanilla
  extract

Dissolve yeast in 1/4 cup warm water in large bowl. Stir in egg, sugar and baking mix. Knead 20 times on floured surface or until smooth. Roll into 9-by-16-inch rectangle. Spread with margarine; sprinkle with brown sugar, raisins and cinnamon. Roll from long side to enclose filling; press edges to seal. Shape seam side down into ring on greased baking sheet, pressing ends to seal. Slice 2/3 of the way through at 1-inch intervals; turn slices to side. Let rise in warm place for 1 hour or until doubled in bulk. Preheat oven to 375 degrees. Bake ring for 15 minutes or until golden brown. Mix confectioners' sugar, 2 teaspoons warm water and vanilla in small bowl. Spread on warm ring. Serve warm. Yield: 12 servings.

Southern Good Luck New Year's Day Party

Hoppin' John
Cabbage Medley — Grits Casserole
Black-Eyed Pea Salad
Poke Sallet or Greens — Corn Bread

See index for similar recipes.

I invited my sorority to feast on traditional Southern "good luck" food on New Year's Day. We have members of both Anglo and Hispanic origins from California as well as members from Minnesota, New York, Germany and Kentucky - that's me. Everyone loved everything except for the member from New York who told me that I could keep my grits! I actually don't care for black-eyed peas myself, so I make Hoppin' John with a package of dried bean soup mix and add ham and onion.

Eddie Cox, Preceptor Delta Gamma
Camarillo, California

CABBAGE MEDLEY

2 tablespoons bacon
  drippings or
  vegetable oil
2 cups shredded cabbage
1 cup thinly sliced celery
1/2 cup chopped green
  bell pepper

1/2 medium onion,
  chopped
2 tomatoes, peeled,
  chopped
1 teaspoon soy sauce
1 teaspoon salt
Pepper to taste

Spread bacon drippings in skillet. Add cabbage, celery, green pepper, onion, tomatoes, soy sauce, salt and pepper. Cook, covered, over medium heat for 10 to 12 minutes or until tender, stirring occasionally. Yield: 8 servings.

GRITS CASSEROLE

1 cup white grits
1/2 teaspoon salt
5 cups water
1 cup sour cream
1 4-ounce can chopped
  green chilies, drained

8 ounces Monterey Jack
  or Cheddar cheese,
  shredded

Preheat oven to 350 degrees. Cook grits with salt in water in saucepan for 15 to 30 minutes or until very thick. Fold in sour cream and chilies. Spread 1/3 of the grits in 8-inch baking dish. Layer cheese and remaining grits 1/2 at a time in prepared dish. Bake for 30 minutes. Let stand for 10 to 20 minutes before serving. Yield: 8 servings.

BLACK-EYED PEA SALAD

2 16-ounce cans black-
  eyed peas, drained
1 cup vegetable oil
1/4 cup vinegar
1 large clove of garlic,
  chopped

1/4 cup chopped onion
1 teaspoon each salt
  and pepper

Combine black-eyed peas, oil, vinegar, garlic, onion, salt and pepper in 1-quart jar; mix well. Chill in refrigerator for up to 2 weeks. Drain before serving. Yield: 8 servings.

Kathleen V. Burk, Xi Lambda Pi, Baldwin, Missouri, makes Red Water Soup by cooking and draining 1 pound ground pork and combining it with one 28-ounce can tomatoes, 2 chopped onions, 6 to 8 peeled chopped potatoes, 1 or 2 stalks celery with leaves, 2 or 3 sliced carrots and salt to taste in soup pot. Simmer, covered, until vegetables are tender, mash with potato masher until vegetables are in small pieces and add sugar to taste. This traditional Christmas Eve soup takes only an hour but tastes as though it had been simmered all day.

❖ Engagement Party

Kir Royale with Raspberries
Salmon Crêpe Appetizers
Leek Soup
Minted Pink Grapefruit Ice
Filet Mignon
Shrimp Salad with Mushrooms
Cardamom Carrots
Ricotta-Almond Torte

See index for similar recipes.

This was served at the engagement party of our youngest daughter. It was the first time we met the groom's family.

Anne Gunn, Laureate Lambda
Sherwood Park, Alberta, Canada

KIR ROYALE WITH RASPBERRIES

1 cup raspberries
1/4 cup Crème de Cassis

3 bottles of brut
Champagne, chilled

Place 3 raspberries in each serving glass. Add 1/2 teaspoon Crème de Cassis to each glass. Fill glasses with Champagne. Yield: 8 servings.

SALMON CRÊPE APPETIZERS

1 16-ounce can salmon
1/2 cup mayonnaise
2 hard-cooked eggs, chopped
2 green onions, chopped
1 teaspoon prepared mustard
1/2 cup all-purpose flour

3 eggs
1/2 cup milk
1/2 teaspoon salt
6 tablespoons melted butter or margarine
1/2 cup sour cream
2 teaspoons capers
Lemon slices (optional)

Combine salmon, mayonnaise, hard-cooked eggs, green onions and mustard in medium bowl; mix well and set aside. Combine flour, eggs, milk and salt in small bowl; mix well. Stir in melted butter. Spoon a small amount at a time into crêpe pan, tilting to coat evenly. Bake crêpes for 2 minutes or until light brown. Cut each crêpe into 8 wedges. Spoon a small amount of salmon filling onto each wedge; roll to enclose filling. Arrange on serving plate; garnish with sour cream, capers and lemon slices. Serve immediately. Yield: 8 servings.

LEEK SOUP

1 chicken
4 large leeks, chopped
1 large onion, chopped
2 cups chopped celery
3 medium potatoes, chopped
Salt and pepper to taste

2 tablespoons butter or margarine
Worcestershire sauce and nutmeg to taste
2 tablespoons all-purpose flour
1 cup milk

Rinse chicken well. Cook in water to cover in saucepan until tender. Strain and reserve stock. Chop chicken into bite-sized pieces, discarding skin and bones. Sauté leeks, onion, celery and potatoes with salt and pepper in butter in saucepan until tender. Add reserved stock, chicken, Worcestershire sauce and nutmeg. Simmer for 45 minutes. Stir in mixture of flour and milk. Cook until thickened, stirring constantly. May purée if desired. Serve hot or chilled. Yield: 8 servings.

MINTED PINK GRAPEFRUIT ICE

Serve this refreshing ice to cleanse the palate before the main course.

Sections of 2 large pink grapefruit
2/3 cup sugar

5 tablespoons white Crème de Menthe
1/4 cup water

Combine all ingredients in blender container; process until smooth. Spoon into freezer container. Freeze until firm. Process again until smooth. Freeze until serving time. Let stand at room temperature for 10 minutes; spoon into small serving bowls. Yield: 8 servings.

SHRIMP SALAD WITH MUSHROOMS

2 tablespoons Dijon mustard
2 tablespoons chopped dill
1/2 cup olive oil
1/2 cup vegetable oil
Lime juice to taste
Salt and pepper to taste
20 large shrimp

Bouillon
16 snow peas
10 mushrooms, sliced
1/2 cup chopped macadamia nuts
3 tablespoons minced red onion
Lettuce

Combine first 7 ingredients in small bowl; mix well. Chill in refrigerator. Peel shrimp, leaving tails intact. Poach in bouillon in saucepan for 3 minutes or until cooked through. Drain, reserving 8 shrimp; slice remaining shrimp. Blanch snow peas in salted water for 3 minutes. Slice each diagonally into 3 pieces. Combine sliced shrimp, snow peas, mushrooms, macadamia nuts and onion in medium bowl. Add salad dressing; toss to coat well. Spoon onto lettuce-lined serving plate; top with reserved shrimp. Yield: 8 servings.

CARDAMOM CARROTS

2 pounds carrots	*1/4 cup unsalted butter*
1 1/2 tablespoons grated	*or margarine*
orange rind	*Salt to taste*
Seed of 4 cardamom	
pods, crushed	

Slice carrots 1/2 inch thick. Steam for 5 to 7 minutes or until tender-crisp. Sauté carrots with orange rind and cardamom seed in butter in skillet for 2 to 3 minutes. Season with salt to taste. Yield: 8 servings.

RICOTTA-ALMOND TORTE

1 3/4 cups ground	*1 tablespoon each*
toasted almonds	*Crème de Cacao and*
1/4 cup sugar	*Amaretto*
1/4 cup unsalted butter	*1 cup whipped cream*
or margarine	*3 tablespoons grated*
1/4 cup water	*baking chocolate*
2/3 cup sugar	*3 ounces semisweet*
20 whole almonds	*chocolate*
2 1/4 cups ricotta cheese	*1 teaspoon butter or*
1/3 cup sugar	*margarine*
1 teaspoon vanilla	
extract	

Preheat oven to 375 degrees. Combine ground almonds, 1/4 cup sugar and 1/4 cup butter in medium bowl; mix well. Press over bottom and side of greased 9-inch springform pan. Bake for 10 minutes. Combine water and 2/3 cup sugar in saucepan. Cook until medium brown. Stir in whole almonds, coating well. Remove almonds with slotted spoon; spread on baking sheet. Drizzle remaining syrup over crust; cool on wire rack. Combine ricotta cheese, 1/3 cup sugar, vanilla and liqueurs in food processor or blender container; process until smooth. Fold in whipped cream and grated chocolate. Spoon into cooled crust. Freeze until firm. Melt semisweet chocolate with 1 teaspoon butter in double boiler, stirring to mix well. Brush onto underside of leaves. Chill until firm. Place torte on serving plate; remove side of pan. Peel leaves from chocolate; arrange chocolate leaves over torte. Garnish with sugared almonds. Yield: 12 servings.

Gary Lou Geddes, Xi Omicron Omega, Fort Worth, Texas, prepares delicious Coffee Punch by combining 16 cups brewed coffee with 2 tablespoons vanilla extract, 1 quart skim milk and sugar to taste in large pitcher. After refrigerating overnight, she pours coffee mixture over 1/2 gallon vanilla ice cream in punch bowl and tops with dollops of whipped cream.

Surprise Birthday Brunch

Cheese Blintzes
Strawberries
Whipped Topping
Sour Cream
Curried Fruit
Coffee
Tea

See index for similar recipes.

We served this menu at one of our member's "Celebration of Life" birthday party.

Rose Marie Netzer, Zeta Beta
Timberon, New Mexico

CHEESE BLINTZES

1 cup cottage cheese	*12 crêpes*
8 ounces cream cheese,	*2 tablespoons vegetable*
softened	*oil*
1 egg yolk	*2 tablespoons melted*
1/3 cup sugar	*margarine*
1 teaspoon grated	*Fresh strawberries*
lemon rind	*Whipped topping or*
1 teaspoon vanilla	*sour cream*
extract	

Combine cottage cheese, cream cheese, egg yolk, sugar, lemon rind and vanilla in medium bowl; mix well. Spoon mixture onto crêpes. Fold sides over and roll to enclose filling. Brown lightly on all sides in oil and margarine in skillet. Serve with strawberries, whipped topping or sour cream. Yield: 12 servings.

CURRIED FRUIT

1 16-ounce can peaches	*Several prunes*
1 16-ounce can apricots	*1/3 cup margarine*
1 16-ounce can	*3/4 cup packed light*
pineapple chunks	*brown sugar*
1 16-ounce can pears	*4 teaspoons curry*
6 maraschino cherries,	*powder*
cut into halves	

Preheat oven to 325 degrees. Drain canned fruits and cherries and pat dry. Combine with prunes in 2-quart baking dish. Melt margarine in saucepan. Stir in sugar and curry powder. Spoon over fruit. Bake for 1 hour. Yield: 12 servings.

Bridesmaids' Luncheon

Chicken Divan Casserole
Tomato Aspic
Whole Wheat Sourdough Rolls
Butter-Pecan Cheesecake

We served this to the bridesmaids for our daughter's wedding. I made red tablecloths and a friend made ruffled skirts for hurricane lamp centerpieces. We glued small cups onto red felt hearts and filled them with small candies for favors. The serving, however, was the problem, and thank heavens for wonderful friends. I prepared all the food for the party in advance, but I just didn't have a place to serve it with 20 people either staying in the house or parked just outside the door in an RV. So our preacher's wife offered to have the luncheon at her house and she and her daughter—bless them—served it and cleaned up.

Soundra Christy, Xi Psi Alpha
Childress, Texas

CHICKEN DIVAN CASSEROLE

1 10-ounce package frozen chopped broccoli, cooked, drained	1/2 cup mayonnaise
	1 teaspoon lemon juice
	1/2 teaspoon curry powder
2 cups chopped cooked chicken breast	1 cup shredded Cheddar cheese
1 10-ounce can cream of chicken soup	1/2 cup crushed butter crackers

Preheat oven to 350 degrees. Layer broccoli and chicken in greased 9-by-9-inch baking dish. Combine soup, mayonnaise, lemon juice and curry powder in small bowl; mix well. Spread over chicken. Top with cheese and cracker crumbs. Bake for 25 to 30 minutes or until heated through. Yield: 6 servings.

TOMATO ASPIC

2 envelopes unflavored gelatin	1 teaspoon onion powder
1/2 cup cold water	1/8 teaspoon white pepper
3 cups tomato juice	Lettuce leaves
2 teaspoons lemon juice	
4 teaspoons minced fresh parsley	

Soften gelatin in water for 1 minute. Bring tomato juice and lemon juice to a boil in saucepan; remove from heat. Stir in gelatin until dissolved. Stir in parsley, onion powder and white pepper. Spoon into molds sprayed with nonstick cooking spray. Chill until firm. Unmold onto lettuce-lined serving plates. Yield: 6 servings.

WHOLE WHEAT SOURDOUGH ROLLS

4 cups whole wheat flour	1 1/2 cups warm water
2 cups (or more) all-purpose flour	1 tablespoon salt
	1 cup Sourdough Starter
1/4 cup sugar	Melted butter or margarine
1/2 cup corn oil	

Combine whole wheat flour, 2 cups all-purpose flour, sugar, oil, water, salt and Sourdough Starter in bowl; mix to form slightly sticky dough. Spray surface with nonstick cooking spray; cover lightly with foil. Let rise for 8 to 12 hours. Knead in a small amount of additional all-purpose flour. Shape into rolls; place in baking pans. Spray tops with nonstick cooking spray. Let rise for 8 to 12 hours. Preheat oven to 350 degrees. Place pans on lowest oven rack. Bake for 20 to 30 minutes or until golden brown. Brush tops with butter. Yield: 3 dozen.

SOURDOUGH STARTER

1 envelope dry yeast	3/4 cup sugar
1 1/2 cups warm water	3 tablespoons potato flakes
3/4 cup sugar	1 cup warm water
3 tablespoons potato flakes	

Dissolve yeast in 1/2 cup warm water in medium bowl. Add 1 cup water, 3/4 cup sugar and 3 tablespoons potato flakes; mix well. Let stand at room temperature for 12 hours. Chill for 3 days. Add 3/4 cup sugar, 3 tablespoons potato flakes and 1 cup warm water; mix well. Store at room temperature in loosely covered container for 8 to 12 hours. Stir mixture well and remove 1 cup for baking. Store remaining mixture in refrigerator. Feed and use or discard 1 cup of the mixture every 3 to 5 days.

BUTTER-PECAN CHEESECAKE

1 1/2 cups graham cracker crumbs	16 ounces sour cream
1/3 cup sugar	1 teaspoon vanilla extract
1/3 cup melted margarine	1/2 teaspoon butter extract
1/2 cup finely chopped pecans	1 cup finely chopped pecans, toasted
24 ounces cream cheese, softened	
1 1/2 cups sugar	
3 eggs	

Preheat oven to 475 degrees. Combine graham cracker crumbs, 1/3 cup sugar, margarine and 1/2 cup pecans in bowl; mix well. Reserve 1/3 cup mixture for topping. Press remaining mixture over bottom of 9-inch springform pan. Beat cream cheese in mixer bowl until light and fluffy. Add 1 1/2 cups sugar, beating until smooth. Beat in eggs 1 at a time. Add sour cream and flavorings; mix well. Stir in 1 cup toasted pecans. Spoon into prepared pan; sprinkle with reserved crumb mixture. Bake for 12 minutes. Reduce oven temperature to 300 degrees. Bake for 50 to 60 minutes longer or until set. Cool on wire rack. Place on serving plate; remove side of pan. Yield: 8 to 10 servings.

Fiftieth Wedding Anniversary Celebration

Ham with Curried Rice
Green Peas and Onions
Apricot Salad
Buttermilk Dinner Rolls
Almond-Vanilla Crunch

See index for similar recipes.

This menu was used at a friend's Golden Anniversary celebration. She and her daughter prepared everything in advance and I was on the church committee to help serve the dinner. These recipes are for a smaller number of servings but were increased to serve the 100 guests who attended.

June Smith, Laureate Nu
Aurora, Nebraska

HAM WITH CURRIED RICE

2 cups cooked rice
1 medium onion, minced
1/4 cup finely chopped parsley
1 tablespoon melted margarine
1/2 teaspoon curry powder
Salt to taste
8 1/4-inch slices boiled ham
1/4 cup margarine
1/2 teaspoon curry powder
2 tablespoons cornstarch
1/2 teaspoon salt
2 cups milk

Preheat oven to 375 degrees. Combine rice, onion, parsley, 1 tablespoon margarine, 1/2 teaspoon curry powder and salt to taste in bowl; mix well. Place 1/3 to 1/2 cup of the mixture on each slice of ham. Roll ham to enclose filling; arrange seam side down in 9-by-13-inch baking dish. Melt 1/4 cup margarine in saucepan. Add 1/2 teaspoon curry powder, cornstarch and 1/2 teaspoon salt; mix well. Stir in milk gradually. Cook over medium heat until thickened, stirring constantly. Spoon over ham rolls. Bake for 30 to 35 minutes or until heated through. Yield: 8 servings.

APRICOT SALAD

1 1/2 cups apricot nectar
1/4 cup grapefruit juice
1 3-ounce package lemon gelatin
Salt to taste
1 cup mandarin orange sections
1/4 cup finely chopped almonds

Bring apricot nectar and grapefruit juice to a boil in saucepan. Stir in gelatin and salt until dissolved. Chill until partially set. Beat until light. Fold in oranges and almonds. Spoon into mold or shallow dish. Chill until set. Unmold onto serving plate or cut into servings. Yield: 8 servings.

BUTTERMILK DINNER ROLLS

2 envelopes dry yeast
2 tablespoons sugar
2 cups lukewarm buttermilk
1/2 cup margarine
1/2 teaspoon baking soda
2 teaspoons salt
5 to 6 cups all-purpose flour

Dissolve yeast and sugar in buttermilk in bowl. Add margarine, baking soda and salt; mix well. Add enough flour to make a medium-stiff dough, mixing well. Place in greased bowl, turning to coat surface. Let rise, covered, for 45 minutes or until doubled in bulk. Punch dough down and shape into balls. Place in 3 greased 8-inch baking pans. Let rise, covered, for 30 minutes. Preheat oven to 400 degrees. Bake for 15 to 20 minutes or until rolls are golden brown. Yield: 2 dozen.

ALMOND-VANILLA CRUNCH

4 ounces slivered almonds or chopped pecans
1/4 cup margarine
1 cup crisp rice cereal
1/2 cup packed light brown sugar
1/2 cup coconut
Salt to taste
1 quart vanilla ice cream, softened

Preheat oven to 375 degrees. Sauté almonds in margarine in skillet for 5 minutes or until golden brown. Add cereal, brown sugar, coconut and salt; mix well. Press into 9-by-13-inch baking pan. Bake for 5 minutes. Cool to room temperature. Spread with ice cream. Freeze until serving time. Yield: 12 to 15 servings.

Easy-Does-It Birthday Dinner

Shrimp Cocktail
Creamy Baked Chicken Breasts
Fluffy Mashed Potatoes
Copper Penny Salad
Pea and Lettuce Salad
Rolls
Banana Split Dessert

See index for similar recipes.

I served this to my family for my son's birthday. Since Banana Split Dessert is his favorite dessert, we had that instead of ice cream and cake. The shrimp cocktail, salads and dessert were all made the day before so I could enjoy the birthday too. When he was leaving, my son told me that it would be worth having a birthday more often to get a wonderful dinner like that.

Dorothy Lee Warren
Princeton, West Virginia

SHRIMP COCKTAIL

1/2 bottle of catsup	*2 tablespoons light*
1/2 bottle of hot catsup	*brown sugar*
2 tablespoons	*1 pound peeled cooked*
horseradish	*shrimp*
2 tablespoons vinegar	

Combine catsup, hot catsup, horseradish, vinegar and brown sugar in medium bowl; mix well. Chill sauce and shrimp in refrigerator. Serve shrimp with sauce. Yield: 6 servings.

CREAMY BAKED CHICKEN BREAST

12 chicken breasts	*1/4 cup dry white wine*
12 4-by-4-inch slices	*1 cup seasoned stuffing*
Swiss cheese	*mix*
1 10-ounce can cream	*1/4 cup melted butter or*
of chicken soup	*margarine*

Preheat oven to 350 degrees. Rinse chicken and pat dry; arrange in lightly greased 9-by-13-inch baking dish. Top with cheese. Spread mixture of soup and wine over cheese. Sprinkle with stuffing mix; drizzle with butter. Bake for 40 to 50 minutes or until tender. Yield: 12 servings.

FLUFFY MASHED POTATOES

11 to 12 potatoes,	*1 5-ounce can*
peeled, chopped	*evaporated milk*
1/4 cup low-fat butter	
or margarine	

Cook potatoes with 2 tablespoons butter in water to cover in large saucepan until tender; drain. Beat in mixer bowl until smooth. Add remaining 2 tablespoons butter and evaporated milk; beat for 5 minutes. Yield: 6 servings.

COPPER PENNY SALAD

2 pounds carrots, sliced	*1/4 cup vegetable oil*
2 medium onions, sliced	*1/2 cup sugar*
1 green bell pepper,	*1 teaspoon*
sliced into rings	*Worcestershire sauce*
1 10-ounce can tomato	*1 teaspoon mustard*
soup	*1/4 teaspoon salt*
1/2 cup vinegar	

Cook carrots in water to cover in saucepan until tender; drain. Combine with onion rings and green pepper rings in salad bowl. Combine remaining ingredients in small bowl; mix well. Add to carrot mixture; mix well. Chill, covered, overnight. Yield: 10 servings.

PEA AND LETTUCE SALAD

1 head lettuce, torn	*2 large cucumbers, sliced*
1 10-ounce package	*3 stalks celery, chopped*
frozen green peas,	*1 onion, chopped*
thawed	*Mayonnaise to taste*
3 hard-cooked eggs,	*Bacon bits and cashews*
chopped	

Layer lettuce, peas, eggs, cucumbers, celery and onion in large salad bowl. Spread with mayonnaise. Top with bacon bits and cashews. May add cheese and sugar to taste if desired. Yield: 6 servings.

BANANA SPLIT DESSERT

2 cups graham cracker	*1 teaspoon vanilla*
crumbs	*extract*
1/2 cup melted butter or	*5 bananas, sliced*
margarine	*1 20-ounce can crushed*
1 1-pound package	*pineapple, drained*
confectioners' sugar	*16 ounces whipped*
2 eggs	*topping*
1 cup butter or	*3/4 cup chopped nuts*
margarine, softened	

Mix graham cracker crumbs with 1/2 cup melted butter in medium bowl. Press into 9-by-13-inch dish. Combine next 4 ingredients in mixer bowl; beat for 5 to 15 minutes or until smooth. Spread in prepared dish. Layer bananas, pineapple, whipped topping and nuts over top. Chill until serving time. Yield: 15 servings.

Make-Ahead Birthday Dinner

Ham Loaf
Hashed Brown Potato Casserole
Almond Green Beans
Lettuce Salad
Congealed Lime Salad
Hot Rolls
German Chocolate Cake
Coffee

See index for similar recipes.

This was the menu for my husband's birthday dinner, and it includes all his favorite foods—especially the German Chocolate Cake. Everything can be prepared the day before, so I can enjoy my guests at party time. I sometimes serve dinners buffet-style, but this time I served family-style. It was a great evening with good friends, good food and good conversation.

Dona Sue Brown, Epsilon Chi
Bolivar, Missouri

HAM LOAF

2 pounds cured ham	1 10-ounce can tomato
1 pound fresh pork	soup
1 pound beef	1 cup (scant) packed
4 eggs, slightly beaten	light brown sugar
1 1/4 cups milk	1 teaspoon mustard
2 1/2 cups graham	1/2 cup water
cracker crumbs	1/2 cup vinegar

Preheat oven to 300 degrees. Ask butcher to grind ham, pork and beef together. Combine eggs, milk and graham cracker crumbs in large bowl. Add ham mixture; mix well. Shape into 2 loaves; place in foil-lined baking pans. Combine remaining ingredients in bowl; mix well. Spoon over loaves. Bake for 2 hours. Yield: 20 to 25 servings.

HASHED BROWN POTATO CASSEROLE

1 32-ounce package	2 cups shredded Cheddar
frozen hashed brown	cheese
potatoes, thawed	1 teaspoon each salt
1/2 cup melted margarine	and pepper
1/2 cup chopped onion	2 cups crushed
1 10-ounce can cream	cornflakes
of chicken soup	1/4 cup melted margarine
8 ounces sour cream	

Preheat oven to 350 degrees. Combine potatoes with 1/2 cup margarine, onion, chicken soup, sour cream, Cheddar cheese, salt and pepper in bowl; mix well. Spoon into baking dish. Top with mixture of cornflakes and 1/4 cup margarine. Bake for 45 minutes. Yield: 10 servings.

ALMOND GREEN BEANS

8 slices bacon	2 16-ounce cans green
1/2 cup sugar	beans, drained
1/4 cup red wine vinegar	1 bunch green onions,
1 small package sliced	chopped
almonds	

Preheat oven to 350 degrees. Fry bacon in skillet until crisp; remove and crumble bacon, reserving drippings in skillet. Stir in sugar, wine vinegar and almonds. Bring to a boil. Pour over beans and green onions in baking dish; top with bacon. Bake for 20 minutes. Yield: 10 servings.

LETTUCE SALAD

1 head lettuce, shredded	1 cup mayonnaise
1 bunch green onions,	1 envelope ranch salad
chopped	dressing mix
1 10-ounce package	1 cup sour cream
frozen green peas,	Chopped hard-cooked
slightly thawed	eggs or deviled eggs
1 pound bacon, crisp-	
fried, crumbled	

Combine lettuce, green onions, peas and bacon in large bowl; mix well. Spoon into 9-by-13-inch dish. Combine mayonnaise, salad dressing mix and sour cream in medium bowl; mix well. Spread over salad. Chill for several hours. Top with eggs.
Yield: 10 servings.

CONGEALED LIME SALAD

1 3-ounce package	1/2 cup drained crushed
lime gelatin	pineapple
7 large marshmallows,	1/2 cup large-curd
chopped	cottage cheese
1 cup boiling water	1/2 cup whipped topping

Dissolve gelatin and marshmallows in boiling water in medium bowl. Cool to room temperature. Stir in pineapple, cottage cheese and whipped topping. Spoon into dish. Chill until firm. Yield: 12 servings.

Lois W. Jensen, Preceptor Alpha Alpha, Pearl River, New York, makes a Light Frozen Pumpkin Dessert by patting a recipe of graham cracker pie crust into a 9-by-13-inch pan, adding a mixture of 2 cups pumpkin purée, 1 1/2 cups packed brown sugar, 1/2 gallon softened vanilla ice cream, 1 teaspoon cinnamon and 1/2 teaspoon each salt, ginger and nutmeg. Freeze overnight and top with whipped cream.

Birthday Bridge Dinner

Polynesian Chicken
Wild Rice Casserole
Mandarin Salad
Igloo Crunch
Coffee — Iced Tea

See index for similar recipes.

I surprised my husband on his birthday with this dinner and bridge party for 12 guests. I chose menu items which could be prepared at least partially in advance and which would please both men and women.

Kathleen Whitney, Beta Kappa
Maryville, Missouri

POLYNESIAN CHICKEN

Chopped meat of 2 cooked chickens	2 3-ounce cans French-fried onions
Salt to taste	1/4 cup mayonnaise
2 16-ounce cans whole green beans, drained	2 10-ounce cans cream of chicken soup
2 7-ounce cans sliced water chestnuts	1/2 cup chicken stock
	1 teaspoon curry powder

Preheat oven to 350 degrees. Season chicken with salt. Layer chicken, green beans, water chestnuts and onions in greased rectangular baking dish. Combine remaining ingredients in bowl; mix well. Spread over layers. Bake, covered, for 45 minutes. Yield: 12 servings.

WILD RICE CASSEROLE

1 cup uncooked wild rice	1 cup chopped green bell pepper
1/2 cup uncooked brown rice	1 cup sliced mushrooms
3 10-ounce cans beef bouillon or broth	1/4 cup margarine
1 10-ounce can water	1 cup whipping cream
1 cup chopped onion	Pepper to taste

Preheat oven to 350 degrees. Cook rice in water and bouillon in saucepan for 20 to 25 minutes or until most of the liquid has been absorbed. Sauté onion, green pepper and mushrooms in margarine in saucepan. Stir in cream, pepper and rice. Spoon into 9-by-13-inch baking dish. Bake for 20 minutes. Yield: 12 servings.

MANDARIN SALAD

1/4 cup vegetable oil	1 head romaine lettuce, torn
2 tablespoons vinegar	3/4 cup chopped celery
2 tablespoons sugar	2 green onions, thinly sliced
2 tablespoons chopped parsley	1/2 cup sliced fresh mushrooms (optional)
Tabasco sauce to taste	1 11-ounce can mandarin oranges, drained
1/2 teaspoon salt	
Pepper to taste	
1/2 cup sliced almonds	
3 tablespoons sugar	

Combine vegetable oil, vinegar, sugar, parsley, Tabasco sauce, salt and pepper in small bowl; mix well. Chill for up to 4 days. Combine almonds and 3 tablespoons sugar in skillet. Cook until sugar melts and coats almonds, stirring constantly. Spread on waxed paper to cool. Combine lettuce, celery, green onions and mushrooms in salad bowl. Add mandarin oranges, almonds and salad dressing at serving time; toss to coat well. Yield: 12 servings.

IGLOO CRUNCH

1 1/2 cups vanilla wafer crumbs	1/4 cup chopped pecans
1/2 cup margarine	1/2 gallon vanilla ice cream, softened
2 1-ounce squares baking chocolate	1/2 cup vanilla wafer crumbs
3 egg yolks	Chopped pecans
2 cups confectioners' sugar	Chocolate ice cream topping
3 egg whites	

Spread 1 1/2 cups cookie crumbs in 9-by-13-inch dish. Melt margarine and chocolate in saucepan, stirring to mix well. Beat egg yolks in mixer bowl. Add confectioners' sugar; mix well. Add to melted chocolate in saucepan; mix well. Simmer for 2 minutes, stirring constantly. Beat egg whites in mixer bowl until stiff peaks form. Fold egg whites and 1/4 cup pecans into chocolate mixture. Spoon into prepared dish. Let stand until cool. Top with ice cream. Sprinkle with 1/2 cup vanilla wafer crumbs and additional pecans. Drizzle with ice cream topping. Freeze until serving time. Let stand at room temperature for several minutes before serving. Yield: 12 servings.

Kay Griffin, Xi Omicron Gamma, Citrus Height, California, prepares Festive Stuffed Bell Peppers with a filling of 1 pound sausage and 1/2 pound bacon cooked and drained, 1 small can crushed pineapple and 1/2 cup chopped nuts. Spoon into 4 green bell pepper cups and bake in preheated 300-degree oven for 20 minutes.

Birthday Dinner for Mom

Beef Burgundy — Noodles
Tossed Green Garden Salad
Chunky Homemade Applesauce
Colonial Pumpkin Pie

See index for similar recipes.

This was the menu prepared for my birthday by my two daughters, who were 10 and 11 years old. I had already made the pie, which is their favorite, and the girls made the rest. It was a simple meal to create but it was elegant when I was led to a candle-lit table and served by two eager waitresses. The food was wonderful, topped off by the pumpkin pie with flickering candles. I'm another year older, but now that I know what good cooks my daughters are, I'm also another year wiser.

Lucinda Joy Robertson, Xi Delta Lambda
Charlton, New York

CHUNKY HOMEMADE APPLESAUCE

This is also good over ice cream for dessert. The secret is to cook the apples over low enough heat for the apples to form their own juice.

8 cups McIntosh apple quarters	1/2 cup (about) sugar Cinnamon to taste

Simmer apples in saucepan over low heat until tender, stirring occasionally. Stir in sugar, breaking up apples slightly. Add cinnamon to taste. Serve warm or cooled. Yield: 8 servings.

COLONIAL PUMPKIN PIE

1 1/2 cups mashed cooked pumpkin	1 teaspoon cinnamon
2 tablespoons unsulphured molasses	1 teaspoon ginger
1 cup packed dark brown sugar	1/8 teaspoon allspice
	3 eggs, slightly beaten
1/2 teaspoon salt	1 cup evaporated milk
	1 unbaked 10-inch pie shell

Preheat oven to 425 degrees. Combine pumpkin with molasses, brown sugar, salt and spices in medium bowl; mix well. Add eggs and evaporated milk; mix until smooth. Spoon into pie shell. Shield edge of pastry with foil strips or moistened pie tape. Bake for 40 to 45 minutes or until knife inserted near center comes out clean. Place on wire rack to cool; remove foil immediately. Yield: 8 servings.

Sorority Supper

Antipasto
Savory Chicken Bites — Date Delights

See index for similar recipes.

I served this menu to my sorority sisters at a meeting. It is casual and easy to serve.

Beverly J. Miller, Gamma Zeta
Princeton, West Virginia

SAVORY CHICKEN BITES

8 ounces cream cheese, softened	1/3 cup finely chopped celery
1/2 teaspoon lemon juice	1 2-ounce jar chopped pimento, drained
1/2 teaspoon basil	2 8-count cans crescent rolls
1/8 teaspoon each oregano and thyme	1 egg, lightly beaten
1/4 teaspoon onion salt	1 1/2 teaspoons sesame seed
1 cup finely chopped cooked chicken	

Preheat oven to 375 degrees. Combine first 6 ingredients in bowl; mix until smooth. Stir in chicken, celery and pimento. Separate roll dough into 8 rectangles; press perforations to seal. Spread with chicken mixture, leaving 1/2 inch edges. Roll from long side to enclose filling; press edges to seal. Brush with egg; sprinkle with sesame seed. Cut each roll into 5 pieces; place seam side down on lightly greased baking sheet. Bake for 12 to 15 minutes or until golden brown. May reheat at 375 degrees for 4 to 6 minutes. Yield: 40 appetizers.

DATE DELIGHT

1 8-ounce package dates, chopped	1/3 cup margarine, softened
1 14-ounce can sweetened condensed milk	3 ounces cream cheese, softened
3 tablespoons margarine	3 cups sifted confectioners' sugar
1 cup chopped pecans	1 teaspoon vanilla extract
60 butter crackers	

Preheat oven to 350 degrees. Combine dates, condensed milk, 3 tablespoons margarine and pecans in skillet. Cook over medium heat until thick. Cool to room temperature. Spread on crackers; place on baking sheet. Bake for 6 minutes. Cool on wire rack. Combine remaining ingredients in bowl; mix well. Spread on cooled crackers. Yield: 5 dozen.

Eighty-Sixth Birthday Party

Chicken Saltimbocca
Wild Rice with Mushrooms
Glazed Carrots
Lush Lettuce Salad
Buns
Lemon-Glazed Angel Food Cake
Chardonnay

See index for similar recipes.

We served this menu at the 86th birthday celebration of my husband's grandmother. The chicken dish is Grandma Lillian's favorite. There were four great-grandchildren and a new puppy in attendance.

Tammy Peterson, Xi Gamma
Minot, North Dakota

CHICKEN SALTIMBOCCA

6 chicken breast filets	*2 tablespoons chopped*
6 thin slices boiled ham	*parsley*
3 slices mozzarella	*2 tablespoons melted*
cheese, cut into halves	*margarine*
1/2 cup fine dry bread	*1 10-ounce can cream*
crumbs	*of chicken soup*
2 tablespoons grated	*Mushrooms*
Parmesan cheese	

Preheat oven to 350 degrees. Rinse chicken and pat dry. Pound flat between plastic wrap. Place 1 slice ham and 1/2 slice cheese on each filet. Fold in sides and roll to enclose filling; secure with wooden pick. Mix bread crumbs, cheese and parsley in dish. Dip chicken rolls in margarine; coat with bread crumb mixture. Arrange in shallow baking dish. Bake for 40 to 45 minutes or until tender. Heat soup and mushrooms in saucepan, stirring to mix well. Serve with chicken. Yield: 6 servings.

WILD RICE WITH MUSHROOMS

1 cup uncooked wild rice	*1 tablespoon chopped*
3 cups boiling water	*parsley*
1 tablespoon chopped	*1/4 cup butter or*
onion	*margarine*
1 tablespoon chopped	*1 7-ounce can sliced*
chives	*water chestnuts,*
1 stalk celery, chopped	*drained*
8 ounces fresh	
mushrooms	

Cook rice in water in saucepan for 30 minutes or until tender. Sauté onion, chives, celery, mushrooms and parsley in butter in saucepan for 3 minutes. Add rice and water chestnuts; mix well. Spoon into glass dish. Microwave for 10 to 15 minutes or until heated through. May bake until heated through.
Yield: 6 servings.

GLAZED CARROTS

2 10-ounce packages	*1/3 cup packed light*
frozen baby carrots	*brown sugar*
2 tablespoons margarine	

Steam carrots until tender. Combine with margarine and brown sugar in saucepan. Cook until carrots are glazed, stirring constantly. Serve immediately.
Yield: 6 to 8 servings.

LUSH LETTUCE SALAD

1/4 cup sugar	*1 cup chow mein*
1/2 cup vegetable oil	*noodles*
2 tablespoons apple	*6 ounces cashews,*
cider vinegar	*coarsely chopped*
2 teaspoons MSG	*4 slices bacon, crisp-*
1 teaspoon salt	*fried, crumbled*
1/2 teaspoon pepper	*2 to 3 tablespoons*
1 head lettuce, torn	*sesame seed*
2 or 3 green onions,	
chopped	

Combine first 6 ingredients in small bowl; mix well. Combine lettuce and green onions in salad bowl. Add noodles, cashews, bacon, sesame seed and salad dressing just before serving; toss to mix well.
Yield: 6 to 8 servings.

LEMON-GLAZED ANGEL FOOD CAKE

We decorate the center of this cake with real yellow flowers and baby's breath.

1 large angel food cake	*1 pint whipping cream,*
Juice of 4 lemons	*whipped*
1/2 cup sugar	*Grated rind of 2 lemons*
1 14-ounce can	*Yellow food coloring*
sweetened condensed	
milk	

Rub crumbs from surface of cake; place cake on serving plate. Combine lemon juice, sugar and condensed milk in mixer bowl; beat for 3 minutes. Fold in whipped cream, lemon rind and food coloring. Drizzle over cake. May store in refrigerator for up to 7 days. Yield: 12 servings.

Cyndi Walters, Gamma, Panora, Iowa, makes Creamy Hot Spaghetti Sauce by heating a can of cream of celery soup with three 1/4-inch slices jalapeño cheese until cheese melts.

Craft Corner

How are you with crafts? Are you nifty at
knitting or needlepoint? Can you wield a glue
gun with the best of them? Or are you more
likely to glue your fingers together? No matter
what your level of skill, if you lead with your
heart, you will find the ability to create. A
dried flower arrangement will reflect your love
of exploring a field of flowers, an ornament
made of seashells will capture forever the
joy of a day at the beach. So don't worry if
you're normally all thumbs when it comes to
crafts. Find something you really enjoy
and throw yourself into it. And be willing to
share your creations. There is nothing more
precious than a gift made with love from the
heart and home of the giver.

Home Sweet Home

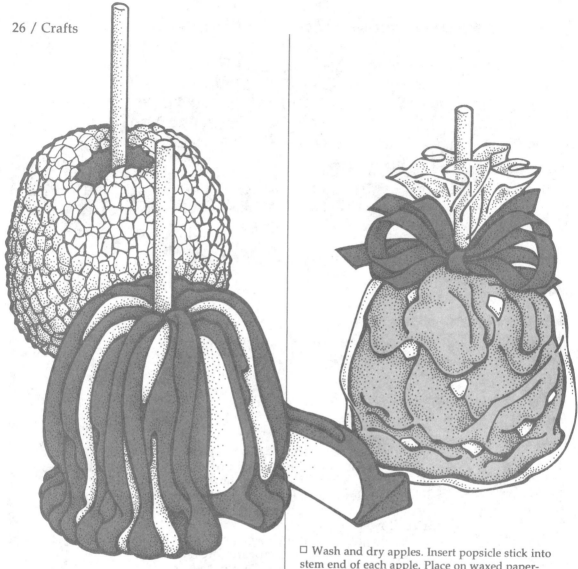

Chocolate-Covered Speckled Apples

Make our Chocolate-Covered Speckled Apples, coat with favorite crunchies, and wrap individually for one-of-a-kind gifts.

8 large Granny Smith apples, stems removed
8 wooden popsicle sticks or skewers
1⅓ cups confectioners' sugar
½ cup Hershey's baking cocoa
½ cup vegetable oil
1 cup Hershey's semisweet or milk chocolate chips
2 cups chopped Hershey's vanilla milk chips

☐ Wash and dry apples. Insert popsicle stick into stem end of each apple. Place on waxed paper-lined tray.

☐ Combine confectioners' sugar, cocoa and oil in glass bowl; mix well. Add chocolate chips.

☐ Microwave on High for 1 minute; mix well. Microwave for 15 to 30 seconds longer if necessary to melt any remaining chips.

☐ Twirl apples in chocolate mixture or spoon mixture over apples; tap popsicle sticks on edge of pan to remove excess coating. Return to tray. Let stand for 5 minutes.

☐ Coat with vanilla milk chips. Chill for 1 to 2 hours or until firm. Store wrapped in plastic wrap.

☐ May drizzle coated apples with melted caramel or milk chocolate or white chocolate and coat with chopped pecans or candy.

☐ Yield: 8 servings.

Santa Pod Ornament

Have a couple of okra pods that didn't wind up in the gumbo? Pull out the paints and make some adorable Santa ornaments.

MATERIALS

Dried okra pod
Acrylic paints: Burnt Sienna, Beige, White, Black, Burnt Umber
Small round paintbrush
Hot glue gun
7 inches thin jute

DIRECTIONS

□ Paint entire pod with burnt sienna paint. Let dry.

□ Paint Santa's face beige approximately 1/3 way down pod.

□ Dab white paint for beard and cap fringe.

□ Dab on black eyes and a burnt sienna mouth. Let dry.

□ Antique ornament by wiping on diluted burnt umber paint.

□ Glue looped jute to back of ornament for hanger.

Popcorn and Gumdrop Ornaments

Create easy ornaments by cutting 12 inches thin wire and threading 4 pieces popped popcorn and 1 gumdrop at a time onto wire until wire is covered. Twist wire ends together. Glue a bow made from a 12-inch length of 7/8-inch wide ribbon over twisted wire.

Artichoke Candle Holders

Use artichokes gilded or not, for unusual candle holders at each place setting at your next dinner party. Or you may choose to group them as a centerpiece for maximum effect.

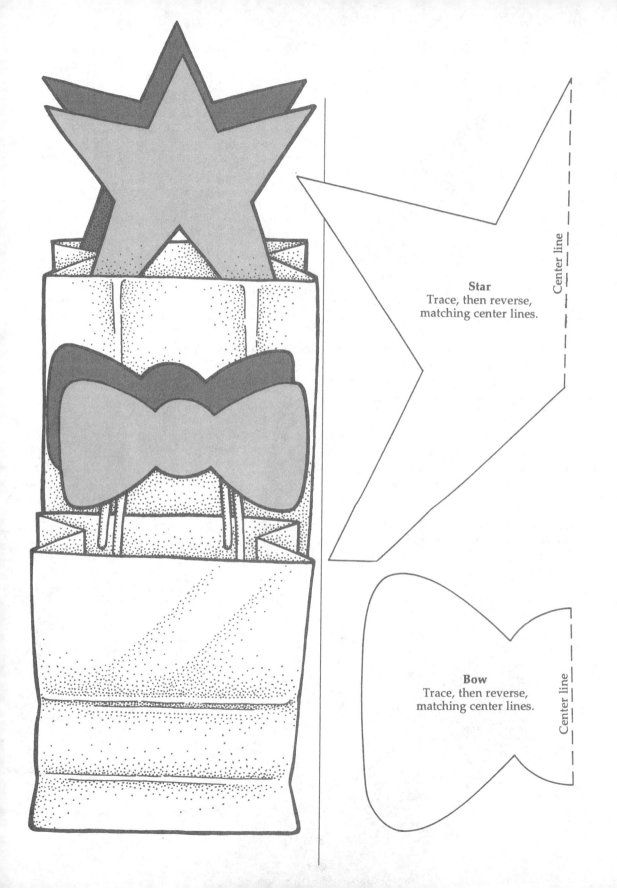

Star
Trace, then reverse,
matching center lines.

Center line

Bow
Trace, then reverse,
matching center lines.

Center line

Gift Bag Handles

Dress up your gift bags with festive handle covers. A bright red bow or a deep blue star change even a plain sack to a lovely goodie bag. Since the handle covers are just cut from heavy paper and glued in place, it's a great way to involve the kids in the fun.

MATERIALS

Heavy-weight paper: Red and Blue
Craft glue
See Pattern

DIRECTIONS

☐ Transfer patterns to paper. Cut out 2 handle covers for each bag.

☐ Position handle covers outside bag handles and just inside top edge of bag for star bags. Glue in place.

☐ Glue 1 bow to each handle for bow, leaving bag handle free at top for carrying.

Cosmetic Travel Bag

Banish any worries about spills in the suitcase with this pretty and practical travel bag. Zip-top bags are the secret. Just secure them under grosgrain ribbon, make a few quick passes with the sewing machine, and you have a bag that will safely transport shampoo and make-up to any port of call.

MATERIALS

1 (12-by-17-inch) piece reversible quilted fabric
6 sandwich-sized zip-top bags
1 yard (1-inch wide) coordinated grosgrain ribbon
24 inches (3/8-inch wide) coordinated satin ribbon

DIRECTIONS

☐ Round corners on fabric piece.

☐ Bind raw edges of fabric with machine set on tight zig-zag stitch.

☐ Mark center line on fabric running parallel to 12-inch sides.

☐ Position 3 bags on 1 half of fabric as follows: Place 1 even with each side and center remaining 1 on top so that all 3 bottoms line up on center mark. Repeat for other side with remaining bags.

☐ Cut a 12½-inch piece of grosgrain ribbon. Turn ends under ¼ inch and pin along center line over bottoms of bags. Stitch along both sides and ends of ribbon securing bags in seams.

☐ Cut remaining grosgrain ribbon in half for handles. Position 1 piece on inside of bag with both ends ⅛ inch from end of bag and loop to inside. Stitch ends to bag, and turn up handle. Repeat for other handle.

☐ Cut satin ribbon in half for ties.

☐ Fold end of 1 satin ribbon piece under ½ inch, and stitch folded end to outside of bag centered between sides of handle. Repeat for other side.

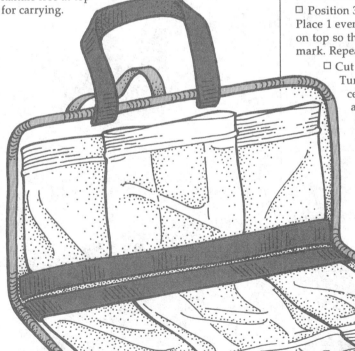

A Memory-Filled Wreath

Collect flowers from special arrangements and occasions throughout the year (example: weddings, birthdays, anniversaries). Dry them and make a keepsake wreath for yourself or a family member. This way you'll have a constant reminder of those special occasions.

Coffee and Mug Samplers

Wrap our Cappucino Mix or Coffee Vienna Mix in pretty mugs and tie on peppermint stick stirrers.

CAPPUCINO MIX

1 (8-quart) package nonfat dry milk powder
1 (16-ounce) jar powdered nondairy creamer
1 (20-ounce) package instant cocoa mix
1 (8-ounce) jar instant coffee powder
1 (1-pound) package confectioners' sugar

□ Combine all ingredients in large container; mix well.

□ Divide into smaller containers; seal tightly.

□ Attach instructions to mix 1/4 cup dry mix with 1 cup boiling water for each serving.

□ Yield: 20 cups mix.

COFFEE VIENNA MIX

2 cups instant cocoa mix
2 cups powdered nondairy creamer
1½ cups instant coffee powder
1½ cups confectioners' sugar
1 teaspoon cinnamon
1 teaspoon nutmeg

□ Combine all ingredients in large container; mix well.

□ Divide into smaller containers; seal tightly.

□ Attach instructions to mix 3 to 4 teaspoons dry mix with 1 cup boiling water for each serving.

□ Yield: 7 cups mix.

Civil War Doll

This doll demonstrates that sweetness comes mostly from inspiration. A man's handkerchief, a bit of stuffing, and scraps of ribbon and lace are all you need. Just gather the center of one end of a handkerchief into a ball, and stuff it firmly with polyester stuffing. Tie the stuffed area off with a string for the head, and tack a length of lace around it to define the face. Knot her hands, tie a pretty ribbon around her neck, and trim the bottom of her dress with lace. Then tack the edges of her hem together to keep baby's skirt tidy.

Reusable Giftwrap

Give the Earth a Christmas present by using recycled or reusable packaging. Some easy ideas include paper bags, dish towels, muslin, brown paper and even newspaper— including the comics! Trim with "biodegradables" such as candy canes and cinnamon sticks.

Bashful Reindeer Shirt

This shy little reindeer will delight any youngster both in the making and in the wearing. Its antlers are made with a child's hand prints! And if you're allergic to needle and thread, this is a safe project to take on. Fusible web fabric, safety pins, and paint work the magic.

MATERIALS

1   (6-by-7-inch) piece brown fabric
Fusible web fabric
Turtleneck shirt in desired color
Red Tulip™ Slick Paint
Newspaper
Silver glitter pen
2 safety pins
1   (1¾-inch diameter) red pom-pom
Ribbon bow
See Pattern

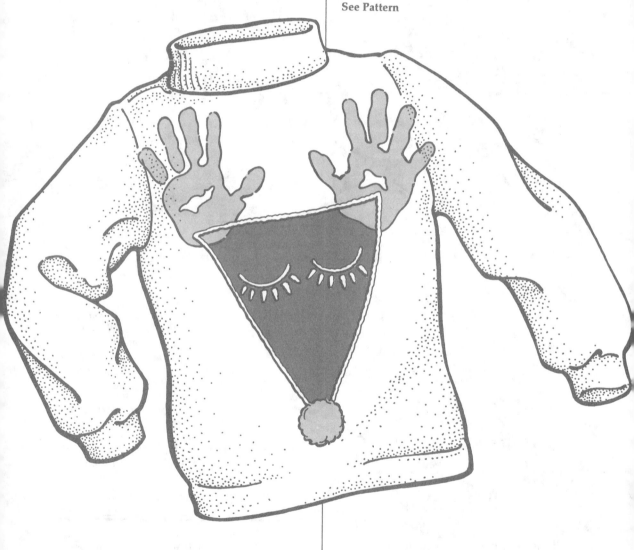

Reindeer head
Cut 1 from brown fabric.
Cut 1 from fusible web fabric.

DIRECTIONS

☐ Transfer pattern to fabric and fusible web and cut out.

☐ Determine placement of triangle reindeer head. Following manufacturer's directions, fuse triangle to shirt.

☐ Coat child's hands with red paint and have child blot them on newspaper to test paint consistency.

Make hand print antlers on reindeer, referring to illustration for placement.

☐ Transfer eye details to face and paint with glitter pen. Outline head with glitter pen.

☐ Attach pom-pom nose to reindeer face with safety pin.

☐ Pin bow to a corner below antler.

Bountiful Tabletop Decoration

Create a beautiful tabletop tree of fruits, vegetables or pasta with greens tucked into empty spaces. It is a great decoration for your sideboard or buffet table.

Sweetheart Frames

Small enough to tuck into a pocket, these little picture frames take on a special charm when their subject is a lovely snippet of lace. If you have an heirloom remnant, show it off on a field of deep cranberry velvet or crimson moire. But if your treasured pieces of lace are intact, you can get the same effect with purchased tatting and lace. Then let your imagination guide your display—prop a grouping on a dresser, loop ribbon around their supports and hang them from the tree, or attach them to a beautiful chain or ribbon and wear them around your neck. Once you've assembled a few of your own, you'll come up with dozens of ways to enjoy them.

No-Fuss Entertainment

If you're in the mood, there's always a good excuse for a party. How long has it been since you've been to a good Arbor Day bash anyway? The point is, parties should be for celebrating good times. And the host and hostess should have as much fun as the guests. The best way to accomplish that is to keep your entertaining no-fuss. Sure, sit-down dinner for twelve with elegant crystal and fine china are lovely, but a backyard barbecue or a pot-luck brunch on the day of the big game can be just as memorable. And if the guests help out by bringing a favorite covered dish, all the better! Just remember, the idea is to have a good time. So relax and have fun. These entertainment ideas will put you in the party mood.

Home Sweet Home

For Starters

ARTICHOKE DIP

1 15-ounce can artichoke hearts, drained	1 cup grated Parmesan cheese
1 cup mayonnaise	Crackers or pita bread

Preheat oven to 350 degrees. Chop artichokes. Combine with mayonnaise and cheese in bowl; mix well. Spoon into small glass baking dish. Bake for 30 to 45 minutes or until golden brown. May process in blender until smooth before baking. Serve with crackers or pita bread. Yield: 8 to 10 servings.

Penelope K. Bowdren, Preceptor Omicron
Rockville, Maryland
*Mildred S. Harward, Laureate Alpha Omega
Fort Pierce, Florida
*Deanne Miller, Chi
Shreveport, Louisiana

CHEDDAR ARTICHOKE DIP

2 6-ounce jars marinated artichoke hearts, drained	2 pounds shredded Cheddar cheese
1 4-ounce can chopped green chilies, drained	Taco chips

Preheat oven to 300 degrees. Chop artichoke hearts into small pieces. Combine with chilies and cheese in bowl; mix well. Spoon into baking dish. Bake until warmed through and cheese is melted. Serve with taco chips. Yield: 8 to 10 servings.

Pat Coontz, Preceptor Eta Kappa
Covina, California

CRAB AND ARTICHOKE DIP

1 13-ounce can water-packed artichoke hearts, drained	1 cup grated Parmesan cheese
1 6-ounce can crab meat, drained	1/2 teaspoon garlic salt
1 cup mayonnaise	1/4 teaspoon lemon-pepper
	Assorted crackers

Preheat oven to 350 degrees. Cut drained artichoke hearts into quarters. Combine artichoke hearts with crab meat, mayonnaise, cheese, garlic salt and lemon-pepper in bowl; toss lightly to mix well. Spoon into lightly greased baking dish. Bake for 20 minutes or until heated through. Serve hot with assorted crackers. Yield: 8 to 10 servings.

Mary Boyle, Xi Epsilon Upsilon
Odessa, Missouri

CREAMY ARTICHOKE DIP

1 15-ounce can artichoke hearts	4 ounces cream cheese, softened
1/2 onion, chopped	1/2 cup grated Parmesan cheese
2 tablespoons mayonnaise	

Preheat oven to 350 degrees. Mash artichoke hearts with fork in bowl. Add onion, mayonnaise and cream cheese; mix well. Spoon into 9-by-9-inch baking dish. Sprinkle with Parmesan cheese. Bake for 15 to 20 minutes or until browned. Yield: 10 servings.

Mary Lou Strohm, Theta Phi
Quinlan, Texas

DRIED BEEF DIP

1 2-ounce jar dried beef
1 cup mayonnaise
1 cup sour cream
1 teaspoon seasoned salt
1 1-pound loaf
  pumpernickel bread

Chop dried beef into small pieces. Combine with mayonnaise, sour cream and seasoned salt in bowl; mix well. Chill for 1 hour. Slice top from loaf. Cut out center of bread, leaving 1/2-inch thick sides to form bread bowl and reserving center and top. Cut reserved bread into bite-sized pieces. Spoon chilled dip into center of loaf. Arrange bread pieces around loaf on serving platter. Yield: 16 servings.

Sue Bastian
Englewood, Ohio

BROCCOLI DIP

2 10-ounce packages
  frozen chopped
  broccoli
1 large onion, chopped
1 cup butter or
  margarine
2 10-ounce cans cream
  of mushroom soup
2 4-ounce packages
  garlic cheese
Salt and pepper to taste
1 8-ounce can
  mushroom pieces,
  drained
1 cup slivered almonds
Tostado chips

Cook broccoli using package directions; drain. Sauté onion in butter in skillet until tender. Combine broccoli, onion, soup, cheese, salt and pepper in slow cooker. Heat until cheese is melted, stirring occasionally. Add mushroom pieces and almonds. Serve warm with tostado chips. May also serve over baked potatoes. Yield: 16 servings.

Sherrie Ricketts
Florence, Alabama

CHILI CHEESE DIP

1 pound ground beef
2 pounds Velveeta
  cheese, cubed
1 8-ounce can green
  chilies and tomatoes
1 8-ounce can tomato
  sauce
4 teaspoons chili
  powder
1/4 cup all-purpose flour
6 tablespoons water
Chips

Brown ground beef in skillet, stirring until crumbly; drain. Combine with cheese, chilies and tomatoes, tomato sauce, chili powder, flour and water in slow cooker; mix well. Cook, covered, for 1 hour or until cheese is melted, stirring occasionally. Serve with chips. Yield: 20 servings.

Carol A. Ruppert, Alpha Delta Lambda
Plano, Texas

HOT BREAD DIP

1 round loaf bread
2 6-ounce cans shrimp
16 ounces cream cheese,
  softened
2 tablespoons grated
  onion
2 tablespoons
  Worcestershire sauce
2 tablespoons lemon
  juice
2 tablespoons beer
1 teaspoon hot pepper
  sauce
1/2 teaspoon salt
Assorted crackers
Assorted bite-sized
  fresh vegetables

Preheat oven to 250 or 300 degrees. Cut top from bread; scoop out center leaving 1- to 2-inch thick shell. Drain shrimp, reserving 1/4 cup liquid. Combine shrimp, reserved liquid, cream cheese, onion, Worcestershire sauce, lemon juice, beer, pepper sauce and salt in bowl; mix well. Spoon into center of bread. Wrap in foil; place on baking sheet. Bake for 1 1/2 to 2 hours. Serve with crackers or fresh vegetables. May substitute canned crab meat or chicken for shrimp. Yield: 16 servings.

Dorothy Dooks, Preceptor Lambda
Porters Lake, Nova Scotia, Canada

CRAB MEAT SALAD DIP

2 6-ounce cans crab
  meat, drained, flaked
1 cup sour cream
4 ounces cream cheese,
  softened, cubed
1 9-ounce jar cocktail
  sauce with
  horseradish
Crackers or chips

Layer crab meat, sour cream, cream cheese and cocktail sauce 1/2 at a time in bowl. Serve with crackers or chips. Yield: 16 servings.

Brenda Keys, Theta
Norcross, Georgia

MUSHROOM CRAB DIP

1/2 cup margarine
1/4 cup all-purpose flour
1 5-ounce can
  evaporated milk
1 10-ounce can cream
  of mushroom soup
1 cup sour cream
1 pound crab meat,
  drained, flaked
Wafer crackers

Melt margarine in saucepan over medium heat. Add flour, stirring until blended. Add evaporated milk. Simmer until thickened, stirring constantly. Add soup and sour cream, stirring until smooth. Stir in crab meat. Serve hot or cold with crackers. Yield: 20 servings.

Rosalie Collins, Laureate Pi
Chesapeake, Virginia

SPICY CRAB MEAT DIP

1/2 cup chili sauce
1/2 cup mayonnaise
1 clove of garlic, finely
    chopped
1/2 teaspoon dry
    mustard
1 tablespoon
    horseradish
1 tablespoon
    Worcestershire sauce
1/8 teaspoon Tabasco
    sauce
1/2 teaspoon salt
2 hard-cooked eggs,
    finely chopped
1 6-ounce can crab
    meat, drained, flaked
Crackers or fresh
    vegetables

Combine chili sauce and mayonnaise in bowl. Stir in garlic, mustard, horseradish, Worcestershire sauce, Tabasco sauce and salt. Add chopped eggs and crab meat, stirring gently. Chill, covered, for 2 hours to overnight. Spoon into serving bowl; serve with crackers or fresh vegetables. Yield: 20 servings.

Marilyn Dubuc, Laureate Alpha
Lavel-sur-le-Lac, Quebec, Canada

CRAB MEAT PIZZA DIP

8 ounces cream cheese,
    softened
1/4 teaspoon garlic
    powder
1 teaspoon hot pepper
    sauce
1/4 teaspoon
    Worcestershire sauce
1 9-ounce bottle of
    seafood cocktail sauce
1 to 2 6-ounce cans
    crab meat, drained,
    flaked
Parsley flakes

Combine cream cheese, garlic powder, pepper sauce and Worcestershire sauce in bowl. Spread evenly over 12-inch pizza pan. Pour cocktail sauce evenly over cream cheese mixture. Top with crab meat and parsley. May substitute shrimp for crab meat, or use 1 can of each. Serve with crackers. Yield: 20 servings.

Peggy Harris, Theta Epsilon
Lacombe, Louisiana

CRAB TREAT

1 large loaf French bread
16 ounces cream cheese,
    softened
1 cup mayonnaise
2 teaspoons dillweed
1 6-ounce can crab
    meat, drained, flaked
1 cup chopped green
    onions
1 cup shredded Cheddar
    cheese
1/2 cup bacon bits

Preheat oven to 350 degrees. Slice top off bread; scoop out center, reserving bread. Combine cream cheese, mayonnaise, dillweed, crab meat, green onions, Cheddar cheese and bacon bits in bowl; mix well. Spoon into bread shell. Wrap with foil; place on baking sheet. Bake for 2 hours. Serve with reserved bread, cut into cubes. Yield: 20 servings.

Faye Saigeon, Preceptor Zeta
Estevan, Saskatchewan, Canada

HOT CRAB DIP

16 ounces cream cheese,
    softened
1 cup sour cream
1 tablespoon
    Worcestershire sauce
1 1/2 teaspoons dry
    mustard
1 teaspoon Old Bay
    Seasoning
2 tablespoons
    mayonnaise
1/4 teaspoon garlic
    powder
1 pound crab meat,
    flaked
2 cups shredded sharp
    Cheddar cheese
Crackers

Preheat oven to 300 degrees. Combine cream cheese, sour cream, Worcestershire sauce, mustard, seafood seasoning, mayonnaise and garlic powder in bowl; mix well. Stir in crab meat. Spoon into greased 9-by-9-inch baking dish. Sprinkle with Cheddar cheese. Bake for 1 hour and 15 minutes. Serve with crackers. Yield: 15 servings.

Clara May Hoff, Laureate Delta Kappa
Montoursville, Pennslyvania

MICROWAVE CRAB DIP

16 ounces cream cheese,
    softened, cubed
1 clove of garlic
1 small onion, cut into
    quarters
1/3 cup mayonnaise
1 teaspoon sugar
Dash of salt
1 6-ounce can crab
    meat, drained, flaked
1/4 cup white wine
Assorted crackers

Combine cream cheese, garlic, onion, mayonnaise, sugar and salt in blender container. Process until smooth. Add crab meat. Process until crab meat is chopped but not puréed. Spoon into glass dish. Microwave on Medium power for 5 minutes or until heated through. Stir in wine. Serve with assorted crackers. Yield: 20 servings.

Roselee Soyka, Preceptor Delta Rho
Caledon East, Ontario, Canada

SEAFOOD DIP

8 ounces cream cheese,
    softened
1 pound Sea Leg
    Supreme, chopped
1 tablespoon finely
    chopped onion
1/2 teaspoon horseradish
1/2 teaspoon garlic salt
Pepper and hot sauce
    to taste
1/2 cup chopped pecans
1 teaspoon butter or
    margarine
Crackers

Preheat oven to 375 degrees. Combine cream cheese, seafood, onion, horseradish, garlic salt, pepper and hot sauce in bowl; mix well. Spoon into 2-quart buttered baking dish. Sauté pecans in butter in skillet. Sprinkle over top. Bake for 25 minutes. Serve with crackers. Yield: 16 servings.

Terri L. Fletcher, Preceptor Beta Zeta
Portsmouth, Virginia

CREAMY CRAB HORS D'OEUVRES

8 ounces cream cheese, softened	8 ounces crab meat, flaked
1 tablespoon milk	Salt and pepper to taste
1 tablespoon minced onion flakes	1 2-ounce package slivered almonds
1/2 teaspoon prepared horseradish	

Preheat oven to 350 degrees. Combine cream cheese, milk, onion flakes and horseradish in bowl; mix well. Stir in crab meat, salt and pepper. Spoon into shallow 1-quart baking dish. Sprinkle with almonds. Bake for 20 minutes or until lightly browned. May substitute 2 tablespoons fresh chopped onion for onion flakes. Yield: 8 servings.

Eleanore Simmons, Preceptor Omicron
Rockville, Maryland
*Lisa Trimble, Pi Omega
Henderson, Texas

FIESTA APPETIZER

1 16-ounce can refried beans	1 4-ounce can chopped green chilies, drained
1 envelope taco seasoning	2 tomatoes, chopped
3 avocados, peeled	6 green onions, chopped
1 tablespoon lemon juice	1 cup shredded Cheddar cheese
1/4 cup sour cream	Tortilla chips
1 2-ounce can sliced black olives, drained	

Combine beans and taco seasoning in small bowl. Spread evenly on round 12-inch serving platter. Mash avocados with lemon juice in bowl. Spread over beans. Cover with sour cream. Top with olives, chilies, tomatoes, green onions and cheese. Serve with tortilla chips. Yield: 20 servings.

Brenda Miller, Epsilon Delta
Cambridge, Ontario, Canada

FOOTBALL FAN'S APPETIZER

1 pound ground beef	1 cup shredded sharp Cheddar cheese
1/2 cup mayonnaise-type salad dressing	1/4 cup chopped onion
1/2 cup taco sauce	Corn chips

Preheat oven to 350 degrees. Brown ground beef in skillet, stirring until crumbly; drain. Combine salad dressing and taco sauce in small bowl. Stir in ground beef. Add 3/4 cup cheese and onion. Spoon into 9-inch pie plate. Top with remaining cheese. Insert chips around edge of pie plate. Bake for 15 minutes. Serve with additional corn chips. Yield: 20 servings.

Julie Whitacre, Preceptor Zeta
Winchester, Virginia

FIVE-LAYER MEXICAN DIP

Always great for a crowd for every occasion.

2 9-ounce cans bean dip	2 tomatoes, chopped
3 avocados, peeled	1/2 cup chopped green onions
1 tablespoon lemon juice	
2 cups sour cream	1 2-ounce can sliced black olives, drained
1 envelope taco seasoning	Chips
1 cup shredded sharp Cheddar cheese	

Spread bean dip in 9-by-13-inch pan. Mash avocados with lemon juice. Combine sour cream with taco seasoning. Layer avocado mixture and sour cream mixture over bean dip. Top with cheese and tomatoes. Sprinkle with green onions and olives. Serve with chips. May substitute prepared guacamole for fresh avocados. Yield: 20 to 30 servings.

Suann Agold, Preceptor Eta Beta
Boerne, Texas
*Kristy L. Vorn, Beta Nu
Encampment, Wyoming

HOT NACHO DIP

1 pound Velveeta cheese, cubed	Chopped jalapeño peppers
1 15-ounce can chili without beans	Tortilla chips

Microwave cheese in glass bowl until melted. Stir in chili and add jalapeño peppers to taste. Serve hot from chafing dish or slow cooker with tortilla chips for dipping. Yield: 20 servings.

Susan J. Seals, Xi Delta Iota
Marshalltown, Iowa

PICANTE SAUCE

12 large ripe tomatoes	1 1/2 tablespoons salt
1 1/2 cups chopped, seeded jalapeño peppers	2 cloves of garlic, chopped
1/2 cup chopped green bell pepper	2 cups chopped celery
2 onions, chopped	1 tablespoon fresh cilantro
1 1/2 cups white vinegar	1 teaspoon ground cumin
1/2 cup water	

Combine tomatoes, jalapeño peppers, green pepper, onions, vinegar, water, salt, garlic, celery, cilantro and cumin in large saucepan. Simmer until of desired thickness, stirring frequently. Pour into hot sterilized jars leaving 1/2 inch headspace. Seal with 2-piece lids. Process in water bath for 35 minutes. Yield: 6 pints.

Vergie Stockton, Laureate Gamma Upsilon
Fort Worth, Texas

PIMENTO CHEESE DIP

1 cup pimento cheese	1 tablespoon dried chives
1 cup sour cream	Dash of hot pepper
1 teaspoon parsley	sauce
flakes	Seasoned salt to taste
1/2 teaspoon	Fresh vegetables,
Worcestershire sauce	crackers or chips

Mix pimento cheese, sour cream, parsley, Worcestershire sauce, chives, hot pepper sauce and seasoned salt in bowl. Chill for several hours. Serve with fresh vegetables, crackers or chips. Yield: 8 to 10 servings.

Joan Clodfelter, Preceptor Alpha Delta
Lexington, North Carolina

HOT SAUERKRAUT DIP

At a Christmas party, two friends "ate the whole thing," but couldn't believe it contained sauerkraut.

1 3/4 pounds ground beef	2 tomatoes, chopped
1 green bell pepper,	1/2 teaspoon garlic salt
chopped	1 teaspoon salt
1 onion, chopped	1/2 teaspoon pepper
1 32-ounce can	1 1/2 cups sour cream
sauerkraut, drained	Tortilla chips

Brown ground beef with green pepper and onion in skillet, stirring until ground beef is crumbly; drain. Combine with next 5 ingredients in slow cooker. Stir in sour cream. Simmer on Low for several hours. Serve with tortilla chips. Yield: 20 servings.

Lynette Stenzel, Mu Phi
Ness City, Kansas

SAUSAGE-HAMBURGER CON QUESO

This was a hit at the office—everyone wanted some.

1 pound sausage	1 10-ounce can cream
1 pound lean ground beef	of mushroom soup
2 pounds Velveeta	1 16-ounce jar picante
cheese, cubed	sauce

Brown sausage and ground beef in skillet, stirring until crumbly; drain. Combine with remaining ingredients in slow cooker. Simmer on Low until cheese is melted, stirring frequently. Yield: 20 to 30 servings.

Nona Fincher, Alpha Mu
Rapid City, South Dakota

SHRIMP DIP

My younger sister served this at Thanksgiving so I always associate it with a holiday feast.

16 ounces cream cheese,	1 8-ounce bottle of
softened	cocktail sauce
1 onion, chopped	1 tablespoon prepared
1 teaspoon	horseradish
Worcestershire sauce	1 cup cooked shrimp
1 teaspoon seasoned salt	

Combine cream cheese, onion, Worcestershire sauce and seasoned salt in bowl; mix well. Spread in 7-by-12-inch pan. Cover with mixture of cocktail sauce and horseradish. Top with shrimp. Chill until firm. Yield: 15 to 20 servings.

Kay Groh, Preceptor Beta Omega
Emporia, Kansas

PUMPERNICKEL SPINACH DIP

Everyone always loves this spinach dip and it's simple to make.

1 cup sour cream	1/4 onion, chopped
1 cup mayonnaise	1 10-ounce package
1 envelope vegetable	frozen chopped
soup mix	spinach, thawed
1 8-ounce can water	1 loaf pumpernickel
chestnuts, drained,	bread
chopped	

Mix sour cream and mayonnaise in bowl. Stir in soup mix, water chestnuts, onion and spinach. Chill for 2 to 4 hours. Slice top off bread; scoop out center, leaving 1-inch shell, reserving scooped out bread. Cut reserved bread into cubes. Spoon spinach mixture into hollowed out bread. Serve dip with bread cubes for dipping. May substitute light mayonnaise and light sour cream to reduce calories. Yield: 12 to 15 servings.

Maxine Geypens, Zeta Theta
Oshawa, Ontario, Canada
*Janice Woodward, Epsilon Delta
Cambridge, Ontario, Canada

TARA'S TORTILLA CHIP DIP

We have this at our Sorority Super Bowl party—a yearly tradition.

1/2 cup margarine	1 pound ground beef
1/2 cup all-purpose	2 to 3 tablespoons
flour	minced onion flakes
2 teaspoons salt	Sliced jalapeño peppers
4 cups milk	to taste
8 ounces Velveeta	Tortilla chips
cheese, cubed	

Melt margarine in saucepan. Add flour and salt, stirring until smooth. Add milk gradually, stirring constantly. Cook until thickened, stirring constantly. Add cheese. Cook over low heat until cheese is melted, stirring frequently. Brown ground beef and onion flakes in skillet, stirring until ground beef is crumbly; drain. Stir into cheese sauce; add jalapeño peppers. Serve with tortilla chips. Yield: 15 to 20 servings.

Tara D. Schnack, Beta
Des Moines, Iowa

BEEFY CHEESE BALL

8 ounces cream cheese, softened	1 8-ounce can crushed pineapple, drained
1 tablespoon mayonnaise	1 4-ounce package chipped beef
1/2 green bell pepper, chopped	Crackers

Mix cream cheese and mayonnaise in bowl until smooth. Add next 3 ingredients. Shape into ball. Chill until firm. Serve with crackers. Yield: 12 servings.

Tama Backlund, Preceptor Mu
Mitchell, South Dakota

SMOKED BEEF CHEESE BALLS

3 to 4 4-ounce packages smoked sliced beef	2 tablespoons MSG
	2 tablespoons Worcestershire sauce
24 ounces cream cheese, softened	Chopped parsley
6 to 8 green onions, chopped	

Chop smoked beef into small pieces, reserving 1 1/2 packages for topping. Combine with cream cheese, green onions, MSG and Worcestershire sauce in bowl. Shape into 2 or 3 balls. Cover with reserved chopped beef. Chill, covered, overnight. Garnish with parsley. Yield: 20 to 30 servings.

Dee Ann Carrouth, Beta Delta Pi
Bellevue, Texas
*Loree Walrath, Alpha Beta Psi
Clinton, Missouri

YUMMY CHEESE BALL

16 ounces cream cheese, softened	1 to 6 green onions, chopped
1 4-ounce can mushroom pieces, drained, chopped	1 2-ounce jar dried beef, chopped
	Crackers
1 4-ounce can chopped black olives	

Combine cream cheese, mushrooms, olives, green onions and dried beef in bowl; mix well. Shape into ball. Chill until firm. Serve with crackers. Yield: 12 to 16 servings.

Shelly Futrell, Xi Gamma Pi
Pocahontas, Arkansas

BOURSIN CHEESE BALL

8 ounces cream cheese, softened	1/4 teaspoon dillweed
	1/4 teaspoon marjoram
1/2 cup margarine, softened	1/4 teaspoon basil
	1/4 teaspoon thyme
1 clove of garlic, minced	Cracked pepper
1/2 teaspoon dried oregano	Crackers

Mix cream cheese and margarine in bowl until smooth. Add garlic and herbs, stirring well. Shape into ball; wrap with waxed paper. Chill until firm. Roll in cracked pepper. Serve with crackers. Yield: 12 servings.

Lillian M. Power, Xi Kappa
Peterborough, New Hampshire

GERMAN CHEESE BALL

6 ounces Roquefort cheese	2 tablespoons dried minced onion
2 5-ounce jars Old English cheese, softened	1 teaspoon Worcestershire sauce
	1/2 cup chopped parsley
12 ounces cream cheese, softened	1 cup ground pecans

Combine cheeses, onion and Worcestershire sauce in bowl, stirring well. Stir in 1/4 cup parsley and 1/2 cup pecans. Shape into a ball; wrap with waxed paper. Chill overnight. Roll in remaining pecans and parsley. Yield: 20 servings.

Helen Cohoe, Preceptor Gamma
Council Bluffs, Iowa

PINE CONE CHEESE BALL

16 ounces cream cheese, softened	1/2 envelope vegetable soup mix
1/2 cup sour cream	1 1/2 teaspoons garlic powder or 1 teaspoon Cajun spice
1 tablespoon mayonnaise	
1 tablespoon honey mustard	1 4-ounce can smoked almonds

Mix cream cheese, sour cream, mayonnaise, mustard, soup mix and garlic powder in bowl. Form into pine cone shape. Cover with smoked almonds. Place on serving plate; top with sprigs of pine or spruce. Yield: 12 servings.

Elaine DePlaunty, Preceptor Gamma Mu
Rochester, Michigan

HOLIDAY CHEESE BALL

16 ounces cream cheese, softened	1/4 to 1 cup drained crushed pineapple
2 tablespoons chopped green bell pepper	1 to 2 teaspoons seasoned salt
2 to 3 tablespoons finely chopped onion	2 cups chopped pecans

Mix cream cheese, green pepper, onion, pineapple, salt and 1 cup pecans in bowl. Shape into ball. Roll in remaining 1 cup pecans. Chill until firm; remove from refrigerator several minutes before serving. Yield: 12 to 15 servings.

Betty Hall, Preceptor Phi
Fort Pierce, Florida
*Helen Tomlin, Laureate Alpha Omega
Fort Pierce, Florida

SMOKED OYSTER CHEESE LOG

This cheese log is our favorite snack on Christmas tree trimming night.

16 ounces cream cheese, softened
2 tablespoons mayonnaise
1 teaspoon soy sauce
1 teaspoon Worcestershire sauce

Dash of Tabasco sauce
1 tablespoon grated onion
2 3-ounce cans smoked oysters, drained
Freshly chopped parsley
Assorted crackers

Mix cream cheese, mayonnaise, soy sauce, Worcestershire sauce, Tabasco sauce and onion in bowl. Spread on heavy-duty foil in 12-inch square. Mash oysters with fork; spread over cream cheese mixture. Chill for 1 hour or until firm. Roll up as for jelly roll. Chill until firm. Roll in chopped parsley just before serving. Place on serving plate. Serve with assorted crackers. Yield: 12 servings.

Elaine Vanderspek, Xi Gamma Tau
Mission, British Columbia, Canada

SALMON CHEESE BALL

1 15-ounce can salmon, drained, flaked
8 ounces cream cheese, softened
1 teaspoon lemon juice

1 tablespoon minced onion
1 teaspoon prepared horseradish
Chopped parsley

Combine salmon, cream cheese, lemon juice, onion and horseradish in bowl; mix well. Shape into ball; roll in parsley. Chill until firm.
Yield: 12 to 15 servings.

Ruth A. Tidd, Eta
Marion, Ohio

SPECIAL CHEESE BALLS

I make this for Christmas gifts for special friends.

1 pound sharp Cheddar cheese, shredded
1 pound mild Cheddar cheese, shredded
1 16-ounce jar Cheez Whiz
16 ounces cream cheese, softened

1 onion, chopped
2 tablespoons Worcestershire sauce
Chili powder
Chopped pecans

Let cheese stand at room temperature until softened. Combine cheeses, onion and Worcestershire sauce in bowl; mix well. Shape into 5 or 6 large balls. Sprinkle with chili powder; roll in pecans. Chill until firm.
Yield: 50 to 60 servings.

Jane Clarke, Alpha Zeta Omicron
Moscow, Texas

SUNSHINE CHEESE BALLS

8 ounces cream cheese, softened
2 cups sharp Cheddar cheese, shredded
1 8-ounce can crushed pineapple, drained

2 tablespoons chopped green onions
1/2 teaspoon curry powder
Crushed granola

Combine cheeses, pineapple, green onions and curry powder in bowl; mix well. Shape into 2 balls. Roll in granola. Chill until serving time.
Yield: 15 to 20 servings.

Barbara J. Neece, Xi Sigma Pi
San Diego, California

CRAB MEAT MOLD

1 teaspoon unflavored gelatin
3 tablespoons cold water
1 10-ounce can cream of mushroom soup
8 ounces cream cheese, softened

1 cup mayonnaise
1 cup finely chopped celery
3 green onions, finely chopped
1 6-ounce can crab meat, drained, flaked

Soften gelatin in cold water in small bowl; set aside. Heat soup and cream cheese over low heat in saucepan, stirring until smooth. Stir in gelatin. Heat until gelatin dissolves, stirring constantly. Add mayonnaise, celery, green onions and crab meat; mix well. Spoon into 6-cup mold. Chill until firm. Unmold onto serving plate before serving.
Yield: 20 servings.

Candice Bockmon, Epsilon Chi
Vancouver, Washington

CRAB MEAT MOUSSE

1 10-ounce can tomato soup
2 envelopes unflavored gelatin
1/4 cup cold water
8 ounces cream cheese, cubed
1/2 cup finely chopped celery

1/2 cup finely chopped onion
1 cup mayonnaise
1 5-ounce can crab meat, drained, flaked
Lettuce leaves

Heat soup in saucepan over low heat. Soften gelatin in cold water; stir into soup. Heat until gelatin dissolves, stirring constantly. Add cream cheese. Cook over low heat until cream cheese is melted, stirring frequently; remove from heat. Add celery, onion, mayonnaise and crab meat, mixing well. Pour into greased 5-cup mold. Chill overnight. Unmold onto serving plate lined with lettuce leaves.
Yield: 20 servings.

Margaret Cheek, Xi Delta Zeta
Etowah, Tennessee

NUTTY CHEESE SPREAD

3 tablespoons chopped
  almonds
3 tablespoons butter or
  margarine
6 tablespoons grated
  Parmesan cheese
3 tablespoons chopped
  parsley

3 tablespoons whipping
  cream or evaporated
  milk
Salt and pepper to taste
1 loaf cocktail rye bread

Preheat oven to 350 degrees. Sauté almonds in butter
in skillet until golden brown. Stir in next 5 ingredients. Spread on rye bread slices. Place on baking
sheet. Heat for 8 to 10 minutes or until bubbly. May
substitute pecans or walnuts for almonds.
Yield: 20 to 40 servings.

Mary Donaldson, Xi Kappa
Peterborough, New Hampshire

BROILED PATÉ

2 onions, sliced
8 ounces chicken livers
1 pound bacon
1 loaf sliced rye bread,
  cut into quarters

1 cup shredded Swiss
  cheese

Preheat broiler. Sauté onions in skillet until tender.
Add chicken livers. Sauté until cooked through. Fry
bacon in skillet until crisp; drain. Process onions,
livers and bacon in food processor for 10 seconds or
until well blended but not puréed. Spread on rye
bread squares. Sprinkle with Swiss cheese. Place on
baking sheet. Broil until cheese is melted. Serve immediately. Yield: 80 servings.

Ann Grassie Hall, Preceptor Beta Theta
Garden Grove, California

QUICKIE SHRIMP SPREAD

8 ounces cream cheese,
  softened
4 6-ounce cans shrimp,
  drained
2 tablespoons sour
  cream

1 tablespoon minced
  onion
1 teaspoon lemon juice
1/2 teaspoon salt
Dash of Tabasco sauce
Crackers

Combine cream cheese, shrimp, sour cream, onion,
lemon juice, salt and Tabasco sauce in bowl; mix
well. Spoon into serving bowl. Serve with crackers.
Yield: 12 to 15 servings.

Linda Scarborough, Xi Delta Gamma
Bealeton, Virginia

Rose La Fountain, Preceptor Alpha, Watertown, New York,
prepares Chili Cheese Dip by spreading 8 ounces cream
cheese over bottom and side of glass pie plate, adding a can of
chili without beans, topping with shredded Cheddar cheese
and microwaving until bubbly. Serve with nacho chips.

SHRIMP BUTTER

8 ounces cream cheese,
  softened
1/2 cup butter or
  margarine
1 small onion, grated
1/4 cup mayonnaise

1/4 cup lemon juice
1/4 cup Worcestershire
  sauce
1 8-ounce can cocktail
  shrimp, drained,
  crumbled

Combine all ingredients in blender container. Process
until smooth. Spoon into serving bowl; chill before
serving. Yield: 15 servings.

Carolyn E. Mitchell
Graniteville, South Carolina

SWISS DIP SPREAD

2 to 3 pounds Swiss
  cheese, grated
1 onion, grated

1 cup mayonnaise
1 round loaf rye or
  wheat bread

Combine cheese and onion with enough mayonnaise
to make of desired consistency in bowl. Chill,
covered, overnight. Slice off top of bread. Scoop out
center, leaving 1-inch shell; cut remaining bread into
cubes. Spoon cheese mixture into bread shell. Place
top over dip; place on serving plate. Arrange bread
cubes around plate. Yield: 20 to 30 servings.

Dorcas Lacey, Preceptor Chi
Myrtle Beach, South Carolina

WHEAT GERM CHEESE SPREAD

2 cups shredded sharp
  Cheddar cheese
1/2 cup chopped apples
1/2 cup chopped walnuts
1/2 cup chopped celery
1/2 cup shredded carrot
1/3 cup mayonnaise
2 tablespoons chopped
  raisins

2 tablespoons chopped
  dates
2 tablespoons chopped
  green bell pepper
1 tablespoon wheat germ
1 teaspoon lemon juice
1 teaspoon
  Worcestershire sauce
Wheat bread or crackers

Combine first 12 ingredients in bowl; mix well.
Spoon into serving bowl. Serve with wheat bread or
crackers. Yield: 30 to 40 servings.

Carol J. Irwin, Alpha Omega Xi
Boerne, Texas

ANGELS

White bread slices,
  crusts trimmed

Cream cheese, softened
Thinly sliced bacon

Preheat oven to 350 degrees. Spread bread with
cream cheese; roll up. Cut roll in half. Cut bacon
slices in half; wrap around rolls. Place on baking
sheet. Bake for 15 minutes. Increase temperature to
375 degrees. Bake until bacon is crisp.
Yield: Variable.

Audra Miller, Preceptor Alpha Upsilon
Bluefield, Virginia

CHEESY ARTICHOKE HEARTS

We used to serve this at our Friday night sing-alongs in Illinois. Lip smacking (or syncing) good!

2 8-count cans
   crescent rolls
3/4 cup shredded
   mozzarella cheese
3/4 cup grated Parmesan
   cheese

1/2 cup mayonnaise
1 14-ounce can
   artichoke hearts,
   drained, chopped
1 4-ounce can chopped
   green chilies

Preheat oven to 375 degrees. Unroll crescent roll dough; press into 10-by-15-inch baking pan, sealing perforations. Bake for 10 minutes. Combine remaining ingredients in bowl; mix well. Spread over prepared crust. Bake for 15 minutes. Let stand for 5 minutes before serving. Yield: 15 servings.

Kelly O'Brien, Xi Zeta Rho
Orangeville, Ontario, Canada

BACON SPREAD APPETIZERS

1 cup mayonnaise
1 teaspoon
   Worcestershire sauce
1/2 teaspoon salad
   seasoning
1/4 teaspoon paprika
2 cups shredded
   Cheddar cheese

8 slices crisp-fried
   bacon, crumbled
1/2 cup chopped peanuts
4 green onions, thinly
   sliced
7 English muffins, split

Preheat oven to 400 degrees. Combine first 4 ingredients in bowl. Stir in cheese, bacon, peanuts and green onions. Spread 3 tablespoons mixture over English muffin halves. Place on baking sheet. Bake for 10 minutes. Cut each muffin half into quarters. Serve hot. Yield: 56 servings.

Judy Hays, Xi Epsilon Theta
Melbourne Beach, Florida

❖ BACON TOMATO CUPS

1 10-count can
   biscuits
1 pound bacon, crisp-
   fried, crumbled
2 tomatoes, seeded,
   chopped

1 onion, chopped
6 ounces Swiss cheese,
   shredded
1 cup mayonnaise
2 teaspoons basil

Preheat oven to 375 degrees. Spray mini-muffin cups with nonstick cooking spray. Separate biscuits; cut into quarters. Spread out in prepared muffin cups. Combine remaining ingredients in bowl; mix well. Spoon mixture into muffin cups. Bake for 20 minutes; remove from oven. Spoon mixture which has overflowed back into muffin cups. Bake for 5 minutes longer. Cool in pan for 5 to 10 minutes before removing. May add two 6-ounce cans minced clams for variety. Yield: 40 servings.

Mary Ellen Sansone, Preceptor Xi
Wallingford, Connecticut

BLITZES

8 ounces cream cheese,
   softened
1 egg yolk
1/4 cup sugar
1/2 teaspoon vanilla
   extract

1 loaf white bread,
   crusts trimmed
1/2 cup melted margarine
2 teaspoons cinnamon
1 cup sugar

Mix cream cheese, egg yolk, 1/4 cup sugar and vanilla in bowl. Flatten bread slices. Spread with cream cheese mixture. Roll up as for jelly roll. Dip in melted margarine. Roll in mixture of cinnamon and 1 cup sugar. Place on baking sheet. Chill overnight. Preheat oven to 350 degrees. Bake for 20 minutes or until lightly browned. Yield: 8 to 10 servings.

Jeanne Curtis, Zeta Nu
Princeton, Missouri

WARMED CRANBERRY BRIE

1/3 cup crushed
   cranberry sauce
2 tablespoons brown
   sugar
1/4 teaspoon rum extract

1/8 teaspoon nutmeg
1 8-ounce round Brie
   cheese
1/4 cup chopped pecans
Crackers

Preheat oven to 500 degrees. Combine cranberry sauce, brown sugar, rum extract and nutmeg in bowl; mix well. Remove rind on top of Brie, leaving 1/4 inch rim. Top with cranberry mixture; sprinkle with pecans. Place in small shallow baking dish. Bake for 5 minutes. Serve with crackers. Yield: 15 servings.

Margaret N. Poston, Preceptor Delta Sigma
Tampa, Florida

❖ HOT WINGS WITH BLEU CHEESE DIP

15 chicken wings
1/2 cup butter or
   margarine
1 4-ounce bottle of
   Durkee's hot sauce
1 tablespoon vinegar
1 teaspoon
   Worcestershire sauce
1 envelope Ranch salad
   dressing mix

4 ounces bleu cheese,
   crumbled
1/4 cup sour cream
1/4 cup mayonnaise
1/8 teaspoon garlic
   powder
1/8 teaspoon onion
   powder

Preheat oven to 375 degrees. Rinse chicken wings; pat dry. Remove tips and disjoint. Melt butter in saucepan. Stir in next 3 ingredients. Dip wings in mixture. Place on baking sheet. Bake for 15 minutes; remove from oven. Dip in remaining sauce mixture; place on baking sheet. Sprinkle with salad dressing mix. Bake for 15 minutes longer. Combine bleu cheese, sour cream, mayonnaise, garlic powder and onion powder in small bowl; mix well. Chill before serving. Serve dip with hot wings. Yield: 15 servings.

Irene G. Berghoff, Laureate Alpha Kappa
Bethalto, Illinois

CRAB APPETIZERS

I am requested to bring this to every sorority social. They are superb!

1/2 cup butter or margarine	1 5-ounce jar Old English cheese spread
2 tablespoons mayonnaise	1/2 teaspoon garlic salt
1 7-ounce can crab meat, drained, flaked	6 English muffins, split

Preheat broiler. Combine butter, mayonnaise, crab meat, cheese and garlic salt in bowl; mix well. Spread over muffin halves. Cut each muffin into 6 wedges. Place on baking sheet. Broil for several minutes or until browned. Serve hot. May make ahead and freeze. Yield: 36 servings.

Dana L. Haley, Preceptor Mu
Mitchell, South Dakota

CRAB FRITTERS

Oil for deep frying	1 teaspoon minced onion
1 cup biscuit mix	Hot pepper sauce to taste
1/2 cup milk	1 7-ounce can crab meat, drained, flaked
1 egg, slightly beaten	
1/2 teaspoon salt	Cocktail sauce, soy sauce or tartar sauce
1/8 teaspoon pepper	

Preheat oil in deep fryer to 375 degrees. Mix next 8 ingredients in bowl. Drop by teaspoonfuls into hot oil. Fry until golden brown; drain. Serve on wooden picks with cocktail sauce, soy sauce or tartar sauce. Yield: 24 servings.

Anna Mary Hughes, Preceptor Delta Omega
Keytesville, Missouri

CRAB PUFF APPETIZERS

1 cup water	Pepper to taste
1/2 cup margarine	1 7-ounce can crab meat, drained, flaked
1 cup sifted all-purpose flour	
4 eggs	1/3 cup slivered almonds
8 ounces cream cheese, softened	2 tablespoons chopped onion
1/2 teaspoon cream-style horseradish	1/4 teaspoon Worcestershire sauce
1 tablespoon milk	1 2-ounce jar chopped pimento, drained
1/4 teaspoon salt	

Preheat oven to 400 degrees. Combine water and margarine in 3-quart saucepan. Bring to a boil. Add flour all at once, stirring constantly until dough pulls away from side of pan and forms a ball; remove from heat. Add eggs 1 at a time beating well after each addition until dough is shiny and smooth. Drop by level tablespoonfuls 2 inches apart onto baking sheet. Bake for 15 minutes or until golden brown and crisp. Cool on wire rack. Slice tops from puffs, removing dough inside. Combine cream cheese, horseradish, milk, salt and pepper in bowl; mix well. Stir in crab meat, almonds, onion, Worcestershire sauce and pimento. Fill puffs with mixture; replace tops. Serve hot. Yield: 36 servings.

Patricia R. Hamilton, Delta Eta
Arco, Idaho

MISSOURI CRAB GRASS

1/2 cup chopped onion	1 7-ounce can crab meat, drained, flaked
1/2 cup butter or margarine	
1 10-ounce package frozen chopped spinach, cooked, drained	3/4 cup grated Parmesan cheese
	Crackers

Sauté onion in butter in skillet until tender. Stir in spinach, crab meat and cheese. Cook over low heat until heated through, stirring frequently. Spoon into chafing dish. Serve with crackers. Yield: 20 servings.

Renée A. Anderson, Mu Epsilon
Jefferson City, Missouri

MAKE-AHEAD FONDUE CUBES

1 large loaf French bread	1/4 teaspoon garlic powder or onion salt
1/2 cup margarine	
8 ounces cream cheese, cubed	2 egg whites, stiffly beaten
8 ounces Cheddar cheese, shredded	

Cube French bread and set aside. Melt margarine and cream cheese in top of double boiler over boiling water. Stir in Cheddar cheese gradually until smooth. Add garlic powder. Remove from heat. Fold in beaten egg whites gently. Dip bread cubes into mixture; place on waxed paper. Let stand for 2 1/2 hours. Freeze in plastic bags. Place on baking sheet to serve. Warm in oven until heated through.
Yield: 6 to 8 servings.

Mary Lou Humber, Xi Upsilon Omicron
Hathaway Pines, California

WRAPPED GOUDA

Men really love this. I never have any leftovers.

1 8-ounce round Gouda cheese	1/2 of 8-count can crescent rolls
Grey Poupon mustard	Sesame seed

Preheat oven to 350 degrees. Remove waxed rind from cheese. Spread layer of mustard on top. Wrap crescent roll dough around cheese, sealing perforations. Sprinkle with sesame seed, pressing in gently. Place in greased round baking pan. Bake for 20 minutes. Let stand for 10 minutes. Slice and serve. Yield: 12 servings.

Patricia Severson, Laureate Omega
Clear Lake, Iowa

HAM AND CHEESE DELIGHTS

3 18-count packages
   brown and serve
   dinner rolls
1 onion, chopped
1 cup margarine
2 tablespoons
   Worcestershire sauce

3 tablespoons poppy seed
3 tablespoons Dijon
   mustard
12 to 16 ounces boiled
   ham, thinly sliced
9 to 12 ounces Swiss
   cheese, thinly sliced

Preheat oven to 350 degrees. Remove rolls from pans; slice in half horizontally. Replace bottom halves in pans. Combine next 5 ingredients in skillet. Sauté until onion is tender. Pour evenly over bottom halves of rolls. Layer with ham and cheese. Replace top layer of rolls. Bake, covered with foil, for 20 minutes. Cut into individual servings to serve. Yield: 54 servings.

Sallie Belperche, Preceptor Eta Chi
Winter Park, Florida
*Beverly Wells, Zeta Alpha
Sheridan, Arkansas

HAM AND CHEESE CRESCENT ROLL-UPS

2 8-count cans
   crescent rolls
8 slices ham
6 ounces soft cream
   cheese with onion
   and chives

1 egg, beaten
Sesame seed

Preheat oven to 375 degrees. Separate crescent roll dough into 8 rectangles, sealing perforations. Place 1 slice ham on each rectangle. Spread with cream cheese. Roll up, pinching seams. Brush with beaten egg; sprinkle with sesame seed. Cut each roll into 6 portions. Place on greased baking sheet. Bake for 12 to 17 minutes or until browned. Yield: 48 servings.

Chris Elm, Zeta Nu
Monroeville, Alabama

TINY HAM-FILLED TOMATOES

1 pint cherry tomatoes
1 4-ounce can deviled
   ham
2 tablespoons sour cream

2 tablespoons prepared
   horseradish

Slice tops from tomatoes. Remove pulp; drain shells upside down on paper towels. Combine remaining ingredients in small bowl; mix well. Spoon into tomatoes. Chill before serving. Yield: 20 servings.

Myrna Ratkovich, Xi Upsilon Omicron
Altaville, California

BOURBON HOT DOGS

1 pound hot dogs
3/4 cup bourbon
1/2 cup catsup
1 tablespoon grated
   onion

1/2 cup packed light
   brown sugar
1 teaspoon minced
   onion flakes

Cut hot dogs into bite-sized pieces. Mix remaining ingredients in large saucepan. Add hot dogs. Simmer on very low heat for 1 hour. Serve in chafing dish with wooden picks. Yield: 50 servings.

Diane Agansky, Preceptor Gamma Mu
Troy, Michigan

HOT DOG APPETIZERS

1 12-ounce jar chili
   sauce
1 6-ounce jar grape
   jelly

1 pound hot dogs, cut
   into bite-sized pieces

Combine chili sauce and grape jelly in glass bowl. Microwave on High for 1 to 2 minutes, stirring to blend. Add hot dogs to sauce. Microwave until hot dogs are heated through. Serve in chafing dish to keep warm. Yield: 50 servings.

Pam Overla
Brookeville, Ohio

CANDIED KIELBASA

2 pounds kielbasa
1 cup packed light
   brown sugar

1/2 cup catsup
1/4 cup prepared
   horseradish

Cut kielbasa into 1-inch slices. Combine brown sugar, catsup and horseradish in slow cooker; mix well. Add kielbasa. Cook on High until sauce begins to boil. Reduce temperature to Low. Cook, covered, for 35 to 50 minutes or until sauce thickens. Cook, uncovered, for 10 minutes longer.
Yield: 50 to 60 servings.

Nancy Taflan, Preceptor Chi
Myrtle Beach, South Carolina

COCKTAIL MEATBALLS

1 pound ground chuck
1 egg, slightly beaten
1/4 cup fine dry bread
   crumbs
1/2 onion, finely chopped
1 teaspoon salt
1/4 teaspoon pepper
2 tablespoons oil

1 teaspoon lemon juice
1 12-ounce jar chili
   sauce
1 10-ounce jar grape
   jelly
2 teaspoons light brown
   sugar

Preheat oven to 350 degrees. Combine ground chuck, egg, bread crumbs, onion, salt, pepper and oil in bowl; mix well. Shape into 1-inch balls; place on baking sheet. Bake for 30 minutes. Drain meatballs well. Combine lemon juice, chili sauce, grape jelly and brown sugar in saucepan; mix well. Bring to a boil, stirring constantly. Add meatballs. Simmer, covered, for 30 minutes, stirring occasionally. Serve warm. Yield: 35 servings.

Helen L. Graham, Xi Xi Xi
Corona, California

HONEY-GARLIC MEATBALLS

2 pounds ground beef	4 cloves of garlic,
1 cup fine bread crumbs	crushed
1/2 cup milk	1 tablespoon butter or
1/2 cup finely chopped	margarine
onion	3/4 cup catsup
2 eggs, beaten	1/2 cup honey
Salt to taste	1/4 cup soy sauce

Preheat oven to 500 degrees. Combine ground beef, bread crumbs, milk, onion, eggs and salt in bowl; mix well. Shape into 1-inch balls. Place in 9-by-13-inch baking pans. Bake for 10 to 12 minutes or until browned; drain. Sauté garlic in butter in large saucepan until tender. Add catsup, honey and soy sauce. Bring to a boil; reduce heat. Simmer, covered, for 5 minutes. Add meatballs to sauce. Simmer, uncovered, for 5 to 10 minutes, stirring occasionally. Yield: 100 meatballs.

Laurie McTaggart, Alpha Upsilon
Fort Frances, Ontario, Canada

STUFFED MUSHROOMS

24 large mushrooms	8 ounces cream cheese,
4 slices bacon, cut up	cubed
1/4 cup finely chopped	1/2 teaspoon
onion	Worcestershire sauce
1/4 cup finely chopped	1 cup soft bread crumbs
green bell pepper	

Remove stems from mushrooms and chop finely; set caps aside. Sauté bacon, onion and green pepper in skillet until bacon is crisp; drain. Add cream cheese and Worcestershire sauce. Cook over low heat until cheese is melted, stirring frequently. Add chopped mushroom stems and bread crumbs. Heat gently for 1 minute, stirring occasionally. Fill mushroom caps with stuffing mixture. Place on microwave-safe tray. Microwave on High for 4 minutes. Yield: 24 servings.

Rose Kasnick, Laureate Alpha Nu
The Dalles, Oregon

CLAM-STUFFED MUSHROOMS

24 mushrooms	2 ounces dry white wine
6 ounces scallions,	1 4-ounce jar chopped
chopped	pimentos, drained
1 clove of garlic, minced	Grated Parmesan cheese
1/4 cup butter or	Dry bread crumbs
margarine	Chopped parsley
1 6-ounce can minced	
clams, drained	

Preheat oven to 350 degrees. Remove stems from mushrooms and chop finely; set caps aside. Sauté stems, scallions and garlic in butter in skillet until tender. Add clams. Simmer for 10 minutes. Add wine and pimentos. Cook, covered, over low heat for 15 minutes, stirring occasionally. Fill mushroom caps with mixture. Sprinkle with cheese, bread crumbs and parsley. Place on baking sheet. Bake for 10 minutes or until lightly browned. Yield: 24 servings.

Marilyn Andreasen, Laureate Alpha Zeta
Cave Creek, Arizona

CRAB-STUFFED MUSHROOMS

12 medium mushrooms	3 tablespoons margarine
2 tablespoons chopped	1/3 cup flaked crab meat
green onions	1/2 cup stuffing mix
1 tablespoon chopped	Grated Parmesan cheese
green bell pepper	

Preheat broiler. Remove stems from mushrooms and chop finely; set caps aside. Sauté stems, green onions and green pepper in margarine in skillet until tender; remove from heat. Add crab meat and stuffing mix, mixing well. May add 1/2 teaspoon water if mixture appears dry. Fill mushroom caps with mixture; sprinkle with Parmesan cheese. Place on baking sheet. Broil for 1 minute or until browned on top. Reduce temperature to 350 degrees. Bake for 10 minutes longer. Yield: 6 servings.

Betty J. Bowers, Laureate Gamma Upsilon
Fort Worth, Texas

GOLDEN STUFFED MUSHROOMS

1 pound mushrooms	1/4 teaspoon
4 slices bacon, cut up	Worcestershire sauce
1/4 cup minced onion	1 tablespoon butter or
2 tablespoons minced	margarine
green bell pepper	1/2 cup soft bread crumbs
1/2 teaspoon salt	Celery salt and garlic
3 ounces cream cheese,	powder to taste
cubed	Grated Parmesan cheese

Preheat oven to 375 degrees. Remove stems from mushrooms and chop finely; set caps aside. Fry bacon in skillet until lightly browned. Add onion. Sauté until tender; drain. Combine sautéed mixture with next 4 ingredients in bowl; mix well. Fill mushroom caps with mixture. Mix butter and bread crumbs in baking pan. Bake for 5 to 8 minutes, stirring occasionally. Spoon over mushrooms; sprinkle with celery salt, garlic powder and Parmesan cheese. Place on baking sheet. Bake at 325 degrees for 20 minutes. Yield: 4 to 6 servings.

Sherri Russell, Preceptor Gamma Rho
Kankakee, Illinois

Pam East, Zeta Alpha, Sheridan, Arkansas, makes Wrapped Water Chestnuts by wrapping whole water chestnuts with half bacon strips, baking in preheated 350-degree oven for 30 minutes, dipping in mixture of 1 cup catsup and 1/2 cup packed brown sugar and baking for 15 minutes longer.

MUSHROOM STRUDEL

Makes a wonderful lunch with salad, fresh fruit and warm bread.

1 pound mushrooms, chopped	1/4 cup freshly chopped parsley
8 ounces cream cheese, softened	Juice of 1 lemon
1 teaspoon salt	1 cup melted butter or margarine
1 teaspoon pepper	10 phyllo leaves
1/2 cup sour cream	1/2 cup fine bread crumbs
1/2 cup plain yogurt	2 tablespoons poppy seed

Preheat oven to 375 degrees. Steam mushrooms in steamer. Drain and squeeze out excess water. Combine with cream cheese in bowl, stirring until cream cheese is melted. Add salt, pepper, sour cream, yogurt, parsley and lemon juice; mix well and set aside. Brush pastry board with melted butter. Spread out 1 leaf phyllo dough. Brush with melted butter; sprinkle with bread crumbs. Repeat using 4 more leaves to form rectangle. Spread half the mushroom filling over bottom half of dough rectangle. Roll up gently. Slash top diagonally 3 times. Sprinkle with poppy seed; place on baking sheet. Repeat procedure for remaining 5 leaves of phyllo dough. Bake for 25 minutes or until lightly browned. Yield: 4 to 8 servings.

Patricia R. Denton, Rho
Waynesboro, Virginia

SPICED PINEAPPLE PICK-UPS

I always serve these at our Christmas Open House and parties. They also make a great gift.

1 13-ounce can pineapple chunks	6 to 8 whole cloves
3/4 cup vinegar	2 sticks of cinnamon
1 1/4 cups sugar	Dash of salt

Drain pineapple, reserving 3/4 cup juice. Mix reserved juice, vinegar, sugar, cloves, cinnamon sticks and salt in saucepan. Simmer for 10 minutes, stirring occasionally. Add pineapple. Bring to a boil; remove from heat. Pour into large bowl. Store in refrigerator for 2 days; drain, reserving cloves and cinnamon for garnish. Serve with wooden picks. May add red food coloring. Yield: 6 to 8 servings.

Barbara Bills, Xi Alpha Alpha Theta
Snyder, Texas

MINI-SAUSAGE PUFFS

1 pound pork sausage	1/2 cup grated Parmesan cheese
8 ounces sharp Cheddar cheese, shredded	1 cup buttermilk biscuit mix
8 ounces Swiss cheese, shredded	1/2 cup hot salsa

Preheat oven to 350 degrees. Combine sausage, cheeses, biscuit mix and salsa in bowl; mix well.

Shape into 1-inch balls. Place on rack in shallow baking pan. Bake for 35 to 40 minutes or until lightly browned. Serve immediately. May freeze and reheat at 350 degrees for 10 minutes. Yield: 50 servings.

Paula Pascoe, Epsilon Phi
Abbotsford, British Columbia, Canada

RANCH SAUSAGE STARS

2 cups cooked crumbled sausage	1 4-ounce can sliced black olives, drained
1 1/2 cups shredded sharp Cheddar cheese	1/2 cup chopped red peppers
1 1/2 cups shredded Monterey Jack cheese	1 14-ounce package wonton wrappers
1 cup prepared Ranch salad dressing	Vegetable oil

Preheat oven to 350 degrees. Combine sausage, cheeses, salad dressing, olives and red peppers in bowl; mix well. Press wonton wrappers in greased muffin cups; brush with oil. Bake for 5 minutes or until golden brown. Remove from muffin cups. Place on baking sheet. Fill with sausage mixture. Bake for 5 minutes or until bubbly. Yield: 48 servings.

Linda Feterl, Preceptor Mu
Mitchell, South Dakota

COFFEE-SAUSAGE BALLS

A real treat for coffee lovers.

1 pound bulk sausage	3 cups brewed coffee

Preheat oven to 300 degrees. Shape sausage into 30 small balls. Place in 9-by-13-inch baking pan. Pour coffee over top. Bake for 2 hours, stirring occasionally. Remove to chafing dish. Serve with wooden picks. Yield: 30 servings.

Marguerite Feist, Mu Kappa
Ellinwood, Kansas

CEVICHE

1 pound mackerel or pompano filets	1/4 cup olive oil
Juice of 6 limes	1 tablespoon white vinegar
1 to 2 tomatoes, chopped	1/4 cup chopped cilantro or parsley
1 small onion, chopped	Salt and pepper to taste
2 jalapeño peppers, seeded, chopped	Green olives

Cut fish filets into small squares. Place in deep dish; cover with lime juice. Marinate in refrigerator for 6 hours, turning once. Drain, reserving marinade. Combine fish, tomatoes, onion, jalapeño peppers, oil, vinegar, cilantro, salt, pepper and reserved marinade in large bowl. Toss gently. Chill until serving time. Garnish with green olives. Yield: 6 servings.

Susana Jauregui, Delta Kappa Psi
San Marcos, California

SHRIMP REMOULADE

2 cups vinegar
1³/4 cups canola oil
1 teaspoon salt
2 teaspoons prepared
  mustard
1 teaspoon paprika
1 to 2 drops of Tabasco
  sauce
5 to 10 pounds cooked,
  shelled shrimp

3 stalks celery, cut into
  1-inch pieces
1 Bermuda onion,
  sliced, separated into
  rings
3 tablespoons parsley
  flakes

Process vinegar, oil, salt, mustard, paprika and Tabasco sauce in blender until smooth. Pour over mixture of shrimp, celery, onion and parsley in large deep bowl. Marinate in refrigerator for 2 to 3 days, stirring occasionally. Serve in sauce with wooden picks. Yield: 25 to 50 servings.

Jane Gerard, Preceptor Eta
Lebanon, New Hampshire

SPINACH AND CHEESE SNACKS

1/4 cup butter or
  margarine
3 eggs, beaten
1 cup all-purpose flour
1 cup milk
1 teaspoon baking
  powder

1 teaspoon salt
1 pound Monterey Jack
  cheese, shredded
2 10-ounce packages
  frozen chopped
  spinach, thawed,
  drained

Preheat oven to 350 degrees. Melt butter in 9-by-13-inch baking pan; set aside. Combine eggs, flour, milk, baking powder and salt in bowl; mix well. Add cheese and spinach. Spread mixture in prepared pan. Bake for 35 minutes; cool. Cut into squares. Yield: 15 to 20 servings.

Barbara E. Downs, Preceptor Epsilon Iota
Naperville, Illinois

"TIROTRIGONA" CHEESE-FILLED TRIANGLES

5 eggs, beaten
2 tablespoons milk
8 ounces feta cheese
8 ounces cottage cheese

16 ounces phyllo dough
12 ounces butter or
  margarine, melted

Preheat oven to 350 degrees. Beat eggs and milk in bowl. Add cheeses, stirring well. Cut phyllo dough into 2¹/2-inch squares; brush with melted butter. Place 1 tablespoon cheese filling on half the pastry square. Fold up to form triangle, sealing edges. Place on baking sheet. Brush with butter. Bake for 20 to 30 minutes or until golden brown. Yield: 12 to 16 servings.

Irene Diane Davis, Laureate Alpha Delta
Cobble Hill, British Columbia, Canada

TUNA ROLL-UPS

1 7-ounce can tuna,
  drained
4 ounces grated cheese
1 tablespoon finely
  minced onion
2 tablespoons lemon
  juice

³/4 teaspoon salt
Dash of pepper
1 tablespoon mustard
1/2 cup mayonnaise
1 loaf bread
Soft butter or margarine

Preheat oven to 425 degrees. Combine tuna, cheese, onion, lemon juice, salt, pepper, mustard and mayonnaise in bowl; mix well. Remove crust from bread slices; roll out thinly with rolling pin. Butter slices; spread with tuna mixture. Roll up as for jelly roll, pressing ends to enclose filling. Place on baking sheet covered with foil. Brush with butter. Bake for 15 minutes or until browned. May prepare ahead and freeze before baking. Yield: 20 servings.

Cynthia Garripoli, Sigma Lambda
New Lenox, Illinois

VEGETABLE PIZZA

1 8-count can
  crescent rolls
8 ounces cream cheese,
  softened
1/2 envelope ranch
  dressing mix
Dillweed and chives to
  taste

1/4 to 1/2 cup mayonnaise
Chopped broccoli,
  cauliflower, onion,
  green bell pepper and
  tomatoes
Sliced black olives

Preheat oven to 350 degrees. Spread crescent roll dough in baking pan, sealing perforations. Bake using package directions until lightly browned. Combine cream cheese, ranch dressing mix, dillweed, chives and mayonnaise in bowl; mix well. Spread over baked layer. Top with mixture of chopped vegetables. Cut into serving pieces. Yield: 8 to 10 servings.

Frances V. Coulter, Preceptor Beta
Seattle, Washington

VISTA BALLS

6 hard-cooked eggs,
  chopped
2 to 6 slices crisp-fried
  bacon, crumbled
1 tablespoon minced
  onion
1/2 teaspoon salt

1/4 teaspoon pepper
1/4 teaspoon prepared
  mustard
1/4 cup mayonnaise
Shredded Cheddar
  cheese
Paprika

Combine eggs, bacon, onion, salt, pepper, mustard and mayonnaise in bowl; mix well. Shape into ³/4-inch balls. Roll in cheese. Sprinkle with paprika. Chill until firm. Yield: 18 to 20 servings.

Sharon Duiguid, Xi Lambda Sigma
Royalton, Illinois

ZUCCHINI APPETIZERS

3 cups thinly sliced zucchini	1/2 teaspoon each salt and seasoned salt
1 cup biscuit mix	1/2 teaspoon dried
1/2 cup chopped onion	marjoram or oregano
1/2 cup grated Parmesan cheese	Dash of pepper
2 tablespoons snipped parsley	1 clove of garlic, minced
	1/2 cup vegetable oil
	4 eggs, slightly beaten

Preheat oven to 350 degrees. Combine all ingredients in large bowl; mix well. Spread in greased 9-by-13-inch baking pan. Bake for 25 minutes or until golden brown. Cut into 2-inch squares. Yield: 48 servings.

Carol Zeiss, Xi Kappa Epsilon
St. Peters, Missouri

CRANBERRY TEA

1 pint fresh cranberries	1 6-ounce can frozen lemonade concentrate
2 cups sugar	
10 whole cloves	1 6-ounce can frozen orange juice concentrate
1 4-ounce package red hot cinnamon candies	

Combine first 4 ingredients in saucepan. Cook, covered, until cranberries pop and candy is melted. Strain through sieve. Add concentrates; mix well. Mix 1 cup cranberry mixture with 2 cups water to serve. Serve hot. Yield: 6 servings.

Pauline Siffring, Gamma Beta
Bellwood, Nebraska

RED HOT CRANBERRY SIPPER

1 quart fresh cranberries	10 whole cloves
1 quart water	1 quart water
3 1/2 cups sugar	Juice of 3 oranges
1/2 cup red hot cinnamon candies	Juice of 3 lemons

Combine cranberries and 1 quart water in large saucepan. Cook, covered, until cranberries split. Strain through sieve, reserving juice. Combine sugar, candies, cloves and remaining 1 quart water in saucepan. Cook until candies are melted and sugar is dissolved. Add juices; mix well. Mix 1 part base with 1 part water to serve. Serve hot. Yield: 24 servings.

Brenda Mansel Reno, Xi Zeta Eta
St. John, Kansas

SNOW BEARS

2 quarts eggnog	1/2 cup Amaretto
1/2 gallon vanilla ice cream	Nutmeg to taste

Combine first 3 ingredients in large container; mix well. Stir in nutmeg. Yield: 10 servings.

Sennie Rhoades, Preceptor Lambda Xi
Lamesa, Texas

ESPRESSO EGGNOG PUNCH

1/4 cup instant espresso coffee	1 pint coffee-flavored ice cream, softened
1 cup boiling water	2 cups half and half
2 cups ice water	3 egg whites, lightly beaten
3 egg yolks	
1 cup coffee-flavored liqueur	Grated chocolate

Mix coffee and boiling water in bowl. Stir in ice water. Chill thoroughly. Beat egg yolks in mixer bowl at high speed until thick and lemon-colored. Add liqueur slowly, beating at medium speed until mixed. Pour into punch bowl. Add coffee mixture, ice cream and half and half; mix gently. Fold in egg whites. Garnish with grated chocolate. Yield: 18 servings.

Janet Cuslidge, Xi Upsilon Omicron
Murphy, California

HOMEMADE EGGNOG

This recipe has been handed down in our family for 4 generations. I did not know eggnog was served cold until we moved to Texas.

1 gallon milk	6 to 8 egg whites, stiffly beaten
6 to 8 egg yolks	
2 to 3 cups sugar	Bourbon, rum or brandy to taste
1/8 cup cinnamon	
1 teaspoon nutmeg	

Heat milk in large saucepan; do not boil. Mix egg yolks, sugar, cinnamon and nutmeg in bowl. Add a small amount of milk gradually until mixture is thin. Add remaining milk; mix well. Fold in egg whites. Stir in liquor. Yield: 8 to 20 servings.

R. Azalynn Mauldin, Preceptor Beta Tau
Dallas, Texas

OLD-FASHIONED EGGNOG

This has become a favorite at our Christmas party. I have rum and brandy that members may add.

1/2 cup sugar	1/4 cup sugar
10 egg yolks, beaten	1 cup whipping cream, whipped
1 quart scalded milk	
1/2 teaspoon salt	Grated nutmeg to taste
10 egg whites	

Mix 1/2 cup sugar and egg yolks in top of double boiler. Stir in milk gradually. Cook over hot water until mixture coats spoon, stirring constantly. Chill thoroughly. Add salt to egg whites in mixer bowl; beat until soft peaks form. Add remaining 1/4 cup sugar gradually, beating until stiff peaks form. Fold egg whites and whipped cream into milk mixture separately. Chill for several hours. Pour into punch bowl. Sprinkle with nutmeg. Yield: 30 servings.

Shirley L. McMillan, Delta Delta Eta
Lake Isabella, California

BANANA SMASH PUNCH

1 12-ounce can frozen
    orange juice
    concentrate
3 cups sugar
6 cups water
5 or 6 ripe bananas,
    mashed
2 tablespoons lemon
    juice

1 46-ounce can
    unsweetened pineapple
    juice
1 2-liter bottle of
    Squirt
Vodka to taste

Prepare orange juice using package directions. Bring sugar and water to a boil in saucepan. Simmer for 5 minutes. Cool completely. Mix bananas and lemon juice in large bowl. Stir in orange juice. Add pineapple juice and sugar mixture; mix well. Fill 5 or 6 freezer containers 3/4 full with punch. Freeze completely. Let stand at room temperature for 2 hours before serving. Combine fruit mixture with Squirt in punch bowl; mix well. Stir in vodka.
Yield: 30 to 40 servings.

Amy McGillvary, Mu Sigma
Mt. Pleasant, Michigan

CHAMPAGNE PUNCH

This is quite delicious and is not as intoxicating as one would think. We use it at some special sorority socials.

1 10-ounce package
    frozen peaches,
    partially thawed
1 10-ounce package
    frozen strawberries,
    partially thawed
1 10-ounce package
    frozen blueberries,
    partially thawed

1 6-ounce bottle of
    lemon juice
1 46-ounce can
    pineapple juice
3 bottles of sparkling
    white wine
Orange slices

Combine peaches, strawberries, blueberries, lemon juice and pineapple juice in large punch bowl. Add wine; mix well. Let stand for 30 minutes, stirring occasionally. Garnish with orange slices. Add more juice or wine as needed. Yield: 50 servings.

Linda Nicol, Xi Gamma Eta
Fernie, British Columbia, Canada

CRAN-APPLE PUNCH

Ice ring
8 cups chilled cran-
    apple juice

2 liters chilled ginger ale
1 quart orange sherbet

Place ice ring in punch bowl. Pour juice and ginger ale gently over ice ring. Add small scoops of sherbet. Stir gently. Serve immediately. Yield: 25 servings.

Rose M. Custer, Preceptor Gamma Pi
Little Orleans, Maryland

CRANBERRY PUNCH

1 1/2 cups water
1 cup sugar
3 cups cranberry juice
1 cup grapefruit juice

1/3 cup lemon juice
3 cups ginger ale
Lemon slices

Bring water and sugar to a boil in saucepan. Simmer until of syrup consistency. Add juices; mix well. Cool completely. Combine with ginger ale and ice in large pitcher or bowl. Garnish with lemon slices. Serve cold. Yield: 10 to 12 servings.

Vivian Hodgson, Laureate Epsilon
Yorkton, Saskatchewan, Canada

❖ GOLDEN PUNCH

This recipe won a contest at my place of employment for the best non-alcoholic drink to be served during the holiday season.

1 24-ounce bottle of
    apple juice
1 16-ounce bottle of
    non-alcoholic
    sparkling white grape
    juice

1 12-ounce can frozen
    apple juice concentrate
1 2-liter bottle of
    lemon-lime soda
1 1-liter bottle of club
    soda

Pour bottled apple juice into gelatin mold for ice ring. Freeze completely. Combine remaining ingredients in punch bowl; mix well. Add ice ring.
Yield: 28 servings.

Janet Clarke, Xi Kappa Gamma
Dayton, Ohio

ORANGE PUNCH

2 12-ounce cans frozen
    orange juice
    concentrate
1 48-ounce can
    pineapple juice

1/2 gallon orange sherbet
1 2-liter bottle of
    ginger ale

Prepare orange juice using package directions. Pour half the juice into mold to make ice ring. Combine remaining orange juice, pineapple juice and sherbet in punch bowl; mix well. Add ice ring. Stir in enough ginger ale to fill bowl. Add additional ginger ale as needed. Yield: 25 servings.

Susan Hood, Preceptor Alpha Zeta
Brantford, Ontario, Canada

SANGRIA

1 bottle of dry red wine
1 bottle of ginger ale
1/2 cup sugar

4 jiggers of brandy
Fruit slices

Combine wine, ginger ale, sugar and brandy in bowl; mix well. Add favorite sliced fruit and lots of ice. Yield: 6 servings.

Susan Clark, Zeta Eta
Derby, Kansas

STRAWBERRY PUNCH

1 12-ounce can frozen orange juice concentrate	1¹/2 quarts boiling water 6 cups sugar 3 quarts cold water
1 6-ounce can frozen lemon juice concentrate	4 12-ounce packages frozen strawberries
8 tablespoons tea	4 quarts ginger ale

Prepare orange juice and lemon juice using package directions. Steep tea in boiling water for 5 minutes. Add sugar, stirring until dissolved. Cool completely. Stir in cold water. Add juices and strawberries; mix well. Stir in ginger ale. Serve cold.
Yield: 20 to 30 servings.

Carol Wehrbein, Xi Beta Gamma
Lincoln, Nebraska

FRIENDSHIP TEA

1 10-ounce package red hot cinnamon candies, crushed	2 cups Tang powder 1¹/2 cups sugar 2 teaspoons ground cloves
1 cup instant tea powder 1 cup instant tea with lemon powder	2 teaspoons ground cinnamon

Combine all ingredients in bowl; mix well. Mix 1 to 2 spoonfuls with 1 cup hot water to serve.
Yield: 80 to 100 servings.

Pamela Cunningham, Omega Epsilon
Tampa, Florida

FRUITED MINT TEA

3 cups boiling water	¹/4 cup lemon juice
4 tea bags	1 cup orange juice
12 fresh mint sprigs	5 cups water
1 cup sugar	Orange slices

Pour boiling water over tea bags and mint. Steep, covered, for 5 minutes. Remove and discard tea bags and mint. Add next 4 ingredients; mix well. Serve over ice. Garnish with orange slices.
Yield: 10 to 12 servings.

Patricia N. Long, Epsilon Kappa
State Road, North Carolina

NANCY'S FRUIT TEA

7 tea bags	1 6-ounce can frozen pineapple juice concentrate
1 quart boiling water	
¹/2 cup Tang powder	
¹/4 cup lemon juice	¹/2 cup sugar

Steep tea bags in boiling water. Pour into 1-gallon container. Stir in Tang. Add lemon juice, pineapple juice concentrate and sugar; mix well. Add enough water to fill container. Yield: 20 servings.

Betty Nash, Preceptor
Elkhorn, West Virginia

WASSAIL

2 gallons apple cider	1 cup sugar
2 cups orange juice	1 cinnamon stick
1 cup lemon juice	1 teaspoon whole cloves
1 cup pineapple juice	

Combine cider, juices, sugar, cinnamon and cloves in large saucepan. Simmer until hot. Strain through sieve. Serve hot. Yield: 50 to 75 servings.

Julia Gonzales, Phi Theta Gamma
Stephenville, Texas

HOLIDAY WASSAIL

This holiday beverage is a tradition for get-togethers at Christmas. It also makes your house smell good!

6 cups apple juice	1 46-ounce can unsweetened pineapple juice
1 cinnamon stick	
¹/4 teaspoon nutmeg	
¹/4 cup honey	1 orange studded with cloves
3 tablespoons lemon juice	

Combine apple juice and cinnamon stick in saucepan. Bring to a boil. Simmer for 5 minutes. Add remaining ingredients. Cook until heated through. Remove and discard orange and cinnamon stick. Serve hot. Yield: 12 servings.

Beverly A. Addis, Alpha Tau
Columbus, Indiana

HOT WASSAIL

My husband's Aunt Marcia concocted this recipe. Having it published will be a nice memorial to her.

1 quart cranberry juice	¹/2 cup lemon juice
1 quart apple cider	1 cup (or more) sugar
1 quart tea	12 whole cloves
2 cups orange juice	Cinnamon sticks

Combine all ingredients in coffee maker or slow cooker. Simmer until heated through; do not boil. Remove and discard cloves and cinnamon sticks. May add rum. Yield: 30 servings.

Mary Pat Willis, Delta Rho
Plainfield, Indiana

SORORITY HOT WINE

1 quart cranberry juice	12 whole cloves
2 cups water	2 quarts Burgundy, rosè or Chianti
1¹/2 cups sugar	
1 cinnamon stick	¹/2 cup lemon juice

Combine cranberry juice, water, sugar, cinnamon and cloves in saucepan. Bring to a boil. Add wine and lemon juice. Cook until heated through.
Yield: 25 to 30 servings.

Deanell Backlund, Preceptor Mu
Mitchell, South Dakota

All Souped-Up

AUTUMN SOUP

1 pound ground beef	1 teaspoon pepper
1 cup chopped onion	1 bay leaf
4 cups water	1/8 teaspoon basil
1 cup chopped carrots	1 quart whole tomatoes
1 cup chopped celery	1 14-ounce can beef
1 cup cubed potatoes	consommé
2 teaspoons salt	

Brown ground beef in skillet, stirring until crumbly; drain. Sauté onion in skillet until tender. Combine ground beef, onion, water, carrots, celery, potatoes, salt, pepper, bay leaf, basil, tomatoes and consommé in large saucepan. Bring to a slow boil. Cook for 30 minutes; reduce heat. Simmer for 2 hours longer. Remove bay leaf before serving. Yield: 10 servings.

Jo Ann Hofhine
Pocatello, Idaho

BEER-CHEESE SOUP

1/2 cup butter or	1/2 cup all-purpose flour
margarine	1/4 cup chives
4 cups chicken broth	1 16-ounce jar Cheez
1 1/2 cups light cream	Whiz
6 ounces beer	1 teaspoon
1/2 teaspoon yellow	Worcestershire sauce
food coloring	

Combine butter, broth, cream, beer, food coloring, flour, chives, Cheez Whiz and Worcestershire sauce in large saucepan; mix with wire whisk. Simmer gently until heated through, stirring frequently; do not boil. Yield: 10 to 12 servings.

Karla Edwards, Xi Eta
Omaha, Nebraska

CHEESE SOUP

4 cups water	1 10-ounce can cream
5 chicken bouillon	of mushroom soup
cubes	1 10-ounce can cream
1 cup chopped onion	of chicken soup
1 cup chopped celery	2 soup cans water
2 1/2 cups cubed	1 4-ounce can sliced
potatoes	mushrooms, drained
1 16-ounce package	16 ounces Velveeta
frozen mixed carrots,	cheese, cubed
broccoli and	
cauliflower	

Combine 4 cups water, bouillon cubes, onion, celery and potatoes in large saucepan. Simmer for 10 minutes, stirring occasionally. Add mixed vegetables. Cook for 10 minutes longer. Add mushroom and chicken soups, 2 cans water and mushrooms. Simmer until heated through. Add Velveeta cheese. Cook over low heat until cheese is melted, stirring frequently. May freeze leftovers.
Yield: 12 to 14 servings.

Rose Richardson, Xi Delta Epsilon
Fort Dodge, Iowa

Patricia Kurtz, Beta Epsilon, Portland, New York, makes Broccoli Cheese Soup by cooking and draining frozen broccoli, blending 1/4 cup melted butter with 2 tablespoons cornstarch and one 10-ounce can chicken broth in saucepan and bringing to a boil, stirring constantly. Then add 1 quart milk, broccoli, salt, pepper, 1/4 teaspoon garlic powder and 4 ounces Cheez Whiz. Heat until cheese melts, stirring constantly.

BENNETT'S BEST CHILI

I won 3rd place in the Compadres Chili Cook-Off in April 1992 with this recipe.

2¹/2 pounds ground beef	1 6-ounce can tomato
1 pound ground pork	paste
3 cloves of garlic,	1 15-ounce can tomato
minced	purée
6 onions, chopped	1 tablespoon fresh
1¹/2 tablespoons olive	oregano
oil	1¹/2 tablespoons each
1¹/2 stalks celery,	cumin, chili powder,
chopped	cilantro and coriander
1 14-ounce can beef	Salt and pepper to taste
broth	
1 10-ounce jar chili	
sauce	

Brown ground beef, ground pork, garlic and onions in olive oil in large soup kettle, stirring until ground beef and pork are crumbly; drain. Add remaining ingredients. Simmer for 2 hours, stirring occasionally. Serve over beans, rice, noodles or spaghetti. May add Tabasco sauce, chili peppers or other spices for desired taste. Yield: 16 servings.

Wendy Bennett, Xi Pi Rho
Napa, California

BLACK BEAN CHILI

3 tablespoons vegetable	2 teaspoons ground
oil	cumin
1 pound chorizo or	1 teaspoon salt
kielbasa, cut into	¹/2 teaspoon freshly
¹/2-inch slices	ground pepper
1¹/2 pounds ground beef	2 16-ounce cans black
1¹/2 pounds ground pork	beans, rinsed, drained
3 onions, chopped	3 cups kernel corn
2 large green bell	40 stuffed green olives,
peppers, chopped	cut into halves
3 cloves of garlic,	Chopped avocado
chopped	Chopped onion
3 jalapeño peppers,	Shredded Cheddar
seeded, chopped	cheese
2 14-ounce cans peeled	Shredded Monterey Jack
tomatoes	cheese
1 12-ounce can beer	Chopped fresh coriander
2 tablespoons chili	Taco chips
powder	

Heat 1 tablespoon oil over medium heat in large soup kettle. Add chorizo. Cook for 10 minutes until browned; remove with slotted spoon to drain. Brown ground beef and ground pork with 1 tablespoon oil in kettle, stirring until crumbly; remove meat and set aside. Sauté onions, bell peppers, garlic and jalapeño peppers in remaining 1 tablespoon oil in kettle for 5 minutes or until tender. Return chorizo, ground beef and ground pork to kettle. Add tomatoes, beer, chili powder, cumin, salt and pepper. Cook over low heat

for 1 hour, stirring occasionally. Stir in black beans, corn and olives. Cook for 15 minutes longer. Ladle into soup bowls; garnish with avocado, onion, cheeses, coriander and chips. Yield: 8 to 10 servings.

Mary Lee Shell, Preceptor Delta Sigma
Temple Terrace, Florida

BLACK HILLS CHILI

2 pounds ground beef	2 tablespoons sugar
1 cup chopped onion	1 bay leaf
1¹/2 cups chopped celery	1 teaspoon salt
¹/2 cup chopped green	1 teaspoon marjoram
bell pepper	¹/2 teaspoon garlic
1 to 2 15-ounce cans	powder
chili beans	1 teaspoon chopped
1 15-ounce can	jalapeño pepper
chopped tomatoes	(optional)
1 15-ounce can tomato	
sauce	

Brown ground beef, onion, celery and bell pepper in large saucepan, stirring until ground beef is crumbly; drain. Add remaining ingredients. Simmer for 3 hours, stirring occasionally. Remove bay leaf before serving. May add tomato juice cocktail for desired consistency. Yield: 10 to 12 servings.

Janis Fisher, Alpha Mu
Rapid City, South Dakota

BAKER'S HOT AND SPICY CHILI

This makes such a large batch that we invite our friends and family over for a card party to eat it up.

5 pounds ground beef	2 16-ounce jars salsa
5 medium onions,	2 15-ounce cans Cajun
chopped	stewed tomatoes
1 tablespoon chili	3 pounds Cheddar
powder	cheese, shredded
1 tablespoon seasoned	2 pounds pinto beans,
pepper	cooked
¹/2 tablespoon garlic	2 tablespoons chili
powder	powder
Salt to taste	2 tablespoons seasoned
5 quarts tomato juice	pepper
4 10-ounce cans Ro-Tel	¹/2 tablespoon garlic
tomatoes	powder

Brown ground beef in large skillet, stirring until crumbly; drain. Combine onions, 1 tablespoon chili powder, 1 tablespoon seasoned pepper, ¹/2 tablespoon garlic powder and salt in 20-quart kettle. Add ground beef, tomato juice, Ro-Tel tomatoes, salsa and stewed tomatoes. Simmer for 1 hour or more, stirring occasionally. Add cheese, beans and remaining seasonings. Simmer until heated through and cheese is melted. Yield: 64 servings.

Donald T. Baker, Eta Beta
Shelbina, Missouri

CHILI

3 pounds ground beef	2 6-ounce cans tomato
2 to 3 medium onions,	paste
chopped	1¹/2 quarts water
1 green bell pepper,	Salt and pepper to taste
chopped	2 to 3 tablespoons chili
1 to 2 cloves of garlic,	powder
chopped	2 15-ounce cans chili
¹/2 teaspoon oregano	beans
¹/4 teaspoon cumin seed	

Brown ground beef in 6-quart kettle, stirring until crumbly; drain. Add onions, bell pepper, garlic, oregano, cumin seed, tomato paste, water, salt, pepper and chili powder; mix well. Simmer for 1¹/2 hours, stirring occasionally. Stir in chili beans. Simmer for 30 minutes longer, adding water for desired consistency. Let stand for several hours before serving. Yield: 24 servings.

Jeanie Felts, Preceptor Alpha Epsilon
Siloam Springs, Arkansas

FAST AND EASY CHILI

2 medium onions,	¹/2 cup catsup
chopped	1 15-ounce can tomato
1 green bell pepper,	sauce
chopped	1 tablespoon chili
1 tablespoon vegetable	powder
oil	2 teaspoons salt
2 pounds ground beef	¹/4 teaspoon pepper
1 16-ounce can	2 15-ounce cans red
tomatoes	kidney beans, drained

Sauté onions and green pepper in oil in large saucepan until tender; drain. Brown ground beef in same saucepan, stirring until crumbly; drain. Add tomatoes, catsup, tomato sauce, chili powder, salt, pepper and beans. Bring to a boil; reduce heat. Simmer for 30 minutes. May add more chili powder or Tabasco sauce for spicier chili. Yield: 10 to 12 servings.

Debbie Young, Mu Lambda
Tarkio, Missouri

HOMEMADE CHILI

2 pounds lean ground	3 tablespoons chili
beef	powder
1 large onion, chopped	2 tablespoons cumin
1 green bell pepper,	1 29-ounce can tomato
chopped	sauce
2 to 3 stalks celery,	2 cups boiling water
chopped	1 15-ounce can ranch-
1 teaspoon salt	style beans
Pepper and minced	
garlic to taste	

Brown ground beef in skillet, stirring until crumbly; drain. Sauté onion, green pepper and celery in small skillet until tender. Combine ground beef, sautéed vegetables, salt, pepper, garlic, chili powder, cumin, tomato sauce and water in large saucepan; mix well. Simmer for 1 hour, stirring occasionally. Add beans. Simmer for 15 minutes longer. Yield: 8 to 10 servings.

Virginia Brown, Laureate Nu
Conway, Arkansas

MOM'S CHILI

1 pound ground beef	¹/2 green bell pepper,
1 28-ounce can crushed	chopped
tomatoes	¹/2 onion, chopped
1 28-ounce can tomato	1 4-ounce can
purée	mushrooms
1 8-ounce can tomato	2 teaspoons chili
paste	powder
2 16-ounce cans kidney	1 teaspoon minced garlic
beans, drained	1 teaspoon oregano
4 ounces pepperoni,	Salt and pepper to taste
sliced (optional)	

Brown ground beef in skillet, stirring until crumbly; drain. Combine with tomatoes, purée, tomato paste, beans, pepperoni, green pepper, onion and mushrooms with juice in slow cooker. Stir in chili powder, garlic, oregano, salt and pepper. Simmer, covered, 5 to 8 hours, stirring occasionally. Yield: 10 servings.

Juliana L. Williams, Xi Alpha Rho
Waterville, Maine

WHITE CHILI

1 pound dried Great	1¹/2 teaspoons dried
Northern beans	oregano, crumbled
2 medium onions,	¹/4 teaspoon cayenne
chopped	pepper
1 tablespoon olive oil	6 cups chicken stock
4 cloves of garlic,	3 cups chopped cooked
minced	chicken breasts
2 4-ounce cans	3 cups shredded
chopped green chilies,	Monterey Jack cheese
drained	Salt and black pepper
2 teaspoons ground	to taste
cumin	Sour cream

Rinse beans. Soak in enough water to cover overnight; drain. Sauté onions in oil in large kettle until tender. Add garlic, chilies, cumin, oregano and cayenne pepper. Sauté for 2 minutes, stirring frequently. Add beans and chicken stock. Bring to a boil; reduce heat. Simmer for 2 hours or until beans are tender, stirring occasionally. Add chicken, 1 cup cheese, salt and black pepper to taste. Simmer until cheese is melted, stirring occasionally. Ladle into soup bowls. Top with remaining cheese and sour cream. May substitute two 16-ounce cans Great Northern beans for dried beans.
Yield: 8 to 10 servings.

Joan Domingue, Zeta Eta
Port Neches, Texas

KRENTJE BREI (Currant Soup)

This recipe is from my late mother-in-law who translated it for me from her native Dutch language.

1/4 cup pre-soaked pearl barley	8 cups water
1 cup currants	1/2 cup sugar
1 to 1 1/2 cups raisins	1 3-ounce package black currant gelatin

Combine first 4 ingredients in large saucepan. Bring to a boil; reduce heat. Simmer over low heat until raisins and currants soften and plump up. Increase heat to high. Add sugar, stirring vigorously. Stir in gelatin; remove from heat. Let stand until cool. Chill overnight; serve cold. Yield: 6 to 8 servings.

Evelyn M. Sennema, Laureate Gamma Delta
Windsor, Ontario, Canada

❖ CHICKEN-CORN CHOWDER

My sister-in-law and I were visiting friends in London who served this up on a cold, blustery October evening.

1 1/2 pounds chicken breast filets, skinned	3 potatoes, cubed
4 1/2 cups frozen whole kernel corn, thawed	1 1/2 quarts chicken stock
2 ounces lean salt pork or bacon, chopped	7 cups whipping cream
6 tablespoons butter or margarine	2 1/4 teaspoons salt
1 cup chopped celery	1/8 teaspoon white pepper
1 cup chopped onion	Black pepper to taste
	3 tablespoons finely chopped fresh parsley

Rinse chicken and pat dry. Cut into 1/2-inch cubes; set aside. Reserve 2 1/2 cups corn. Process remaining 2 cups corn in blender until puréed. Sauté pork in 6-quart saucepan until browned. Add butter, celery and onion. Sauté until tender. Add chicken, puréed corn and reserved corn. Cook until chicken is cooked through. Add potatoes and chicken stock. Bring to a boil; reduce heat. Simmer, partially covered, over low heat for 30 minutes or until potatoes and corn are tender. Add cream. Simmer for 2 to 3 minutes. Season with salt and peppers; garnish with parsley. Yield: 6 to 8 servings.

Belva L. Novodvorsky, Laureate Sigma
Long Beach, California

HOME-STYLE CHICKEN NOODLE SOUP

1 4-pound fryer chicken	1 teaspoon seasoned salt
12 cups water	1 bay leaf
3 teaspoons chicken bouillon granules	1/4 teaspoon celery salt
1 1/2 teaspoons salt	1/4 teaspoon basil
3/4 teaspoon pepper	1 large green bell pepper, chopped
1 1/2 teaspoons onion powder	4 carrots, chopped
1/4 teaspoon garlic powder	1 8-ounce package wide egg noodles
	1 1/2 cups milk

Rinse chicken and pat dry. Cover with water in large kettle. Add bouillon and seasonings. Bring to a boil; reduce heat. Simmer for 1 hour or until chicken is tender. Remove chicken, reserving broth; let stand to cool. Cut into bite-sized pieces, discarding skin and bones; set aside. Add bell pepper and carrots to reserved broth. Boil for 8 minutes. Add noodles. Cook until tender. Add chicken and milk. Simmer over low heat for 5 minutes longer. Remove bay leaf before serving. Yield: 10 servings.

Debra Ezell, Xi Zeta Lambda
Ft. Stockton, Texas

CHICKEN GUMBO

3/4 cup canola oil	1 cup chopped onion
1 cup all-purpose flour	3 cloves of garlic, chopped
3 pounds chicken, skinned	1/2 cup sliced green onions
1 gallon water	Seasonings to taste
1/2 cup chopped green bell pepper	Cooked rice

Heat oil in skillet over low heat. Add flour gradually. Cook until roux is smooth and dark brown, stirring constantly; remove from heat. Place paper towels over roux to remove excess oil. Rinse chicken and pat dry. Bring water to a boil in large kettle. Add chicken and next 4 ingredients. Bring to a boil; reduce heat. Stir in roux; add seasonings to taste. Simmer for 45 minutes. Serve over rice. Yield: 8 to 10 servings.

Brenda Boudreaux, Xi Beta Omega
New Iberia, Louisiana

MICROWAVE CHICKEN AND SAUSAGE GUMBO

2/3 cup canola oil	3 cups chicken stock
2/3 cup all-purpose flour	4 cups hot water
2 cups chopped onion	2 teaspoons salt
1 cup chopped celery	1/2 teaspoon black pepper
1/2 cup chopped green bell pepper	1/4 teaspoon cayenne pepper
4 cloves of garlic, chopped	2 cups chopped cooked chicken
1/4 cup chopped parsley	1 pound link sausage, cut into small pieces
1/4 cup chopped green onions	Cooked rice
Hot water	

Mix oil and flour in 4-cup microwave-safe bowl. Microwave on High for 6 to 7 minutes or until dark brown, stirring frequently. Add onion, celery and green pepper. Microwave for 3 minutes longer; stir. Add garlic, parsley and green onions. Microwave for 2 minutes longer; skim off excess oil. Stir in enough hot water to make 4 cups of roux. Combine with chicken stock, 4 cups hot water and seasonings in 5-quart microwave-safe bowl. Microwave, covered, on High for 10 minutes. Add chicken and sausage.

Microwave for 10 minutes longer, stirring occasionally. Serve over cooked rice.
Yield: 6 to 8 servings.

Faye Harper, Xi Delta Beta
Edinburg, Texas

SHRIMP AND SAUSAGE GUMBO

2 tablespoons vegetable
  oil
2 leeks, trimmed,
  chopped
2 stalks celery, sliced
  1/4-inch thick
1 green bell pepper,
  chopped
1 red bell pepper,
  chopped
2 cloves of garlic,
  crushed
8 ounces smoked turkey
  or ham, cut into strips

8 ounces spicy
  pepperoni sausage,
  sliced
2 cups uncooked rice
6 cups chicken broth
3/4 teaspoon fennel seed
1/2 teaspoon each black
  pepper and cayenne
  pepper
1/4 teaspoon salt
8 ounces zucchini, sliced
12 ounces large shrimp,
  peeled

Heat oil over medium-low heat in large deep skillet. Sauté leeks, celery, bell peppers and garlic until leeks are tender, stirring occasionally. Add turkey, pepperoni and rice, stirring to coat rice. Add chicken broth, seasonings and zucchini. Bring to a boil; reduce heat. Simmer, covered, for 30 minutes or until rice is tender. Add shrimp. Simmer, covered, for 3 to 5 minutes or until shrimp is tender.
Yield: 8 to 10 servings.

Gloria Johnston, Preceptor Delta Rho
Orangeville, Ontario, Canada

SCOTT'S PRIZE GUMBO

This is one dish my husband doesn't mind helping with. Great for football games or informal get-togethers.

2 large onions, chopped
2 stalks celery, chopped
2 green bell peppers,
  chopped
5 pounds chicken
  drumettes
2 pounds frozen okra
2 pounds peeled shrimp

1 pound Cajun sausage,
  cut up
2 pounds crab meat
4 bay leaves
2 16-ounce cans
  tomato sauce
Water
3 tablespoons filé

Sauté onions, celery and green peppers in skillet until tender; set aside. Cook chicken drumettes in skillet until browned; set aside. Fry okra in skillet until dark brown; set aside. Combine sautéed vegetables, chicken, okra, shrimp, sausage, crab meat, bay leaves, tomato sauce and enough water to cover in large stock pot. Simmer for 2 to 4 hours, stirring occasionally. Sprinkle with filé just before serving; remove bay leaves. Yield: 15 servings.

Deborah Lewis, Preceptor Xi Alpha
Atwater, California

SEAFOOD GUMBO

3 tablespoons
  shortening
1/2 cup all-purpose flour
1 large onion, chopped
3 green onions, chopped
1 medium green bell
  pepper, chopped
1 stalk celery, chopped
1/2 cup chopped celery
  leaves
3 sprigs of parsley
2 cloves of garlic,
  minced

2 cups sliced okra
6 cups chicken broth
Salt and pepper to taste
2 tablespoons
  Worcestershire sauce
1 tablespoon thyme
Hot pepper sauce to
  taste
2 pounds shrimp, peeled
1 6-ounce can crab
  meat, drained, flaked
1 tablespoon filé

Heat shortening in large stockpot. Stir in flour gradually. Cook until roux is dark brown, stirring constantly. Add onion, green onions, green pepper, celery, celery leaves, parsley, garlic and okra. Sauté until tender. Add chicken broth, salt, pepper, Worcestershire sauce, thyme, hot pepper sauce, shrimp and crab meat. Simmer until shrimp are tender, stirring occasionally. Add filé 10 minutes before serving.
Yield: 8 servings.

Dixie Mulhollan, Preceptor Eta Beta
Boerne, Texas

LOUISIANA-STYLE JAMBALAYA

1 3-pound chicken,
  cut up
1/2 teaspoon salt
1/4 teaspoon black
  pepper
2 tablespoons bacon
  drippings
2 tablespoons all-
  purpose flour
1 pound smoked
  sausage, sliced
2 medium onions,
  chopped
1 green bell pepper,
  chopped

3 cups chopped peeled
  tomatoes
1 clove of garlic,
  chopped
3 cups water
3/4 teaspoon thyme
1/2 teaspoon salt
1/2 teaspoon red pepper
2 cups cooked long
  grain rice
1 pound peeled shrimp
1/4 cup chopped parsley
1/3 cup chopped green
  onions

Rinse chicken and pat dry; sprinkle with 1/2 teaspoon salt and 1/4 teaspoon black pepper. Brown in bacon drippings in large skillet; remove and set aside. Add flour gradually to pan drippings. Cook until roux is dark brown, stirring constantly. Add chicken, sausage, onions, green pepper, tomatoes and garlic. Simmer for 10 minutes, stirring occasionally. Add water, thyme, 1/2 teaspoon salt, red pepper and rice. Bring to a boil; reduce heat. Simmer, covered, for 15 minutes. Add shrimp. Simmer for 1 minute longer. Add parsley and green onions. Simmer for 5 minutes longer or until rice is tender. Yield: 8 servings.

Esperanza Gallinger
Barstow, California

SEAFOOD JAMBALAYA

1 14-ounce can beef broth	1 medium green bell pepper, chopped
1 4-ounce can mushrooms, drained, chopped	1/2 cup melted margarine
	1 pound shrimp, crab meat or crayfish
1 jalapeño pepper, chopped	2 1/2 cups uncooked rice
1 medium onion, chopped	Salt and cayenne pepper to taste

Combine all ingredients in 8- to 10-cup electric rice cooker. Do not add water. Set on cook cycle; at end of cycle, keep on warm cycle for 30 minutes longer. May use up to 2 pounds seafood. Do not use smaller rice cooker and do not double recipe.
Yield: 8 to 10 servings.

Claudette LeBlanc, Laureate Eta
Lafayette, Louisiana

JAMBALAYA

2 pounds ham with bone	3 8-ounce cans tomato sauce
1 1/2 to 2 pounds Polish sausage, sliced	3/4 teaspoon basil
1 medium onion, chopped	3/4 teaspoon thyme
2 carrots, sliced	1/4 teaspoon cayenne pepper
3 stalks celery with leaves, sliced	1 teaspoon black pepper
1 green bell pepper, chopped	1 teaspoon parsley
	1 clove of garlic, minced
2 bay leaves	Worcestershire sauce to taste

Chop ham into bite-sized pieces. Combine all ingredients in large stockpot. Add enough water to cover. Simmer for 2 hours, stirring occasionally. Remove bay leaves. Yield: 12 to 15 servings.

Teresa Hampton, Beta
Lincoln, Nebraska

HEARTY MINESTRONE

Great served on cold winter nights.

1 teaspoon vegetable oil	2 teaspoons salt
1 pound lean ground beef	1/4 teaspoon freshly ground pepper
1 cup chopped onion	
1 cup chopped celery	1 teaspoon Worcestershire sauce
1 cup chopped green bell pepper or zucchini	2 bay leaves
1 cup shredded cabbage	1 14-ounce can red kidney beans, drained
1 cup sliced carrots	1/2 cup macaroni
1 28-ounce can tomatoes	Grated Parmesan cheese
6 cups water	

Coat large stockpot with oil. Brown ground beef in stockpot, stirring until crumbly; drain. Add next 11 ingredients. Bring to a boil; reduce heat. Simmer, covered, for 1 hour, stirring occasionally. Add beans and macaroni. Simmer for 30 minutes longer. Remove bay leaves. Ladle into soup bowls; sprinkle with Parmesan cheese. Yield: 14 servings.

Diane Burgess, Delta Rho
Caledon East, Ontario, Canada

MINESTRONE

8 chicken or beef bouillon cubes	1 10-ounce package frozen green beans
8 cups water	1 6-ounce can tomato paste
1 medium onion, chopped	2 cloves of garlic, minced
1 teaspoon salt	
3 carrots, sliced	1/2 cup chopped parsley
2 potatoes, sliced	1/2 cup grated Parmesan cheese
3 zucchini, sliced	
1 16-ounce can kidney beans, drained	1 tablespoon dried basil
	1/4 cup olive oil

Mix bouillon cubes, water, onion and salt in 5-quart saucepan. Bring to a boil. Add next 5 ingredients. Simmer over medium heat for 1 1/2 hours or until vegetables are tender. Mix tomato paste, garlic, parsley, cheese, basil and olive oil in bowl. Stir into soup. Simmer for 30 minutes longer. Yield: 8 servings.

Danalee Fregulia, Beta Nu
Enterprise, Oregon

MAIN-DISH MINESTRONE

3 large carrots, sliced	2 teaspoons Worcestershire sauce
2 medium onions, chopped	1/4 teaspoon oregano
2 stalks celery, sliced	4 medium potatoes, peeled, cubed
1 clove of garlic, crushed	
1 small head cabbage, coarsely sliced	4 beef bouillon cubes
	2 large zucchini, cubed
6 tablespoons butter or margarine	2 15-ounce cans red kidney beans, drained
1 10-ounce can tomatoes	1 10-ounce package frozen chopped spinach
1/3 cup uncooked long grain rice	1/2 cup grated Parmesan cheese or grated Romano cheese
2 teaspoons salt	
1/4 teaspoon pepper	

Sauté carrots, onions, celery, garlic and cabbage in butter in 8-quart saucepan for 20 minutes or until tender, stirring frequently. Add undrained tomatoes and next 7 ingredients. Bring to a boil; reduce heat to low. Simmer, covered, for 30 minutes or until rice and vegetables are tender. Add zucchini, beans and spinach. Cook over medium heat until heated through, adding water if necessary. Ladle into soup bowls; sprinkle with Parmesan cheese.
Yield: 9 to 18 servings.

Gertrude M. Jarvis, Laureate Omicron
Eugene, Oregon

PLAZA II STEAK SOUP

2 pounds ground beef	1 cup chopped celery
1/2 cup margarine	1 15-ounce can
1 cup all-purpose flour	tomatoes
2 quarts water	1 tablespoon MSG
2 16-ounce cans mixed	2 tablespoons beef
vegetables	concentrate
1 cup chopped onion	1 tablespoon pepper

Brown ground beef in skillet, stirring until crumbly; drain. Melt margarine in large saucepan. Add flour, stirring to make smooth paste. Add water, ground beef, mixed vegetables, onion, celery, tomatoes, MSG, beef concentrate and pepper, stirring well. Simmer for 30 minutes or until vegetables are tender. May be frozen for later use. Yield: 8 servings.

Julie Fox, Xi Zeta Eta
St. John, Kansas

HEARTY TACO SOUP

2 pounds lean ground	1 16-ounce can red
beef	kidney beans, drained
1 small onion, chopped	1 envelope taco
1 to 2 4-ounce cans	seasoning
chopped green chilies,	1 to 1 1/2 cups water
drained	1 envelope ranch
1 teaspoon each salt	dressing mix
and pepper	1 to 2 15-ounce cans
1 16-ounce can pinto	stewed tomatoes
beans, drained	Shredded Cheddar
1 16-ounce can lima	cheese
beans, drained	Tortilla chips

Brown ground beef with onion in 6-quart saucepan, stirring frequently; drain. Add next 10 ingredients, stirring to mix. Simmer over low heat for 30 minutes, stirring occasionally. Ladle into soup bowls; garnish with cheese and chips. Yield: 8 servings.

Melva Wilkie, Beta Pi
Lakeview, Oregon

SPICY TACO SOUP

2 pounds ground beef	2 16-ounce cans whole
1 onion, chopped	kernel corn, drained
3 10-ounce cans Ro-Tel	2 16-ounce cans
chilies and tomatoes	hominy, drained
2 16-ounce cans ranch-	2 envelopes taco
style beans	seasoning
1 15-ounce can	1 envelope ranch
Jalapinto beans,	dressing mix
drained	

Brown ground beef in 8-quart stockpot, stirring until crumbly; drain. Add remaining ingredients. Simmer for 45 minutes, stirring occasionally. May cook on Low in slow cooker overnight. Yield: 14 to 16 servings.

Chis Bawcom, Laureate Delta Tau
Amarillo, Texas

TACO SOUP

Good to have on hand when family and friends drop by at Christmastime.

1 pound lean ground beef	2 16-ounce cans pinto
2 onions, chopped	beans, drained
1 envelope ranch	2 16-ounce cans
dressing mix	hominy, drained
1 envelope taco	2 16-ounce cans
seasoning	tomatoes
2 4-ounce cans	Shredded Longhorn or
chopped green chilies,	Colby cheese
drained	Corn bread

Brown ground beef in large saucepan, stirring until crumbly; drain. Stir in onions, dressing mix and taco seasoning. Simmer for 10 minutes. Add chilies, beans, hominy and tomatoes. Simmer for 20 minutes longer, stirring occasionally. Ladle into soup bowls; garnish with cheese. Serve with corn bread. Yield: 8 servings.

Nancy Carlton, Preceptor Lambda Phi
Lamesa, Texas

TORTILLA SOUP

1 green bell pepper,	1 14-ounce can stewed
chopped	tomatoes
1 onion, chopped	1 10-ounce package
2 cloves of garlic,	frozen whole kernel
minced	corn
1 4-ounce can chopped	2 teaspoons
green chilies, drained	Worcestershire sauce
2 tablespoons vegetable	1 teaspoon ground
oil	cumin
6 cups chicken broth	1 teaspoon chili powder
3 cups chopped cooked	Salt and pepper to taste
chicken	1 8-ounce package
1 10-ounce can tomato	tortilla chips
soup	Shredded Monterey Jack
1 10-ounce can Ro-Tel	cheese
tomatoes	Avocado slices

Sauté green pepper, onion, garlic and chilies in oil in large saucepan until tender. Add chicken broth, chicken, soup, tomatoes, corn, Worcestershire sauce, cumin, chili powder, salt and pepper. Simmer for 3 hours, stirring occasionally. Place tortilla chips in soup bowls. Ladle in soup; garnish with cheese and avocado. Yield: 10 to 12 servings.

Dana Quisenberry, Alpha Epsilon Epsilon
Seminole, Texas

Toni Riley, Xi Lambda Beta, Waco, Texas, makes Easy Soup by browning 1 pound lean ground beef with 1 chopped onion and 1 clove of garlic and combining with 2 cans of minestrone, 2 cans of ranch-style pinto beans and a can of Ro-Tel tomatoes in slow cooker. Cook all day.

MARTY'S TURKEY-BARLEY SOUP

2 pounds ground turkey	1 cup chopped celery
1 28-ounce can	2 carrots, sliced
chopped tomatoes	1 large potato, cubed
1 6-ounce can tomato	2 teaspoons garlic
juice	2 tablespoons light soy
7 cups water	sauce
1/2 cup pearl barley	1 bay leaf
1 green bell pepper,	1/2 teaspoon paprika
chopped	1/2 teaspoon thyme
8 ounces fresh green	Salt and pepper to taste
beans	

Brown ground turkey in 10-quart saucepan, stirring until crumbly. Add tomatoes, juice, water, barley, vegetables and seasonings. Simmer for 1 1/2 hours, stirring occasionally. Remove bay leaf before serving. Yield: 10 servings.

Marty Wilson, Xi Alpha Eta
Grass Valley, California

CHICKEN AND WILD RICE SOUP

1 onion, chopped	2 14-ounce cans
1/4 cup butter or	chicken broth
margarine	1 6-ounce package long
1/4 cup all-purpose flour	grain and wild rice
1 8-ounce can sliced	1 chicken, cooked, cut up
mushrooms, drained	1 1/2 cups half and half

Sauté onion in butter in large saucepan. Stir in flour. Cook until browned, stirring constantly. Add mushrooms and chicken broth. Simmer several minutes, stirring occasionally. Cook rice using package directions. Add rice, cooked chicken and half and half to broth. Cook over low heat until heated through. Yield: 8 servings.

Mary Lu Grappe, Kappa Psi
Levelland, Texas

BEAN CHOWDER

1 pound bulk sausage	1 1/2 teaspoons garlic
2 16-ounce cans red	salt
beans, drained	1 1/2 teaspoons thyme
1 16-ounce can	1/8 teaspoon red pepper
tomatoes, chopped	1 bay leaf
1 quart water	1 cup cubed potatoes
1 large onion, chopped	1/2 green bell pepper,
1 1/2 teaspoons seasoned	chopped
salt	

Brown sausage in skillet, stirring until crumbly; drain. Combine with next 9 ingredients in large saucepan. Simmer, covered, for 1 hour, stirring occasionally. Add potatoes and green pepper. Cook, covered, for 15 to 20 minutes longer or until potatoes are tender. Remove bay leaf before serving. Yield: 8 servings.

Russanna Metzger, Chi Alpha
Hayti, Missouri

EASY-FUN-GOOD-CHEAP-AND-FAST SOUP

1 28-ounce can	1 14-ounce can green
chopped tomatoes	beans, drained
1 14-ounce can each	1 onion, chopped
garbanzo beans, red	3/4 cup uncooked rice
kidney beans and	Pepper, salt and garlic
yellow beans,	powder to taste
drained	2 quarts chicken or beef
3 carrots, chopped	broth
3 stalks celery, chopped	

Combine all ingredients in large kettle. Bring to a boil; reduce heat. Simmer for 1 hour. Serve with salad and rolls for complete dinner. Yield: 10 to 12 servings.

Linda Schwarz, Xi Gamma Tau
Maple Ridge, British Columbia, Canada

CREAM OF BROCCOLI-PLUS SOUP

I often refer to this as "Cream of Kitchen Sink Soup" because I use anything I find in the kitchen.

1 cup sliced carrots	1 10-ounce package
2 stalks celery,	frozen chopped
chopped	broccoli, thawed
1/4 cup chopped onion	4 to 8 ounces Velveeta
1 10-ounce can cream	cheese, cubed
of chicken soup	Salt, black pepper,
3 to 4 cups milk	cayenne pepper, celery
1 10-ounce package	salt and dry mustard
frozen corn, thawed	to taste

Sauté carrots, celery and onion in nonstick skillet until tender. Combine with remaining ingredients in large saucepan. Cook over low heat until cheese is melted and vegetables are tender, stirring frequently. Yield: 8 to 10 servings.

Kelly Jensen-Webster, Beta Kappa
Meeteetse, Wyoming

BROCCOLI-CHEESE SOUP

3/4 to 1 cup chopped	2 10-ounce packages
onion	frozen chopped
2 tablespoons vegetable	broccoli
oil	1/8 teaspoon garlic
6 cups water	powder
6 chicken bouillon cubes	6 cups milk
1 8-ounce package egg	16 ounces Velveeta
noodles	cheese, cubed
1 teaspoon salt	Pepper to taste

Sauté onion in oil in 6-quart saucepan for 3 minutes. Add water and bouillon cubes. Bring to a boil. Add noodles and salt gradually. Cook for 3 minutes. Add broccoli and garlic powder. Cook for 4 minutes. Add remaining ingredients. Simmer until cheese melts, stirring frequently. Yield: 12 to 15 servings.

Darlene Johnson, Preceptor Alpha Phi
Altus, Oklahoma

RICH BROCCOLI-CHEESE SOUP

3 tablespoons butter or margarine	3/4 cup chopped carrots
3 tablespoons all-purpose flour	1/2 cup chopped celery
4 cups chicken broth	1 small onion, chopped
1/2 teaspoon salt	1 small clove of garlic, minced
1/8 teaspoon pepper	1 egg yolk
1/4 teaspoon thyme	1 cup whipping cream
2 cups chopped broccoli	1 1/2 cups shredded Cheddar cheese

Melt butter in large saucepan. Stir in flour. Cook for several minutes until smooth paste forms, stirring constantly; remove from heat. Add broth gradually. Bring to a boil, stirring constantly. Add salt, pepper, thyme, broccoli, carrots, celery, onion and garlic. Simmer for 8 minutes or until vegetables are tender. Beat egg yolk with cream in small bowl. Stir a small amount of soup into cream mixture. Add cream mixture to soup gradually. Simmer over very low heat until thickened, stirring constantly. Add cheese, stirring until melted. Yield: 6 to 8 servings.

Mary M. Doucette, Laureate Gamma
Pittsfield, Massachusetts

❖ HUNGARIAN MUSHROOM SOUP

6 shallots, thinly sliced	2 quarts chicken stock
1 cup butter or margarine	10 cups sliced fresh mushrooms
3 tablespoons Hungarian paprika	4 cups sour cream
3 tablespoons Spanish paprika	1 tablespoon dried dillweed
6 tablespoons all-purpose flour	Salt and pepper to taste Croutons

Sauté shallots in butter over medium heat in large saucepan until tender. Stir in paprikas; reduce heat to low. Add flour. Cook for 3 minutes, stirring constantly. Stir in chicken stock and mushrooms. Bring to a boil. Cook for 20 minutes, stirring occasionally. Add sour cream 1/2 cup at a time, stirring well. Add dillweed, salt and pepper. Serve in deep bowls, garnished with croutons. Yield: 12 to 15 servings.

Kimberly Crawford, Alpha Alpha
Anthony, Kansas

MUSHROOM SOUP

1/2 onion, chopped	6 cups chicken broth
2 tablespoons butter or margarine	1/2 teaspoon salt
1 pound fresh mushrooms, ground	1 teaspoon lemon juice
	1 lemon, thinly sliced

Sauté onion in butter in large saucepan until tender. Add mushrooms. Cook for 5 minutes, stirring occasionally. Add chicken broth. Bring to a boil; reduce heat. Simmer for 30 minutes. Strain through sieve, pressing mushrooms to extract all liquid. Season with salt and lemon juice. Serve in bowls garnished with lemon slices. Yield: 6 servings.

Hedda Orr, Xi Pi Nu
Chico, California

HOMEMADE ONION SOUP

6 cups thinly sliced onions	3 14-ounce cans beef broth
3 tablespoons butter or margarine	1 cup Burgundy or white wine
1 tablespoon vegetable oil	1 bay leaf
1 teaspoon salt	1/2 teaspoon sage
1/2 teaspoon sugar	Mushrooms
3 tablespoons all-purpose flour	Sliced bread
	Shredded mozzarella cheese

Cook onions in butter and oil over low heat in covered saucepan for 15 minutes or until tender. Sprinkle with salt and sugar. Cook over high heat for 20 minutes or until onions are brown. Stir in flour. Cook over medium heat for 2 minutes. Stir in 1 cup broth gradually. Add remaining broth, wine, bay leaf and sage. Simmer, covered, for 30 minutes. Add mushrooms. Cook for 5 minutes; remove bay leaf. Preheat oven to 350 degrees. Ladle soup into ovenproof bowls. Top with bread and cheese. Bake for 10 minutes. Yield: 6 to 8 servings.

Nancy Metcalfe, Zeta Epsilon
Cuyahoga Falls, Ohio

ONION SOUP

2 pounds onions, sliced	2 14-ounce cans beef broth
1/2 small head cabbage, sliced	1/4 cup dry sherry
1/4 cup margarine	6 3/4-inch slices Italian bread
1 tablespoon all-purpose flour	1/2 cup shredded Swiss cheese
1/4 teaspoon salt	

Preheat oven to 450 degrees. Brown onions and cabbage in margarine in large saucepan until tender. Add flour, salt, broth and sherry. Simmer for 10 minutes, stirring occasionally. Toast bread on both sides in oven. Ladle soup into ovenproof bowls; place on baking sheet. Top with toast; sprinkle with cheese. Bake for 20 minutes. Yield: 6 servings.

Judith Blair, Preceptor Lambda Xi
Lamesa, Texas

Doreen Wheeler, Xi Delta Lambda, Gig Harbor, Washington, makes The Best Clam Chowder by heating a 6-ounce can clams, a chopped potato, chopped onion and 2 chopped partially cooked slices bacon in saucepan. When vegetables are tender, add 4 cups milk, season and heat to serving temperature.

PEA-COTTAGE CHEESE SOUP

1 medium potato, chopped	1/2 teaspoon basil
2 stalks celery, chopped	Salt and pepper to taste
1 medium onion, chopped	2 cups cottage cheese
1/2 cup chicken broth	1 8-ounce can peas, drained
	1 cup milk

Combine potato, celery, onion, broth, basil, salt and pepper in 2-quart saucepan. Bring to a boil; reduce heat. Simmer, covered, until vegetables are tender. Process cottage cheese, peas and milk in blender until smooth. Stir into vegetables. Cook until heated through. Yield: 6 servings.

Sharon Bittner, Xi Upsilon Omicron
Altaville, California

"GOOD LUCK" BLACK-EYED PEA SOUP WITH RELISH

1 16-ounce package dried black-eyed peas	1 cup cooked rice
2 slices bacon	1 large tomato, chopped
1 small onion, sliced	1 large green bell pepper, chopped
3 cloves of garlic, chopped	1 medium onion, chopped
Salt and pepper to taste	1 teaspoon sugar
Water	Vinegar and oil salad dressing

Combine peas, bacon, onion, garlic, salt and pepper with enough water to cover in large saucepan. Bring to a boil; reduce heat. Simmer for 2 to 2 1/2 hours, stirring occasionally. Add water as needed for desired consistency. Add rice. Simmer until heated through. Ladle into soup bowls. Top with mixture of tomato, green pepper, onion and sugar; sprinkle with salad dressing. Yield: 8 servings.

Dee Dorman, Preceptor Kappa Xi
San Antonio, Texas

POTATO SOUP

6 cups cubed potatoes	2 chicken bouillon cubes
2 cups water	1 teaspoon salt
1 cup sliced celery	1/2 teaspoon pepper
1 cup sliced carrots	3 cups milk
1/2 cup chopped onion	1/4 cup all-purpose flour
2 teaspoons parsley flakes	12 ounces Cheddar cheese, shredded

Combine potatoes, water, celery, carrots, onion, parsley, bouillon cubes, salt and pepper in 2-quart saucepan. Bring to a boil; reduce heat. Simmer, covered, for 8 minutes or until vegetables are tender. Mix 1/4 cup milk with flour in small bowl, stirring to form paste. Stir into soup. Add remaining milk and cheese. Simmer over medium heat until thickened, stirring frequently. Yield: 9 servings.

Liz Byrom, Xi Kappa Mu
Keystone Heights, Florida

CROCKED CREAM OF POTATO SOUP

1 32-ounce package frozen Tater Tots	1 10-ounce can cream of mushroom soup
1 pound cooked chopped ham	1/2 cup finely chopped onion
1 cup shredded Cheddar cheese	1 cup sour cream
2 cups milk	Salt and pepper to taste

Combine all ingredients in slow cooker; mix well. Cook on High for 4 hours or on Low for 5 to 7 hours, stirring occasionally. Add milk or water as necessary for desired consistency. Yield: 6 to 8 servings.

Jennifer Burch, Delta Delta
McPherson, Kansas

JACK-O'-LANTERN SOUP

Our International Women's Club celebrates Halloween by carving pumpkins into jack-o'-lanterns, then cooking the pumpkin in different ways. The addition of peanut butter makes this a really American dish.

4 onions, chopped	2 cups beef broth
4 cloves of garlic, minced	2 cups chicken broth
1 1/2 teaspoons Italian seasoning	3 cups cooked pumpkin
1/4 teaspoon nutmeg	4 cups milk
3 tablespoons vegetable oil	1 cup smooth peanut butter
	1 teaspoon Tabasco sauce
	1/2 cup chopped peanuts

Sauté onions and garlic with Italian seasoning and nutmeg in oil in large saucepan until onions are tender. Add beef broth, chicken broth and pumpkin, stirring until mixed. Add milk, peanut butter and Tabasco sauce. Simmer for 10 minutes. Ladle into soup bowls. Garnish with chopped peanuts.
Yield: 12 servings.

Ruby L. Cheaney, Beta Epsilon Omicron
Brackettville, Texas

ZUCCHINI SOUP

7 zucchini	2 cups water
2 tablespoons instant chicken bouillon	1 cup cream
	1 tablespoon lemon juice

Slice 6 zucchini; chop remaining zucchini and set aside. Combine chicken bouillon and water in saucepan. Bring to a boil. Add sliced zucchini. Cover and turn off heat. Let stand on stovetop until cooled. Remove zucchini with slotted spoon to blender container. Add cream and 1 cup broth. Process until smooth and creamy. Add lemon juice and additional broth for desired consistency. Return to saucepan. Cook over low heat until heated through. Ladle into soup bowls; garnish with chopped zucchini.
Yield: 6 servings.

Susan Shoemaker, Xi Chi
Scottsdale, Arizona

BANANA SALAD

1 cup sugar	1/2 teaspoon vanilla
2 tablespoons all-	extract
purpose flour	1/2 cup melted margarine
1/4 teaspoon baking	16 ounces whipped
powder	topping
1/2 teaspoon salt	3 bananas, sliced
1/2 cup coconut	1/2 cup chopped pecans
1/2 cup oats	Whipped topping
1 egg, beaten	

Preheat oven to 350 degrees. Combine sugar and next 5 ingredients in bowl; mix well. Stir in egg, vanilla and margarine. Spread into greased and floured 9-by-13-inch baking pan. Bake for 25 to 30 minutes or until golden brown. Let stand until cool; crumble. Layer whipped topping, bananas, baked crumbs and pecans 1/2 at a time into large glass salad bowl. Top with additional whipped topping. Chill for 4 hours. Yield: 10 to 12 servings.

Toni Koch, Omicron Beta
Bosworth, Missouri

CONGEALED CONCORD GRAPE SALAD

2 3-ounce packages	2 cups sour cream
grape gelatin	8 ounces cream cheese,
2 cups boiling water	softened
1 21-ounce can	1/2 cup sugar
blueberry pie filling	1 teaspoon vanilla
1 8-ounce can crushed	extract
pineapple, drained	Walnuts or pecans

Dissolve gelatin in boiling water in bowl. Stir in pie filling and pineapple. Spoon into glass bowl. Chill until set. Top with mixture of sour cream, cream cheese, sugar and vanilla. Sprinkle with walnuts. Yield: 12 servings.

Betty Fielding, Preceptor Lambda
Ely, Nevada

FRUIT SALAD

1 12-ounce can	2 bananas, sliced
pineapple chunks	1 cup strawberries,
1 cantaloupe, cut into	sliced
bite-sized pieces	2 kiwifruit, sliced
1 cup seedless grapes	1 to 2 tablespoons sugar
1 navel orange,	
cut into sections	

Combine undrained pineapple, cantaloupe, grapes and orange sections in large bowl, stirring gently. Chill overnight. Stir in remaining ingredients. Serve immediately. May substitute any preferred fruit according to availability. Yield: 10 to 12 servings.

Teri Bycroft, Xi Delta Chi
Broken Arrow, Oklahoma

LEMON SALAD

3 3-ounce packages	3 cups vanilla ice cream
lemon gelatin	1 can crushed pineapple,
2 cups boiling water	drained
1 large can lemon	1 1/4 cups shredded
pudding	Colby cheese

Dissolve gelatin in boiling water in bowl. Stir in pudding, ice cream, pineapple and 1 cup cheese. Spoon into serving dish. Sprinkle with remaining cheese. Chill until set. Yield: 10 to 12 servings.

Anne Nelson, Xi Zeta Omega
Kanawha, Iowa

MANDARIN ORANGE SALAD

1 15-ounce can crushed	1/2 cup mayonnaise
pineapple	1/4 cup whipping cream
1 11-ounce can	1 tablespoon grated
mandarin oranges	orange peel
1 6-ounce package	1 teaspoon sugar
orange gelatin	1/4 teaspoon mace
1 1/2 cups hot tea	
1 8-ounce can water	
chestnuts, drained,	
chopped	

Drain pineapple and mandarin oranges, reserving liquid. Add enough water to reserved liquid to measure 1 1/2 cups. Dissolve gelatin in hot tea in bowl. Stir in fruit juice mixture, drained fruit and water chestnuts. Spoon into 9-by-11-inch dish. Chill until set. Mix mayonnaise and remaining ingredients in small bowl. Chill, covered, in refrigerator. Serve mayonnaise mixture with congealed salad. Yield: 12 servings.

Edna Roundy, Beta Nu
Joseph, Oregon

ORANGE SALAD SUPREME

1 11-ounce can	1 3-ounce package
mandarin oranges	tapioca pudding
1 3-ounce package	mix
orange gelatin	2 cups whipped topping
1 3-ounce package	
vanilla instant	
pudding mix	

Drain mandarin oranges, reserving liquid. Add enough hot water to reserved liquid to measure 2 cups. Combine with gelatin and pudding mixes in saucepan. Cook over medium heat until clear and thickened. Let stand until cool. Fold in drained mandarin oranges and whipped topping. Spoon into glass serving dish. Chill until set. Yield: 8 to 10 servings.

Carol Jones, Alpha Delta
Knoxville, Tennessee

ORANGE CIRCUS PEANUT GELATIN SALAD

1 7-ounce package peanut-shaped orange candy	1 6-ounce package orange gelatin
1 16-ounce can mandarin oranges	2 cups boiling water 2 cups whipped topping

Cut orange candy into small pieces. Drain mandarin oranges, reserving liquid. Add enough water to measure 1³/4 cups. Dissolve gelatin in boiling water in bowl. Add orange candy, stirring until dissolved. Stir in mandarin orange liquid mixture. Chill until partially set. Fold in drained mandarin oranges and whipped topping. Spoon into 9-by-13-inch dish. Chill until set. May substitute crushed pineapple for mandarin oranges. Yield: 8 to 10 servings.

Carol Sylvis, Xi Gamma Nu
Hendersonville, Tennessee

PINEAPPLE SALAD SUPREME

1 29-ounce can juice-pack pineapple chunks	2 tablespoons sugar
1 16-ounce package marshmallows, chopped	2 tablespoons cornstarch
1 pound walnuts, chopped	2 eggs, beaten 2 tablespoons melted butter or margarine

Drain pineapple, reserving 1 cup juice. Combine marshmallows, walnuts and pineapple in medium bowl. Mix sugar and cornstarch in small saucepan. Add reserved pineapple juice, eggs and butter. Cook over medium heat until thickened, stirring constantly. Pour over pineapple mixture; toss gently. Yield: 10 to 12 servings.

Jean A. Wiyatt, Xi Alpha
Fargo, North Dakota

SAWDUST SALAD

1 20-ounce can crushed pineapple	2 tablespoons all-purpose flour
1 package orange gelatin	1 egg
1 package lemon gelatin	¹/2 cup sugar
2 cups boiling water	8 ounces whipped topping
1¹/2 cups cold water	8 ounces cream cheese, softened
8 ounces miniature marshmallows	8 ounces sharp Cheddar cheese, shredded
3 or 4 bananas, mashed	

Drain pineapple, reserving 1 cup liquid. Dissolve gelatins in boiling water in bowl. Add cold water. Stir in marshmallows, bananas and drained pineapple. Spoon into 9-by-13-inch dish. Chill until set. Combine reserved pineapple liquid, flour, egg and sugar in saucepan. Cook over medium heat until thickened, stirring constantly. Let stand until cooled.

Spread over congealed layer. Chill thoroughly. Mix whipped topping and cream cheese in small bowl. Spread over chilled layers. Sprinkle with cheese. Yield: 10 to 12 servings.

Minnie K. Stapleton, Xi Alpha Tau
Morristown, Tennessee

PRETZEL SALAD

2 cups crushed pretzels	¹/4 cup crushed pineapple, drained
2 tablespoons sugar	
¹/4 cup melted margarine	1 6-ounce package strawberry gelatin
8 ounces cream cheese, softened	2 cups boiling water
8 ounces whipped topping	2 10-ounce packages frozen strawberries
1 cup sugar	

Preheat oven to 400 degrees. Combine pretzel crumbs, sugar and margarine in bowl. Press into 9-by-13-inch baking dish. Bake for 8 minutes. Combine cream cheese and next 3 ingredients in bowl; mix well. Spread over baked layer. Dissolve gelatin in boiling water in bowl. Add frozen strawberries; mix well. Pour over cream cheese layer. Chill overnight. Yield: 8 to 12 servings.

Lonna S. Crouch, Preceptor Theta
Virginia Beach, Virginia

STRAWBERRY-CREAM CHEESE GELATIN

1 6-ounce package strawberry gelatin	6 ounces cream cheese, softened
2 cups boiling water	¹/2 cup chopped walnuts
2 10-ounce packages frozen strawberries, thawed	

Dissolve gelatin in boiling water in bowl. Stir in strawberries. Spoon into 9-by-13-inch dish. Shape cream cheese into small balls. Roll each ball in walnuts. Drop into gelatin. Chill until firm. Yield: 8 to 12 servings.

Catherine Rostoczynski
Wyandotte, Michigan

STRAWBERRY-PECAN SALAD

2 3-ounce packages strawberry gelatin	1 20-ounce can crushed pineapple
1 cup boiling water	3 medium bananas, mashed
2 10-ounce packages frozen strawberries, thawed	1 cup chopped pecans Whipped topping

Dissolve gelatin in boiling water in bowl. Stir in strawberries, pineapple, bananas and pecans. Let stand until cool. Spoon into 9-by-13-inch dish. Top with whipped topping. Chill until set. Yield: 10 to 12 servings.

Dorothy Davis, Laureate Mu
Vienna, West Virginia

WHITE SALAD

1 cup crushed pineapple	1 tablespoon all-
2 cups shredded cabbage	purpose flour
1 16-ounce package	1 tablespoon vinegar
miniature	1 tablespoon lemon juice
marshmallows	1/4 cup sugar
1/2 cup chopped pecans	1 cup whipping cream,
1 egg white	whipped

Drain pineapple, reserving liquid. Combine pineapple, cabbage, marshmallows and pecans in bowl. Beat egg white until stiff peaks form. Combine with flour, reserved pineapple liquid, vinegar, lemon juice and sugar in double boiler. Cook over hot water until thickened, stirring constantly. Let stand until cool. Pour over pineapple mixture; toss. Fold in whipped cream just before serving. Yield: 8 to 10 servings.

Donna Haley, Alpha Alpha
Hartselle, Alabama

YUM-YUM SALAD

1 20-ounce can crushed	1 cup chopped celery
pineapple	1 cup chopped apple
2/3 cup sugar	1/2 cup chopped pecans
1 6-ounce package	2 cups whipped topping
lemon gelatin	
8 ounces cream cheese,	
softened	

Combine undrained pineapple and sugar in saucepan. Cook for 3 minutes. Add gelatin and cream cheese, stirring until gelatin dissolves. Let stand until cool. Add celery, apple and pecans. Fold in whipped topping gently. Spoon into 9-by-12-inch dish. Chill until set. Yield: 15 servings.

Patty Moore, Alpha Beta Psi
Clinton, Missouri

HAM SALAD

1 10-ounce package	2 tablespoons chopped
frozen peas	onion
2 cups chopped smoked	3/4 cup mayonnaise
ham	1 1/2 teaspoons prepared
1 cup shredded Cheddar	mustard
cheese	Salad Bowl Puff

Rinse frozen peas under cold water until separated; drain. Combine with next 5 ingredients in bowl; mix well. Chill for 2 hours. Fill Salad Bowl Puff with ham salad. Cut into wedges. Yield: 6 to 8 servings.

SALAD BOWL PUFF

2/3 cup water	1 cup baking mix
1/4 cup margarine or	4 eggs
butter	

Preheat oven to 400 degrees. Bring water and margarine to boiling point in 2-quart saucepan. Add baking mix all at once. Stir vigorously over low heat for 1 1/2 minutes or until mixture forms a ball. Remove from heat. Beat in eggs 1 at a time until mixture is smooth. Spread over bottom of greased 9-inch pie plate. Bake for 35 to 40 minutes or until puffed and dry in center. Let stand until cool. Yield: 6 to 8 servings.

Sandra L. Utz, Psi Beta
Plattsburg, Missouri

CHICKEN-CRANBERRY SALAD

1 tablespoon unflavored	3/4 cup cold water
gelatin	1 cup mayonnaise
1/4 cup cold water	3/4 teaspoon salt
2 cups whole cranberry	3 tablespoons lemon
sauce	juice
1 cup crushed pineapple	2 cups chopped cooked
2 tablespoons lemon	chicken
juice	1/2 cup chopped celery
1/2 cup chopped almonds	1/2 tablespoon chopped
1 tablespoon unflavored	parsley
gelatin	Lettuce leaves

Soften 1 tablespoon gelatin in 1/4 cup cold water in double boiler. Place over hot water, stirring until dissolved. Stir in cranberry sauce and next 3 ingredients. Spoon into 9-by-12-inch dish. Chill until set. Soften 1 tablespoon gelatin in 1/4 cup cold water in double boiler. Place over hot water, stirring until dissolved. Stir in remaining 1/2 cup water and remaining ingredients. Pour over congealed layer. Chill until firm. Serve on lettuce leaves. Yield: 8 servings.

Donelda F. Anderson, Laureate Sigma
King Hill, Idaho

CHICKEN SALAD DELIGHT

2 cups chopped cooked	2 tablespoons chicken
chicken	broth
1/2 cup chopped celery	1/4 cup mayonnaise
1/2 cup chopped sweet	1 tablespoon pickle juice
pickle	8 lettuce leaves
1/2 large apple, chopped	Pimento strips
4 hard-cooked eggs,	
chopped	

Combine chicken with next 7 ingredients in bowl; mix well. Arrange on lettuce leaves. Garnish with pimento. Yield: 8 servings.

Sandy Miller, Xi Pi Alpha
Tuscola, Texas

Edith Bowman, Alpha Omega Xi, Boerne, Texas, dissolves a large package strawberry gelatin in 1 cup boiling water, adds a large can crushed pineapple, sliced strawberries, 3 mashed bananas and 1 cup nuts, chills half the mixture in pan, adds layers of 1 pint sour cream and remaining gelatin mixture and chills until firm for Yummy Strawberry Salad.

FRUITED CHICKEN SALAD

4 cups chopped cooked
  chicken
1 15-ounce can
  pineapple chunks,
  drained
1 11-ounce can
  mandarin oranges,
  drained
1/2 cup sliced black
  olives
1 cup chopped celery

1/2 cup chopped green
  bell pepper
2 tablespoons grated
  onion
1 cup mayonnaise-type
  salad dressing
1 tablespoon prepared
  mustard
1 5-ounce can chow
  mein noodles
Lettuce leaves

Combine chicken, pineapple chunks, orange segments, olives, celery, green pepper and onion in bowl. Toss gently with mixture of salad dressing and mustard. Chill, covered, for several hours. Toss with chow mein noodles just before serving. Spoon into lettuce-lined salad bowl. Yield: 8 servings.

Marie Weedin, Delta Sigma
Lexington, Missouri

CABBAGE-CHICKEN SALAD

1 cup slivered almonds
3 tablespoons sesame
  seed
2 3-ounce packages
  chicken-flavored
  ramen noodles
1 head cabbage,
  shredded
2 bunches green onions,
  chopped

2 cups chopped cooked
  chicken
1/4 cup vegetable oil
1/4 cup tarragon vinegar
2 tablespoons soy sauce
4 packets artificial
  sweetener
1/2 teaspoon pepper

Toast almonds and sesame seed in skillet coated with nonstick cooking spray until golden brown. Let stand until cool. Crumble noodles, reserving seasoning packets for salad dressing. Combine noodles with cabbage, green onions and chicken in bowl. Add almonds and sesame seed. Combine oil with reserved seasoning packets and remaining ingredients in small bowl; mix well. Pour over cabbage mixture; mix well. Chill until serving time. Yield: 10 servings.

SWEET AND SOUR STIR-FRY

2/3 cup unsweetened
  pineapple juice
1/4 cup rice vinegar
4 teaspoons cornstarch

1 tablespoon soy sauce
4 cups Cabbage-Chicken
  Salad

Combine pineapple juice, rice vinegar, cornstarch and soy sauce in wok. Cook until thickened, stirring constantly. Add Cabbage-Chicken Salad. Cook until heated through, stirring constantly. Yield: 2 servings.

Sarah Morra, Phi
Moscow, Idaho

SUPERB CHICKEN SALAD

4 chicken breasts,
  boned, skinned
1 cup sour cream
2 cups toasted slivered
  almonds
1/2 cup snipped chives
2 eggs

21/2 cups safflower oil
2 tablespoons white
  wine vinegar
1 teaspoon salt
1 teaspoon white pepper
1 cup sour cream

Preheat oven to 450 degrees. Rinse chicken; pat dry. Cut into 3/4-by-3-inch pieces. Coat pieces with 1 cup sour cream. Arrange in single layer on baking sheet. Bake for 10 to 12 minutes or until just cooked. Cut into bite-sized pieces. Combine with almonds and chives in bowl. Set aside. Combine next 5 ingredients in blender container. Process until smooth. Stir in remaining 1 cup sour cream. Spoon over chicken mixture; mix well. Yield: 10 servings.

Jackie Vogler, Preceptor Kappa Rho
Hilltop Lakes, Texas

CITRUS-SHRIMP SALAD

1 pound cooked peeled
  shrimp
2 peeled oranges, thinly
  sliced
1 peeled lime, thinly
  sliced
1 peeled lemon, thinly
  sliced
3/4 cup cider vinegar
1/4 cup lemon juice
1/4 cup olive oil
2 tablespoons catsup
1 teaspoon sugar

2 tablespoons finely
  chopped parsley
2 tablespoons capers,
  drained
2 cloves of garlic, finely
  chopped
2 tablespoons mustard
  seed
1/4 teaspoon celery seed
1/4 teaspoon pepper
Mixed salad greens
1 small purple onion,
  thinly sliced

Combine shrimp, oranges, lime and lemon in glass bowl. Mix vinegar with next 10 ingredients in bowl. Pour over shrimp mixture; toss. Chill, covered, for 2 to 4 hours. Arrange salad greens in bowl; top with onion. Spoon shrimp mixture over top. Yield: 8 servings.

Vernie Monty, Preceptor Gamma Theta
Arlington, Washington

SHRIMP SALAD

1 envelope unfavored
  gelatin
1 10-ounce can cream
  of chicken soup
3/4 cup mayonnaise

8 ounces cream cheese,
  softened
1 cup chopped fresh
  vegetables
1 cup cooked shrimp

Soften gelatin in soup in saucepan. Heat over medium heat until gelatin dissolves, stirring constantly. Let stand until cool. Stir in mayonnaise, cream cheese, vegetables and shrimp. Spoon into 6-cup mold. Chill until firm. Yield: 8 to 10 servings.

Carilerene Harper, Xi Beta Phi
Bend, Oregon

BROCCOLI SALAD

Flowerets of 1 bunch
  broccoli
8 ounces crisp-fried
  bacon, crumbled
8 ounces raisins
1/2 red onion, chopped

1 cup sliced water
  chestnuts
1/3 cup sugar
1 tablespoon vinegar
1 cup mayonnaise

Combine broccoli and remaining ingredients in large
bowl; mix well. Spoon into salad bowl.
Yield: 8 servings.

Jessie Terrill, Laureate Iota
Oklahoma City, Oklahoma

BROCCOLI-PEANUT SALAD

1 cup mayonnaise
2 tablespoons vinegar
1/4 cup sugar
Flowerets of 1 bunch
  broccoli

1 cup raisins
6 green onions, chopped
Crisp-fried bacon,
  crumbled
Peanuts

Combine all ingredients in large bowl; mix well.
Spoon into salad bowl. May substitute bacon bits for
bacon. Yield: 10 to 12 servings.

Nancy L. East, Xi Kappa
Harrisonburg, Virginia

PINE TREE SALAD

4 to 5 cups chopped
  broccoli
1 cup raisins
1 cup salted sunflower
  seed
12 strips crisp-fried
  bacon, crumbled

1 onion, chopped
1/2 cup mayonnaise-
  type salad dressing
1 tablespoon vinegar
3 tablespoons sugar
Milk

Combine broccoli with next 4 ingredients in bowl;
mix well. Mix salad dressing, vinegar and sugar in
small bowl. Add milk to make of desired consistency.
Pour over broccoli mixture; toss. Chill until serving
time. Yield: 6 to 8 servings.

Doneen Clark, Beta Theta
Hulett, Wyoming

BROCCOLI-CAULIFLOWER SALAD

Flowerets of 1 bunch
  broccoli
Flowerets of 1 head
  cauliflower
1 medium onion, thinly
  sliced
1 cup shredded Cheddar
cheese

1 5-ounce can sliced
  water chestnuts,
  drained
1/2 cup mayonnaise
1/2 cup sugar
2 teaspoons vinegar

Combine broccoli and next 4 ingredients in salad
bowl; mix well. Add mixture of mayonnaise, sugar
and vinegar; toss lightly. Yield: 8 to 10 servings.

Marguerite Eberly, Laureate Eta
Bel Air, Maryland

CARROT SALAD

5 cups thinly sliced
  carrots
1 cup finely chopped
  celery
1 medium onion, thinly
  sliced
1 cup finely chopped
  green bell pepper

1 10-ounce can tomato
  soup
3/4 cup sugar
1/4 cup vinegar
1 teaspoon mustard
1 teaspoon
  Worcestershire sauce
1/2 cup vegetable oil

Cook carrots with water to cover in saucepan for 5
minutes; drain. Mix carrots with next 8 ingredients
in large bowl. Let stand until cool. Add oil; mix well.
Chill, covered, overnight. Yield: 8 to 10 servings.

Doris C. Williams, Preceptor Epsilon Tau
Englewood, Florida

ANITA'S SLAW

1 medium head cabbage,
  shredded
1/2 cup sugar
6 green olives, sliced
1 medium onion, grated
1/2 green bell pepper,
  chopped

1/2 cup vegetable oil
1 cup white vinegar
1 teaspoon celery seed
1 teaspoon prepared
  mustard
1 teaspoon salt
1/8 teaspoon pepper

Combine first 5 ingredients in large bowl; mix well.
Mix oil and next 5 ingredients in small bowl. Pour
over cabbage mixture; toss lightly.
Yield: 8 to 12 servings.

Evelyn Fenton, Preceptor Pi
Columbia, Missouri

NAPPA SALAD

1 head Nappa cabbage,
  sliced
6 green onions, sliced
2 3-ounce packages
  ramen noodles,
  crumbled
1 tablespoon margarine

1 cup slivered almonds
2 to 4 tablespoons
  sesame seed
1 cup vegetable oil
1 cup sugar
1/2 cup vinegar
3 tablespoons soy sauce

Combine cabbage and green onions in large bowl.
Chill, covered, for several hours. Sauté noodles in
margarine with almonds and sesame seed in saucepan. Let stand until cool. Chill until serving time.
Mix oil with remaining ingredients in small bowl.
Combine cabbage mixture and sautéed mixture in
salad bowl. Add enough salad dressing to coat; toss
lightly. Yield: 10 to 12 servings.

Sandra Balhoff, Preceptor Beta Phi
Adrian, Michigan

Claire Holland, Xi Phi Alpha Omega, Wichita Falls, Texas,
uses a can of seasoned English peas, drained, 1 teaspoon
onion flakes, 1 tablespoon salad dressing and 8 ounces
cubed Colby cheese for Quick and Easy Pea Salad.

CHINESE COLESLAW

1 3-ounce package ramen noodles	4 green onions, chopped
1/2 cup sunflower seed	1/2 cup vegetable oil
1/2 cup slivered almonds	1/4 cup vinegar
4 to 6 cups coleslaw	1/4 cup sugar

Reserve seasoning packet for salad dressing. Combine noodles and next 4 ingredients in large bowl. Mix reserved seasoning packet with oil, vinegar and sugar in small bowl. Pour over coleslaw mixture; toss. Spoon into salad bowl. Yield: 8 to 10 servings.

Lynn Henle, Preceptor Phi
Sioux Falls, South Dakota

RAMEN NOODLE SALAD

This was served to me by a dear sorority sister when I visited her new retirement home in New Mexico. She and her husband made us feel at home in their home.

1 package beef-flavored ramen noodles	1 small package slivered almonds, toasted
1 package coleslaw mix	
1 small package salted sunflower seed	1/3 cup apple cider vinegar
2 or 3 green onions, chopped	1/2 cup vegetable oil
	1/2 cup sugar

Break noodles into pieces; reserve seasoning packet for salad dressing. Combine noodles with coleslaw mix in bowl. Add next 3 ingredients; toss. Mix vinegar, oil, sugar and reserved seasoning packet in small bowl until sugar dissolves. Pour over noodle mixture; toss. Yield: 12 to 15 servings.

Peggy Walker, Gamma Xi
Apple Valley, Minnesota

HOT SLAW MEXICANA

1/4 medium head cabbage, sliced	1/2 cup cooked whole kernel corn, drained
1 medium carrot, sliced	1 cup shredded sharp or jalapeño pepper cheese
1/2 medium green bell pepper, sliced	
1 cup cherry tomatoes, sliced	2 tablespoons milk
	1 tablespoon celery seed
1/2 cup pitted black olives, sliced	1/4 teaspoon dry mustard
	1 peeled avocado, sliced

Combine first 6 ingredients in large glass bowl; toss. Set aside. Combine cheese, milk, celery seed and dry mustard in glass bowl. Microwave on Medium-Low for 2 1/2 to 3 minutes or until cheese melts, stirring twice. Stir until smooth. Pour over cabbage mixture; toss gently. Microwave, covered, on High for 4 minutes or until heated through, stirring once. Garnish with avocado. Serve immediately. Yield: 6 to 8 servings.

Janie Kurth, Preceptor Alpha
Missoula, Montana

OVERNIGHT COLESLAW

1 medium head cabbage, shredded	2 teaspoons sugar
	3/4 cup vegetable oil
1 cup sugar	1 cup vinegar
1 green bell pepper, chopped	1 teaspoon dry mustard
	1 teaspoon celery seed
2 carrots, shredded	1 teaspoon salt

Combine cabbage with next 3 ingredients in large bowl. Sprinkle with 2 teaspoons sugar. Set aside. Combine oil, vinegar, dry mustard, celery seed and salt in saucepan. Bring to a boil. Pour over cabbage mixture; toss until covered evenly. Chill, covered, overnight. Stir before serving. Yield: 12 to 16 servings.

Marilyn Kelley, Laureate Beta Xi
Findlay, Ohio

CUCUMBER SALAD

1 3-ounce package lemon gelatin	1 small onion, finely chopped
1 3-ounce package lime gelatin	1 green bell pepper, finely chopped
1 1/3 cups boiling water	Radishes, finely chopped
3/4 cup mayonnaise	1 cup cottage cheese
1 cucumber, finely chopped	Maraschino cherries
	Lettuce leaves

Dissolve gelatins in boiling water in bowl. Let stand until cooled to room temperature. Stir in mayonnaise and next 5 ingredients. Spoon into 8-by-13-inch dish. Chill until firm. Cut into squares; place a cherry on each serving. Serve on lettuce-lined salad plates. Yield: 10 to 12 servings.

Rosemary Grunewald, Nu Delta
Clinton, Iowa

GERMAN POTATO SALAD

1 pound thinly sliced bacon	1 cup vinegar
	1 1/2 cups water
3/4 cup sugar	12 cups sliced cooked potatoes
1/4 cup cornstarch	
1 teaspoon salt	1 onion, finely chopped
1/4 teaspoon pepper	

Fry bacon in skillet until crisp; drain. Crumble bacon; return to skillet. Add mixture of sugar, cornstarch, salt and pepper. Add vinegar and water. Cook until clear, stirring constantly. Add potatoes and onion. Serve warm. Yield: 12 to 14 servings.

Judy Cox, Preceptor Alpha
Missoula, Montana

EASY GERMAN POTATO SALAD

5 pounds potatoes, boiled, peeled	1/4 to 1/2 cup vinegar
	1 1/2 teaspoons salt
1 medium onion, chopped	1/2 teaspoon pepper
	1 pound sliced bacon

Cut potatoes into slices. Combine with onion, vinegar, salt and pepper in large bowl. Cut bacon crosswise into 1/4-inch strips. Fry bacon in skillet until crisp. Pour bacon and pan drippings over potato mixture; mix well. Add more vinegar if mixture is dry. Serve warm. Yield: 10 to 12 servings.

Barbara Ordner, Kappa Omicron
Victoria, Texas

SAUERKRAUT SALAD

5 large cans sauerkraut	3 tablespoons finely
6 strips bacon	chopped parsley
6 tablespoons olive oil	3 tablespoons finely
1 large onion, finely	chopped celery
chopped	2 cans tomato sauce
3 cloves of garlic, finely	Salt and pepper to taste
chopped	

Rinse sauerkraut with water; drain. Fry bacon in skillet until crisp; drain. Combine bacon with olive oil and next 4 ingredients in skillet. Sauté until golden brown. Add sauerkraut. Cook for 20 minutes longer. Stir in tomato sauce and enough water to cover. Add salt and pepper. Bring to a boil. Reduce heat. Simmer, covered, for 2 hours.
Yield: 10 to 12 servings.

Beverly Mosich, Preceptor Eta Kappa
Covina, California

CHINESE SPINACH SALAD

1 pound fresh spinach,	1 small onion, chopped
torn into pieces	1/2 cup oil
1 8-ounce can water	7 tablespoons sugar
chestnuts, thinly sliced	1/4 cup catsup
2 hard-cooked eggs	2 tablespoons vinegar
3/4 cup bean sprouts	2 tablespoons
8 to 12 ounces bacon,	Worcestershire sauce
crisp-fried, crumbled	

Combine spinach with next 4 ingredients in large bowl. Chill, covered, until serving time. Combine onion with next 5 ingredients in small bowl; mix well. Chill for 2 hours or longer. Pour over salad just before serving; toss. Yield: 8 servings.

Eva Letha Lucas, Preceptor Alpha Phi
Elmer, Oklahoma

SPINACH SALAD

2 packages spinach,	1 teaspoon salt
torn into pieces	1/2 teaspoon pepper
1/2 cup herb-seasoned	1 large Bermuda onion,
stuffing mix	coarsely chopped
2 hard-cooked eggs,	1 tablespoon prepared
sliced	mustard
6 to 8 strips crisp-fried	1/2 cup cider vinegar
bacon, crumbled	1 cup vegetable oil
2/3 cup sugar	

Combine spinach, stuffing mix, eggs and bacon in large salad bowl. Combine remaining ingredients in blender container. Process until smooth. Pour over salad just before serving; toss. Yield: 8 servings.

Michelle Tressel, Gamma Theta
Cedar Rapids, Iowa

TOMATO ASPIC

2 cups tomato juice	1/2 cup finely chopped
1 package lemon gelatin	celery
1 1/2 teaspoon lemon	1/2 cup finely chopped
juice	small sweet pickle
1 teaspoon	Chopped onion
Worcestershire sauce	Salt and pepper to taste

Bring tomato juice to a boil in saucepan. Add gelatin, stirring until gelatin dissolves. Stir in remaining ingredients. Spoon into mold. Chill until firm.
Yield: 12 servings.

Nancy G. Gallivan, Eta Master
Las Cruces, New Mexico

ANTIPASTO SALAD BOWL

1/2 head iceberg lettuce	1/2 cup sliced black
1/2 head romaine lettuce	olives
1 cup thinly sliced	3/4 to 1 cup Italian
unpeeled zucchini	salad dressing
1/2 cup thinly sliced	1/2 cup grated Parmesan
mushrooms	cheese
6 green onions, sliced	8 ounces pepperoni, cut
2 stalks celery, thinly	into strips
sliced	Cherry tomato halves

Tear lettuces into bite-sized pieces. Combine with next 5 ingredients in salad bowl. Add salad dressing; toss gently. Combine with Parmesan cheese and pepperoni. Garnish with tomato halves. Serve immediately. Yield: 6 to 8 servings.

Ethel Dougherty, Xi Epsilon Epsilon
Hazelton, Pennsylvania

ANTIPASTO-PASTA SALAD

1 16-ounce package	1 small can black olives
shell-shaped pasta	8 ounces Genoa salami,
2 green bell peppers,	cut into cubes
chopped	8 ounces provolone
1 medium onion,	cheese, cut into cubes
chopped	Sliced pepperoni
3 stalks celery, chopped	1 8-ounce bottle of
1 package cherry	Italian salad dressing
tomatoes	Salt and pepper to taste

Cook pasta using package directions; drain. Combine pasta with remaining ingredients in large bowl; mix well. Chill, covered, overnight.
Yield: 20 servings.

Joanne R. Lim, Xi Zeta Psi
Stroudsburg, Pennsylvania

CAESAR SALAD

This recipe was shared with me by one of my co-workers who is a very good cook. He often makes Caesar Salad for the "gals in the office" as a special treat for lunch.

4 medium heads romaine lettuce	1 egg, beaten (at room temperature)
3 to 4 large cloves of garlic, crushed	1 cup grated Parmesan cheese
1 cup virgin olive oil	4 ounces mushrooms, sliced or cut into quarters
1 can diced anchovies	
Juice of 2 lemons	4 ounces cherry tomato halves
Freshly ground pepper	

Wash lettuce; pat dry. Tear into bite-sized pieces. Place in salad bowl. Chill until serving time. Mix garlic, olive oil, anchovies, lemon juice and pepper in small bowl. Add egg; mix well. Let stand for 5 to 10 minutes. Pour salad dressing over lettuce; toss. Add Parmesan cheese; toss again. Serve immediately. Yield: 4 to 6 servings.

Louise T. Moore, Xi Alpha Chi
Boise, Idaho

❖ LETTUCELESS SALAD

1 bunch broccoli, finely chopped	4 ounces shredded Cheddar cheese
1 head cauliflower, finely chopped	1 egg, beaten
2 carrots, finely chopped	3 ounces cream cheese, softened
1 cucumber, finely chopped	2 tablespoons vinegar
2 apples, finely chopped	2 tablespoons vegetable oil
1/2 cup raisins	1 tablespoon prepared mustard
1 green bell pepper, finely chopped	
1/2 cup finely chopped celery	Garlic salt to taste
	Salt and pepper to taste
	Croutons

Combine first 9 ingredients in large bowl; mix well. Combine beaten egg with cream cheese, vinegar, oil, mustard, garlic salt, salt and pepper in saucepan. Cook until thickened, stirring constantly. Cool. Pour over salad. Chill overnight. Top with croutons. May double dressing. Yield: 8 servings.

Margaret T. Tanner, Lambda Master
Harrisburg, Illinois

CREAMED LETTUCE SALAD

1 head lettuce	Vinegar
2 stalks celery, chopped	1/2 cup mayonnaise
1 sweet onion, sliced	8 ounces bacon, crisp-fried
1 cup sour cream	
1/2 cup sugar	Parmesan cheese

Tear lettuce into bite-sized pieces. Arrange in 9-by-13-inch dish. Layer celery and onion over lettuce.

Top with mixture of sour cream and sugar. Mix a small amount of vinegar with mayonnaise in small bowl. Pour over sour cream layer. Crumble bacon over top; sprinkle with Parmesan cheese. Chill, covered with plastic wrap, for 4 hours or longer. Yield: 6 to 8 servings.

Carol Sylvis, Xi Gamma Nu
Hendersonville, Tennessee

SUPER BOWL SALAD

Flowerets of 1 bunch broccoli	10 cherry tomatoes, cut into halves
Flowerets of 1 head cauliflower	1/2 cup canola oil
2 or 3 carrots, diagonally sliced	1/3 cup white vinegar
	1/4 cup sugar
8 ounces asparagus	2 cloves of garlic, crushed
6 to 8 red radishes, sliced	Red pepper flakes to taste
1 cucumber, sliced	1/2 teaspoon each salt and white pepper
1 red bell pepper, coarsely chopped	
1 jar marinated artichoke hearts	10 mushrooms, cut into halves
1/2 cup small black olives	1 avocado, sliced
	3 ounces grated Parmesan cheese

Blanch broccoli and next 3 ingredients in boiling water in saucepan for 30 seconds. Rinse with cold water; drain. Combine blanched vegetables with radishes, cucumber, red pepper, artichoke hearts, black olives and tomatoes in glass bowl. Mix oil, vinegar, sugar, garlic, red pepper flakes, salt and white pepper in small bowl. Pour over vegetable mixture; toss. Marinate in refrigerator for 8 hours or longer. Add mushrooms and avocado just before serving. Top with Parmesan cheese. Yield: 10 servings.

Nancy Chaney, Xi Pi
Moscow, Idaho

COUNTERPOINT SALAD

3 large peeled avocados	1/2 cup yogurt, buttermilk or milk
1/2 cup lemon juice	
11/2 pounds alfalfa sprouts	1/4 cup chopped chives
	11/2 tablespoons Worcestershire sauce
6 large tomatoes, cut into 1/3-inch slices	
11/2 pounds bacon, crisp-fried, crumbled	1/2 teaspoon freshly ground pepper
1 cup mayonnaise	1/4 teaspoon Tabasco sauce

Cut each avocado into 8 wedges; sprinkle with lemon juice. Layer alfalfa sprouts, tomatoes, avocados and bacon 1/3 at a time into glass salad bowl. Chill, covered, until serving time. Combine mayonnaise with next 5 ingredients in bowl; mix well. Pour over salad; toss. Serve immediately. Yield: 8 to 10 servings.

Margo Jakobs, Tau Pi
Sterling, Illinois

SIX-LAYER LETTUCE SALAD

1 head lettuce, broken into pieces	2 cups mayonnaise
1 white onion, sliced into thin rings	Shredded Cheddar cheese
1 10-ounce package frozen peas	3/4 jar bacon bits

Spread lettuce in 9-by-13-inch dish. Layer remaining ingredients in order listed over lettuce. Chill, covered with plastic wrap, for 24 hours. Yield: 12 servings.

Candis Thornton, Laureate Alpha Zeta
Weston, Colorado

CHINESE SALAD

3 cups cooked rice	6 green onions, chopped
2 cups frozen peas, cooked	1/2 cup vegetable oil
1 8-ounce can water chestnuts, chopped	3 tablespoons soy sauce
	Celery salt to taste

Toss rice, peas, water chestnuts and green onions together in large bowl. Pour mixture of oil and soy sauce over top. Add celery salt. Yield: 6 to 8 servings.

Denise M. Gorham, Epsilon Chi
Kingman, Arizona

INDIAN RICE SALAD

2/3 cup uncooked brown rice	1 1/2 tablespoons white vinegar
1/2 cup raisins	1 clove of garlic, finely chopped
10 whole almonds, toasted, coarsely chopped	1 teaspoon curry powder
1/4 cup chopped celery	1/2 teaspoon ground cumin
2 tablespoons chopped onion	1/4 teaspoon cinnamon
3 tablespoons vegetable oil	1/4 teaspoon salt
	1/8 teaspoon pepper

Cook rice using package directions omitting salt. Combine with raisins, almonds, celery and onion in medium bowl; toss. Mix oil with remaining ingredients in small bowl. Pour over rice mixture; toss. Chill, covered, for 2 hours. Yield: 4 servings.

Juanita Lunn, Alpha Kappa
Mount Vernon, Ohio

Sandy Duncan, Xi Omicron, Cresapton, Maryland, combines 1 1/4 cups sugar, 1 1/2 teaspoons salt, 3 heaping tablespoons flour, 2 eggs, 3/4 cup vinegar and 3/4 cup water in saucepan, cooks over medium heat until thickened, stirring constantly and then blends in 2 tablespoons margarine, 2 tablespoons prepared mustard and 1 cup salad dressing to make Delicious Cooked Dressing for Potato Salad.

LINGUINE SALAD SUPREME

16 ounces linguine	1 bunch green onions, chopped
1 8-ounce bottle of zesty Italian salad dressing	1 large tomato, chopped
1 cucumber, sliced	1/2 jar Salad Supreme seasoning

Cook linguine using package directions; drain, rinse with cold water and drain well. Place in large bowl. Add salad dressing and vegetables; toss to mix. Add seasoning; toss lightly. Chill, covered, overnight. Yield: 16 servings.

Sharon A. Lewis, Laureate Alpha Epsilon
Williamsburg, Virginia

SPAGHETTI SALAD

2 envelopes Italian salad dressing mix	1 package favorite frozen vegetables
1 16-ounce package spaghetti, cooked, cooled	1/4 teaspoon chili powder
1/4 cup chopped onion	Salt, pepper and garlic salt to taste
1 red bell pepper, finely chopped	Hard-cooked eggs, sliced
2 tablespoons parsley flakes	Paprika to taste

Prepare salad dressing mix using package directions. Combine spaghetti with next 8 ingredients in large bowl. Pour prepared salad dressing over top; toss. Chill, covered, for several hours to overnight. Toss before serving. Garnish with eggs and paprika. Yield: 12 servings.

Karla Wheeler, Laureate Alpha Theta
Rifle, Colorado

RASPBERRY SALAD DRESSING

1 cup Raspberry Vinegar	1 cup maple syrup
1 cup olive oil	1 tablespoon tarragon leaves
1 cup vegetable oil	1 teaspoon salt
1 tablespoon Dijon mustard	

Combine Raspberry Vinegar with remaining ingredients in blender container. Process for 3 minutes or until smooth. Yield: 4 cups.

RASPBERRY VINEGAR

3 cups fresh raspberries, mashed	2 cups white wine vinegar

Combine raspberries and wine vinegar in glass jar. Let stand, covered, in cool place for 2 days or longer. Yield: 3 cups.

Betty Zimbeck, Gamma Iota
Berlin, Maryland

Mostly Meats

BAKED CORNED BEEF PASTIES

1/4 cup chopped onion
2 tablespoons butter or margarine
2 tablespoons all-purpose flour
1 16-ounce can stewed tomatoes
1 12-ounce can corned beef, chopped
Parsley to taste

2 cups all-purpose flour
1 teaspoon baking powder
1/2 teaspoon salt
6 tablespoons shortening
1 egg yolk, beaten
1/3 cup milk
1 8-ounce jar Cheez Whiz

Preheat oven to 400 degrees. Sauté onion in butter in skillet. Stir in 2 tablespoons flour. Add tomatoes gradually. Cook until thickened, stirring constantly. Stir in corned beef. Cook for 10 minutes. Stir in parsley; cool. Mix 2 cups flour, baking powder and salt in medium bowl. Cut in shortening with pastry blender. Add egg yolk and milk; stir until mixture forms ball. Roll 1/4 inch thick on floured surface. Cut into squares. Press into muffin cups. Fill cups 3/4 full with corned beef mixture. Pinch corners together at tops to enclose filling. Bake for 20 minutes. Serve with Cheez Whiz. Yield: 12 servings.

Naomi D. Rhine, Zeta Master
Carlisle, Pennsylvania

HOT CORNED BEEF SANDWICHES

1 12-ounce can corned beef
1 10-ounce can cream of mushroom soup
1/4 cup pickle relish
3 hard-cooked eggs, chopped

Pepper to taste
12 hamburger buns
Softened butter or margarine
Garlic salt to taste

Preheat oven to 400 degrees. Combine corned beef with soup, relish, eggs and pepper in bowl; mix well. Split buns; spread cut surfaces with butter; sprinkle with garlic salt. Spread corned beef mixture evenly over prepared buns; wrap in foil. Bake for 20 minutes. Serve hot. Yield: 12 servings.

Joann J. Huth, Laureate Tau
Butler, Pennsylvania

BEEF BURGUNDY

This is great after a day on the ski slopes.

5 medium onions, sliced
2 tablespoons corn oil
2 pounds lean beef, cut into 1-inch cubes
1 cup unsalted beef broth
2 cups dry red wine
1/4 teaspoon thyme

Freshly ground pepper to taste
8 ounces fresh mushrooms, sliced
2 tablespoons cornstarch
1/2 cup water
Cooked noodles

Sauté onions in oil in heavy saucepan; remove with slotted spoon. Brown beef in drippings in saucepan. Stir in 1/2 cup beef broth, 1 cup wine, thyme and pepper. Simmer for 1 1/2 hours, adding remaining 1/2 cup beef broth and 1 cup wine as needed to cover beef. Add onions and mushrooms. Simmer for 20 minutes. Dissolve cornstarch in water. Stir into beef mixture. Cook until thickened, stirring constantly. Serve beef mixture over hot cooked noodles. Add salad and French bread for a full hearty meal. Yield: 8 servings.

Patricia W. Mecaughey, Eta Chi
Basye, Virginia

BEEF FRANÇAIS

3 pounds lean beef
  chuck, cubed
4¹/2 tablespoons all-
  purpose flour
5 tablespoons vegetable
  oil
1 tablespoon parsley
  flakes
³/4 teaspoon thyme
1 tablespoon salt
³/4 teaspoon pepper
1¹/2 bay leaves

2 10-ounce cans beef
  consommé
2 6-ounce cans tomato
  paste
³/4 cup red cooking wine
1¹/2 cups sliced celery
8 to 10 small potatoes,
  peeled
1 pound carrots, peeled
3 8-ounce jars whole
  onions, drained

Preheat oven to 325 degrees. Shake beef in flour in bag, coating well. Brown in oil in saucepan; remove to large roasting pan. Sprinkle with mixture of parsley flakes, thyme, salt and pepper. Top with bay leaves. Combine consommé, tomato paste and wine in small bowl. Pour over beef; sprinkle with celery. Bake, covered, for 1¹/2 hours. Add potatoes, carrots and onions. Bake, covered, for 45 minutes longer. Chill overnight. Bake at 325 degrees for 1 hour to serve; discard bay leaves. Serve with bread, salad and a simple dessert. Yield: 6 servings.

Debbie Farrar, Eta Tau
Bluefield, Virginia

CHUCK'S CHOW

2 pounds beef cubes
3 10-ounce cans cream
  of chicken soup
3 10-ounce cans cream
  of mushroom soup
1 10-ounce can cream
  of celery soup
1¹/2 soup cans water
1 green bell pepper,
  chopped

1 cup chopped carrots
1 cup chopped celery
1 16-ounce can peas
  (optional)
1 teaspoon paprika
Salt and pepper to taste
Steamed rice or cooked
  noodles
Garlic bread

Preheat oven to 250 degrees. Combine first 12 ingredients in large bowl; mix well. Spoon into large baking dish. Bake for 4 hours or longer. Serve over rice or noodles with garlic bread for dipping. May add mushrooms if desired. Yield: 10 servings.

Diana L. Bunce, Pi Eta
Castalia, Ohio

Christina R. Stafford, Preceptor Alpha Gamma, Sterling, Colorado, makes wonderful Oven-Barbecued Beef by baking a 6-pound trimmed brisket with 2 cups water, salt and pepper in preheated 325-degree oven for 4 hours then shredding. She cooks 4 chopped onions in 3 tablespoons Worcestershire sauce, 1/4 cup sugar, 3 tablespoons chili powder, 5¹/4 cups tomato purée, a large bottle of barbecue sauce, adds shredded beef and roast pan juices and simmers. Flavor improves if prepared and frozen ahead of time.

FIVE-HOUR BEEF STEW

This is as easy to clean up after as it is to prepare, with only one dish to wash. It is a favorite of family and friends for gatherings or for the holidays.

3 pounds beef cubes
1 29-ounce can
  tomatoes
1 10-ounce package
  frozen peas
6 carrots, sliced
3 medium potatoes,
  chopped
3 medium onions,
  coarsely chopped

1 cup chopped celery
3 tablespoons minute
  tapioca
1 tablespoon sugar
¹/4 cup red wine
Thyme, oregano and
  rosemary to taste
1 tablespoon salt
Pepper to taste

Preheat oven to 225 degrees. Combine all ingredients in 5-quart baking dish. Bake, covered tightly, for 5 hours. Yield: 8 to 10 servings.

Kristy K. Launtz, Mu Tau
Huntingdon, Pennsylvania

OVEN STEW

2 pounds stew beef
1¹/2 cups chopped
  carrots
4 large potatoes,
  chopped
¹/2 cup chopped celery
1 onion, sliced
¹/2 green bell pepper,
  chopped

3 tablespoons tapioca
1 tablespoon sugar
1 24-ounce can mixed
  vegetable juice cocktail
1 teaspoon Beau Monde
  seasoning
1 teaspoon minced garlic
Salt and pepper to taste

Preheat oven to 250 degrees. Combine all ingredients in large bowl; mix well. Spoon into large baking pan. Bake for 5 hours. Yield: 8 to 10 servings.

Mary Manis, Delta Iota
West Frankfort, Ilinois

OVEN BEEF STEW

3 pounds stew beef
4 large carrots, coarsely
  chopped
4 potatoes, coarsely
  chopped
1 16-ounce can onions
1 16-ounce can
  tomatoes
1 16-ounce can peas
¹/2 10-ounce can beef
  consommé

6 tablespoons minute
  tapioca
1 tablespoon light
  brown sugar
¹/2 cup bread crumbs
1 bay leaf
1¹/4 teaspoons salt
Pepper to taste

Preheat oven to 250 degrees. Combine beef with remaining ingredients in large bowl; mix well. Spoon into heavy baking pan. Bake, covered, for 7 to 8 hours. Discard bay leaf. Yield: 8 to 10 servings.

Darlene Gumfory, Laureate Alpha Sigma
Iola, Kansas

SLOW-COOKED BEEF STEW

1 1/2 pounds stew beef	1 16-ounce can stewed
All-purpose flour	tomatoes
1 onion, chopped	2 tablespoons tapioca
Margarine	1 tablespoon sugar
3 potatoes, chopped	Mushrooms
6 carrots, chopped	1 cup wine
1 cup chopped celery	
1 10-ounce can beef	
gravy	

Preheat oven to 275 degrees. Coat beef with flour. Brown beef and onion in margarine in Dutch oven. Add remaining ingredients; mix well. Bake for 6 hours. May add 1 can beef broth if needed for desired consistency. Yield: 8 servings.

Marilyn A. Reitmeyer, Preceptor Gamma Nu
Pittsburgh, Pennsylvania

DRIP BEEF

1 5-pound boneless	Salt and pepper to taste
rump roast	3 bouillon cubes
1/2 teaspoon each	Hard rolls or sandwich
savory, oregano and	buns
rosemary	Catsup or mustard
1 tablespoon garlic salt	

Combine beef with seasonings, bouillon cubes and water to cover in heavy saucepan. Simmer for 7 to 8 hours or until very tender. Shred beef into cooking liquid. Serve on hard rolls or sandwich buns with catsup and mustard. May drain some of the cooking liquid for desired consistency. Yield: 10 to 12 servings.

Kaye Beilue, Preceptor Gamma Gamma
Tulsa, Oklahoma

OLD-COUNTRY ITALIAN POT ROAST

1 2-pound boneless	1/2 teaspoon basil
chuck roast, 2 inches	1/8 teaspoon cinnamon
thick	1 teaspoon salt
1 large clove of garlic,	1/4 teaspoon pepper
cut into quarters	2 6-ounce cans tomato
2 tablespoons olive oil	paste
2 tablespoons butter or	3 1/2 cups water
margarine	16 ounces spaghetti,
1 clove of garlic, minced	cooked
1 small onion, chopped	Grated Parmesan or
2 teaspoons oregano	Romano cheese
1 teaspoon thyme	

Tie roast if necessary to hold shape. Insert garlic quarters into slits in roast. Brown roast on all sides in olive oil and butter in large saucepan; remove roast and reduce heat. Add minced garlic, onion and seasonings to drippings in saucepan. Cook for 5 minutes, stirring frequently. Return beef to

saucepan. Add mixture of tomato paste and water. Bring to a full boil; reduce heat. Simmer, covered, for 2 hours or until beef is tender and sauce is thickened to desired consistency, turning beef occasionally. Slice beef. Spoon cooking sauce over spaghetti in large shallow serving dish; lift with forks to mix gently. Arrange sliced beef on spaghetti. Sprinkle with cheese. Yield: 8 servings.

Frances Kucera, Laureate Omicron
Eugene, Oregon

❖ WESTERN POT ROAST

All four of my daughters cook this and insist it's a family all-together night, just as I did when they were younger.

1 cup water	1 1/2 cups chopped onions
1 cup dried apricots	2 cloves of garlic, finely
1 5-pound boneless	chopped
beef roast	1 6-ounce can pitted
1/2 teaspoon ginger	black olives, drained
2 teaspoons salt	2 cups sliced mushrooms
1/4 teaspoon pepper	1/2 cup red wine or water
1 tablespoon vegetable	
oil	

Preheat oven to 325 degrees. Combine water and apricots in small bowl; let stand for several minutes until plumped. Rub beef with mixture of ginger, salt and pepper. Brown on all sides in oil in Dutch oven; drain. Add apricots, onions, garlic, black olives, mushrooms and red wine; mix well. Bake, covered, for 3 hours. May bake in slow cooker on Low for 8 hours if preferred. Yield: 12 to 16 servings.

Sandy Dumont, Preceptor Epsilon Mu
Shorewood, Illinois

YANKEE POT ROAST

1 5-pound (about)	5 cups beef bouillon
bottom round roast	1 teaspoon Kitchen
1/3 cup corn oil	Bouquet
1 cup chopped onion	3 bay leaves
1/2 cup chopped celery	1 teaspoon salt
1/2 cup all-purpose flour	1/2 teaspoon pepper

Preheat oven to 400 degrees. Brown roast on all sides in oil in Dutch oven; remove to plate. Add onion and celery to drippings in Dutch oven. Sauté for 5 minutes. Stir in flour. Simmer for 8 minutes. Add beef bouillon, Kitchen Bouquet, bay leaves, salt and pepper. Cook until thickened, stirring constantly. Add roast. Roast for 2 hours. Remove roast to serving platter; strain cooking juices to serve as gravy. Serve with potatoes and an additional vegetable of choice. Yield: 10 servings.

Dottie Holbrook, Preceptor Epsilon Kappa
Winter Park, Florida

LAZY TEXAS BRISKET

1 4 to 5-pound brisket	1/2 teaspoon cumin,
1 large clove of garlic,	crumbled sage, sugar
minced	and oregano
1 tablespoon chili	1/4 teaspoon each red
powder	pepper and black
1 teaspoon each	pepper
paprika and salt	

Preheat oven to 200 degrees. Rub brisket with garlic. Rub with mixture of remaining seasonings. Place fat side up on large piece of foil; seal tightly. Place in shallow roasting pan. Roast for 8 hours or until tender. Yield: 12 servings.

La Donna Smith, Preceptor Kappa Xi
Schertz, Texas

OVEN-BAG BRISKET

1 4 to 5-pound brisket	1 envelope onion soup
Garlic powder,	mix
Worcestershire sauce	2 cups beef broth or Port
and pepper to taste	
1 tablespoon all-	
purpose flour	

Preheat oven to 300 degrees. Rub brisket with garlic powder, Worcestershire sauce and pepper. Shake with flour and soup mix in bag. Place fat side up in oven-baking bag; place in 2-inch deep baking pan. Add beef broth to bag. Secure opening and cut 6 slits in bag. Roast for 4 hours. Serve with cooking juices. Yield: 12 to 15 servings.

Evelyn Schlueter, Iota Master
New Braunfels, Texas

BONELESS BIRDS

2 pounds round steak,	1 small onion, sliced
1/4 inch thick	2 tablespoons all-
1 teaspoon salt	purpose flour
1/2 teaspoon allspice	2 tablespoons butter or
4 ounces mushrooms,	margarine
chopped	1/2 cup beef broth
4 ounces bacon, chopped	1/2 cup half and half
2 tablespoons chopped	
parsley	

Preheat oven to 300 degrees. Cut steak into 8 serving pieces. Pound very thin between waxed paper with flat side of meat mallet. Sprinkle with salt and allspice. Top with mushrooms, bacon, parsley and onion. Roll tightly to enclose filling; secure with wooden picks. Coat with flour. Brown on all sides in butter in heavy skillet; remove to 9-by-13-inch baking dish. Add mixture of beef broth and half and half. Bake, covered, for 1 hour. Yield: 8 servings.

Margaret S. Poll, Omega Nu
Lakeland, Florida

OVEN-BARBECUED STEAKS

3 pounds beef round	1 tablespoon light
steak	brown sugar
2 tablespoons vegetable	1 tablespoon prepared
oil	mustard
3 tablespoons instant	1 tablespoon
onion	Worcestershire sauce
3/4 cup catsup	1/2 teaspoon salt
3/4 cup water	1/8 teaspoon pepper
1/2 cup vinegar	

Preheat oven to 350 degrees. Cut steak into 10 serving pieces. Brown in oil in large skillet over medium heat; remove to baking pan. Add remaining ingredients to skillet; mix well. Simmer for 5 minutes. Pour over steak. Bake, covered, for 1 1/2 to 2 hours or until tender. Yield: 10 servings.

Marcia Nestler, Xi Zeta Mu
Eldridge, Iowa

BEEF TOURNEDOS IN WINE SAUCE

6 slices French bread	1/4 teaspoon seasoned
1 1/2 pounds medium	pepper
mushrooms	6 1 1/4-inch thick beef
1/4 teaspoon seasoned	loin steaks
salt	2 tablespoons butter or
1/8 teaspoon seasoned	margarine
pepper	1/4 cup water
1/4 cup butter or	1/4 cup red or rosé wine
margarine	Parsley
1 teaspoon seasoned salt	

Toast bread slices for 3 minutes or until golden brown on both sides. Sauté mushrooms with 1/4 teaspoon seasoned salt and 1/8 teaspoon seasoned pepper in 1/4 cup butter in 12-inch skillet over medium heat until tender. Remove to 1 end of warm platter. Sprinkle 1 teaspoon seasoned salt and 1/4 teaspoon pepper over steaks. Add 2 tablespoons butter to skillet. Brown steaks for 5 minutes on each side in butter. Arrange on toast on warm platter. Stir water and wine into drippings in skillet. Bring to a boil; pour over steaks. Garnish with parsley. Yield: 6 servings.

Margaret Titus, Xi Alpha Epsilon
Durango, Colorado

Rae Brewer, Waynesboro, Pennsylvania, prepares Easy Hungarian Goulash by layering 2 pounds of 1-inch lean beef cubes and 1 large sliced onion in slow cooker, adding mixture of 1 minced clove of garlic, 1/2 cup catsup, 2 tablespoons Worcestershire sauce, 1 tablespoon brown sugar, 1 teaspoon salt, 2 teaspoons paprika, 1/2 teaspoon dry mustard and 1 cup water. Cook on Low for 9 to 10 hours and stir in 1/4 cup flour mixed with a small amount of water. Cook on High for 10 to 15 minutes to thicken and serve over noodles, rice or mashed potatoes.

DEVILED SWISS STEAK

3 pounds beef round steak	2 tablespoons corn oil
1¹/2 teaspoons dry mustard	1 6-ounce can mushrooms
1¹/2 teaspoons salt	1 tablespoon Worcestershire sauce
¹/4 teaspoon pepper	

Trim steak; rub with mixture of dry mustard, salt and pepper. Pound with meat mallet. Brown on both sides in hot oil in large heavy skillet; drain. Drain mushrooms, reserving liquid. Add reserved liquid and Worcestershire sauce to skillet. Simmer, tightly covered, over very low heat for 1¹/2 hours or until tender. Add mushrooms. Cook until heated through. Skim off fat. Serve with baked potatoes and green salad. Yield: 8 servings.

Paula M. Duncan
Bastrop, Louisiana

STEAK STEW

1 2¹/2 to 3-pound sirloin steak or inexpensive roast, grilled	¹/2 cup Worcestershire sauce
Water	4 or 5 large carrots, chopped
Tomato juice	4 or 5 medium potatoes, chopped
2 medium onions, chopped	1 10-ounce package frozen corn
4 or 5 stalks celery, chopped	1 10-ounce package frozen peas
2 16-ounce cans tomatoes, chopped	Salt and pepper to taste

Cut steak into pieces. Combine with equal parts water and tomato juice in large saucepan. Add onions, celery, tomatoes and Worcestershire sauce. Simmer over low heat until steak is tender. Add remaining ingredients; mix well. Simmer, covered, for 1 hour or until vegetables are tender. Yield: 8 servings.

Frances Gumpert
Dallas, Texas

WET BURRITOS

2 pounds ground beef	Chopped tomatoes
Garlic salt and salt to taste	1 12-ounce can tomato sauce
1 16-ounce can refried beans	3 cups water
1 envelope burrito seasoning mix	2 beef bouillon cubes
10 to 12 tortillas	1¹/2 tablespoons chili powder
Shredded lettuce	Shredded cheese

Preheat oven to 375 degrees. Brown ground beef with garlic salt and salt in skillet, stirring until crumbly; drain. Stir in beans and burrito seasoning mix. Reserve 1 cup mixture. Spoon remaining meat mixture onto tortillas; add lettuce and tomatoes. Roll tortillas to enclose filling; arrange in two 8-by-12-inch baking dishes. Combine reserved meat mixture with remaining ingredients in medium bowl; mix well. Spoon over burritos; sprinkle with cheese. Yield: 10 to 12 servings.

Roberta Waters, Xi Lambda Mu
Camdenton, Missouri

MEXICAN STACK

4 pounds ground beef	Cooked rice (optional)
1 onion, chopped	Chopped onion
2 29-ounce cans tomatoes	Picante sauce
2 6-ounce cans tomato purée	1 pound cheese, shredded
1 29-ounce can ranch-style beans	2 heads lettuce, chopped
2 to 3 tablespoons garlic powder	Chopped avocado or avocado dip
3 tablespoons chili powder	2 pints sour cream
2 packages corn chips, crushed	7 tomatoes, chopped
	1 jar chopped black olives
	1 10-ounce package pecans, chopped
	1 7-ounce can coconut

Brown ground beef with 1 onion in skillet, stirring until ground beef is crumbly; drain. Add tomatoes, tomato purée, beans, garlic powder and chili powder; mix well. Simmer for 1 hour, adding water if necessary for desired consistency. Place remaining ingredients in individual serving bowls. Arrange in order listed on serving table, placing meat sauce after rice. Allow guests to assemble their own stacks, using ingredients of choice. Yield: 15 to 20 servings.

Beth Peyton, Laureate Psi
Altus, Oklahoma

PIZZA BURGERS

2 pounds ground beef	¹/4 teaspoon red pepper
1 pound extra-lean sausage	15 English muffins, split into halves
Chopped onion	12 ounces mozzarella cheese, shredded
1 16-ounce can tomato sauce	8 ounces Cheddar cheese, shredded
1 6-ounce can tomato paste	8 ounces Swiss cheese, shredded
¹/2 teaspoon each oregano and garlic salt	

Preheat oven to 350 degrees. Brown ground beef and sausage with onion in large skillet, stirring frequently; drain. Add tomato sauce, tomato paste and seasonings; mix well. Spread on muffins; sprinkle with cheeses. Place on baking sheet. Bake for 20 to 25 minutes or until cheese melts. Yield: 30 servings.

Vicky Osmundson, Beta Delta
Calmar, Iowa

ZUCCHINI-HAMBURGER MELT

8 ounces (or more) Velveeta cheese	2 small tomatoes, chopped
1 pound ground beef	2 small zucchini, sliced
1 cup drained canned corn	1 small onion, chopped
1 cup cooked rice	1 cup croutons

Preheat oven to 350 degrees. Slice 2 slices of cheese; chop remaining cheese. Combine ground beef, corn, rice, tomatoes, zucchini, onion, chopped cheese and half the croutons in bowl; mix well. Spread in 8-by-8-inch glass baking dish. Top with remaining croutons and cheese slices. Microwave on High for 10 minutes or until cooked through. Bake in oven for 15 minutes or until brown. Yield: 12 servings.

Teresa L. Sickels, Xi Delta Epsilon
St. Peters, Missouri

GROUND BEEF CASSEROLE

1 pound ground beef	1 10-ounce can cream of chicken soup
1 cup chopped celery	
2 onions, chopped	1 10-ounce can cream of mushroom soup
3 tablespoons shortening	
	1/4 cup soy sauce
1 cup instant rice	1 3-ounce can Chinese noodles
1 cup water	

Preheat oven to 350 degrees. Brown ground beef with celery and onions in shortening in large skillet, stirring until ground beef is crumbly; drain. Add rice and next 4 ingredients; mix well. Spoon into large baking dish; sprinkle with noodles. Bake for 30 minutes. Yield: 8 servings.

Ann E. Garner, Xi Delta Lambda
Gig Harbor, Washington

BEEF DRESSING CASSEROLE

1 small onion, minced	1 cup milk
1/4 cup minced celery	2 pounds ground beef
12 slices dry bread, torn into small pieces	1 tablespoon mustard
	1 tablespoon Worcestershire sauce
1 tablespoon poultry seasoning	
	1/4 teaspoon pepper
1 10-ounce can cream of mushroom soup	1 10-ounce can cream of mushroom soup

Combine onion, celery, bread and poultry seasoning in medium bowl. Add mixture of 1 can soup and milk; mix well. Chill, covered, overnight. Preheat oven to 350 degrees. Brown ground beef in skillet, stirring until crumbly; drain. Add ground beef, mustard, Worcestershire sauce and pepper to bread mixture; mix well. Press into 9-by-13-inch baking dish. Spread remaining can soup over top. Bake for 1 hour. Yield: 8 to 10 servings.

Barbara Robertson, Preceptor Epsilon Epsilon
Belvidere, Illinois

MAKE-AHEAD LAYERED MEXICAN CASSEROLE

2 pounds ground beef	1 pound Monterey Jack cheese, shredded
1 onion, chopped	
2 tablespoons chili powder	1 10-ounce can Ro-Tel tomatoes
Garlic powder, cumin, salt and pepper to taste	1 cup shredded Cheddar cheese
6 to 8 corn tortillas	1 10-ounce can cream of chicken or cream of mushroom soup
1 16-ounce can ranch-style beans	

Brown ground beef with onion and seasonings in large skillet, stirring frequently; drain. Spread half the mixture in very large baking dish. Top with tortillas. Mix beans with remaining beef mixture; spread over tortillas. Layer Monterey Jack cheese, tomatoes, Cheddar cheese and soup over top. Chill, covered, for 24 hours. Preheat oven to 350 degrees. Bake casserole for 1 hour. Yield: 6 to 8 servings.

Betty Borchardt, Xi Omicron
Harlingen, Texas

BEEF AND MUSHROOM CASSEROLE

This is good cold the next day.

2 pounds lean ground chuck	1 cup sour cream
	1/4 cup chopped pimento (optional)
1/2 cup chopped onion	
1 10-ounce can cream of mushroom soup	3 cups cooked curly noodles
1 10-ounce can cream of chicken soup	3/4 teaspoon salt
	1/4 teaspoon pepper
1 4-ounce can sliced mushrooms (optional)	Buttered bread crumbs

Preheat oven to 350 degrees. Brown ground chuck in skillet, stirring until crumbly. Add onion. Cook until onion is tender; drain. Stir in soups, mushrooms, sour cream, pimento, noodles, salt and pepper. Spoon into 2-quart baking dish; top with bread crumbs. Bake until golden brown. Yield: 8 to 10 servings.

Cathy L. Thomas, Phi Beta Omega
Boynton, Oklahoma

BEEFY TATER TOT CASSEROLE

2 pounds ground beef	1 10-ounce can golden mushroom soup
1 small onion, chopped	
1 10-ounce can cream of chicken soup	1 32-ounce package frozen Tater Tots

Preheat oven to 350 degrees. Spread beef in 9-by-13-inch baking dish. Sprinkle with onion. Spread mixture of soups evenly over onion. Sprinkle with Tater Tots. Bake for 1 1/2 hours. Yield: 8 servings.

Loree Walrath, Alpha Beta Psi
Clinton, Missouri

BEEFY NOODLE DELIGHT

This recipe was given to me by a very loving grandmother many years ago. I still have the original card she wrote by hand.

1¹/2 pounds ground beef	*8 ounces cream cheese,*
2 8-ounce cans tomato	*softened*
sauce	*¹/2 cup chopped onion*
1 8-ounce package	*1 teaspoon sugar*
noodles, cooked,	*(optional)*
drained	*¹/2 cup shredded*
8 ounces sour cream	*Cheddar cheese*

Preheat oven to 350 degrees. Brown ground beef in skillet, stirring until crumbly; drain. Stir in tomato sauce. Simmer for 15 minutes. Spread noodles in greased 9-by-13-inch baking dish. Spoon beef mixture over noodles. Combine sour cream, cream cheese, onion and sugar in bowl; mix well. Spread over beef mixture; top with Cheddar cheese. Bake until cheese melts and casserole is heated through. Yield: 8 or more servings.

Jerry S. Inscho, Laureate Alpha Beta
Ft. Myers, Florida

POTLUCK CASSEROLE

This casserole is better on the second day.

1 pound ground beef	*1 8-ounce package*
1 medium onion,	*noodles, cooked*
chopped	*Salt and pepper to taste*
1 10-ounce can cream	*1 cup shredded cheese*
of mushroom soup	*1 small bottle of stuffed*
1 10-ounce can cream	*green olives, sliced*
of chicken soup	
¹/2 10-ounce can	
tomato soup	

Preheat oven to 350 degrees. Brown ground beef with onion in skillet, stirring until ground beef is crumbly; drain. Add soups, noodles, salt and pepper; mix well. Spoon into 2-quart baking dish. Bake for 30 minutes. Add cheese and undrained olives. Bake for 10 minutes longer. Yield: 10 to 12 servings.

Irma Heiser, Preceptor Beta Kappa
Bowling Green, Ohio

BEEFY HASHED BROWN CASSEROLE

1 pound ground beef	*1¹/2 to 2 cups cubed*
¹/4 cup chopped onion	*Velveeta cheese*
24 to 32 ounces frozen	*4 cups crushed*
shredded hashed	*cornflakes*
brown potatoes	*3 tablespoons melted*
8 ounces cream cheese,	*margarine*
softened	
1 10-ounce can cream	
of chicken soup	

Preheat oven to 350 degrees. Brown ground beef with onion in skillet, stirring until ground beef is crumbly; drain. Layer hashed brown potatoes and ground beef in 9-by-13-inch baking dish. Combine cream cheese, soup and Velveeta cheese in glass dish. Microwave until cheeses melt. Spread over beef. Sprinkle with cornflakes; drizzle with margarine. Bake for 1 hour. Yield: 8 servings.

Brenda Houge, Beta Gamma
Huron, South Dakota

GRANNY'S CABBAGE PATCH STEW

2 pounds ground beef	*1 small head cabbage,*
1 cup chopped onion	*chopped*
1 cup chopped celery	*1 clove of garlic, minced*
1 29-ounce can	*2 cups water*
tomatoes	*1 teaspoon each chili*
1 29-ounce can pinto	*powder and salt*
beans	*¹/2 teaspoon pepper*

Brown ground beef in saucepan, stirring until crumbly; drain. Add remaining ingredients; mix well. Simmer for 1¹/2 hours. Yield: 8 servings.

Becky Guthrie, Mu Omega
Tahlequah, Oklahoma

OLD-TIME STUFFED PEPPERS

8 medium green bell	*1 teaspoon*
peppers	*Worcestershire sauce*
Salt to taste	*³/4 teaspoon salt*
1 pound ground beef	*¹/2 teaspoon MSG*
¹/2 cup chopped onion	*2 cups shredded sharp*
1¹/2 cups fresh or canned	*process cheese*
corn kernels	*1 cup soft buttered*
1 8-ounce can seasoned	*bread crumbs*
tomato sauce	

Preheat oven to 350 degrees. Cut off tops of peppers, discarding seed and membrane. Cook in water to cover in large saucepan for 5 minutes; drain. Sprinkle insides of peppers with salt. Brown ground beef with onion in skillet, stirring until ground beef is crumbly; drain. Add corn, tomato sauce, Worcestershire sauce, salt and MSG; mix well. Simmer for 5 minutes. Stir in cheese until melted. Spoon into peppers. Stand upright in 7-by-11-inch baking dish; sprinkle tops with bread crumbs. Add ¹/2 inch water to dish. Bake for 40 minutes or until heated through. Yield: 8 servings.

Brenda Bebee, Xi Zeta Eta
St. John, Kansas

Marcia McCoy, Xi Zeta Tau, El Dorado, Kansas, breads her Chicken Fried Steak by dipping tenderized round steak into egg beaten with ¹/4 cup milk and coating with mixture of 1 cup each saltine, Ritz and club cracker crumbs.

STUFFED SHELLS

1 pound ground beef
1 pound Italian sausage
1 16-ounce package
  frozen spinach,
  cooked, drained
6 cloves of garlic, minced
3 eggs, beaten
1¹/4 cups small curd
  cottage cheese, drained

1 teaspoon oregano
Salt and pepper to taste
1 package large pasta
  shells, cooked
1 15-ounce jar
  spaghetti sauce
1 cup shredded Swiss
  cheese

Preheat oven to 350 degrees. Cook ground beef and sausage in skillet, stirring until crumbly; drain. Stir in next 7 ingredients. Spoon into shells; arrange in 9-by-13-inch baking dish. Spread spaghetti sauce over top; sprinkle with cheese. Bake for 45 to 60 minutes or until bubbly and light brown. Yield: 8 to 12 servings.

Deborah Crawford, Zeta Theta
Olathe, Kansas

LASAGNA

1 pound ground beef
1 28-ounce can whole
  tomatoes
1 12-ounce can tomato
  paste
1¹/2 teaspoons oregano
1 teaspoon basil
2 teaspoons garlic salt
12 ounces mozzarella
  cheese, shredded

2 cups cream-style
  cottage cheese
¹/2 cup grated Parmesan
  cheese
12 ounces lasagna
  noodles, cooked
¹/2 cup grated Parmesan
  cheese

Preheat oven to 350 degrees. Brown ground beef in saucepan, stirring frequently; drain. Stir in next 5 ingredients. Bring to a boil, stirring occasionally; reduce heat. Simmer, uncovered, for 20 minutes. Reserve 1 cup meat sauce and ¹/2 cup mozzarella cheese. Mix cottage cheese with ¹/2 cup Parmesan cheese in bowl. Layer noodles, remaining meat sauce, remaining mozzarella cheese and cottage cheese mixture ¹/3 at a time in 9-by-13-inch baking dish. Top with reserved meat sauce, remaining ¹/2 cup Parmesan cheese and reserved mozzarella cheese. Bake for 45 minutes. Yield: 8 servings.

Lena Korpela, Preceptor Eta
Lebanon, New Mexico

LASAGNA FOR THE WEEKEND

8 wide lasagna noodles
1 teaspoon olive oil
1¹/2 pounds ground beef
2 tablespoons minced
  onion
1 whole clove of garlic
1 6-ounce can tomato
  paste

1 8-ounce can tomato
  sauce
¹/2 teaspoon oregano
¹/4 teaspoon salt
8 ounces mozzarella
  cheese, sliced
¹/4 cup grated Parmesan
  cheese

Preheat oven to 350 degrees. Cook noodles with oil in water to cover in large saucepan until tender; drain.

Brown ground beef with onion and garlic in skillet, stirring frequently; drain. Add next 4 ingredients. Alternate layers of noodles, mozzarella cheese and meat sauce in 8-by-12-inch baking dish until all ingredients are used. Top with Parmesan cheese. Bake for 45 minutes. Let stand for 15 minutes before serving. Yield: 9 to 12 servings.

Kara Roth, Alpha Nu
Sidney, Nebraska

BEEF AND SAUSAGE LASAGNA

1 pound ground beef
1 pound pork sausage
1 16-ounce can
  tomatoes
1 12-ounce can tomato
  sauce
2 6-ounce cans tomato
  paste
1 cup each chopped
green bell pepper, onion
  and celery
1 tablespoon sugar

2 tablespoons Italian
  seasoning
2 tablespoons oregano
Salt and pepper to taste
1 16-ounce package
  lasagna noodles,
  cooked
4 cups cottage cheese
4 cups shredded
  mozzarella cheese
Grated Parmesan
  cheese to taste

Preheat oven to 350 degrees. Brown ground beef and sausage in saucepan, stirring until crumbly; drain. Stir in next 11 ingredients. Simmer until of desired consistency. Alternate noodles, sauce, cottage cheese and mozzarella cheese in 11-by-13-inch baking pan until all ingredients are used. Top with Parmesan cheese. Bake for 30 to 45 minutes or until cheese is brown. Yield: 12 servings.

Linda Bailey, Nu Delta
Clinton, Iowa

BETH'S LASAGNA

This recipe came from a special lady who is no longer with us.

1¹/2 to 2 pounds ground
  beef
1 medium onion, chopped
1 cup chopped celery
  leaves and parsley
4 16-ounce cans whole
  tomatoes
1 8-ounce can tomato
  sauce
1 zucchini, chopped

1 teaspoon cinnamon
¹/4 teaspoon sage
³/4 teaspoon nutmeg
¹/8 teaspoon cloves
2 or 3 bay leaves
Salt and pepper to taste
1 package lasagna
  noodles, cooked
2 to 3 cups shredded
  mozzarella cheese

Preheat oven to 375 degrees. Brown ground beef, stirring until crumbly. Add onion. Sauté until onion is tender. Add next 11 ingredients; mix well. Simmer for 2¹/2 to 3 hours or until thickened to desired consistency; discard bay leaves. Alternate layers of noodles, meat sauce and cheese in large baking dish until all ingredients are used. Bake for 45 minutes. Yield: 8 to 12 servings.

Jami Bevans, Xi Eta Nu
College Station, Texas

EASY LASAGNA

1 pound ground beef	1 tablespoon Italian
1/2 cup chopped onion	herb seasoning
3 cups shredded	2 teaspoons parsley
mozzarella cheese	flakes
2 cups water	1 teaspoon sugar
1 15-ounce can tomato	1/2 teaspoon garlic
sauce	powder
1 6-ounce can tomato	1 teaspoon salt
paste	1/2 teaspoon pepper
1/4 cup dry red wine	8 ounces uncooked
(optional)	lasagna noodles
2 tablespoons	Grated Parmesan
Worcestershire sauce	cheese to taste

Preheat oven to 350 degrees. Brown ground beef with onion, stirring frequently. Mix with next 12 ingredients in bowl. Spread 2 cups mixture in 9-by-13-inch baking dish. Layer noodles and remaining meat sauce 1/2 at a time in prepared dish. Top with Parmesan cheese. Bake, tightly covered with foil, for 1 hour. Let stand for 30 minutes before serving. Yield: 8 servings.

Terri Duhon, Chi
Shreveport, Louisiana

GRANDMA H'S LASAGNA

2 pounds ground beef	1 pound ricotta cheese
2 cups tomatoes	2 eggs, beaten
2 cups tomato sauce	1 2-ounce can grated
1 tablespoon parsley	Parmesan cheese
flakes	2 tablespoons parsley
Garlic, salt and pepper	flakes
to taste	1 pound mozzarella
1 16-ounce package	cheese, sliced
lasagna noodles	

Preheat oven to 375 degrees. Brown ground beef in skillet over low heat, stirring until crumbly; drain. Stir in next 6 ingredients; mix well. Simmer for 45 to 60 minutes or until of desired consistency, stirring occasionally. Cook noodles using package directions; rinse in cold water. Combine next 4 ingredients in medium bowl; mix well. Layer meat sauce, noodles, ricotta cheese mixture and mozzarella cheese 1/2 at a time in 9-by-13-inch baking dish. Bake for 30 minutes. Yield: 8 to 10 servings.

Suzette Evert, Epsilon Pi
Centerville, Iowa

Kris Krumland, Gamma Beta, Columbus, Nebraska, makes Sandwich Loaf by cutting Italian bread lengthwise into halves, shaping mixture of 1 1/2 pounds lean ground beef, 1/3 cup milk, 1/2 cup cracker crumbs, 1 egg, 1/2 cup chopped onion, 1 tablespoon mustard, 2 cups shredded American cheese, salt and pepper to fit bottom of loaf, wrapping bread in foil, leaving mixture exposed and baking in preheated 350-degree oven for 45 minutes.

BARBECUED MEATBALLS

3 pounds ground beef	2 cups catsup
1 5-ounce can	1 cup packed light
evaporated milk	brown sugar
2 cups oats	1 tablespoon minced
2 eggs	onion
2 tablespoons minced	1 tablespoon liquid
onion	smoke
2 teaspoons chili powder	1/2 teaspoon garlic
1/2 teaspoon garlic	powder
powder	

Preheat oven to 350 degrees. Combine ground beef with next 6 ingredients in large bowl; mix well. Shape into meatballs. Arrange in single layer in two 9-by-13-inch baking dishes. Combine catsup, brown sugar, 1 tablespoon onion, liquid smoke and 1/2 teaspoon garlic powder in medium bowl; mix well. Spoon over meatballs. Bake for 1 hour. Yield: 42 large or 80 small meatballs.

Leigh Ann Lawrence, Mu Lambda
Fairfax, Missouri

❖ REUBEN MEATBALLS

1 1/2 pounds ground beef	2 cups drained
or lamb	sauerkraut
1 cup cooked white rice	1 10-ounce can cream
1 egg, beaten	of mushroom soup
1/4 cup chopped parsley	1 cup mayonnaise-type
1 small onion, minced	salad dressing
1/3 cup bread crumbs	Caraway seed to taste
1/3 cup cornflake crumbs	4 ounces Swiss cheese,
Salt and pepper to taste	shredded

Preheat oven to 350 degrees. Combine ground beef with next 8 ingredients in large bowl; mix well. Shape into 1 1/2-inch meatballs; place in large baking dish. Spread sauerkraut over meatballs. Combine soup, salad dressing and caraway seed in medium bowl; mix well. Spread over sauerkraut; top with cheese. Bake for 1 hour. Yield: 8 servings.

Debby Chesterman, Xi Alpha Iota
Nebraska City, Nebraska

MEAT LOAF IN PASTRY

You may make this meat loaf with ground pork, ham, lamb, veal or any combination you choose.

1/4 cup butter or	1 cup milk
margarine	1 cup shredded Cheddar
3/4 cup minced	or Swiss cheese
mushrooms	1 recipe pie pastry
3 pounds finely ground	1 egg
beef	2 tablespoons milk
1/3 cup minced onion	Sour cream
1/4 cup minced parsley	

Preheat oven to 375 degrees. Heat butter in 10- to 12-inch skillet until foam subsides. Add mushrooms. Sauté over medium heat for 6 to 8 minutes or until golden brown. Add ground beef. Cook until beef is brown and crumbly, stirring constantly. Combine with onion, parsley, 1 cup milk and cheese in large bowl; mix well. Roll pastry into rectangle on floured surface. Spoon beef mixture onto pastry; fold pastry over to enclose filling, pressing edges to seal. Place on baking sheet; brush with mixture of egg and 2 tablespoons milk. Bake for 45 minutes. Serve with sour cream. May make individual pastries using crescent roll dough and bake for 20 minutes. Yield: 6 to 8 servings.

Shirley L. Turnbull, Preceptor Laureate Gamma Delta
Windsor, Ontario, Canada

❖ CAJUN MEAT LOAF

1/2 teaspoon each cumin and nutmeg	*1/2 cup minced green bell pepper*
2 bay leaves	*1/4 cup minced green onions*
1 tablespoon salt	
1 teaspoon each cayenne pepper and black pepper	*1 tablespoon each Tabasco sauce and Worcestershire sauce*
1/2 teaspoon white pepper	*1/2 cup each evaporated milk and catsup*
1/4 cup butter or margarine	*1 1/2 pounds ground beef*
2 teaspoons minced garlic	*8 ounces ground pork*
3/4 cup minced onion	*2 eggs*
1/2 cup minced celery	*1 cup fine dry bread crumbs*

Preheat oven to 350 degrees. Mix first 7 seasonings together. Melt butter in skillet. Add seasoning mixture, garlic, minced vegetables, Tabasco sauce and Worcestershire sauce. Sauté for 6 minutes; mixture will stick. Stir in evaporated milk and catsup. Cook for 2 minutes longer; cool to room temperature. Remove bay leaves. Combine with ground beef, ground pork, eggs and bread crumbs in large bowl; mix well. Shape into loaf; place in 9-by-13-inch baking pan. Bake for 1 hour or until cooked through. Serve with baked potatoes. Yield: 8 servings.

Cynthia Albert, Beta Phi
Wilber, Nebraska

MOZZARELLA MEAT LOAF

1 1/2 to 2 pounds ground beef	*1 teaspoon salt*
1 medium onion, grated	*1 15-ounce jar spaghetti sauce*
1 cup cracker crumbs	*1 pound mozzarella cheese, shredded*
1/2 cup water	

Preheat oven to 350 degrees. Combine ground beef, onion, cracker crumbs, water, salt and half the spaghetti sauce in medium bowl; mix well. Press half the mixture into loaf pan. Spread with half the cheese and remaining beef mixture. Bake for 1 hour. Top with remaining spaghetti sauce and cheese. Bake just until cheese melts. Yield: 8 servings.

Tammy Grossman, Mu Lambda
Fairfax, Missouri

SICILIAN MEAT LOAF

2 eggs, beaten	*1/4 teaspoon pepper*
3/4 cup soft bread crumbs	*2 pounds lean ground beef*
1/2 cup tomato juice	*8 thin slices ham*
2 tablespoons chopped parsley	*6 ounces mozzarella cheese, shredded*
1 small clove of garlic, minced	*3 slices mozzarella cheese, sliced diagonally*
1/2 teaspoon oregano	
1 teaspoon salt	

Preheat oven to 350 degrees. Combine eggs, bread crumbs, tomato juice, parsley, garlic, oregano, salt and pepper in large bowl. Add ground beef; mix well. Shape into 10-by-12-inch rectangle on waxed paper or foil. Arrange ham slices over beef mixture, leaving edges free; sprinkle with shredded cheese. Roll beef from narrow edge to enclose filling, lifting edge with paper or foil; seal edges. Place seam side down in 9-by-13-inch baking dish. Bake for 1 1/4 hours or until done to taste. Top with sliced cheese. Bake for 5 minutes or until cheese melts. Yield: 8 servings.

Jolynn A. Dowling, Zeta Eta
Derby, Kansas

HEARTY CRESCENT PIES

2 pounds lean ground beef	*2 16-ounce cans green beans, drained*
1 tablespoon garlic powder	*2 teaspoons cumin seed*
1 green bell pepper, chopped	*2 8-count cans crescent rolls*
1 onion, chopped	*2 eggs*
1 16-ounce can tomato sauce	*2 cups shredded Cheddar cheese*

Preheat oven to 375 degrees. Brown ground beef with garlic powder, green pepper and onion in large skillet, stirring frequently; drain. Add tomato sauce, beans and cumin seed. Simmer for several minutes. Line bottoms and sides of 2 pie plates with roll dough. Beat 1 egg with 1/4 cup cheese for each pie; spread in prepared plates. Spoon ground beef mixture into pastries. Bake for 20 minutes. Sprinkle with remaining cheese. May substitute two 10-count cans biscuits for crescent rolls. Yield: 12 servings.

Margo Zinszer, Preceptor Alpha Eta
Pocatello, Idaho

NATCHITOCHES MEAT PIES

1¹/2 pounds ground beef
1¹/2 pounds ground pork
1 cup chopped green
  onions
1 teaspoon each
  cayenne pepper and
  black pepper
1 tablespoon salt
¹/2 cup all-purpose flour
¹/3 cup shortening
2 cups self-rising flour
1 egg, beaten
³/4 cup milk
Vegetable oil for deep
  frying

Brown ground beef and ground pork with green onions and seasonings in heavy saucepan over medium heat, stirring frequently. Sift ¹/2 cup flour over mixture; stir to mix well. Drain and cool in colander. Cut shortening into 2 cups self-rising flour in medium bowl. Add egg and milk; mix to form dough. Roll ¹/3 of the dough at a time on lightly floured surface. Cut into 5 to 5¹/2-inch circles. Place 1 heaping tablespoonful of beef mixture on each circle. Moisten edge and fold pastry over filling. Seal edge and prick top with fork. Deep-fry pies in 350-degree oil until golden brown. May cut circles with biscuit cutter for appetizer-sized pies.
Yield: 26 to 28 pies.

Shanna Andrews, Epsilon Eta
Jonesboro, Louisiana

CRAZY CRUST PIZZA

1 cup plus 2
  tablespoons self-
  rising flour
2 eggs
²/3 cup milk
1 teaspoon oregano
1 8-ounce can tomato
  sauce
1 4-ounce can
  mushrooms
1 small onion, chopped
1 pound ground beef,
  crumbled
1 cup shredded
  mozzarella cheese

Preheat oven to 425 degrees. Combine flour, eggs, milk and oregano in medium bowl; mix well. Spoon into greased 9-by-13-inch baking dish. Spread tomato sauce over top. Sprinkle with mushrooms, onion, ground beef and half the cheese. Bake for 25 to 30 minutes or until golden brown. Top with remaining cheese. Bake for 5 minutes longer.
Yield: 12 servings.

Toby L. Cook, Xi Gamma Iota
Cabot, Arkansas

Dolores C. Montgomery, Xi Delta Psi, Westland, Michigan, makes Oven Chop Suey with 1 pound cooked and drained ground beef mixed with 1 cup chopped celery, 1 chopped onion, ¹/2 cup instant rice, 1 can each cream of mushroom and cream of chicken soup, 1 can bean sprouts and ¹/4 cup soy sauce poured into 9-by-13-inch baking pan, topped with 2 cans chow mein noodles and baked in preheated 350-degree oven for 1¹/2 hours.

SLOW-COOKER SPAGHETTI SAUCE

My mother-in-law made good spaghetti sauce but never used a recipe. This is my version, created by watching her and asking lots of questions.

1 pound ground beef
Minced onion, chili
  powder, salt and
  black pepper to taste
1 pound Italian
  sausage, cut into
  1-inch pieces
1 46-ounce can tomato
  juice
2 6-ounce cans tomato
  paste
1 8-ounce can tomato
  sauce
1 small onion, minced
¹/4 cup minced green bell
  pepper
Garlic powder to taste
¹/2 teaspoon each basil,
  oregano, ground cloves
  and cayenne pepper
Cooked spaghetti

Combine ground beef with minced onion, chili powder, salt and pepper to taste in bowl; mix well. Shape into meatballs. Combine with sausage, tomato juice, tomato paste, tomato sauce, onion, green pepper and seasonings in slow cooker; mix well. Cook on Low all day. Serve over hot cooked spaghetti.
Yield: 10 to 12 servings.

Wilma E. Jolly, Laureate Zeta
Arvada, Colorado

SPAGHETTI BOWL

I once served this to a friend who is a commentator at a local radio station. Quite often he has mentioned on the radio that he loves my spaghetti.

1 8-ounce can Italian-
  style stewed tomatoes
2 8-ounce cans Italian-
  style tomato sauce
2 envelopes spaghetti
  sauce mix
¹/4 cup olive oil
1 teaspoon oregano
1 pound ground sirloin
  or turkey
1 small onion, grated
¹/2 cup Italian bread
  crumbs
¹/4 cup chopped parsley
1 egg
¹/8 teaspoon marjoram
1 16-ounce package
  spaghetti, cooked,
  drained
Grated Romano or
  Parmesan cheese

Combine tomatoes, tomato sauce, spaghetti sauce mix, olive oil and oregano in 12-inch skillet. Bring to a boil over medium-high heat; reduce heat. Simmer, covered, for 30 minutes. Combine ground sirloin or turkey with onion, bread crumbs, parsley, egg and marjoram in bowl; mix well. Shape into small balls. Place in simmering sauce. Simmer, covered, for 30 minutes. Spoon over spaghetti in serving bowl. Serve with cheese. Yield: 8 to 10 servings.

June Lombard, Preceptor Kappa Upsilon
Yucca Valley, California

SPAGHETTI AND BEEF CASSEROLE

2 pounds ground beef	8 ounces cream cheese,
2 medium onions,	softened
chopped	2 cups cottage cheese
8 ounces fresh	1/2 cup sour cream
mushrooms, chopped	1 container chopped
2 8-ounce cans tomato	fresh or frozen chives
sauce	2 7-ounce packages
1 6-ounce can tomato	spaghetti, cooked
paste	1/2 cup Italian bread
1 teaspoon each oregano	crumbs
and garlic powder	

Preheat oven to 350 degrees. Brown ground beef with onions in skillet, stirring until ground beef is crumbly and onions are tender; drain. Add mixture of next 5 ingredients; mix well. Simmer for 15 minutes. Combine cream cheese, cottage cheese, sour cream and chives in bowl; mix well. Layer half the spaghetti, cream cheese mixture, remaining spaghetti and meat sauce in buttered large baking dish. Top with bread crumbs. Bake for 30 minutes.
Yield: 12 servings.

Ginny Spann, Preceptor Laureate Gamma Theta
Katy, Texas

BEST HAM LOAF

1 1/2 pounds ground ham	1 teaspoon dry mustard
1 pound ground turkey	1 tablespoon onion
2 eggs, beaten	flakes
1/2 cup milk	1/8 teaspoon pepper
1 cup soft bread crumbs	

Preheat oven to 350 degrees. Combine all ingredients in large bowl; mix well. Press lightly into greased 5-by-9-inch loaf pan. Bake for 1 hour.
Yield: 8 to 10 servings.

Marty Todd, Preceptor Kappa
Montrose, Colorado

TEXAS STUFFED HAM

2 pounds shelled pecans	1 12-ounce can ginger
8 cups dry bread crumbs	ale
2 tablespoons cinnamon	1/2 cup honey
1 tablespoon ginger	1/2 cup bourbon or
18 ounces honey	ginger ale
4 eggs	1/4 cup Dijon mustard
1/2 cup bourbon or	Watercress
ginger ale	Orange wedges
1 15-pound whole	
ham, fully cooked	

Preheat oven to 350 degrees. Process pecans 1/4 at a time in food processor until finely chopped. Combine with bread crumbs, cinnamon and ginger in large bowl; mix well. Whisk 18 ounces honey, eggs and 1/2 cup bourbon in medium bowl until smooth. Add to bread crumb mixture; mix well. Trim excess fat from ham. Score remaining fat in diamond pattern. Remove bone from ham. Spoon 1 to 2 cups stuffing mixture into bone cavity. Place in shallow roasting pan. Pour ginger ale over top. Heat 1/2 cup honey, 1/2 cup bourbon and mustard in small saucepan until bubbly. Brush over ham. Spoon remaining stuffing mixture into baking dish. Bake ham and stuffing for 30 minutes or until ham is glazed, basting several times. Let ham stand, tented with heavy-duty foil, for 30 minutes or longer. Place ham on heated serving platter. Cut into thin slices. Garnish with watercress and orange wedges.
Yield: 30 servings.

Penelope Willan, Preceptor Chi
Sarnia, Ontario, Canada

PEACHY PORK CHOPS AND STUFFING

This was what I served the first time I had my grandparents to supper when I was a young bride.

1 8-ounce can sliced	Salt and pepper to taste
peaches	1 tablespoon corn oil
1/4 cup packed light	1 package stove-top
brown sugar	stuffing mix for pork
1/4 cup catsup	1 1/2 cups very hot water
2 tablespoons vinegar	
6 3/4-inch thick pork	
chops	

Preheat oven to 350 degrees. Drain peaches, reserving 1/3 cup syrup. Combine reserved syrup with brown sugar, catsup and vinegar in saucepan. Simmer for several minutes. Sprinkle pork chops with salt and pepper. Brown on both sides in oil in large skillet; remove to 9-by-13-inch baking dish. Brush with glaze. Bake for 35 minutes. Prepare stuffing mix with water in same skillet using package directions. Move pork chops to end of baking dish. Spoon stuffing into baking dish. Arrange peaches around chops; brush with remaining glaze. Bake for 20 minutes longer. Yield: 6 servings.

Karen L. Jackson, Xi Phi Alpha Omega
Wichita Falls, Texas

BARBECUED LEG OF LAMB

1 7 to 8-pound leg of	1/4 cup coarsely chopped
lamb	onion
Salt and pepper to taste	1 tablespoon light
1 8-ounce can tomato	brown sugar
sauce	1 tablespoon vegetable
1/2 cup catsup	oil

Preheat coals. Sprinkle lamb with salt and pepper. Skewer and place on spit 8 inches above coals. Grill for 30 minutes. Combine remaining ingredients in medium bowl; mix well. Brush on lamb. Grill for 25 to 30 minutes per pound or until done to taste, brushing with sauce. Yield: 12 servings.

Josephine Pascoe, Laureate Beta Psi
Oshawa, Ontario, Canada

Fowl Play

❖ AMARETTO CHICKEN

5 whole chicken breasts,
  boned, cut into halves
3 tablespoons all-
  purpose flour
2 teaspoons paprika
1¹/₂ teaspoons each
  garlic salt, salt and
  pepper
1 tablespoon vegetable
  oil

3 tablespoons butter or
  margarine
1 6-ounce can frozen
  orange juice
  concentrate, thawed
1 cup Amaretto
1¹/₂ tablespoons Dijon
  mustard

Preheat oven to 350 degrees. Rinse chicken; pat dry.
Coat with mixture of next 5 ingredients. Sauté in oil
and butter in skillet until brown; remove to baking
dish. Add remaining ingredients to skillet, stirring to
deglaze. Increase heat. Cook until thickened, stirring
constantly. Pour over chicken. Bake for 45 minutes.
Yield: 10 servings.

June Sine, Laureate Alpha Eta
Belleville, Ontario, Canada

APRICOT-GLAZED CHICKEN

2¹/₂ to 3 pounds cut-up
  chicken, skinned
¹/₂ cup Russian salad
  dressing

³/₄ cup apricot preserves
2 ¹/₂-ounce packets
  instant onion soup
  mix

Preheat oven to 350 degrees. Rinse chicken and pat
dry. Arrange in 8-by-12-inch baking dish. Combine
remaining ingredients in small saucepan. Cook until
heated through, stirring to mix well. Spoon over
chicken. Bake for 1 hour and 20 minutes or until
tender, basting after 30 minutes. Yield: 4 servings.

Muriel W. Kimball, Preceptor Xi
Bath, Maine

CORN BREAD UPSIDE-DOWN CHICKEN

1¹/₄ cups chicken broth
1¹/₄ cups all-purpose
  flour
4 teaspoons salt
¹/₂ teaspoon pepper
2 10-ounce cans
  chicken broth soup

4 cups half and half
6 cups chopped cooked
  chicken
Chopped celery, sautéed
Frozen peas and carrots
1 large package corn
  bread mix

Preheat oven to 400 degrees. Blend 1¹/₄ cups chicken
broth, flour, salt and pepper in medium saucepan.
Cook over low heat until bubbly, stirring constantly.
Stir in chicken soup and half and half. Bring to a boil
and boil for 1 minute, stirring constantly. Stir in
chicken, celery and peas and carrots. Spoon into 13-
by-15-inch baking dish. Prepare corn bread using
package directions. Spread over casserole. Bake for
20 minutes. Yield: 8 to 10 servings.

Millie Redding, Preceptor Zeta
Orange, California

CRAB-STUFFED CHICKEN

4 whole boneless
  chicken breasts,
  skinned
¹/₄ cup all-purpose
  flour
3 tablespoons melted
  butter or margarine
³/₄ cup milk
³/₄ cup chicken broth
¹/₃ cup white wine
¹/₄ cup chopped onion
1 tablespoon butter or
  margarine

1 7-ounce can crab
  meat, drained, flaked
4 ounces mushrooms,
  chopped
¹/₂ cup coarsely crushed
  crackers
2 tablespoons chopped
  parsley
¹/₂ teaspoon salt
Pepper to taste
1 cup shredded Swiss
  cheese
¹/₂ teaspoon paprika

Preheat oven to 350 degrees. Cut chicken breasts into halves; rinse and pat dry. Pound 1/8 inch thick with meat mallet. Stir flour into 3 tablespoons melted butter in medium saucepan. Add milk, broth and wine. Cook until thickened, stirring constantly; set aside. Sauté onion in 1 tablespoon butter in skillet until tender. Add crab meat, mushrooms, cracker crumbs, parsley, salt and pepper; mix well. Stir in 2 tablespoons cream sauce. Spoon 1/4 cup crab meat mixture onto each chicken breast. Roll to enclose filling; place seam side down in 7-by-12-inch baking pan. Spoon remaining cream sauce over top. Bake, covered with foil, for 1 hour. Sprinkle with cheese and paprika. Bake for 2 minutes longer. Yield: 8 servings.

Deborah Crawford, Zeta Theta
Olathe, Kansas

CREOLE CHICKEN WITH GARLIC

2 3¹/₂-pound chickens, cut up	Salt and pepper to taste
2 tablespoons vegetable oil	1/2 cup white wine
3 green bell peppers, cut into 1-inch pieces	1 cup drained canned tomatoes
2 onions, chopped	2 teaspoons oregano
10 cloves of garlic, chopped	1/4 teaspoon cayenne pepper

Rinse chicken and pat dry. Brown on all sides in oil in large heavy saucepan; remove to platter. Sauté green peppers, onions and garlic with salt and pepper in drippings in saucepan over medium heat for 10 minutes or until tender. Increase heat to high. Add wine to saucepan, stirring to deglaze. Cook until liquid has evaporated. Add tomatoes, oregano, cayenne pepper and chicken. Simmer, covered, for 45 to 60 minutes or until chicken is tender. Place chicken on serving platter. Spoon sauce over top. May cook sauce longer if necessary to reduce to desired consistency. Yield: 8 servings.

Deborah Pulley, Epsilon Sigma
Chesapeake, Virginia

❖ CHICKEN DIJONNAISE

8 chicken breast filets or skinned chicken pieces	1 teaspoon Dijon mustard
1 10-ounce can cream of mushroom or chicken soup	1/2 cup dry white wine
	1/2 teaspoon salt
1 cup reduced-fat sour cream	1/8 teaspoon white pepper
2 tablespoons Dijonnaise	2 tablespoons grated Parmesan cheese
	Cooked rice

Preheat oven to 375 degrees. Rinse chicken and pat dry. Arrange in 9-by-13-inch baking pan sprayed with nonstick cooking spray. Combine soup, sour cream, Dijonnaise, Dijon mustard, wine, salt and white pepper in medium bowl; mix well. Spread evenly over chicken. Bake, tightly covered with foil, for 1 hour or until tender. Sprinkle with cheese. Broil for 3 minutes or until light brown. Serve sauce over rice. Serve with green beans and angel biscuits. Yield: 8 servings.

Nancy H. McCreary, Xi Epsilon Beta
Maurertown, Virginia

DRAMBUIE POULET

2 cups chopped cooked ham	8 slices Cheddar cheese
8 chicken breast filets	1 cup cream of mushroom soup
1/4 cup white wine	1 cup sour cream
1/4 cup Drambuie	Cooked noodles or rice
8 slices Swiss cheese	

Preheat oven to 375 degrees. Spread ham in shallow baking dish. Rinse chicken and pat dry; arrange over ham. Pour mixture of wine and liqueur over top. Bake for 1 hour or until tender. Place 1 slice of Swiss cheese and 1 slice of Cheddar cheese on each filet. Spread with mixture of soup and sour cream. Bake until cheese melts. Serve with noodles or rice. Yield: 8 servings.

Liliane Digilio, Xi Delta Gamma
Milledgeville, Georgia

CHICKEN ENCHILADAS

1 package tortilla chips	Green or red chili peppers to taste
1 can whole boned chicken	2 10-ounce cans cream of mushroom soup
1 onion, chopped	1 soup can water
3 to 4 stalks celery, chopped	Shredded longhorn cheese and Monterey Jack cheese to taste
1 green bell pepper, chopped	

Preheat oven to 350 degrees. Layer half the chips, chicken, onion, celery, green pepper, chili peppers and remaining chips in 9-by-13-inch baking dish. Spread mixture of soup and water over layers. Top with additional chili peppers and cheeses. Bake, covered with foil, for 45 to 60 minutes or until heated through. Yield: 8 to 10 servings.

Jeanne DiNardo, Eta Chi
Edinburg, Virginia

Kari Lee Smith, Gamma Xi, Apple Valley, Minnesota, stuffs her Swiss Enchiladas with mixture of 8 ounces cream cheese, 1/4 cup milk, 2 cups chopped cooked chicken, 1/2 cup sliced green onions, 1/4 cup slivered almonds and 1/2 cup shredded Monterey Jack cheese, tops with enchilada or picante sauce and additional cheese, then bakes in preheated 375-degree oven for 15 minutes and serves with guacamole and sour cream.

SOUR CREAM GREEN ENCHILADAS

2 cups chopped cooked
  chicken
1/4 cup chopped onion
2 cups shredded
  Cheddar cheese
12 flour tortillas
1/2 cup vegetable oil
1/4 cup all-purpose flour
1/4 cup melted butter or
  margarine
2 cups chicken broth
1 1/2 cups sour cream
1 cup chopped green
  chilies
Parmesan cheese to
  taste

Preheat oven to 400 degrees. Combine chicken, onion and Cheddar cheese in bowl; mix well. Soften tortillas in hot oil in skillet; drain. Spoon chicken mixture onto tortillas; roll to enclose filling. Arrange in 9-by-13-inch baking dish. Blend flour into melted butter in medium saucepan. Cook until smooth. Stir in chicken broth. Cook until thickened, stirring constantly. Stir in sour cream and green chilies. Spoon over enchiladas; sprinkle with Parmesan cheese. Bake for 20 minutes. Yield: 8 servings.

Cathy Simmelink, Epsilon
Wichita, Kansas

CREAMY CHILI AND CHICKEN ENCHILADAS

4 cups chopped cooked
  chicken
1 1/2 cups sour cream
6 ounces low-fat cream
  cheese, softened
1 cup shredded longhorn
  cheese
1 cup salsa
Chopped green chilies
  to taste
Salt to taste
16 flour tortillas
Vegetable oil
1 cup salsa
1 cup shredded longhorn
  cheese

Preheat oven to 350 degrees. Combine chicken, sour cream, cream cheese, 1 cup longhorn cheese, 1 cup salsa, green chilies and salt in bowl; mix well. Soften tortillas in hot oil in skillet; drain. Spoon chicken mixture onto tortillas; roll to enclose filling. Arrange in 9-by-13-inch baking dish. Spoon 1 cup salsa over top; sprinkle with 1 cup longhorn cheese. Bake for 30 minutes or until bubbly. Yield: 8 servings.

Michele S. Donnell, Zeta Eta
North Bend, Washington

GARLIC CHICKEN

2 chickens, cut up
1 cup melted butter
Garlic powder to taste
1/2 cup all-purpose flour
2 stacks crackers,
  crushed
Salt and pepper to taste

Preheat oven to 350 degrees. Rinse chicken and pat dry. Cook in water to cover in large saucepan for 15 minutes; drain. Mix butter and garlic powder in medium bowl. Mix flour, cracker crumbs, salt and pepper in shallow dish. Dip chicken into butter mixture; coat with cracker crumb mixture. Arrange in greased 9-by-13-inch baking dish. Bake for 30 to 60

minutes or until tender and golden brown. Yield: 8 to 10 servings.

Norma Bennett, Xi Lambda Sigma
Royalton, Illinois

HAWAIIAN CHICKEN

30 pieces chicken thighs
  and legs
Vegetable oil
6 tablespoons light
  brown sugar
1/4 cup cornstarch
1/4 cup light vinegar
1 cup catsup
1 15-ounce can
  pineapple chunks or
  crushed pineapple
2 tablespoons soy sauce
1 teaspoon salt
Cooked rice

Preheat oven to 325 degrees. Rinse chicken and pat dry. Brown lightly in oil in skillet; remove to 9-by-13-inch baking dish. Stir next 7 ingredients into skillet. Simmer for 10 to 20 minutes or until slightly thickened. Spoon over chicken. Bake for 30 to 40 minutes or until heated through. Serve with rice. Yield: 10 servings.

Carolyn Bolton, Preceptor Delta Rho
Orangeville, Ontario, Canada

JALAPEÑO CHICKEN

1 medium onion,
  chopped
1 10-ounce can
  cream of mushroom
  soup
1 10-ounce can cream
  of chicken soup
1 10-ounce can cream
  of celery soup
1 15-ounce can
  evaporated milk
2 cups chopped cooked
  chicken
1 jalapeño pepper,
  finely chopped
1 package tortilla chips,
  crushed
Shredded cheese

Preheat oven to 350 degrees. Sauté onion in medium saucepan sprayed with nonstick cooking spray until light brown. Add soups, evaporated milk and chicken; mix well. Cook until heated through. Stir in pepper. Layer tortillas chips, chicken mixture and cheese in 9-by-13-inch baking pan. Bake for 45 minutes. Yield: 12 to 16 servings.

Laura Fluke, Laureate Iota
Oklahoma City, Oklahoma

CHICKEN MARINATED IN SOUR CREAM

2 cups sour cream
1 clove of garlic, minced
1 tablespoon
  Worcestershire sauce
Tabasco sauce to taste
1 teaspoon paprika
10 chicken breast filets
2 teaspoons salt
Bread crumbs
Butter or margarine

Combine sour cream, garlic, Worcestershire sauce, Tabasco sauce and paprika in shallow dish. Rinse chicken and pat dry; sprinkle with salt. Add to sour cream mixture, coating well. Marinate in refrigerator overnight. Remove chicken from marinade, wiping off excess. Coat with bread crumbs. Chill for 2 hours or longer. Preheat oven to 350 degrees. Arrange chicken in greased 10-by-13-inch baking dish. Dot with butter. Bake, covered, for 30 minutes. Bake, uncovered, for 30 minutes longer. Yield: 5 to 10 servings.

Helen C. Warwick, Laureate Delta
Caldwell, Idaho

PARTY CHICKEN

1 4-ounce package	1 cup sour cream
chipped beef	1 10-ounce can cream
8 chicken breast filets	of mushroom soup
8 slices bacon	

Preheat oven to 275 degrees. Spread chipped beef in greased 9-by-13-inch baking dish. Rinse chicken and pat dry. Wrap each piece with 1 slice of bacon. Arrange in prepared dish. Spread mixture of sour cream and soup over chicken. Bake for 3 hours. Yield: 8 servings.

Bev Corron, Xi Gamma Delta
Grimes, Iowa

CHICKEN IN SPICY CREAM SAUCE

I took this dish to a sister who was ill and later learned that her father, who does not like chicken, loved it!

2 cloves of garlic, crushed	1 cup half and half
1/2 teaspoon paprika	2 tablespoons lemon
1 tablespoon salt	juice
3 pounds chicken breasts	1 tablespoon chopped
3 tablespoons vegetable	parsley
oil	

Mix garlic, paprika and salt in bowl. Rinse chicken and pat dry. Rub with garlic mixture; let stand for 15 minutes. Cook in hot oil in large skillet for 7 to 8 minutes or until brown on both sides. Spoon mixture of half and half and lemon juice over chicken. Simmer, covered, for 1 hour or until tender, turning once. Place chicken on warm serving dish. Spoon sauce over top; garnish with parsley. Yield: 4 servings.

Kimberly A. Gurdak, Psi Kappa
Ft. Lauderdale, Florida

CHICKEN BREASTS WITH SPINACH DRESSING

4 whole boned chicken	3 cups fresh bread crumbs
breasts, skinned	1 cup ricotta cheese
1 teaspoon salt	1 egg
1 10-ounce package	1/2 cup melted butter or
chopped spinach,	margarine
thawed	1 tablespoon minced
4 ounces mushrooms,	parsley
chopped	1/2 teaspoon poultry
1 cup chopped celery	seasoning
1/2 cup chopped onion	1/8 teaspoon pepper
1/4 cup melted butter or	Melted butter or
margarine	margarine

Preheat oven to 325 degrees. Cut chicken breasts into halves; rinse and pat dry. Pound 1/4 inch thick; sprinkle with salt. Press spinach to remove moisture. Sauté mushrooms, celery and onion in 1/4 cup butter in medium skillet over medium heat until tender; remove from heat. Stir in spinach and next 7 ingredients; mix well. Spoon onto chicken filets. Roll chicken to enclose filling; secure with wooden picks. Arrange on rack in 10-by-14-inch baking pan; brush with additional butter. Bake for 45 to 60 minutes. May slice to serve if desired. Yield: 8 servings.

Dot Lovell, Laureate Gamma
Rome, Georgia

CHICKEN BOING-BOING

This dish was always a treat for my children when they were little.

4 chicken breast filets	1 small package
2 cups low-fat sour	stuffing mix
cream	
2 10-ounce cans cream	
of mushroom soup	

Rinse chicken well. Cook in water to cover in medium saucepan until tender; drain. Chop chicken; place in 9-by-13-inch baking dish. Spread mixture of sour cream and soup over top. Prepare stuffing mix using half the water called for in package directions. Sprinkle over chicken. Preheat oven to 325 degrees. Bake for 45 minutes. Yield: 4 to 6 servings.

Barbara Black, Tau Eta
Hemet, California

CHICKEN AND CROUTONS

8 chicken breast filets	1/2 cup milk
8 slices Swiss cheese	1 6-ounce package
1 10-ounce can cream	herb-seasoned
of chicken soup	croutons
1 8-ounce can	1/4 cup melted butter or
mushrooms, drained	margarine

Preheat oven to 350 degrees. Rinse chicken and pat dry; arrange in 9-by-13-inch baking dish. Top each filet with slice of cheese. Combine soup, mushrooms and milk in bowl; mix well. Spread over chicken. Toss croutons with melted butter in small bowl. Sprinkle over casserole. Bake, covered with foil, for 1 hour. Bake, uncovered, for 15 minutes longer or until brown. Yield: 8 servings.

Cheryl L. Shewach, Preceptor Gamma Mu
Birmingham, Michigan

Julie Yemm, Tau Pi, Sterling, Illinois, makes Easy Chicken Potpie by heating 2 cans chicken, 2 cans mixed vegetables and 2 cans cream of chicken soup to serve over baked refrigerator biscuits.

EASY-BAKE BONELESS CHICKEN

I made this dish for a sorority brunch at a Kentucky Derby Party.

8 chicken breast filets	1¹/2 cups seasoned
8 Swiss cheese slices	stuffing mix, crushed
¹/4 cup dry white wine	3 tablespoons melted
1 10-ounce can cream	butter or margarine
of chicken soup	Parsley

Preheat oven to 350 degrees. Cut chicken filets into quarters; rinse and pat dry. Arrange in lightly greased 9-by-13-inch baking dish. Cut cheese slices into quarters; arrange over chicken. Spoon mixture of wine and soup over top. Sprinkle with stuffing mix; drizzle with butter. Bake for 45 minutes. Garnish with parsley. Yield: 8 to 10 servings.

Madeline Britnell, Preceptor Omicron
Gaithersburg, Maryland

PECAN-BREADED CHICKEN WITH MUSTARD

2 whole boned chicken	2 tablespoons
breasts, skinned	sunflower oil
Salt and freshly ground	¹/4 cup melted butter or
pepper to taste	margarine
2 tablespoons Dijon	²/3 cup sour cream
mustard	1 tablespoon Dijon
6 tablespoons melted	mustard
butter or margarine	
5 to 6 ounces pecans,	
ground	

Preheat oven to 200 degrees. Cut chicken breasts into halves; rinse and pat dry. Pound lightly with meat mallet; season with salt and pepper. Whisk 2 tablespoons mustard into 6 tablespoons butter in bowl. Dip chicken into butter mixture; coat with pecans, pressing down firmly. Sauté chicken in mixture of oil and ¹/4 cup butter in medium skillet for 3 minutes on each side; remove to platter in warm oven. Drain skillet. Whisk sour cream and 1 tablespoon mustard into skillet. Cook just until heated through. Serve with chicken. Yield: 4 servings.

Alvena Spangenberg, Xi Zeta Eta
St. John, Kansas

❖ COLD CHICKEN IN CURRY SAUCE

I got this recipe while living in Australia in the 70s. It has always been a hit with the family.

2 3-pound chickens	¹/4 cup catsup
2 medium white onions,	1 tablespoon apricot jam
chopped	1 tablespoon sweet
3 tablespoons vegetable	chutney
oil	¹/2 cup mayonnaise
1 tablespoon curry	¹/2 cup whipping cream,
powder	lightly whipped

Rinse chicken and pat dry. Steam in a small amount of water in large saucepan until tender but not dry; drain. Chop chicken into bite-sized pieces, discarding skin and bones. Sauté onions in oil in large skillet until tender. Stir in curry powder. Cook for 1 minute; remove from heat. Stir in catsup, jam and chutney. Cool to room temperature. Fold in mayonnaise and lightly whipped cream. Spoon a portion of the sauce into serving dish. Spread chicken in sauce; top with remaining sauce. Chill for up to 12 hours. Serve with rice or salad. Yield: 6 servings.

Lyn Massey, Xi Gamma Nu
Dallas, Texas

CHICKEN STEW WITH DUMPLINGS

2 to 2¹/2 pounds chicken	Salt and pepper to taste
breasts	1¹/2 cups all-purpose
5 cups water	flour
4 potatoes, chopped	2 teaspoons baking
3 carrots, cut into	powder
quarters	³/4 teaspoon salt
2 stalks celery, sliced	3 tablespoons butter or
1 medium onion, cut	margarine, softened
into eighths	1 cup milk
1 10-ounce package	¹/2 cup chopped parsley
frozen peas	

Rinse chicken well; combine with water in heavy saucepan. Cook, covered, over medium heat for 50 to 60 minutes or until tender. Remove and chop chicken, discarding skin and bones. Return chicken to broth. Add potatoes, carrots, celery, onion and peas. Simmer, covered, over medium heat for 15 to 20 minutes or until vegetables are fork tender. Season with salt and pepper to taste. Mix flour, baking powder and ³/4 teaspoon salt in large bowl. Cut in butter until crumbly. Stir in milk and parsley. Drop by rounded tablespoonfuls into hot stew. Cook, uncovered, for 10 minutes. Cook, covered, for 8 to 10 minutes longer or until dumplings are cooked through. Yield: 8 servings.

Bobbie Austin, Preceptor Iota Omicron
San Angelo, Texas

EGG ROLLS

1 small head cabbage,	1 egg yolk
shredded	1 package original-
1 cup chopped cooked	flavor Shake'n Bake
chicken	coating mix
1 7-ounce can crab	18 egg roll wrappers
meat, drained	1 egg white
1 medium onion,	Vegetable oil for deep-
chopped	frying

Blanch cabbage; drain well. Combine with chicken, crab meat, onion, egg yolk and coating mix in bowl; mix well. Spoon chicken mixture onto egg roll wrappers. Wrap to enclose filling, sealing with egg white.

Deep-fry in hot oil until golden brown.
Yield: 18 egg rolls.

Brenda L. Jacobs, Xi Beta Lambda
Brookfield, Missouri

CHICKEN LOAF WITH MUSHROOM SAUCE

1 4-pound chicken	1/4 cup all-purpose flour
1 cup cooked rice	1/4 cup milk
4 eggs, beaten	1/2 teaspoon lemon juice
2 cups dry bread crumbs	1/2 teaspoon chopped
1 1/2 teaspoons salt	parsley
1 cup sliced mushrooms	1/8 teaspoon paprika
1/4 cup melted butter or	Salt and pepper to taste
margarine	

Rinse chicken well. Cook in water to cover in large saucepan until tender. Drain, reserving 5 cups stock. Chop chicken into bite-sized pieces, discarding skin and bones. Combine chicken with rice, eggs, bread crumbs, 3 cups reserved chicken stock and 1 1/2 teaspoons salt in bowl; mix well. Spoon into 9-by-13-inch baking dish. Preheat oven to 300 degrees. Bake for 1 hour. Sauté mushrooms in butter in skillet for 5 minutes. Stir in flour. Add remaining 2 cups reserved chicken stock gradually. Cook until thickened, stirring constantly. Add remaining ingredients. Cook until heated through. Serve over chicken loaf. Yield: 8 servings.

Colette Iberg, Rho Chi
Pocahontas, Illinois

HOOSIER HEN LOAF

This recipe is a church favorite and was given credit with helping the church to rebuild after it burned in the 1930s.

1 stewing hen	6 hard-cooked eggs,
8 ounces crackers, finely	chopped
crushed	Salt and pepper to taste
4 eggs, beaten	

Rinse hen well. Cook in water to cover in large saucepan until tender. Drain, reserving 4 cups broth. Cut chicken cross grain into 1/2-inch pieces, discarding skin and bones. Combine chicken with cracker crumbs, beaten eggs, hard-cooked eggs, reserved chicken broth, salt and pepper in bowl; mix well. Spoon into greased 9-by-13-inch baking pan. Preheat oven to 350 degrees. Bake for 45 minutes. Yield: 8 to 12 servings.

Doris Grigsby Byers, Preceptor Chi
Terre Haute, Indiana

HOT CHICKEN SANDWICHES

4 cups chopped cooked	2 cups broth
chicken	3 eggs
6 slices soft bread, torn	24 sandwich buns

Combine chicken, bread, broth and eggs in double boiler. Cook for 25 minutes, stirring occasionally. Serve hot or cold on sandwich buns. May cook on low in electric skillet. Yield: 24 servings.

Sharon M. Rhodehamel, Mu Pi
Ft. Wayne, Indiana

CHICKEN PIE

1 large chicken	1 10-ounce can cream
2 10-count cans	of chicken soup
Hungry Jack	2 teaspoons pepper
buttermilk	4 hard-cooked eggs,
biscuits	chopped
1 10-ounce can cream	1 16-ounce can peas
of celery soup	and carrots

Rinse chicken well. Cook in water to cover in large saucepan. Drain, reserving 6 cups broth. Chop chicken, discarding skin and bones. Bring reserved broth to a boil in saucepan. Pinch 15 biscuits into thumb-sized pieces; drop into broth. Add soups, pepper, chicken, eggs and peas and carrots; mix gently. Spoon into 11-by-16-inch baking pan sprayed with nonstick cooking spray. Place remaining 5 biscuits on floured surface. Roll into rectangle; cut into strips. Arrange over pie. Preheat oven to 350 degrees. Bake for 25 minutes. Yield: 10 servings.

Cynthia Manning-McCall, Alpha Xi
Tyler, Texas

CHICKEN AND CHEDDAR ROLLS

1/2 cup chopped	1 1/4 cups shredded
mushrooms	Cheddar cheese
2 tablespoons butter or	4 whole boned chicken
margarine	breasts, skinned
2 tablespoons all-	1/3 cup all-purpose flour
purpose flour	2 eggs, beaten
1/2 cup light cream	2/3 cup dry bread crumbs
1/8 teaspoon each	1/4 teaspoon each thyme,
salt and cayenne	nutmeg and salt
pepper	Vegetable oil for frying

Sauté mushrooms in butter in skillet. Stir in 2 tablespoons flour. Add cream, 1/8 teaspoon salt and cayenne pepper. Cook until very thick, stirring constantly. Stir in cheese until melted. Spoon into 5-by-9-inch loaf pan. Chill until firm. Cut crosswise into 8 sticks. Preheat oven to 350 degrees. Cut chicken breasts into halves; rinse and pat dry. Pound 1/4 inch thick with meat mallet. Place 1 cheese stick on each filet. Tuck in edges and roll chicken to enclose cheese; secure with skewer. Coat chicken rolls with 1/3 cup flour. Dip into egg; roll in mixture of next 4 ingredients. Brown in 1/4 inch oil in skillet over medium heat; drain. Place in 9-by-13-inch baking dish. Bake for 20 to 25 minutes. Yield: 8 servings.

Delores J. Munson, Xi Gamma Alpha
Norfolk, Nebraska

POULTRY WITH PASTA AND PEAS

1 10-ounce package
  frozen peas
1 24-ounce package
  curly pasta
2 5-ounce cans chuck
  chicken packed in
  water

Chopped parsley, basil,
  garlic salt and pepper
  to taste
Shredded sharp Cheddar
  cheese (optional)

Place peas in colander. Cook pasta using package directions. Drain over peas in colander. Place in large bowl. Add undrained chicken, breaking up large pieces. Season with parsley, basil, garlic salt and pepper; mix well. Top with cheese. Yield: 8 servings.

Laura A. Cooley, Beta Alpha Psi
Converse, Texas

CHICKEN LASAGNA

I prepared this for a church supper which included several people who couldn't eat tomatoes.

1/2 cup all-purpose flour
1/2 cup melted butter or
  margarine
2 to 3 cups chicken broth
1/2 teaspoon basil
1/2 teaspoon salt
2 to 3 cups chopped
  cooked chicken
8 ounces lasagna
  noodles, cooked

1 10-ounce package
  chopped frozen
  spinach or broccoli
16 ounces cottage
  cheese or ricotta
  cheese
1 cup shredded
  mozzarella cheese
1/4 cup grated Parmesan
  cheese

Preheat oven to 375 degrees. Blend flour into melted butter in saucepan. Stir in chicken broth, basil and salt. Cook until thickened, stirring constantly. Layer chicken, noodles, spinach, cottage cheese, cream sauce and mozzarella cheese 1/2 at a time in 9-by-13-inch baking dish. Top with Parmesan cheese. Bake for 1 hour. Yield: 8 to 10 servings.

Marjorie Orr, Laureate Alpha
Roseburg, Oregon

CHICKEN SPAGHETTI

1 chicken or chicken
  breasts
2 quarts water
1 12-ounce package
  spaghetti
1 medium onion,
  chopped
1 medium green bell
  pepper, chopped
2 stalks celery, chopped
1/2 cup butter or
  margarine

1 10-ounce can Ro-Tel
  tomatoes
1 16-ounce stewed
  tomatoes
1 16-ounce can tiny
  peas (optional)
1 pound Velveeta
  cheese, chopped
Salt and pepper to taste

Rinse chicken well. Cook in water in large saucepan until tender. Drain, reserving broth. Chop chicken into bite-sized pieces, discarding skin and bones.

Cook spaghetti in reserved broth in saucepan until tender; drain. Sauté onion, green pepper and celery in butter in skillet until tender. Combine chicken, spaghetti, sautéed vegetables and remaining ingredients in large saucepan. Cook until cheese melts, stirring occasionally. Spoon into 13-by-15-inch baking dish. Preheat oven to 350 degrees. Bake spaghetti until bubbly. Yield: 12 to 15 servings.

Ginny Fewell, Xi Gamma Kappa
Slidell, Louisiana

CHICKEN SPAGHETTI CASSEROLES

1 chicken
1 medium onion,
  chopped
1 cup chopped celery
1 green bell pepper,
  chopped
1 16-ounce package
  spaghetti
1 10-ounce can Ro-Tel
  tomatoes, chopped
1 10-ounce can cream
  of mushroom soup

1 10-ounce can cream
  of chicken soup
1 4-ounce jar chopped
  pimentos
1 4-ounce can
  mushrooms
1 pound Velveeta
  cheese, chopped
1 cup shredded Cheddar
  cheese

Rinse chicken well. Cook in water to cover in large saucepan until tender. Drain and bone chicken, reserving broth. Cook onion, celery and green pepper in reserved broth in saucepan until tender. Add spaghetti. Cook until tender; drain. Add chicken, tomatoes, soups, pimentos, mushrooms and Velveeta cheese; mix well. Cook until Velveeta cheese melts. Spoon into two 9-by-13-inch baking dishes. Top with Cheddar cheese. Preheat oven to 350 degrees. Bake casseroles for 30 minutes. Yield: 18 to 24 servings.

Pamela K. Pomajzl, Xi Beta Chi
Grand Island, Nebraska

SPANISH PAELLA

1 21/2- to 3-pound
  chicken
1/4 cup all-purpose flour
1 teaspoon salt
Pepper to taste
1/4 cup olive oil
1 stalk celery with
  leaves, chopped
2 carrots, sliced
2 onions, cut into
  quarters
1 clove of garlic, minced

2/3 cup uncooked long
  grain rice
1/4 cup chopped pimento
2 cups chicken broth
1/4 teaspoon each
  saffron and oregano
1 9-ounce package
  frozen artichoke
  hearts, thawed
12 ounces peeled shrimp
12 small clams in shells

Rinse chicken and pat dry. Coat with mixture of flour, salt and pepper. Brown in hot olive oil in heavy skillet for 20 minutes. Remove to large saucepan. Add next 9 ingredients; mix well. Simmer, covered, for 30 minutes. Add artichoke hearts, shrimp and

clams. Simmer for 15 to 20 minutes longer.
Yield: 6 to 8 servings.

Doris Mates, Laureate Alpha Rho
St. Petersburg, Florida

SWEET AND SOUR CHICKEN WINGS

6 pounds chicken wings	Vegetable oil for frying
Garlic powder and salt	2 cups sugar
to taste	1 cup vinegar
2 cups cornstarch	1/4 cup catsup
6 eggs, beaten	2 tablespoons soy sauce

Preheat oven to 325 degrees. Cut each chicken wing into 3 portions, discarding tip portions. Rinse chicken and pat dry. Sprinkle with garlic powder and salt; let stand for 20 minutes. Coat with cornstarch; dip in eggs. Fry in hot oil in skillet until golden brown. Arrange close together on 2 foil-lined baking sheets. Combine remaining ingredients in saucepan. Cook until bubbly, stirring constantly. Spoon over chicken. Bake for 1 hour. Yield: 60 to 80 wings.

Jan D. Moser, Tau Pi
Sterling, Illinois

CHICKEN CASSEROLE

4 cups chopped cooked	3/4 cup mayonnaise
chicken	1 cup cooked rice
2 tablespoons lemon	2/3 cup sliced almonds
juice	1 tablespoon salt
2 cups chopped celery	1 cup shredded Cheddar
1 10-ounce can cream	cheese
of chicken soup	1 1/2 cups crushed potato
1 tablespoon grated onion	chips

Preheat oven to 400 degrees. Combine chicken with next 9 ingredients in large bowl; mix well. Spoon into 2-quart baking dish. Top with potato chips. Bake for 15 to 20 minutes or until heated through. May prepare in advance, adding potato chips at baking time. Yield: 6 to 8 servings.

Vicki L. Unruh, Alpha Rho
Havana, Illinois

CHICKEN AND SHRIMP CASSEROLE

3 cups shredded cooked	2 tablespoons melted
chicken	margarine
1 cup shrimp (optional)	Salt and pepper to taste
1 10-ounce can cream	1/3 cup grated Parmesan
of chicken soup	cheese
3 cups cooked fettucini	1/3 cup shredded
2/3 cup milk	mozzarella cheese

Preheat oven to 350 degrees. Combine first 8 ingredients in large bowl; mix well. Spoon into 9-by-11-inch baking dish. Sprinkle with cheese. Bake for 35 to 40 minutes or until heated through. Yield: 8 to 10 servings.

Juanita Carlsen, Laureate Xi
Coos Bay, Oregon

CHICKEN AND ALMOND CASSEROLE

I served this to a church youth group; even teenagers like it!

2 cups chopped cooked	3/4 cup slivered almonds
chicken	4 hard-cooked eggs,
2 cups cooked rice	chopped
1 10-ounce can cream	2 tablespoons lemon
of chicken soup	juice
1 10-ounce can cream	1 tablespoon onion
of mushroom soup	flakes
1 cup mayonnaise	1 teaspoon salt
1 1/2 cups chopped celery	Buttered bread crumbs

Combine chicken with next 10 ingredients in large bowl; mix well. Spread evenly in 9-by-13-inch baking dish. Chill, covered, overnight. Let stand at room temperature for 45 to 60 minutes. Preheat oven to 350 degrees. Top casserole with buttered bread crumbs. Bake for 45 minutes. Yield: 10 to 12 servings.

Sharon Bady, Xi Alpha Rho
Grand Island, Nebraska

SOUPER CHICKEN CASSEROLE

1/2 cup melted margarine	1 10-ounce can cream
1 small package corn	of celery soup
bread dressing mix	2 cups water or chicken
Chopped meat of 1	stock
cooked chicken	
1 10-ounce can cream	
of chicken soup	

Preheat oven to 350 degrees. Mix margarine with dressing mix in bowl. Spread half the mixture in 2-quart baking dish. Arrange chicken in prepared dish. Combine soups and water in saucepan. Heat until bubbly, stirring to mix well. Spread over chicken; top with remaining dressing mixture. Bake until brown and bubbly. Yield: 8 servings.

Louise Garrett, Laureate Pi
Chesapeake, Virginia

RITZY CHICKEN CASSEROLE

3 stacks Ritz crackers,	Salt and pepper to taste
crushed	1 10-ounce can cream
1/2 cup butter or	of mushroom soup
margarine	1 10-ounce can cream
6 chicken breasts,	of chicken soup
cooked, chopped	1 cup sour cream

Preheat oven to 350 degrees. Spread half the cracker crumbs in 9-by-13-inch baking dish; dot with half the butter. Sprinkle chicken, salt and pepper in prepared dish. Mix soups with sour cream in medium bowl. Spread over chicken. Top with remaining cracker crumbs; dot with remaining butter. Bake for 45 to 60 minutes or until bubbly. Yield: 8 servings.

Mary Jo Kennel, Xi Beta Delta
Midlothian, Virginia

CHICKEN AND MACARONI CASSEROLE

2³/4 cups chopped
  cooked chicken
2 cups uncooked
  macaroni
1 10-ounce can cream
  of mushroom soup
1 soup can milk
1³/4 cups chicken broth
1 small onion, finely
  chopped
¹/2 green bell pepper,
  chopped

1 2-ounce jar chopped
  pimento
1 5-ounce can water
  chestnuts, drained,
  chopped
8 ounces Cheddar
  cheese, shredded
¹/2 teaspoon each salt,
  garlic powder and
  pepper

Combine all ingredients in large bowl in order listed, mixing well. Spread in greased 9-by-13-inch baking dish. Chill overnight. Preheat oven to 350 degrees. Bake casserole for 1 hour. Yield: 12 to 14 servings.

Margaret M. Fisher, Laureate Alpha Alpha
Maryville, Missouri

CRUNCHY CHICKEN CASSEROLE

1 12-ounce package
  Escort crackers,
  crushed
¹/2 cup butter or
  margarine
6 chicken breasts,
  cooked, chopped
1 cup sour cream
1 10-ounce can cream
  of chicken soup

1 10-ounce can cream
  of mushroom soup
1 5-ounce can sliced
  water chestnuts,
  drained
1 4-ounce jar chopped
  pimentos

Preheat oven to 350 degrees. Spread half the cracker crumbs in buttered 9-by-13-inch baking dish; dot with half the butter. Combine chicken, sour cream, soups, water chestnuts and pimentos in large bowl; mix well. Spread in prepared dish. Top with remaining cracker crumbs; dot with remaining butter. Bake for 45 minutes. May add chopped onion and celery if desired. Yield: 10 servings.

Joyce Kirk, Preceptor Laureate Tau
Corpus Christi, Texas

CLUB CHICKEN CASSEROLE

¹/4 cup all-purpose flour
¹/4 cup melted butter or
  margarine
1 cup chicken broth
¹/2 cup water
1 15-ounce can
  evaporated milk
2¹/2 cups chopped
  cooked chicken

3 cups cooked rice
1 4-ounce can
  mushrooms
¹/3 cup chopped green
  bell pepper
¹/4 cup chopped pimento
1¹/2 teaspoons salt

Preheat oven to 350 degrees. Blend flour into melted butter in medium saucepan. Add chicken broth, water and evaporated milk. Cook over low heat until

thickened, stirring constantly. Add chicken, rice, vegetables and salt; mix well. Spoon into greased 8-by-12-inch baking dish. Bake for 30 minutes. Yield: 8 to 10 servings.

Imogene Reasor, Preceptor Lambda
Oliver Springs, Tennessee

CORKEY CHICKEN

3 or 4 chicken breasts
3 bay leaves
1 medium onion,
  chopped
1 7-ounce package long
  grain and wild rice
  mix, cooked
¹/4 cup mayonnaise

¹/4 cup milk
1 10-ounce can cream
  of celery soup
1 5-ounce can sliced
  water chestnuts,
  drained
1 3-ounce can French-
  fried onions

Rinse chicken well. Cook with bay leaves and onion in water to cover in large saucepan; drain. Chop chicken into bite-sized pieces, discarding skin and bones. Combine with rice, mayonnaise, milk, soup and water chestnuts in large bowl; mix well. Spoon into 9-by-13-inch baking dish. Preheat oven to 350 degrees. Bake casserole for 40 minutes. Top with onions. Bake for 5 minutes longer. Yield: 12 servings.

Denise Emory, Xi Kappa Lambda
Fountain Valley, California

ONE-HOUR CHICKEN CASSEROLE

3 pounds cut-up
  chicken or 5 to 6
  whole chicken
  breasts
Salt to taste
1 or 2 packages chicken-
  flavored stove-top
  stuffing mix

2 or 3 10-ounce
  packages frozen
  broccoli, cooked,
  drained
2 10-ounce cans cream
  of chicken soup
1 cup shredded Cheddar
  cheese

Preheat oven to 350 degrees. Rinse chicken well. Cook in salted water to cover in large saucepan until tender. Drain, reserving broth. Chop chicken into bite-sized pieces, discarding skin and bones. Prepare stuffing mix using package directions and substituting reserved chicken broth for water. Layer broccoli, stuffing mixture, chicken and soup in 9-by-13-inch baking dish; top with cheese. Bake for 30 minutes. Yield: 10 servings.

Jerri Phillips, Xi Lambda Gamma
Sesser, Illinois

Sue Trammel, Alpha Alpha, Hartselle, Alabama, makes Chicketti with 8 ounces spaghetti cooked and drained and mixed with ¹/4 cup shredded cheese, 2 cups chopped cooked chicken, 1 can mushroom soup, ¹/2 cup milk, 2 tablespoons minced green pepper and half of a 3-ounce can French-fried onions, topped with remaining onions and ¹/4 cup cheese and bake in preheated 350-degree oven for 40 minutes.

THREE-CHEESE CHICKEN BAKE

1¹/2 cups chopped onions	¹/2 teaspoon basil
1¹/2 cups chopped green bell peppers	8 ounces lasagna noodles
1 10-ounce can cream of chicken soup	1¹/2 cups cream-style cottage cheese
¹/3 cup milk	3 cups chopped cooked chicken breast
1 6-ounce can mushroom stems and pieces, drained	2 cups shredded American cheese
¹/4 cup drained chopped pimento	¹/2 cup grated Parmesan cheese

Preheat oven to 350 degrees. Microwave onions and green peppers on High in glass dish for 2 minutes. Stir in soup, milk, mushrooms, pimento and basil; mix well. Layer noodles, mushroom sauce, cottage cheese, chicken, American cheese and Parmesan cheese ¹/2 at a time in lightly greased 9-by-13-inch baking dish. Bake for 45 minutes. Let stand for 10 minutes before serving. Yield: 9 to 10 servings.

Diana Witt, Zeta Beta
Parkersburg, West Virginia

FORGOTTEN CHICKEN

2 cups uncooked instant rice	1 cup water
	4 chicken breasts
1 10-ounce can cream of mushroom soup	1 envelope onion soup mix
1 10-ounce can cream of celery soup	

Preheat oven to 350 degrees. Sprinkle rice in 9-by-13-inch baking dish. Heat soups and water in medium saucepan, stirring until smooth. Spoon over rice. Rinse chicken and pat dry. Arrange in prepared dish; sprinkle with soup mix. Bake, covered, with foil for 2¹/4 hours; do not "peek" during baking time. Yield: 4 servings.

Mary E. Loveks, Xi Gamma Mu
Grinnell, Iowa

BROCCOLI AND CHICKEN CASSEROLE

4 chicken breasts or 1 chicken, cooked, chopped	¹/2 cup mayonnaise
	¹/2 teaspoon curry powder
1 10-ounce can cream of chicken soup	1 16-ounce package herb-seasoned stuffing mix
2 10-ounce packages frozen chopped broccoli, cooked, drained	³/4 cup melted margarine

Preheat oven to 350 degrees. Combine chicken, soup, broccoli, mayonnaise and curry powder in large bowl; mix well. Spoon into 9-by-13-inch baking dish. Top with mixture of stuffing mix and margarine.

Bake for 20 to 30 minutes or until heated through. Yield: 6 to 10 servings.

Kay Schwartz, Preceptor Gamma Gamma
Broken Arrow, Oklahoma

SHERRY'S CHICKEN BROCCOLI

6 chicken breasts, cooked, chopped	1 cup sour cream
	¹/2 package potato chips, crushed
1 10-ounce package frozen chopped broccoli, cooked	Shredded Cheddar cheese
1 10-ounce can cream of mushroom soup	Chopped tomato

Preheat oven to 400 degrees. Combine chicken, broccoli, soup, sour cream and most of the potato chips in medium bowl; mix well. Spoon into 8-by-8-inch baking dish. Bake for 20 to 30 minutes or until bubbly. Top with cheese. Bake just until cheese melts. Garnish with remaining potato chips and chopped tomato. Yield: 8 servings.

Christi Boulware, Mu Omega
Tahlequah, Oklahoma

BROCCOLI AND CHICKEN BAKE

1 10-ounce package frozen chopped broccoli, cooked, drained	¹/2 cup mayonnaise
	1 teaspoon lemon juice
	¹/4 teaspoon curry powder
3 chicken breasts, cooked, chopped	1 cup shredded Cheddar cheese
2 10-ounce cans cream of chicken soup	¹/2 cup buttered bread crumbs

Preheat oven to 350 degrees. Layer broccoli and chicken in greased 7-by-11-inch baking dish. Combine soup, mayonnaise, lemon juice and curry powder in medium bowl; mix well. Spread over chicken. Top with cheese and bread crumbs. Bake for 30 to 40 minutes or until golden brown. Yield: 8 servings.

Kathleen Burgher, Beta Nu
Butte, Montana

CHICKEN DIVAN

2 10-ounce packages frozen broccoli spears, cooked, drained	4 cups cooked rice
	2 10-ounce cans cream of mushroom soup
1¹/2 pounds chicken breasts, cooked, chopped	²/3 cup water
	1 cup shredded Cheddar cheese

Preheat oven to 450 degrees. Layer broccoli, chicken and rice in 9-by-13-inch baking dish. Spread with mixture of soup and water; top with cheese. Bake for 15 minutes. Yield: 8 servings.

Ann F. Phillips, Mu Pi
Ft. Wayne, Indiana

CHICKEN DIVAN CASSEROLE

1 large bunch fresh broccoli	2 cups shredded Cheddar cheese
2 cups chopped cooked chicken	1 teaspoon lemon juice
2 10-ounce cans cream of chicken soup	Croutons
1/2 cup mayonnaise	Melted butter or margarine

Preheat oven to 350 degrees. Cook broccoli partially using package directions; drain. Layer chicken and broccoli 1/2 at a time in 9-by-13-inch baking dish. Combine soup, mayonnaise, cheese and lemon juice in medium bowl; mix well. Spread over layers. Bake for 25 minutes. Toss croutons with melted butter. Sprinkle over casserole. Bake for 15 minutes longer. Yield: 8 to 10 servings.

Mary Jean Baker, Tau Pi
Sterling, Illinois

JANET'S CHICKEN DIVAN

This is a delicious recipe from a beloved deceased sister.

2 pounds fresh asparagus or broccoli, cooked	1/2 teaspoon curry powder
4 cups chopped cooked chicken	2 teaspoons lemon juice
2 10-ounce cans cream of chicken soup	11/2 cups shredded Cheddar cheese
1/2 cup mayonnaise	1 tablespoon melted butter or margarine
1/2 cup sour cream	Paprika to taste
	Slivered almonds

Preheat oven to 350 degrees. Layer asparagus and chicken in buttered baking dish. Combine soup, mayonnaise, sour cream, curry powder and lemon juice in medium bowl; mix well. Spread over layers; top with cheese. Drizzle with butter; sprinkle with paprika and almonds. Bake for 30 minutes. Yield: 8 servings.

Virginia M. Firda, Xi Kappa
Peterborough, New Hampshire

CHICKEN AND DRESSING CASSEROLE

4 large chicken breasts or 1 21/2- to 3-pound cut-up chicken	1 8-ounce package herb-seasoned stuffing mix
2 10-ounce cans creamy chicken-mushroom soup	1/2 cup melted butter or margarine

Rinse chicken well. Cook in water to cover in large saucepan until tender. Strain broth, reserving 22/3 cups. Chop chicken into bite-sized pieces, discarding skin and bones. Mix soup with reserved broth. Combine stuffing mix with melted butter in medium bowl; mix well. Reserve 1/4 cup stuffing mixture. Layer remaining stuffing mixture, chicken and soup mixture 1/2 at a time in lightly greased 9-by-13-inch baking dish. Top with reserved stuffing mixture. Chill covered, overnight. Preheat oven to 350 degrees. Let casserole stand at room temperature for 15 minutes. Bake for 30 to 45 minutes or until heated through. Yield: 8 to 10 servings.

Marilyn Summers, Xi Delta
Vincennes, Indiana

HOT CHICKEN SALAD

This was served at my mother's 95th birthday party on June 24, 1992.

1 cup chopped cooked chicken	3 hard-cooked eggs, chopped
1 10-ounce can cream of chicken soup	1 cup chopped celery
3/4 cup mayonnaise	1 to 11/2 cups cooked rice

Preheat oven to 450 degrees. Combine all ingredients in bowl; mix well. Spoon into 9-by-9-inch baking dish. Bake for 10 minutes or until heated through. Yield: 8 to 9 servings.

Jean Harris, Laureate Lambda
Ogden, Utah

MEXICAN CHICKEN CASSEROLE

Corn tortillas, cut into quarters	Garlic salt to taste
1 10-ounce can cream of chicken soup	6 chicken breasts, cooked, chopped
1 small green bell pepper, chopped	1 to 2 cups shredded cheese
1 small onion, chopped	1 10-ounce can Ro-Tel tomatoes, drained, chopped
11/2 to 2 tablespoons chili powder	

Preheat oven to 300 degrees. Line bottom and side of 2-quart baking dish with tortillas. Combine soup, green pepper, onion, chili powder and garlic salt in medium bowl; mix well. Layer half the soup mixture, chicken and cheese in prepared dish. Add layers of remaining tortillas, soup mixture, chicken and cheese. Top with tomatoes. Bake for 1 hour. Yield: 8 servings.

Carolyn D. Lee, Xi Gamma Pi
Imperial, Nebraska

CHICKEN AND RICE

1 chicken	2 cups instant rice, cooked
1 10-ounce can cream of mushroom soup	1 4-ounce can mushrooms, drained
1 10-ounce can cream of celery soup	1 envelope onion soup mix
1 10-ounce can cream of chicken soup	
1/4 cup butter or margarine	

Rinse chicken well. Cook in water to cover in large saucepan until tender. Drain, reserving 1 cup broth. Chop chicken into bite-sized pieces, discarding skin and bones. Combine reserved broth with soups and butter in saucepan. Heat until bubbly, stirring to mix well. Stir in rice, mushrooms, chicken and soup mix. Spoon into 9-by-13-inch baking dish. Preheat oven to 350 degrees. Bake casserole for 15 minutes or until light brown. Yield: 8 to 10 servings.

Alice M. Rufenacht, Preceptor Epsilon Epsilon
Belvidere, Illinois

JUDY'S CHICKEN AND RICE

4 pieces chicken	1 10-ounce can creamy
4 cups water	chicken and
4 cups instant rice	mushroom soup
1/2 cup chopped onion	Garlic salt, celery salt
1/2 cup butter or	and pepper to taste
margarine	

Rinse chicken well. Cook in water in saucepan until tender. Remove and bone chicken. Return to broth. Bring to a boil. Stir in rice, onion, butter, soup and seasonings; remove from heat. Let stand, covered, for 5 minutes. Yield: 8 servings.

Leslie Bridges, Mu Omega
Tahlequah, Oklahoma

CHICKEN SUPREME

1 large chicken	1/4 teaspoon curry
1 10-ounce can cream	powder
of chicken soup	2 cups rice, cooked
1 cup shredded sharp	1 13-ounce package
Cheddar cheese	frozen broccoli,
4 teaspoons lemon juice	cooked, drained
1/4 cup mayonnaise	

Rinse chicken well. Cook in water to cover in large saucepan until tender. Drain and chop chicken, reserving 1/2 cup broth. Combine reserved broth with soup, cheese, lemon juice, mayonnaise and curry powder in medium bowl; mix well. Alternate layers of chicken, broccoli, rice and soup mixture in baking dish until all ingredients are used. Preheat oven to 350 degrees. Bake casserole for 20 minutes. Yield: 10 servings.

Doris LaFond, Preceptor Gamma Xi
Weslaco, Texas

CHICKEN TETRAZZINI

4 chicken breasts,	1/2 cup margarine
skinned	2 10-ounce cans cream
8 ounces uncooked	of chicken soup
spaghetti	2 cups sour cream
1 8-ounce can	(optional)
mushrooms, drained	Grated Parmesan cheese
1/4 cup chopped onion	Paprika to taste
1/4 cup chopped celery	

Preheat oven to 350 degrees. Rinse chicken and pat dry; place on baking sheet. Bake for 30 minutes or until tender. Chop into bite-sized pieces, discarding bones. Break spaghetti into halves. Cook using package directions. Spread in buttered baking dish. Sauté mushrooms, onion and celery in margarine in skillet, Stir in chicken, soup and sour cream. Spoon over spaghetti. Top with cheese and paprika. Bake for 40 minutes. Yield: 6 servings.

Melanie Stockdale, Sigma Lambda
Chicago Ridge, Illinois

PHEASANT CASSEROLE

This is a unique way to prepare pheasant, but it is just as delicious with chicken or turkey.

12 ounces mild sausage	Juice of 1/2 lemon
1 large onion, chopped	1 teaspoon salt
8 ounces mushrooms	1/8 teaspoon pepper
Chopped meat of 1	1/4 cup all-purpose flour
cooked pheasant	1/2 cup melted butter or
1 16-ounce package	margarine
wild rice mix, cooked	1/2 cup milk
1 8-ounce can water	13/4 cups chicken broth
chestnuts, drained,	1/2 cup toasted slivered
chopped	almonds

Preheat oven to 350 degrees. Brown sausage in skillet, stirring until crumbly; drain. Add onion and mushrooms. Sauté until vegetables are tender. Stir in pheasant, rice, water chestnuts, lemon juice, salt and pepper. Spoon into large baking dish. Blend flour into butter in small saucepan. Stir in milk and chicken broth. Cook until thickened, stirring constantly. Spread over pheasant mixture. Bake for 1 hour. Top with almonds. Yield: 8 to 10 servings.

Vicky Leitnaker, Epsilon
Wichita, Kansas

FRENCH TURKEY STUFFING

My mom and dad were both born in Canada and this was a family tradition.

8 medium potatoes,	1 cup finely chopped
peeled, chopped	onion
Heart, liver and gizzard	1 cup sliced celery
of turkey	Poultry seasoning, salt
Vegetable oil	and pepper to taste

Boil potatoes in water to cover in saucepan until tender. Grind turkey parts together. Brown in a small amount of oil in skillet. Add onion, celery and enough water to cover. Cook until vegetables are tender. Stir in seasonings. Mash potatoes in bowl. Add cooked vegetable mixture; mix well. Use to stuff turkey. Yield: 8 servings.

Evelyn H. Mowry, Nu Delta
Clinton, Iowa

TURKEY BREAST CUTLETS WITH ARTICHOKE HEARTS

4 turkey breast cutlets
1 cup Italian bread
  crumbs
2 to 6 tablespoons
  butter-flavored
  margarine
1 cup reduced-sodium
  chicken broth
1 large onion, sliced
  into half-rings

1 16-ounce can
  artichokes hearts,
  drained
1/2 cup white wine
Pepper to taste
3 tablespoons chopped
  fresh parsley

Preheat oven to 300 degrees. Rinse cutlets and pat dry. Coat with bread crumbs. Brown lightly on both sides in 2 tablespoons margarine in cast-iron skillet over medium heat, adding additional margarine as needed and removing to shallow baking dish. Add chicken broth to skillet, stirring to deglaze. Add onion. Cook for 2 minutes. Add artichokes, wine and pepper. Cook until heated through. Remove artichokes and onion to top of cutlets; pour cooking liquid over top. Bake, covered, for 20 minutes. Garnish with parsley. Yield: 4 servings.

Myrna Bernstein, Preceptor Omicron
Bethesda, Maryland

TURKEY MEXICANA

My nephew always called when he was coming to remind me to prepare this favorite dish.

1 pound Louis Rich
  barbecued breast of
  turkey
1 8-ounce jar salsa
1/2 cup shredded cheese

1/4 cup sliced black
  olives
1/2 cup sour cream
Chopped fresh parsley

Cut turkey into 1/4-inch slices; arrange in overlapping layer in large skillet. Add salsa. Bring to a boil; reduce heat. Simmer, covered, for 10 minutes. Add cheese and olives. Cook, covered, for 1 minute or until cheese melts. Remove to serving plate. Garnish with sour cream and parsley. May microwave on High for 8 to 10 minutes; add cheese and olives and microwave for 1 1/2 to 2 minutes longer. May substitute oven-roasted or hickory-smoked turkey for barbecued turkey. Yield: 4 servings.

Gertrude Pontius, Zeta Beta
Timberon, New Mexico

Shanda S. Dyke, Xi Lambda Tau, Garden City, Missouri, flakes 2 cans drained chicken breast to roll up in refrigerator crescent rolls and places in casserole, tops with mixture of cream of chicken soup and 1 soup can water, dollops 1 small jar Cheez Whiz on top and bakes in preheated 375-degree oven for 15 minutes for Crescent Casserole.

TURKEY STUFF-A-RONI

2 medium onions,
  chopped
1 pound ground turkey
2 tablespoons corn oil
1 10-ounce package
  frozen chopped
  spinach, thawed,
  drained
8 ounces ricotta cheese
3/4 cup grated Parmesan
  cheese

1 cup shredded
  mozzarella cheese
16 to 20 uncooked
  stuff-a-roni shells
3 tablespoons all-
  purpose flour
1/4 cup melted butter or
  margarine
2 1/4 cups milk
1/2 teaspoon salt

Preheat oven to 350 degrees. Sauté onions and turkey in oil in skillet, stirring until turkey is brown and crumbly; cool to room temperature. Stir in spinach, ricotta cheese, Parmesan cheese and half the mozzarella cheese. Cook pasta *al dente* using package directions; drain. Stuff with turkey mixture; arrange in 9-by-13-inch baking dish. Blend flour into melted butter in 1-quart saucepan. Cook for 1 minute. Add milk and salt gradually. Cook until thickened, stirring constantly. Spoon over pasta; sprinkle with remaining mozzarella cheese. Bake for 40 minutes or until brown. Yield: 8 servings.

Beverly J. Smith, Laureate Epsilon Beta
Fresno, California

TURKEY TETRAZZINI

This recipe was given to me many years ago by my dear friend Betty Eisenberger. It is still as special for my family as she is 25 years later.

8 ounces spaghetti,
  cooked
1/2 cup all-purpose flour
1/4 cup melted butter or
  margarine
2 1/2 cups chicken broth
1 cup half and half
1/4 cup cooking sherry
1 6-ounce can
  mushroom stems and
  pieces

1/4 cup chopped green
  bell pepper
2 cups chopped cooked
  turkey
1/2 teaspoon MSG
  (optional)
1 1/4 teaspoons salt
  (optional)
Pepper to taste
1/2 cup grated Parmesan
  cheese

Preheat oven to 350 degrees. Spread spaghetti in 9-by-13-inch baking dish. Blend flour into melted butter in large skillet. Stir in chicken broth and half and half gradually. Cook until thickened, stirring constantly. Add wine, mushrooms, green pepper, turkey and seasonings; mix well. Spoon evenly over spaghetti; sprinkle with cheese. Bake for 35 minutes. Yield: 8 to 10 servings.

Camilla M. Emmons, Preceptor Eta Kappa
Azusa, California

Under the Sea

CRAB AND BROCCOLI CASSEROLE

2 10-ounce packages
   frozen broccoli spears
   in butter sauce
1/4 onion, chopped
1 10-ounce can cream
   of mushroom soup

3/4 cup shredded sharp
   Cheddar cheese
1 pound frozen crab
   meat or imitation
   crab meat

Preheat oven to 350 degrees. Cook broccoli using package directions. Drain butter sauce into small saucepan. Add onion. Sauté until onion is tender. Stir in soup and cheese. Layer broccoli, crab meat and soup mixture in 9-by-13-inch baking dish. Bake for 30 minutes. Yield: 8 to 10 servings.

Marienne Sisko, Laureate Theta
Medicine Hat, Alberta, Canada

❖ EDISTO CRAB CASSEROLE

This recipe is best made with fresh crab caught in a tidal creek at Edisto Beach, South Carolina.

1 package stuffing mix
1 pound crab meat
2 cups cream
3 hard-cooked eggs,
   sliced
2 cups mayonnaise

2 tablespoons chopped
   onion
2 tablespoons chopped
   parsley
1/2 cup sherry

Preheat oven to 300 degrees. Reserve 1/2 cup stuffing mix. Combine remaining stuffing mix with crab meat and remaining ingredients in medium bowl; mix well. Spoon into baking dish; sprinkle with reserved stuffing. Bake for 45 minutes. Yield: 8 servings.

Rosanne Willis, Laureate Theta
Aiken, South Carolina

CAJUN SHRIMP BALLS

2 tablespoons chopped
   parsley
2 tablespoons chopped
   scallions
2 tablespoons butter or
   margarine
2 tablespoons all-
   purpose flour
1/2 cup milk
1/2 teaspoon salt

1/4 teaspoon hot pepper
   sauce
8 ounces cooked shrimp,
   finely chopped
2 cups fine dry bread
   crumbs
2 eggs, beaten
Vegetable oil for deep
   frying

Sauté parsley and scallions in butter in medium saucepan for 1 minute. Stir in flour. Add milk, salt and pepper sauce. Cook until thickened, stirring constantly; remove from heat. Stir in shrimp. Shape by tablespoonfuls into balls. Coat balls with bread crumbs. Dip into eggs; coat again with bread crumbs. Chill for 30 minutes. Deep-fry 4 at a time in 350-degree oil for 2 to 3 minutes or until golden brown; remove to warm serving bowl. Yield: 2 dozen.

Ann Doucet, Preceptor Alpha Omicron
Deer Park, Texas

Dorothy K. Clements, Preceptor Gamma Mu, Twenty-Nine Palms, California, makes delicious Crab and Shrimp Casserole by mixing 3/4 cup milk, 3/4 cup mayonnaise and 1 can crab bisque in large saucepan, adding half to three-fourths 8-ounce bag noodles, cooked, 1 pound steamed shelled shrimp and 1 pound crab meat, pouring into 3-quart casserole and topping with 1 cup shredded Cheddar cheese. Bake in preheated 350-degree oven for 45 minutes.

SHRIMP À L'ACADIAN

3 pounds large shrimp in shells	1 pound margarine
Cayenne pepper, black pepper and garlic powder to taste	Juice of 2 lemons
	1/2 teaspoon Tabasco sauce
1/3 cup Worcestershire sauce	2 teaspoons salt
	French bread

Rinse and drain shrimp; sprinkle generously with cayenne pepper, black pepper and garlic powder. Place in glass dish. Combine margarine, Worcestershire sauce, lemon juice and Tabasco sauce in glass measure. Microwave on High for 1 to 1 1/2 minutes. Pour over shrimp; cover with waxed paper. Microwave on High for 10 to 12 minutes or until cooked through, stirring several times. Stir in salt. Let stand for 3 minutes. Serve with French bread for dipping. Yield: 6 servings.

Frances Reynolds, Delta Kappa
Ellisville, Mississippi

BAVARIAN SHRIMP

1 cup uncooked rice	1/4 cup butter or margarine
2 tablespoons butter or margarine	2 tablespoons all-purpose flour
3 tablespoons onion soup mix	1/8 teaspoon Tabasco sauce
2 cups water	1 1/2 teaspoons salt
1/2 teaspoon salt or to taste	1 cup beer
1/8 teaspoon pepper	1 bay leaf
2 pounds peeled shrimp	2 teaspoons minced parsley
3 tablespoons minced onion	Cooked rice

Sauté rice lightly in 2 tablespoons butter in skillet. Stir in soup mix, water, 1/2 teaspoon salt and pepper. Simmer, covered, for 30 minutes. Rinse shrimp and pat dry. Sauté with onion in 1/4 cup butter in skillet for 2 minutes. Stir in flour, Tabasco sauce and 1 1/2 teaspoons salt. Add beer. Bring to a boil, stirring constantly. Add bay leaf. Simmer for 5 minutes. Spoon into serving dish, discarding bay leaf; sprinkle with parsley. Serve with rice. Yield: 4 servings.

Clara H. Evans, Preceptor Delta Sigma
Tampa, Florida

SHRIMP CREOLE

2 large onions, chopped	2 16-ounce cans tomatoes
2 green bell peppers, chopped	2 tablespoons vinegar
2 cloves of garlic, chopped	2 teaspoons curry powder
Shortening	1 teaspoon oregano
1 cup chopped celery	2 pounds shrimp
2 8-ounce cans tomato sauce	Cooked rice

Sauté onions, green peppers and garlic in a small amount of shortening in large saucepan. Add celery, tomato sauce, tomatoes, vinegar, curry powder and oregano; mix well. Simmer for 1 1/2 hours. Clean and devein shrimp. Parboil for several minutes. Add to saucepan. Simmer just until shrimp are cooked through. Serve over rice. May chop shrimp if preferred. Yield: 6 servings.

Margaret Garrett, Preceptor Gamma Xi
Weslaco, Texas

DRUNKEN CAJUN SHRIMP

We have enjoyed this recipe during many family gatherings and we can fondly recall those who are no longer with us who also enjoyed this dish.

2 pounds black tiger shrimp	1 12-ounce can beer, at room temperature
2 or 3 cubes fish bouillon	White pepper and cayenne pepper to taste
1 cup butter or margarine	6 cups cooked rice

Clean, devein and butterfly shrimp. Bring bouillon, half the butter and half the beer to a boil in large skillet. Simmer for 5 minutes. Add remaining butter and beer. Bring to a simmer. Stir in white pepper and cayenne pepper. Add shrimp. Cook until shrimp turn pink, turning once; remove from heat. Place shrimp on bed of rice on serving platter. Spoon sauce into bowl to serve with shrimp. Serve with green salad and steamed broccoli. Yield: 4 servings.

Cindy L. Kane, Preceptor Alpha Omicron
Dillard, Oregon

❖ SHRIMP FETTUCINI

1 large onion, chopped	4 teaspoons all-purpose flour
1 green bell pepper, chopped	2/3 cup half and half
1 clove of garlic, chopped	8 ounces process jalapeño cheese
1/2 cup margarine	12 ounces fettucini, cooked, drained
4 teaspoons parsley flakes	1 cup shredded cheese
1 pound shrimp or crawfish	

Sauté onion, green pepper and garlic in margarine in medium saucepan. Add parsley flakes and shrimp. Stir in flour, half and half and jalapeño cheese. Simmer for 30 minutes, stirring occasionally. Add pasta; mix gently. Spoon into baking dish; top with shredded cheese. Preheat oven to 350 degrees. Bake casserole for 20 minutes. Yield: 4 servings.

Gwen Newburn, Preceptor Beta Gamma
Jacksonville, Texas

SHRIMP IN CREAM SAUCE

6 jumbo shrimp
3 leeks, sliced
2 carrots, finely chopped
1/2 each red and green
bell pepper, sliced
2 ounces Drambuie
2 tablespoons cream
1 teaspoon butter or
margarine

Sauté shrimp in nonstick skillet over low heat for 2 minutes. Turn shrimp and add leeks, carrots and bell peppers. Sauté until vegetables are tender-crisp. Add Drambuie. Ignite sauce and let flame subside. Stir in cream and butter. Cook for 1 to 2 minutes or just until heated through. Spoon vegetables onto serving plate; spoon shrimp and sauce over top. Yield: 2 servings.

Deborah Mann, Zeta Theta
Oshawa, Ontario, Canada

SEAFOOD CASSEROLE

1 cup chopped onion
2 cups chopped celery
1 cup chopped green bell
pepper
1/4 cup butter or
margarine
2 pounds shrimp,
cooked, chopped
1 pound crab meat
4 cups cooked rice
2 cups mayonnaise
2 cups half and half
4 ounces mushrooms,
sliced
1 2-ounce jar chopped
pimento
Salt and pepper to taste

Preheat oven to 375 degrees. Sauté onion, celery and green pepper in butter in skillet. Add shrimp and crab meat; mix well. Mix remaining ingredients in bowl. Add seafood mixture; mix well. Spoon into 9-by-13-inch baking dish sprayed with nonstick cooking spray. Bake for 30 minutes. Yield: 12 servings.

Beverly Stewart, Xi Alpha Gamma Gamma
Huntsville, Texas

NANA'S SEAFOOD CASSEROLE

This favorite recipe of my mother's also became a favorite with her grandchildren, who call her Nana.

1/2 cup each chopped
celery, onion and
green bell pepper
1 clove of garlic, minced
1/4 cup corn oil
1 10-ounce can Ro-Tel
tomatoes, crushed
1 10-ounce can cream
of mushroom soup
1 4-ounce can sliced
mushrooms
1 pound peeled shrimp
1 pound crab meat
2 cups (or more) cooked
rice
1 tablespoon
Worcestershire sauce
1/4 teaspoon paprika
Salt and pepper to taste
1 cup shredded cheese

Preheat oven to 350 degrees. Sauté celery, onion, green pepper and garlic in oil in saucepan until onion is tender. Add tomatoes, soup and mushrooms. Simmer for 5 minutes. Add shrimp. Cook over low heat until shrimp are cooked through. Add crab meat. Simmer for several minutes, stirring occasionally. Stir in rice and seasonings. Spoon into 11-by-13-inch baking dish. Bake for 20 minutes. Top with cheese. Bake for 5 minutes longer or until cheese melts. Yield: 10 to 12 servings.

Barbara Gerami, Laureate Eta
Lafayette, Louisiana

SEAFOOD CRÊPES

1 cup all-purpose flour
2 cups milk
6 eggs
Salt and pepper to taste
2 stalks celery, chopped
2 green bell peppers,
chopped
1/2 cup butter or
margarine
1/4 cup all-purpose flour
1 pound Velveeta
cheese, cubed
2 cups milk
2 pounds mixed shrimp,
crawfish and crab
meat
2 tablespoons crab boil
seasoning

Combine 1 cup flour, 2 cups milk, eggs, salt and pepper in mixer bowl; beat until smooth. Let stand for 4 hours. Sauté celery and green peppers in butter in saucepan until tender. Stir in 1/4 cup flour. Add cheese, stirring until melted. Add 2 cups milk; mix well. Add mixture of seafood and crab boil seasoning. Simmer until thickened to desired consistency. Ladle 1/4 cup crêpe batter at a time into heated skillet or crêpe pan, swirling to coat pan evenly. Bake for 1 minute; turn crêpe. Bake for 30 seconds longer. Fill crêpes with seafood filling; fold over to enclose filling. Yield: 12 servings.

Donna Estes, Iota Epsilon
Baton Rouge, Louisiana

SEAFOOD ENCHILADAS

12 6-inch flour tortillas
1/2 cup vegetable oil
1 pound Monterey Jack
cheese, shredded
1 medium onion, chopped
2 cups crab meat or
imitation crab meat
1 cup shrimp
1/4 cup all-purpose flour
1/4 cup melted butter or
margarine
4 cups chicken broth
1 cup sour cream
1 cup finely chopped
green bell pepper
Green chili sauce

Preheat oven to 350 degrees. Soften tortillas 1 at a time in hot oil in skillet for 5 seconds; layer between paper towels. Place 1 spoonful of cheese, onion, crab meat and shrimp on each tortilla. Fold in ends; roll to enclose filling. Arrange in 9-by-13-inch baking dish. Blend flour into melted butter in saucepan. Stir in broth gradually. Cook until thickened, stirring constantly. Stir in sour cream; remove from heat. Add green pepper. Spoon over enchiladas. Bake for 30 minutes. Sprinkle with remaining cheese; spread with chili sauce. Bake for 5 minutes longer. Yield: 12 enchiladas.

Wendy Lawrence, Epsilon Omega
Mission, British Columbia, Canada

SEAFOOD LASAGNA

1 onion, minced	1 pound shrimp
2 tablespoons margarine	8 ounces crab meat
8 ounces cream cheese, softened	8 ounces scallops
8 ounces ricotta cheese	1/2 cup white wine
1 egg, beaten	8 noodles, cooked
2 teaspoons basil	1/2 cup grated Parmesan cheese
Fresh mushrooms	1/2 cup shredded sharp Cheddar cheese
2 10-ounce cans cream of mushroom soup	

Preheat oven to 350 degrees. Sauté onion in margarine in skillet until tender; reduce heat. Stir in cream cheese, ricotta cheese, egg and basil; remove from heat. Sauté mushrooms in nonstick skillet until tender. Combine with soup, seafood and wine in medium bowl; mix well. Layer noodles, cheese mixture and seafood mixture 1/2 at a time in greased baking dish. Top with Parmesan cheese. Bake for 45 minutes. Top with Cheddar cheese. Yield: 8 servings.

Ali MacMillan, Xi
Victoria, British Columbia, Canada

SEAFOOD LINGUINE

1 cup minced clams	1/2 teaspoon oregano
2 cloves of garlic, minced	Salt and pepper to taste
1/2 cup olive oil	1 pound linguine
1 tablespoon chopped parlsey	1 pound ricotta cheese
	1/2 cup milk

Drain clams, reserving liquid. Sauté garlic in olive oil in skillet until light brown. Add parsley, oregano, salt, pepper and reserved clam liquid. Heat for 2 minutes. Stir in clams and set aside. Cook linguine using package directions to desired degree of doneness; drain and return to pan. Add ricotta cheese and milk. Heat to serving temperature, stirring gently. Pour pasta onto serving platter. Ladle sauce over top. Yield: 4 servings.

Della Mimico, Laureate Xi
Fairmont, West Virginia

MARINATED FISH

1/2 cup vegetable oil	2 tablespoons chopped onion
3 tablespoons soy sauce	2 pounds walleye or other fish
2 tablespoons wine vinegar	

Combine oil, soy sauce, vinegar and onion in skillet. Add fish. Marinate in refrigerator as desired. Simmer until fish flakes easily. Yield: 4 servings.

Tami Schaufler, Pi Eta
Castalia, Ohio

SWEET AND SOUR SEAFOOD

2 pounds thick cod or other fish filets	Vegetable oil for frying
1 chicken bouillon cube	2 onions, sliced
1 cup water	4 stalks celery, sliced diagonally
1 tablespoon tomato paste	1 small red bell pepper, cut into strips
1 tablespoon soy sauce	2 shallots, sliced diagonally
3 tablespoons white wine	2 teaspoons cornstarch
1 teaspoon ginger	Salt and pepper to taste
1 pound shrimp	Cooked rice
Cornstarch for coating fish	

Cut fish into bite-sized pieces. Heat bouillon cube in water in saucepan, stirring to dissolve well; cool. Combine half the bouillon mixture with tomato paste, soy sauce, wine and ginger in bowl. Add fish and shrimp. Marinate in refrigerator for 1 hour. Drain, reserving marinade. Toss seafood with cornstarch, coating well. Fry in hot oil in skillet until golden brown; remove to warm platter. Drain skillet, reserving a small amount of oil. Sauté onions in reserved oil in skillet. Add celery, bell pepper and shallots. Sauté for 3 to 4 minutes. Add seafood; keep hot. Blend 2 teaspoons cornstarch into remaining bouillon mixture in saucepan. Stir in reserved marinade. Bring to a boil, stirring constantly. Season with salt and pepper. Spoon over seafood; mix gently. Serve with rice. Yield: 8 servings.

Carolyn P. Zaza, Preceptor Lambda
Waterbury, Connecticut

HALIBUT CASSEROLE

2 1/2 pounds halibut	1 7-ounce can water chestnuts, drained
1/2 cup all-purpose flour	Salt and seasoned pepper to taste
1/2 cup melted margarine	
4 cups milk	1 cup shredded sharp Cheddar cheese
2 tablespoons chopped pimento	Buttered bread crumbs or Wheaties
2 tablespoons chopped onion	
2 tablespoons minced green bell pepper	

Preheat oven to 400 degrees. Wrap fish in foil. Bake for 15 to 20 minutes or until fish flakes easily. Blend flour into melted margarine in saucepan. Cook for several minutes. Stir in milk. Cook until thickened, stirring constantly. Add fish and next 6 ingredients. Spoon into buttered 9-by-13-inch baking dish. Sprinkle with cheese and bread crumbs. Bake for 20 minutes. Yield: 12 servings.

Genevieve Bingham, Laureate Lambda
Ogden, Utah

BAKED SALMON

1 medium-large onion, sliced	Lemon pepper, parsley and salt to taste
1 10 to 15-pound salmon	

Preheat gas grill. Place onion slices in cavity of fish; sprinkle with lemon pepper, parsley and salt. Place piece of heavy-duty foil on each side of fish. Wrap with another piece of foil; seal securely. Place on grill with ball of foil under tail portion. Grill for 30 minutes or until fish flakes easily, checking every 5 minutes after first 30 minutes of grilling time. Yield: 10 servings.

Dulcy Berry, Preceptor Xi
Sherwood Park, Alberta, Canada

❖ SALMON SALAD TART

1 10-ounce package frozen chopped broccoli, cooked	1/4 cup sliced green onions
1 unbaked 9-inch pie shell	3 hard-cooked eggs, finely chopped
1 7-ounce can red salmon or tuna, drained, flaked	1 cup shredded Swiss cheese
1 cup minced celery	1/2 teaspoon dillweed
	1/8 teaspoon pepper
	1 cup mayonnaise

Preheat oven to 375 degrees. Arrange broccoli in pie shell. Combine salmon, celery, green onions, eggs, Swiss cheese, dillweed and pepper in bowl; mix well. Fold in mayonnaise. Spoon into pie shell. Bake for 30 minutes or until set. Serve hot or cold. Yield: 6 to 8 servings.

Jean F. Weir, Preceptor Beta
Butte, Montana

SALMON LOAF

This is good hot or cold, for picnics or holiday gatherings. For parties, cut into very thin slices and garnish with cherry tomatoes and fresh cilantro.

3 17-ounce cans red salmon	6 eggs
1 large onion, chopped	2 tablespoons chopped garlic
1/2 cup chopped cilantro	1/2 teaspoon herb seasonings
2 cups corn bread stuffing mix	

Preheat oven to 350 degrees. Drain salmon and flake into medium bowl, discarding skin and bones. Add onion, cilantro, stuffing mix, eggs, garlic and herb seasonings; mix well. Shape into loaf in baking pan. Bake for 1 hour. Yield: 10 to 12 servings.

Pat Salgado, Tau Eta
Hemet, California

BAKED ALMOND TROUT

1/4 cup white wine or white sherry	1/4 teaspoon each salt and pepper
1/3 cup corn oil	4 trout
1/2 teaspoon each garlic powder, dried green onions or dry mustard	1/4 to 1/2 cup melted butter or margarine
	Slivered almonds

Preheat oven to 325 degrees. Combine first 7 ingredients in shallow baking dish; mix well. Add trout. Marinate in refrigerator for 8 to 10 hours, turning often and spooning marinade over trout. Drain and reserve half the marinade. Bake trout in remaining marinade for 50 minutes, basting with reserved marinade if necessary. Spread with mixture of butter and almonds. Bake for 10 minutes longer. Yield: 4 servings.

Judy Kutcher, Xi Zeta Mu
Eldridge, Iowa

POTLUCK PASTA PLEASER

1/2 cup chopped onion	1 28-ounce can tomatoes, chopped
Vegetable oil	
1/3 cup each finely chopped green and red bell pepper	1 7-ounce can chunk light tuna
Salt, cayenne pepper and black pepper to taste	3 cups penne, cooked
	1 1/2 cups shredded mozzarella cheese

Preheat oven to 350 degrees. Sauté onion in oil in skillet. Add bell pepper, salt, cayenne pepper and black pepper. Sauté lightly. Add tomatoes. Simmer for 10 minutes. Stir in tuna. Layer pasta, tuna mixture and cheese in 3-quart baking dish. Bake for 30 minutes. Serve with crisp spinach or Caesar salad and hot rolls. Yield: 8 servings.

Patricia Philpotts, Laureate Gamma Rho
Oxford Mills, Ontario, Canada

QUICK TUNA OR SALMON CASSEROLE

1 large can tuna or salmon	1 tablespoon melted butter or margarine
2 eggs, beaten	1 cup crushed potato chips
1 cup milk	
2 tablespoons minced green bell pepper	1 cup cracker crumbs
2 tablespoons minced onion	

Preheat oven to 350 degrees. Flake tuna in bowl. Add eggs beaten with milk, green pepper, onion and butter; mix well. Alternate layers of tuna mixture, potato chips and cracker crumbs in buttered baking dish. Bake for 35 to 45 minutes or until brown and bubbly. Yield: 4 servings.

E. Renee Soward, Epsilon Chi
Kingman, Arizona

Rise'n Shine Brunch

BANANA-MACADAMIA BREAD

2 cups all-purpose flour
3/4 cup sugar
1/2 cup butter or
 margarine, softened
2 eggs
1 teaspoon baking soda
1 tablespoon grated
 orange rind

1/2 teaspoon salt
1 teaspoon vanilla
 extract
2 bananas, mashed
1/4 cup orange juice
3/4 cup chopped
 macadamia nuts
1 cup coconut

Preheat oven to 350 degrees. Combine flour and next 7 ingredients in large mixer bowl. Beat at low speed for 2 to 3 minutes. Add bananas and orange juice; beat for 1 minute. Stir in macadamia nuts and coconut. Spoon into greased loaf pan. Bake for 1 hour or until bread tests done. Cool in pan for 10 minutes. Remove to wire rack to cool completely. Yield: 1 loaf.

Deb Vitek, Alpha Gamma
Marshalltown, Iowa

❖ BRAIDED STUFFED BREAD

My mother-in-law's recipe was a big hit at the rehearsal party before our wedding! Now it's a regular feature for brunch or a late midnight snack in our home.

2 1/2 cups all-purpose
 flour
1 envelope rapid-rising
 yeast
1 tablespoon sugar
1 tablespoon butter or
 margarine
1 cup warm water
1 teaspoon salt
350 grams corned beef

1/4 cup mayonnaise
2 teaspoons mustard
1 cup shredded Swiss
 cheese
2 teaspoons sauerkraut
 (optional)
1 egg, beaten
2 tablespoons sesame
 seed

Combine first 6 ingredients in large bowl; stir just until moistened. Let stand, covered with towel, in warm place for 10 minutes. Combine corned beef, mayonnaise, mustard, cheese and sauerkraut in bowl; mix well. Roll dough into 9-by-12-inch rectangle on floured surface; place on baking sheet. Spread filling down center of dough. Make diagonal cuts down sides of dough at 1-inch intervals. Alternate strips over top, leaving filling partially visible. Let rise for 30 minutes. Preheat oven to 400 degrees. Brush braid with beaten egg; sprinkle with sesame seed. Bake for 25 minutes. Cool for 15 to 20 minutes before slicing. Yield: 10 to 15 servings.

Ham Filling: Combine 2 cups chopped deli-style ham, 1 cup shredded sharp cheese, 2 tablespoons pickle relish, 1 tablespoon mustard and 1 tablespoon mayonnaise for filling and proceed as above.

Salmon Filling: Combine 220 grams red salmon, 1 cup shredded Cheddar cheese and 1 tablespoon mayonnaise for filling. Layer thinly sliced dill pickle over filling and proceed as above.

Robyn Wolfe, Alpha
Winnipeg, Manitoba, Canada

PEACH BREAD

3 cups chopped fresh
 peaches or 16 ounces
 frozen peaches
2 1/4 cups sugar
1/2 cup shortening
2 eggs
1 teaspoon vanilla
 extract

2 cups all-purpose flour
1 teaspoon each baking
 powder, baking soda
 and salt
1 teaspoon (heaping)
 cinnamon
1 cup chopped nuts
 (optional)

Preheat oven to 325 degrees. Process peaches with 6 tablespoons sugar in blender until smooth. Cream remaining sugar with shortening in medium mixer bowl. Beat in eggs. Add peaches and remaining ingredients; mix well. Spoon into 2 greased and floured 5-by-9-inch loaf pans. Bake for 55 to 65 minutes or until bread tests done. May soften shortening in microwave. Yield: 2 loaves.

Daryl Rodway, Xi Alpha
Albuquerque, New Mexico

SAUSAGE AND APPLE BRUNCH CAKE

1 pound pork sausage links	1 cup all-purpose flour
1/2 cup pancake or maple syrup	1 cup baking mix
	2 tablespoons sugar
1/2 cup water	1 tablespoon baking powder
1/2 teaspoon cinnamon	1 teaspoon salt
1/4 teaspoon nutmeg	1 egg
6 apples, peeled, sliced	1 cup milk

Preheat oven to 400 degrees. Brown sausage in skillet; remove sausage, reserving drippings. Arrange sausage in pinwheel design in greased 8-inch springform pan. Bring syrup, water, cinnamon and nutmeg to a boil in medium saucepan; reduce heat. Simmer for several minutes. Add apples. Simmer for 2 minutes. Remove apples with slotted spoon, reserving syrup; arrange apples between sausages. Combine flour, baking mix, sugar, baking powder and salt in mixer bowl. Combine egg, 3 tablespoons reserved sausage drippings and milk in mixer bowl; beat until smooth. Add to dry ingredients; mix well. Spoon into prepared pan. Bake for 20 to 25 minutes or until golden brown. Invert onto serving plate. Serve with warm reserved syrup. Yield: 8 servings.

Mary Anne Watson, Xi Epsilon Xi
Stouffville, Ontario, Canada

BAKED STUFFED EGGS

The kids always know that there will be company after church when the bowl of hard-cooked eggs in the refrigerator has a note "Do Not Eat/For Company." This is also a good way to use eggs after Easter.

6 hard-cooked eggs	1/2 cup butter or margarine
1/4 cup sour cream	
1 teaspoon mustard	1 10-ounce can cream of mushroom or celery soup
Salt and pepper to taste	
1/4 cup chopped green onions	
	1 cup sour cream
1/4 cup chopped green bell pepper	1 cup shredded Cheddar cheese
1/4 cup chopped pimento	

Preheat oven to 350 degrees. Slice eggs lengthwise into halves and remove yolks to medium bowl. Add 1/4 cup sour cream, mustard, salt and pepper to

yolks; mash until smooth. Spoon into white halves; arrange in shallow 9-inch baking dish. Sauté green onions, green pepper and pimento in butter in skillet; remove from heat. Stir in soup and 1 cup sour cream. Spoon over eggs; sprinkle with cheese. Bake for 25 minutes or until bubbly. Yield: 6 servings.

Linda Zibell, Preceptor Alpha Lambda
Rochester, Michigan

BAKED DENVER SANDWICHES

8 slices bread	2 small green onions, chopped
Softened butter or margarine	
	3 eggs, slightly beaten
1/2 cup shredded Cheddar cheese	2 cups milk
	1/2 teaspoon salt
1 cup ground ham	Cayenne pepper to taste
1/4 cup chopped green bell pepper	

Trim crusts from bread and spread with butter. Place 4 slices buttered side down in 9-by-9-inch baking dish. Sprinkle with cheese, ham, green pepper and green onions. Arrange remaining bread buttered side up over filling. Beat eggs with milk, salt and cayenne pepper in small mixer bowl. Pour over bread; press down with spatula. Chill, covered, overnight. Preheat oven to 375 degrees. Bake sandwiches for 35 to 45 minutes or until set. Yield: 4 servings.

Patti Soard, Theta Psi
Cookeville, Tennessee

BREAKFAST EGG CASSEROLE

9 slices sourdough bread	1 4-ounce can chopped green chilies
6 eggs	
3 cups milk	Sliced fresh mushrooms
2 cups each shredded Cheddar and Monterey Jack cheese	1 4-ounce can sliced black olives
	1 8-ounce jar salsa

Arrange bread in 9-by-13-inch baking dish. Pour mixture of eggs and milk over bread; top with cheese. Chill overnight. Preheat oven to 350 degrees. Spread chilies, mushrooms and olives over casserole; top with salsa. Bake for 45 to 60 minutes or until set. Yield: 12 servings.

Hazel Rafferty, Laureate Gamma
Great Falls, Montana

Nancy Wright, Xi Nu Kappa, Keystone Heights, Florida, makes BLT Pie by filling unbaked deep-dish pie shell with 6 slices crumbled crisp-fried bacon, 1/2 cup shredded Monterey Jack cheese, 1 1/2 cups chopped tomato, 1 cup chopped onion and 1/4 cup chopped parsley, adding 2 eggs beaten with 1 cup evaporated milk and 1 thinly sliced tomato. Bake in preheated 350-degree oven for 35 minutes. Let stand for 15 minutes and garnish with shredded lettuce and additional bacon.

WINDRIFT FARM SCRAMBLED EGGS

1 7-ounce package frozen shrimp	1 tablespoon chopped chives
1 7-ounce can crab meat	12 eggs
3 1/2 tablespoons dry sherry	Tabasco sauce to taste
	Tarragon and pepper to taste
2 tablespoons all-purpose flour	1 teaspoon salt
2 tablespoons melted butter or margarine	1/4 cup melted butter or margarine
3/4 cup milk	Chopped parsley and paprika to taste

Cook shrimp using package directions. Rinse and drain shrimp and crab meat; chop shrimp. Combine seafood with wine in bowl. Blend flour into 2 tablespoons melted butter in medium saucepan. Stir in milk. Cook until thickened, stirring constantly. Stir in chives and seafood mixture. Beat eggs with next 4 ingredients in medium bowl. Cook eggs in 1/4 cup butter in skillet until soft-set, stirring constantly. Add seafood mixture. Cook until set. Sprinkle with parsley and paprika. Yield: 6 servings.

Julie Dirks
Amherst, Colorado

❖ BAJA QUICHE

8 ounces Italian sausage	2 tablespoons chopped green chilies
6 corn tortillas	3 eggs, beaten
1/2 cup refried beans	1 1/2 cups half and half
1 cup shredded Monterey Jack cheese	1 teaspoon cilantro

Preheat oven to 375 degrees. Brown sausage in skillet, stirring until crumbly; drain. Line 9-inch deep-dish pie plate with tortillas. Spread beans over tortillas. Sprinkle with cheese, sausage and green chilies. Beat eggs with half and half and cilantro in medium bowl. Pour over sausage filling. Bake for 40 to 45 minutes or until knife inserted in center comes out clean. May cover edge with foil to prevent over-browning. Yield: 6 to 8 servings.

Barbara J. Neece, Xi Sigma Pi
San Diego, California

BREAKFAST QUICHE

I served this at my first Founder's Day brunch. It is good to take to brunches because it needs to stand for a while before being served.

1 unbaked 9-inch pie shell	1 pound fresh asparagus
5 slices bacon	1/2 cup each shredded Cheddar and Monterey Jack cheese
8 ounces sausage	2 eggs
1/2 cup chopped onion	1 cup half and half
8 ounces fresh mushrooms	1/4 teaspoon nutmeg
Butter or margarine	Salt and pepper to taste

Preheat oven to 375 degrees. Bake pie shell for 7 minutes. Fry bacon in skillet until crisp; remove and crumble into pie shell. Brown sausage in skillet, stirring until crumbly; drain and set aside. Sauté onion and mushrooms in a small amount of butter in skillet; drain well. Combine with sausage in small bowl; mix well. Spread over bacon. Steam asparagus just until tender. Arrange over sausage mixture; sprinkle with cheese. Beat eggs with remaining ingredients in medium bowl. Pour over filling. Bake for 50 minutes or until knife comes out clean. Let stand for 15 minutes before serving. May substitute other vegetables for asparagus. Yield: 8 servings.

Frances DiDavide, Psi Beta
Plattsburg, Missouri

EASY-AS-PIE QUICHE

1 cup chopped fresh spinach	8 ounces bacon or breakfast strips, crisp-fried, crumbled
1 medium red bell pepper, chopped	1 unbaked 10-inch pie shell
1 medium bunch scallions, chopped	2 cups beaten eggs or egg substitute
1/2 small zucchini, chopped	1/2 cup nonfat milk
6 ounces shredded Swiss cheese	1 cup sour cream
	1 teaspoon white pepper
6 ounces grated Parmesan cheese	

Combine spinach with next 6 ingredients in large bowl; mix well. Chill overnight. Preheat oven to 375 degrees. Spread vegetable mixture in pie shell. Beat eggs with milk, sour cream and white pepper in medium bowl. Pour over vegetables; bake for 15 minutes. Reduce oven temperature to 325 degrees. Bake for 45 minutes longer or until knife inserted in center comes out clean. Yield: 6 to 8 servings.

Stefanie Brimacomb, Xi Alpha Tau
Twin Falls, Idaho

HOLIDAY QUICHE

Our social committee has used this recipe at Christmas. I also serve it to the electric crew, of which I am the only female member, of the local utility company. The guys always ask for the dish and the recipe.

1 1/2 cups butter cracker crumbs	4 ounces pimentos
2/3 cup butter-flavored shortening	2 cups shredded Swiss cheese
1 1/2 cups all-purpose flour	3/4 cup chopped green onions
1/2 cup water	5 eggs
2/3 cup sausage	1 cup whipping cream
2/3 cup each chopped ham, pepperoni and bacon	1 cup half and half
	1/2 teaspoon each salt and pepper

Preheat oven to 350 degrees. Combine cracker crumbs, shortening, flour and water in medium bowl; mix well. Press into 9-by-13-inch baking dish. Brown sausage in skillet, stirring until crumbly; drain. Sprinkle sausage, ham, pepperoni, bacon, pimentos, Swiss cheese and onions over crust. Beat eggs with remaining ingredients in bowl. Pour over filling. Bake for 30 minutes. Cool for 10 minutes before serving. Yield: 12 servings.

Janice M. Stimpson, Laureate Beta
Trenton, Missouri

ITALIAN SAUSAGE-VEGETABLE QUICHE

1 unbaked 10-inch pie shell	*1 teaspoon Italian seasoning*
10 ounces mild or hot Italian sausage	*3/4 teaspoon garlic salt*
1 10-ounce package frozen Italian-style vegetables, thawed	*1 1/2 cups shredded sharp Cheddar cheese*
	4 eggs
	1 cup half and half

Preheat oven to 350 degrees. Bake pie shell for 10 to 15 minutes or just until it begins to brown. Remove casings and crumble sausage. Brown in skillet over medium heat; remove sausage with slotted spoon, reserving 1 tablespoon drippings. Add vegetables, Italian seasoning and garlic salt to reserved drippings in skillet. Sauté for 2 minutes; remove from heat. Stir in sausage and cheese. Spread evenly in pie shell. Beat eggs with half and half in bowl. Pour over sausage filling. Bake for 30 minutes. Cool for 5 to 10 minutes. Yield: 6 servings.

JoAnn J. Kresky, Laureate Alpha Chi
Lansing, Michigan

LASAGNA FLORENTINE

I prepare this in advance when our daughter and her friends are coming on visits from college.

3/4 cup chopped onion	*1/2 cup grated Parmesan cheese*
2 cloves of garlic, minced	*1 10-ounce package frozen chopped spinach, thawed, drained*
2 tablespoons olive oil	
2 26-ounce jars spaghetti sauce	*2 eggs*
15 ounces ricotta cheese	*1 16-ounce package lasagna noodles, cooked, drained*
1 pound mozzarella cheese, shredded	

Preheat oven to 350 degrees. Sauté onion and garlic in olive oil in saucepan. Add spaghetti sauce. Simmer for 15 minutes. Spread 2 cups of the mixture in 10-by-15-inch baking dish. Mix ricotta cheese, 1 cup mozzarella cheese, Parmesan cheese, spinach and eggs in bowl. Layer half the noodles, half the remaining spaghetti sauce mixture and all the spinach mixture in prepared dish. Top with half the remaining mozzarella cheese, remaining noodles and

remaining spaghetti sauce mixture. Bake for 45 minutes. Sprinkle with remaining mozzarella cheese. Bake for 15 minutes longer. Yield: 8 servings.

Kathy Hubbard, Sigma
Wellington, Kansas

SOUTHWESTERN LASAGNA

2 medium onions, coarsely chopped	*1 tablespoon cumin*
2 cloves of garlic, minced	*1/2 teaspoon each salt and pepper*
2 tablespoons olive oil	*1 16-ounce package lasagna noodles*
1 28-ounce can whole tomatoes	*8 ounces Monterey Jack cheese, shredded*
1 4-ounce can chopped green chilies	*3/4 cup grated Parmesan cheese*
3 tablespoons chili powder	*1 pound small curd cottage cheese*

Sauté onions and garlic in olive oil in medium saucepan over medium-high heat for 5 minutes. Add next 6 ingredients; mix well. Bring to a simmer over medium heat; reduce heat. Simmer for 35 minutes, stirring occasionally. Cook noodles using package directions for 10 to 12 minutes; rinse with cold water and drain well. Mix Monterey Jack cheese and Parmesan cheese in bowl. Preheat oven to 350 degrees. Spoon enough cooked sauce into 9-by-13-inch baking dish to cover bottom. Layer noodles, cottage cheese, remaining sauce and mixture of shredded cheeses 1/3 at a time in prepared dish. Bake for 35 minutes. Yield: 8 servings.

Robin Keating, Alpha Delta Lambda
Plano, Texas

BREAKFAST CASSEROLE

1 pound Monterey Jack cheese, shredded	*7 eggs, slightly beaten*
	1 3/4 cups milk
12 ounces fresh mushrooms, sliced	*1/2 cup all-purpose flour*
1/2 large onion, chopped	*1 tablespoon parsley flakes*
1/4 cup butter or margarine	*1 1/2 teaspoons seasoned salt*
1 cup chopped cooked ham	

Preheat oven to 350 degrees. Sprinkle half the cheese in 9-by-13-inch baking dish sprayed with nonstick cooking spray. Sauté mushrooms and onion in butter in skillet until tender. Sprinkle over cheese in dish. Layer ham and remaining cheese over vegetables. Beat eggs with remaining ingredients in medium mixer bowl. Pour over casserole. Bake for 45 minutes. Yield: 10 to 12 servings.

Anna C. Walker, Mu Omega
Houstonia, Missouri

BRUNCH CASSEROLE IN PHYLLO

1 package frozen phyllo dough	1 green bell pepper, chopped
Melted margarine	1 onion, chopped
2 cups shredded Cheddar cheese	4 eggs, beaten
1 cup chopped cooked ham	

Preheat oven to 375 degrees. Thaw phyllo dough using package directions. Layer 7 sheets of dough in buttered 8-by-10-inch baking dish, brushing each layer with melted margarine. Spread cheese, ham and vegetables in prepared dish. Layer 6 or 7 sheets of phyllo dough over filling, brushing each sheet with margarine; tuck in edges to seal. Cut into serving sizes. Pour eggs over top, tilting pan to spread evenly. Bake on lowest oven shelf for 10 minutes. Move casserole to center shelf of oven. Bake for 15 minutes. May prepare layered ingredients the night before and add eggs before baking. Yield: 6 to 8 servings.

Deb Vitek, Alpha Gamma
Marshalltown, Iowa

RUBY'S MEXICAN CASSEROLE

7 eggs	2 cups shredded Monterey Jack cheese
1¼ cups milk	
¼ cup all-purpose flour	1 7-ounce can each chopped green chilies and jalapeño peppers
¼ teaspoon salt	
2 cups shredded Cheddar cheese	

Preheat oven to 350 degrees. Beat eggs with milk, flour and salt in medium bowl until smooth. Stir in cheeses and peppers. Spoon into 9-by-13-inch baking dish. Bake for 45 minutes or until set in center. Yield: 12 servings.

Shirley Lusher-Weingarten, Gamma Delta
Aurora, Colorado

BRUNCH BAKED EGGS

6 cups shredded Monterey Jack cheese	8 ounces cooked ham, sliced or julienned
12 ounces mushrooms, sliced	8 eggs, beaten
½ medium onion, chopped	1¾ cups milk
¼ cup thinly sliced red bell pepper	½ cup all-purpose flour
¼ cup butter or margarine	Chopped chives and parsley to taste

Sprinkle half the cheese in large baking dish. Sauté next 3 ingredients in butter in saucepan; drain. Spread over cheese. Arrange ham over vegetables; top with remaining cheese. Chill overnight. Preheat oven to 350 degrees. Mix eggs with remaining ingredients in bowl. Pour over casserole. Bake for 45

minutes. Let stand for 10 minutes before serving. Yield: 12 servings.

Theresa Gober, Xi Omicron Upsilon
San Angelo, Texas

BRUNCH SKILLET PIZZA

This is a simple one-dish meal that is easy to serve outdoors on a lazy weekend.

2 cups julienned cooked ham	½ cup chopped onion
	Salt and pepper to taste
1½ tablespoons corn oil	3 eggs, beaten
3 medium potatoes, thinly sliced	½ cup shredded sharp American cheese
½ cup chopped green bell pepper	Parsley

Reserve ¼ cup ham. Pour oil into 10-inch skillet. Layer potato slices, green pepper, onion and remaining ham ½ at a time in prepared skillet, sprinkling layers with salt and pepper to taste. Cook, covered, over low heat for 20 minutes or until potatoes are tender. Pour eggs evenly over layers; arrange reserved ham in spoke design over top. Cook, covered, for 10 minutes or until eggs are set. Top with cheese. Let stand, covered, until cheese melts. Garnish with parsley. Cut into wedges to serve. Yield: 5 or 6 servings.

Delores Overacker, Xi Nu
Weiser, Idaho

COUNTRY MORNING OMELET

½ cup butter or margarine	5 eggs, beaten
	2 cups milk
8 slices bread, cubed	½ teaspoon garlic salt
2 cups shredded Cheddar cheese	1 10-ounce can cream of mushroom soup
1½ cups chopped cooked ham	½ cup milk
½ onion, finely chopped	2 cups crushed cornflakes

Melt butter in 9-by-13-inch baking pan. Layer bread cubes, cheese, ham and onion in prepared pan. Beat eggs with 2 cups milk and garlic salt in mixer bowl. Pour over layers. Chill overnight or freeze until needed. Preheat oven to 350 degrees. Top casserole with mixture of soup and ½ cup milk; sprinkle with cornflakes. Bake for 1 hour. Yield: 6 to 8 servings.

Kim Wilmes, Xi Eta Alpha
Calmar, Iowa

Anna Broughton, Omicron Beta, Bosworth, Missouri, makes Sticky Biscuits by mixing 2 tablespoons butter or margarine, ¼ cup packed brown sugar, ¼ cup pancake syrup, ¼ cup pecans and ¼ teaspoon cinnamon in baking pan, arranging one 10-count can refrigerator biscuits on top and baking using package directions. Invert onto serving plate.

EASY BRUNCH BENEDICT

May heat sauce, cook ham and poach eggs in microwave, using microwave instructions, for a quick and easy dish for company.

1 10-ounce can cream of chicken soup	6 English muffin halves, toasted
1/4 cup mayonnaise	6 slices cooked ham or
1/3 cup milk	Canadian bacon
1/2 to 1 tablespoon lemon juice	6 eggs, poached
	Parsley

Heat soup, mayonnaise, milk and lemon juice in saucepan until heated through, stirring until smooth. Top each muffin half with 1 slice ham and 1 egg. Place on serving plates. Spoon sauce over top. Garnish with parsley; serve with fruit.
Yield: 6 servings.

Angeline Fincher, Xi Alpha Pi
Albuquerque, New Mexico

FANCY EGG SCRAMBLE

2 tablespoons all-purpose flour	1/4 cup chopped green onions
1/2 teaspoon salt	3 tablespoons butter or
1/8 teaspoon pepper	margarine
2 tablespoons melted butter or margarine	12 eggs, beaten
	3 ounces mushrooms
2 cups milk	2 1/4 cups soft bread
1 cup shredded American cheese	crumbs
1 cup chopped Canadian bacon or ham	4 teaspoons melted butter or margarine
	1/8 teaspoon paprika

Blend flour, salt and pepper into 2 tablespoons melted butter in saucepan. Stir in milk. Cook until thickened, stirring constantly. Stir in cheese until melted. Cook Canadian bacon and green onions in 3 tablespoons butter in large skillet until onions are tender but not brown. Add eggs. Cook just until eggs are set, stirring constantly. Fold eggs into cheese sauce with mushrooms. Spoon into 9-by-13-inch baking pan. Toss bread crumbs with 4 teaspoons melted butter and paprika in bowl. Sprinkle over casserole. Chill, covered in refrigerator. Preheat oven to 350 degrees. Bake casserole, covered, for 30 minutes. Serve with fresh fruit and coffee cake or muffins. Yield: 10 servings.

Connie L. McGill, Preceptor Alpha Kappa
North Vancouver, British Columbia, Canada

Kelly K. Gruenwald, Xi Delta Gamma, Leesburg, Virginia, coats buttermilk biscuits with mixture of 1/4 cup melted margarine, 1 1/2 teaspoons parsley flakes, 1/2 teaspoon dillweed and 1/4 teaspoon onion flakes and bakes in preheated 425-degree oven for 12 minutes to make Easy Herbed Rolls.

ASPARAGUS AND HAM BRUNCH

6 slices whole wheat bread	2 teaspoons minced onion
1 1/2 cups shredded Cheddar cheese	3/4 teaspoon Worcestershire sauce
1 pound fresh asparagus, chopped, cooked	3/4 teaspoon dry mustard
1 cup chopped cooked ham	1/4 teaspoon each garlic powder and salt
5 eggs	Cayenne pepper to taste
1 3/4 cups milk	1 cup shredded Cheddar cheese

Trim crusts from bread. Arrange bread in lightly buttered 9-by-13-inch baking dish. Layer 1 1/2 cups cheese, asparagus and ham in prepared dish. Beat eggs with milk, onion, Worcestershire sauce, dry mustard, garlic powder, salt and cayenne pepper in bowl. Pour over layers. Chill, covered, overnight. Preheat oven to 350 degrees. Bake casserole for 30 minutes. Sprinkle 1 cup cheese over top. Bake for 10 minutes longer. Yield: 6 to 8 servings.

Mary Lou Burgess, Xi Masters
Kennewick, Washington

HAM AND BROCCOLI BRUNCH ROLL-UPS

1 medium onion, sliced	1 teaspoon dry mustard
1 cup sliced fresh mushrooms or	2 9-ounce packages frozen broccoli spears,
1 4-ounce can mushroom pieces, drained	thawed
	8 thin ham slices
3 tablespoons margarine	1 red bell pepper, cut into 16 strips
8 eggs, beaten	2 cups shredded Swiss
1/4 cup milk	cheese

Preheat oven to 350 degrees. Reserve 8 medium onion rings; chop enough remaining onion to measure 1/3 cup. Sauté chopped onion and mushrooms in margarine in large skillet until onion is tender-crisp. Combine eggs, milk and dry mustard in medium bowl; beat until smooth. Stir in mushroom mixture. Place broccoli spears on ham slices; roll ham to enclose broccoli. Slide 1 onion ring over each roll-up; insert 1 red bell pepper strip into each end of roll-ups. Arrange in lightly greased 9-by-13-inch baking dish. Spoon sauce over top. Bake for 25 minutes. Sprinkle with cheese. Bake for 10 to 15 minutes longer or until done to taste. May prepare roll-ups in advance and chill, individually wrapped in plastic wrap, for up to 24 hours. Add sauce at baking time. Yield: 8 servings.

Bonnie Wold, Xi Gamma Mu
Grinnell, Iowa

HAM AND CHEESE STRATA

12 slices bread	6 eggs, slightly beaten
12 ounces sharp process cheese, sliced	3¹/2 cups milk
1 10-ounce package frozen broccoli, cooked, drained	1 teaspoon onion powder
	¹/4 teaspoon each dry mustard and salt
2 cups chopped cooked ham	

Preheat oven to 325 degrees. Trim crusts from bread. Arrange 6 slices in 9-by-13-inch baking dish. Layer cheese, broccoli and ham in prepared dish; top with remaining bread. Beat eggs with remaining ingredients in mixer bowl. Pour over layers. Bake for 55 minutes. Yield: 12 servings.

Mildred Franta, Xi Upsilon Epsilon
Hallettsville, Texas

HAM-PANCAKE PIE

3 tablespoons light brown sugar	3 medium apples, peeled, sliced
¹/4 teaspoon curry powder	¹/3 cup apple juice or water
¹/2 teaspoon salt	1 cup pancake mix
¹/4 teaspoon pepper	1 cup milk
2 medium sweet potatoes, peeled, thinly sliced	¹/2 teaspoon dry mustard
3 cups chopped cooked ham	2 tablespoons melted butter or margarine

Preheat oven to 375 degrees. Mix brown sugar with curry powder, salt and pepper in small bowl. Layer sweet potatoes, ham, apples and brown sugar mixture ¹/2 at a time in 2-quart baking dish. Pour apple juice over layers. Bake for 40 minutes or until sweet potatoes are tender. Combine remaining ingredients in mixer bowl; mix until smooth. Spoon over sweet potato mixture. Bake for 20 minutes or until puffed and golden brown. Yield: 6 servings.

Ann M. Lobenstein, Xi Sigma
Tomah, Wisconsin

BEST BRUNCH CASSEROLE

This is our traditional Christmas morning treat, prepared the night before. You may substitute ham, shrimp or chicken for bacon.

12 slices bread	4 eggs
Butter or margarine, softened	2 cups milk
1 pound Swiss cheese, shredded	2 teaspoons mustard
8 ounces fresh mushrooms, sliced	1 teaspoon Worcestershire sauce
1 to 2 cups crumbled crisp-fried bacon	1 teaspoon Beau Monde seasoning
	Salt to taste

Trim crusts from bread. Spread both sides with butter. Layer bread, cheese, mushrooms and bacon ¹/2 at a time in 9-by-13-inch baking dish. Combine remaining ingredients in mixer bowl; mix until smooth. Pour over layers. Chill overnight. Preheat oven to 325 degrees. Bake casserole for 1 hour. Let stand for 15 minutes before serving. Serve with fresh fruit. Yield: 12 servings.

Cynthia G. Young, Gamma Delta
Martinsville, Virginia

BRUNCH CASSEROLE

This was first served at a family reunion at the beach 6 years ago. It was easy to prepare the night before, serve and clean up.

Crisp rice cereal	2 10-ounce cans cream of celery soup
1 pound bulk pork sausage	5 eggs, beaten
1 large onion, chopped	1 cup mayonnaise
2 cups cooked rice	
2 cups shredded sharp Cheddar cheese	

Spread ¹/2 inch cereal in 9-by-13-inch baking pan sprayed with nonstick cooking spray. Brown sausage with onion in skillet, stirring until sausage is crumbly; drain. Spread in prepared pan. Layer rice and cheese over sausage. Combine remaining ingredients in bowl; whisk until smooth. Pour over layers. Preheat oven to 350 degrees. Bake casserole for 30 minutes or until set. Yield: 8 to 12 servings.

Candace R. M. Promowicz, Xi Alpha Phi
Niagara Falls, New York

CHEESY EGGS FANTASTIC

1 pound bulk sausage	¹/3 to ¹/2 cup salsa
4 ounces fresh mushrooms, sliced	8 ounces Velveeta cheese, sliced
1 medium onion, chopped	8 ounces medium Cheddar cheese, sliced
Salt and pepper to taste	
6 eggs	8 ounces mozzarella cheese, sliced
3 tablespoons sour cream	

Preheat oven to 400 degrees. Brown sausage with next 4 ingredients in skillet, stirring until sausage is crumbly; drain. Process eggs and sour cream in blender for 1 minute. Pour into greased 7-by-11-inch baking dish. Bake for 8 to 10 minutes or until set in center. Reduce oven temperature to 300 degrees. Layer salsa, sausage mixture, Velveeta cheese, Cheddar cheese and mozzarella cheese over eggs. Bake for 45 minutes longer. Let stand for 5 to 10 minutes before serving. Serve with muffins and fruit. May bake egg mixture, layer remaining ingredients and chill or freeze prior to second baking step. Yield: 6 to 8 servings.

Jo Hicks, Xi Gamma Mu
Ontario, Oregon

COME BACK BREAKFAST

This was named by guests who said "We're coming back for more of this" the first time I served it.

8 slices bread, crusts
  trimmed, cubed
1 pound bulk sausage or
  2 cups chopped cooked
  ham
4 eggs
2 cups milk
1/4 cup chopped green or
  red bell pepper
1 2-ounce can sliced
  mushrooms

1/4 cup chopped onion
1 10-ounce can cream
  of mushroom or celery
  soup
3 1/2 cups shredded
  Cheddar cheese
1 teaspoon each dry
  mustard, salt and
  pepper
1/2 cup shredded
  Cheddar cheese

Preheat oven to 350 degrees. Spread bread cubes in 9-by-13-inch baking dish. Brown sausage in skillet, stirring until crumbly; drain. Combine sausage with next 10 ingredients in large bowl; mix well. Spoon into prepared dish. Top with 1/2 cup cheese. Bake, covered with foil, for 45 minutes. Bake, uncovered, for 15 minutes longer. May chill overnight before serving. Yield: 12 servings.

Mary Helen Goldberg, Psi Beta
Plattsburg, Missouri

LIGHT AND RICH BREAKFAST DELIGHT

10 slices light wheat
  bread
1 pound light bulk
  sausage
1 cup shredded fat-free
  Swiss cheese
1 cup shredded fat-free
  Cheddar cheese
Egg substitute equal to
  8 eggs

2 egg whites
1/2 cup skim milk
Cinnamon and nutmeg
  to taste
2 21-ounce cans light
  apple pie filling
2 to 4 packets artificial
  sweetener

Preheat oven to 350 degrees. Trim crusts from bread. Process crusts in food processor until finely crumbled; cut bread into cubes. Spread bread cubes in buttered 9-by-13-inch baking dish. Brown sausage in skillet, stirring until crumbly; drain. Spread over bread. Layer cheeses over sausage. Beat egg substitute, egg whites and milk in mixer bowl. Pour over layers. Sprinkle bread crumbs, cinnamon and nutmeg over top. Bake, covered, for 45 minutes. Heat pie filling with cinnamon and nutmeg in saucepan; remove from heat. Stir in sweetener. Cut casserole into squares. Spoon apple mixture over servings. May prepare casserole and chill overnight prior to baking. Yield: 12 servings.

Merline McCoy, Laureate Beta Psi
Village Mills, Texas

MEXICAN BREAKFAST

This can also be prepared in a Dutch oven set in coals for a campers' breakfast.

3 pounds pork sausage
2 4-ounce cans
  chopped green chilies
6 to 8 medium potatoes,
  peeled, cut into
  1/2-inch cubes
1/2 medium onion,
  chopped

18 eggs
Salt and pepper to taste
2 cups shredded
  Cheddar cheese
Salsa
Sour cream

Preheat oven to 350 degrees. Brown sausage in skillet, stirring frequently; drain. Stir in green chilies. Remove to 9-by-13-inch baking dish sprayed with nonstick cooking spray. Drain skillet, reserving a small amount of drippings. Sauté potatoes and onion in drippings in skillet. Spread over sausage. Beat eggs with salt and pepper in mixer bowl. Pour over layers. Bake for 45 minutes or until set. Sprinkle with cheese. Bake for 1 to 2 minutes or until cheese melts. Serve with salsa and sour cream. Yield: 15 servings.

Lynn E. Acord, Beta Nu
Encampment, Wyoming

SAUSAGE RING WITH SCRAMBLED EGGS

2 eggs
1 cup fine dry bread
  crumbs
2 tablespoons grated
  onion
1/4 cup chopped parsley
1 1/2 pounds sage or hot
  sausage
1/3 cup chopped onion
1/4 cup chopped green
  bell pepper
3/4 cup sliced mushrooms
3 tablespoons vegetable
  oil

1 16-ounce can
  tomatoes
1 tablespoon cornstarch
2 teaspoons sugar
1 teaspoon salt
Cayenne pepper and
  black pepper to taste
8 eggs
2 tablespoons light
  cream
1/2 teaspoon salt
Pepper to taste
3 tablespoons butter or
  margarine

Preheat oven to 350 degrees. Beat 2 eggs in bowl. Add bread crumbs, 2 tablespoons onion, parsley and sausage; mix well. Press into ring mold. Bake for 20 minutes; drain. Bake for 20 minutes longer. Sauté 1/3 cup onion, green pepper and mushrooms in oil in skillet. Drain 2 tablespoons juice from tomatoes. Blend drained juice with cornstarch in cup. Add to skillet with remaining tomatoes and juice, sugar, 1 teaspoon salt, cayenne pepper and black pepper. Cook over low heat until thickened, stirring constantly. Beat 8 eggs with cream, 1/2 teaspoon salt and pepper in bowl. Cook in butter in skillet, stirring until soft-set. Drain sausage ring; invert onto warm platter. Spoon eggs into center of ring. Serve with sauce. Yield: 8 servings.

Anita M. Wilson, Laureate Alpha Mu
Mansfield, Ohio

CRAB NEWBERG CRÊPES

3 eggs
2 tablespoons melted
  butter or margarine
1 1/2 cups milk
1 cup all-purpose flour
1/2 teaspoon salt
2 tablespoons butter or
  margarine
1/4 cup all-purpose flour
1 1/2 cups whipping
  cream
1/2 cup milk
3 egg yolks, beaten
1/4 cup dry sherry
2 1/2 cups cooked crab
  meat or imitation crab
  meat
Salt and pepper to taste

Combine first 5 ingredients in blender container; process for 1 minute or until smooth. Let stand at room temperature for 1 hour. Spoon a small amount of batter at a time into heated crêpe pan or 8-inch skillet, tilting pan to coat evenly. Bake until light brown. Melt 2 tablespoons butter in double boiler over simmering water. Stir in 1/4 cup flour. Cook for 2 to 3 minutes. Stir in cream and milk gradually. Cook until thickened, stirring frequently. Stir a small amount of hot mixture into egg yolks; stir egg yolks into hot mixture. Stir in wine, crab meat and salt and pepper to taste. Cook until heated through. Spoon crab mixture onto crêpes, reserving some of the mixture for topping. Roll crêpes to enclose filling. Arrange in 9-by-13-inch baking dish; top with reserved crab meat mixture. Preheat oven to 350 degrees. Bake crêpes for 10 to 15 minutes or until heated through. Yield: 6 servings.

Pat Sawka, Preceptor Beta Sigma
Magalia, California

SEAFOOD QUICHE

1 8-ounce can tiny
  shrimp
4 eggs
1 cup sour cream
1 cup light cream
6 to 8 ounces each
  shredded Monterey
  Jack and sharp
  Cheddar cheese
1/3 cup finely chopped
  green onions
1 8-ounce can crab
  meat, drained
Salt, cayenne pepper
  and black pepper to
  taste
1 unbaked 9-inch pie
  shell

Preheat oven to 425 degrees. Soak shrimp in ice water in bowl for several minutes; drain. Beat eggs in bowl. Stir in shrimp and next 9 ingredients. Pour into pie shell. Bake for 15 minutes. Reduce oven temperature to 350 degrees. Bake for 30 minutes longer or until set in center. Serve with fresh fruit compote or frozen strawberry yogurt. Yield: 6 to 8 servings.

Martha C. Carter, Laureate Alpha Beta
Ft. Myers, Florida

SOUTHWESTERN SUNRISE

4 large bananas
1/3 cup unsalted butter
  or unsalted margarine
1/4 cup sugar
1 cup whipping cream
1/4 cup sugar
2 tablespoons rum
3/4 teaspoon vanilla
  extract
5 to 6 plum tomatoes
3 4-ounce cans
  chopped green chilies,
  drained
1 pound Cheddar
  cheese, shredded
5 green onions, thinly
  sliced
1 can medium black
  olives, sliced
1 pound crab meat
9 eggs
2 1/2 cups milk
1 cup all-purpose flour
12 ounces jalapeño
  cheese, shredded
Ground cloves to taste

Sauté bananas in butter in skillet; drain and cool. Sprinkle with 1/4 cup sugar. Whip cream in mixer bowl until soft peaks form. Fold in 1/4 cup sugar, rum and vanilla. Place bananas on platter. Spoon whipped cream over bananas. Chill in refrigerator. Preheat oven to 350 degrees. Cut plum tomatoes into halves crosswise. Squeeze out and discard seed and juice; chop tomatoes. Layer green chilies, Cheddar cheese, green onions, olives, tomatoes and crab meat 1/2 at a time in 9x13-inch baking dish. Process eggs, milk and flour in blender until smooth. Spoon over layers; top with jalapeño cheese. Bake for 30 to 40 minutes or until nearly set in center. Let stand for 10 minutes. Place bananas on casserole; sprinkle with cloves. Yield: 10 to 12 servings.

Diane M. Polansky Ward, Xi Gamma Psi
Ankeny, Iowa

❖ TURKEY POCKETS

5 tablespoons melted
  margarine
6 ounces cream cheese,
  softened
4 cups chopped cooked
  turkey
1/2 cup milk
2 tablespoons each
  chopped onion and
  pimento
1/2 teaspoon salt
1/2 teaspoon pepper
2 8-count cans crescent
  rolls
2 tablespoons melted
  margarine
1/2 cup crushed croutons
1 10-ounce can cream
  of mushroom soup
1/3 cup milk
2 tablespoons sour cream

Preheat oven to 350 degrees. Blend 5 tablespoons margarine and cream cheese in bowl. Add next 6 ingredients; mix well. Separate roll dough into 8 squares, pressing perforations to seal. Spoon turkey mixture onto squares; roll dough to enclose filling. Place on baking sheet sprayed with nonstick cooking spray. Brush with 2 tablespoons margarine; sprinkle with croutons. Bake for 12 minutes. Heat soup, 1/3 cup milk and sour cream in saucepan until bubbly. Serve over pockets. Yield: 8 servings.

Donna L. Smith, Laureate Alpha Psi
Council Bluffs, Iowa

The Vegetable Patch

❖ ARTICHOKE TORTA

2 6-ounce jars marinated artichoke hearts	1/4 teaspoon salt
1 small onion, chopped	1/8 teaspoon each pepper, oregano and Tabasco sauce
1 clove of garlic, chopped	2 cups shredded sharp Cheddar cheese
4 eggs, beaten	2 tablespoons minced parsley
1/4 cup bread crumbs	

Preheat oven to 325 degrees. Drain artichokes, reserving liquid. Chop artichokes; sauté with onion and garlic in reserved liquid in skillet for 5 minutes. Combine with eggs, bread crumbs, salt, pepper, oregano, Tabasco sauce, cheese and parsley in bowl; mix well. Spoon into 8-by-12-inch baking dish. Bake for 30 minutes. Yield: 8 to 10 servings.

Mattie Vierra, Xi Upsilon Omicron
Altaville, California

BEAN CASSEROLE

1 10-ounce package frozen green beans	1/16 teaspoon Tabasco sauce
1 10-ounce package frozen green peas	1 tablespoon Worcestershire sauce
1 10-ounce package frozen lima beans	1 1/2 cups mayonnaise
Juice of 1 lemon	3 hard-cooked eggs, grated
1/16 teaspoon garlic powder	1 red onion, sliced in rings
1 teaspoon prepared mustard	

Cook frozen vegetables separately; drain. Combine lemon juice, garlic powder, mustard, Tabasco sauce, Worcestershire sauce and mayonnaise in small bowl; mix well. Stir in grated egg gently. Layer vegetables in 2-quart dish. Pour sauce over top; garnish with onion rings. Yield: 8 servings.

Evelyn Morehead, Preceptor Lambda
Oak Ridge, Tennessee

BAKED BEAN CASSEROLES

1 16-ounce can garbanzo beans, drained	2/3 cup hot catsup
1 16-ounce can kidney beans, drained	1/2 cup packed light brown sugar
1 16-ounce can lima beans, drained	1 medium onion, chopped
1 16-ounce can pork and beans	1 teaspoon vinegar
8 ounces Cheddar cheese, cubed	3 tablespoons Worcestershire sauce
	1 pound cooked ham, cubed
	Parmesan cheese

Preheat oven to 350 degrees. Combine beans, cheese, catsup, brown sugar, onion, vinegar, Worcestershire sauce and ham in large bowl; mix well. Spoon into two 2-quart baking dishes. Sprinkle with Parmesan cheese. Bake for 45 minutes. Yield: 16 servings.

Debbie Lee, Xi Theta
Nelson, British Columbia, Canada

Janet E. Dittman, Xi Mu Nu, Ocala, Florida, browns 1 pound ground beef with 1/2 cup chopped onion in skillet, drains, adds 1 can tomato paste, two 16-ounce cans pork and beans and serves hot over rice for Skillet Beans.

DAD'S HUNTIN' CAMP BEANS

My dad concocted this recipe about 20 years ago.

1 pound dried small red beans	1 10-ounce can cream of mushroom soup
1 pound sliced bacon	1 15-ounce can tomato sauce
1 pound lean ground round	1 14-ounce can stewed tomatoes
1 large onion, chopped	

Soak beans in water to cover in Dutch oven overnight; drain. Add enough water to cover plus 1 inch. Bring to a boil; reduce heat. Simmer, covered, for 15 to 20 minutes, stirring occasionally. Preheat oven to 325 degrees. Cut bacon slices into 4 pieces. Fry in skillet until almost done but not crisp; drain. Add to beans. Brown ground round and onion in skillet, stirring until ground round is crumbly; drain. Add mushroom soup and tomato sauce; mix well. Simmer for 20 to 30 minutes. Stir ground round mixture into beans; add stewed tomatoes. Bake, covered, for 4 to 5 hours. May also cook in slow cooker on Low for 7 to 8 hours. Yield: 10 servings.

Colleen Ann Smith, Laureate Psi
Challis, Idaho

GREEN BEAN BUNDLES

1 12-ounce package sliced bacon	1/4 cup melted butter or margarine
2 16-ounce cans whole green beans, drained	1/4 cup packed light brown sugar
	Garlic powder to taste

Preheat oven to 350 degrees. Cut bacon slices in half. Wrap each slice around 4 to 5 beans. Place bundles in 9-by-13-inch baking dish. Mix butter and brown sugar in bowl; pour over beans. Sprinkle with garlic powder. Bake for 30 to 40 minutes or until bacon is cooked through. Yield: 8 to 10 servings.

Janelle Persall, Beta Zeta Alpha
Canyon, Texas

GREEN BEAN CASSEROLE

1 medium onion, sliced	1/8 teaspoon Tabasco sauce
1 pound fresh mushrooms	1 teaspoon salt
1/2 cup butter or margarine	1/2 teaspoon pepper
1/4 cup all-purpose flour	1 5-ounce can sliced water chestnuts, drained
2 cups milk	2 12-ounce packages frozen green beans, cooked, drained
1 cup cream	
1 1/2 cups shredded Cheddar cheese	1/2 cup toasted almonds
2 teaspoons soy sauce	

Preheat oven to 350 degrees. Sauté onion and mushrooms in skillet in butter until tender. Add flour, stirring until blended with butter. Add milk and

cream. Simmer until thickened, stirring constantly. Add cheese, soy sauce, Tabasco sauce, salt, pepper, water chestnuts and beans; mix well. Spoon into greased 9-by-13-inch baking dish. Sprinkle with almonds. Bake for 35 to 45 minutes or until bubbly. Yield: 8 to 10 servings.

Shizuko Hironaka, Gamma Master
Lethbridge, Alberta, Canada

BROCCOLI-CHEESE SQUARES WITH HOLLANDAISE SAUCE

Great for breakfast or brunch.

1 tablespoon melted butter or margarine	10 eggs
8 ounces sharp Cheddar cheese, shredded	1 10-ounce package frozen chopped broccoli, thawed, drained
8 ounces Monterey Jack cheese, shredded	3 tablespoons melted butter or margarine
1/2 cup all-purpose flour	4 egg yolks
1 teaspoon baking powder	4 teaspoons lemon juice
1/2 teaspoon salt	2/3 cup melted butter or margarine
2 cups small curd cottage cheese	1 tablespoon hot water

Preheat oven to 350 degrees. Coat bottom and sides of 3-quart oblong baking dish with 1 tablespoon melted butter. Combine cheeses, flour, baking powder and salt in large bowl, tossing to coat; set aside. Mash cottage cheese with fork in small bowl; set aside. Beat eggs in large bowl with wire whisk. Stir in cheese mixture, cottage cheese, broccoli and 3 tablespoons butter, mixing well. Spoon into prepared dish. Bake for 40 to 45 minutes or until knife inserted near center comes out clean. Cool for 10 minutes; cut into squares. Process egg yolks and lemon juice in blender until smooth. Add 2/3 cup butter slowly while blender is running. Process until thickened; add water. Process until smooth. Spoon over broccoli-cheese squares. May make sauce up to 2 days in advance. Reheat in top of double boiler, stirring constantly. Yield: 12 servings.

Joanne Morgan, Alpha Alpha Beta
Houston Lake, Missouri

BROCCOLI-RICE CASSEROLE

1/2 cup chopped celery	1 8-ounce jar Cheez Whiz
1/2 cup chopped onion	1 1/2 cups rice, cooked
1 tablespoon butter or margarine	1 16-ounce package frozen broccoli, cooked
1 10-ounce can cream of mushroom soup	2 6-ounce cans chunked ham
1 10-ounce can cream of chicken soup	Shredded Cheddar cheese

Preheat oven to 350 degrees. Sauté celery and onion in butter in skillet until tender. Stir in soups and Cheez Whiz. Cook over low heat until cheese is melted, stirring frequently. Layer rice, broccoli, ham and soup mixture in 9-by-13-inch baking dish. Top with Cheddar cheese. Bake for 5 minutes or until heated through. Yield: 8 servings.

Amy Crowley, Beta Zeta Alpha
Canyon, Texas

BROCCOLI PUFF

2 10-ounce packages frozen chopped broccoli	1 cup mayonnaise
	1 cup shredded Cheddar cheese
2 eggs, beaten	1 cup butter cracker crumbs
1 10-ounce can cream of mushroom soup	

Preheat oven to 350 degrees. Cook broccoli using package directions; drain. Combine eggs, soup, mayonnaise and cheese in bowl; mix well. Stir in broccoli. Spoon into 8-by-10-inch baking dish; top with cracker crumbs. Bake for 30 minutes. Yield: 8 servings.

Juanita Corkwell, Laureate Chi
Ellenton, Florida

MARINATED BROCCOLI

1 teaspoon each onion salt, garlic salt and oregano	3 tablespoons distilled white vinegar
	2/3 cup vegetable oil
1/2 teaspoon each thyme, pepper and dry mustard	Flowerets of 1 bunch broccoli

Combine onion salt, garlic salt, oregano, thyme, pepper, mustard, vinegar and oil in small bowl; mix well. Place broccoli flowerets in large bowl. Pour marinade over, tossing to coat. Chill, covered, for 4 hours to overnight, stirring occasionally. Yield: 6 servings.

Gayle Carlson, Preceptor Omicron
Gaithersburg, Maryland

RIGATONI-BROCCOLI BAKE

A creamy, colorful dish.

1 8-ounce package rigatoni	1 teaspoon salt
	1/2 teaspoon garlic salt
2 quarts boiling water	1/8 teaspoon each nutmeg and thyme
1 tablespoon vegetable oil	
2 teaspoons salt	1 1/2 cups shredded Cheddar cheese
1/3 cup margarine	
1/3 cup all-purpose flour	1 1/2 pounds fresh broccoli flowerets, cooked
3 cups milk	
3/4 cup grated Parmesan cheese	3/4 cup shredded Swiss cheese

Preheat oven to 350 degrees. Cook rigatoni in boiling water, oil and 2 teaspoons salt in large saucepan for 12 to 15 minutes or until tender; drain and replace in saucepan. Melt margarine in saucepan. Blend in flour; add milk. Cook over low heat stirring until smooth and thickened. Add Parmesan cheese, 1 teaspoon salt, garlic salt, nutmeg, thyme and Cheddar cheese; mix well. Pour over cooked rigatoni. Stir in broccoli. Spoon into greased 9-by-13-inch baking dish; sprinkle with Swiss cheese. Bake for 20 minutes. Yield: 12 to 15 servings.

Darlene Radomske, Preceptor Gamma Theta
Richmond, British Columbia, Canada

SAUCY BRUSSELS SPROUTS

2 pints Brussels sprouts	1 tablespoon light brown sugar
1/2 cup chopped onion	
2 tablespoons butter or margarine	1/2 teaspoon dry mustard
	1/2 cup milk
1 tablespoon all-purpose flour	1 cup sour cream
1 teaspoon salt	

Cook Brussels sprouts in small amount of boiling water in medium saucepan until tender; drain. Sauté onion in butter in large saucepan until tender. Stir in flour, salt, brown sugar and mustard. Cook over low heat, stirring constantly. Add milk slowly, stirring until thickened. Stir in sour cream. Add Brussels sprouts. Cook over low heat until heated through. Yield: 6 to 8 servings.

Jeanne S. Gordon, Xi Zeta Omicron
Trenton, Ontario, Canada

CARROT CASSEROLE

5 to 6 cups chopped carrots	1/4 cup sugar
	Salt to taste
2 tablespoons chopped onion	2 tablespoons all-purpose flour
2 tablespoons chopped green bell pepper	1 cup milk
1 tablespoon vegetable oil	

Preheat oven to 350 degrees. Cook carrots in water in saucepan until tender; mash. Sauté onion and green pepper in oil in skillet until tender. Stir in sugar, salt and flour. Add milk. Cook over low heat until thickened, stirring constantly. Add carrots, mixing well. Pour into 3-quart baking dish. Bake for 30 minutes. Yield: 8 to 10 servings.

Ruth Fugitt, Laureate Iota
Oklahoma City, Oklahoma

Lynn Nicklow, Laureate Kappa, York, Pennsylvania, makes delicious Fried Cabbage by layering a head of finely cut cabbage alternately with 2 sliced onions in well buttered saucepan and steaming until tender. Season with butter, salt and pepper.

COPPER PENNY CARROTS

2 pounds carrots, sliced	1 cup sugar
1 green bell pepper, sliced	3/4 cup vinegar
1 medium onion, sliced	1 teaspoon prepared mustard
1 10-ounce can tomato soup	1 teaspoon Worcestershire sauce
1/2 cup vegetable oil	Salt and pepper to taste

Cook carrots in boiling salted water until tender-crisp; rinse in ice water. Layer carrots, green pepper and onion in large bowl. Combine soup, oil, sugar, vinegar, mustard, Worcestershire sauce, salt and pepper in small bowl; mix well. Pour over vegetable layer. Chill, covered, overnight, stirring occasionally. May store up to 1 week in refrigerator. Yield: 8 to 10 servings.

Carole B. Bolling, Xi Tau
Northport, Alabama

CARROT-PECAN CASSEROLE

3 pounds carrots, sliced	1 tablespoon vanilla extract
2/3 cup sugar	1 teaspoon grated orange rind
1/2 cup butter or margarine, softened	1/4 teaspoon ground nutmeg
1/2 cup chopped pecans, toasted	Carrot curls and fresh parsley sprigs
1/4 cup milk	
2 eggs, slightly beaten	
3 tablespoons all-purpose flour	

Preheat oven to 350 degrees. Cook carrots in boiling water in medium saucepan for 12 to 15 minutes or until tender; drain and mash. Stir in sugar, butter, pecans, milk, eggs, flour, vanilla, orange rind and nutmeg; mix well. Spoon into greased 2-quart baking dish. Bake for 40 minutes. Garnish with carrot curls and parsley. Yield: 10 to 12 servings.

Maudelle Swanzy, Laureate Epsilon Gamma
Center, Texas

CAULIFLOWER-GO-ROUND

Flowerets of 1 medium head cauliflower	1/3 cup mayonnaise
1 bunch broccoli, separated into stalks	1 tablespoon chopped onion
1 pound small carrots, peeled	1/4 teaspoon dry mustard
1/3 cup water	8 ounces Cheddar cheese, sliced

Parboil cauliflower, broccoli and carrots until tender-crisp in large saucepan; drain. Arrange cauliflower in middle of 12-inch round microwave-safe dish. Surround with broccoli, placing stalks under cauliflower. Place carrots around edge; sprinkle with water. Microwave on High until tender. Combine mayonnaise, onion and mustard in small bowl; mix well. Spread over vegetables. Arrange overlapping slices of cheese over vegetables. Microwave for 2 to 3 minutes or until cheese is melted. Let stand for 3 minutes before serving. Yield: 6 to 8 servings.

Nancy Huelsman, Xi Gamma Sigma
Toccoa, Georgia

FRENCH-FRIED CAULIFLOWER

This treasured recipe was handed down from my grandmother to my mother and then to me. We love it in our family.

1 head cauliflower	2 tablespoons chopped celery leaves
1 cup bread crumbs	1 teaspoon salt
1 tablespoon grated Parmesan cheese	Pepper to taste
1 clove of garlic, minced	2 eggs, beaten
2 tablespoons chopped parsley	Vegetable oil for frying

Cook cauliflower in boiling salted water until tender-crisp; drain and separate into flowerets. Combine bread crumbs, cheese, garlic, parsley, celery, salt and pepper in bowl; mix well. Dip cauliflowerets into eggs; coat with bread crumb mixture. Fry in hot oil in skillet until golden brown; drain. Yield: 6 servings.

Mary D. Behan, Xi Beta Xi
Ocala, Florida

CELERY ORIENTAL

2 cups diagonally sliced celery	1 10-ounce can cream of chicken soup
1 8-ounce can sliced water chestnuts, drained	1/2 cup herb-seasoned stuffing mix
1 cup chopped red bell pepper	1/2 cup slivered almonds
	2 tablespoons melted butter or margarine

Preheat oven to 350 degrees. Combine celery, water chestnuts, red pepper and soup in bowl; mix well. Spoon into greased 1 1/2-quart baking dish. Mix stuffing mix, almonds and melted butter in bowl. Sprinkle over celery mixture. Bake for 45 minutes. Yield: 6 to 8 servings.

Pidgin Trapp, Preceptor Omicron
Silver Spring, Maryland

CHILI-CORN CASSEROLE

My family often asks for this at our Sunday get-togethers. It's so-o-o easy!

1/2 cup margarine	1 7-ounce can Mexicorn, drained
8 ounces cream cheese, softened	1 4-ounce can chopped green chilies, drained
2 16-ounce cans whole kernel corn, drained	

Microwave margarine in 2-quart microwave-safe dish until melted. Add cream cheese, stirring until blended. Add corn and chilies, mixing well. Microwave, covered, on High for 5 minutes. Yield: 8 to 10 servings.

Cornelia Kridler, Preceptor Gamma Sigma
Gonzales, Texas

CORN CASSEROLE

1 17-ounce can cream-   1/2 cup melted margarine
   style corn   1 8-ounce package
1 12-ounce can niblet   corn bread mix
   corn   1 cup sour cream
2 eggs, beaten

Preheat oven to 350 degrees. Combine cream-style corn, whole kernel corn, eggs, melted margarine, corn bread mix and sour cream in large bowl; mix well. Spoon into 9-by-13-inch baking dish. Bake for 45 minutes. Yield: 12 servings.

Josephine Palumbo, Laureate Alpha Beta
Fort Myers, Florida

CREOLE CORN CASSEROLE

1 1/2 cups uncooked rice   2 eggs, beaten
1 large onion, chopped   1 2-ounce jar chopped
1 large green bell   pimento, drained
   pepper, chopped   Creole seasoning and
1/2 cup margarine   pepper to taste
2 17-ounce cans cream-   2 cups shredded
   style corn   Cheddar cheese

Preheat oven to 350 degrees. Cook rice using package directions. Combine rice, onion, green pepper, margarine, corn, eggs, pimento, Creole seasoning, pepper and 1 cup cheese in bowl; mix well. Spoon into 2-quart baking dish sprayed with nonstick cooking spray. Bake for 30 to 40 minutes or until bubbly. Sprinkle with remaining cheese. Bake until cheese is melted. Yield: 8 to 10 servings.

Cherry L. Ford, Preceptor Delta Zeta
Beaumont, Texas

EASY BAKED CORN

2 8-ounce packages   1 16-ounce can whole
   corn bread muffin   kernel corn, drained
   mix   4 eggs, beaten
1 17-ounce can cream-   1 cup melted margarine
   style corn   2 cups sour cream

Preheat oven to 325 degrees. Combine muffin mix, cream-style corn, whole kernel corn, eggs, melted margarine and sour cream in large bowl; mix well. Spoon into greased 9-by-13-inch baking dish. Bake for 1 hour or until knife inserted in center comes out clean. Yield: 12 servings.

Kay Hessong, Alpha Sigma Psi
Edna, Texas

SCALLOPED CORN

3 eggs, beaten   3 tablespoons light
1 16-ounce can whole   brown sugar
   kernel corn   1/3 teaspoon salt
1 17-ounce can cream-   1 cup milk
   style corn   3 tablespoons melted
1/4 cup all-purpose flour   butter or margarine

Preheat oven to 350 degrees. Combine all ingredients in large bowl; mix well. Spoon into greased 7-by-9-inch glass baking dish. Place dish in pan half-filled with water in oven. Bake for 1 1/2 hours. Yield: 10 servings.

Linda Hart, Preceptor Alpha Chi
Oneonta, New York

FABULOUS SHOE PEG CORN CASSEROLE

At least one person in my sorority brings this dish to all covered dish dinners!

8 ounces cream cheese,   3 16-ounce cans Shoe
   softened   Peg corn, drained
1/2 cup margarine   Salt and pepper to taste
1/2 cup milk   Shredded American
1 4-ounce can chopped   cheese
   green chilies

Preheat oven to 350 degrees. Heat cream cheese, margarine and milk over low heat in saucepan, stirring until blended. Add green chilies and liquid, corn, salt and pepper; mix well. Spoon into 9-by-12-inch baking dish. Top with cheese. Bake for 20 to 30 minutes or until heated through. Yield: 10 to 12 servings.

Audine Ekiss, Laureate Alpha
Guthrie, Oklahoma

CORN AND BEAN CASSEROLE

1 16-ounce can   1/2 cup chopped celery
   Shoe Peg corn,   1/2 cup chopped onion
   drained   1/4 cup chopped green
1 16-ounce can French-   bell pepper
   style green beans,   1 roll butter crackers,
   drained   crushed
1 10-ounce can cream   1/2 cup melted butter or
   of celery soup   margarine
1 cup sour cream
1/2 cup shredded sharp
   Cheddar cheese

Preheat oven to 350 degrees. Combine corn, beans, soup, sour cream, cheese, celery, onion and green pepper in bowl; mix well. Spoon into 2-quart baking dish. Toss cracker crumbs with butter in bowl; sprinkle over vegetable mixture. Bake for 45 minutes. Yield: 8 to 10 servings.

Linda D. Weingeroff, Xi Alpha Alpha
Jacksonville, Florida

CORN PUDDING CASSEROLE

1/2 cup vegetable oil	*1 8-ounce package corn*
1 cup sour cream	*muffin mix*
1 17-ounce can cream-	*2 eggs, beaten*
style corn	

Preheat oven to 350 degrees. Combine oil, sour cream, corn, corn muffin mix and eggs in bowl; mix well. Spoon into greased glass pie plate. Bake for 45 minutes or until knife inserted in center comes out clean. Yield: 8 to 10 servings.

Norma Jean Lesperance, Xi Lambda Delta
Penetang, Ontario, Canada

CORN AND RICE CASSEROLE

1 5-ounce package	*1 cup shredded Cheddar*
saffron rice, cooked	*cheese*
1 11-ounce can	*1/2 cup butter or*
Mexicorn, drained	*margarine*

Preheat oven to 350 degrees. Mix rice, Mexicorn, Cheddar cheese and butter in bowl. Spoon into 1-quart baking dish. Bake for 30 minutes. Yield: 6 servings.

Jackie Johnson, Alpha Zeta
Oviedo, Florida

❖ CREAM CHEESE AND MUSHROOM ENCHILADAS

1/2 cup chopped onion	*Ground red pepper to*
1 clove of garlic, minced	*taste*
1 tablespoon vegetable	*12 ounces fresh*
oil	*mushrooms, sliced*
1 28-ounce can Italian	*1 1/2 teaspoons chili*
seasoned tomatoes,	*powder*
cut up	*2 tablespoons margarine*
1 tablespoon honey	*8 ounces cream cheese*
1 tablespoon chili	*1 cup sour cream*
powder	*3/4 cup thinly sliced*
1/2 teaspoon ground	*green onions*
cumin	*8 7-inch flour tortillas*
1/2 teaspoon ground	*3/4 cup shredded*
coriander	*Monterey Jack cheese*

Preheat oven to 350 degrees. Sauté onion and garlic in oil in skillet until tender. Stir in undrained tomatoes, honey, 1 tablespoon chili powder, cumin, coriander and pepper. Bring to a boil; reduce heat. Simmer for 30 minutes or until thickened, stirring occasionally. Cook mushrooms with 1 1/2 teaspoons chili powder and margarine in saucepan over medium-high heat for 4 minutes or until liquid has evaporated; reduce heat. Add cream cheese, stirring until melted. Stir in sour cream and green onions. Spoon 1/3 cup cream cheese mixture into center of each tortilla; roll up. Place seam side down in 7-by-12-inch baking dish. Spoon tomato mixture over

tortillas. Sprinkle with Monterey Jack cheese. Bake, covered, for 30 minutes. Yield: 8 servings.

Linda L. Perkins, Preceptor Alpha Mu
Ephrata, Washington

FESTIVE MUSHROOMS

This dish is always a hit and a must-have at Christmas dinner.

2 pounds fresh	*2 tablespoons all-*
mushrooms, sliced	*purpose flour*
3 tablespoons butter or	*2 tablespoons butter or*
margarine	*margarine*
1 5-ounce jar sliced	*1/2 cup soft bread crumbs*
olives, drained	*1 tablespoon melted*
1 cup shredded Old	*butter or margarine*
Cheddar cheese	

Preheat oven to 350 degrees. Sauté mushrooms in 3 tablespoons butter in skillet until tender. Layer half the mushrooms, olives and cheese in 2-quart baking dish. Sprinkle with flour; dot with 2 tablespoons butter. Repeat layers. Toss bread crumbs with melted butter; sprinkle over top. Bake for 30 minutes. Yield: 8 to 10 servings.

Jane Langridge, Xi Alpha Psi
Airdrie, Alberta, Canada

STUFFED MUSHROOMS

1 pound fresh	*2 tablespoons butter or*
mushrooms	*margarine, softened*
2 cloves of garlic,	*12 ounces shredded*
minced	*Cheddar cheese*

Preheat oven to 350 degrees. Remove stems from mushrooms and chop finely. Place caps on baking sheet. Mix chopped mushroom stems, garlic and butter in small bowl to form thick paste. Fill caps with mixture; top with cheese. Bake for 20 minutes. Yield: 25 servings.

Rosie Sulak, Beta Zeta Beta
Carrollton, Texas

❖ ONION SHORTCAKE CASSEROLE

My best friend shared this recipe with me. It's different, wonderful and easy!

1 8-ounce package corn	*1 cup sour cream*
bread mix	*1 cup shredded Cheddar*
1/3 cup milk	*cheese*
1/4 cup melted butter or	*1/2 cup mayonnaise*
margarine	*1 teaspoon salt*
1 egg, beaten	*Cayenne pepper or*
2 large onions, sliced	*Tabasco sauce to taste*
1 17-ounce can cream-	
style corn	

Preheat oven to 350 degrees. Combine corn bread mix, milk, butter and egg in bowl; mix well. Spread evenly in 9-by-13-inch baking dish. Sauté onions in nonstick skillet until tender. Arrange over corn bread mixture. Combine corn, sour cream, 3/4 cup Cheddar cheese, mayonnaise, salt and cayenne pepper in bowl; mix well. Spoon over onion layer. Top with remaining 1/4 cup cheese. Bake for 30 minutes. Yield: 8 to 12 servings.

Diane Jones, Theta Rho
Seminole, Florida

BAKED POTATO SALAD

10 medium potatoes,
  cooked, peeled, cubed
1/4 cup chopped onion
12 to 16 ounces Velveeta
  cheese, cubed

1 to 1 1/2 cups
  mayonnaise
8 slices bacon, crisp-
  fried, crumbled

Preheat oven to 350 degrees. Combine potatoes, onion, Velveeta cheese and mayonnaise in bowl; mix well. Spoon into 9-by-13-inch baking dish. Top with crumbed bacon. Bake for 45 minutes. May substitute unpeeled new red potatoes for potatoes. Yield: 10 to 12 servings.

Carol Sue Brewer, Preceptor Alpha Rho
Charleston, West Virginia

CRAB-STUFFED POTATOES

This recipe was given to me by a good friend who lives in Louisiana. I always think of her when I prepare this.

3 large potatoes, baked
1/2 cup shredded sharp
  Cheddar cheese
1/4 cup half and half
1 6-ounce can crab
  meat, drained, flaked
2 tablespoons grated
  onion

1/4 cup butter or
  margarine, softened
Salt, pepper and
  paprika to taste
Green onion tops, finely
  chopped

Preheat oven to 350 degrees. Slice baked potatoes into halves. Scoop out centers, leaving shells intact; place shells on baking sheet. Combine potatoes, cheese, half and half, crab meat, onion and butter in bowl; mix well. Season with salt and pepper. Spoon mixture into shells. Sprinkle with paprika and green onions. Bake for 30 minutes. Yield: 6 servings.

Anne Hough, Laureate Omicron
Mount Pleasant, North Carolina

CREAMY POTATOES ROMANOFF

4 to 5 large potatoes,
  boiled
1 cup sour cream
1 medium onion, chopped

1 teaspoon salt
8 ounces Velveeta
  cheese, shredded

Preheat oven to 350 degrees. Peel and grate potatoes. Mix with sour cream, onion, salt and Velveeta

cheese, reserving 1/2 cup cheese. Spoon into 2-quart baking dish. Top with reserved cheese. Bake, covered, for 30 minutes. May substitute low-fat sour cream and cheese. May prepare ahead and store in refrigerator before baking. Yield: 8 servings.

Dinah Mashburn, Theta Rho
Franklin, North Carolina

POTATOES ROMANOFF

6 to 8 large potatoes,
  boiled
2 cups sour cream
1 bunch green onions,
  chopped

1 2/3 cups shredded Old
  Cheddar cheese
Salt and pepper to taste

Peel and mash potatoes in large bowl. Add sour cream, green onions, cheese, salt and pepper, mixing well. Spoon into greased 2 1/2-quart baking dish. Chill, covered, for 2 hours to overnight. Preheat oven to 350 degrees. Bake for 30 to 40 minutes or until heated through. Yield: 8 to 10 servings.

Patricia Reid, Preceptor Delta Rho
Orangeville, Ontario, Canada

POTATO AND SAUSAGE CASSEROLE

4 large potatoes, peeled,
  sliced 1/2 inch thick
1 pound smoked
  sausage, cut into
  bite-sized pieces
1 envelope ranch salad
  dressing mix

1 10-ounce can cream
  of mushroom soup
1/2 soup can water
1 8-ounce jar Cheez
  Whiz

Preheat oven to 350 degrees. Boil potatoes until tender in water in saucepan; drain. Layer potato slices and sausage in 4-by-7-inch glass baking dish. Combine salad dressing mix, soup, water and Cheez Whiz in bowl; mix well. Spoon over potato mixture. Bake for 30 minutes or until cheese is melted. Yield: 6 to 8 servings.

Estelline Mikeworth, Laureate Gamma Upsilon
Bellevue, Texas

POTATO WEDGES

2 cups crushed
  cornflakes
1/2 teaspoon seasoned
  salt

1/8 teaspoon each onion
  salt and garlic salt
4 to 6 medium potatoes
Vegetable oil

Preheat oven to 400 degrees. Combine cornflakes, seasoned salt, onion salt and garlic salt in small bowl; mix well and set aside. Cut each unpeeled potato into 8 wedges. Dip in vegetable oil; roll in cornflake mixture. Place on greased baking sheet. Bake for 30 minutes or until tender. Yield: 6 to 8 servings.

Audrey Schumacher, Beta Delta
Havre, Montana

COMPANY HASHED BROWN POTATOES

1/4 to 1/2 cup chopped onion	1 10-ounce can cream of chicken soup
1/2 cup margarine	1 2-pound package frozen hashed brown potatoes, thawed
1 to 2 cups sour cream	
2 cups shredded Cheddar cheese	Salt and pepper to taste

Sauté onion in margarine in skillet until tender. Combine with sour cream, 1 cup cheese, soup, potatoes, salt and pepper in large bowl; mix well. Spoon into greased 9-by-13-inch baking dish. Bake for 30 minutes. Top with remaining 1 cup cheese. Bake for 30 minutes longer. May substitute cream of celery soup or cream of mushroom soup for cream of chicken soup. May add all of cheese to potato mixture and top with cornflake crumbs dotted with butter or crushed potato chips. Yield: 10 to 12 servings.

Evelyn H. Finnegan, Laureate Theta
Aiken, South Carolina
*Brenda Moody, Preceptor Tau
Bowling Green, Kentucky
*Burdene Olson, Zeta Master
Colorado Springs, Colorado

CHEESY HASHED BROWN POTATOES FOR-A-CROWD

1 2-pound package frozen hashed brown potatoes, thawed	6 ounces cream cheese, softened
1 cup butter or margarine, softened	2 cups cubed Velveeta cheese
1 10-ounce can cream of mushroom soup	4 to 5 cups rice cereal or cornflakes, crushed
2 tablespoons minced onion flakes	1/2 cup melted margarine

Preheat oven to 350 degrees. Spread hashed brown potatoes in greased 9-by-13-inch baking dish. Combine butter, soup, onion flakes, cream cheese and Velveeta cheese in saucepan; mix well. Cook over low heat until cheese is melted, stirring constantly. Pour over hashed brown potatoes. Top with mixture of cereal and melted margarine. Bake for 1 hour. Yield: 10 to 12 servings.

Lea J. Moran, Preceptor Mu
Mitchell, South Dakota

FLUFFY POTATO CASSEROLE

4 cups mashed potatoes	2 eggs, beaten
8 ounces cream cheese, softened	3 tablespoons all-purpose flour
1 tablespoon minced onion flakes	1 3-ounce can French-fried onions

Preheat oven to 300 degrees. Beat mashed potatoes, cream cheese, onion, eggs and flour in mixer bowl at high speed for 3 to 5 minutes or until light and fluffy. Spoon into greased 7-by-11-inch baking dish. Bake

for 45 minutes. Sprinkle French-fried onions over top. Bake for 15 to 20 minutes longer or until browned. Yield: 12 to 15 servings.

Margaret Marks, Preceptor Kappa Upsilon
Yucca Valley, California

INSTANT POTATO KNISHES

Instant mashed potatoes	Salt and pepper to taste
1 3-ounce can French-fried onions	1 10-count can refrigerator biscuits

Preheat oven to 325 degrees. Prepare instant mashed potatoes for 1 serving using package directions, omitting 1/2 cup milk. Combine next 3 ingredients in small bowl; mix well. Divide biscuits into halves; roll out. Spoon 1/2 teaspoon potato mixture into center of each biscuit. Fold up to enclose filling, sealing edges. Place on ungreased baking sheet. Bake for 8 to 10 minutes or until lightly browned. Yield: 20 servings.

Toby R. Heller, Preceptor Iota
Albuquerque, New Mexico

MAKE-AHEAD MASHED POTATOES

Mom makes this recipe for holiday dinners because it's so convenient. It's a cross between twice-baked potatoes and mashed potatoes, but we think it's the best of both.

8 large potatoes	1/2 cup sour cream
1 medium onion, chopped	1 egg, beaten
1/2 cup margarine	Salt and pepper to taste
8 ounces cream cheese, softened	2 to 4 tablespoons butter or margarine
	Paprika to taste

Preheat oven to 350 degrees. Peel and cut potatoes into thick slices. Place in large saucepan with onion and enough water to cover. Bring to a boil; reduce heat. Simmer for 20 minutes or until tender; drain. Combine with margarine, cream cheese, sour cream, egg, salt and pepper in mixer bowl. Beat at high speed until smooth. Spoon into greased 2-quart baking dish. Dot with butter; sprinkle with paprika. Bake for 30 to 35 minutes or until heated through. May make up to 2 to 3 days ahead of time and refrigerate until ready to bake. Yield: 8 to 10 servings.

Michelle L. Cotton, Xi Gamma Tau
McPherson, Kansas

BROCCOLI AND TATER TOT CASSEROLE

1 10-ounce can cream of mushroom soup	1/4 teaspoon pepper
1/2 cup cottage cheese	2 cups chopped broccoli
1/3 cup sour cream	4 cups Tater Tots
1 cup shredded Cheddar cheese	1 1/2 cups cubed ham

Preheat oven to 350 degrees. Combine soup, cottage cheese, sour cream, Cheddar cheese and pepper in bowl; mix well. Fold in broccoli and Tater Tots. Spoon into greased 9-by-13-inch baking dish. Top with cubed ham. Bake for 45 to 50 minutes or until browned. Let stand for 5 to 10 minutes before serving. Yield: 8 to 10 servings.

Sandy McCune, Xi Zeta Rho
Wichita, Kansas

FESTIVE TATER TOT CASSEROLE

1 2-pound package frozen Tater Tots, thawed	1 10-ounce can cream of mushroom soup
1 pound ground beef	1/2 cup chopped green bell pepper
1 10-ounce can cream of chicken soup	1/2 cup chopped onion
	Shredded Cheddar cheese

Preheat oven to 350 degrees. Mash Tater Tots in bowl with fork. Brown ground beef in skillet, stirring until crumbly; drain. Combine with Tater Tots and soups, mixing well. Spread into 9-by-13-inch casserole. Top with green pepper, onion and cheese. Bake for 50 minutes. Yield: 8 servings.

April A. Wood, Alpha Beta Rho
Windsor, Missouri

TATER TOT CASSEROLE

1 2-pound package frozen Tater Tots	1 soup can milk
1 pound ground beef	Shredded Cheddar cheese
2 10-ounce cans cream of chicken soup	

Preheat oven to 350 degrees. Place Tater Tots in single layer in 9-by-13-inch casserole. Brown ground beef in skillet, stirring until crumbly; drain. Spoon over Tater Tots. Mix soup and milk in bowl; pour over top. Sprinkle with cheese. Bake, covered with foil, for 1 hour. Remove foil. Bake for 30 minutes longer or until bubbly and browned. Yield: 8 servings.

Michelle Miller, Xi Gamma Xi
Oroville, California

SPINACH MADELINE

2 10-ounce packages frozen chopped spinach	1/2 cup milk
1 cup chopped onion	6 ounces jalapeño cheese
1/4 cup butter or margarine	1/2 teaspoon pepper
1 tablespoon all-purpose flour	3/4 teaspoon each celery salt and garlic salt
	1 teaspoon Worcestershire sauce

Cook spinach using package directions; drain. Sauté onion in butter in skillet until tender. Add flour, stirring until blended. Add remaining ingredients. Cook over low heat, stirring until cheese is melted. Add spinach, stirring well. Spoon into serving dish. Serve immediately. May place in baking dish, topped

with bread crumbs, and bake at 350 degrees for 5 to 10 minutes. Yield: 8 servings.

Jewell Wainwright, Xi Alpha Gamma Gamma
Huntsville, Texas

SPINACH QUICHES

1 recipe 2-crust pie pastry	2 tablespoons milk
1 10-ounce package frozen spinach soufflé, thawed	2 or 3 eggs, beaten
	3/4 cup cooked sausage
	3/4 cup shredded Swiss or mozzarella cheese
2 tablespoons chopped onion	4 ounces fresh or canned mushrooms, sliced

Preheat oven to 400 degrees. Line two 9-inch pie plates with pie pastry. Combine remaining ingredients in bowl; mix well. Spoon into pie shells. Bake for 25 to 30 minutes or until knife inserted near center comes out clean. Let stand for 5 minutes before cutting into serving portions. Yield: 10 to 12 servings.

Pauline P. LeDuc, Preceptor Eta
Lebanon, New Hampshire

SPINACH SIDE DISH

My sons are very picky eaters but they love this because the spinach is disguised by the cheese.

2 eggs, beaten	16 ounces cottage cheese
2 tablespoons all-purpose flour	1 10-ounce package frozen chopped spinach, thawed
2 cups shredded Cheddar cheese	

Preheat oven to 350 degrees. Combine first 4 ingredients in bowl; mix well. Fold in spinach. Spoon into 1 1/2-quart baking dish. Bake for 35 to 40 minutes or until golden and puffed. Yield: 6 to 8 servings.

Christine Stutzman, Theta Theta
Goshen, Indiana

SQUASH CASSEROLE

I created this recipe to encourage my husband to eat squash!

1 pound yellow squash	4 ounces Cheddar cheese, shredded
1 onion, chopped	
1 teaspoon lemon pepper	1/2 cup seasoned bread crumbs
1 pound bulk sausage	

Preheat oven to 350 degrees. Steam squash and onion in steamer for 15 minutes. Drain and sprinkle with lemon pepper. Brown sausage in skillet, stirring until crumbly; drain. Combine squash, onion, sausage and cheese in bowl; mix well. Spoon into 2-quart baking dish. Bake for 15 minutes. Sprinkle with bread crumbs. Bake for 15 minutes longer. May also microwave on High for 10 minutes. Yield: 8 servings.

Madeline Watson, Xi Alpha Beta Omega
Jasper, Texas

CREAMY SQUASH CASSEROLE

Christmas in Alabama with my in-laws is always a feasting delight as we eat vegetables harvested from their garden. This is a simple way to prepare garden-fresh squash.

1¹/2 pounds yellow squash, sliced	2 medium onions, chopped
1 10-ounce can cream of chicken soup	6 tablespoons melted margarine
1 cup sour cream	¹/2 8-ounce package herb-seasoned stuffing mix
1 4-ounce can pimentos, drained, sliced	2 tablespoons margarine

Preheat oven to 350 degrees. Cook squash in water in saucepan until tender; drain. Combine with soup, sour cream, pimentos and onions in bowl; mix well. Toss melted margarine and stuffing mix together. Add to squash mixture, reserving ¹/2 cup. Spoon into 2-quart baking dish. Top with reserved stuffing mixture; dot with margarine. Bake for 30 minutes. Yield: 8 servings.

Linda Abbott, Preceptor Alpha Chi
Friendswood, Texas

SWEET POTATO PUDDING

3 16-ounce cans mashed sweet potatoes	1 tablespoon cinnamon
	¹/2 teaspoon vanilla extract
1 cup packed dark brown sugar	2 eggs, beaten
2 tablespoons butter or margarine	¹/2 cup coconut
	¹/2 cup chopped walnuts
¹/2 teaspoon salt	8 ounces marshmallows, cut into halves
1 tablespoon nutmeg	

Preheat oven to 325 degrees. Combine sweet potatoes, brown sugar, butter, salt, nutmeg, cinnamon, vanilla, eggs, coconut, walnuts and marshmallows in bowl; mix well, adding water for desired consistency. Spoon into 2-quart baking dish. Bake for 25 minutes. Yield: 10 servings.

Marilyn Alvaro, Laureate Xi
Fairmont, West Virginia

LAURA'S SWEET POTATO CASSEROLE

This was a favorite of my mother and we always serve it for family Christmas dinners.

6 medium sweet potatoes	1 teaspoon grated orange rind
1¹/4 cups packed light brown sugar	1 cup apricot juice
1¹/2 tablespoons cornstarch	1 cup drained apricots
	2 tablespoons butter or margarine
¹/8 teaspoon cinnamon	¹/2 cup pecans

Preheat oven to 375 degrees. Boil or bake sweet potatoes in their skins. Cool, peel and slice. Arrange in buttered 9-by-13-inch baking dish. Combine brown sugar, cornstarch, cinnamon, orange rind and apricot juice in saucepan. Cook over low heat until thickened, stirring frequently. Add apricots, butter and pecans. Pour mixture over sweet potatoes. Bake for 25 minutes. Yield: 8 to 10 servings.

Jo Ann Spinks, Laureate Gamma
Columbus, Mississippi

MUSHROOM-STUFFED TOMATOES

6 large tomatoes	2 cups soft bread crumbs
Salt to taste	¹/2 teaspoon salt
8 slices bacon	¹/8 teaspoon pepper
³/4 cup coarsely chopped mushrooms	¹/2 teaspoon sugar
¹/4 cup chopped onion	¹/2 teaspoon MSG

Preheat oven to 375 degrees. Cut tops from tomatoes. Scoop out centers leaving thick shells. Drain and reserve pulp. Sprinkle shells with salt; invert on paper towels to drain. Fry bacon in skillet until crisp; drain and crumble. Sauté mushrooms and onion in pan drippings for 3 minutes. Combine with reserved tomato pulp, crumbled bacon, bread crumbs, salt, pepper, sugar and MSG in bowl; mix well. Spoon into tomato shells; place in shallow baking pan. Bake for 20 minutes. Yield: 6 servings.

Evelyn Bemis, Laureate Alpha Eta
Belleville, Ontario, Canada

ITALIAN ZUCCHINI

8 to 10 small zucchini, sliced ¹/8 inch thick	²/3 cup grated Parmesan cheese
²/3 cup chopped onion	1¹/2 cups tomato paste
4 ounces sliced mushrooms	1 teaspoon salt
	¹/2 teaspoon garlic salt
3 tablespoons olive oil	¹/8 teaspoon pepper

Preheat oven to 350 degrees. Cook zucchini, onion and mushrooms in olive oil in covered saucepan over low heat for 10 to 15 minutes, stirring occasionally; remove from heat. Add half the cheese, tomato paste, salt, garlic salt and pepper, mixing gently. Spoon into 2-quart baking dish. Sprinkle with remaining cheese. Bake for 20 to 30 minutes or until browned. May also add 1 pound cooked ground beef for complete meal. Yield: 8 to 10 servings.

Willmetta Felton, Beta Pi
Lakeview, Oregon

Carol N. Buckner, Pi Zeta, Inverness, Florida, makes Zucchini Squares by baking mixture of 3 cups sliced zucchini, 1 cup baking mix, ¹/2 cup each onions, Parmesan cheese and oil, 4 eggs, oregano, salt, parsley and pepper in 9-by-13-inch pan in preheated 350-degree oven for 30 to 35 minutes. Serve hot or cold.

ZUCCHINI CASSEROLE

This dish is an all-around family favorite.

1 pound zucchini, chopped	1/8 cup water
1 onion, chopped	1/2 cup Cheez Whiz
1/4 cup butter or margarine	1 10-ounce can cream of chicken soup
Salt and pepper to taste	1/4 cup milk
	1 cup quick-cooking rice

Preheat oven to 350 degrees. Sauté zucchini and onion in butter in skillet until tender. Season with salt and pepper. Add water, Cheez Whiz, soup, milk and rice, mixing gently. Spoon into 9-by-12-inch baking dish. Bake for 40 to 45 minutes or until bubbly. Yield: 8 servings.

Kyle Elaine Harris, Xi Zeta Omicron
Columbia, Missouri

ZUCCHINI-NOODLE BAKE

2 medium zucchini, diagonally sliced	2 medium green bell peppers, sliced
3 cups cooked elbow macaroni	8 ounces Velveeta cheese, sliced
1 large sweet onion, thinly sliced	Salt and pepper to taste
3 to 4 ripe tomatoes, peeled, sliced	

Preheat oven to 375 degrees. Spray 2-quart baking dish with nonstick cooking spray. Line bottom and sides of dish with zucchini. Layer macaroni, onion, tomatoes, green peppers and Velveeta cheese 1/2 at a time in prepared dish, seasoning layers with salt and pepper. Cover tightly with foil. Bake for 1 hour and 10 minutes or until onion is tender. Yield: 6 servings.

Yolanda Flory, Preceptor Epsilon
Swartz Creek, Michigan

SPICY ZUCCHINI-POTATO CASSEROLE

My parents retired to a small farm and grew so many zucchini that they didn't know what to do with them. My mother developed this recipe.

8 to 10 medium potatoes, peeled, thinly sliced	3 cups spicy tomato sauce
1 cup finely chopped onion	1 cup grated Parmesan or Romano cheese
4 medium zucchini, peeled, sliced	1 bay leaf

Preheat oven to 350 degrees. Layer potatoes, onion, zucchini, tomato sauce and cheese, 1/4 at a time, in greased 2-quart baking dish, placing bay leaf in center of top layer. Bake for 40 minutes. Remove bay leaf before serving. Yield: 4 to 6 servings.

Hollis Wheaton, Xi Delta Iota
Cranbrook, British Columbia, Canada

STUFFED ZUCCHINI

I use this recipe for the zucchini that hide in the garden and become extra large!

1 extra large zucchini	2 tablespoons vegetable oil
2 slices fresh bread, crumbled	1 tablespoon chopped parsley
1 pound ground beef	1/2 teaspoon oregano
1 clove of garlic, chopped	Salt and pepper to taste
1/2 large green bell pepper, chopped	4 8-ounce cans tomato sauce
1 medium onion, chopped	Grated Parmesan cheese

Preheat oven to 350 degrees. Cut zucchini into 4-inch long quarters. Scoop out pulp and chop; set shells aside. Mix bread crumbs with zucchini pulp in small bowl and set aside. Brown ground beef, garlic, green pepper and onion in oil in skillet, stirring until ground beef is crumbly; drain. Stir in zucchini mixture, parsley, oregano, salt, pepper and 2 cans tomato sauce; mix well. Stuff zucchini shells with mixture. Place in 9-by-12-inch baking dish. Pour remaining tomato sauce over top; sprinkle with cheese. Bake for 1 hour. Yield: 9 servings.

Opal Baert, Laureate Eta
Klamath Falls, Oregon

ZUCCHINI LASAGNA

8 ounces sweet Italian sausage, sliced	16 ounces low-fat cottage cheese
1 large onion, chopped	2 eggs, beaten
1 28-ounce can tomato purée	1/2 cup grated Parmesan cheese
8 ounces mushrooms, sliced	6 large zucchini, thinly sliced
1 teaspoon salt	1 1/2 cups shredded low-fat mozzarella cheese
1 teaspoon leaf oregano, crushed	
1 teaspoon mixed Italian herbs, crumbled	

Preheat oven to 350 degrees. Brown sausage in large skillet. Push to one side; drain, reserving 1 tablespoon pan drippings. Sauté onion in reserved pan drippings until tender. Add tomato purée, mushrooms, salt, oregano and herbs; mix well. Simmer, covered, for 15 minutes. Mix cottage cheese, eggs and Parmesan cheese in small bowl. Layer 1/2 of the sausage mixture, half the remaining zucchini, all the cottage cheese mixture, 1/3 of the zucchini, remaining sausage mixture and remaining zucchini in 9-by-13-inch baking pan. Bake, covered with foil, for 45 minutes. Sprinkle with mozzarella cheese. Bake, uncovered, for 15 minutes longer. Yield: 8 servings.

Cris Bourbois, Preceptor Alpha Phi
Altus, Oklahoma

CHILI VERDE

2 pounds green chilies, chopped	1 tablespoon cumin
8 cups water	1 tablespoon coriander
1 16-ounce can stewed tomatoes	1 tablespoon white pepper
2 tablespoons beef bouillon granules	8 ounces ground pork
1 tablespoon oregano	1/2 onion, chopped
	3/4 cup margarine
	1/2 cup all-purpose flour

Combine chilies, water, tomatoes, beef bouillon granules, oregano, cumin, coriander and pepper in large kettle. Simmer, stirring occasionally, until chilies are tender. Brown ground pork and onion in 1 tablespoon margarine in skillet, stirring until ground pork is crumbly; drain. Add to chili mixture. Simmer for 30 minutes. Melt remaining margarine over low heat in skillet. Add flour, stirring to form roux. Add slowly to chili mixture. Simmer, stirring until thickened. May serve as chili before adding roux or as sauce for enchiladas after adding roux. Yield: 12 servings.

Barbara Pash, Alpha Nu
Farmington, New Mexico

VEGETABLE PIZZA

A great make-ahead supper or snack.

2 cups biscuit mix	1 teaspoon prepared horseradish
1/2 cup water	Tabasco sauce to taste
8 ounces cream cheese, softened	Chopped carrots, broccoli, cauliflower, mushrooms and tomatoes
1/2 cup mayonnaise-type salad dressing	
1 6-ounce can water-pack tuna, drained	
1/2 cup sliced green onions	

Preheat oven to 450 degrees. Combine biscuit mix and water in bowl, stirring to form dough. Press out on ungreased pizza pan. Bake for 8 minutes; let cool. Combine cream cheese, salad dressing, tuna, green onions, horseradish and Tabasco sauce in bowl; mix well. Spread over cooled crust. Top with variety of chopped vegetables. Yield: 6 to 8 servings.

Gloria Brown, Preceptor Lambda
Dartmouth, Nova Scotia, Canada

Cathy Stevenson, Zeta Eta, Derby, Kansas, makes Beans and Corn Bread with a package of 13-bean soup mix soaked overnight as directed, drained and combined with 1 chopped onion, 1 can tomato soup, 1/2 soup can water, 1 small can tomatoes, 3 tablespoons Worcestershire sauce and 1 cup chopped ham in slow cooker. Cook all day and serve over favorite corn bread.

VEGETARIAN LASAGNA

2 tablespoons vegetable oil	1/2 cup water
2 tablespoons olive oil	1 8-ounce package lasagna noodles
2 large onions, chopped	2 pounds fresh spinach, rinsed, drained
3 cloves of garlic, minced	3 cups cream-style cottage cheese
Minced parsley to taste	12 ounces Monterey Jack cheese, sliced
4 4-ounce cans sliced mushrooms, drained	16 ounces mozzarella cheese, sliced
1/2 cup black olives	2 ounces Parmesan cheese, grated
2 cups grated carrots	
3 to 4 15-ounce cans tomato sauce	
Sweet basil, salt, black pepper and red pepper to taste	

Preheat oven to 350 degrees. Heat vegetable oil and olive oil over medium heat in large saucepan. Sauté onions, garlic and parsley until tender. Add mushrooms, olives and carrots. Sauté until tender. Add next 5 ingredients. Simmer for 30 minutes. Cook lasagna noodles in boiling water for 10 minutes; drain. Spoon a small amount of sauce in 9-by-13-inch baking pan. Layer noodles, remaining sauce, spinach, cottage cheese, Monterey Jack cheese, mozzarella cheese and Parmesan cheese alternately in prepared dish until all ingredients are used, ending with sauce. Bake for 1 hour. Yield: 6 servings.

Lilia Hansen, Xi Gamma
Minot, North Dakota

VEGETABLES AND PASTA

1 medium yellow squash	1/4 teaspoon salt
1 medium zucchini	1/4 teaspoon dried basil, crushed
2 tablespoons olive oil	1/4 teaspoon dried tarragon, crushed
1 medium red bell pepper, cut into thin strips	1/4 teaspoon crushed red pepper
1 1/2 cups sliced fresh mushrooms	6 ounces uncooked linguini or fusilli
2 to 3 cloves of garlic, minced	1/4 cup grated Parmesan cheese
1/4 cup dry white wine	

Cut squash and zucchini into 1/4-inch thick slices; cut slices into strips. Heat oil over high heat in wok or large skillet. Add squash, zucchini, bell pepper, mushrooms and garlic. Stir-fry for 2 to 3 minutes or until vegetables are tender-crisp. Combine wine, salt, basil, tarragon and red pepper in small bowl; mix well. Drizzle over vegetables, tossing to coat. Cook linguini using package directions; drain. Toss with vegetables; place on serving platter. Sprinkle with Parmesan cheese. Yield: 6 to 8 servings.

Pat DeVries, Xi Zeta
Rock Rapids, Iowa

MIXED VEGETABLE CASSEROLE

1 10-ounce package frozen mixed vegetables	2 10-ounce cans cream of mushroom soup
1 10-ounce package frozen peas	8 ounces Velveeta cheese, cubed
1 10-ounce package frozen French-style green beans	4 slices bread, cubed
	1/2 cup melted butter or margarine

Preheat oven to 350 degrees. Cook mixed vegetables, peas and green beans using package directions; drain slightly. Place in buttered 2-quart baking dish. Spread soup over vegetables. Top with Velveeta cheese cubes and bread; drizzle with butter. Bake for 40 minutes. Yield: 6 to 8 servings.

Sherry Vogt, Xi Lambda Tau
Urich, Missouri

CHEESY VEGETABLE CASSEROLE

1 16-ounce package frozen mixed vegetables	1 cup cubed sharp Cheddar cheese
1 8-ounce can sliced water chestnuts, sliced	3/4 cup mayonnaise
	1/4 cup sour cream
1 cup finely chopped onion	1 roll butter crackers, crushed
	1/2 cup melted margarine

Preheat oven to 350 degrees. Cook vegetables using package directions; drain. Combine with water chestnuts, onion, cheese, mayonnaise and sour cream, mixing well. Spoon into 3-quart baking dish. Sprinkle with cracker crumbs; drizzle with margarine. Bake for 30 minutes. Yield: 8 servings.

Rebecca J. Meek, Laureate Theta
Aiken, South Carolina

ESTHER'S CHILI RELLENO SOUFFLÉ

This is one of my favorite things to take to potluck suppers—never any leftovers!

4 eggs	10 to 12 long green chili peppers, roasted, peeled and seeded
1 1/2 cups milk	
2 cups biscuit mix	
1/2 cup chopped onion	Milk
1 teaspoon crushed garlic	8 ounces Provolone cheese, sliced
1/2 cup chopped parsley	8 ounces mozzarella cheese, shredded
1/2 teaspoon salt	8 ounces ricotta cheese
1/4 teaspoon pepper	2 cups mild salsa

Preheat oven to 375 degrees. Combine eggs, milk, biscuit mix, onion, garlic, parsley, salt, pepper and 1 chili pepper in blender container. Process on high until blended. Add enough milk to make 2 quarts of sauce. Pour enough sauce to cover bottom of greased 9-by-13-inch baking dish. Layer remaining chilies, Provolone cheese, mozzarella cheese and ricotta cheese in prepared dish until all ingredients have been used, ending with sauce. Bake for 1 1/2 hours or until browned and knife inserted in center comes out clean. Cover with salsa. Bake for 5 minutes longer. Cut into squares to serve. Yield: 12 servings.

Esther L. Wyatt, Laureate Mu
Sierra Vista, Arizona

CHEESE GRITS

6 cups water	Tabasco sauce to taste
2 teaspoons salt	Paprika to taste
1 1/2 cups hominy grits	1/2 cup margarine, cut into pieces
16 ounces longhorn cheese, shredded	3 eggs, beaten
3 teaspoons seasoned salt	

Preheat oven to 250 degrees. Bring water and 2 teaspoons salt to boil in large saucepan. Add grits slowly. Cook over low heat for 10 minutes, stirring frequently; remove from heat. Add cheese, seasoned salt, Tabasco sauce, paprika, margarine and eggs, beating well. Pour into greased 9-by-13-inch baking dish. Bake for 1 to 1 1/2 hours or until set. Yield: 12 to 15 servings.

Mary Ann Wheat, Preceptor Nu
Higgins, Texas

SCALLOPED HOMINY

1/4 cup chopped green bell pepper	2 1/2 cups canned hominy, drained
1/4 cup chopped onion	1 cup soft bread crumbs
1/4 cup butter or margarine	1 cup shredded Swiss cheese
1/4 cup all-purpose flour	1 cup shredded Cheddar cheese
2 cups milk	
3/4 teaspoon salt	Paprika and melted butter or margarine to taste
1/4 teaspoon white pepper	
1 teaspoon sugar	

Preheat oven to 375 degrees. Sauté bell pepper and onion in butter in saucepan until tender. Stir in flour to make a roux. Cook for 1 minute, stirring frequently. Add milk, salt, pepper and sugar. Simmer for 5 minutes, stirring occasionally. Stir in hominy; remove from heat. Pour half the hominy mixture into shallow 2-quart baking dish. Layer bread crumbs, remaining hominy, Swiss cheese and Cheddar cheese 1/2 at a time until all ingredients are used. Sprinkle with paprika; dot with butter. Bake for 20 to 25 minutes or until browned. Yield: 8 servings.

Ruth Bearden, Preceptor Beta Gamma
Jacksonville, Texas

CHILI HOT HOMINY

1 16-ounce can white hominy, drained	1 cup sour cream
1 16-ounce can yellow hominy, drained	1/4 teaspoon cumin
	1/2 teaspoon salt
1 4-ounce can chopped green chilies, drained	20 black olives, chopped
	1 cup shredded Monterey Jack cheese

Preheat oven to 350 degrees. Combine hominy, chilies, sour cream, cumin, salt and olives in bowl; mix well. Spoon into 2-quart baking dish. Top with cheese. Bake, covered, for 30 minutes. Let stand for 5 minutes before serving. Yield: 8 to 10 servings.

Doris Renfroe, Kappa Pi
Mt. Pleasant, Texas

MACARONI AND CHEESE

2 cups small macaroni	Salt and pepper to taste
3 eggs	10 ounces Cheddar cheese, shredded
1 12-ounce can evaporated milk	3 tablespoons margarine
1 12-ounce can water	

Preheat oven to 350 degrees. Spray 9-by-13-inch baking dish with nonstick cooking spray. Cook macaroni using package directions; drain. Beat eggs with evaporated milk, water, salt and pepper in bowl. Layer macaroni and Cheddar cheese in prepared dish, 1/2 at a time. Pour egg mixture over top; dot with margarine. Bake for 1 hour. May use 8 ounces egg substitute in place of eggs and skim evaporated milk for reduced cholesterol. Yield: 12 servings.

Roseanne H. Cooper, Laureate Theta
Aiken, South Carolina

THE BEST MACARONI AND CHEESE

2 cups uncooked macaroni	8 ounces mozzarella cheese, shredded
2 cups small-curd cottage cheese	1 egg, beaten
1 cup sour cream	1 cup milk
12 ounces sharp Cheddar cheese, shredded	1 1/2 teaspoons salt
	Pepper and paprika to taste

Preheat oven to 350 degrees. Cook macaroni using package directions; drain. Combine cottage cheese, sour cream, Cheddar cheese, mozzarella cheese, egg, milk, salt and pepper in bowl; mix well. Stir in macaroni. Spoon into buttered 9-by-13-inch baking dish. Sprinkle with paprika. Bake for 45 to 60 minutes or until browned. Yield: 8 to 10 servings.

Lynn Caylor, Beta Eta
Lebanon, Indiana

MACARONI CASSEROLE

1/4 cup chopped green bell pepper	8 ounces Velveeta cheese, cubed
1/4 cup chopped onion	1 cup mayonnaise
1/4 cup chopped pimento	1 8-ounce package elbow macaroni
1 cup water	
1 10-ounce can cream of chicken soup	

Preheat oven to 350 degrees. Steam bell pepper, onion and pimento in water in saucepan until tender. Stir in soup and Velveeta cheese. Simmer until cheese is melted, stirring constantly. Stir in mayonnaise; remove from heat. Cook macaroni using package directions; drain. Add to cheese mixture, stirring well. Pour into 2-quart baking dish. Bake for 25 to 30 minutes or until bubbly. Yield: 8 to 10 servings.

Carolyn Mathews Richburg, Zeta Eta
Goshen, Alabama

CHEESE-STUFFED MANICOTTI

18 jumbo manicotti shells	3/4 teaspoon dried dillweed
3 eggs, beaten	1/4 cup butter or margarine
1 1/2 cups cottage cheese	
1 1/2 cups shredded mozzarella cheese	1/2 cup all-purpose flour
	1 teaspoon pepper
3/4 cup grated Parmesan cheese	2 1/2 cups milk
	Paprika to taste

Preheat oven to 350 degrees. Cook manicotti using package directions, reducing cooking time by 1/4; drain and rinse. Combine eggs, cottage cheese, mozzarella cheese, 1/4 cup Parmesan cheese and dillweed in bowl; mix well. Spoon mixture into manicotti shells. Place in large greased baking pan. Melt butter in saucepan. Stir in flour and pepper. Add milk gradually. Cook over low heat until thickened, stirring constantly. Stir in remaining 1/2 cup Parmesan cheese; remove from heat. Pour over manicotti; sprinkle with paprika. Bake, covered, for 20 to 25 minutes or until sauce is bubbly. Yield: 9 servings.

Suzanne Bouchard, Lambda Gamma
Windsor, Ontario, Canada

GRANDMA'S DRY NOODLES

These noodles are a family tradition. I prepare this recipe for every holiday meal just like my grandmother used to do.

5 eggs	3 cans water
2/3 cup milk	2 tablespoons chicken bouillon granules
2 1/2 teaspoons salt	
5 cups all-purpose flour	1/2 cup butter
2 10-ounce cans chicken broth	

Beat eggs with milk and salt in bowl. Add enough flour to make stiff dough. Divide dough into halves. Roll out each portion thinly on floured surface. Let stand for 2 hours, turning occasionally to dry. Roll up dough; slice thinly with sharp knife. Spread out dough slices to dry. Combine chicken broth, water and chicken bouillon in large kettle. Bring to a boil. Drop in noodles, reserving 1 cup. Cook for 20 to 25 minutes or until broth is absorbed, stirring occasionally. Fry reserved noodles in butter in skillet until browned. Arrange over cooked noodles before serving. Do not substitute margarine for butter in this recipe. Yield: 6 servings.

Bonnie Guenthner, Preceptor Beta Psi
Dodge City, Kansas

OUR FAVORITE SPAGHETTI

1 pound sliced bacon	2 15-ounce cans
1 medium onion,	tomato sauce
chopped	1¹/₂ pounds spaghetti

Cut bacon into ¼-inch pieces. Sauté in large pan over medium heat until partially cooked. Add onion. Cook until onion is tender. Add tomato sauce. Simmer until of desired consistency. Cook spaghetti using package directions; drain. Add to sauce in pan; toss until coated with sauce. Yield: 6 to 10 servings.

Rosemary Dougherty, Beta Mu
San Manuel, Arizona

WINNER'S SPAGHETTI

¹/₂ cup chopped green	1 19-ounce package
bell pepper	spaghetti with meat
¹/₃ cup chopped onion	sauce dinner
1 tablespoon margarine	¹/₄ cup grated Parmesan
8 ounces cream cheese,	cheese
cubed	1 3-ounce can French-
¹/₄ cup milk	fried onions

Preheat oven to 350 degrees. Sauté green pepper and onion in margarine in saucepan until tender. Add cream cheese and milk, mixing until well blended. Prepare spaghetti dinner using package directions. Combine half the meat sauce with spaghetti. Pour spaghetti mixture into 6-by-10-inch baking dish. Top with cream cheese mixture. Spread remaining meat sauce over top. Sprinkle with Parmesan cheese. Bake for 25 minutes. Top with French-fried onions and bake for 5 minutes longer. Yield: 6 servings.

Cynthia P. Lane, Iota Eta
Chesapeake, Virginia

RICE PILAF

¹/₂ cup margarine	2 cans chicken broth
1 cup long grain rice	1 small can mushrooms,
¹/₃ cup chopped onion	drained
Chopped bacon to taste	

Preheat oven to 325 degrees. Melt margarine in skillet. Add rice, onion and bacon. Cook over low heat until lightly browned, stirring frequently. Pour into casserole. Stir in broth and mushrooms. Bake for 1¹/₂ hours, stirring after 40 minutes and 80 minutes. May add chopped parsley, cooked shredded carrots, cooked celery and/or almonds in any amounts or combinations if desired. Yield: 6 to 8 servings.

Susan H. Minard, Eta
Marion, Ohio

RICE CASSEROLE

1 large onion, chopped	2 4-ounce cans
2 stalks celery, chopped	mushrooms
1 2-ounce package	2 10-ounce cans beef
slivered almonds	bouillon
³/₄ cup margarine	Salt to taste
1¹/₂ cups uncooked	
long grain rice	

Preheat oven to 300 degrees. Sauté onion, celery and almonds in margarine in skillet for 3 minutes. Add rice and undrained mushrooms. Cook for 1 minute longer, stirring occasionally. Stir in bouillon and salt. Spoon into 4-quart baking dish. Bake for 1 hour. Yield: 8 servings.

Karen Nifeneger, Xi Epsilon
Newport News, Virginia

MUSHROOMS AND RICE

1 10-ounce can French	1¹/₂ cups uncooked
onion soup	minute rice
1 14-ounce can beef	¹/₄ cup margarine
consommé	
1 4-ounce can sliced	
mushrooms, drained	

Combine soup, consommé, mushrooms and rice in bowl; mix well. Spoon into 9-by-13-inch baking dish. Dot with margarine. Bake for 20 minutes, covered, for moister rice, or uncovered for crunchy top. May also prepare in microwave on High for 5 minutes; let stand for 5 minutes before serving. Yield: 12 servings.

Joy E. Brooks, Preceptor Beta Omega
Emporia, Kansas

SAVORY RICE

¹/₄ cup orzo	2 tablespoons onion
2 tablespoons butter or	soup mix
margarine	3 cups chicken bouillon
1 cup long grain rice	

Sauté orzo in butter in saucepan, stirring until browned. Add rice, onion soup mix and bouillon. Bring to a boil, stirring frequently; reduce heat. Cook, covered, for 25 minutes. Yield: 8 servings.

Phyllis Beveridge, Laureate Alpha Rho
St. Petersburg, Florida

BEET PICKLES

My dear neighbor of 40 years shared this recipe with me.

1 quart beets	2 cups beet juice
1 cup sugar	2 tablespoons whole
1 cup vinegar	cloves

Cook beets in water in saucepan until tender; drain, reserving 2 cups juice. Peel beets and cut into chunks. Place in canning jars. Combine sugar, vinegar, beet juice and cloves in saucepan. Pour over beets, leaving 1/2 inch headspace. Process in hot water bath; seal with 2-piece lids. Yield: 20 servings.

Imogene L. Geiger, Laureate Alpha Nu
Sedro Woolley, Washington

MY FAVORITE PICKLES

6 cups thinly sliced	1/2 teaspoon salt
cucumbers	1/2 teaspoon mustard
2 cups thinly sliced	seed
onions	1/2 teaspoon celery seed
1 1/2 cups sugar	1/2 teaspoon ground
1 1/2 cups vinegar	turmeric

Layer cucumbers and onions in large heavy bowl. Combine sugar, vinegar, salt, mustard seed, celery seed and turmeric in saucepan. Bring to a boil, stirring until sugar is dissolved. Pour over cucumbers and onions. Let stand until cool. Spoon into sterilized jars; seal with 2-piece lids. Store in refrigerator for up to 1 month. Yield: 6 to 7 cups pickles.

Mary Ann Gibson, Preceptor Lambda Alpha
Vallejo, California

CORN RELISH

16 to 20 ears sweet corn	2 cups vinegar
4 cups chopped celery	2 tablespoons salt
2 cups chopped red bell	1 teaspoon celery seed
peppers	1/4 cup all-purpose flour
2 cups chopped green	1 teaspoon turmeric
bell peppers	2 tablespoons dry
1 cup chopped onion	mustard
2 cups sugar	1/2 cup water
2 cups water	

Cook corn in boiling water for 5 minutes; plunge into cold water and drain. Cut kernels from corn. Combine celery, bell peppers, onion, sugar, 2 cups water, vinegar, salt and celery seed in large saucepan. Bring to a boil. Cook for 5 minutes, stirring occasionally. Blend flour, turmeric, mustard and 1/2 cup water in small bowl; stir into boiling mixture. Add corn. Cook for 5 minutes, stirring frequently. Pack hot mixture into sterilized jars, leaving 1/2 inch headspace. Process in hot water bath for 15 minutes; seal with 2-piece lids. Yield: 7 pints.

Janet Sanders, Laureate Eta
Eagle Grove, Iowa

CRANBERRY-APPLE RELISH

This relish is fantastic by itself, long after the turkey and dressing are gone. Try it and you'll throw away your cranberry sauce!

1 navel orange	1/4 teaspoon cinnamon
1 pound fresh	1 large apple, cored,
cranberries	chopped
1 1/4 cups packed light	1 tablespoon lemon juice
brown sugar	1/2 cup chopped pecans

Peel orange, removing white outer membrane and center core. Process orange and half the cranberries in food processor with metal blade until desired consistency. Pour into bowl. Process remaining cranberries and add to mixture. Stir in brown sugar, cinnamon, apple, lemon juice and pecans. Chill, covered, for 12 hours or longer.
Yield: 3 to 4 cups relish.

Carol Sassin, Xi Psi Beta
Beeville, Texas

SLOW-COOKER APPLES

When cooking, this delicious recipe makes the whole house smell heavenly.

7 medium tart apples,	1 teaspoon cinnamon
cored	3 tablespoons margarine
1/4 cup raisins	1/2 cup apple cider
1/2 cup packed light	(optional)
brown sugar	

Place apples in slow cooker. Combine raisins and brown sugar. Fill cored centers of apples with mixture. Sprinkle with cinnamon; dot with margarine. Pour in cider or substitute water. Cook, covered, on Low overnight. Yield: 7 servings.

Debra Principe, Iota Eta
Chesapeake, Virginia

ORANGE-YOGURT SAUCE

1 tablespoon butter or	1/4 cup orange juice
margarine	1/4 cup plain yogurt
1 tablespoon all-	Dried tarragon to taste
purpose flour	

Melt butter in saucepan over medium heat. Add flour, stirring for 1 minute. Add orange juice slowly, stirring constantly until smooth. Stir in yogurt and tarragon. Serve over cooked broccoli or asparagus. May add additional orange juice for desired consistency. Yield: 1/2 cup sauce.

Olga Tombs, Preceptor Delta Rho
Orangeville, Ontario, Canada

Let it Rise!

CHEESE DROPS

I first made this recipe for a Super Bowl party at a sorority sister's home.

2 cups all-purpose flour	8 ounces sharp Cheddar
1/2 teaspoon cayenne	cheese, grated
pepper	1 cup chopped pecans
1/2 teaspoon salt	1 3/4 teaspoons caraway
1 cup butter or	seed
margarine, softened	

Preheat oven to 350 degrees. Sift flour, cayenne pepper and salt together. Cream butter and cheese in mixer bowl. Add dry ingredients; mix well. Fold in pecans and caraway seed. Drop by rounded teaspoonfuls onto ungreased baking sheets. Bake for 15 to 18 minutes or until brown. Yield: 5 dozen.

Nancy McDaniel Galkowski
River Ridge, Louisiana

CHEESE-GARLIC BISCUITS

2 cups baking mix	1/4 cup melted margarine
2/3 cup milk	1/4 teaspoon garlic
1/2 cup shredded	powder
Cheddar cheese	
1/4 teaspoon garlic	
powder	

Preheat oven to 450 degrees. Combine baking mix, milk, cheese and 1/4 teaspoon garlic in mixer bowl; mix until soft dough forms. Beat for 30 seconds. Drop by rounded spoonfuls onto ungreased baking sheets. Bake for 8 to 10 minutes or until golden brown. Combine margarine and 1/4 teaspoon garlic powder in bowl; brush over warm biscuits. Serve immediately. Yield: 10 to 12 servings.

Patricia Theiss, Zeta Nu
Princeton, Missouri

GARLIC BISCUITS

2 cups baking mix	1/4 cup melted margarine
2/3 cup milk	1/4 teaspoon garlic
1/2 cup shredded	powder
Cheddar cheese	

Preheat oven to 450 degrees. Combine all ingredients in medium bowl; mix well. Drop by tablespoonfuls onto nonstick baking sheet. Bake for 10 minutes. Yield: 1 dozen.

Betty Paulus, Preceptor Eta Kappa
Cherry Valley, California

SISTERS' ZESTY ZINGERS

2 cups baking mix	Melted butter or
1/2 teaspoon sugar	margarine
3/4 cup zesty ranch	Garlic salt or Mrs. Dash
shredded cheese	seasoning
1 cup milk	

Preheat oven to 400 degrees. Combine baking mix, sugar and cheese in medium bowl; mix well. Stir in milk. Drop by teaspoonfuls onto greased baking sheets. Brush tops with melted butter; sprinkle with garlic salt. Bake for 12 minutes or until golden brown. Yield: 2 dozen.

Patricia Cable, Eta Beta
Almond, North Carolina

AUNT LAURA'S SCONES

My favorite Canadian aunt always had these on hand when we visited. They bring back some happy childhood memories.

1/2 cup raisins	1 egg white, slightly
3 cups all-purpose flour	beaten
1 tablespoon baking	1 teaspoon vanilla
powder	extract
1/2 teaspoon salt	1/2 cup milk
1/2 cup sugar	1 egg yolk, beaten
1/2 cup shortening	1/2 cup coarse sugar

Preheat oven to 350 degrees. Plump raisins in warm water to cover in small bowl for 10 minutes. Drain, reserving raisins. Combine flour, baking powder, salt and sugar in large bowl. Cut in shortening until crumbly. Add raisins, egg white, vanilla and milk; mix until soft dough forms. Roll dough 1/2 inch thick on floured surface. Spread with egg yolk and 1/2 cup coarse sugar. Cut into diamond shapes. Place on greased baking sheets. Bake for 10 to 15 minutes or until light brown. Yield. 2 to 3 dozen.

Christine Kinnaman
Hamilton, Ohio

SCONES

I have been making this recipe since the late fifties. My family loves them and each has the recipe. I still make them for my husband.

3 cups sifted all-	3/4 cup butter or
purpose flour	margarine, softened
2 teaspoons baking	1 cup chopped raisins
powder	1 egg, beaten
1 cup sugar	Milk
1/4 teaspoon salt	

Preheat oven to 450 degrees. Sift flour, baking powder, sugar and salt in large bowl. Cut in butter until crumbly. Add raisins; mix well. Combine egg and enough milk to measure 1 cup. Stir into batter. Knead on floured surface 15 to 20 times. Roll 3/4 inch thick; cut into triangles or circles. Place 1/2 inch apart on nonstick baking sheets. Bake for 10 to 12 minutes or until light brown. Yield: 20 to 24 servings.

Doreen Gray, Xi Beta
Yarker, Ontario, Canada

APPLE BREAD

3 eggs	2 teaspoons baking soda
1 1/2 cups vegetable oil	1 teaspoon baking
1 1/2 cups sugar	powder
2 cups chopped apples	1/2 teaspoon cloves or
1 teaspoon vanilla	nutmeg
extract	1 teaspoon cinnamon
3 1/2 cups all-purpose	2/3 cup chopped nuts
flour	

Preheat oven to 350 degrees. Beat eggs, oil and sugar in mixer bowl for 1 minute. Add remaining ingredients; mix well. Spread batter in 2 greased 5-by-9-inch loaf pans. Bake for 1 hour. Yield: 2 loaves.

Cathy Switzer, Alpha Beta Psi
Clinton, Missouri

APRICOT BREAD

I always serve this at Christmas breakfast and at family reunions.

2 cups dried apricots	4 cups all-purpose flour
2 cups sugar	4 teaspoons baking
1/4 cup margarine,	powder
softened	1/2 teaspoon baking soda
2 eggs	3/4 teaspoon salt
1/2 cup water	1 cup chopped nuts
1 cup orange juice	(optional)

Preheat oven to 350 degrees. Soak apricots in water to cover in small bowl for 15 minutes. Drain; cut into quarters. Combine sugar, margarine, eggs, water and orange juice in medium bowl; mix until blended. Add mixture of flour, baking powder, baking soda and salt; mix well. Fold in apricots and nuts. Spread batter in 2 greased 5-by-9-inch loaf pans. Bake for 55 to 65 minutes or until loaves test done. Yield: 2 loaves.

Nancy Blackman, Xi Lambda Mu
Sunrise Beach, Missouri

BANANA BREAD

1 cup butter or	4 cups sifted all-
margarine, softened	purpose flour
2 cups sugar	2 teaspoons baking soda
1 teaspoon vanilla	6 ripe bananas, mashed
extract	Butter, margarine or
4 eggs, beaten	cream cheese

Preheat oven to 350 degrees. Cream 1 cup butter, sugar, vanilla and eggs in mixer bowl until light and fluffy. Add mixture of flour and baking soda alternately with bananas, mixing well after each addition. Spread batter in 3 greased 5-by-9-inch loaf pans. Bake for 1 1/4 hours. Serve warm with butter, margarine or cream cheese. Yield: 3 loaves.

Krista Campbell, Epsilon Tau
Louisville, Kentucky

BANANA-MOLASSES BREAD

3 ripe bananas, mashed	4 teaspoons light brown
1/4 cup melted butter or	sugar substitute
margarine	1 tablespoon molasses
1 egg, beaten	2 teaspoons vanilla
1/4 cup sugar	extract
1 teaspoon baking soda	1 1/2 cups all-purpose
1 teaspoon salt	flour
1/2 cup chopped nuts	

Preheat oven to 350 degrees. Combine bananas and butter in medium bowl. Add next 8 ingredients; mix well. Stir in flour; mix well. Spread batter in 5-by-10-inch glass loaf pan sprayed with nonstick cooking spray. Bake for 1 hour and 10 minutes. Yield: 1 loaf.

Louis Johnston, Laureate Alpha Epsilon
Williamsburg, Virginia

RICH AND WONDERFUL BANANA BREAD

It is the best banana bread I have ever tasted.

1/2 cup shortening	4 eggs
1/2 cup margarine, softened	31/2 cups all-purpose flour
3 cups sugar	2 teaspoons baking soda
6 to 7 ripe bananas, mashed	1/2 teaspoon salt
	1/2 cup buttermilk
2 tablespoons vanilla extract	1 cup chopped nuts

Preheat oven to 325 degrees. Cream shortening, margarine and sugar in mixer bowl until light and fluffy. Add bananas, vanilla and eggs; mix until blended. Add 1/2 of the mixture of flour, baking soda and salt to batter; mix well. Stir in buttermilk and remaining flour mixture. Fold in nuts. Spread batter in 2 greased and floured 5-by-9-inch loaf pans. Bake for 11/4 to 11/2 hours or until loaves test done. Yield: 2 loaves.

Elaine Wendel, Mu Kappa
Ellinwood, Kansas
*Erika Perkins, Xi Gamma Rho
Cornville, Arizona

BANANA-NUT BREAD

4 bananas, mashed	11/2 teaspoons baking soda
2 cups sugar	
3 eggs, beaten	1 teaspoon vanilla extract
1/2 cup vegetable oil	
1/3 cup buttermilk	1 cup chopped nuts
2 cups all-purpose flour	

Preheat oven to 325 degrees. Combine bananas and next 7 ingredients in medium bowl; mix well. Fold in nuts. Spread batter in 2 greased and floured 5-by-9-inch loaf pans. Bake for 1 hour. Yield: 2 loaves.

Molly Anne Polvado
Alamo, Texas

BANANA TEA BREAD

13/4 cups sifted all-purpose flour	1 cup raisins
	1/3 cup shortening
2 teaspoons baking powder	2/3 cup sugar
	2 eggs
1/4 teaspoon baking soda	1 cup mashed ripe bananas
1/2 teaspoon salt	

Preheat oven to 350 degrees. Sift flour, baking powder, baking soda and salt into medium bowl. Stir in raisins. Cream shortening in mixer bowl. Add sugar gradually, beating until light and fluffy. Add eggs; mix well. Add flour mixture alternately with bananas, stirring well after each addition. Spread batter in greased 5-by-9-inch loaf pan. Bake for 1 hour and 10 minutes or until loaf tests done. Yield: 1 loaf.

M. Violet Roberts, Laureate Zeta
Burnaby, British Columbia, Canada

CARROT-PINEAPPLE BREAD

Our family can have a holiday banquet "fit for a King," but all my husband looks for is this bread.

3 cups all-purpose flour	1 8-ounce can crushed pineapple
1 tablespoon cinnamon	
1 teaspoon salt	2 cups grated carrots
1 teaspoon baking soda	1 cup chopped walnuts (optional)
3 eggs, beaten	
2 cups sugar	1 tablespoon vanilla extract
1 cup vegetable oil	

Preheat oven to 325 degrees. Sift flour, cinnamon, salt and baking soda together. Combine eggs and sugar in medium bowl; mix well. Stir in oil, undrained pineapple, carrots and walnuts. Add dry ingredients; mix well. Stir in vanilla. Spread batter in 2 greased and floured 5-by-9-inch loaf pans. Bake for 60 to 70 minutes or until loaves test done. Yield: 2 loaves.

Leslie Carman, Xi Gamma Sigma
Rocky Ford, Colorado

PINEAPPLE-COCONUT LOAVES

1 2-layer package yellow cake mix with pudding	1/2 teaspoon nutmeg
	1/2 cup flaked coconut
	11/2 cups confectioners' sugar
1 cup evaporated milk	
1 8-ounce can crushed pineapple	1 to 2 tablespoons water
	2 tablespoons toasted coconut
2 eggs	

Preheat oven to 325 degrees. Combine cake mix, evaporated milk, undrained pineapple, eggs and nutmeg in mixer bowl; beat at low speed until moistened. Beat at high speed for 2 minutes. Stir in flaked coconut. Spread batter in 2 buttered 5-by-9-inch loaf pans. Bake for 45 to 50 minutes or until loaves test done. Cool in pans for 15 minutes. Invert onto wire rack to cool completely. Combine confectioners' sugar and enough water in medium bowl to make of spreading consistency. Drizzle over cooled loaves. Sprinkle with toasted coconut. Yield: 2 loaves.

Roxanne Saathoff, Preceptor Alpha Pi
Beatrice, Nebraska

HAWAIIAN BREAD

4 cups all-purpose flour
1 teaspoon salt
1 teaspoon baking soda
10 ounces flaked coconut
2 20-ounce cans
   crushed pineapple
1¹/2 cups sugar
4 eggs

Preheat oven to 375 degrees. Sift flour, salt and baking soda together. Mix remaining ingredients in medium bowl. Stir in dry ingredients. Spoon into 2 greased 5-by-9-inch loaf pans. Bake for 1 hour or until loaves test done. Store in refrigerator. Yield: 2 loaves.

Georgia Gilley, Theta Delta
Burlington, Colorado

AUNT LIZIE'S GINGERBREAD

This is a recipe from my great aunt. She was a great cook, and we loved going to her farm for Sunday dinner.

2 teaspoons baking soda
1 cup boiling water
¹/2 cup sugar
¹/2 cup butter or
   margarine, softened
1 cup molasses
1 teaspoon cinnamon
1 teaspoon ginger
1 teaspoon cloves
¹/2 teaspoon salt
3¹/2 cups all-purpose
   flour
2 eggs, beaten

Preheat oven to 350 degrees. Dissolve baking soda in boiling water; set aside. Cream sugar and butter in mixer bowl until light and fluffy. Add molasses, spices and salt; mix well. Stir in baking soda mixture. Add flour; mix well. Add eggs; mix well. Spread batter in greased 9-by-13-inch baking pan. Bake for 30 minutes. Yield: 18 to 20 servings.

Helen R. Cranor, Laureate Zeta
Wheat Ridge, Colorado

LEMON BREAD

3 cups all-purpose flour
¹/2 teaspoon salt
¹/2 teaspoon baking
   powder
¹/2 teaspoon baking soda
1 cup butter or
   margarine, softened
2 cups sugar
4 eggs
1 cup buttermilk
Grated rind of 1 lemon
1 cup chopped nuts
1 cup sugar
Juice of 3 lemons

Preheat oven to 325 degrees. Combine flour, salt, baking powder and baking soda together. Cream butter and 2 cups sugar in mixer bowl until light and fluffy. Beat in eggs 1 at a time. Add dry ingredients alternately with buttermilk, mixing well after each addition. Stir in lemon rind and nuts. Spoon batter into 3 greased and floured 5-by-9-inch loaf pans. Bake for 1 hour. Invert onto wax paper-lined baking sheet. Drizzle with mixture of 1 cup sugar and lemon juice. Yield: 3 loaves.

Jane A. Ross, Iota Masters
Carrollton, Missouri
*Ruthie Little, Preceptor Mu
Las Vegas, Nevada

LEMON-PISTACHIO BREAD

¹/2 cup sugar
¹/2 cup chopped nuts
1¹/2 teaspoons cinnamon
1 4-ounce package
   pistachio instant
   pudding mix
1 2-layer package
   lemon cake mix
4 eggs
¹/2 cup vegetable oil
³/4 cup water

Preheat oven to 350 degrees. Combine sugar, nuts and cinnamon in small bowl; set aside. Combine pudding mix, cake mix, eggs, oil and water in mixer bowl; mix until smooth. Layer batter and nut mixture half at a time in three 5-by-9-inch loaf pans sprayed with nonstick cooking spray. Bake for 40 minutes or until loaves test done. Yield: 3 loaves.

Sue L. Rice, Xi Gamma Nu
Richardson, Texas

❖ MANGO BREAD

I was taught how to make this bread when we lived in Kaneohe, Hawaii in 1973.

4 cups all-purpose flour
4 teaspoons baking soda
4 teaspoons cinnamon
1 teaspoon salt
¹/2 cup macadamia nuts
2¹/2 cups sugar
2 cups vegetable oil
2 teaspoons vanilla
   extract
4 cups diced mangos
6 eggs, beaten
1 tablespoon lemon juice
1 cup grated coconut

Preheat oven to 350 degrees. Sift flour, baking soda, cinnamon and salt in large bowl. Make well in center of dry ingredients. Add remaining ingredients; mix well. Spread batter in 2 greased 5-by-9-inch loaf pans. Bake for 1 hour. May substitute fresh peaches for mangos. May bake in 4 to 5 miniature loaf pans. Yield: 2 loaves.

Chris Judt, Xi Gamma Alpha
Norfolk, Nebraska

❖ MACADAMIA NUT LOAVES

I got this recipe from my mother. I've made it many times for friends, family and church.

3 cups all-purpose flour
¹/4 teaspoon salt
¹/2 teaspoon baking
   powder
1 cup butter or
   margarine, softened
¹/2 cup shortening
3 cups sugar
1 teaspoon lemon
   extract
1 teaspoon coconut
   extract
1 teaspoon vanilla
   extract
1 teaspoon almond
   extract
5 eggs
1 cup milk
1 20-ounce can crushed
   pineapple, drained
5 ounces macadamia
   nuts
1 cup shredded coconut

Preheat oven to 325 degrees. Sift flour, salt and baking powder in bowl, reserving ¹/2 cup. Cream butter, shortening and sugar in mixer bowl until light and fluffy. Add flavorings; mix well. Add eggs 1 at a time, beating well after each addition. Add dry ingredients alternately with milk to creamed mixture, mixing well after each addition. Combine reserved 1/2 cup flour mixture with pineapple, macadamia nuts and coconut in medium bowl; toss until coated. Stir into batter. Spoon into 3 greased and floured 5-by-9-inch loaf pans. Bake for 1 hour. Yield: 3 loaves.

Jan Black, Xi Chi Sigma
Flint, Texas

PEACH-NUT BREAD

1 1/2 cups sugar	1 teaspoon baking
2 eggs	powder
1/2 cup shortening	1/8 teaspoon salt
2 cups mashed drained	1 teaspoon vanilla
peaches	extract
2 cups all-purpose flour	1 cup chopped walnuts
1 teaspoon cinnamon	(optional)
1 teaspoon baking soda	

Preheat oven to 350 degrees. Cream sugar, eggs and shortening in mixer bowl until light and fluffy. Add peaches, flour, cinnamon, baking soda, baking powder and salt; mix well. Stir in vanilla and walnuts. Spread batter in 2 greased 5-by-9-inch loaf pans. Bake for 35 to 40 minutes or until loaves test done. Yield: 2 loaves.

Carolyn J. Cummings, Theta Psi
Cookeville, Tennessee

PEAR BREAD

This recipe was received from a sorority sister who invents different ways to use her bumper crop of pears each year.

4 cups sifted all-	1 1/3 cups chopped
purpose flour	pecans (optional)
1 1/2 teaspoons baking	1 cup vegetable oil
soda	4 eggs, slightly beaten
1/2 teaspoon baking	2 1/2 cups sugar
powder	2 1/2 cups grated pears
1 teaspoon salt	2 1/4 teaspoons vanilla
1 1/2 tablespoons	extract
cinnamon	

Preheat oven to 325 degrees. Combine flour, baking soda, baking powder, salt, cinnamon and pecans in large bowl. Combine oil, eggs, sugar, pears and vanilla in medium bowl; mix well. Make well in flour mixture. Pour pear mixture into well; mix just until moistened. Spoon into 2 greased 5-by-9-inch loaf pans. Bake for 1 1/4 hours or until loaves test done. Yield: 2 loaves.

Ginger Lake, Preceptor Kappa Xi
Universal City, Texas

ICEBOX NUT BREAD

These rolls have been prepared for Christmas morning by the women in my family for the last six generations.

1 envelope dry yeast	4 egg whites
1/4 cup lukewarm milk	2/3 cup sugar
3/4 cup milk, scalded	1 teaspoon vanilla
1 cup shortening	extract
4 cups sifted all-	1/2 teaspoon almond
purpose flour	extract
1/2 cup sugar	1 pound walnuts,
1 teaspoon salt	ground
4 egg yolks	

Dissolve yeast in lukewarm milk. Combine scalded milk and shortening in small bowl; mix until shortening melts. Combine flour, 1/2 cup sugar, salt, egg yolks and part of the milk-shortening mixture in bowl; mix well. Add the yeast mixture and the remaining milk-shortening mixture; mix well. Knead on floured surface until smooth and elastic. Chill, covered, overnight. Beat egg whites in mixer bowl until stiff peaks form. Beat in 2/3 cup sugar and flavorings. Stir in walnuts; set aside. Divide dough into four portions. Roll each into a rectangle on floured surface. Spread with walnut mixture. Roll as for jelly roll, sealing edge and ends. Place on non-stick baking sheets. Let rise for 1 hour. Preheat oven to 350 degrees. Bake for 35 to 40 minutes or until loaves tests done. Yield: 4 loaves.

Sue Troino, Alpha Iota
Coral Springs, Florida

ORANGE-WALNUT BREAD

I took this bread to our Sweetheart cocktail party.

2 1/2 cups all-purpose	1/4 cup melted butter or
flour	margarine
1 1/4 cups sugar	1/2 cup orange juice
2 teaspoons baking	2 tablespoons grated
powder	orange rind
1/2 teaspoon baking soda	3 tablespoons water
1/2 teaspoon salt	1 cup chopped walnuts
2 eggs, beaten	

Preheat oven to 350 degrees. Combine flour, sugar, baking powder, baking soda and salt in medium bowl. Combine eggs, butter, orange juice, orange rind and water in medium bowl; mix until blended. Stir mixture into dry ingredients, mixing just until moistened. Fold in walnuts. Spread batter in greased and floured 5-by-9-inch loaf pan. Bake for 1 hour or until bread tests done. Yield: 1 loaf.

Patty Truskolaski, Delta Gamma Psi
San Jose, California

PERSIMMON BREAD

2¹/2 cups sugar
1 teaspoon salt
3 cups all-purpose
  flour
1 teaspoon baking
  powder
1 teaspoon baking soda
1 tablespoon cinnamon
1 cup chopped nuts
3 eggs, beaten
1 cup vegetable oil
1 cup grated zucchini
1 cup persimmon pulp
1 tablespoon vanilla
  extract

Preheat oven to 350 degrees. Combine sugar and next 6 ingredients in medium bowl. Combine eggs and oil in medium bowl; mix until blended. Stir in zucchini, persimmon pulp and vanilla. Add flour mixture to batter, stirring just until moistened. Spread batter in 2 greased 5-by-9-inch loaf pans. Bake for 1 hour or until loaves test done. Yield: 2 loaves.

Virginia Guy
Clovis, California

LEMON POPPY SEED BREAD

My grandmother's favorite recipe.

1 2-layer package
   lemon cake mix
1 4-ounce package
   lemon instant
   pudding mix
1 cup water
1 teaspoon lemon
  extract
¹/2 cup vegetable oil
4 eggs
¹/4 cup poppy seed

Preheat oven to 350 degrees. Combine all ingredients in medium bowl; mix well. Spread batter in 2 greased 5-by-9-inch loaf pans. Bake for 45 minutes or until loaves test done. May bake in 4 miniature loaf pans. Yield: 2 loaves.

Teresa A. Garton, Theta Lambda
Colorado Springs, Colorado
*Melissa Vogel, Tau Pi
Sterling, Illinois

MELT-IN-YOUR-MOUTH PUMPKIN BREAD

2 cups all-purpose flour
2 cups sugar
2 4-ounce packages
   coconut instant
   pudding mix
1 teaspoon baking soda
1 teaspoon salt
1 teaspoon cinnamon
1¹/4 cups vegetable oil
5 eggs
2 cups canned pumpkin

Preheat oven to 325 degrees. Combine flour, sugar, pudding mix, baking soda, salt and cinnamon in bowl. Combine oil, eggs and pumpkin in large bowl; mix well. Add flour mixture; mix well. Spread batter in 2 greased 5-by-9-inch loaf pans. Bake for 1 hour. Yield: 2 loaves.

Ihlia Weno, Alpha Beta Rho
Windsor, Missouri

QUICK GRAHAM BREAD

This recipe was passed down from my great-grandmother. My mother remembers her mother-in-law making this bread when they were in a hurry. Hence the name "Quick" Graham Bread.

1 teaspoon baking soda
1¹/4 cups sour milk or
  buttermilk
¹/2 cup sugar
¹/2 to 1 teaspoon salt
1¹/2 cups graham flour
¹/2 cup all-purpose flour
1 egg
2 tablespoons
  shortening

Preheat oven to 350 degrees. Dissolve baking soda in a small amount of lukewarm water. Combine baking soda mixture and remaining ingredients in medium bowl; mix by hand just until moistened. Spread batter in greased 5-by-9-inch loaf pan. Bake for 50 minutes. Yield: 1 loaf.

Jean Hanson, Preceptor Nu
Apple Valley, Minnesota

COLONIAL SEED CAKE

¹/2 cup poppy seed
³/4 cup milk
6 tablespoons butter or
  margarine, softened
3 eggs, at room
  temperature
1¹/4 cups sugar
1 teaspoon vanilla
  extract
2 teaspoons baking
  powder
2 cups all-purpose flour
Confectioners' sugar or
  whipped cream

Preheat oven to 350 degrees. Combine poppy seed and milk in small bowl. Let stand for 3 to 4 hours. Combine poppy seed mixture with next 6 ingredients in mixer bowl. Beat for 1 minute. Spoon batter into greased and floured 5-by-9-inch loaf pan. Bake for 1 hour or until loaf tests done. Cool in pan. Invert onto serving platter. Sprinkle with confectioners' sugar or garnish with whipped cream. Yield: 1 loaf.

Carole M. Steen, Xi Iota Rho
Yucca Valley, California

POPPY SEED BREAD

It was a special treat that my mother made.

¹/2 cup confectioners'
  sugar
¹/4 cup orange juice
¹/2 teaspoon vanilla
  extract
¹/2 teaspoon butter
  extract
¹/2 teaspoon almond
  extract
3 cups all-purpose
  flour
2¹/2 cups sugar
1¹/2 teaspoons salt
1¹/2 teaspoons baking
  powder
3 eggs
1¹/2 cups milk
1 cup plus 2
  tablespoons vegetable
  oil
1¹/2 teaspoons poppy
  seed
1¹/2 teaspoons each
  vanilla extract, butter
  extract and almond
  extract

Preheat oven to 325 degrees. Combine first 5 ingredients in small bowl, mixing until smooth; set aside.

Combine flour and remaining ingredients in large bowl; mix well. Spread batter in 2 greased 5-by-9-inch loaf pans. Bake for 70 minutes. Cool slightly. Invert loaves onto serving platter. Pour glaze over warm bread. Yield: 2 loaves.

Diana Thames, Preceptor Alpha Beta
Hampton, Georgia

PARTY PUMPKIN BREAD

I took this pumpkin bread and cream cheese sandwiches to my first Beta Sigma Phi social. I came home with an empty platter, and many requests for the recipe.

4 eggs	1/2 teaspoon baking
3 cups sugar	powder
1 cup vegetable oil	1 teaspoon cinnamon
2 cups canned pumpkin	1 teaspoon cloves
2/3 cup water	1 teaspoon nutmeg
3 cups all-purpose flour	1 teaspoon allspice
2 teaspoons baking soda	1/8 teaspoon salt

Preheat oven to 350 degrees. Combine eggs and remaining ingredients in large bowl; mix well. Pour batter into 10 greased soft drink cans. Bake for 1 hour or until toothpick inserted in center comes out clean. Invert cans onto wire racks to cool. Serve plain or with cream cheese. Yield: 10 loaves.

Lestina Kalali, Xi Nu Zeta
Ponte Vedra Beach, Florida

SHERRY-FIG-NUT BREAD

1 cup dried figs, cut up	2/3 cup sugar
1/2 cup sherry	1 egg, beaten
1/2 cup boiling water	1/2 cup melted
2 cups sifted all-	shortening
purpose flour	1/2 cup chopped pecans
1 1/2 teaspoons salt	1/2 teaspoon maple
1 tablespoon baking	extract
powder	

Preheat oven to 350 degrees. Combine figs, sherry and boiling water in small bowl; set aside. Sift flour, salt, baking powder and sugar in medium bowl. Add fig mixture, egg, shortening, pecans and flavoring; mix just until moistened. Spread batter in greased 5-by-9-inch loaf pan. Bake for 1 hour. Cool in pan for 10 minutes. Invert onto wire rack to cool completely. Yield: 1 loaf.

Janet Shaw, Laureate Beta Eta
Avon Lake, Ohio

STRAWBERRY BREAD

3 cups all-purpose flour	1 cup vegetable oil
1 teaspoon baking soda	2 10-ounce packages
1 1/2 teaspoons cinnamon	frozen sliced
2 cups sugar	strawberries, thawed
3 eggs, beaten	

Preheat oven to 350 degrees. Combine flour, baking soda, cinnamon and sugar in medium bowl. Combine eggs, oil and strawberries in medium bowl; mix well. Add flour mixture; mix well. Spread batter in 2 greased 5-by-9-inch loaf pans. Bake for 1 hour or until bread tests done. Yield: 2 loaves.

Paula Murphy, Epsilon Alpha
Coppell, Texas
*Nadeen Steffey, Preceptor Tau
Erie, Pennsylvania
*Linda Wolf, Lambda Epsilon
Auburn, Indiana

BEVERLY'S EARTH BREAD

A very dear friend shared this recipe with me.

2 cups whole wheat	3 eggs
flour	1 cup vegetable oil
1 cup all-purpose flour	1 teaspoon vanilla
1 teaspoon baking	extract
powder	2 cups sugar
1/2 teaspoon baking soda	1 cup finely grated
1 teaspoon salt	zucchini
1/4 teaspoon cinnamon	1/2 cup grated carrots
3/4 teaspoon pumpkin	1/2 cup mashed banana
pie spice	1/2 cup chopped nuts

Preheat oven to 375 degrees. Mix flours, baking powder, baking soda, salt and spices together. Combine eggs, oil, vanilla and sugar in bowl; mix well. Add dry ingredients; mix well. Stir in zucchini, carrots, banana and nuts. Spread batter in 2 greased 5-by-9-inch loaf pans. Bake for 1 hour. Yield: 2 loaves.

Suzanne Best Wyman, Xi Beta Sigma
Pecos, Texas

ZUCCHINI BREAD

3 cups all-purpose flour	2 cups sugar
1 teaspoon salt	2 teaspoons vanilla
1 teaspoon baking soda	extract
1 1/2 teaspoons cinnamon	1 cup vegetable oil
1/2 teaspoon baking	3 cups grated zucchini
powder	1 cup chopped pecans
3 eggs, beaten	(optional)

Preheat oven to 350 degrees. Mix flour, salt, baking soda, cinnamon and baking powder together. Combine eggs, sugar, vanilla and oil in mixer bowl; mix until smooth. Stir in zucchini. Add dry ingredients; mix well. Fold in pecans. Spread batter in 2 greased and floured 5-by-9-inch loaf pans. Bake for 50 to 60 minutes or until loaves test done. Remove to wire rack to cool. Cut into slices. Yield: 2 loaves.

Loree Dienstbier, Preceptor Alpha Pi
Beatrice, Nebraska
*Kathleen Dixon, Xi Epsilon Epsilon
Hazelton, Pennsylvania
*Kathy Andrews, Preceptor Epsilon Epsilon
Marengo, Illinois

ZUCCHINI-NUT BREAD

3 cups all-purpose flour
1/2 teaspoon baking
  powder
2 teaspoons baking soda
1/8 teaspoon salt
4 eggs, beaten
1 cup sugar
1 cup vegetable oil

2 teaspoons vanilla
  extract
2 cups drained shredded
  zucchini
1 8-ounce can crushed
  pineapple, drained
1 cup chopped nuts

Preheat oven to 375 degrees. Mix flour, baking powder, baking soda and salt in medium bowl. Combine eggs, sugar, oil and vanilla in mixer bowl; mix until smooth. Stir in zucchini. Add to dry ingredients; mix well. Stir in pineapple and nuts. Spread batter in 2 greased 5-by-9-inch loaf pans. Bake for 45 to 60 minutes or until loaves test done. Cool in pans for 20 minutes. Invert onto wire rack to cool completely. Yield: 2 loaves.

Rebecca Podoba, Preceptor Gamma Delta
Bedford, Ohio

❖ FANTASY CHEESE BREAD

1 cup sour cream
1/2 cup sugar
1 teaspoon salt
1/2 cup melted butter or
  margarine
2 envelopes dry yeast
1 teaspoon sugar
1/2 cup lukewarm water
2 eggs, beaten
4 cups all-purpose flour
16 ounces cream cheese,
  softened

3/4 cup sugar
1 egg
1 teaspoon salt
2 teaspoons vanilla
  extract
2 cups confectioners'
  sugar
2 teaspoons milk
2 teaspoons vanilla
  extract

Heat sour cream in saucepan over low heat. Add 1/2 cup sugar, 1 teaspoon salt and butter; mix well. Cool to lukewarm. Dissolve yeast and 1 teaspoon sugar in lukewarm water in medium bowl. Add 2 beaten eggs and flour to yeast mixture; mix well. Stir into sour cream mixture. Knead on floured surface until smooth. Place in greased bowl, turning to coat surface. Let rise, covered, for 1 hour. Combine cream cheese and next four ingredients in medium bowl; mix until smooth. Divide dough into four portions. Roll each portion into circle on lightly floured surface. Spread with cream cheese mixture. Fold over to enclose filling; seal edge. Place on nonstick baking sheet. Let rise for 1 hour. Cut diagonal slashes in top. Preheat oven to 350 degrees. Bake for 15 to 20 minutes or until light brown. Remove to wire rack to cool. Frost with mixture of confectioners' sugar, milk and 2 teaspoons vanilla. Yield: 4 loaves.

Ceressa Kent, Psi Rho
St. Joseph, Missouri

BACON-CHEESE-ONION BREAD

When my husband and I lived in a small Eskimo community in the High Arctic, this was his favorite treat.

2 tablespoons dry yeast
1 teaspoon sugar
1/2 cup lukewarm water
8 slices bacon, chopped
1/2 cup finely grated
  onion
2 tablespoons margarine

2 cups grated cheese
1 cup sugar,
1 tablespoon salt
4 cups warm water
11 cups all-purpose flour

Dissolve yeast and 1 teaspoon sugar in lukewarm water. Cook bacon in skillet until light brown; drain. Saute onion in margarine in skillet until tender; cool. Combine cheese, 1 cup sugar, salt, warm water, bacon and onion in large bowl; mix well. Stir in yeast mixture and flour. Knead on floured surface until smooth and elastic. Place in greased bowl, turning to coat surface. Let rise, covered, in warm place until doubled in bulk. Punch dough down. Let rise, covered, until doubled in bulk. Knead on floured surface until smooth and elastic. Shape into 3 loaves. Place in 3 greased 5-by-9-inch loaf pans. Let rise until doubled in bulk. Preheat oven to 325 degrees. Bake for 1 hour or until loaves are golden brown. Yield: 3 loaves.

Flora Neave, Kappa Phi
Carleton Place, Ontario, Canada

SOFT AND SWEET BREAD DOUGH

A sister shared this recipe at the chapter Christmas party. I was impressed with the ease of preparation and the delicious results.

3 envelopes dry yeast
11/4 cups sugar
5 cups lukewarm water
1 cup shortening
11/4 cups dry milk
  powder

11/2 tablespoons salt
12 to 121/2 cups all-
  purpose flour

Dissolve yeast and sugar in lukewarm water in large bowl. Add shortening; mix well. Combine milk powder, salt and 6 cups flour in medium bowl. Add to yeast mixture gradually, mixing well after each addition. Beat for 5 minutes or until smooth. Place in greased bowl, turning to coat surface. Let rise, covered, until doubled in bulk. Punch dough down. Shape into 4 loaves. Place in 4 greased 5-by-9-inch loaf pans. Let rise until doubled in bulk. Preheat oven to 350 degrees. Bake for 30 to 40 minutes or until golden brown. May also shape into rolls if desired. Yield: 4 loaves or 4 to 6 dozen rolls.

Sandi Thrasher, Preceptor Beta Mu
Prineville, Oregon

COTTAGE CHEESE DILL BREAD

3 envelopes dry yeast
3/4 cup lukewarm water
24 ounces cottage cheese
2 tablespoons dillweed
1 tablespoon salt
3/4 teaspoon baking soda
3 eggs
3 tablespoons minced
  onion
6 tablespoons sugar
3 tablespoons
  margarine, softened
7 to 71/2 cups all-
  purpose flour

Dissolve yeast in lukewarm water. Combine cottage cheese and next 7 ingredients in large bowl; mix well. Stir in yeast. Add flour; mix well. Knead in bowl for 5 minutes. Let rise, covered, until doubled in bulk. Punch dough down. Shape into loaves. Place in 3 greased 5-by-9-inch loaf pans. Let rise in warm place for 45 to 50 minutes. Preheat oven to 350 degrees. Bake for 30 minutes. Yield: 3 loaves.

Helen Fisk, Delta Kappa Psi
Escondido, California

CRUSTY FRENCH BREAD

4 envelopes dry yeast
11/2 tablespoons sugar
1 cup lukewarm water
1/4 cup sugar
1/4 cup shortening
4 teaspoons salt
4 cups boiling water
12 cups (about) all-
  purpose flour
1 egg
1 tablespoon water

Combine yeast and 11/2 tablespoons sugar in lukewarm water in bowl. Let stand until foamy. Blend 1/4 cup sugar, shortening, salt and boiling water in large bowl. Cool to lukewarm. Beat in yeast mixture and 4 cups flour. Stir in enough remaining flour to make a medium dough. Knead on floured surface until elastic. Place in greased bowl, turning to coat surface. Let rise, covered, for 10 to 15 minutes. Punch dough down. Repeat 4 times. Divide into 6 portions; let rest for 10 minutes. Shape into 6 long loaves. Place on greased baking sheets. Cut 3 or 4 diagonal slashes in top. Brush with mixture of egg and 1 tablespoon water. Preheat oven to 400 degrees. Bake for 25 minutes or until golden brown. Cool on wire racks. Yield: 6 loaves.

Sandra Moldenhauer, Preceptor Mu
Williston, North Dakota

GARLIC-BACON-CHEESE BREAD

1/2 cup sugar
1 teaspoon salt
2 envelopes dry yeast
2 cups water
1/2 cup butter or
  margarine
1 egg
2 tablespoons garlic
  powder
2 tablespoons minced
  onion
6 cups (about) all-
  purpose flour
2 cups grated Cheddar
  cheese
1 pound bacon, crisp-
  fried, crumbled
1 egg
3 tablespoons water

Combine sugar, salt and yeast in large bowl. Microwave 2 cups water and butter in microwave-safe bowl until lukewarm. Pour over yeast mixture; mix until blended. Beat in 1 egg; mix well. Stir in garlic powder and onion. Let stand for 15 minutes. Add 3 cups flour, cheese and bacon; mix well. Add enough remaining flour 1 cup at a time to make an easily handled dough. Knead on floured surface for 15 minutes or until smooth. Let rise, covered, in warm place for 30 minutes. Punch dough down. Shape into 2 loaves. Place on greased baking sheets. Let rise until doubled in bulk. Brush with mixture of 1 egg and 3 tablespoons water. Preheat oven to 400 degrees. Bake for 15 to 20 minutes or until golden brown. Yield: 2 loaves.

Jill Hanson, Nu
Montrose, Colorado

GOOD HOMEMADE BREAD

This bread recipe was passed down from my mother, who was born in 1875. My grandfather taught her how to bake bread.

1 medium potato,
  cooked, mashed
3 cups (about) milk,
  scalded
1/4 cup shortening
2 teaspoons salt
3 tablespoons sugar
11/2 envelopes dry yeast
1/3 cup lukewarm water
91/2 cups (about) sifted
  all-purpose flour

Combine mashed potato with enough scalded milk in medium bowl to measure 3 cups. Combine potato mixture with shortening, salt and sugar in medium bowl. Cool to lukewarm. Dissolve yeast in lukewarm water. Add to potato mixture; mix well. Add enough flour to make an easily handled dough. Knead on floured surface until smooth and elastic. Place in greased bowl, turning to cover surface. Let rise, covered, in warm place until doubled in bulk. Punch dough down. Let rise, covered, in warm place for 45 minutes. Knead on floured surface until smooth and elastic. Shape into 3 loaves. Place on greased baking sheets; brush with additional melted shortening. Let rise until doubled in bulk. Preheat oven to 375 degrees. Bake for 1 hour. Invert onto wire rack to cool completely. Yield: 3 loaves.

Mabel E. Muir, Preceptor Beta Kappa
Bowling Green, Ohio

Kathy Suker, Preceptor Omega, Sleepy Eye, Minnesota, makes 2 loaves of delicious Peasant Bread of 2 envelopes yeast dissolved in 21/4 cups warm water, 6 to 61/2 cups flour, 1/4 cup molasses, 1 tablespoon salt, 2 tablespoons oil, 1 tablespoon Kitchen Bouquet, 1 cup crumbled shredded wheat cereal and 2 cups All-Bran cereal. Rise, shape loaves, rise and brush with mixture of Kitchen Bouquet and water. Bake in preheated 400-degree oven for 30 minutes.

ITALIAN MOZZARELLA CHEESE BREAD RING

I have made this recipe for 10 years. It is always a hit!

1 cup shredded mozzarella cheese	1/4 cup sugar
1/2 teaspoon Italian seasoning	1 1/2 teaspoons salt
1/4 teaspoon garlic powder	2 envelopes dry yeast
1/4 cup butter or margarine, softened	1 cup water
2 1/2 cups all-purpose flour	1 cup milk
	1/2 cup butter or margarine
	2 eggs
	2 to 3 cups all-purpose flour

Combine cheese, Italian seasoning, garlic powder and 1/4 cup butter in medium bowl; mix well. Combine 2 1/2 cups flour, sugar, salt and yeast in mixer bowl; mix well. Heat water, milk and 1/2 cup butter in saucepan until blended. Stir into flour mixture. Add eggs; beat at low speed just until moistened. Beat at medium speed for 3 minutes. Stir in enough remaining flour to make stiff dough. Spread half of batter in greased bundt pan. Spoon cheese mixture over batter to within 1/2 inch of side of pan. Spread remaining batter over cheese layer. Let rise, covered, until doubled in bulk. Preheat oven to 350 degrees. Bake for 30 to 40 minutes or until golden brown. Invert onto wire rack to cool. Yield: 16 servings.

Tammy Nicks, Xi Beta Kappa
Salmon, Idaho

KUCHEN

I have fond memories of my grandmother teaching me to make chocolate chip cookies and kuchen.

2 envelopes dry yeast	2 eggs, slightly beaten
1 teaspoon sugar	2 teaspoons salt
1/4 cup lukewarm water	4 cups (about) all-purpose flour
1 cup milk, scalded	Melted butter or margarine
1 cup lukewarm water	Sugar
3 cups all-purpose flour	Cinnamon
1 cup sugar	
1/2 cup melted shortening	

Dissolve yeast and 1 teaspoon sugar in 1/4 cup lukewarm water. Combine yeast mixture, scalded milk, 1 cup lukewarm water and 3 cups flour in large bowl; mix until smooth. Let sponge rise in warm place until doubled in bulk. Stir down and add next 4 ingredients. Stir in enough flour to make medium dough. Let stand for 10 minutes. Knead in remaining flour until smooth and elastic. Let rise, covered, in warm place until doubled in bulk. Punch dough down. Divide into 4 portions. Pat each portion into 4 greased 8-inch baking pans. Let rise in warm place

until doubled in bulk. Brush with melted butter. Sprinkle with sugar and cinnamon. Preheat oven to 375 degrees. Bake for 20 minutes. Yield: 20 servings.

Darlene R. Rohlfsen, Xi Eta
Omaha, Nebraska

OATMEAL BREAD

1 envelope dry yeast	2 tablespoons melted shortening
1/2 cup lukewarm water	1 tablespoon salt
2 cups milk, scalded	5 to 6 cups all-purpose flour
2 cups oats	
1/2 cup packed light brown sugar	

Dissolve yeast in lukewarm water. Combine scalded milk, oats, brown sugar, shortening and salt in large bowl. Cool to lukewarm. Stir in yeast. Add half the flour; mix well. Add enough remaining flour to make an easily handled dough. Place on lightly floured surface. Let rise, covered, for 10 minutes. Knead until smooth and elastic. Place in greased bowl, turning to coat surface. Let rise, covered, until doubled in bulk. Punch dough down. Divide into 4 portions. Shape each into loaf. Place in 4 greased 5-by-9-inch loaf pans. Let rise, covered, until doubled in bulk. Preheat oven to 400 degrees. Bake for 30 to 40 minutes or until loaves test done. Yield: 4 loaves.

Shannon Cline, Chi Alpha
Portageville, Missouri

HONEY-OATMEAL BREAD

3 cups quick-cooking oats	1/3 cup honey
1 tablespoon salt	2 envelopes dry yeast
3 cups boiling water	1/2 cup lukewarm water
1/3 cup vegetable oil	7 cups all-purpose flour
1/3 cup packed light brown sugar	Melted butter or margarine

Combine oats, salt and boiling water in large bowl; mix well. Stir in oil, brown sugar and honey. Cool for 30 minutes, stirring occasionally. Dissolve yeast in lukewarm water. Add yeast to oat mixture; mix well. Stir in 3 cups flour. Add 2 cups of flour 1 cup at a time; mix well. Knead in remaining 2 cups flour. Place in greased bowl, turning to coat surface. Let rise, covered, in warm place until doubled in bulk. Punch dough down. Divide into 3 portions. Shape each into loaf. Place in 3 greased 5-by-9-inch loaf pans. Let rise, covered, until doubled in bulk. Preheat oven to 350 degrees. Bake for 45 minutes or until loaves test done. Brush hot loaves with melted butter. Remove to wire rack to cool. Yield: 3 loaves.

Valerie Herriges, Preceptor Alpha Epsilon
The Dalles, Oregon

GRANDMA'S WEEKLY POTATO BREAD

1 medium potato, peeled, sliced	2 envelopes dry yeast
4 cups water	1/4 cup lukewarm water
1 cup shortening	Water
2 cups sugar	14 cups all-purpose
1 tablespoon salt	flour

Cook potato in 4 cups water in saucepan until tender. Drain potato, reserving liquid. Mash potato in large bowl with a small amount of reserved liquid. Cool to lukewarm. Stir in shortening, sugar and salt. Dissolve yeast in 1/4 cup lukewarm water. Add to potato mixture. Add enough water to remaining reserved potato liquid to measure 6 cups. Add flour and potato water alternately to potato mixture, mixing well after each addition. Let rise in warm place until doubled in bulk. Punch dough down. Knead on floured surface for 20 minutes. Let rise in warm place until doubled in bulk. Punch dough down. Shape into 5 or 6 loaves. Place on nonstick baking sheets. Let rise until doubled in bulk. Preheat oven to 350 degrees. Bake for 45 minutes. Yield: 5 to 6 loaves.

Iva M. Smith, Laureate Alpha Epsilon
Tucson, Arizona

REUBEN LOAF

This homemade reuben bread is a meal within itself. Served with a fresh tossed green salad and iced tea, it's hard to beat.

3 1/4 cups all-purpose flour	7 ounces thinly sliced corned beef
1 tablespoon sugar	4 ounces thinly sliced Swiss cheese
1 teaspoon salt	1 8-ounce can sauerkraut, drained
1 envelope RapidRise dry yeast	1 egg white, beaten
1 cup hot water	Sesame seed
1 tablespoon margarine	
1/2 cup Thousand Island salad dressing	

Reserve 1 cup flour. Combine remaining flour, sugar, salt and yeast in large bowl. Stir in hot water and margarine. Add enough reserved flour to make a soft dough. Knead on floured surface for 4 to 5 minutes. Place on greased baking sheet. Roll into 10-by-14-inch rectangle. Spread salad dressing down center third of dough. Top with corned beef, cheese, and sauerkraut. Cut 1-inch strips from outer edge to filling. Fold strips alternately across filling to create a braided appearance. Let rise, covered, in warm place for 15 to 20 minutes. Brush with egg white; sprinkle with sesame seed. Preheat oven to 400 degrees. Bake for 25 minutes or until golden brown. Serve warm. Yield: 10 to 12 servings.

Peggy Patton, Kappa Kappa
Meriden, Kansas

SPECIAL OCCASION BREAD

1 envelope dry yeast	1/2 cup milk
3 tablespoons sugar	3 egg whites
1/2 cup lukewarm water	3/4 cup sugar
4 cups all-purpose flour	1 1/2 teaspoons cinnamon
1 cup shortening	Chopped nuts, chopped
1 teaspoon salt	dates and/or raisins
3 egg yolks	

Dissolve yeast and sugar in lukewarm water in large bowl. Combine flour, shortening and salt in medium bowl. Add to yeast mixture, mixing well. Stir in mixture of egg yolks and milk. Place in greased bowl, turning to coat surface. Store in refrigerator. Beat egg whites with 3/4 cup sugar and 1 1/2 teaspoons cinnamon in mixer bowl; set aside. Divide chilled dough into 3 or 4 portions. Roll each into 8-by-18-inch rectangle on lightly floured surface. Brush with egg white mixture; sprinkle with nuts, dates and\or raisins. Roll as for jelly roll, sealing edge and ends. Shape into crescent. Place on greased baking sheet. Let rise until doubled in bulk. Preheat oven to 350 degrees. Bake for 25 minutes. May frost with confectioners' sugar icing. Yield: 12 to 14 servings.

Clara Kunkel, Laureate Phi
Phoenix, Arizona

SWEDISH RYE BREAD

2 envelopes dry yeast	1 cup dark molasses
1/4 teaspoon sugar	11 to 12 cups all-purpose flour
4 cups 105- to 115-degree water	3 cups rye flour
1/4 cup packed dark brown sugar	1 tablespoon salt (optional)
1/4 cup melted shortening	Melted margarine

Sprinkle yeast and sugar over warm water in mixer bowl; stir until dissolved. Beat in brown sugar, shortening, molasses and 2 cups all-purpose flour at low speed until smooth. Let rise, covered, in warm place for 20 minutes or until bubbly. Beat in rye flour, salt and 1 cup all-purpose flour at low speed until blended. Beat at medium speed for 3 minutes. Stir in enough remaining all-purpose flour to make a soft dough. Knead on lightly floured surface until smooth and elastic. Place in greased bowl, turning to cover surface. Let rise, covered, in warm place until doubled in bulk. Punch dough down. Divide into 4 portions. Let rise, covered, for 10 minutes. Shape into loaves. Place in 4 greased 5-by-9-inch loaf pans. Let rise, covered, until doubled in bulk. Preheat oven to 375 degrees. Bake for 35 minutes or until loaves are golden brown. Remove from pans. Brush with margarine. Cool completely on wire rack. Yield: 4 loaves.

Connie K. Berggren, Preceptor Upsilon
Red Oak, Iowa

HONEY WHOLE WHEAT BREAD

A dear friend gave me this recipe 12 years ago. It makes a month's supply for my family, and is great for fundraisers!

1/2 cup lukewarm water	2 tablespoons salt
1 tablespoon honey	1/2 cup sugar
3 envelopes dry yeast	6 to 7 cups whole wheat
41/2 cups warm water	flour
2/3 cup vegetable oil	8 cups all-purpose flour
2/3 cup honey	

Combine 1/2 cup lukewarm water and 1 tablespoon honey in small bowl. Add yeast, stirring until dissolved. Combine warm water, oil, 2/3 cup honey, salt and sugar in large bowl; mix until blended. Add whole wheat flour 1 cup at a time, mixing well after each addition. Stir in all-purpose flour; mix well. Knead on floured surface until smooth and elastic. Place in greased bowl, turning to coat surface. Let rise, covered with damp cloth, in warm place until doubled in bulk. Punch dough down. Let rise, covered, until doubled in bulk. Divide into 5 portions. Shape into loaves. Place in 5 greased 5-by-9-inch loaf pans. Spray tops with nonstick cooking spray. Let rise, covered, until doubled in bulk. Preheat oven to 350 degrees. Bake for 20 minutes. Reduce oven temperature to 325 degrees. Bake for 20 minutes longer. Invert onto wire rack. Cover with dry cloth. Cool completely before slicing. Yield: 5 loaves.

Hope Franz, Preceptor Zeta
Boise, Idaho

WHOLE WHEAT BRAN BREAD

This is a great recipe for beginners. A scrumptious, hearty, healthy homemade bread.

1/4 cup honey	3/4 cup vegetable oil
1/4 cup (about) molasses	1 tablespoon salt
3 cups very warm water	4 cups wheat bran cereal
4 envelopes RapidRise	4 cups whole wheat
yeast	flour
1 cup skim milk powder	4 to 6 cups all-purpose
4 eggs, beaten	flour

Combine honey, molasses and warm water in large bowl, stirring until blended. Add yeast; mix well. Let stand for 2 minutes. Stir in milk powder. Add eggs, oil, salt, cereal and whole wheat flour; mix well. Add enough all-purpose flour to make an easily handled dough. Knead on floured surface for 10 minutes or until smooth and elastic. Place in greased bowl, turning to coat surface. Let rise, covered with damp cloth, in warm place until doubled in bulk. Punch dough down. Divide into 4 portions. Roll each portion into rectangle on lightly floured surface; fold into thirds. Shape into loaves; tuck ends under. Place in four 5-by-9-inch loaf pans sprayed with nonstick cooking spray. Punch 3 holes in each loaf with sharp knife.

Let rise, covered, in warm place until doubled in bulk. Preheat oven to 375 degrees. Bake for 30 to 40 minutes or until golden brown. Let stand for 5 minutes in pan. Invert onto wire rack to cool completely. Yield: 4 loaves.

Kathy Weber, Lambda
Yorkton, Saskatchewan, Canada

GRANDMA'S BUTTERHORNS

1 cup milk, scalded	3 eggs, beaten
1/2 cup butter or	41/2 cups all-purpose
margarine	flour
1/2 cup sugar	Melted butter or
1 teaspoon salt	margarine
1 envelope dry yeast	

Combine scalded milk, 1/2 cup butter, sugar and salt in large bowl; cool to lukewarm. Add yeast; mix well. Stir in eggs. Add flour; mix until soft dough forms. Knead lightly on floured surface. Place in greased bowl, turning to coat surface. Let rise, covered, until doubled in bulk. Divide into 3 portions. Roll into 9-inch circle on lightly floured surface. Brush with melted butter. Cut into 12 to 16 wedges. Roll from wide end to narrow end. Place rolls with point down on greased baking sheets. Preheat oven to 375 degrees. Bake for 10 to 15 minutes or until light brown. Yield: 3 to 4 dozen.

Joyce A. Scharf, Rho Chi
Highland, Illinois
*Jeanne Byquist, Xi Eta Delta
Salina, Kansas

BUTTERHORNS WITH LOVE

Many warm and special memories are associated with this recipe. It has been in the family for many years. Instead of "giving" me the recipe, my husband's Aunt Betty chose to "lovingly" show me how to make this delightful treat.

1 envelope dry yeast	3 egg yolks, beaten
1/2 teaspoon sugar	1 cup lukewarm milk
1/4 cup lukewarm water	1/4 cup butter or
4 cups all-purpose flour	margarine, softened
3 tablespoons (scant)	1/2 cup packed light
sugar	brown sugar
1 teaspoon salt	1/2 teaspoon vanilla
1 cup butter or	extract
margarine	1/2 cup chopped pecans

Dissolve yeast and 1/2 teaspoon sugar in lukewarm water in small bowl. Let rise. Sift flour, 3 tablespoons sugar and salt in large bowl. Cut in 1 cup butter until crumbly. Combine egg yolks and warm milk in medium bowl; mix well. Stir in yeast mixture. Add to flour mixture; mix well. Chill, covered, for 3 hours. Divide into 4 portions. Roll each portion into circle on lightly floured surface. Cut into 8 wedges. Spread with mixture of 1/4 cup butter, brown sugar, vanilla and pecans. Roll up from wide end to narrow end. Shape into crescents on nonstick baking sheets. Let rise, covered, until doubled in bulk. Preheat oven to 375 degrees. Bake for 10 to 12 minutes or until light brown. Remove to wire rack to cool. May frost with butter icing. Yield: 32 servings.

Arlene K. Brauns, Preceptor Beta
Clinton, Wisconsin

SUPERB GOLDEN CRESCENT ROLLS

These are a favorite of my 3 children.

1/2 cup sugar	2 envelopes dry yeast
1/2 cup shortening	4 cups sifted all-
1 teaspoon salt	purpose flour
2 eggs	Melted margarine
3/4 cup lukewarm milk	

Beat sugar, shortening, salt and eggs in mixer bowl until smooth. Add lukewarm milk; mix well. Stir in yeast until dissolved. Add flour 1 cup at a time, mixing well after each addition. Scrape dough from side of bowl. Let rise, covered with damp cloth, until doubled in bulk. Divide dough into 2 portions. Roll each into 1/4-inch thick circle on floured surface. Cut into 16 wedges. Roll from wide end to narrow end. Shape into crescents on lightly greased baking sheets. Let rise, covered with damp cloth, for 1 hour or until impression remains when lightly touched. Preheat oven to 400 degrees. Bake for 10 to 15 minutes or until golden brown. Brush with melted margarine. Yield: 32 servings.

Dolores Curry, Delta Lambda
Graham, Texas

CRESCENT DINNER ROLLS

2 envelopes dry yeast	1/2 cup margarine,
1/4 cup lukewarm water	softened
2 cups lukewarm milk	2 eggs
2 teaspoons salt	6 to 7 cups all-purpose
1/4 cup sugar	flour

Dissolve yeast in lukewarm water in small bowl. Pour lukewarm milk over salt and sugar in mixer bowl; mix well. Beat in margarine until blended. Add eggs and yeast; mix well. Add 1 cup flour, beating for 5 minutes. Add remaining flour; mix well. Place in greased bowl, turning to coat surface. Chill, covered with damp cloth, for 1 hour. Punch dough down. Let rise, covered, for 1 to 2 hours. Divide into 5 portions. Roll into circle on lightly floured surface. Cut into 8 wedges. Roll from wide end to narrow end. Shape into crescents on nonstick baking sheets. Let rise until doubled in bulk. Preheat oven to 375 degrees. Bake for 20 to 25 minutes or until light brown. Yield: 40 servings.

Mary Ann Cavalier, Xi Kappa Beta
Follansbee, West Virginia

GRANDMA'S CRESCENT POTATO ROLLS

1/2 cup mashed potatoes	1 teaspoon salt
1/2 cup sugar	1 teaspoon baking
1/2 cup butter or	powder
margarine, softened	1/2 teaspoon baking soda
2 cups milk, scalded	3 to 4 cups all-purpose
1 envelope dry yeast	flour
2 eggs, beaten	Melted butter or
2 cups all-purpose flour	margarine

Combine mashed potatoes, sugar and butter in mixer bowl; mix well. Stir in scalded milk. Cool to lukewarm. Add yeast, eggs, 2 cups flour, salt, baking powder and baking soda, beating until mixed. Stir in enough remaining flour to make a medium soft dough. Knead on floured surface for 2 minutes. Place in greased bowl, turning to coat surface. Chill, covered, overnight. Divide dough into 4 portions. Roll into 1/4-inch thick circle on lightly floured surface. Cut into 12 wedges. Brush with melted butter. Roll from wide end to narrow end. Shape into crescents on nonstick baking sheets. Let rise, covered, for 2 hours. Preheat oven to 400 degrees. Bake until golden brown. Yield: 48 servings.

Dawn M. Starr, Xi Delta Chi
Tulsa, Oklahoma

ORANGE-BUTTER CRESCENTS

1 envelope dry yeast	Melted butter or
1 teaspoon sugar	margarine
1/4 cup lukewarm	3/4 cup sugar
water	3/4 cup coconut
6 tablespoons melted	2 tablespoons orange
margarine	rind
1/2 cup sour cream	3/4 cup sugar
1 teaspoon salt	1/2 cup sour cream
2 eggs	2 tablespoons orange
1/4 cup sugar	juice
2 3/4 to 3 1/4 cups all-	1/4 cup melted butter or
purpose flour	margarine

Dissolve yeast and sugar in lukewarm water in small bowl. Let stand for 10 minutes. Mix 6 tablespoons melted margarine, 1/2 cup sour cream, salt, eggs and 1/4 cup sugar in large bowl. Stir in yeast mixture. Stir in enough flour to make a stiff dough. Knead lightly on floured surface. Let rise, covered, for 2 hours. Divide into 2 portions. Roll into 12-inch circle on floured surface. Brush with melted butter. Spread with mixture of 3/4 cup sugar, coconut and orange rind. Cut into 12 wedges. Roll from wide end. Place close together in greased 9-by-13-inch baking pan. Let rise until doubled in bulk. Preheat oven to 350 degrees. Bake for 30 minutes. Glaze with mixture of 3/4 cup sugar, 1/2 cup sour cream, orange juice and 1/4 cup melted butter. Yield: 2 dozen.

Janet Lawrance, Lambda
Yorkton, Saskatchewan, Canada

ONE-HOUR ITALIAN DINNER ROLLS

Delicious as a cold snack.

1¹/2 cups all-purpose flour	1 egg
2 tablespoons sugar	¹/2 cup grated Parmesan cheese
2 envelopes dry yeast	2 to 4 cups all-purpose flour
2 teaspoons garlic salt	
1 teaspoon Italian seasoning	2 tablespoons melted margarine
1 cup milk	¹/4 cup grated Parmesan cheese
¹/2 cup warm water	
2 tablespoons margarine	

Combine 1¹/2 cups flour, sugar, yeast, garlic salt and Italian seasoning in mixer bowl; mix well. Heat milk, warm water and 2 tablespoons margarine to 120 to 130 degrees in saucepan. Add to flour mixture; mix well. Add egg, mixing at low speed just until moistened. Beat at medium speed for 3 minutes. Stir in ¹/2 cup Parmesan cheese and enough remaining flour to make a firm dough. Knead on floured surface until smooth and elastic. Place in greased bowl, turning to coat surface. Let rise, covered, in warm oven for 15 minutes. Punch dough down. Shape into 16 rolls. Dip each top into mixture of 2 tablespoons melted margarine and ¹/4 cup Parmesan cheese. Place in greased 9-by-13-inch baking pan or two 9-inch baking pans. Let rise in warm oven for 10 minutes. Preheat oven to 375 degrees. Bake for 20 to 25 minutes or until golden brown. Remove to wire rack to cool completely. Yield: 16 servings.

Eddie G. Nichols, Preceptor Phi
Great Bend, Kansas

REFRIGERATOR ROLLS

1 cake of yeast	7 cups sifted all-purpose flour
¹/4 cup sugar	
2 cups lukewarm milk	3 tablespoons melted shortening
¹/2 teaspoon salt	
1 egg, beaten	

Crumble yeast cake in large mixer bowl. Add sugar, lukewarm milk and salt; mix well. Add egg; mix well. Add 3¹/2 cups flour, beating until mixed. Add shortening and remaining flour; mix well. Let rise until doubled in bulk. Punch dough down. Knead on floured surface. Store, covered, in refrigerator. Shape desired amount of dough into rolls as needed. Place on nonstick baking sheets. Let rise for 30 to 60 minutes, or until doubled in bulk. Preheat oven to 400 degrees. Bake for 20 to 25 minutes or until golden brown. Yield: 4 to 5 dozen.

Jimmie McGhee, Psi Master
Victoria, Texas

OLD COUNTRY SAFFRON BUNS

My great-grandmother made these buns on special holidays. They are still very special because Spanish Saffron is hard to find and very expensive.

2 cups milk, scalded	²/3 cup sugar
¹/16 ounce Pure Spanish Saffron	2 eggs, beaten
	3 cups all-purpose flour
¹/4 cup hot water	¹/2 teaspoon salt
3 envelopes dry yeast	1 cup Sultanas or golden raisins
2 tablespoons sugar	
3 cups all-purpose flour	
¹/2 cup butter or margarine, softened	

Let scalded milk stand until cooled to lukewarm. Steep Spanish Saffron in hot water for 20 minutes; set aside. Combine scalded milk, yeast and 2 tablespoons sugar in large bowl, mixing until dissolved. Add 3 cups flour; mixing well to make sponge. Let rise, covered, in warm place for 1 hour or until light. Cream butter and ²/3 cup sugar in mixer bowl until light and fluffy. Add eggs and Spanish Saffron infusion; mix well. Stir in remaining 3 cups flour and salt. Fold in Sultanas. Shape into buns. Place on nonstick baking sheets. Let rise until doubled in bulk. Preheat oven to 350 degrees. Bake for 20 minutes. Yield: 3 dozen.

Margie E. Miller
Quincy, California

TOMATO-CHEESE ROLLS

1 envelope dry yeast	2¹/4 cups all-purpose flour
1 tablespoon sugar	
³/4 cup lukewarm tomato juice	2 tablespoons melted margarine
3 tablespoons melted margarine	³/4 cup shredded sharp cheese
1 teaspoon salt	1 tablespoon celery seed

Dissolve yeast and sugar in lukewarm tomato juice in large bowl. Stir in 3 tablespoons margarine and salt. Add half the flour; mix until blended. Add remaining flour; mix well. Place in greased bowl; brush with 2 tablespoons melted margarine. Let rise, covered, until doubled in bulk. Knead on lightly floured surface for 3 minutes. Roll into ¹/4-inch thick circle on floured surface. Brush with additional melted margarine; sprinkle with cheese and celery seed. Cut into 16 wedges. Roll each wedge from wide end to narrow end. Place, point side down, on greased baking sheets. Brush with additional melted margarine. Let rise until doubled in bulk. Preheat oven to 350 degrees. Bake for 15 minutes or until golden brown. Yield: 16 servings.

Soundra Christy, Xi Psi Alpha
Childress, Texas

BASIC SWEET DOUGH

2 envelopes dry yeast	2 teaspoons salt
1/2 cup sugar	1/4 cup shortening
2 1/4 cups lukewarm water	2 eggs, beaten
	8 cups all-purpose flour

Dissolve yeast and 2 teaspoons sugar in 1/4 cup lukewarm water. Let stand for 15 minutes. Combine remaining lukewarm water, remaining sugar, salt, shortening, eggs and yeast mixture in medium bowl; mix well. Sift flour into large bowl; make well in center. Pour liquid mixture into well until liquid is absorbed. Mix by hand in circular motion to form smooth ball. Place in large greased bowl, turning to coat surface. Brush with melted shortening. Store, covered with greased waxed paper, for up to 1 week. May shape into rolls, buns, tea rings or loaves. Yield: 2 to 3 dozen rolls.

JELLY BRAID

1/4 recipe Basic Sweet Dough	1 tablespoon milk
1 tablespoon melted butter or margarine	1/4 teaspoon vanilla extract
1/2 cup packed confectioners' sugar	1 teaspoon chopped nuts Jelly or jam

Roll dough into 6-by-12-inch rectangle on greased baking sheet using greased rolling pin. Cut lengthwise into 3 strips to within 2 inches of 1 end. Braid strips, sealing end. Drizzle melted butter in crevices. Let rise, covered, for 2 hours. Preheat oven to 375 degrees. Bake for 20 minutes. Mix confectioners' sugar, milk, vanilla and nuts in small bowl. Drizzle over warm loaf. Garnish with jelly or jam. Yield: 1 loaf.

Eleanor H. Hillman, Preceptor Beta Lambda
Mississauga, Ontario, Canada

CINNAMON ROLLS

This is my mother's recipe.

1 cup butter, margarine or shortening	3/4 cup sugar
2 cups lukewarm milk	6 cups all-purpose flour
2 envelopes dry yeast	1 teaspoon salt
1 tablespoon sugar	Cinnamon
1/2 cup lukewarm water	Light brown sugar
2 eggs, beaten	Butter or margarine

Combine margarine and lukewarm milk in medium bowl; mix well. Stir yeast and 1 tablespoon sugar into lukewarm water in medium bowl. Let stand for 5 minutes. Add eggs, 3/4 cup sugar and yeast mixture to milk mixture; mix well. Stir in flour and salt. Beat with spoon until mixed. Let rise, covered, until doubled in bulk. Roll into 1/2-inch thick rectangle on floured surface. Spread with mixture of cinnamon, brown sugar and butter. Roll as for jelly roll, sealing

edge and ends. Cut into 1-inch slices. Place on greased baking sheets. Let rise until doubled in bulk. Preheat oven to 400 degrees. Bake for 20 to 30 minutes or until light brown. Yield 2 dozen.

Margaret Weese, Xi Delta Tau
Dove Creek, Colorado

DANISH KRINGLE ROLLS

This recipe was created by my great aunt.

1 envelope dry yeast	1 cup milk
1/2 cup lukewarm water	1/2 cup packed light brown sugar
4 cups all-purpose flour	
3 tablespoons sugar	1/2 cup chopped pecans
1 1/2 teaspoons salt	1/4 cup melted butter or margarine
1 cup shortening	
2 eggs, beaten	1 teaspoon cinnamon

Dissolve yeast in lukewarm water. Combine flour, sugar and salt in large bowl; mix well. Cut in shortening until crumbly. Add eggs, milk and yeast; mix well. Chill, covered, overnight. Divide dough into 2 portions. Roll into 1/2-inch thick rectangle on floured surface. Sprinkle with mixture of brown sugar, pecans, butter and cinnamon. Roll as for jelly roll, sealing edge and ends. Cut into 1-inch slices. Flatten each slice; roll in additional sugar. Place 1 inch apart on greased baking sheets. Let rise for 2 hours or until doubled in bulk. Preheat oven to 325 degrees. Bake until light brown. Yield: 24 servings.

Nancy Anderson, Xi Kappa Gamma
Galva, Illinois

GRANDMA WELLS' CINNAMON ROLLS

Easiest way to learn a secret to your husband's heart—ask his mother!

2 envelopes dry yeast	2 teaspoons salt
1/2 cup lukewarm water	4 eggs, beaten
2 cups margarine, softened	2 cups milk, scalded, cooled
1/2 cup sugar	8 cups all-purpose flour
1 tablespoon vanilla extract	Cinnamon and sugar

Dissolve yeast in lukewarm water. Cream margarine, sugar, vanilla and salt in mixer bowl until light and fluffy. Add eggs, cooled milk and yeast along with flour to creamed mixture; mix well. Chill, covered, for several hours to overnight. Divide dough into 2 portions. Roll into rectangle on floured surface. Sprinkle with cinnamon and sugar. Roll as for jelly roll, sealing edge and ends. Cut into 1-inch slices. Flatten and place on nonstick baking sheets. Let rise until doubled in bulk. Preheat oven to 425 degrees. Bake for 10 to 15 minutes or until light brown. Yield: 24 servings.

Susan Wells, Xi Epsilon Mu
Junction City, Kansas

MOM'S FAVORITE CINNAMON ROLLS

These are a family favorite. If there are any leftovers warm them in the oven wrapped in foil.

2 envelopes dry yeast	2¹/₂ teaspoons salt
2¹/₂ cups lukewarm water	¹/₂ cup margarine
³/₄ cup melted margarine, cooled	2 teaspoons light corn syrup
³/₄ cup sugar	²/₃ cup packed light brown sugar
2 eggs	Chopped nuts
8 to 8¹/₂ cups all-purpose flour	Cinnamon and sugar

Dissolve yeast in lukewarm water in small bowl. Combine ³/₄ cup melted margarine, sugar and eggs in large bowl; mix by hand. Stir in yeast. Add mixture of flour and salt gradually; mix well. Let rise until doubled in bulk. Punch dough down. Let rise until doubled in bulk. Combine ¹/₂ cup margarine, corn syrup and brown sugar in medium saucepan; mix well. Bring to a boil, stirring constantly. Remove from heat. Sprinkle chopped nuts into 2 greased 9-by-13-inch baking pans. Pour topping over nuts. Divide dough into 4 portions. Roll into rectangle on floured surface. Sprinkle with cinnamon and sugar. Roll as for jelly roll, sealing edge and ends. Cut into 1-inch slices. Place in prepared pan. Let rise until doubled in bulk. Preheat oven to 350 degrees. Bake until light brown. Yield: 40 servings.

Lois Foell, Alpha Pi
Clare, Michigan

QUICK CINNAMON ROLLS

4 envelopes RapidRise yeast	1 teaspoon salt
2¹/₂ cups lukewarm water	¹/₃ cup melted margarine
¹/₂ cup melted margarine	¹/₂ cup sugar
6 to 7 cups all-purpose flour	¹/₂ cup packed light brown sugar
2 small boxes Golden Egg Custard pudding mix	1 tablespoon cinnamon
	Raisins or chopped nuts

Dissolve yeast in lukewarm water in large bowl. Add ¹/₂ cup melted margarine and next 3 ingredients; mix until smooth and elastic. Divide dough into 3 portions. Roll into 14-inch rectangle. Spread with mixture of ¹/₃ cup melted margarine, sugar, brown sugar and cinnamon. Sprinkle with raisins or chopped nuts. Roll as for jelly roll, sealing edge and ends. Cut into 1-inch slices. Place in greased 9-by-13-inch baking pan. Let rise for 30 minutes. Preheat oven to 350 degrees. Bake for 15 to 20 minutes or until light brown. Yield: 36 to 45 servings.

Rhonda Atkins, Xi Alpha Theta
Berryton, Kansas

SWEET ROLLS

These are wonderful to take as a gift for special occasions. Add raisins, prunes and dried apricots to the filling.

1 envelope dry yeast	2 eggs
¹/₄ cup 110- to 115-degree water	¹/₄ cup orange juice
1 cup milk, scalded	3¹/₄ cups all-purpose flour
¹/₂ cup margarine	³/₄ cup sugar
¹/₃ cup sugar	³/₄ cup chopped walnuts
¹/₂ teaspoon salt	¹/₂ cup margarine, softened
2 cups all-purpose flour	1 teaspoon cinnamon

Dissolve yeast in warm water. Mix milk, ¹/₂ cup margarine, ¹/₃ cup sugar and salt in large bowl. Cool to lukewarm. Stir in 2 cups flour. Add eggs; mix well. Stir in yeast and orange juice. Add remaining flour; mix well. Let stand for 10 minutes. Knead on floured surface for 6 to 8 minutes or until smooth and elastic. Place in greased bowl, turning to coat surface. Let rise until doubled in bulk. Punch dough down. Let rise for 10 minutes. Divide into 3 portions. Roll into ¹/₄-inch thick rectangle on floured surface. Spread with mixture of ³/₄ cup sugar, walnuts, ¹/₂ cup margarine and cinnamon. Roll as for jelly roll, sealing edge and ends. Cut into 1-inch slices. Place in greased muffin cups. Let rise until doubled in bulk. Preheat oven to 400 degrees. Bake for 12 minutes. May glaze with confectioners' sugar icing. Yield: 30 servings.

Laura Jurek, Gamma Zeta
Mobridge, South Dakota

HOMEMADE CHILI BREAD

For extra hot chili bread use jalapeño peppers. Serve hot from the oven.

1 loaf sourdough French bread	¹/₈ teaspoon garlic powder
¹/₃ cup butter or margarine, softened	8 ounces Monterey Jack cheese, shredded
1 4-ounce can green chilies	1 cup mayonnaise

Split French bread into halves lengthwise. Combine butter, green chilies and garlic powder in medium bowl; mix well. Spread over each half. Top with mixture of cheese and mayonnaise. Place on nonstick baking sheets. Broil until bubbly. Cut into strips. Yield: 24 servings.

Suzanne High, Alpha Nu
Mesa, Arizona

Norma Bradley, Xi Eta Nu, Bryan, Texas, makes Hearty Beer Bread using a hot roll mix and package directions, adding 1 cup beer, 1 envelope yeast, ¹/₄ cup margarine, 2 tablespoons sugar, ¹/₂ teaspoon salt and ¹/₂ cup wheat germ.

GARLIC BREAD

2 loaves frozen white
  bread dough, thawed
1/3 cup melted butter or
  margarine, lukewarm
1/4 teaspoon basil

2 tablespoons chopped
  parsley
5 cloves of garlic,
  minced
1 small onion, chopped

Cut dough into 1-inch pieces. Arrange half in greased 10-inch bundt pan. Combine butter and remaining ingredients in medium bowl; mix well. Pour half the butter mixture over the dough. Top with remaining dough and butter mixture. Let rise, covered, for 1½ hours or until doubled in bulk. Preheat oven to 375 degrees. Bake for 30 to 35 minutes or until golden brown. Yield: 20 servings.

June Jones, Psi Zeta
Okeechobee, Florida

PARMESAN BREAD

First tasted at a salad supper at church. Have made for parties and other functions.

2 loaves frozen bread
  dough, thawed
1 cup melted butter or
  margarine
2 teaspoons dillweed

2 teaspoons oregano
2 teaspoons garlic salt
2 teaspoons parsley
  flakes
Grated Parmesan cheese

Slice each loaf into 12 slices. Combine butter and next 4 ingredients in small bowl; mix well. Dip slices in butter mixture; coat with cheese. Stand upright in 2 nonstick bundt pans. Let rise, covered with damp cloth, for 3 to 4 hours. Preheat oven to 350 degrees. Bake for 35 to 40 minutes or until golden brown. Yield: 24 servings.

Lisa Karen Turner, Epsilon Beta
Brookfield, Wisconsin

SAUSAGE BREAD

2 loaves frozen bread
  dough, thawed
1 pound bacon
2 pounds sausage
1 bunch green onions,
  chopped

1 can sliced black olives
4 eggs, beaten
3/4 cup grated Parmesan
  cheese
1 cup sliced mushrooms

Let dough rise using package directions. Cook bacon and sausage in skillet until brown; drain. Add remaining ingredients; mix well. Punch dough down. Roll each loaf as thin as possible on floured surface. Spoon bacon-sausage mixture onto dough. Roll as for jelly roll, sealing edge and ends. Place on nonstick baking sheet. Let rise until doubled in bulk. Preheat oven to 350 degrees. Bake for 25 to 35 minutes or until golden brown. Freezes well. Yield: 24 servings.

Deborah A. Miller, Gamma Pi
Hutchinson, Kansas

APPLE COFFEE CAKE

1 tablespoon margarine
1½ cups chopped apples
1 10-count can
  buttermilk biscuits,
  cut into quarters
1 tablespoon margarine,
  softened
1/3 cup packed light
  brown sugar
1/4 teaspoon cinnamon

1/3 cup light corn syrup
1½ teaspoons whiskey
  (optional)
1 egg
1/2 cup chopped pecans
1/3 cup confectioners'
  sugar
1/4 teaspoon vanilla
  extract
1 to 2 teaspoons milk

Preheat oven to 350 degrees. Grease 8-inch square baking pan with 1 tablespoon margarine. Sprinkle with 1 cup apples. Arrange biscuit pieces point-side up in prepared pan. Top with remaining apples. Combine 1 tablespoon margarine and next 5 ingredients in mixer bowl; beat for 2 to 3 minutes. Fold in pecans. Spoon over biscuits. Bake for 35 to 45 minutes or until brown. Drizzle warm coffee cake with mixture of confectioners' sugar, vanilla and milk. Yield: 6 to 8 servings.

Pam Williams, Epsilon Nu
Corning, Arkansas

CINDY'S BLUEBERRY COFFEE CAKE

1½ cups all-purpose
  flour
2 teaspoons baking
  powder
1/4 teaspoon salt
1/2 cup margarine,
  softened
1/2 cup sugar
1 egg

1/2 cup milk
2 cups blueberries
1/2 cup sugar
1/2 cup all-purpose flour
1/2 teaspoon cinnamon
1/4 teaspoon allspice
1/4 teaspoon cardamom
1/4 cup butter or
  margarine, softened

Preheat oven to 375 degrees. Mix 1½ cups flour, baking powder and salt together. Cream margarine and ½ cup sugar in mixer bowl until light and fluffy. Add egg; mix well. Add flour mixture alternately with milk to creamed mixture, beating well after each addition. Fold in blueberries. Spread in greased and floured 8-inch square baking pan. Combine ½ cup sugar and next 4 ingredients in medium bowl. Cut in butter until crumbly. Sprinkle crumb mixture over batter. Bake for 40 to 45 minutes or until coffee cake tests done. Serve warm. Yield: 6 servings.

Sharon L. Saus, Xi Lambda Lambda
Canton, Ohio

Shari Goode, Gamma Eta, Soda Springs, Idaho, makes Zorro Bread by spreading split French bread with mixture of 3/4 cup mayonnaise, 1/2 cup butter or margarine, 6 minced green onions, 1 minced clove of garlic and a small can each of sliced green and black olives. Broil until bubbly.

CINNAMON COFFEE BREAD

1 cup vegetable oil	*8 cups all-purpose flour*
3 cups sugar	*2 teaspoons salt*
4 eggs	*1/4 cup cinnamon*
4 cups buttermilk	*2 cups sugar*
4 teaspoons baking soda	

Preheat oven to 350 degrees. Combine first 7 ingredients in large bowl; mix well. Mix cinnamon and 2 cups sugar in small bowl. Layer batter and cinnamon-sugar mixture half at a time in 6 foil loaf pans sprayed with nonstick cooking spray. Cut through layers to marbleize. Bake for 1 hour. Yield: 6 loaves.

Marie Barter, Sigma Lambda
Inverness, Florida

ORANGE-CREAM CHEESE COFFEE CAKES

This is my favorite Christmas recipe because it makes 4 coffee cakes to share with my boss and friends.

2 envelopes dry yeast	*8 ounces cream cheese,*
2/3 cup sugar	*softened*
1 cup 105- to 115-degree	*1/4 cup margarine,*
water	*softened*
1 teaspoon salt	*1/4 cup orange*
1/2 cup margarine,	*marmalade*
softened	*1/4 cup sugar*
1/2 cup shortening	*1/2 cup orange juice*
1 cup boiling water	*1 1-pound package*
2 eggs, beaten	*confectioners' sugar*
6 to 7 cups all-purpose	
flour	

Dissolve yeast and 1 tablespoon sugar in warm water. Let stand for 3 minutes. Combine remaining sugar, salt, 1/2 cup margarine and shortening in large mixer bowl; mix well. Add boiling water, mixing until margarine and shortening have melted. Stir in eggs and yeast mixture. Add 3 cups flour. Beat at medium speed until blended. Add enough remaining flour to make a soft dough. Place in greased bowl, turning to coat surface. Let rise, covered, until doubled in bulk. Beat cream cheese and next 3 ingredients in mixer bowl at medium speed. Punch dough down. Divide into 4 portions. Knead 4 to 5 times on lightly floured surface. Roll each into 9-by-12-inch rectangle. Cut lengthwise into 3 strips. Spread filling down center of each strip. Roll to enclose filling, sealing edges. Braid 3 ropes together; seal ends. Place on greased baking sheets. Let rise, covered, until doubled in bulk. Preheat oven to 325 degrees. Bake for 35 to 45 minutes or until loaves sound hollow when tapped. Remove to wire racks to cool. Drizzle with mixture of orange juice and confectioners' sugar. Yield: 4 coffee cakes.

Anita Lockhart, Alpha Upsilon Rho
Breckenridge, Texas

CINNAMON-APPLE TEA RINGS

In 1965 I baked tea rings and gave them as Christmas gifts. Today, 27 years later, my gift has become family tradition to 36 families. I deliver them a day or two before Christmas; however, one is mailed next day air to North Carolina.

3/4 cup milk, scalded	*1 egg, beaten*
1/2 cup sugar	*4 cups all-purpose flour*
2 teaspoons salt	*Melted margarine*
1/2 cup margarine	*1 1/2 cups chopped apples*
2 envelopes dry yeast	*1 cup sugar*
1/2 cup 105- to	*1/2 cup chopped pecans*
115-degree water	*2 teaspoons cinnamon*

Combine milk, 1/2 cup sugar, salt and margarine in medium bowl; mix well. Cool to lukewarm. Sprinkle yeast over warm water in large warm bowl; stir until dissolved. Stir in milk mixture, egg and 2 cups flour; mix well. Stir in remaining flour. Chill, covered, for 2 hours or to 3 days. Divide dough in 2 portions. Roll into 7-by-14-inch rectangle on floured surface. Brush with melted margarine. Spread mixture of apples, 1 cup sugar, pecans and cinnamon over dough. Roll as for jelly roll, sealing edge. Place seam side down on greased baking sheet. Shape into ring; seal ends. Cut 2/3 through ring from outside edge at 1-inch intervals. Turn slices cut side down. Let rise, covered, for 1 hour. Preheat oven to 350 degrees. Bake for 20 to 25 minutes. May frost warm tea ring with confectioners' sugar icing. Yield: 12 servings.

Donna Kay Garver, Gamma Psi
Paris, Illinois

GRANDMA BEYLAND'S COFFEE CAKE

This is great-grandmother's recipe. My grandmother, 92 years young, still bakes this coffee cake.

2 loaves frozen bread	*3/4 cup chopped pecans*
dough, thawed	*1 14-ounce can*
1/2 cup margarine, cut up	*sweetened condensed*
1 1/2 cups packed dark	*milk*
brown sugar	
2 tablespoons (about)	
cinnamon	

Pat dough to cover bottom of 9-by-13-inch glass baking dish sprayed with nonstick cooking spray. Let rise, covered, until doubled in bulk. Punch dough down. Sprinkle with margarine. Sprinkle with mixture of brown sugar, cinnamon and pecans. Let rise, covered, until doubled in bulk. Pour condensed milk over top. Preheat oven to 300 degrees. Bake for 1 hour or until toothpick inserted in center comes out clean. Yield: 15 servings.

Carole A. Terry, Eta
Marion, Ohio

Grand Finales

APPLE PUDDING

This recipe was a favorite of my family in Ontario. After we moved to the States, we found that this dessert is called Apple Crisp.

1/4 cup sugar	1/2 cup packed light
1 tablespoon all-	brown sugar
purpose flour	1/2 cup butter or
1/8 teaspoon salt	margarine, softened
1/2 teaspoon cinnamon	1/4 teaspoon baking soda
4 cups sliced apples	1/4 teaspoon baking
1 cup oats	powder
3/4 cup all-purpose flour	

Preheat oven to 375 degrees. Sift sugar, 1 tablespoon flour, salt and cinnamon together. Combine with apples in bowl; mix well. Spread in greased 9-by-9-inch baking dish or 2-quart casserole. Combine oats, remaining 3/4 cup flour, brown sugar, butter, baking soda and baking powder in bowl; mix well. Sprinkle over apple mixture. Bake for 35 to 40 minutes or until bubbly and heated through. Serve hot or cold with milk. Yield: 4 to 6 servings.

Gay Lehman, Theta Theta
Goshen, Indiana

SOUR CREAM-APPLE SQUARES

2 cups all-purpose flour	1/2 teaspoon salt
2 cups packed light	1 cup sour cream
brown sugar	1 teaspoon vanilla
1/2 cup butter or	extract
margarine, softened	1 egg
1 cup chopped nuts	2 cups finely chopped
1 1/2 teaspoons cinnamon	apples
1 teaspoon baking soda	

Preheat oven to 350 degrees. Combine flour, brown sugar and butter in mixer bowl. Beat at low speed until crumbly. Stir in nuts. Press 2 3/4 cups of mixture into ungreased 9-by-13-inch baking pan. Add cinnamon, baking soda, salt, sour cream, vanilla and egg to remaining mixture; mix well. Stir in apples. Spread over base. Bake for 25 to 30 minutes or until bubbly and heated through. Serve with whipped cream or ice cream. Yield: 12 servings.

Beverly Moreland, Preceptor Gamma Omicron
Geneseo, Illinois

APRICOT DUMPLING SURPRISE

12 fresh apricots	Salt to taste
12 sugar cubes	1/4 cup butter or
8 ounces farmer cheese	margarine
1/4 cup butter or	1/2 cup fine dry bread
margarine, softened	crumbs
1 egg	Superfine sugar
1 cup all-purpose flour	

Remove pits from apricots, leaving fruit whole. Insert sugar cube into each apricot. Beat cheese in mixer bowl. Add 1/4 cup butter and egg; beat well. Blend in flour. Shape into ball. Roll out on floured surface with floured stockinette-covered rolling pin. Shape into 12x16-inch rectangle. Cut into twelve 4-inch squares. Place apricot on each square. Roll up, sealing edges. Shape into small balls. Drop gently into boiling salted water in 6-quart saucepan. Boil for 10 minutes or until dumplings test done, turning occasionally. Remove with slotted spoon. Melt remaining 1/4 cup butter in large skillet. Add bread crumbs. Cook until lightly browned, stirring frequently. Add warm dumplings, turning gently to coat. Remove from skillet. Sprinkle generously with sugar. Serve hot. May be frozen and reheated. Yield: 12 dumplings.

Susan Miller, Preceptor Mu Phi
Auburn, California

BROKEN GLASS TORTE

24 graham wafers, crushed	4¹/2 cups hot water
¹/2 cup butter or margarine, softened	2 envelopes unflavored gelatin
¹/2 cup sugar	¹/4 cup cold water
1 3-ounce package raspberry gelatin	1 cup hot pineapple juice
1 3-ounce package lemon gelatin	2 cups whipping cream, whipped
1 3-ounce package lime gelatin	¹/2 cup sugar
	1 teaspoon vanilla extract

Mix wafer crumbs, butter and ¹/2 cup sugar in bowl. Pat ²/3 of the mixture into 9-by-13-inch serving dish. Dissolve each package of gelatin in 1¹/2 cups hot water. Chill until firm. Cut into cubes or ¹/2-inch strips. Soften unflavored gelatin in cold water. Add pineapple juice, stirring until gelatin is dissolved. Let stand to cool. Combine whipped cream, remaining ¹/2 cup sugar, vanilla and pineapple juice mixture in bowl; mix gently. Fold in gelatin cubes. Spread in prepared dish. Top with remaining wafer crumb mixture. Chill for 6 to 12 hours to overnight. Yield: 12 servings.

Kathy Deane-Freeman, Alpha Chi
Vancouver, British Columbia, Canada

CARAMEL DELIGHT

For any special occasion, my family always asks for this dessert that started out like a big cookie.

1 cup margarine, softened	¹/2 cup chopped pecans
2 cups all-purpose flour	1 12-ounce jar caramel ice cream topping
¹/2 cup packed light brown sugar	¹/2 gallon butter brickle or vanilla ice cream, softened
¹/2 cup oats	

Preheat oven to 350 degrees. Combine margarine, flour and brown sugar in bowl; mix well. Stir in oats and pecans. Spread as flat as possible on large baking sheet. Bake for 20 minutes. Let stand to cool; crumble. Layer half the crumbs, half the ice cream topping, ice cream, remaining crumbs and remaining topping in 9-by-13-inch pan. Freeze until firm. Yield: 16 to 20 servings.

Helen V. Still, Mu Alpha
Smithville, Missouri

CLASSIC LEMON CHARLOTTE

16 to 20 ladyfingers, cut into halves lengthwise	¹/2 cup sugar
	¹/4 teaspoon salt
1 envelope unflavored gelatin	1 teaspoon freshly grated lemon rind
¹/2 cup freshly squeezed lemon juice	4 egg whites
	¹/2 cup sugar
4 egg yolks	1 cup whipping cream, whipped

Trim ¹/2 inch from 1 end of each ladyfinger. Line bottom and side of springform pan with ladyfingers, using trimmings for bottom. Soften gelatin in lemon juice. Combine egg yolks, ¹/2 cup sugar and salt in top of double boiler. Beat well with electric mixer. Beat in gelatin mixture gradually. Cook over simmering water for 4 to 6 minutes or until mixture begins to thicken, stirring constantly. Remove from heat. Stir in lemon rind. Pour into bowl. Place bowl in larger bowl filled with ice. Stir for 5 minutes or until thickened. Beat egg whites in mixer bowl until foamy. Add remaining ¹/2 cup sugar gradually, beating until soft peaks form. Fold egg whites and whipped cream into lemon mixture. Pour into prepared pan. Chill, covered, for 4 hours to overnight. Remove carefully from pan. Garnish with lemon rind curls and fresh mint. Yield: 10 servings.

Lois Kimes, Xi Lambda Mu
Laurie, Missouri

AMARETTO CHEESECAKE

There is never a slice of this cheesecake left!

2 cups vanilla wafer crumbs	2 eggs
2 tablespoons sugar	¹/4 cup Amaretto
¹/2 cup melted butter or margarine	2 cups sour cream
	³/4 cup sugar
32 ounces cream cheese, softened	2 tablespoons Amaretto
	¹/2 cup sliced almonds (optional)
1 cup sugar	

Preheat oven to 350 degrees. Mix wafer crumbs, 2 tablespoons sugar and melted butter in bowl. Press into 10-inch springform pan. Bake for 5 minutes. Beat cream cheese in mixer bowl. Add 1 cup sugar; mix well. Add eggs 1 at a time, beating well after each addition. Stir in ¹/4 cup Amaretto. Pour into prepared pan. Bake for 40 minutes. Beat sour cream in mixer bowl at medium speed for 2 minutes. Add remaining ³/4 cup sugar and 2 tablespoons Amaretto; beat for 1 minute. Pour over cheesecake. Bake for 10 minutes. Cool to room temperature. Chill for 8 hours. Sprinkle almonds around edge. Remove springform. Yield: 10 to 12 servings.

Teresa Murray Brown, Beta Sigma
Clemmons, North Carolina

APPLE BAVARIAN CHEESECAKE

¹/2 cup butter or margarine, softened	1 egg
	¹/2 teaspoon vanilla extract
¹/3 cup sugar	
¹/4 teaspoon vanilla extract	4 cups sliced apples
	¹/2 teaspoon cinnamon
1 cup all-purpose flour	¹/4 cup sugar
¹/4 cup sugar	¹/4 to ¹/2 cup slivered almonds
8 ounces cream cheese, softened	

Preheat oven to 400 degrees. Combine butter, 1/3 cup sugar and 1/4 teaspoon vanilla in bowl; beat well. Add flour; stir until crumbly. Press into 8-by-10-inch baking pan. Beat 1/4 cup sugar, cream cheese, egg and 1/2 teaspoon vanilla in mixer bowl until light and fluffy. Spread over crust. Mix apples, cinnamon and remaining 1/4 cup sugar in bowl. Spoon over cream cheese mixture. Top with almonds. Bake for 20 minutes. Reduce oven temperature to 300 degrees. Bake for 10 minutes. Yield: 8 to 10 servings.

Rita Reid, Preceptor Alpha Zeta
Brantford, Ontario, Canada
*Trese Arends, Xi Beta Upsilon
Belmond, Iowa

CHOCOLATE-ALMOND CHEESECAKE

2 1/2 cups chocolate cookie crumbs	1 cup sour cream
1/2 cup melted butter or margarine	1/2 cup Amaretto
	1/4 cup melted butter or margarine
3/4 cup sugar	1 teaspoon vanilla extract
24 ounces cream cheese, softened	1 cup sour cream
4 eggs	2 tablespoons Amaretto
1 cup melted milk chocolate chips	Sliced toasted almonds

Preheat oven to 350 degrees. Mix cookie crumbs and 1/2 cup melted butter in bowl. Press onto bottom and 2 inches up side of 9-inch springform pan. Chill completely. Beat sugar and cream cheese in mixer bowl until light and fluffy. Add eggs 1 at a time, beating well after each addition. Add melted chocolate, 1 cup sour cream, 1/2 cup Amaretto, 1/4 cup melted butter and vanilla; beat well. Pour into prepared pan. Bake for 1 hour and 5 minutes. Mix remaining 1 cup sour cream and 2 tablespoons Amaretto in bowl. Spread over cheesecake. Bake for 3 minutes longer. Let stand to cool. Garnish with almonds. Chill, covered, until serving time. Yield: 8 servings.

Mary Lou Short, Beta Theta
Oak Hill, West Virginia

NO-BAKE AMARETTO CHEESECAKE

1 cup crushed almonds	1/4 teaspoon almond extract
1 cup finely crushed vanilla wafers	1/3 cup Amaretto
1/3 cup melted butter or margarine	3 egg whites
1 1/2 tablespoons unflavored gelatin	1/4 cup sugar
	2 cups whipping cream, whipped
1/4 cup water	2 tablespoons confectioners' sugar
3 egg yolks	3 tablespoons Amaretto
1 cup sugar	1/4 cup sliced toasted almonds
1 cup warm milk	
16 ounces cream cheese, softened	

Mix first 3 ingredients in bowl. Press into 9 or 10-inch springform pan. Chill thoroughly. Sprinkle gelatin into water in heavy saucepan. Let stand for 5 minutes. Cook over low heat until gelatin is dissolved. Beat egg yolks and 1 cup sugar in mixer bowl until lemon-colored. Add milk gradually; beat well. Stir gelatin into milk mixture. Cook over low heat until thickened, stirring frequently. Let stand for 5 minutes. Beat cream cheese, flavoring and 1/3 cup Amaretto in mixer bowl. Add to cooked mixture; mix well. Pour into mixer bowl set in bowl of ice cubes. Beat well, stirring occasionally. Let stand until thick and syrupy. Beat egg whites in small mixer bowl until soft peaks form. Add remaining 1/4 cup sugar gradually, beating constantly until stiff peaks form. Fold into cream cheese mixture. Fold in 2/3 of the whipped cream. Spoon over crust. Chill for 8 hours. Whip remaining whipped cream, confectioners' sugar and 3 tablespoons Amaretto together in bowl until stiff. Spread over cheesecake. Top with sliced almonds. Yield: 16 servings.

L. Amy Clark, Preceptor Pi
Kindersley, Saskatchewan, Canada

BLACK FOREST CHEESECAKES

18 to 24 vanilla wafers	1/2 teaspoon almond extract
16 ounces cream cheese, softened	1 cup sour cream
1 1/4 cups sugar	1/4 cup sugar
1/3 cup baking cocoa	2 tablespoons baking cocoa
2 tablespoons all-purpose flour	1/2 teaspoon vanilla extract
3 eggs	1 21-ounce can cherry pie filling, chilled
1 cup sour cream	

Preheat oven to 325 degrees. Line muffin cups with 2 1/2-inch foil-laminated baking cups. Place a vanilla wafer in each. Beat cream cheese in mixer bowl until light and fluffy. Add 1 1/4 cups sugar, 1/3 cup baking cocoa and flour; beat well. Add eggs 1 at a time, beating well after each addition. Stir in 1 cup sour cream and almond extract. Fill cups 2/3 full with batter. Bake for 20 minutes or until set. Remove from oven. Let stand for 5 to 10 minutes. Combine remaining 1 cup sour cream, 1/4 cup sugar, 2 tablespoons baking cocoa and 1/2 teaspoon vanilla in bowl; mix well. Spread 1 teaspoonful over each cheesecake. Cool completely in muffin cups. Chill until serving time. Top with pie filling. Yield: 18 to 24 servings.

Gill Barnett, Delta Phi
North Platte, Nebraska

Linda L. Yount, Epsilon Xi, Hickory, North Carolina, layers any kind of cookies dipped into milk alternately with whipped cream for Cookie Delight.

CANDY BAR CHEESECAKE

1¹/₄ cups graham cracker crumbs	3 eggs
3 tablespoons sugar	2 10-ounce English toffee candy bars, finely chopped
6 tablespoons melted margarine	³/₄ cup sour cream
8 ounces cream cheese, softened	³/₄ teaspoon vanilla extract
1¹/₄ cups sugar	¹/₂ cup hot fudge topping
3 tablespoons baking cocoa	¹/₄ cup sour cream

Preheat oven to 325 degrees. Mix graham cracker crumbs, 3 tablespoons sugar and melted margarine in bowl. Press onto bottom and side of 9-inch spring-form pan. Beat cream cheese in mixer bowl until light and fluffy. Add mixture of 1¹/₄ cups sugar and baking cocoa gradually; beat well. Add eggs 1 at a time, beating well after each addition. Stir in candy. Add ³/₄ cup sour cream and vanilla; beat well. Pour into prepared pan. Bake for 1 hour. Turn off oven. Let cheesecake stand in closed oven for 45 minutes. Remove from oven. Cool to room temperature. Chill thoroughly. Remove sides of pan. Combine fudge topping and remaining ¹/₄ cup sour cream in bowl; mix well. Spread over top of cheesecake. Chill until serving time. Yield: 8 servings.

Kathy Whitley, Mu Phi
Ness City, Kansas

COOKIES AND CREAM CHEESECAKE

1¹/₂ cups crushed Oreo cookies	1 cup whipping cream
2 tablespoons unsalted butter or unsalted margarine, softened	2 tablespoons melted butter or margarine
	2 teaspoons vanilla extract
24 ounces cream cheese, softened	1 cup coarsely chopped Oreo cookies
1 cup sugar	Whipped cream
3 eggs	Crushed Oreo cookies

Preheat oven to 325 degrees. Place shallow pan half full of hot water on lower rack. Mix 1¹/₂ cups cookie crumbs and 2 tablespoons butter in bowl. Press onto bottom and up side of 10-inch springform pan. Chill thoroughly. Beat cream cheese and sugar in mixer bowl until light and fluffy. Add eggs 1 at a time, beating well after each addition. Add whipping cream, 2 tablespoons butter and vanilla; beat well. Stir in remaining 1 cup cookie crumbs. Pour into pan. Bake for 50 minutes. Turn off oven. Let stand with oven door open approximately 4 inches for 30 minutes or until center is set. Remove from oven. Cool to room temperature. Chill overnight. Garnish with whipped cream and additional cookie crumbs. Yield: 16 servings.

Sue Kuca, Xi Alpha Eta
Grass Valley, California

GIANT CHOCOLATE BAR CHEESECAKE

My sorority sisters love this rich, special cheesecake and encouraged me to send in the recipe. It is a popular item at our annual Christmas auction.

³/₄ cup graham cracker crumbs	Salt to taste
²/₃ cup chopped walnuts	2 eggs
2 tablespoons sugar	¹/₂ teaspoon vanilla extract
¹/₄ cup melted margarine	1 8-ounce milk chocolate bar, melted
12 ounces cream cheese, softened	¹/₂ cup sour cream
³/₄ cup sugar	2 tablespoons sugar
2 tablespoons baking cocoa	¹/₂ teaspoon vanilla extract

Preheat oven to 325 degrees. Combine graham cracker crumbs, walnuts, 2 tablespoons sugar and melted margarine in bowl; mix well. Press onto bottom and side of 8-inch springform pan. Beat cream cheese in mixer bowl until light and fluffy. Mix ³/₄ cup sugar, baking cocoa and salt in bowl. Add to cream cheese; beat well. Beat in eggs and ¹/₂ teaspoon vanilla. Add melted chocolate; beat just until blended. Pour into prepared pan. Bake for 40 minutes. Turn off oven. Let stand in closed oven for 40 minutes. Chill for 8 hours. Combine sour cream, remaining 2 tablespoons sugar and ¹/₂ teaspoon vanilla in bowl; mix well. Spread over cheesecake. Chill until serving time. Yield: 20 servings.

Nadine Meacham, Xi Zeta Nu
Edwardsville, Illinois

FUDGE TRUFFLE CHEESECAKE

1¹/₂ cups vanilla wafer crumbs	1 14-ounce can sweetened condensed milk
¹/₂ cup confectioners' sugar	2 cups melted semisweet chocolate chips
¹/₃ cup baking cocoa	
¹/₃ cup melted butter or margarine	4 eggs
24 ounces cream cheese, softened	1 teaspoon vanilla extract

Preheat oven to 300 degrees. Combine wafer crumbs, confectioners' sugar, baking cocoa and melted butter in bowl; mix well. Press onto bottom of 9-inch springform pan. Beat cream cheese in mixer bowl until light and fluffy. Add condensed milk gradually; beat well. Add melted chocolate, eggs and vanilla; beat well. Pour over crumb mixture. Bake for 1 hour and 5 minutes or until set. Cool to room temperature. Chill until serving time. Yield: 16 servings.

Tamara Leigh Kuhn, Xi Beta Rho
Eau Claire, Wisconsin
*Teresa Euken, Xi Gamma Theta
Red Oak, Iowa

MOCHA-CHOCOLATE CHEESECAKE

2 cups graham cracker
  crumbs
1/2 cup sugar
1/3 cup plus 1
  tablespoon melted
  butter or margarine
24 ounces cream cheese,
  softened
1 cup sugar
2 tablespoons whipping
  cream
2 eggs
1 cup sour cream
1/8 cup strong coffee
1/4 cup dark rum
1 teaspoon vanilla
  extract
8 ounces melted
  semisweet chocolate
  chips
1/4 cup sour cream

Preheat oven to 350 degrees. Mix graham cracker crumbs, sugar and melted butter in bowl. Press onto bottom and side of 10-inch springform pan. Mix cream cheese, sugar, whipping cream, eggs, 1 cup sour cream, coffee, rum and vanilla in bowl. Stir in melted chocolate. Pour into prepared pan. Bake for 40 minutes. Spread with thin layer of sour cream. Bake for 5 to 15 minutes longer or until set. Let stand for 15 minutes. Chill thoroughly. Yield: 12 servings.

Sheri Wierzbicki, Gamma Eta
Soda Springs, Idaho

NO-BAKE MOCHA-CHOCOLATE CHEESECAKE

1 cup melted semisweet
  chocolate chips
1 tablespoon shortening
1 tablespoon sifted
  confectioners' sugar
8 ounces cream cheese,
  softened
1/3 cup sugar
1 cup sour cream
8 ounces whipped
  topping
2 tablespoons Swiss
  mocha coffee powder
1 tablespoon chocolate
  syrup
1/2 cup crushed
  semisweet chocolate
  chips

Combine melted chocolate, shortening and confectioners' sugar in bowl; mix well. Spread in foil-lined 9-inch pie plate. Chill until firm. Remove foil; return crust to pie plate. Chill thoroughly. Beat cream cheese in mixer bowl until light and fluffy. Add sugar and sour cream; beat well. Reserve 1/4 of sour cream mixture. Add whipped topping to remaining sour cream mixture; mix well. Spread over crust. Chill thoroughly. Add coffee powder and syrup to reserved mixture; mix well. Spread over cheesecake. Swirl with knife. Sprinkle with crushed chocolate. Chill for 2 hours. Yield: 8 servings.

M. Janelle Andrus, Alpha
Springfield, Missouri

Silvia M. Savin, Xi Alpha Beta, Aiken, South Carolina, makes Cheesecake Crust using 12 finely crushed Zwieback slices mixed with 1/4 cup melted butter or margarine and 1/2 cup sugar.

PEACHES AND CREAM CHEESECAKE

This recipe came from my mother-in-law, Alice Koenig, a wonderful cook and a great lady.

3/4 cup all-purpose flour
1 teaspoon baking
  powder
1/2 teaspoon salt
3 tablespoons butter or
  margarine, softened
1 egg
1/2 cup milk
1 4-ounce package
  vanilla pudding mix
1 15- to 20-ounce can
  peaches
8 ounces cream cheese,
  softened
3 tablespoons peach
  juice
1/2 cup sugar
1/2 teaspoon cinnamon
1 tablespoon sugar

Preheat oven to 350 degrees. Combine flour, baking powder, salt, butter, egg, milk and pudding mix in mixer bowl. Beat at medium speed for 2 minutes. Pour into greased 10-inch pie plate. Drain peaches, reserving 3 tablespoons juice. Arrange peaches over batter. Combine cream cheese, reserved peach juice and 1/2 cup sugar in mixer bowl; beat for 3 minutes. Spoon over peaches to within 1/2 inch of edge. Sprinkle with cinnamon and remaining 1 tablespoon sugar. Bake for 30 to 35 minutes or until golden brown. Yield: 10 servings.

Crystal Koenig, Beta Zeta Alpha
Canyon, Texas

FROZEN PEACH DELIGHT CHEESECAKE

1/4 cup sugar
1 1/2 cups graham wafer
  crumbs
1/3 cup melted butter or
  margarine
16 ounces cream cheese,
  softened
3 cups chopped canned
  or fresh peaches
1 cup plus 3
  tablespoons sweetened
  condensed milk
2 tablespoons lemon
  juice
16 ounces whipped
  topping

Mix sugar, graham wafer crumbs and melted butter in bowl. Press into 9-inch springform pan. Beat cream cheese in mixer bowl until light and fluffy. Stir in peaches. Add condensed milk gradually; beat well. Stir in lemon juice. Fold in whipped topping. Pour into prepared pan. Freeze until firm. Let stand 15 minutes before serving. Yield: 12 to 16 servings.

Beverley R. Lane, Alpha Rho
Estevan, Saskatchewan, Canada

Melissa Robinson, Xi Alpha Beta Omega, Jasper, Texas, makes Mallow Cheese Dip by beating 8 ounces cream cheese with a jar of marshmallow creme until creamy. She serves it with fresh strawberries and freshly sliced apples.

PEPPERMINT CHEESECAKE

1¹/2 cups Oreo cookie
   crumbs
¹/4 cup sugar
¹/4 cup butter or
   margarine
8 ounces cream cheese,
   softened
1 14-ounce can
   sweetened condensed
   milk

1 cup crushed
   peppermint candy
¹/2 cup miniature milk
   chocolate chips
2 cups whipping cream,
   whipped
Crushed peppermint
   candy or mint leaves

Press mixture of first 3 ingredients into 9-by-13-inch pan or 9-inch springform pan. Beat cream cheese in mixer bowl until light and fluffy. Add condensed milk; beat well. Stir in candy and chocolate chips. Fold in whipped cream. Pour over prepared layer. Freeze, covered, until firm. Garnish with additional crushed candy or mint leaves. Yield: 16 servings.

Glenda Berry, Gamma Psi
Paris, Illinois

PIÑA COLADA CHEESECAKE

1¹/2 cups graham
   cracker crumbs
¹/2 cup toasted coconut
3 tablespoons sugar
¹/4 cup melted butter or
   margarine
5 eggs
32 ounces cream cheese,
   softened

1 cup sugar
1 cup crushed pineapple,
   drained
1 teaspoon rum extract
1 teaspoon coconut
   extract
¹/4 cup crushed
   pineapple, drained

Preheat oven to 325 degrees. Mix graham cracker crumbs, coconut, 3 tablespoons sugar and melted butter in bowl. Press into 9 or 10-inch springform pan. Bake for 10 minutes. Cream eggs and cream cheese in mixer bowl until light and fluffy. Beat in remaining 1 cup sugar, 1 cup pineapple and flavorings. Pour into prepared pan. Bake for 60 to 70 minutes or until set. Top with remaining ¹/4 cup pineapple. Yield: 16 servings.

Starla M. Atcheson, Beta Nu
Butte, Montana

PRALINE-PECAN CHEESECAKE

We have a friend who is a chef. He introduced this recipe to us and we have served it on many occasions.

1 2-layer package
   butter-recipe yellow
   cake mix
¹/2 cup butter or
   margarine, softened
¹/3 cup sugar
24 ounces cream cheese,
   softened
1¹/2 teaspoons rum
   extract

3 tablespoons all-
   purpose flour
3 eggs, lightly beaten
6 Heath bars, crushed
¹/2 cup firmly packed
   light brown sugar
1 cup chopped pecans
1 cup caramel topping

Preheat oven to 325 degrees. Combine cake mix and butter in mixer bowl. Beat at low speed until crumbly. Reserve 1 cup mixture. Press remaining mixture onto bottom and side of 9-inch springform pan. Cream sugar, cream cheese, flavoring and flour in mixer bowl until light and fluffy. Add eggs 1 at a time, beating well after each addition. Stir in candy. Pour into prepared pan. Combine reserved mixture, brown sugar and pecans in bowl; mix well. Sprinkle evenly over filling. Bake for 1 hour and 10 minutes to 1 hour and 25 minutes or until center is set and topping is golden brown. Pour caramel topping over cheesecake. Bake for 10 minutes longer. Cool for 30 minutes. Loosen from side of pan with knife. Chill for 5 hours or overnight. Yield: 16 to 20 servings.

Cameila Anderson, Xi Delta Lambda
Windsor, Ontario, Canada

ORANGE CHEESECAKE

3 10-ounce cans
   mandarin oranges
1¹/2 cups graham wafer
   crumbs
¹/2 cup melted butter or
   margarine
¹/4 cup firmly packed
   light brown sugar
1 teaspoon cinnamon
4 eggs

16 ounces cream cheese,
   softened
³/4 cup sugar
1 teaspoon vanilla extract
1 cup sour cream
¹/4 cup sugar
Frozen orange juice
   concentrate
¹/4 cup cornstarch
¹/4 cup sugar

Preheat oven to 325 degrees. Drain mandarin oranges, reserving juice. Combine wafer crumbs, melted butter, brown sugar and cinnamon in bowl; mix well. Press into greased 9-by-13-inch baking dish. Cream eggs, cream cheese, ³/4 cup sugar and vanilla in mixer bowl until light and fluffy. Pour into prepared dish. Bake for 25 minutes. Mix sour cream and ¹/4 cup sugar in bowl. Spread over hot cheesecake. Bake for 5 minutes longer. Let stand to cool. Arrange mandarin orange slices over cheesecake. Combine mandarin orange juice and enough juice concentrate to measure 2 cups in saucepan. Add cornstarch and remaining ¹/4 cup sugar. Cook over medium heat for 3 minutes or until thickened, stirring constantly. Pour over cheesecake. Chill until serving time. Yield: 15 servings.

Joan Craig, Preceptor Alpha Zeta
Brantford, Ontario, Canada

Claire M. Evangelista, Westlake, Ohio, makes Two-Crust Cheesecake by lining a 9-by-13-inch pan with a can of refrigerator crescent rolls, spreading with mixture of 16 ounces cream cheese, 1 cup sugar, 1 egg and 1 teaspoon vanilla and topping with another can rolls. Bake in preheated 350- degree oven for 30 to 35 minutes and drizzle with confectioners' sugar glaze.

ORANGE SUPREME CHEESECAKE

At age 60 I began a 2-year culinary arts course at Pennsylvania College of Technology. This cheesecake is one of the many assignments I really liked and enjoyed!

³/4 cup all-purpose flour	*1 cup sugar*
3 tablespoons sugar	*3 eggs*
1 teaspoon finely shredded orange rind	*¹/4 cup orange juice*
	2 tablespoons sugar
6 tablespoons butter or margarine	*1 tablespoon cornstarch*
	1 cup orange juice
1 egg yolk, lightly beaten	*2 tablespoons orange marmalade*
24 ounces cream cheese, softened	*1 tablespoon orange liqueur (optional)*
1 teaspoon finely shredded orange rind	*Orange sections*
	Orange peel
¹/4 teaspoon vanilla extract	

Preheat oven to 400 degrees. Combine flour, 3 tablespoons sugar and 1 teaspoon orange rind in bowl. Cut in butter until crumbly. Stir in egg yolk. Pat ¹/3 of the dough onto bottom of 9-inch springform pan. Bake for 7 minutes or until golden brown. Cool in pan. Reduce oven temperature to 375 degrees. Butter side of pan; attach to bottom. Pat remaining dough 1³/4 inches up side of pan. Beat cream cheese, remaining 1 teaspoon orange rind and vanilla in mixer bowl until light and fluffy. Stir in 1 cup sugar. Add eggs all at once. Beat at low speed just until blended; do not overbeat. Stir in ¹/4 cup orange juice. Pour into prepared pan. Bake for 35 to 45 minutes or until center is set. Cool for 15 minutes. Loosen sides of cheesecake from pan with spatula. Cool for 30 minutes. Remove side of pan. Cool for 2 hours. Combine remaining 2 tablespoons sugar and cornstarch in saucepan. Stir in remaining 1 cup orange juice. Cook until bubbly, stirring constantly. Cook for 2 minutes longer, stirring constantly. Cool slightly. Stir in marmalade and liqueur. Spread over cheesecake. Chill thoroughly. Arrange orange sections over cheesecake. Garnish with twist of orange peel. Yield: 12 to 14 servings.

Mary E. Lyons, Laureate Delta Kappa
Montoursville, Pennsylvania

CHERRIES JUBILEE SAUCE FLAMBÉ

This sauce is delicious served over plain white cake, or over white cake into which you stirred lightly floured pitted cherries before baking.

2 cups canned pitted Bing cherries	*¹/4 teaspoon salt*
	¹/3 cup brandy
2 tablespoons quick-cooking tapioca	*¹/2 cup rum*
	Vanilla ice cream
¹/2 cup sugar	

Drain cherries, reserving juice. Add enough water to juice to measure 1¹/2 cups liquid. Combine juice mixture, cherries, tapioca, sugar and salt in saucepan. Bring to a boil over medium heat, stirring constantly. Remove from heat. Let stand for 15 minutes. Stir in half the brandy. Mix remaining brandy and rum in bowl. Pour over warm sauce. Ignite carefully. Spoon flaming sauce over ice cream. Yield: 4 servings.

June Cavanaugh, Preceptor Alpha Phi
Altus, Oklahoma

CHERRIES JUBILEE

This is a simple, elegant dessert that always impresses guests. It can be made ahead and microwaved before serving.

1 16-ounce can pitted sweet dark cherries	*2 shots of brandy*
	1 shot of Triple Sec
1 shot of brandy	*1 shot of cherry brandy*
1 tablespoon melted butter or margarine	*¹/2 teaspoon cinnamon*
	1 tablespoon confectioners' sugar
2 lemon slices	
2 orange slices	*4 servings vanilla ice cream*
Juice of ¹/2 lime	

Drain cherries, reserving juice. Combine 1 shot of brandy and melted butter in large sauté pan. Hold lighted match over edge of pan; let steam ignite. Add fruit slices. Stir in lime juice and cherry juice. Remove fruit slices. Add remaining brandy, triple sec and cherry brandy. Ignite again. Add cinnamon, confectioners' sugar and cherries. Cook until heated through. Spoon over ice cream. Yield: 4 servings.

Cindy Ammondson, Beta Nu
Butte, Montana

CHOCOLATE FONDUE

For the 1990 Heart in Hand, we used the theme "Gifts from the Heart." We served chocolate fondue, champagne and strawberries in a room filled with over 300 red and white balloons.

1¹/2 cups semisweet chocolate chips	*1 pineapple, cut into chunks*
¹/2 cup whipping cream	*4 mandarin oranges, cut into chunks*
¹/2 cup light corn syrup	
Vanilla extract to taste	*4 kiwifruit, cut into chunks*
1 tablespoon coffee-orange liqueur	
	¹/2 pound cake, cut into chunks
1 pint strawberries	
4 bananas, sliced	

Combine first 3 ingredients in large microwave-safe bowl. Microwave on High for 2¹/2 minutes, stirring twice. Add vanilla and liqueur. Microwave for 5 minutes longer, stirring 3 times. Pour into fondue pot. Serve with fruit and cake. Yield: 12 servings.

Janet Cuslidge, Xi Upsilon Omicron
Altaville, California

BITTER CHOCOLATE PAVÉ WITH MINT

10 ounces semisweet chocolate	4¹/3 cups milk
10 ounces unsweetened chocolate	8 egg yolks
	1 cup sugar
¹/2 cup unsalted butter	7 tablespoons crème de menthe
2 cups whipping cream, whipped	Chocolate shavings
	Confectioners' sugar
1 cup chopped fresh wild mint	Mint leaves

Melt chocolates in double boiler over hot but not boiling water. Stir in butter. Cool to lukewarm. Fold in whipped cream. Pour into lightly greased 4-by-8-inch dish. Chill for 4 to 6 hours or overnight. Combine chopped mint and milk in large saucepan. Bring to a boil over high heat. Beat egg yolks with sugar in bowl until pale and thickened. Add a small amount of boiling milk to egg mixture; add egg mixture to boiling milk, stirring constantly. Return mixture to saucepan. Cook over medium-low heat for 15 minutes or until thickened, stirring constantly; do not boil. Cool, covered, to room temperature. Stir in crème de menthe. Strain through a fine sieve. Unmold pavé onto plate. Cut into 1-inch slices. Place 1 slice in center of each dessert plate. Surround with chocolate shavings. Sprinkle with confectioners' sugar. Spoon cream sauce around pavé. Sprinkle with chopped mint leaves or with whole leaves. Yield: 8 to 16 servings.

Kimberly L. Birch, Eta Nu
Charles City, Iowa

CRÊPES WITH SAUCE

1¹/2 cups milk	16 to 36 ounces ice cream, softened
1 cup all-purpose flour	
2 eggs	Melba Sauce or Chocolate Sauce
2 tablespoons sugar	
1 tablespoon vegetable oil or melted butter or margarine	16 to 18 peach or banana slices
	Whipped cream
¹/8 teaspoon salt	

Combine milk, flour, eggs, sugar, oil and salt in bowl. Beat with wire whisk until completely blended. Place 2 tablespoons batter in lightly greased 6-inch skillet. Lift and tilt skillet to spread batter. Return to heat. Brown on 1 side. Invert pan over paper toweling; allow crêpe to fall out. Repeat to make 16 to 18 crêpes, greasing skillet occasionally. Place crêpes on work surface. Scoop 1 to 2 ounces ice cream onto each crêpe; roll to desired shape. Top with Melba Sauce and peach slice or Chocolate Sauce and diagonally cut banana slice. Garnish with whipped cream. Yield: 16 to 18 servings.

MELBA SAUCE

1 cup frozen raspberries	1 teaspoon cornstarch
1 teaspoon sugar	¹/2 cup currant jelly

Thaw raspberries, reserving juice. Combine all ingredients in saucepan. Cook over low heat until syrup is clear. Strain through sieve; cool. Yield: 2 cups.

CHOCOLATE SAUCE

4 ounces semisweet chocolate	5 teaspoons sugar
	1¹/2 tablespoons butter or margarine
¹/2 cup milk	
2 teaspoons whipping cream	

Melt chocolate in double boiler. Bring milk to a boil in saucepan. Add whipping cream; return to boil. Remove from heat. Stir in sugar, melted chocolate and butter. Boil over low heat for a few seconds. Pour into bowl. Serve warm or cold. Yield: 1¹/2 cups.

Ann Grassie Hall, Preceptor Beta Theta
Garden Grove, California

ALMA'S ICE CREAM

9 eggs, beaten	2 tablespoons vanilla extract
1¹/2 cans evaporated milk	
	Few grains of salt
1¹/2 cups sugar	Homogenized milk

Combine first 5 ingredients in bowl; beat well. Pour into freezer container. Add enough homogenized milk to bring to fill line. Freeze using manufacturer's directions. Yield: 12 to 15 servings.

Sandi Davison, Preceptor Gamma Upsilon
Kansas City, Missouri

BANANA SPLIT ICE CREAM

4 eggs	4 cups milk
2 cups sugar	2 bananas, chopped
¹/4 teaspoon salt	1 6-ounce can crushed pineapple, drained
1¹/2 teaspoons vanilla extract	
	1 cup sliced frozen strawberries, drained
1 4-ounce package vanilla instant pudding mix	¹/2 cup chocolate syrup
	¹/2 to 1 cup chopped nuts
4 cups half and half	

Beat eggs in bowl. Stir in next 4 ingredients. Stir in half and half and milk. Add remaining ingredients; mix well. Pour into freezer container. Freeze using manufacturer's directions. Yield: 12 to 15 servings.

Lynette Stenzel, Mu Phi
Ness City, Kansas

FROSTY CHOCOLATE MALT ICE CREAM

2/3 cup sugar	4¹/2 teaspoons vanilla extract
4 eggs, beaten	
1 cup malt	1 16-ounce can chocolate syrup
3 cups whipping cream	
2 to 4 cups half and half	Milk

Add sugar gradually to beaten eggs in bowl. Stir in malt. Add whipping cream, half and half, vanilla and syrup; mix well. Pour into freezer container. Add enough milk to reach fill line. Freeze using manufacturer's directions. Yield: 24 servings.

Kim Roozeboom, Alpha Kappa
Oskaloosa, Iowa

CURRIED BAKED FRUIT

1 16-ounce can pear halves, drained	12 maraschino cherries
1 16-ounce can cling peaches, drained	2/3 cup blanched slivered almonds
1 16-ounce can pineapple chunks, drained	3/4 cup packed light brown sugar
1 16-ounce can apricot halves, drained	1 tablespoon curry powder
	1/3 cup melted butter or margarine

Preheat oven to 325 degrees. Arrange fruit and almonds in 9-by-13-inch baking dish. Add brown sugar and curry powder to melted butter in bowl; mix well. Pour over fruit mixture. Bake for 1 hour. Cool. Chill overnight. Reheat at 350 degrees before serving. Yield: 10 to 12 servings.

Mary Ann Richard, Xi Alpha Delta
Metairie, Louisiana

SIX-FRUIT SURPRISE

1 16-ounce can sliced peaches, drained	1 16-ounce can pitted dark cherries, drained
1 16-ounce can apricots, drained	1 21-ounce can cherry pie filling
1 16-ounce can pear halves, drained	1 16-ounce package coconut macaroons, crushed
1 16-ounce can pineapple chunks, drained	1/2 cup Amaretto, Triple Sec or other compatible liqueur

Alternate layers of fruit in glass bowl until all fruit is used, finishing with pie filling on top. Sprinkle with macaroon crumbs. Pour liqueur over all. Chill, covered, overnight. Yield: 8 to 10 servings.

Jane K. Hardage, Psi Sigma
Palm Beach Gardens, Florida

HONEY-FUDGE PARFAITS

8 tablespoons baking cocoa	1/2 teaspoon vanilla extract
2/3 cup hot water	1/4 cup bourbon
1 tablespoon butter or margarine	1 quart vanilla ice cream
1/2 cup honey	Whipped cream
1/3 cup light corn syrup	

Combine baking cocoa, water, butter, honey and corn syrup in saucepan. Bring to a boil, stirring occasionally. Remove from heat. Stir in vanilla and bourbon. Alternate layers of ice cream and cocoa mixture in parfait glasses. Place in freezer until serving time. Top with whipped cream. Yield: 6 to 8 servings.

Diana R. Hobbs, Laureate Alpha Rho
St. Petersburg, Florida

GREEK MARMALADE-CUSTARD DESSERT

1 large box baby Zwieback crackers	3 cups milk
1 16-ounce jar orange marmalade	1 tablespoon vanilla extract
3/4 cup sugar	8 ounces whipped topping
1 1/2 cups hot water	1/2 cup chopped toasted almonds
3/4 cup sugar	1 8-ounce jar maraschino cherries
6 tablespoons cornstarch	

Line 9-by-13-inch dish with crackers. Combine marmalade, 3/4 cup sugar and hot water in saucepan. Cook until marmalade is melted and sugar is dissolved. Pour over crackers. Combine remaining 3/4 cup sugar, cornstarch, milk and vanilla in saucepan. Cook over medium heat until thickened. Pour over dessert. Chill until set. Cut into squares. Top each piece with whipped topping. Sprinkle with almonds. Top with cherries. Yield: 12 servings.

KiKi Fhiaras, Xi Epsilon
Gulfport, Mississippi

CALIFORNIA LEMON CRUNCH DESSERT

1 7-ounce package shredded coconut	3/4 teaspoon cinnamon
1 cup butter or margarine, softened	1/2 teaspoon baking soda
1/2 cup firmly packed light brown sugar	8 ounces whipped topping
1 1/2 cups oats	2 cups lemon low-fat yogurt
3/4 cup all-purpose flour	2 teaspoons grated lemon rind
1/2 cup chopped nuts	Lemon twists

Preheat oven to 350 degrees. Arrange coconut in single layer in 9-by-13-inch baking pan. Bake for 18 to 20 minutes or until lightly toasted, stirring after 12 minutes. Cool completely. Beat butter and brown sugar in mixer bowl until creamy. Add oats, flour, nuts, cinnamon and baking soda; beat well. Reserve 1 cup toasted coconut for topping. Stir remaining coconut into oat mixture. Press onto bottom of 9-by-13-inch baking pan. Bake for 18 to 20 minutes or until golden brown. Cool completely. Combine whipped topping, yogurt and lemon rind in bowl; mix well. Spread over crust. Sprinkle with reserved coconut. Chill, covered, until serving time. Garnish with lemon twists. Yield: 12 servings.

June Laughlin, Preceptor Beta Sigma
Paradise, California

MANGO CREAM WITH ALMONDS

1 14-ounce can sweetened condensed milk	2 oranges, peeled, sectioned
2 cups whipping cream	1 4-ounce package flaked almonds
Juice of 1 lemon	
1 30-ounce can mango pulp	

Cream condensed milk and whipping cream in mixer bowl until light and fluffy. Stir in lemon juice. Fold in mango and orange sections. Spoon into individual serving dishes. Top with almonds. May substitute one 7-ounce can pineapple chunks for oranges. Yield: 8 servings.

Beverley Singer, Xi Gamma
Saskatoon, Saskatchewan, Canada

PAVLOVA

This sweet is popular is Australia, where it was originally served to the ballerina Pavlova. I lived in South Australia for almost three years in the mid 1970s. Although whipped topping is acceptable in this recipe, Aussies seldom use it as a substitute for real whipped cream.

2 egg whites	1 teaspoon baking powder
1 cup sugar	
3 tablespoons boiling water	2 cups whipping cream, whipped
1 teaspoon vanilla extract	1 to 2 cups strawberries, pineapple or bananas
1 teaspoon vinegar	

Preheat oven to 300 degrees. Pour egg whites onto sugar in mixer bowl. Let stand for 1 hour. Beat for 2 minutes. Add boiling water, vanilla, vinegar and baking powder. Beat for 7 minutes or until peaks form. Pile onto foil-lined pizza pan. Shape evenly. Bake for 10 minutes. Reduce oven temperature to 250 degrees. Bake for 1 hour and 20 minutes. Cool completely. Spread with whipped cream. Cover with fruit. Chill until serving time. Cut into quarters, then eighths. Remove from pan with spatula to serve. May substitute other fruit in season.
Yield: 8 servings.

Sue Legate, Zeta Beta
Timberon, New Mexico

PEACH BRULÉE

6 fresh peaches, peeled	1 tablespoon confectioners' sugar
1/2 teaspoon cinnamon	
1 cup whipping cream, chilled	1 cup packed dark brown sugar

Preheat broiler. Cut peaches into halves, discarding pits; place cut side down in 9-by-13-inch baking dish. Sprinkle with cinnamon. Whip cream with confectioners' sugar in mixer bowl until soft peaks form.

Spread over peaches. Sprinkle evenly with brown sugar. Broil until topping is brown and bubbly. Cool to room temperature. Chill for 2 hours.
Yield: 12 servings.

Arlene Chynoweth, Preceptor Pi
Kindersley, Saskatchewan, Canada

BOHEMIAN PLUM DUMPLINGS

4 eggs	1 1/4 to 1 1/2 cups whipping cream
1 cup butter or margarine, softened	Italian blue plums, pitted
4 cups all-purpose flour	
Salt to taste	

Combine eggs, butter, flour, salt and cream in bowl; mix to form stiff dough. Roll on floured surface. Cut into squares large enough to enclose plums. Place 1 plum on each square; press dough around plums, enclosing completely. Drop into boiling water in saucepan. Cook for 20 minutes. Serve dumplings with butter and sugar. May freeze prepared dumplings and cook as needed. Yield: about 16 servings.

Jeannette Srozinski, Xi Psi
Jamestown, North Dakota

AMARETTO-BREAD PUDDING

1 loaf French bread, torn into small pieces	2 tablespoons unsalted butter, softened
4 cups half and half	1 cup confectioners' sugar
3 eggs	
1 1/2 cups sugar	1/2 cup unsalted butter or margarine, softened
2 tablespoons almond extract	1 egg, beaten
3/4 cup each golden raisins and sliced almonds	1/4 cup Amaretto

Preheat oven to 325 degrees. Combine bread with half and half in bowl. Let stand, covered, for 1 hour. Beat 3 eggs, sugar and almond extract in bowl. Add to bread mixture; mix well. Fold in raisins and almonds. Spread in 9-by-13-inch baking dish greased with 2 tablespoons butter. Bake for 50 minutes. Combine confectioners' sugar and 1/2 cup butter in double boiler. Cook over simmering water until butter melts, stirring to mix well; remove from heat. Whisk a small amount of hot mixture into 1 egg; whisk egg into hot mixture. Whisk in liqueur. Serve over pudding. Yield: 15 servings.

Marcia Carter, Theta
Vincennes, Indiana

Gwen Boardman, Alpha Psi Kappa, Atascocita, Texas, lines a pan with crushed Oreo cookies, adds partially set lime gelatin mixed with whipped topping, chills until firm and garnishes with grated semisweet chocolate for delicious Emerald Fluff.

BREAD PUDDING TO DIE FOR

People always rave over this dish; just don't put it in the diet section!

1 cup raisins	1 13-ounce can
6 to 7 slices stale bread,	evaporated milk
torn	2 cups milk
1 7-ounce can crushed	3 or 4 eggs, beaten
pineapple, drained	1 teaspoon vanilla
Cinnamon to taste	extract
1/2 cup butter or	Whipped cream or
margarine	A Good Lemon Sauce
2 cups sugar	

Soak raisins in hot water to cover in bowl for several minutes. Layer bread, raisins and pineapple in 9-by-9-inch baking dish. Sprinkle generously with cinnamon. Melt butter in saucepan. Stir in sugar until dissolved. Add evaporated milk and milk. Bring to a boil; cool to room temperature. Add eggs and vanilla; mix well. Spoon over layers; let stand for 30 minutes. Preheat oven to 350 degrees. Bake pudding for 30 minutes. Serve warm or cool with whipped cream or A Good Lemon Sauce. Yield: 12 servings.

A GOOD LEMON SAUCE

1 cup sugar	1/4 cup butter or
2 tablespoons	margarine
cornstarch	3 tablespoons lemon
2 cups boiling water	juice
Salt to taste	Grated rind of 1 lemon

Mix sugar and cornstarch in double boiler. Stir in 2 cups boiling water gradually. Cook over boiling water for 5 minutes or until thickened and clear, stirring constantly; remove from heat. Stir in remaining ingredients. Serve hot. Yield: 2 cups.

Janice W. Craig, Beta Master
Ormond Beach, Florida

TENNESSEE BREAD PUDDING WITH BOURBON SAUCE

2 cups hot water	1 teaspoon vanilla
1 1/2 cups sugar	extract
1 12-ounce can	1/2 teaspoon nutmeg
evaporated milk	9 slices white bread,
4 eggs	crusts trimmed, cubed
1 cup flaked coconut	1 cup light corn syrup
1/2 cup drained crushed	1/2 cup butter or
pineapple	margarine
1/2 cup raisins	1/4 cup bourbon
1/3 cup melted butter or	1/2 teaspoon vanilla
margarine	extract

Mix water and sugar in medium bowl until sugar dissolves. Whisk in evaporated milk and eggs. Stir next 7 ingredients. Let stand for 30 minutes, stirring occasionally. Preheat oven to 350 degrees. Spoon pudding mixture into greased 9-by-13-inch baking pan. Bake for 45 minutes or until knife inserted in center comes out clean. Bring corn syrup to a boil in saucepan; remove from heat. Cool slightly. Whisk in 1/2 cup butter, bourbon and 1/2 teaspoon vanilla. Serve warm over pudding. Yield: 12 servings.

Christine J. Murr, Preceptor Alpha Alpha
Macon, Georgia

BAKED MOCHA-CHOCOLATE PUDDING

1 cup sifted all-purpose	2 tablespoons butter or
flour	margarine
2 teaspoons baking	1 teaspoon vanilla extract
powder	1/4 cup baking cocoa
4 1/2 teaspoons baking	1/2 cup each sugar and
cocoa	packed light brown
3/4 cup sugar	sugar
1/2 teaspoon salt	1 cup cold double-
1/2 cup milk	strength coffee

Preheat oven to 350 degrees. Sift first 5 ingredients into large bowl. Combine butter, milk and vanilla in small bowl; mix well. Add to dry ingredients; mix well. Spoon into greased 8-by-8-inch baking dish. Sprinkle with mixture of 1/4 cup baking cocoa, 1/2 cup sugar and brown sugar. Pour coffee over top. Bake for 40 minutes. Serve with whipped topping. Yield: 6 to 8 servings.

Dayle Nelson, Laureate Beta
Cheyenne, Wyoming

CHOCOLATE-PEAR FLAN

3 1/2 ounces all-purpose	1/2 ounce all-purpose
flour	flour
1 ounce chocolate drink	1/2 cup milk
mix	3 ounces dark
4 ounces butter or	chocolate, melted
margarine, softened	1 15-ounce can pear
2 ounces castor sugar	halves, drained
2 1/2 ounces desiccated	Toasted desiccated
coconut	coconut
1 egg yolk	Whipped cream
1 ounce castor sugar	

Preheat oven to 325 degrees. Sift 3 1/2 ounces flour and chocolate drink mix into medium bowl. Cut in butter. Stir in 2 ounces sugar and 2 1/2 ounces coconut. Press into 8-inch flan pan; prick bottom. Bake for 40 minutes. Cool to room temperature. Beat egg yolk with 1 ounce sugar in medium bowl until thick. Add 1/2 ounce flour and milk; mix well. Spoon into saucepan. Cook until thickened, stirring constantly. Simmer for 3 minutes; remove from heat. Stir in melted chocolate. Cool to room temperature. Spread in prepared flan pan. Arrange pears over chocolate; sprinkle with toasted coconut. Top with whipped cream. Yield: 6 servings.

Moira Williams, Epsilon Omega
Brampton, Ontario, Canada

CAMILLA'S DANISH RUM PUDDING

3 egg yolks
6 tablespoons sugar
Salt to taste
2 tablespoons dark rum
1 tablespoon unflavored
  gelatin
3/4 cup cold water
1 cup whipping cream,
  whipped

2 cups thawed frozen
  sweetened red
  raspberries
1/2 cup water
1 tablespoon cornstarch
1/4 teaspoon vanilla
  extract

Beat egg yolks, sugar and salt in medium bowl. Stir in rum. Soften gelatin in cold water in double boiler. Heat until gelatin dissolves, stirring to mix well. Stir into egg yolk mixture. Chill until partially set. Fold in whipped cream. Spoon into serving bowls. Chill until set. Bring raspberries and water to a boil in saucepan; reduce heat. Simmer, covered, for 5 minutes. Strain, reserving syrup. Blend reserved syrup with cornstarch and vanilla in saucepan. Cook until thickened, stirring constantly. Serve warm or chilled over pudding. Yield: 12 servings.

Dolores Therkilsen, Preceptor Gamma Mu
Troy, Michigan

VANILLA BLANCMANGE

This was my grandmother's favorite dessert.

1 quart milk
6 tablespoons
  cornstarch
1/2 cup milk
2 eggs
3/4 cup sugar

1/2 teaspoon each
  vanilla and orange
  flavoring
Whipped cream
Jelly

Scald 1 quart milk in medium saucepan. Blend cornstarch with 1/2 cup milk in small bowl. Stir into scalded milk. Cook for 15 minutes, stirring constantly. Beat eggs with sugar in small bowl. Stir a small amount of hot mixture into eggs; stir eggs into hot mixture. Cook for several minutes; remove from heat. Stir in flavorings. Spoon into mold. Chill until set. Unmold onto serving plate. Serve with whipped cream and dollop of jelly. Yield: 8 servings.

Beverly Steele, Xi Alpha Alpha
Havana, Illinois

RHUBARB COBBLER

4 cups chopped rhubarb
1 cup sugar
1 3-ounce package
  strawberry gelatin
1 1/2 cups all-purpose
  flour
2 teaspoons baking
  powder
1/2 teaspoon salt

1/2 cup butter or
  margarine, softened
1 cup (scant) sugar
1 egg, beaten
3/4 cup milk
1 teaspoon vanilla
  extract
1 teaspoon cinnamon
1 tablespoon sugar

Preheat oven to 350 degrees. Combine rhubarb, 1 cup sugar and dry gelatin in large bowl; mix well. Spread in 9-by-13-inch baking dish. Sift flour, baking powder and salt together. Cream butter and 1 cup sugar in mixer bowl until light and fluffy. Beat in egg. Add dry ingredients, milk and vanilla; mix until smooth. Spread over rhubarb mixture. Sprinkle with mixture of cinnamon and 1 tablespoon sugar. Bake for 35 to 40 minutes or until golden brown. Yield: 12 servings.

Georgia Schaefer, Beta Nu
Joseph, Oregon

ANGEL FOOD CAKE À L'ORANGE

This is a light and fat-free dessert.

2 seedless oranges
1/2 cup orange juice
1/4 cup sugar

2 teaspoons cornstarch
1 cinnamon stick
6 slices angel food cake

Peel outer rind of 1/2 orange with vegetable peeler. Chop rind into strips to measure 1/4 cup. Pour boiling water over strips in bowl. Peel and thinly slice oranges. Combine orange juice, sugar, cornstarch and cinnamon stick in small saucepan. Drain orange rind; add rind to saucepan. Bring to a boil, stirring constantly. Cook for 1 minute. Add orange slices. Cook just until heated through; discard cinnamon stick. Serve orange sauce over cake. Yield: 6 servings.

Merle Sherwin, Laureate Epsilon
Yorkton, Saskatchewan, Canada

SOPA BORRACHA

It is customary in the Republic of Panama, where I was born and still live, to make this cake for weddings. It was served at my own wedding. It can be decorated with tiny silver balls and tiny candles. Melted marshmallows can also be poured over cake prior to decorating.

1 pound seedless raisins
1 pound pitted prunes
2 cups sherry
2 cups rum
3 pounds sugar

6 cups water
2 large cinnamon sticks
2 lemon or lime slices
1 large sponge cake, cut
  into pieces

Soak raisins and prunes in mixture of sherry and rum in bowl overnight. Bring sugar, water, cinnamon sticks and lemon slices to a boil in saucepan. Cook until syrup is thickened to desired consistency. Drain fruit, reserving wine mixture. Stir fruit into syrup; remove from heat. Cool to room temperature. Stir in reserved wine mixture. Dip cake pieces into syrup; arrange on platter. Spoon fruit over top, discarding cinnamon stick; drizzle with remaining syrup. Chill until serving time. Serve cold. Yield: 24 servings.

Lydia I. Garrido, Xi Alpha
Republic of Panama

SCHAUM TORTE

A co-worker brought this dessert for the boss's birthday on the first day of my first job. It has been my favorite dessert for 30 years now.

1 pint strawberries	1 teaspoon vanilla
Sugar to taste	extract
9 egg whites	2 cups whipped cream
3 cups sugar	
3/4 teaspoon cream of	
tartar	

Preheat oven to 275 degrees. Sweeten strawberries with sugar to taste in bowl; let stand to form juice. Beat egg whites in mixer bowl until stiff peaks form. Add 3 cups sugar, cream of tartar and vanilla gradually, beating constantly. Spoon into buttered 9-by-13-inch baking pan. Bake for 1 hour; turn off oven. Let stand in closed oven for 2 hours or until cool; crust will fall. Push any firm edges into pan. Spread with whipped cream; top with strawberries and juice. Yield: 20 servings.

Ruth E. Hawkins, Xi Eta Gamma
DuQuoin, Illinois

PRONTO SHORTCAKES

1 8-count can	1 cup whipping cream,
refrigerator cinnamon	whipped
rolls with icing	2 16-ounce cans sliced
1 cup sour cream	peaches or fruit
2 tablespoons sugar	cocktail

Preheat oven to 375 degrees. Reserve icing from cinnamon rolls for another use. Bake rolls using package directions. Blend sour cream and sugar in medium bowl. Fold in whipped cream. Split warm cinnamom rolls into halves crosswise with fork. Drain peaches, reserving 2 tablespoons juice. Drizzle reserved juice over rolls. Spoon fruit mixture between halves and over tops of rolls. Yield: 8 servings.

Sister Rita Lewis, Laureate Alpha Gamma
Alamogordo, New Mexico

RUM-CREAM TORTE

2 cups Oreo cookie	1 cup sugar
crumbs	2 cups whipping cream,
1/2 cup melted butter or	whipped
margarine	3 kiwifruit, peeled,
1 tablespoon unflavored	sliced
gelatin	1 11-ounce can
1/4 cup cold water	mandarin oranges,
1/4 cup light rum	drained
6 egg yolks	

Mix cookie crumbs and butter in medium bowl. Press over bottom and side of 9-inch springform pan. Soften gelatin in water in double boiler. Bring to a simmer, stirring to dissolve gelatin completely. Stir in rum. Cool to room temperature. Beat egg yolks in

mixer bowl until thickened. Add sugar gradually, beating constantly. Fold in gelatin mixture and whipped cream gently. Spoon into prepared pan. Chill for several hours or until set. Place on serving plate; remove side of pan. Decorate with ring of kiwifruit and ring of mandarin oranges; finish with kiwifruit in center. May freeze this for unexpected guests and serve frozen. Yield: 10 servings.

Sherrie Bennett, Preceptor Gamma Zeta
North Delta, British Columbia, Canada

STRAWBERRY DESSERT

This very light and delicious dessert recipe was given to me by my wonderful mother-in-law more that 35 years ago.

20 graham crackers,	1 cup confectioners'
crushed	sugar
1/2 cup melted margarine	1 package whipped
1/2 cup sugar	topping mix
8 ounces cream cheese,	1 21-ounce can
softened	strawberry pie filling
2 to 3 tablespoons milk	

Mix graham cracker crumbs, margarine and sugar in medium bowl. Press into 9-by-13-inch dish. Chill for 10 to 15 minutes. Combine cream cheese, milk and confectioners' sugar in mixer bowl; beat until smooth. Spread in prepared dish. Prepare whipped topping using package directions. Spread over cream cheese layer. Top with pie filling. Chill for several hours to overnight. Yield: 12 to 15 servings.

Jeannine Severeid, Preceptor Alpha Phi
Niles, Michigan

SWEET STRAWBERRY SOUP

2 10-ounce packages	1/2 teaspoon grated lime
frozen strawberries	rind
8 ounces nonfat plain	1/2 teaspoon vanilla
yogurt	extract
1 cup peach nectar	Grated lime rind
1 tablespoon lime juice	

Process strawberries in food processor or blender until smooth. Add yogurt, peach nectar, lime juice, 1/2 teaspoon grated lime rind and vanilla; process until smooth. Chill until serving time. Spoon into serving dishes; garnish with additional lime rind. Serve with cookies. Yield: 4 to 6 servings.

Bonnie Marsh, Preceptor Beta Chi
Breckenridge, Texas

Sharon Hoeppner, Kappa Chi, Aurora, Ontario, Canada, makes Easy Chocolate Mousse by processing 1 cup chocolate chips with 5 tablespoons boiling water, 4 egg yolks and 2 teaspoons dark rum in blender, folding into 4 stiffly beaten egg whites, spooning into wine glasses and chilling.

ALMOND ANGEL CAKE MOSAIC ON RASPBERRY SAUCE

1 cup sugar
1/2 cup sifted all-
  purpose flour
4 egg yolks, beaten
1/8 teaspoon salt
2 cups milk
1 tablespoon unflavored
  gelatin
2 tablespoons milk
2 cups whipping cream
1 teaspoon almond
  extract

1 angel food cake
2 cups fresh raspberries
1/4 cup sugar
1 1/2 teaspoons fresh
  lemon juice
1 1/2 cups whipping
  cream
6 tablespoons
  confectioners' sugar
1 teaspoon vanilla
  extract

Mix 1 cup sugar and flour in medium bowl; beat in egg yolks and salt. Scald 2 cups milk in double boiler. Stir a small amount of hot milk into egg yolk mixture; stir egg yolks into hot milk. Cook over simmering water until thickened, stirring constantly. Soften gelatin in 2 tablespoons milk in small bowl. Add to hot custard, stirring to dissolve completely. Chill until partially set. Chill 2 cups whipping cream and beaters. Beat cream until soft peaks form. Fold into custard with almond extract. Chill in refrigerator. Tear or cut cake into bite-sized pieces. Fold into custard. Spoon into buttered 10-inch tube pan. Chill, covered, for 1 to 2 hours or until set. Process raspberries in food processor until smooth. Strain into bowl with 1/4 cup sugar and lemon juice; mix well. Chill in refrigerator. Whip 1 1/2 cups whipping cream with confectioners' sugar and vanilla in mixer bowl until soft peaks form. Wrap tube pan briefly in hot towel; run knife around edge of pan and tube. Unmold onto serving plate. Frost with whipped cream mixture. Spoon raspberry sauce onto serving plates. Slice cake; place in sauce. Yield: 16 servings.

Kathy Garraway, Alpha Nu
Leduc, Alberta, Canada

ANGEL FOOD-LEMON DESSERT

1 2-envelope package
  Sheriff lemon pie
  filling mix
4 egg yolks

4 egg whites
1/2 cup sugar
1 angel food cake, torn

Prepare both envelopes of lemon pie filling mix with 4 egg yolks, using package directions for pie. Beat egg whites with sugar according to package directions for meringue; fold into lemon mixture. Spread 1/3 of the lemon mixture in large dish. Layer cake and remaining lemon mixture 1/2 at a time in dish. Chill overnight. Yield: 16 or more servings.

Linda Smith, Preceptor Alpha Zeta
Brantford, Ontario, Canada

LIGHT AND FANCY TRIFLE

1 angel food cake
Fruit liqueur to taste
3 85-gram packages
  vanilla pudding mix
1 16-ounce can peaches
1 11-ounce can
  mandarin oranges

1 16-ounce can
  pineapple chunks
1/2 16-ounce package
  whole frozen
  strawberries
1 cup whipping cream
Sugar to taste

Cut cake into bite-sized pieces. Toss with liqueur in bowl. Prepare and cook pudding using package directions; cool. Drain fruit well. Layer half the cake and all of the mandarin oranges and pineapple in punch bowl. Spread with half the pudding. Add layers of remaining cake, peaches, strawberries and remaining pudding. Chill, covered, for up to 3 days. Whip cream with a small amount of sugar in mixer bowl until soft peaks form. Spread over trifle. Garnish with fruit as desired. Yield: 10 to 12 servings.

Judith Buck, Preceptor Theta
Winnipeg, Manitoba, Canada

BROWNIE TRIFLE

1 large package fudge
  brownie mix
1/4 cup coffee liqueur
1 4-ounce package
  instant chocolate
  mousse mix

8 1 1/2-ounce toffee
  candy bars, crushed
12 ounces whipped
  topping
Chocolate curls

Prepare and bake brownie mix using package directions for 9-by-13-inch baking pan. Pierce baked layer at 1-inch intervals with long fork. Brush with liqueur; let stand until cool and crumble. Prepare mousse using package directions, omitting cooling step. Layer brownie crumbs, mousse, candy and whipped topping 1/2 at a time in 3-quart trifle dish. Chill for 8 hours. Garnish with chocolate curls. Yield: 16 to 18 servings.

Mary Jo Bent, Epsilon Master
Kansas City, Missouri

DEATH BY CHOCOLATE

1 2-layer package
  chocolate cake mix
1 cup Kahlua
4 small packages
  chocolate mousse mix

2 12-ounce containers
  whipped topping
6 Skor candy bars,
  crushed

Prepare and bake cake using package directions for 9-by-13-inch cake pan. Pierce top of cake with fork. Pour liqueur over cake; let stand until cool and crumble. Prepare mousse using package directions. Layer cake, mousse, whipped topping and candy 1/2 at a time in large glass bowl. Chill until serving time. Yield: 18 servings.

Christine Richardson, Preceptor Pi
Baton Rouge, Louisiana

PUNCH BOWL DESSERT

1 2-layer package yellow cake mix	1 21-ounce can cherry pie filling
1 6-ounce package vanilla instant pudding mix	8 ounces whipped topping
1 16-ounce can crushed pineapple, drained	1 cup chopped nuts
	2 cups coconut

Prepare and bake cake mix using package directions. Cool and tear into bite-sized pieces. Prepare pudding mix using package directions. Layer cake, pudding, pineapple, pie filling, whipped topping, nuts and coconut 1/2 at a time in punch bowl. Chill until serving time. Yield: 10 to 12 servings.

Jenny Reynolds, Iota Phi
Pleasanton, Kansas

LEMON CUSTARD ROYALE

1 angel food cake	6 egg whites
1 envelope unflavored gelatin	3/4 cup sugar
1/4 cup water	1 cup whipping cream
6 egg yolks, beaten	1/2 cup confectioners' sugar
3/4 cup sugar	Cherries and thin lemon slices
3/4 cup lemon juice	
1 1/2 teaspoons grated lemon rind	

Trim brown sides from cake; tear into medium-sized pieces. Soften gelatin in water in double boiler. Add egg yolks, 3/4 cup sugar, lemon juice and lemon rind; mix well. Cook for 10 minutes, stirring to dissolve gelatin. Beat egg whites with 3/4 cup sugar in mixer bowl until stiff peaks form. Fold into custard. Layer cake and custard 1/3 at a time in 10-inch tube pan. Chill overnight. Place in pan of hot water for 2 seconds. Unmold onto serving plate. Beat whipping cream with confectioners' sugar in mixer bowl until soft peaks form. Spread over dessert. Garnish with cherries and lemon slices. Chill until serving time. Yield: 10 or more servings.

Dawn Lorrie Mongeau, Xi Delta Lambda
Windsor, Ontario, Canada

TWINKIES AT ATTENTION

2 packages ladyfingers	2 cups whipping cream, whipped
11 ounces cream cheese, softened	Blueberries, strawberries, raspberries or other favorite fruit
3/4 cup sugar	
2 teaspoons vanilla extract	

Line bottom and side of 9 or 10-inch springform pan with ladyfingers. Beat cream cheese in mixer bowl until light. Add sugar and vanilla, beating until fluffy. Fold in whipped cream. Spoon half the mixture into prepared pan. Add layer of ladyfingers and remaining cream cheese mixture. Top with blueberries. Chill until serving time. Place on serving plate; remove side of pan. Yield: 12 servings.

Marcella Ridenour, Laureate Beta Eta
Lorain, Ohio

CRÈME DE MENTHE ANGEL FOOD CAKE

2 1/2 cups marshmallows	2 cups whipping cream
1/2 cup milk	1 angel food cake
1/4 cup green Crème de Menthe	1 milk chocolate bar, melted

Heat marshmallows with milk in saucepan for 5 minutes or until melted. Cool for 20 to 25 minutes. Stir in Crème de Menthe. Beat whipping cream in mixer bowl until soft peaks form. Fold into marshmallow mixture. Split cake horizontally into 3 layers. Spread marshmallow mixture between layers and over top and side of cake. Drizzle top and down side with chocolate. Chill until serving time. Yield: 16 servings.

Patricia Spence, Laureate
Goderich, Ontario, Canada

APRICOT BRANDY POUND CAKE

1 cup margarine, softened	1/2 cup apricot or peach brandy
3 cups sugar	1 teaspoon orange extract
6 eggs	
3 cups all-purpose flour	1/2 teaspoon each rum and lemon extract
1/4 teaspoon baking soda	
1/2 teaspoon salt	1/4 teaspoon almond extract
1 cup sour cream	

Preheat oven to 325 degrees. Grease and flour bottom of tube pan. Cream margarine and sugar in mixer bowl until light and fluffy. Beat in eggs 1 at a time. Sift flour, baking soda and salt together. Mix sour cream, brandy and flavorings in small bowl. Add dry ingredients to creamed mixture alternately with sour cream mixture, mixing well after each addition. Spoon into prepared tube pan. Bake for 1 hour and 10 minutes or until cake tests done. Cool in pan for 20 minutes. Remove to wire rack to cool completely. Yield: 16 servings.

Corrinne Luna, Preceptor Eta Epsilon
Stanton, Texas

Gina Wood, Preceptor Gamma Rho, Kankakee, Illinois, makes Pop Cake by baking a yellow cake mix using package directions, dissolving strawberry gelatin in 1 cup boiling water and adding 1 cup strawberry pop. She pokes holes in cake, pours gelatin over cake and ices with prepared French vanilla pudding mixed with whipped topping. Chill for 2 to 3 hours.

APRICOT CAKE WITH BUTTERCREAM ICING

This special cake was served on a special occasion when my niece made it for my sister and me when we visited her in Alaska. She had written on it: Welcome to Alaska.

1 2-layer package yellow cake mix	1/2 cup shortening
6 ounces dried apricots	1 teaspoon vanilla extract
1/2 cup drained crushed pineapple	4 cups sifted confectioners' sugar
1/4 to 1/2 cup sugar	1/4 cup milk
1/2 cup margarine, softened	

Prepare and bake cake mix in tube pan using package directions. Cool completely. Bring apricots to a boil in water to cover in saucepan; reduce heat. Simmer for 30 minutes; drain. Process in blender until smooth. Combine with pineapple and sugar in bowl; mix well. Chill in refrigerator. Cream margarine and shortening in mixer bowl until light. Add vanilla. Add confectioners' sugar gradually, beating until fluffy; mixture will appear dry. Beat in milk. Store, covered with damp cloth, in refrigerator until cake is assembled. Cut cake horizontally into 3 layers. Spread apricot mixture between layers. Frost top and side with buttercream icing. Yield: 10 to 12 servings.

*Geraldine Ricker, Laureate Kappa
Lewiston, Maine*

DUTCH ALMOND BUTTER CAKE

1 cup all-purpose flour	2 tablespoons almond extract
1/2 cup butter or margarine, softened	1/2 can almond paste
1/2 cup sugar	1 egg white
1 egg yolk	Chocolate chips, melted

Preheat oven to 350 degrees. Combine flour, butter, sugar, egg yolk and almond extract in large mixer bowl; mix by hand to form ball. Press evenly into 8-inch round or square baking pan. Spread almond paste evenly over top; brush with egg white. Bake for 20 to 30 minutes or until golden brown. Drizzle with chocolate; cool to room temperature. Cut into wedges to serve. Yield: 8 to 16 servings.

*Judith R. H. Barton, Beta Gamma Kappa
Bay City, Texas*

Kathy Cook, Xi Omega Nu, Needville, Texas, makes Easy Apple Cake by mixing a yellow cake mix with 2/3 cup water, 2 tablespoons oil, 1 teaspoon vanilla, 1/2 teaspoon cinnamon and a can of apple pie filling. Top with mixture of 1/2 cup packed brown sugar, 1 cup pecans and 3 tablespoons melted margarine. Pour into 9-by-13-inch cake pan. Bake in preheated 350-degree oven for 40 minutes.

APPLE-RAISIN-SPICE CAKE

This cake is especially good in the fall with cider, hot tea, coffee or milk.

2 cups sugar	1 cup raisins
2 cups all-purpose flour	2 cups chopped apples or unsweetened applesauce
4 eggs	
2 teaspoons baking soda	
1 1/2 cups vegetable oil	1 cup chopped black walnuts
1 teaspoon cinnamon	
1/2 teaspoon each nutmeg and cloves	Whipped cream

Preheat oven to 325 degrees. Combine sugar, flour, eggs, baking soda, oil, cinnamon, nutmeg and cloves in large bowl; mix well. Add raisins, applesauce and black walnuts; mix well. Spoon into 10-by-13-inch cake pan. Bake for 1 hour or until cake tests done. Cool on wire rack. Serve with whipped cream. Yield: 24 servings.

Carrot Cake: Combine first 6 ingredients as above. Add 1 1/2 cups grated carrots, 1 1/2 cups drained crushed pineapple and 1 cup chopped black walnuts and bake as above. Frost with mixture of 1/2 cup softened butter or margarine, 8 ounces softened cream cheese, 1 teaspoon vanilla and enough confectioners' sugar to make of spreading consistency.

*Cathy Clark, Iota Sigma
Hiawatha, Kansas*

JEWISH APPLE CAKE

My mother made this cake when the new crop of apples was ripe. Serve it with whipped topping or ice cream.

4 eggs	2 teaspoons vanilla extract
2 cups sugar	
1 cup vegetable oil	5 large apples, peeled, sliced
2 cups all-purpose flour, sifted	
4 teaspoons baking powder	1 cup finely chopped pecans
4 teaspoons cinnamon	2 tablespoons sugar
1/2 teaspoon salt	1 teaspoon cinnamon

Preheat oven to 350 degrees. Beat eggs in large mixer bowl. Add 2 cups sugar gradually, beating for 5 minutes. Beat in oil, flour, baking powder, 4 teaspoons cinnamon, salt and vanilla; mix well. Fold in apples and pecans. Spoon into greased 9-by-13-inch cake pan; sprinkle with 2 tablespoons sugar and 1 teaspoon cinnamon. Bake for 50 to 60 minutes or until cake tests done. Cool on wire rack. Yield: 15 servings.

*Roberta T. White, Eta Master
Las Cruces, New Mexico*

OLD-FASHIONED APPLE STACK CAKE

We had lots of apples on our farm and made lots of desserts using them. This one represents lots of hard work and hard times and soothed the soul. The apples were dried at home and the entire family took part in the process.

3 cups cooked dried apples	1 cup sugar
2 teaspoons allspice	2 teaspoons baking powder
Cinnamon and nutmeg to taste	1/2 teaspoon each baking soda, ginger and salt
1/4 cup butter or margarine	3/4 cup shortening
3/4 cup sugar	1/2 cup molasses
31/2 cups (or more) all-purpose flour	3 eggs
	1/2 to 3/4 cup buttermilk

Combine apples, spices, butter and 3/4 cup sugar in saucepan. Simmer for 30 minutes. Cool completely. Preheat oven to 375 degrees. Mix flour, 1 cup sugar, baking powder, baking soda, ginger and salt in bowl. Cut in shortening. Add molasses; mix well. Stir in eggs and buttermilk. Shape into 6 balls. Press each ball into a greased and floured 8-inch cake pan. Bake in 2 batches for 18 minutes. Remove to wire rack to cool. Stack layers on serving plate, spreading apple mixture between layers. Let stand for 6 hours or longer before serving. May substitute chunky applesauce for cooked dried apples.
Yield: 12 to 18 servings.

Ann O. Barkalow, Laureate Omicron
Old Hickory, Tennessee

CANDY-APPLE CAKE

2 teaspoons baking soda	1 teaspoon ground cloves
1/2 cup sweetened applesauce	1 cup raisins
1/2 cup shortening	1 cup chopped walnuts
1 cup sugar	1 tablespoon light corn syrup
1 teaspoon vanilla extract	1 tablespoon water
21/2 cups all-purpose flour	3 tablespoons red hot cinnamon candies
2 teaspoons nutmeg	1 egg white
2 teaspoons cinnamon	

Preheat oven to 350 degrees. Mix baking soda with applesauce in small bowl. Cream shortening in mixer bowl until light. Beat in sugar until fluffy. Add applesauce mixture and vanilla. Sift in flour and spices. Fold in raisins and walnuts. Spoon into greased 8-by-8-inch cake pan. Bake for 30 to 35 minutes or until cake tests done. Cool on wire rack. Bring corn syrup, water and candies to a boil in small saucepan over medium heat, stirring constantly; remove from heat. Candies may not be completely dissolved. Beat egg white at high speed in mixer bowl until stiff peaks form. Add syrup mixture in thin stream, beating constantly until soft peaks form. Spread over cake. Yield: 9 to 12 servings.

Jean Gretsch, Xi Xi Omicron
Palm Desert, California

SUPER DUPER TRIPLE LAYER APPLE-NUT CAKE WITH CARAMEL GLAZE

This rich cake is a must for special birthdays.

11/2 cups vegetable oil	11/2 teaspoons salt
2 cups sugar	6 cups chopped apples
3 eggs	1 cup chopped walnuts
11/2 teaspoons vanilla extract	1/2 cup butter or margarine
31/4 cups all-purpose flour	1/4 cup milk
11/2 teaspoons baking soda	1 cup packed light brown sugar
	1 teaspoon vanilla extract

Preheat oven to 350 degrees. Combine oil, sugar and eggs in mixer bowl; beat until smooth. Add 11/2 teaspoons vanilla, flour, baking soda and salt; mix well. Fold in apples and walnuts. Spoon into 3 greased and floured 10-inch cake pans. Bake for 30 minutes. Cool in pans for several minutes; remove to wire rack to cool completely. Combine remaining ingredients in small saucepan. Cook over medium heat for 2 to 3 minutes. Cool until slightly thickened. Spread between layers and over top of cake.
Yield: 20 servings.

Sharon Veith, Eta
Marion, Ohio

GRAND FINALE APPLE-SPICE CAKE

4 cups chopped unpeeled apples	1/2 teaspoon each nutmeg and cloves
2 cups sugar	1 cup vegetable oil
3 cups all-purpose flour	2 eggs beaten
2 teaspoons baking soda	1 tablespoon Worcestershire sauce
1 teaspoon each salt and allspice	1 cup chopped walnuts
2 teaspoons cinnamon	1 cup raisins

Preheat oven to 325 degrees. Mix apples and sugar in medium bowl; let stand for 15 minutes. Sift flour, baking soda, salt, allspice, cinnamon, nutmeg and cloves into large bowl. Stir in oil, eggs and Worcestershire sauce. Add apple mixture; mix well. Fold in walnuts and raisins. Spoon into greased and floured 10-inch tube pan. Bake for 11/4 hours or until cake tests done. Cool in pan for several minutes. Invert onto wire rack to cool completely.
Yield: 10 servings.

Beverly Cooper, Alpha Zeta
Los Alamos, New Mexico

BANANA CAKE WITH CARAMEL ICING

2 cups sugar
3/4 cup shortening
3 cups sifted cake flour
1 1/2 teaspoons each
    baking powder and
    baking soda
1 teaspoon salt
1 1/2 teaspoons vanilla
    extract
3/4 cup sour milk

1 cup mashed banana
3 eggs
1/2 cup butter or
    margarine, softened
1 cup packed light
    brown sugar
1/4 cup milk
1 3/4 cups confectioners'
    sugar

Preheat oven to 350 degrees. Line 3 round cake pans with waxed paper; grease and flour waxed paper. Cream sugar and shortening in mixer bowl until light and fluffy. Add cake flour, baking powder, baking soda, salt, vanilla, sour milk, banana and eggs; beat for 2 minutes. Spoon into prepared cake pans. Bake for 35 to 40 minutes or until layers test done. Cool in pans for several minutes; remove to wire rack to cool completely. Cook butter and brown sugar in saucepan for 2 minutes, stirring constantly. Add milk. Bring to a boil. Cool to room temperature. Add confectioners' sugar; beat until of spreading consistency. Spread between layers and over top and side of cake. Yield: 16 servings.

Jan Vanderveer, Theta Theta
Goshen, Indiana

BANANA AND ZUCCHINI CAKE

4 eggs
2 cups sugar
1 cup vegetable oil
1 cup banana purée
1 1/2 cups shredded
    zucchini
3 cups all-purpose
flour
1 teaspoon salt

1 1/2 teaspoons each
    baking powder,
    baking soda and
    cinnamon
1 1/2 cups chopped
    walnuts
1 cup raisins (optional)
Confectioners' sugar

Preheat oven to 350 degrees. Beat eggs in large mixer bowl. Add sugar and oil; beat for 1 minute. Add banana and zucchini; mix well. Sift in dry ingredients; mix well. Fold in walnuts and raisins. Spoon into greased 10-inch tube pan. Bake for 1 hour or until cake tests done. Cool in pan for 20 minutes. Invert onto serving plate. Sprinkle with confectioners' sugar. Yield: 12 servings.

Kay Ellis, Xi Zeta Eta
St. John, Kansas

Alice Johnson, Zeta Nu, Princeton, Missouri, makes a Better-Than-Sex Cake with a baked German chocolate cake mix. Punch holes in the cake and pour caramel syrup over the top. Frost with whipped topping and sprinkle with crushed Heath bar.

BLACKBERRY JAM CAKE

This was originally made in the summer with 1 1/2 cups fresh blackberries. Now we enjoy it year-round made with jam. We still serve it in the summer with ice cream.

1 cup butter or
    margarine, softened
2 cups sugar
4 eggs
3 cups all-purpose flour
1 teaspoon each baking
    powder, baking soda,
    allspice, nutmeg and
    cinnamon
1/2 cup sour cream
1 1/2 cups blackberry jam

1/2 cup butter or
margarine
1 cup packed light
    brown sugar
1/4 teaspoon salt
1/4 cup milk
2 1/2 cups sifted
    confectioners' sugar
1/2 teaspoon vanilla
    extract

Preheat oven to 350 degrees. Cream 1 cup butter in large mixer bowl until light. Add sugar and eggs; beat until smooth. Sift dry ingredients together. Add to creamed mixture alternately with sour cream and jam, mixing well after each addition. Spoon into greased and floured 9-by-13-inch cake pan. Bake for 45 to 60 minutes or until cake tests done. Cool on wire rack. Melt 1/2 cup butter in saucepan. Blend in brown sugar and salt. Cook over low heat for 2 minutes, stirring constantly. Add milk. Bring to a boil; remove from heat. Beat in confectioners' sugar and vanilla gradually. Spread over cake. May thin frosting with a small amount of cream if necessary for desired consistency. Yield: 15 servings.

Dorothy Davis, Laureate Mu
Vienna, West Virginia

SMOKY MOUNTAIN BLACKBERRY CAKE

This is from a cookbook featuring old-fashioned recipes from the Smoky Mountains.

1 cup margarine,
    softened
2 cups sugar
4 eggs, beaten
3 cups self-rising flour
1 teaspoon each
    cinnamon, nutmeg,
    ground cloves and salt

2 cups blackberries
    with juice
1 cup peach preserves
1 cup raisins
1/2 cup buttermilk
2 teaspoons baking
soda
Confectioners' sugar

Preheat oven to 350 degrees. Cream margarine and sugar in mixer bowl until light and fluffy. Beat in eggs. Add next 8 ingredients; mix just until moistened. Add mixture of buttermilk and baking soda. Spoon into 3 greased and floured 8-inch cake pans. Bake for 25 to 30 minutes or until layers test done. Cool in pans for several minutes; remove to wire rack to cool. Sprinkle confectioners' sugar between layers and over top of cake. May use one 16-ounce can blackberries. Yield: 16 servings.

Jean H. Daley, Laureate Zeta
Augusta, Georgia

BLACKBERRY WINE CAKE

Members of the DuVall family have traveled hundreds of miles all over the state of Arkansas and made many long-distance calls, including to the Jell-O Corporation, to obtain the blackberry gelatin for this favorite family recipe.

1/2 cup chopped nuts	1/2 cup confectioners'
1 2-layer package	sugar
white cake mix	1 3-ounce package
1 3-ounce package	blackberry gelatin
blackberry gelatin	1/2 cup blackberry wine
4 eggs	1/2 cup butter or
1/2 cup vegetable oil	margarine
1 cup blackberry wine	Confectioners' sugar

Preheat oven to 350 degrees. Sprinkle chopped nuts into greased and floured bundt pan. Combine cake mix, 1 package gelatin, eggs, oil and 1 cup wine in large mixer bowl; mix until smooth. Spoon into prepared cake pan. Bake for 45 to 50 minutes or until cake tests done. Combine next 4 ingredients in saucepan. Bring to a boil, stirring until smooth. Spoon half the glaze mixture over hot cake in pan. Let stand for 30 minutes. Remove to serving plate. Blend enough additional confectioners' sugar with remaining glaze mixture to make of desired consistency. Spread over cake. Yield: 16 servings.

Ginger DuVall, Xi Alpha Theta
Conway, Arkansas

BLACKBERRY YUMMY CAKE

I used blackberries from my own blackberry bushes to make this cake to take to a dinner-play at a friend's house.

2 cups all-purpose flour	1 cup (or more)
1 1/2 cups sugar	blackberries
2 teaspoons baking	16 ounces cream cheese,
powder	softened
1 teaspoon salt	2 cups sifted
2/3 cup butter or	confectioners' sugar
margarine, softened	2 to 3 teaspoons vanilla
1 cup milk	extract
2 eggs	

Preheat oven to 350 degrees. Mix first 7 ingredients in large mixer bowl; beat at low speed until ingredients are moistened. Beat at medium speed for 3 minutes. Spoon into greased and floured 9-by-13-inch cake pan; arrange blackberries over top. Bake for 40 to 50 minutes or until cake springs back when lightly touched. Cool slightly on wire rack. Combine cream cheese, confectioners' sugar and vanilla in medium mixer bowl; mix until smooth. Spread over cake. Yield: 12 to 15 servings.

Dolores G. Magee, Preceptor Theta Chi
Argyle, Texas

BURNT SUGAR CAKE

2 cups sugar	2 teaspoons baking
2 cups boiling water	powder
1/2 cup butter or	1 teaspoon vanilla extract
margarine, softened	2 cups sugar
1 1/2 cups sugar	1 cup cream
2 egg yolks	1 tablespoon butter or
2 1/2 cups cake flour	margarine
1 cup cold water	1 teaspoon vanilla extract
2 egg whites	

Sprinkle 2 cups sugar in skillet. Cook until sugar is dark, stirring constantly. Stir in 2 cups boiling water. Store in refrigerator until needed. Preheat oven to 350 degrees. Cream butter and 1 1/2 cups sugar in mixer bowl until light and fluffy. Beat in egg yolks. Add flour alternately with 1 cup cold water, mixing well after each addition. Beat egg whites with baking powder, 1 teaspoon vanilla and 5 teaspoons burnt sugar mixture in medium bowl. Stir into batter. Spoon into greased and floured cake pans. Bake for 35 minutes. Cool in pans for several minutes. Cool on wire rack. Combine remaining ingredients and 1 tablespoon burnt sugar mixture in saucepan. Cook until of desired consistency. Spread between layers and over top and side of cake. Yield: 12 servings.

Connie McQuern, Laureate Sigma
New Whiteland, Indiana

BUTTER PECAN POUND CAKE

1 1/2 cups butter or	1 teaspoon baking
margarine, softened	powder
1 cup sugar	1 cup milk
2 1/4 cups packed light	1 cup chopped pecans
brown sugar	1 cup butter or
5 eggs	margarine
1 teaspoon vanilla	2 cups sugar
extract	1 cup evaporated milk
3 cups all-purpose flour	1 teaspoon vanilla
1/2 teaspoon salt	extract

Preheat oven to 325 degrees. Cream first 3 ingredients in mixer bowl until light and fluffy. Beat in eggs 1 at a time. Add 1 teaspoon vanilla. Sift flour, salt and baking powder together. Add to batter alternately with milk, mixing well after each addition. Stir in pecans. Spoon into greased and floured tube pan. Bake for 1 1/2 hours. Cool in pan for 10 minutes; remove to wire rack to cool completely. Melt 1 cup butter in saucepan over medium heat. Stir in 2 cups sugar and evaporated milk. Cook to 324 degrees on candy thermometer, soft-ball stage, stirring constantly; remove from heat. Add 1 teaspoon vanilla; do not stir. Cool for 10 minutes. Beat at medium speed for 10 minutes or until of spreading consistency. Spread on cooled cake. Yield: 20 servings.

Oleta Clifton, Laureate Alpha Rho
Anson, Texas

WAYNE'S FAVORITE CANNOLI CAKE

I won second place in a local recipe contest in 1992 with this recipe, which is also my son's favorite cake.

6 egg whites	1 teaspoon vanilla
1/2 cup sugar	extract
6 egg yolks	1/3 cup orange juice
3/4 cup all-purpose flour	2 tablespoons orange
1 tablespoon baking	liqueur
powder	3 tablespoons milk
1/2 cup sugar	13/4 cups confectioners'
1/2 teaspoon salt	sugar
1 teaspoon vanilla	3 tablespoons butter or
extract	margarine, softened
2 tablespoons water	3/4 teaspoon vanilla
32 ounces ricotta cheese	extract
8 ounces cream cheese,	2 cups whipping cream
softened	1/2 cup semisweet
2 teaspoons grated	chocolate chips,
orange rind	melted
1 cup confectioners'	
sugar	

Preheat oven to 375 degrees. Beat egg whites at high speed in mixer bowl until soft peaks form. Add 1/2 cup sugar 2 tablespoons at a time, beating constantly until stiff peaks form. Combine egg yolks, flour, baking powder, 1/2 cup sugar, salt, 1 teaspoon vanilla and water in small mixer bowl; beat at low speed. Fold 1/3 of the egg whites into egg yolk mixture; fold egg yolk mixture into remaining egg whites. Spoon into ungreased 10-inch springform pan. Bake for 30 to 35 minutes or until golden brown. Cool on wire rack. Beat ricotta cheese and cream cheese at low speed in large mixer bowl. Add orange rind, 1 cup confectioners' sugar and 1 teaspoon vanilla; mix well. Loosen cake from pan with knife and remove from pan. Cut horizontally into 2 layers. Brush cut sides with mixture of orange juice and liqueur. Place 1 layer cut side up on serving plate. Spread with ricotta mixture, spreading to edge and mounding slightly in center. Place remaining layer cut side down on top. Combine milk, 13/4 cups confectioners' sugar, butter and 3/4 teaspoon vanilla in small mixer bowl; beat until of spreading consistency. Whip cream in large mixer bowl until soft peaks form. Fold in confectioners' sugar mixture. Spread over top and side of cake. Drizzle with chocolate; swirl with wooden pick. Chill overnight.
Yield: 10 to 12 servings.

Peggy Zimmerman, Laureate Delta Iota
Tamaqua, Pennsylvania

Janet M. Spearly, Mu Chi, DuBois, Pennsylvania, makes a Sour Cream Glaze for pound cake by heating 3/4 cup confectioners' sugar and 2 tablespoons sour cream over low heat and adding 1 teaspoon lemon juice and 1/4 teaspoon vanilla.

CHERRY CAKE WITH HOT CHERRY SAUCE

1/3 cup shortening	2 to 21/4 cups pitted
11/2 cups sugar	sour cherries, well
2 eggs, beaten	drained
21/4 cups all-purpose	1/2 cup sugar
flour	2 tablespoons
11/2 teaspoons baking	cornstarch
powder	3/4 cup cherry juice
1/2 teaspoon baking soda	1 cup water
1/2 teaspoon salt	Salt to taste
1 cup milk	1/4 teaspoon almond
1/2 cup chopped walnuts	flavoring

Preheat oven to 350 degrees. Cream shortening in mixer bowl until light. Add 11/2 cups sugar gradually, beating until fluffy. Beat in eggs. Sift flour, baking powder, baking soda and 1/2 teaspoon salt together. Add to batter alternately with milk, mixing well after each addition. Stir in walnuts and cherries. Spoon into greased and floured 9-by-13-inch cake pan. Bake for 50 minutes. Blend next 5 ingredients in saucepan. Cook until thickened, stirring constantly; remove from heat. Stir in almond flavoring. Serve cake warm with sauce spooned over servings. Yield: 12 servings.

Connie J. Hawkshaw, Beta Tau
Woodslee, Ontario, Canada

BETTY C'S BANANA CHIFFON CAKE

21/4 cups all-purpose	1 cup mashed bananas
flour	1 teaspoon lemon juice
11/2 cups sugar	8 or 9 egg whites
1 tablespoon baking	1 teaspoon cream of
powder	tartar
1/2 teaspoon salt	1/4 teaspoon salt
6 egg yolks	Chopped walnuts or
1/2 cup vegetable oil	pecans
1 teaspoon grated	Lemon glaze or
lemon rind	confectioners' sugar
1 teaspoon vanilla	
extract	

Preheat oven to 350 degrees. Sift flour, sugar, baking powder and 1/2 teaspoon salt together 2 or 3 times; make well in center. Add egg yolks, oil, lemon rind, vanilla and mixture of bananas and lemon juice to well; set aside. Beat egg whites in mixer bowl until soft peaks form. Add cream of tartar and 1/4 teaspoon salt, beating until stiff peaks form. Beat banana mixture for 2 minutes. Fold gradually into egg whites with wooden spoon. Spoon into ungreased tube pan; sprinkle with walnuts. Bake for 15 minutes; reduce oven temperature to 325 degrees. Bake for 40 minutes longer. Invert onto funnel or bottle to cool. Remove to serving plate. Drizzle with lemon glaze or sprinkle with confectioners' sugar. Yield: 16 servings.

Mary C. Henchon, Laureate Beta
Trenton, New Jersey

CHIFFON BIRTHDAY CAKE

2 cups all-purpose flour	Grated rind of 1 lime
1 cup sugar	7 egg whites
1 3-ounce package	1 teaspoon lime juice
lime gelatin	1/2 teaspoon salt
1 tablespoon baking	11/2 cups confectioners'
powder	sugar
1/2 cup vegetable oil	2 teaspoons lime juice
3 egg yolks	11/2 tablespoons milk
3/4 cup water	

Preheat oven to 325 degrees. Line bottom of 10-inch tube pan with waxed paper. Mix flour, sugar, gelatin and baking powder in large mixer bowl. Add oil, egg yolks, water and lime rind; beat until smooth. Beat egg whites in large mixer bowl until frothy. Add 1 teaspoon lime juice and salt; beat until soft peaks form. Fold into batter. Spoon evenly into prepared pan. Bake for 60 to 65 minutes or until cake springs back when lightly touched. Invert onto funnel or bottle; cool completely. Loosen edge of cake with spatula; remove to serving plate. Combine remaining ingredients in small bowl; mix well. Drizzle over top and side of cake; smooth top. Yield: 16 servings.

Joan Herbert, Preceptor Alpha Zeta
Brantford, Ontario, Canada

CHIFFON CAKE

2 cups all-purpose flour	1 cup egg whites
3/4 cup sugar	1/2 teaspoon cream of
1 tablespoon baking	tartar
powder	1 cup finely chopped
1 teaspoon salt	nuts
3/4 cup packed light	1/4 cup butter or
brown sugar	margarine
3/4 cup cold water	2 cups sifted
2 teaspoons maple	confectioners' sugar
extract	2 tablespoons cream
1/2 cup vegetable oil	1 teaspoon vegetable oil
6 egg yolks	1 teaspoon hot water

Preheat oven to 325 degrees. Sift flour, sugar, baking powder and 1 teaspoon salt together. Add brown sugar; sift into large bowl. Add 3/4 cup cold water, maple extract, 1/2 cup oil and egg yolks, beating until smooth. Beat egg whites with cream of tartar in large mixer bowl until very stiff peaks form. Fold in batter and nuts. Spoon into ungreased tube pan. Bake for 1 hour and 5 minutes. Invert onto funnel or bottle to cool. Remove to serving plate. Melt butter in saucepan. Cook until golden brown. Add remaining ingredients; mix well. Spread over cake. Yield: 16 servings.

Beverly Nuebel, Preceptor Mu
Mitchell, South Dakota

BIT O' CHOCOLATE CHIFFON CAKE

My best friend's mother always made this cake for my birthday and it is still my favorite. I make it but it is never as good as hers.

2 cups all-purpose	2 teaspoons vanilla
flour	extract
13/4 cups sugar	1 ounce unsweetened
1 tablespoon baking	baking chocolate,
powder	grated
1 teaspoon salt	7 egg whites
1/2 cup vegetable oil	1/2 teaspoon cream of
7 egg yolks	tartar
3/4 cup cold water	

Preheat oven to 325 degrees. Mix flour, sugar, baking powder and salt in large mixer bowl. Add oil, egg yolks, cold water and vanilla; beat until smooth. Beat in chocolate. Beat egg whites with cream of tartar in large mixer bowl until very stiff peaks form. Fold in batter gently. Spoon into ungreased tube pan. Bake for 55 minutes; increase oven temperature to 350 degrees. Bake for 10 minutes longer. Invert onto funnel or bottle to cool. Remove to serving plate. Yield: 12 servings.

Kim Davis, Theta Delta
Burlington, Colorado

MAPLE-PECAN CHIFFON CAKE

21/4 cups sifted cake	7 egg yolks
flour or 2 cups sifted	3/4 cup cold water
all-purpose flour	2 teaspoons maple
3/4 cup sugar	extract
3/4 cup packed light	1 cup egg whites
brown sugar	1/2 teaspoon cream of
1 tablespoon baking	tartar
powder	1 cup finely chopped
1 teaspoon salt	pecans
1/2 cup vegetable oil	

Preheat oven to 325 degrees. Sift flour, sugar, brown sugar, baking powder and salt into large bowl; make well in center. Add oil, egg yolks, cold water and maple extract to well in order listed; beat until smooth. Beat egg whites and cream of tartar in mixer bowl until very stiff peaks form. Fold in batter gently with rubber spatula. Fold in pecans. Spoon into ungreased 10-inch tube pan. Bake for 55 minutes; increase oven temperature to 350 degrees. Bake for 10 minutes longer. Invert onto funnel or bottle to cool. Remove to serving plate. Yield: 16 servings.

Mildred L. Neel, Laureate Gamma Alpha
Nokomis, Florida

ALMOND JOY CAKE

1 2-layer package pudding-recipe chocolate cake mix	1/2 cup margarine
1 cup evaporated milk	1 1/2 cups sugar
1 cup sugar	1 cup evaporated milk
26 large marshmallows	2 cups semisweet chocolate chips
1 14-ounce package coconut	1 3 1/2-ounce package almonds

Preheat oven to 350 degrees. Prepare and bake cake mix using package directions for 9-by-13-inch cake pan. Combine 1 cup evaporated milk, 1 cup sugar, marshmallows and coconut in saucepan. Cook until marshmallows melt, stirring to mix well. Spread over hot cake. Melt margarine in saucepan. Stir in 1 1/2 cups sugar and 1 cup evaporated milk. Bring to a boil. Stir in chocolate chips until melted. Add almonds. Spread evenly over marshmallow layer. Yield: 15 to 20 servings.

Sharon Bittner, Xi Upsilon Omicron
Altaville, California

REINE DE SABA CHOCOLATE-ALMOND CAKE

4 1-ounce squares semisweet chocolate	Salt to taste
2 tablespoons rum	8 ounces sweet chocolate, broken
1/2 cup margarine, softened	2 tablespoons margarine
2/3 cup sugar	6 tablespoons water
3 egg yolks	2 cups sifted confectioners' sugar
1/3 cup ground almonds	2 teaspoons vanilla extract
3 egg whites	
1 tablespoon sugar	1/4 cup ground almonds
3/4 cup sifted cake flour	

Preheat oven to 350 degrees. Combine semisweet chocolate and rum in small glass bowl. Microwave on High just until chocolate melts; do not mix. Cream 1/2 cup margarine and 2/3 cup sugar in mixer bowl until light and fluffy. Beat in egg yolks, chocolate mixture and 1/3 cup almonds. Beat egg whites in mixer bowl until soft peaks form. Sprinkle with 1 tablespoon sugar; beat until stiff peaks form. Fold egg whites into chocolate mixture alternately with flour and salt. Spoon into greased and floured 8-inch cake pan. Bake for 25 minutes. Cool in pan for 10 minutes; remove to wire rack to cool completely. Combine sweet chocolate, 2 tablespoons margarine and water in saucepan. Cook until chocolate melts, stirring to mix well; remove from heat. Beat in confectioners' sugar and vanilla. Spread on cake; sprinkle with 1/4 cup almonds. Yield: 12 servings.

Jane Mercer, Preceptor Delta Phi
Ada, Oklahoma

CHOCOLATE-APRICOT CAKE

5 tablespoons walnuts, toasted	6 egg yolks, at room temperature
6 tablespoons bourbon	1 cup all-purpose flour
12 ounces semisweet chocolate, coarsely chopped	6 egg whites, at room temperature
1 cup unsalted butter, softened	1/2 teaspoon cream of tartar
2 cups sugar	6 ounces dried apricots, slivered

Preheat oven to 350 degrees. Butter 10-inch spring-form pan and dust lightly with baking cocoa. Soak walnuts in bourbon in small bowl for 20 minutes; drain, reserving walnuts and bourbon. Melt chocolate with reserved bourbon in double boiler over simmering water, stirring until smooth. Cool to lukewarm. Cream butter and sugar in medium mixer bowl until light and fluffy. Beat in egg yolks 1 at a tim. Blend in flour. Beat egg whites with cream of tartar in large mixer bowl until stiff but not dry. Fold 1/4 of the egg whites into chocolate mixture; fold in remaining egg whites, creamed mixture, walnuts and apricots. Spoon into prepared pan. Bake for 55 minutes or until top forms cracked crust and center is still moist. Cool on wire rack. Place on serving plate; remove side of pan. Yield: 8 to 10 servings.

Catherine Luchsinger, Xi Upsilon Omicron
Angels Camp, California

ABSOLUTELY DIVINE CHOCOLATE CAKE

I served this cake to my son on his first birthday and all the guests enjoyed watching him eat with his hands.

3 1-ounce squares unsweetened chocolate, chopped	2 teaspoons vanilla extract
1 8-ounce can julienned beets	2 cups all-purpose flour
1/2 cup unsalted butter, softened	2 teaspoons baking soda
	1/2 teaspoon salt
2 1/2 cups packed light brown sugar	1/2 cup buttermilk
	2 cups whipping cream
3 eggs, at room temperature	1 pound semisweet chocolate, chopped
	2 teaspoons vanilla extract

Preheat oven to 350 degrees. Melt unsweetened chocolate in double boiler; let stand until cool. Drain beets, reserving juice. Cut beets into small pieces and return to juice; set aside. Combine butter, brown sugar, eggs and 2 teaspoons vanilla in large mixer bowl; beat for 5 minutes. Add chocolate; mix well. Add mixture of dry ingredients alternately with buttermilk, mixing well after each addition. Stir in beets. Spoon into 2 greased and floured 9-inch cake pans. Bake for 30 to 35 minutes or until cake tester comes out clean. Cool in pans for 10 minutes; remove to wire rack to cool completely. Bring whipping cream just to a simmer in saucepan; remove from heat. Stir in semisweet chocolate until melted. Add 2 teaspoons vanilla. Spoon into glass bowl. Chill for 50 minutes or until thickened to pudding consistency, stirring every 10 minutes. Spread between layers and over top and side of cake. Yield: 10 to 12 servings.

Alison Maartensen
Eureka, California

GRANDMA'S CHOCOLATE CAKE

My Grandma and her church friends sold this recipe for 10 cents back in the 30s.

1/2 cup margarine, softened	2 cups all-purpose flour
21/4 cups packed light brown sugar	2 teaspoons baking soda
	1/2 teaspoon salt
3 eggs	1/2 cup sour milk
3 1-ounce squares baking chocolate, melted	2 teaspoons vanilla extract
	1 cup boiling water

Preheat oven to 375 degrees. Cream first 2 ingredients in mixer bowl until light and fluffy. Beat in eggs and chocolate. Add mixture of dry ingredients alternately with sour milk and vanilla, mixing well after each addition. Stir in water. Spoon into greased 10-by-14-inch cake pan. Bake for 25 minutes or until cake tests done. Cool on wire rack. May frost with chocolate frosting or seven-minute frosting. Yield: 20 servings.

Virginia Kirschner, Preceptor Alpha Chi
Kendallville, Indiana

CHOCOLATE CAKE

This was a favorite of my mother's and started a wonderful friendship with the lady who was buying the house next door. She came to see our house, as it was like the one she was to purchase, and never got out of the kitchen when she saw the tomato juice going into the chocolate cake. Their friendship lasted through 40 years and many cakes.

1/3 cup shortening	1 cup all-purpose flour
1 cup sugar	1 teaspoon baking powder
1 egg, beaten	
1 teaspoon baking soda	1/2 cup baking cocoa
1 cup tomato juice	Salt to taste

Preheat oven to 350 degrees. Cream shortening and sugar in mixer bowl until light and fluffy. Beat in egg. Dissolve baking soda in a small amount of boiling water. Stir into batter. Beat in tomato juice. Sift in remaining ingredients; mix well. Spoon into greased and floured 9-by-9-inch cake pan. Bake for 30 to 35 minutes or until cake tests done. Cool on wire rack. Yield: 9 servings.

Margaret Counsell, Laureate Alpha Lambda
Kelowna, British Columbia, Canada

BUTTERCREAM RIBBON CHOCOLATE FUDGE CAKE

8 ounces cream cheese, softened	2 cups all-purpose flour
	1 teaspoon baking powder
1 egg	
1/4 cup sugar	1/2 teaspoon baking soda
3 tablespoons milk	1/4 teaspoon salt
2 tablespoons butter or margarine, softened	11/3 cups milk
1 tablespoon cornstarch	4 1-ounce squares unsweetened baking chocolate, melted, cooled
1/2 teaspoon vanilla extract	
1/2 cup butter or margarine, softened	1 teaspoon vanilla extract
2 cups sugar	Chocolate frosting
2 eggs	

Preheat oven to 350 degrees. Beat cream cheese, 1 egg and 1/4 cup sugar in mixer bowl until smooth. Add 3 tablespoons milk, 2 tablespoons butter, cornstarch and 1/2 teaspoon vanilla; mix well and set aside. Cream 1/2 cup butter and 2 cups sugar in mixer bowl until light and fluffy. Beat in 2 eggs. Mix next 4 ingredients together. Add to creamed mixture alternately with 11/3 cups milk, mixing well after each addition. Stir in chocolate and 1 teaspoon vanilla. Spoon half the mixture into greased 9-by-13-inch cake pan. Spread with cream cheese mixture and remaining chocolate mixture. Bake for 55 to 60 minutes or until cake tests done. Cool on wire rack. Frost with chocolate frosting. Yield: 12 servings.

Janice Watts, Laureate Xi
Fairmont, West Virginia

COCOA-POTATO CAKE

2 cups all-purpose flour, sifted	1/8 teaspoon salt
	2 egg yolks
2 teaspoons baking powder	1 cup pecan pieces
	1 cup raisins
1/4 cup baking cocoa	1 teaspoon vanilla extract
1 teaspoon nutmeg	
1 teaspoon ground cloves	1/2 cup applesauce
	1 cup hot unseasoned mashed potatoes
1 teaspoon cinnamon	
2 cups sugar	2 egg whites, beaten
1 cup vegetable oil	

Preheat oven to 350 degrees. Sift flour and next 5 ingredients together. Mix sugar with next 6 ingredients in large bowl. Add sifted dry ingredients and applesauce alternately, mixing well after each addition. Add mashed potatoes. Fold in beaten egg whites. Pour into greased and floured bundt pan. Bake for 1 hour. Cool in pan for several minutes. Invert onto serving plate. Serve plain or frosted with favorite glaze. Yield: 12 to 16 servings.

Cheri Clark, Preceptor Eta Beta
Boerne, Texas

MAYONNAISE CAKE

2 cups all-purpose flour	1 cup sugar
1/2 teaspoon salt	3/4 cup mayonnaise
1 teaspoon baking powder	1 cup water
1 teaspoon baking soda	1/2 teaspoon vanilla extract
1/4 cup baking cocoa	Elegant Fudge Frosting

Sift flour and next 5 ingredients together 4 times. Combine with mayonnaise, water and vanilla in bowl; stir well. Pour into 2 greased and floured 9-inch cake pans. Bake for 30 to 40 minutes or until cake tests done. Cool in pans for 10 minutes. Remove to wire rack to cool completely. Spread Elegant Fudge Frosting between layers and over top and side of cooled cake. Yield: 12 servings.

ELEGANT FUDGE FROSTING

2 tablespoons shortening	2 ounces unsweetened and semisweet chocolate
1 1/2 cups sugar	
1 tablespoon light corn syrup	1/8 teaspoon salt
7 tablespoons milk	1 teaspoon vanilla extract
2 tablespoons butter or margarine	

Combine shortening with next 6 ingredients in saucepan. Bring to a boil over low heat. Boil for 1 minute. Cool to room temperature. Stir in vanilla. Beat until smooth and of desired spreading consistency. Yield: 12 servings.

Barbara Howe, Xi Omicron Gamma
Sacramento, California

SWISS CHOCOLATE CAKE

1 2-layer package Swiss chocolate cake mix	1/2 cup sugar
	1 cup confectioners' sugar
3 eggs	1/2 cup chopped pecans
1 cup vegetable oil	12 ounces whipped topping
1 package vanilla instant pudding mix	1/2 cup chopped milk chocolate candy
1 1/2 cups milk	
8 ounces cream cheese, softened	

Preheat oven to 325 degrees. Combine cake mix with next 4 ingredients in bowl; mix well. Pour into 2 greased and floured 9-inch cake pans. Bake for 25 to 30 minutes or until cake tests done. Cool in pans for 10 minutes. Remove to wire rack to cool completely. Beat cream cheese with sugar and confectioners' sugar in bowl until smooth. Add pecans, whipped topping and chocolate; mix well. Spread between layers and over top and side of cooled cake. Yield: 12 servings.

Lillie Mae Merriman, Gamma Delta
Martinsville, Virginia

TRIPLE LAYER FUDGE CAKE

3 cups sifted all-purpose flour	2 cups buttermilk
2 teaspoons baking soda	3/4 cup butter or margarine, softened
1 teaspoon salt	5 ounces unsweetened chocolate, melted
1 cup butter or margarine, softened	1 tablespoon vanilla extract
1 cup sugar	
1 cup packed light brown sugar	5 tablespoons milk
3 eggs	6 cups confectioners' sugar, sifted
4 ounces unsweetened chocolate, melted	Sliced almonds
2 teaspoons vanilla extract	

Preheat oven to 350 degrees. Sift flour, baking soda and salt together. Cream 1 cup butter with sugar and brown sugar in bowl until light and fluffy. Add eggs and next 2 ingredients; mix well. Add sifted dry ingredients and buttermilk alternately, mixing well after each addition. Pour into 3 greased and floured 9-inch cake pans. Bake for 30 to 35 minutes or until cake tests done. Cool in pans for 10 minutes. Remove to wire rack to cool completely. Cream 3/4 cup butter with 5 ounces melted chocolate and vanilla in bowl. Add milk and confectioners' sugar alternately, beating constantly until creamy. Spread frosting between layers and over top and side of cake. Sprinkle almonds around top edge of cake.
Yield: 12 to 16 servings.

Rita H. Mullen, Psi
Taylors, South Carolina

HEATH BAR CAKE

1 2-layer package German chocolate cake mix	16 ounces whipped topping
	4 large Heath candy bars, broken into small pieces
1 14-ounce can sweetened condensed milk	
1 jar caramel ice cream topping	

Prepare and bake cake mix using package directions for 9-by-13-inch cake. Make holes in hot cake with large fork. Mix condensed milk and caramel sauce in bowl. Pour evenly over cake. Cool completely. Spread whipped topping over top. Sprinkle with candy pieces. Chill for 2 to 3 hours before serving. Yield: 12 servings.

Juanita Brillhart, Gamma Rho
Perryton, Texas
*Patti A. Langel, Omicron
Norfolk, Nebraska
*Kamie Mielke, Beta Eta
Alcester, South Dakota

SNICKER CAKE

1 2-layer package chocolate cake mix	1/3 cup milk
1 package caramels	3/4 cup semisweet chocolate chips
1/2 cup margarine	

Preheat oven to 350 degrees. Prepare cake using package directions. Pour half the batter in greased 9-by-13-inch cake pan. Bake for 20 minutes. Melt caramels with margarine and milk in saucepan. Pour over cake. Sprinkle with chocolate chips. Drop remaining batter by spoonfuls over baked layer. Reduce oven temperature to 250 degrees. Bake for 20 minutes. Increase oven temperature to 350 degrees. Bake for 10 minutes longer. Yield: 12 servings.

Kay Thomas, Beta Kappa
Meeteetse, Wyoming

CHOCOLATE-RUM CAKE

1 2-layer package yellow cake mix	1 cup sour cream
	4 eggs
3/4 cup uncooked chocolate-flavored cereal	1/2 cup vegetable oil
	1/2 cup rum
	1 cup chopped nuts
1 package chocolate instant pudding mix	Confectioners' sugar

Preheat oven to 350 degrees. Combine cake mix with cereal, pudding mix, sour cream, eggs, oil and rum in large bowl; mix well. Stir in nuts. Pour into greased and floured 12-cup bundt pan. Bake for 1 hour. Cool in pan for 10 minutes. Invert onto serving plate. Sprinkle with confectioners' sugar. Yield: 16 servings.

Myrna Russell, Delta
Bozeman, Montana

CHOCOLATE CHIP CAKE

1 2-layer package devil's food cake mix	1/2 cup vegetable oil
	1/2 cup water
1 4-ounce package chocolate instant pudding mix	4 eggs
	2 cups semisweet chocolate chips
1 cup sour cream	

Preheat oven to 350 degrees. Combine cake mix with pudding mix, sour cream, oil, water and eggs in bowl. Beat for 5 minutes. Fold in chocolate chips gently. Pour into greased and floured bundt pan. Bake for 50 to 55 minutes or until cake tests done. Cool in pan for 5 minutes. Invert onto serving plate. Yield: 8 servings.

Carol Hayes, Delta Delta Chi
Rancho Cucamonga, California

CHOCOLATE CHIP-DATE CAKE

1 1/4 cups boiling water	1 teaspoon baking soda
1 8-ounce package chopped dates	2 teaspoons baking cocoa
3/4 cup shortening	1/2 teaspoon salt
1 cup sugar	1/2 cup sugar
2 eggs, beaten	1/2 cup walnuts
1 1/2 cups all-purpose flour	1 cup semisweet chocolate chips

Preheat oven to 350 degrees. Pour boiling water over dates in bowl; stir. Let stand until cool. Cream shortening, 1 cup sugar and eggs in mixer bowl until light and fluffy. Stir in date mixture. Sift in flour, baking soda, baking cocoa and salt; mix well. Pour into greased and floured 9-by-13-inch cake pan. Sprinkle with mixture of 1/2 cup sugar, walnuts and chocolate chips. Bake for 35 to 40 minutes or until cake tests done. Yield: 24 servings.

Carilerene Harper, Xi Beta Phi
Bend, Oregon

OLD-FASHIONED DARK CHOCOLATE CAKE

2 1/2 cups all-purpose flour	4 eggs
	1 cup sour milk
1/4 teaspoon salt	3/4 cup baking cocoa
1 tablespoon baking soda	2/3 cup boiling water
	1 teaspoon vanilla extract
1 cup shortening	
2 cups sugar	Caramel Frosting

Preheat oven to 350 degrees. Mix flour, salt and baking soda. Mix shortening, sugar and eggs in large bowl. Add sour milk and dry ingredients alternately, mixing well after each addition. Stir baking cocoa into boiling water until dissolved. Add to cake batter; mix well. Stir in vanilla. Pour into 3 greased and floured 8-inch cake pans. Bake for 35 to 40 minutes or until layers test done. Cool in pans for 10 minutes. Remove to wire rack to cool completely. Spread Caramel Frosting between layers and over top and side of cooled cake. Yield: 16 to 20 servings.

CARAMEL FROSTING

3/4 cup margarine	9 tablespoons milk
1 1/2 cups packed light brown sugar	4 1/2 cups confectioners' sugar
3/8 teaspoon salt	

Melt margarine in 2-quart saucepan over low heat. Stir in brown sugar and salt. Boil for 2 minutes, stirring constantly. Remove from heat. Add milk, stirring vigorously. Return to heat. Bring to a boil. Remove from heat. Let stand until lukewarm. Add confectioners' sugar; beat until smooth and of spreading consistency. Yield: 16 to 20 servings.

Phylis Hyland, Xi Epsilon Rho
Sturgis, Michigan

COCONUT CAKE

1 2-layer package yellow cake mix	1 12-ounce package frozen fresh coconut,
2 cups sour cream	thawed, or 1 16-ounce
2 cups sugar	can cream of coconut

Prepare and bake cake mix using package directions for two 9-inch cakes. Cut cooled layers into halves horizontally. Combine sour cream, sugar and coconut in bowl; mix well. Stack layers, spreading coconut mixture between layers and on top. Chill, wrapped in plastic wrap, for 3 days before serving. Yield: 12 servings.

Patricia A. Siron, Preceptor Delta Rho
Mexico, Missouri

COCONUT-BLACK WALNUT POUND CAKE

This recipe was given to me by my next-door neighbor, Miss Bessie. She is a dear woman who cooks like a master chef. This is one of the best cakes I have ever eaten.

3 cups all-purpose flour	1 cup flaked coconut
1/2 teaspoon salt	2 teaspoons coconut
1/2 teaspoon baking soda	extract
1/2 teaspoon baking powder	1 teaspoon vanilla extract
2 cups sugar	1 cup sugar
1 cup vegetable oil	1/2 cup water
4 eggs, beaten	2 tablespoons butter or
1 cup buttermilk	margarine
1 cup chopped black walnuts	1 teaspoon coconut extract

Preheat oven to 325 degrees. Sift flour, salt, baking soda and baking powder together. Combine 2 cups sugar, oil and eggs in mixer bowl; mix well. Add sifted dry ingredients and buttermilk alternately, mixing well after each addition. Stir in walnuts, coconut and flavorings. Spoon into greased and floured 10-inch tube pan. Bake for 65 minutes. Combine 1 cup sugar with remaining ingredients in saucepan. Cook until of syrup consistency, stirring constantly. Pour syrup over hot cake. Cool in pan for 3 to 4 hours. Invert onto serving plate. Yield: 16 servings.

Gwen Beaver, Zeta Phi
Wingate, North Carolina

PUMPKIN-COCONUT CAKE

2 cups all-purpose flour	2 cups canned pumpkin
1 teaspoon cinnamon	1/2 cup chopped walnuts
1 teaspoon baking powder	1/2 cup flaked coconut
1 teaspoon salt	8 ounces cream cheese
2 cups sugar	1/4 cup margarine,
11/4 cups vegetable oil	softened
4 eggs, beaten	13/4 cups confectioners' sugar

Preheat oven to 350 degrees. Combine flour with next 3 ingredients. Beat sugar and oil together in bowl. Add eggs and pumpkin; mix well. Add dry ingredients, walnuts and coconut in order listed, stirring well after each addition. Pour into greased 9-by-13-inch cake pan. Bake for 35 minutes. Cool completely. Beat cream cheese with remaining ingredients in small bowl until of spreading consistency. Spread evenly over cake. Yield: 12 to 15 servings.

Sharon Base, Preceptor Gamma Mu
Troy, Michigan

COCONUT-SPICE CAKE

21/2 cups all-purpose flour	1 teaspoon vanilla extract
1 teaspoon baking soda	1 cup flaked coconut
1 teaspoon cinnamon	1 cup chopped pecans
1 teaspoon nutmeg	8 ounces cream cheese,
1/2 teaspoon salt	softened
1 cup packed light brown sugar	1/4 cup butter or margarine, softened
1 cup sugar	1 1-pound package
1 cup vegetable oil	confectioners' sugar
2 eggs	1 cup chopped pecans
1 cup buttermilk	1 cup coconut

Preheat oven to 350 degrees. Combine flour with next 4 ingredients. Combine brown sugar with next 2 ingredients in mixer bowl; mix well. Add eggs 1 at a time, beating well after each addition. Add dry ingredients and buttermilk alternately, beginning and ending with dry ingredients and mixing well after each addition. Stir in vanilla, 1 cup coconut and 1 cup pecans. Spoon into 2 greased and floured 9-inch round cake pans. Bake for 25 minutes. Cool in pans for 10 minutes. Remove to wire rack to cool completely. Beat cream cheese, butter and confectioners' sugar in bowl until smooth. Stir in 1 cup pecans. Frost cake. Sprinkle 1 cup coconut and additional chopped pecans over top. Yield: 12 servings.

Sue Bretschneider, Xi Gamma Alpha
Norfolk, Nebraska

RAVE REVIEWS COCONUT CAKE

1 2-layer package yellow cake mix	2 cups flaked coconut
1 3-ounce package vanilla instant pudding mix	2 tablespoons butter or margarine, softened
	8 ounces cream cheese, softened
11/3 cups water	2 teaspoons milk
4 eggs	31/2 cups sifted
1/4 cup vegetable oil	confectioners' sugar
2 cups flaked coconut	1/2 teaspoon vanilla
1 cup chopped pecans or walnuts	extract
2 tablespoons butter or margarine	

Preheat oven to 350 degrees. Combine cake mix with next 4 ingredients in mixer bowl; beat at medium speed for 4 minutes. Stir in coconut and pecans. Spoon into 3 greased and floured 8-inch round cake pans. Bake for 35 minutes. Cool in pans for 15 minutes. Remove to wire rack to cool completely. Melt 2 tablespoons butter in skillet. Add 2 cups coconut. Cook over low heat until golden brown; stirring constantly. Spread coconut on paper towel to cool. Cream 2 tablespoons butter with cream cheese in bowl until light and fluffy. Add milk, confectioners' sugar and vanilla; mix well. Stir in 1³/4 cups toasted coconut. Spread between layers and over top of cooled cake. Sprinkle with remaining coconut. Yield: 15 or 16 servings.

Polly A. Patton, Xi Epsilon Beta
Woodstock, Virginia

FUZZY NAVEL CAKE

1 28-ounce can sliced peaches, drained	1 2-layer package yellow cake mix
¹/2 cup peach schnapps	4 eggs
1 cup sugar	²/3 cup vegetable oil
¹/4 cup frozen orange juice concentrate	1 cup chopped pecans
1 3-ounce package vanilla instant pudding mix	¹/4 cup frozen orange juice concentrate
	2 cups confectioners' sugar

Combine peaches with next 3 ingredients in glass container. Let stand, covered, at room temperature for 24 hours. Drain, reserving liquid. Chop peaches. Combine pudding mix, cake mix, eggs, oil, 1¹/2 cups chopped peaches and ¹/2 cup reserved liquid in large bowl; mix well. Stir in pecans. Pour into greased and floured bundt pan. Bake for 1 hour or until cake tests done. Combine ¹/4 cup reserved liquid, ¹/4 cup orange juice concentrate and confectioners' sugar in bowl; beat until of spreading consistency. Spread over cake. Garnish with additional chopped peaches. Yield: 12 servings.

June Underkoffler, Laureate Iota
Oklahoma City, Oklahoma

GREAT-GRANDMOTHER'S GINGERBREAD

This recipe, over 150 years old, brings back wonderful memories of being in Grandmother's kitchen. She served gingerbread warm with lemon sauce.

2¹/1 cups all-purpose flour, sifted	¹/2 cup butter or margarine, softened
1 teaspoon cinnamon	¹/2 cup sugar
1 teaspoon ginger	1 egg, beaten
¹/2 teaspoon cloves	1 cup molasses
1¹/2 teaspoons baking soda	1 cup hot water
¹/2 teaspoon salt	Lemon Sauce

Preheat oven to 350 degrees. Sift flour and next 5 ingredients together. Cream butter and sugar in mixer bowl until light and fluffy. Add egg; mix well. Add sifted dry ingredients and mixture of molasses and water alternately, mixing well after each addition. Spoon into 9-inch square waxed paper-lined cake pan. Bake for 45 minutes. Serve warm with Lemon Sauce. Yield: 16 servings.

LEMON SAUCE

¹/2 cup sugar	2 tablespoons lemon juice
1 tablespoon cornstarch	Nutmeg to taste
1 cup boiling water	Grated lemon rind to taste
Salt to taste	
2 tablespoons butter or margarine	

Combine sugar and cornstarch in top of double boiler. Stir in boiling water and salt. Cook over direct heat until thickened and clear, stirring constantly. Place pan over hot water. Cook for 20 minutes. Beat in butter and remaining ingredients. Yield: 16 servings.

Miere K. Harris, Laureate Phi
Tonkawa, Oklahoma

VINARTARTA (Icelandic Cake)

3¹/2 cups all-purpose flour	3 tablespoons cream
1 teaspoon baking powder	1 teaspoon almond extract
1 cup butter or margarine, softened	1 pound prunes
1¹/2 cups sugar	³/4 cup sugar
2 eggs, beaten	1 tablespoon cinnamon
	1 tablespoon vanilla extract

Preheat oven to 350 degrees. Mix flour and baking powder. Cream butter, 1¹/2 cups sugar and eggs in bowl until light and fluffy. Sift in dry ingredients; mix well. Stir in cream and flavoring. Knead on floured surface. Divide into 5 portions. Place each portion in greased 9-inch round cake pan. Bake until golden brown. Remove to wire rack to cool. Combine prunes, sugar and cinnamon with water to cover in saucepan. Bring to a boil. Stir in vanilla. Cool slightly. Stack layers, spreading prune filling between layers. Yield: 12 servings.

Brenda I. Caine, Xi Alpha Delta
Fort St. John, British Columbia, Canada

Julie Meeker, Alpha, Sioux Falls, South Dakota, adds ¹/4 cup green Crème de Menthe to a white cake mix and bakes using package directions. Frost with canned chocolate frosting and top with mixture of 12 ounces whipped topping and 3 tablespoons Crème de Menthe for a delicious Crème de Menthe Cake.

INDIAN FRUIT CAKE

This is an Indian recipe handed down from generation to generation. It is at least 100 years old.

4³/4 cups all-purpose flour	1¹/2 cups sugar
1 teaspoon salt	2 eggs
1 teaspoon baking soda	2 teaspoons vanilla extract
1 teaspoon baking powder	1 cup sour cream
¹/2 teaspoon nutmeg	Dried peaches or other favorite fruit
1 cup butter or margarine, softened	

Sift flour and next 4 ingredients together. Cream butter in bowl until light and fluffy. Beat in sugar gradually. Add eggs 1 at a time, beating well after each addition. Stir in vanilla. Add sifted dry ingredients and sour cream alternately, mixing well after each addition. Chill, covered, for several hours to overnight or until firm enough to roll. Preheat oven to 375 degrees. Roll dough into 6 to 8-inch circles on floured surface. Place 2 at a time on baking sheet. Bake for 10 to 12 minutes or until layers test done. Cool on wire rack. Cook peaches using package directions. Stack baked layers on serving plate, spooning peaches between layers. Yield: 20 servings.

Linda Stacey, Preceptor Delta Phi
Ada, Oklahoma

JACK DANIELS CAKE

1 2-layer package yellow cake mix	¹/2 cup milk
1 package vanilla instant pudding mix	³/4 cup margarine, softened
5 eggs, slightly beaten	1 cup black walnuts
¹/2 cup Jack Daniels whiskey	16 ounces butterscotch chips

Preheat oven to 350 degrees. Sift cake mix and pudding into large bowl. Add next 4 ingredients; mix well. Reserve ¹/2 cup each walnuts and butterscotch chips. Stir remaining walnuts and butterscotch chips into batter. Spoon into greased and floured 9-by-13-inch cake pan. Sprinkle with reserved walnuts and butterscotch chips. Bake for 45 to 60 minutes or until cake tests done. Yield: 15 servings.

Janice Ray, Mu Lambda
Fairfax, Missouri

Mary Lou Claussen, Xi Alpha Tau, Martin, South Dakota, makes Pineapple-Nut Cake by mixing 2 cups sugar, 2 cups all-purpose flour, 2 eggs, 2 tablespoons baking soda, 1 teaspoon vanilla, one 20-ounce can crushed pineapple and 1 cup chopped nuts with spoon. Bake in 9-by-13-inch cake pan in preheated 350-degree oven for 30 to 40 minutes. Frost with cream cheese frosting.

LADY BALTIMORE CAKE

When my family lived on a farm, my mother made many cakes but this one was my favorite. She would often add chopped figs, raisins, pecans and candied cherries between the layers.

³/4 cup vegetable shortening	¹/2 teaspoon lemon extract
2 cups sugar	1 cup milk
3 cups sifted cake flour	6 egg whites, stiffly beaten
³/4 teaspoon salt	Lemon-flavored filling
1 tablespoon baking powder	Seven-minute frosting
³/4 teaspoon vanilla extract	

Preheat oven to 350 degrees. Cream shortening and sugar in bowl until light and fluffy. Sift in mixture of flour, salt and baking powder. Add flavorings and milk alternately, beating well after each addition. Fold in beaten egg whites gently. Spoon into 2 greased and floured 9-inch round cake pans. Bake for 30 to 35 minutes or until cake tests done. Spread lemon-flavored filling between layers. Frost top and side with 7-minute frosting. Yield: 12 servings.

Mavis A. Stromme, Preceptor Xi
Devils Lake, North Dakota

LEMON-RICOTTA CAKE

1 2-layer package lemon or yellow cake mix	2 teaspoons vanilla extract
4 eggs	Pineapple, cherry or blueberry pie filling
4 cups ricotta cheese	Confectioners' sugar
³/4 cup sugar	

Preheat oven to 325 degrees. Prepare cake mix using package directions. Spoon into greased and floured 9-by-13-inch cake pan. Beat eggs, ricotta cheese, sugar and vanilla in bowl until creamy. Spread over cake batter. Bake for 1¹/2 hours. Cool in pan. Cut into squares. Serve plain or garnish with pie filling or confectioners' sugar. Yield: 16 servings.

Carmel-Beth Kemerling, Mu Lambda
Tarkio, Missouri

MANGO CAKE

3 eggs, well-beaten	¹/2 cups chopped nuts
1³/4 cups sugar	2 tablespoons butter or margarine, softened
1 cup vegetable oil	
2 cups all-purpose flour	2 cups confectioners' sugar
1 teaspoon salt	
1 teaspoon baking soda	2 tablespoons mashed mango
2 cups mashed mangos	

Mix eggs, sugar and oil in bowl. Sift in flour, salt and baking soda; mix well. Stir in 2 cups mangos and nuts. Spoon into greased and floured 9-by-13-inch cake pan. Bake for 1 hour or until cake tests done.

Cream butter in bowl. Add confectioners' sugar and 2 tablespoons mango; beat until of spreading consistency. Spread on cooled cake. Yield: 12 servings.

Margaret A. Bohls, Laureate Alpha Lambda
Arvada, Colorado

MINCEMEAT CAKE

2 cups all-purpose flour	6 ounces cream cheese,
2 cups sugar	softened
1 teaspoon baking soda	1 tablespoons butter or
1/2 teaspoon salt	margarine, softened
1 teaspoon pumpkin pie	2 teaspoons vanilla
spice	extract
3 eggs	4 cups sifted
1 cup vegetable oil	confectioners' sugar
1 cup mincemeat	1/2 cup chopped pecans
1 cup chopped pecans	

Preheat oven to 300 degrees. Mix first 5 ingredients. Beat eggs in large bowl. Add oil, mincemeat and pecans. Add dry ingredients gradually, stirring well after each addition. Spoon into greased and floured 9-by-13-inch cake pan. Bake for 1 hour. Cool in pan. Beat cream cheese, butter and vanilla in bowl at low speed until light and fluffy. Add confectioners' sugar gradually, beating well after each addition. Stir in pecans. Spread over cake. Yield: 12 servings.

Clara Christine Farmer, Preceptor Alpha
Richmond, Indiana

MOCHA-OATMEAL CAKE

2 tablespoons instant	3/4 teaspoon salt
coffee powder	1 1/4 teaspoons baking
1 1/3 cups boiling water	soda
1 cup oats	3 tablespoons baking
3/4 cup butter or	cocoa
margarine, softened	1 1/2 tablespoons butter
1 cup sugar	or margarine, softened
1 cup packed light	1 cup confectioners' sugar
brown sugar	1 1/2 tablespoons liquid
2 eggs	coffee
1 1/2 teaspoons vanilla	1/2 teaspoon vanilla
extract	extract
2 cups all-purpose flour	Salt to taste

Dissolve coffee powder in boiling water. Pour over oats in bowl. Let stand, covered, for 20 minutes. Beat 3/4 cup butter with sugar, brown sugar and eggs in mixer bowl until light and fluffy. Stir in vanilla and oats mixture. Sift in next 4 ingredients; stir until moistened. Pour into greased bundt pan. Bake for 50 minutes or until cake tests done. Cool in pan for 10 minutes. Cool on wire rack. Beat 1 1/2 tablespoons butter in bowl until creamy. Add confectioners' sugar and remaining ingredients; beat until smooth. Drizzle over cooled cake. Yield: 16 servings.

Evelyn T. Roy, Preceptor Eta
Lebanon, New Hampshire

KENTUCKY ORANGE CAKE

3 cups sifted all-	5 eggs, at room
purpose flour	temperature
1 tablespoon baking	3/4 cup fresh orange juice
powder	Grated rind of 1 orange
1/4 teaspoon salt	1 cup melted butter or
1 cup butter or	margarine
margarine, softened	2/3 cup sugar
2 cups sugar	1/2 cup bourbon

Preheat oven to 350 degrees. Sift flour, baking powder and salt together. Cream butter in bowl. Add 2 cups sugar gradually, beating until light and fluffy. Add eggs 1 at a time, beating well after each addition. Add sifted dry ingredients and orange juice alternately, beating well after each addition. Stir in grated rind. Pour into greased and floured bundt pan. Bake for 1 hour or until cake tests done. Remove to wire rack. Combine melted butter with 2/3 cup sugar in small saucepan. Heat until sugar dissolves, stirring constantly. Stir in bourbon. Drizzle over hot cake. Cool completely. Invert onto serving plate. Yield: 16 servings.

Lillian P. Richards, Xi Epsilon Beta
Woodstock, Virginia

GRAM'S ORANGE CAKE

My grandmother used to make this cake for all her grandchildren's birthdays and when we were sick. This cake was our cure-all. Now my mother carries on the tradition with her grandchildren.

5 egg yolks	2 teaspoons baking
1 1/2 cups sugar	powder
Grated rind of 1 orange	1 egg white
1 cup orange juice	1 teaspoon butter or
2 cups sifted all-	margarine, softened
purpose flour	1/4 cup orange juice
5 egg whites	Confectioners' sugar

Preheat oven to 350 degrees. Beat egg yolks in bowl. Add sugar; mix until creamy. Add orange rind; mix well. Add orange juice and flour alternately, beginning with orange juice and mixing well after each addition. Beat egg whites with baking powder in mixer bowl until stiff peaks form. Fold into egg yolk mixture gently. Pour into greased and floured 9-by-12-inch cake pan. Bake for 45 to 50 minutes or until cake tests done. Beat remaining egg white in bowl. Add butter, orange juice and enough confectioners' sugar to make of spreading consistency, beating until smooth. Spread over cooled cake. Yield: 12 servings.

Denise K. Cressman, Iota Zeta
Danville, Pennsylvania

ORANGE BLOSSOMS

2 2-layer packages lemon cake mix	2 1-pound packages confectioners' sugar
Juice of 4 lemons	Grated rind of 2 lemons
Juice of 4 oranges	Grated rind of 2 oranges

Preheat oven to 350 degrees. Prepare cake mix using package directions. Fill greased miniature muffin cups 2/3 full. Bake for 10 to 12 minutes or until muffins test done. Remove to wire rack to cool. Mix lemon juice with remaining ingredients in bowl; stir until of syrup consistency. Dip muffins into syrup. Place on waxed paper to drain. Yield: 9 to 10 dozen.

Lucille Buttrum, Laureate Pi
LaGrange, Georgia

ORANGE MANDARIN CAKE

Every time I make this cake for an occasion, I've learned to bring copies of the recipe along to hand out. Make ahead of time for rush days or sorority meetings.

2 11-ounce cans mandarin oranges	1 large package vanilla instant pudding mix
1 2-layer package yellow cake mix	1 20-ounce can crushed pineapple
4 eggs	16 ounces whipped topping
1/2 cup vegetable oil	
1/8 teaspoon baking soda	

Preheat oven to 350 degrees. Drain mandarin oranges, reserving 3/4 cup liquid. Mix cake mix, eggs, oil, reserved liquid, baking soda and half the mandarin oranges in large bowl. Pour into 3 greased and floured 9-inch round cake pans. Bake for 25 to 30 minutes or until cake tests done. Cool in pans for 10 minutes. Remove to wire rack to cool completely. Combine pudding mix, pineapple and whipped topping in bowl; mix well. Spread between layers and over top and side of cake. Garnish top with remaining mandarin oranges. Chill overnight. Yield: 12 servings.

Connie Arabie John, Xi Psi
Crowley, Louisiana

ORANGE MARBLE SURPRISE

1 2-layer package white or yellow cake mix	1 ounce semisweet chocolate
1 cup water	1 tablespoon margarine
1/3 cup vegetable oil	3/4 cup sifted confectioners' sugar
3 eggs	2 tablespoons hot milk
3 ounces semisweet chocolate, melted	Grated orange rind
3 tablespoons grated orange rind	

Preheat oven to 350 degrees. Combine cake mix with next 3 ingredients in mixer bowl. Beat at medium-high speed for 4 minutes. Divide batter into 2 portions. Stir 3 ounces melted chocolate into one portion. Stir grated orange rind into the other. Alternate chocolate and orange batters in greased and floured bundt pan. Cut through with knife in zigzag pattern to marbleize. Bake for 35 to 40 minutes or until cake tests done. Cool in pan for 10 minutes. Remove to serving plate to cool completely. Melt 1 ounce chocolate with margarine in saucepan. Let stand until cool. Stir in confectioners' sugar and milk gradually. Beat until smooth and shiny. Drizzle over cooled cake. Garnish with additional grated orange rind. Yield: 16 servings.

Sandra E. Todd, Alpha Epsilon
Carman, Manitoba, Canada

FRESH PEAR CAKE

4 cups finely chopped peeled pears	2 teaspoons baking soda
2 cups sugar	1/2 teaspoon salt
1 cup chopped nuts	1 cup vegetable oil
3 cups all-purpose flour	2 eggs, beaten
1/2 teaspoon cinnamon	1 teaspoon vanilla extract

Preheat oven to 350 degrees. Combine pears, sugar and nuts in large bowl. Let stand for 1 hour, stirring often. Stir flour and next 3 ingredients with spoon. Stir in oil, vanilla and eggs. Pour into greased and floured tube pan. Bake for 1 1/4 hours. Cool in pan for several minutes. Invert onto serving plate. Yield: 12 servings.

Maxine Ball, Pi Master
Texarkana, Texas

PINEAPPLE-CARROT CAKE

1 8-ounce can crushed pineapple, drained	1 1/2 cups chopped walnuts
1 1/4 cups vegetable oil	8 ounces cream cheese, softened
4 eggs	1/4 cup butter or margarine
2 cups all-purpose flour	2 teaspoons vanilla extract
2 cups sugar	
2 teaspoons cinnamon	1 1-pound package confectioners' sugar
2 teaspoons baking soda	
2 teaspoons baking powder	
1 teaspoon salt	
3 cups finely shredded carrots	

Preheat oven to 325 degrees. Reserve 1/3 can pineapple for frosting. Combine remaining pineapple with next 10 ingredients in large bowl; mix well. Pour into greased 9-by-13-inch glass cake pan. Bake for 1 1/4 hours. Cool completely. Mix reserved pineapple with cream cheese and remaining ingredients in bowl until of desired spreading consistency. Spread over cooled cake. Yield: 12 servings.

Gail Daviault, Preceptor Alpha Zeta
Paris, Ontario, Canada

PIÑA COLADA CAKE

1/4 cup vegetable oil	1 15-ounce can cream
1 2-layer package	of coconut
white cake mix	1 cup shredded coconut
1 1/2 cups water	16 ounces whipped
2 eggs	topping
1 cup shredded coconut	

Preheat oven to 350 degrees. Pour oil into 9-by-13-inch cake pan. Spread oil over bottom and sides of pan. Place cake mix in pan. Top with water, eggs and 1 cup coconut; stir well. Mixture will be lumpy. Bake for 30 minutes. Pierce top with fork. Spread coconut cream evenly over top of hot cake. Chill for 1 hour. Mix remaining coconut with whipped topping. Spread over cake. Chill until serving time. Yield: 12 servings.

Laurie Steinberg, Gamma Eta
Lighthouse Point, Florida

HOT FUDGE SUNDAE CAKE

1 cup all-purpose flour	1/2 cup milk
3/4 cup sugar	1 teaspoon vanilla
2 tablespoons baking	extract
cocoa	1 cup packed light
2 teaspoons baking	brown sugar
powder	1/4 cup baking cocoa
1/4 teaspoon salt	1 3/4 cups hot water
2 tablespoons vegetable	Vanilla ice cream
oil	

Preheat oven to 350 degrees. Mix first 5 ingredients in bowl. Stir in oil, milk and vanilla until smooth. Spread into 9-inch square cake pan. Sprinkle with brown sugar and 1/4 cup baking cocoa. Pour hot water over top. Bake for 40 minutes. Cool for 15 minutes. Spoon each cake portion into serving dish. Top with ice cream and self-made sauce. Yield: 6 servings.

Shannon Bell, Xi Xi
Weyburn, Saskatchewan, Canada

LEMON PUDDING-CAKE SUPREME

This is a special treat for sorority nights and card parties. A light cake forms on top and a creamy jelly on the bottom.

1 cup sugar	2 egg yolks, beaten
1 tablespoon butter or	Juice and grated rind of
margarine, softened	1 lemon
2 tablespoons all-	1 cup milk
purpose flour	2 egg whites, beaten

Preheat oven to 300 degrees. Cream sugar and butter in bowl. Add flour, beaten egg yolks, lemon juice and grated rind; mix well. Add milk gradually, beating constantly. Fold in beaten egg whites. Pour into custard cups placed in pan of water. Bake for 45 minutes. Yield 4 to 6 servings.

Dorothy H. Ebert, Laureate Zeta
Hope, Idaho

MOCHA-WALNUT PUDDING CAKE

3/4 cup sugar	1/2 cup milk
1 cup all-purpose flour	1 1/2 teaspoons vanilla
3 tablespoons baking	extract
cocoa	1/2 cup chopped walnuts
2 teaspoons baking	1/2 cup sugar
powder	1/2 cup packed light
1 teaspoon cinnamon	brown sugar
1/4 teaspoon salt	1/4 cup baking cocoa
1/3 cup melted butter or	1 1/4 cups hot water
margarine	

Preheat oven to 350 degrees. Blend 3/4 cup sugar with next 5 ingredients in bowl. Add butter, milk, vanilla and walnuts; mix well. Pour into ungreased 9-inch square cake pan. Mix 1/2 cup sugar, brown sugar and 1/4 cup baking cocoa in small bowl. Sprinkle over batter. Pour hot water over top. Do not stir. Bake for 35 to 40 minutes or until set in center. Let stand for 15 minutes. Spoon cake into serving dishes. Top with pudding from pan and ice cream. Yield: 8 servings.

Rose Tuttle, Eta
Winter Springs, Florida

OLD-FASHIONED ICE CREAM CAKE ROLL

For a nice holiday variation, substitute strawberry ice cream for vanilla ice cream. Top with sliced strawberries and additional whipped cream.

4 eggs	1/2 gallon vanilla ice
3/4 teaspoon baking	cream, softened
powder	1 cup packed light
1/4 teaspoon salt	brown sugar
3/4 cup sugar	1/2 cup sugar
3/4 cup all-purpose flour	1/2 teaspoon salt
1 teaspoon vanilla	1/2 cup light corn syrup
extract	1 cup whipping cream

Preheat oven to 375 degrees. Beat eggs with baking powder and salt in large bowl. Add 3/4 cup sugar gradually, mixing until mixture is thick and lemony. Add flour gradually, beating well after each addition. Stir in vanilla. Spoon into greased and waxed paper-lined 10-by-15-inch cake pan. Bake for 10 to 12 minutes or until golden brown. Turn onto towel sprinkled with confectioners' sugar. Remove waxed paper. Roll in towel as for jelly roll; cool. Unroll cake, removing towel. Spread with ice cream; reroll. Freeze until firm. Combine brown sugar, remaining sugar, salt and corn syrup in heavy saucepan. Bring to a boil. Remove from heat. Cool slightly. Stir in whipping cream. Cut cake roll into slices. Serve with sauce. Yield: 10 servings.

Lynne Byram, Preceptor Xi
Devils Lake, North Dakota

DELICIOUS NUT ROLL

7 eggs, separated	1 1/2 cups ground nuts
3/4 cup sugar	Confectioners' sugar
1 teaspoon baking powder	2 cups whipped topping

Preheat oven to 350 degrees. Brush 10-by-15-inch jelly roll pan with oil; line with waxed paper. Beat egg yolks with sugar in large bowl until thick and lemon-colored. Beat in baking powder and nuts. Beat egg whites in bowl until fluffy. Fold into egg yolk mixture gently. Spread in prepared pan. Bake for 15 to 20 minutes or until golden brown. Cover with damp towel. Cool in pan. Chill completely. Remove towel. Sprinkle with enough confectioner's sugar to cover top. Spread with whipped topping. Roll up as for jelly roll, removing waxed paper. Place on serving plate. Sprinkle with additional confectioners' sugar. Yield: 12 servings.

Carol Jarman, Beta Sigma
New Bern, North Carolina

CHOCO-MINT JELLY ROLL

6 tablespoons all-purpose flour	2 tablespoons cold water
1 cup confectioners' sugar	1 cup whipping cream
1/4 cup baking cocoa	1/2 cup confectioners' sugar
1 teaspoon baking powder	Peppermint extract to taste
6 eggs, separated	Green food coloring
1 tablespoon unflavored gelatin	

Preheat oven to 350 degrees. Sift flour and next 3 ingredients together. Beat egg yolks until light and lemon-colored. Beat egg whites until stiff peaks form. Fold gently into egg yolks. Fold sifted dry ingredients in gradually. Spread batter in greased and waxed paper-lined 10-by-15-inch jelly roll pan. Bake for 15 minutes. Invert onto damp towel. Roll as for jelly roll. Cool completely. Soften gelatin in cold water in saucepan. Whip whipping cream with 1/2 cup confectioners' sugar in bowl. Boil gelatin water for 1 minute. Stir in a small amount of whipped cream; stir gelatin mixture into whipped cream. Unroll cake; remove towel. Spread with whipped cream mixture, working quickly because mixture sets fast. Reroll. Yield: 12 servings.

Cynthia Wardle, Alpha Mu
Preeceville, Saskatchewan, Canada

Ann Nuzum, Laureate Xi, Fairmont, West Virginia, makes Easy Fluffy Icing by beating 1 egg white, 2 cups confectioners' sugar, 1 cup shortening and 1 teaspoon vanilla extract for 15 minutes.

PUMPKIN AND CREAM CHEESE ROLL-UP

I won first place with this recipe in our county fair. Everyone raves about it. One regular-sized can of pumpkin will make 3 roll-ups. I make 3 at a time, freezing 2 for later.

3/4 cup sifted all-purpose flour	2/3 cup canned pumpkin
1 teaspoon baking powder	1 cup chopped walnuts
2 teaspoons cinnamon	Confectioners' sugar
1 teaspoon pumpkin pie spice	8 ounces cream cheese, softened
1/2 teaspoon nutmeg	1 cup sifted confectioners' sugar
1/2 teaspoon salt	6 tablespoons butter or margarine, softened
3 eggs, slightly beaten	1 teaspoon vanilla extract
1 cup sugar	

Preheat oven to 375 degrees. Grease 10-by-15-inch jelly roll pan. Line with waxed paper; grease and flour waxed paper. Sift flour with next 5 ingredients. Beat eggs with sugar in large bowl until thick and fluffy. Beat in pumpkin. Stir in sifted dry ingredients. Spread evenly in prepared pan. Sprinkle with walnuts. Bake for 15 minutes. Invert onto damp towel dusted with confectioners' sugar. Peel off waxed paper. Trim 1/4 inch from sides of cake. Roll in towel as for jelly roll. Place seam side down. Cool completely. Beat cream cheese with remaining ingredients in bowl until smooth. Unroll cake, removing towel. Spread with cream cheese mixture. Reroll. Chill until serving time. Yield: 12 servings.

Connie Morgenstein, Preceptor Beta Phi
Fort Lauderdale, Florida

STRAWBERRY ROLL

1 cup all-purpose flour	3/4 cup sugar
1 teaspoon baking powder	2 cups strawberries
3 eggs	1 1/2 cups whipping cream
	Sugar to taste

Preheat oven to 450 degrees. Line 10-by-15-inch jelly roll pan with foil; coat with butter. Mix flour with baking powder. Beat eggs with 3/4 cup sugar in bowl until light and fluffy. Fold in flour mixture gently. Spread in prepared pan. Bake for 5 minutes. Invert onto waxed paper sprinkled with additional sugar. Remove foil. Let stand, covered, until cool. Reserve several strawberries for garnish. Slice remaining strawberries; place in bowl. Beat whipping cream with sugar to taste in mixer bowl until soft peaks form. Spoon half the whipped cream over sliced strawberries; mix well. Spread cake with whipped cream mixture. Roll as for jelly roll. Top with remaining plain whipped cream. Garnish with reserved strawberries. Yield: 12 servings.

Cherokee Carter, Zeta Master
Medford, Oregon

MARGARET'S RUM CAKE

1 cup chopped pecans	1/2 cup dark rum
1 2-layer package yellow cake mix	1/2 cup vegetable oil
1 3-ounce package vanilla instant pudding mix	1/2 cup butter or margarine, melted
4 eggs	1/4 cup water
1/2 cup cold water	1 cup sugar
	1/2 cup dark rum

Preheat oven to 325 degrees. Sprinkle pecans over bottom of greased and floured 12-cup bundt pan. Mix cake mix with next 5 ingredients in bowl. Spoon into prepared bundt pan. Bake for 1 hour. Let stand until cool. Invert onto cake plate. Prick top with fork or handle of wooden spoon. Melt butter in saucepan. Stir in water and sugar. Boil for 5 minutes, stirring constantly. Remove from heat. Stir in remaining rum. Spoon mixture evenly over top and side of cake. Allow cake to absorb glaze. Repeat process until all glaze is absorbed. Yield: 16 servings.

Diane E. Frame, Xi Delta Gamma
Manassas, Virginia

UPSIDE-DOWN STRAWBERRY SHORTCAKE

This is a perfect summertime dessert to take to picnics.

1 cup miniature marshmallows	1 tablespoon baking powder
2 10-ounce packages frozen strawberries, thawed	1 cup milk
1 3-ounce package strawberry gelatin	1/2 cup shortening
2 1/4 cups all-purpose flour	1 1/2 cups sugar
	1 teaspoon vanilla extract
	3 eggs

Preheat oven to 350 degrees. Line greased 9-by-13-inch cake pan with marshmallows. Combine strawberries and gelatin in bowl. Set aside. Mix flour with remaining ingredients in large bowl. Pour into prepared pan. Top with strawberry mixture. Bake for 45 to 50 minutes or until cake tests done. Cut into squares. Invert squares onto serving plates. Yield: 15 servings.

Debbie Bellesine, Xi Zeta Tau
El Dorado, Kansas

SUMMER CAKE

1 3-ounce package strawberry gelatin	Cream cheese, softened
3/4 cup boiling water	2 teaspoons lemon juice
1 2-layer package fudge marble cake mix	1 can creamy vanilla frosting
	Fresh strawberries, sliced

Dissolve gelatin in boiling water in bowl. Let stand at room temperature. Prepare and bake cake mix using package directions for 9-by-13-inch cake pan. Let cake cool for 25 minutes. Pierce cake deeply with fork. Pour gelatin over top. Chill in refrigerator. Mix cream cheese and lemon juice in bowl until smooth. Stir in frosting. Spread over cake. Garnish with strawberries. Yield: 12 servings.

Victoria L. Bernatchy, Xi Lambda Lambda
Oceanside, California

TROPICAL DREAM CAKE

1 2-layer package yellow cake mix with pudding	1 15-ounce can crushed pineapple, drained
1 cup water or pineapple juice	1 3-ounce package vanilla or coconut cream instant pudding mix
1/3 cup vegetable oil	
3 eggs	8 ounces cream cheese, softened
1 14-ounce can sweetened condensed milk	8 ounces whipped topping
2 teaspoons rum extract	

Preheat oven to 350 degrees. Combine cake mix with water or pineapple juice, oil and eggs in large bowl. Beat for 2 minutes at high speed. Pour into greased 9-by-13-inch cake pan. Bake for 25 to 35 minutes or until cake tests done. Cool for 5 minutes. Pierce top with fork every 1 to 2 inches. Pour mixture of condensed milk and 1 teaspoon rum flavoring slowly over top. Chill for 2 hours or longer. Combine pineapple, pudding mix, cream cheese and remaining rum flavoring in bowl. Mix until of desired spreading consistency. Spread evenly over chilled cake just before serving. Top with whipped topping. Yield: 15 servings.

Frances M. Buck, Epsilon Alpha
Mesquite, Texas

VANILLA WAFER CAKE

2 cups sugar	1/2 cup milk
1 cup butter or margarine, softened	1 cup chopped pecans
6 eggs	1 cup coconut
2 teaspoons vanilla extract	1 12-ounce package vanilla wafers, crushed

Preheat oven to 350 degrees. Cream sugar and butter in bowl until light and fluffy. Add eggs 1 at a time, mixing well after each addition. Add vanilla, milk, pecans, coconut and cookie crumbs; mix well. Spoon into greased tube pan. Bake for 1 1/2 hours. Cool in pan for several minutes. Remove to wire rack to cool completely. Yield: 16 servings.

Jewell Nitzsche, Epsilon Chi
Kingman, Arizona

WHITE PEPPER AND LEMON-GINGER CAKE

1/4 cup fine dry bread crumbs	3/4 teaspoon baking powder
Grated rind of 2 large lemons	1/2 teaspoon salt
2 tablespoons lemon juice	1 teaspoon white pepper
1/2-by-1-inch piece of ginger, grated	1 cup butter or margarine, softened
3 cups all-purpose flour	13/4 cups sugar
3/4 teaspoon baking soda	3 eggs
	1 cup buttermilk
	Lemon glaze

Preheat oven to 325 degrees. Grease bundt pan; sprinkle with bread crumbs. Combine lemon rind, lemon juice and ginger in small bowl. Set aside. Sift flour with next 4 ingredients. Beat butter in bowl until light and fluffy. Add sugar; beat for 1 minute. Add eggs 1 at a time, mixing well after each addition. Add sifted dry ingredients and buttermilk alternately, beating well after each addition. Stir in lemon juice mixture. Spoon into prepared pan. Place on rack in bottom third of oven. Bake for 1 1/4 hours. Cool in pan for 5 to 10 minutes. Remove to wire rack placed over foil. Brush surface with lemon glaze until all is absorbed. Yield: 16 servings.

Donna Gilligan, Preceptor Gamma
Pierrefonds, Quebec, Canada

WHISKEY CAKE

1 2-layer package yellow cake mix	1 1/2 ounces whiskey
1 package vanilla instant pudding mix	1 cup crushed walnuts
4 eggs	1/2 cup butter or margarine
1/2 cup vegetable oil	1 cup sugar
1 cup milk	1/2 cup whiskey

Preheat oven to 350 degrees. Combine cake mix with next 6 ingredients in large bowl. Mix for 3 minutes. Pour into greased tube pan. Bake for 50 to 60 minutes or until cake tests done. Pierce top of cake with fork. Melt butter in saucepan. Add sugar and remaining 1/2 cup whiskey. Cook until sugar dissolves and mixture resembles syrup. Drizzle part of syrup over cake. Cool in pan for 15 to 20 minutes. Remove to wire rack. Brush top and sides with remaining syrup. Yield: 16 servings.

Jane Myers, Xi Eta Theta
Arlington, Ohio

BEST ITALIAN WINE CAKE EVER

1 to 2 quarts wine	Baking powder
1 cup butter or margarine	1 teaspoon baking soda
1 teaspoon sugar	Lemon juice
2 large eggs	Brown sugar
1 cup dried fruit	Nuts

Before you start, sample the wine to check for quality. Good, isn't it? Now go ahead. Select a large mixing bowl, measuring cup, etc. Check the wine again. It must be just right. To be sure wine is of the highest quality, pour 1 level cup of wine into a glass and drink it as fast as you can. Repeat. With an electric mixer beat 1 seaspoon of thugar and beat again. Meanwhile, make sure that the wine is of the finest quality. Try another cup. Open second quart if necessary. Add 2 large eggs, 2 cups fried druit and beat till high. If druit gets stuck in beaters, just pry it loose with a drewscriver. Sample the wine again, checking for tonscisticity. Next, sift 3 cups of pepper or salt (it really doesn't matter). Sample the wine again. Sift 1/2 pint of lemon juice. Fold in chopped butter and strained nuts. Add 1 babblespoon of brown thugar, or whatever color you can find. Wix mel. Grease oven and turn cake pan to 350 gredees. Now pour the whole mess into the coven, and ake. Check the wine again, and bo to ged.

Patty Boyd, Preceptor Alpha Upsilon
Northfork, West Virginia

ZUCCHINI-ALMOND CAKE

3 cups all-purpose flour	1 teaspoon almond extract
2 teaspoons baking powder	3 cups shredded peeled zucchini
1 teaspoon baking soda	1 cup ground almonds
1 teaspoon salt	Thin vanilla icing
4 eggs	Ground almonds
3 cups sugar	
1 1/2 cups vegetable oil	

Preheat oven to 350 degrees. Mix flour with baking powder, baking soda and salt. Beat eggs in large bowl until thick and lemony. Add sugar 1/4 cup at a time, beating well after each addition. Stir in oil and almond flavoring. Add dry ingredients, stirring until smooth. Stir in zucchini and 1 cup ground almonds. Bake for 1 hour and 25 minutes. Cool in pan. Invert onto serving plate. Drizzle with vanilla icing. Garnish with additional ground almonds. Yield: 12 to 14 servings.

Arlene Stormoen, Xi Alpha Psi
Airdrie, Alberta, Canada

GREAT PUDDING ICING

1 3-ounce package vanilla instant pudding mix	8 ounces chocolate whipped topping
3/4 cup milk	4 Heath candy bars, crushed

Prepare pudding mix using package directions reducing milk to 3/4 cup. Fold in whipped topping and crushed candy bars. Yield: 3 to 4 cups.

Susan Secoy, Preceptor
Bryan, Ohio

FRESH APPLE TORTE

3 cups sifted all-
  purpose flour
1 teaspoon baking soda
1 teaspoon baking
  powder
1½ teaspoons salt
1 teaspoon cinnamon
¾ cup vegetable oil
4 cups finely chopped
  apples

1 teaspoon vanilla
  extract
2 eggs
2 cups sugar
1 cup finely chopped
  nuts
Maple-flavored
  buttercream icing

Preheat oven to 350 degrees. Sift flour, baking soda, baking powder, salt and cinnamon into large bowl. Add oil, apples and vanilla. Beat with electric mixer at medium speed for 2 minutes. Beat eggs in another bowl until light and fluffy. Beat in sugar. Fold into batter gently. Fold in nuts. Spoon into lightly greased 10-inch tube pan. Bake for 1 to 1½ hours or until top springs back when lightly touched. Cool in pan for several minutes. Remove to serving plate. Frost with buttercream icing. Yield: 16 servings.

Verna Killam, Preceptor Alpha Zeta
Brantford, Ontario, Canada

BLITZ-N-TORTE

1½ cups all-purpose
  flour
1 teaspoon baking
  powder
½ teaspoon (or less)
  salt
½ cup butter or
  margarine, softened
5 egg yolks
¾ cup sugar
5 egg whites

⅛ teaspoon cream of
  tartar
¼ to ½ cup sugar
Pecans, walnuts or
  cherries
½ cup whipping cream,
  stiffly beaten
¼ cup sugar
1 can crushed pineapple,
  drained

Preheat oven to 350 degrees. Mix flour, baking powder and salt. Beat butter with egg yolks and ¾ cup sugar until light and fluffy. Add dry ingredients gradually, beating constantly. Spread into two 9-inch round cake pans. Beat egg whites until stiff peaks form. Add cream of tartar and ¼ to ½ cup sugar; mix well. Spread over batter in pans. Garnish with pecans, walnuts or cherries. Bake for 20 to 25 minutes or until layers test done. Cool in pans for several minutes. Remove to wire rack to cool completely. Combine whipped cream and remaining ¼ cup sugar in small bowl. Stir in pineapple. Spread between baked layers on serving plate. Chill until serving time. Yield: 12 servings.

Margaret Von Lukawiecki, Preceptor Alpha Zeta
Brantford, Ontario, Canada

BLITZ TORTE

½ cup shortening
½ cup sugar
⅛ teaspoon salt
4 egg yolks
3 tablespoons milk
1 teaspoon vanilla
  extract
1 cup sifted cake flour

1 teaspoon baking
  powder
4 egg whites
¾ cup sugar
½ cup sliced almonds
1 tablespoon sugar
½ teaspoon cinnamon
Whipped cream

Preheat oven to 350 degrees. Cream shortening with ½ cup sugar and salt in large bowl until light and fluffy. Add egg yolks 1 at a time, mixing well after each addition. Add milk and vanilla; mix well. Sift in flour and baking powder; mix well. Spread in two 9-inch round cake pans. Beat egg whites until soft peaks form. Add ¾ cup sugar gradually, beating constantly. Spread over batter in cake pans. Sprinkle with almonds, 1 tablespoon sugar and cinnamon. Bake for 30 minutes. Cool in pans for several minutes. Remove to wire rack to cool completely. Spread whipped cream between layers on serving plate. Yield: 12 servings.

Caroline Arner, Preceptor Alpha Zeta
Brantford, Ontario, Canada

BROWNIE-FRUIT TORTE

1 cup all-purpose flour
¼ cup baking cocoa
1 teaspoon baking
  powder
¼ teaspoon baking soda
¼ cup margarine,
  softened
⅔ cup sugar
¾ teaspoon vanilla
  extract
⅔ cup ice water

2 egg whites
1 11-ounce can
  mandarin oranges
8 ounces cream cheese,
  softened
1 tablespoon sugar
¼ cup sliced
  strawberries
2 kiwifruit, peeled,
  sliced

Preheat oven to 375 degrees. Combine flour with next 3 ingredients. Set aside. Beat margarine in large bowl until smooth. Add ⅔ cup sugar and vanilla; mix well. Add dry ingredients and cold water alternately, beating at low speed after each addition. Beat egg whites until stiff peaks form. Fold into batter gently. Spoon into 8-inch round pan coated with non-stick cooking spray. Bake for 25 minutes. Cool in pan. Split torte into halves horizontally. Drain mandarin oranges, reserving 2 tablespoons liquid. Combine reserved liquid with cream cheese and 1 tablespoon sugar in small bowl; mix until smooth. Layer mixture and mandarin oranges over torte layers. Stack layers on serving plate. Garnish top with strawberries and kiwifruit. Yield: 8 servings.

June Smathers Jolley, Xi Beta Tau
Canton, North Carolina

STRAWBERRY-BROWNIE TORTE

1 21-ounce package brownie mix	1 3-ounce package French vanilla instant pudding mix
1 14-ounce can sweetened condensed milk	4 ounces whipped topping
1/2 cup water	4 cups strawberries, sliced

Preheat oven to 350 degrees. Grease two 9-inch round cake pans. Line with waxed paper, extending up sides of pans. Grease waxed paper. Prepare brownie mix using package directions for cake-like brownies. Pour into prepared pans. Bake for 20 minutes or until brownies test done. Cool in pans. Mix condensed milk and water in large bowl. Beat in pudding mix. Chill for 5 minutes. Fold in whipped topping gently. Place 1 brownie layer on serving plate. Top with half the pudding mixture and half the strawberries. Repeat layers. Chill until serving time. Yield: 8 to 10 servings.

Alice L. Duba, Preceptor Alpha Kappa
Fresno, California

CHOCOLATE PASTRY CAKE

8 ounces German's sweet chocolate	1 3/4 cups all-purpose flour
1/2 cup sugar	1 teaspoon salt
1/2 cup water	1/2 cup vegetable oil
1 1/2 teaspoons instant coffee powder	8 ounces whipped topping
1 1/2 teaspoons vanilla extract	Peppermint stick candy

Preheat oven to 425 degrees. Combine chocolate, sugar, water and coffee powder in saucepan. Cook over low heat until smooth, stirring constantly. Stir in vanilla. Cool to room temperature. Combine flour, salt and oil in bowl. Stir in 3/4 cup chocolate mixture. Divide pastry into 6 portions. Press each over bottom to within 1/2 inch of edge of inverted 9-inch cake pan. Bake for 5 minutes. Loosen edge of layers with tip of knife. Remove carefully to wire rack to cool completely. Fold remaining chocolate mixture into whipped topping in bowl. Stack baked layers on serving plate, spreading whipped topping mixture between layers and over top. Chill for 8 hours to overnight. Garnish with candy before serving. Yield: 8 to 10 servings.

Darlene Gumfory, Laureate Alpha Sigma
Iola, Kansas

Deborah K. Marriott, Zeta Nu, Monroeville, Alabama, makes Mom's Fudge Icing by cooking 2 cups sugar, 1/3 cup baking cocoa, 1/2 cup margarine and 1/2 cup evaporated milk to soft-ball stage. Stir in 1 teaspoon vanilla extract, cool and spread on cake.

CHOCOLATE-RUM TORTE

1 cup butter or margarine, softened	1 teaspoon butter or margarine
1 cup sugar	2 teaspoons baking cocoa
1 egg	2 egg yolks
2 cups all-purpose flour	1 teaspoon vanilla extract
1/4 teaspoon baking soda	1/4 cup butter or margarine
1/2 cup sugar	1 cup sugar
1 tablespoon cornstarch	1/4 cup baking cocoa
1 1/2 cups milk	1/4 cup milk
1/2 cup rum	

Preheat oven to 375 degrees. Cream butter and 1 cup sugar in bowl until light and fluffy. Add egg, flour and baking soda. Stir until mixture forms a ball. Divide dough into 5 portions. Pat into greased 8-inch pans. Bake for 10 minutes or until golden brown. Remove carefully to wire rack. Combine 1/2 cup sugar with next 7 ingredients in top of double boiler. Cook over hot water until thickened. Spread between layers. Combine butter with remaining ingredients in saucepan. Boil for 1 1/2 minutes. Let stand until cool. Beat until shiny. Drizzle over top of torte. Chill for 1 to 2 days. Yield: 8 to 10 servings.

Maureen Attridge, Preceptor Gamma Rho
Kemptville, Ontario, Canada

CHOCOLATE VIENNA TORTE

1 angel food cake	1/3 cup cold milk
1 cup butter or margarine, softened	1/3 cup boiling water
1 1/4 cups confectioners' sugar	1/2 teaspoon rum flavoring
1 4-ounce package chocolate instant pudding mix	Unsweetened chocolate shavings

Split cake into 3 layers horizontally. Cream butter in mixer bowl until light and fluffy. Blend in confectioners' sugar, pudding mix and cold milk; beat until fluffy. Add boiling water gradually, beating constantly until smooth and creamy. Spread between layers and over top. Garnish with chocolate shavings. Chill until serving time. Yield: 10 to 12 servings.

Janice M. Fluker, Beta Iota
Owen Sound, Ontario, Canada

DOBOS TORTE

5 eggs, separated	2 egg yolks
2/3 cup sugar	2 1/2 to 3 cups sifted confectioners' sugar
1 teaspoon vanilla extract	1/2 cup half and half
2/3 cup sifted cake flour	1 tablespoon vanilla extract
4 ounces unsweetened chocolate	12 lace cookies
1 cup butter or margarine, softened	Brandy-flavored whipped cream

Preheat oven to 350 degrees. Grease and line two 10-by-15-inch cake pans with waxed paper. Grease waxed paper. Beat egg whites in large bowl until foamy. Add 1/3 cup sugar 1 tablespoon at a time, beating until soft peaks form. Beat egg yolks in small bowl with remaining sugar and vanilla until thick and fluffy. Fold in flour gently. Stir in 1/3 of the beaten egg whites. Fold mixture into remaining egg whites. Spread evenly in prepared pans. Bake for 12 minutes or until center springs back when lightly touched. Invert onto wire rack; remove waxed paper. Cool completely. Cut each baked layer crosswise into four 4-by-10-inch strips. Melt chocolate in top of double boiler over hot water. Remove from heat. Beat in butter and 2 egg yolks. Beat in confectioners' sugar and half and half alternately until smooth and of desired spreading consistency. Stir in vanilla. Stack layers on serving plate, spreading 1/4 cup frosting between layers. Spread remaining frosting over top and sides. Prepare favorite recipe lace cookies, shaping each into a cone. Pipe whipped cream into cones. Arrange filled cookies on top of torte. Garnish with piped whipped cream. Yield: 12 servings.

Vicki Fugate, Delta Phi
North Platte, Nebraska

MIDNIGHT TORTE

1 cup semisweet chocolate chips, melted	3 eggs
1 1/4 cups water	1/4 cup baking cocoa
2 1/4 cups all-purpose flour	1/4 cup sugar
1 teaspoon baking soda	2 cups whipping cream
3/4 teaspoon salt	6 tablespoons butter or margarine
1 1/2 cups sugar	1/3 cup light corn syrup
3/4 cup butter or margarine, softened	2 tablespoons water
1 teaspoon vanilla extract	2 cups semisweet chocolate chips

Preheat oven to 375 degrees. Blend 1 cup melted chocolate chips with 1/4 cup water. Set aside. Blend flour with next 2 ingredients. Beat 1 1/2 cups sugar with 3/4 cup butter and vanilla in large mixer bowl until creamy. Add eggs 1 at a time, beating well after each addition. Add chocolate mixture, beating until blended. Add flour and 1 cup water alternately, beating well after each addition. Pour into 2 greased and floured 9-inch round cake pans. Bake for 30 to 35 minutes or until top springs back when lightly touched. Cool in pans for 10 minutes. Remove to wire racks to cool completely. Split layers into halves horizontally. Blend baking cocoa and 1/4 cup sugar in small mixer bowl. Add whipping cream. Beat at medium speed until soft peaks form. Place 1 torte layer on serving plate. Spread with 1/3 of the filling. Repeat with remaining torte layers and filling, ending with torte layer. Combine 6 tablespoons butter with

corn syrup and 2 tablespoons water in saucepan. Bring to a boil over low heat, stirring constantly. Remove from heat. Stir in 2 cups chocolate chips until smooth. Let stand until cool. Spread over top and sides of torte. Chill for several minutes or until glaze is set. Store in refrigerator. Yield: 10 to 12 servings.

Denise Flanders, Delta Phi
North Platte, Nebraska

NUTCRACKER SWEET

6 eggs, separated	1 cup finely crushed graham crackers
1 cup sugar	1 ounce unsweetened chocolate, grated
1/4 cup all-purpose flour	1 cup finely chopped nuts
1 1/4 teaspoons baking powder	4 cups whipping cream
1/2 teaspoon ground cloves	1/2 cup confectioners' sugar
2 teaspoons cinnamon	2 teaspoons rum extract
2 tablespoons vegetable oil	Grated chocolate
1 tablespoon rum extract	

Preheat oven to 350 degrees. Beat egg whites until frothy. Add 1/2 cup sugar gradually, beating until stiff peaks form. Stir in remaining sugar and next 4 ingredients. Combine egg yolks, oil and 1 tablespoon rum extract in bowl; beat for 1 minute at medium speed. Pour mixture over beaten egg whites; fold in gently. Fold in graham cracker crumbs, 1 ounce chocolate and nuts gently. Pour into 2 waxed paper-lined 8-inch round cake pans. Bake for 30 to 35 minutes or until layers test done. Invert immediately to cool by resting edges of each pan on 2 other inverted pans. Loosen with spatula when completely cooled. Tap bottom of pan to release cake. Split layers into halves horizontally. Whip whipping cream with confectioners' sugar and 2 teaspoons rum extract. Place 1 layer on serving plate; spread with whipped cream mixture. Repeat with remaining layers. Garnish with grated chocolate. Yield: 12 servings.

Linda Jonsson, Eta
Marion, Ohio

BAVARIAN MINTS

2 cups each semisweet chocolate chips and milk chocolate chips	1 14-ounce can sweetened condensed milk
1 tablespoon butter or margarine	1 teaspoon peppermint extract
1 teaspoon vanilla extract	

Microwave chocolate chips with butter in glass bowl until melted. Add remaining ingredients; stir until smooth. Spoon into buttered 9-by-13-inch dish. Cool. Cut into squares. Yield: 36 servings.

Lonne Kay Mackie, Epsilon Iota
Blair, Nebraska

CHERRY MASH CANDY

2 cups sugar	1 teaspoon vanilla
2/3 cup evaporated milk	extract
Salt to taste	2 cups semisweet
12 marshmallows	chocolate chips
1/2 cup margarine	1 10-ounce can
1 cup cherry-flavored	peanuts, crushed
chips	3/4 cup peanut butter

Combine sugar with next 4 ingredients in saucepan. Boil for 5 minutes. Remove from heat. Stir in cherry chips and vanilla until smooth. Pour into buttered 9-by-14-inch dish. Melt chocolate chips in saucepan over low heat, stirring constantly. Stir in remaining ingredients. Pour over cherry layer. Chill until firm. Yield: 36 servings.

Susan J. Seals, Xi Delta Iota
Marshalltown, Iowa

CHOCOLATE-AMARETTO TRUFFLES

2 cups milk chocolate	2/3 cups finely chopped
chips	toasted almonds
1/4 cup sour cream	
2 tablespoons Amaretto	

Melt chocolate chips in double boiler over hot water. Stir until smooth. Remove from heat. Stir in sour cream. Add liqueur; mix well. Spoon into small bowl. Chill until firm. Drop by rounded teaspoonfuls onto waxed paper-lined baking sheets. Shape into balls. Roll in almonds. Chill for 30 minutes or until firm. Yield: 30 servings.

Brandi Fleischmann, Xi Upsilon Omicron
Murphys, California

DARK CHOCOLATE FUDGE

3 cups semisweet	Salt to taste
chocolate chips	1 cup pecans, chopped
1 14-ounce can	1 1/2 teaspoons almond
sweetened condensed	extract
milk	

Melt chocolate chips with condensed milk and salt in heavy saucepan over low heat. Remove from heat. Stir in pecans and almond flavoring. Spread evenly in wax paper-lined 8-inch square pan. Chill for 2 hours or until firm. Invert pan; remove waxed paper. Cut into squares. Store, loosely covered, at room temperature. Yield: 24 servings.

Virginia A. Phillips
Brandon, Mississippi

MICRO-RAVE FUDGE

2 1-pound packages	1/2 cup milk
confectioners' sugar	1 1/2 cups chopped nuts
1 cup baking cocoa	2 tablespoons vanilla
1 cup butter or	extract
margarine	

Sift confectioners' sugar and baking cocoa into large glass bowl. Make well in center. Add butter and milk in well. Do not stir. Microwave on High for 4 1/2 to 6 minutes or until butter melts. Add nuts and vanilla. Stir until smooth. Pour into greased 8-by-12-inch dish. Chill until firm. Cut into squares. Yield: 36 servings.

Carol M. Wyatt, Delta Nu
West Columbia, South Carolina

PEANUT BUTTER-CHOCOLATE FUDGE PINWHEELS

1 cup peanut butter	1 teaspoon vanilla
chips	extract
1 14-ounce can	1/2 cup chocolate
sweetened condensed	sprinkles
milk	
1 cup semisweet	
chocolate chips	

Cover baking sheet with foil. Grease lightly a 10-by-12-inch area on foil. Melt peanut butter chips with half the condensed milk in saucepan over low heat, stirring occasionally. Spread mixture over greased area of prepared pan. Cool slightly. Pat gently with hands to distribute evenly. Let stand for 30 minutes. Melt chocolate chips with remaining condensed milk in medium saucepan over low heat, stirring occasionally. Remove from heat. Stir in vanilla. Cool slightly. Spread evenly over peanut butter layer. Let stand for 30 minutes. Roll layers together gently as for jelly roll, lifting long side of foil. Roll log in chocolate sprinkles. Store, tightly wrapped in plastic wrap, in cool place for up to 2 weeks. Bring to room temperature; cut into 1/4-inch slices. Yield: 48 servings.

Janette Annis, Preceptor Pi
Kindersley, Saskatchewan, Canada

MARTHA WASHINGTON CANDY

1/2 cup melted butter or	1 teaspoon vanilla
margarine	extract
2 1-pound packages	2 cups chopped pecans
confectioners' sugar	2 cups semisweet
1 14-ounce can	chocolate chips
sweetened condensed	1 bar paraffin wax
milk	

Combine butter with next 4 ingredients in bowl; mix well with hands. Shape into small balls. Melt chocolate with paraffin in top of double boiler over hot water, stirring occasionally. Dip balls into chocolate; place on waxed paper. Let stand until set. Store in refrigerator. Yield: 60 servings.

Cindy Haden, Alpha Lambda
Parker, Colorado

DATE-NUT ROLL

2 cups sugar
1 cup evaporated milk
1 package dates, finely
    chopped

2 cups chopped pecans
1 cup finely chopped
    pecans

Combine sugar and evaporated milk in saucepan. Cook over low heat to 234 to 240 degrees on candy thermometer, soft-ball stage. Add dates, stirring until dates are very soft. Cool slightly. Beat until creamy. Stir in 2 cups chopped pecans. Pour mixture onto damp towel. Roll, forming a roll 1¹/₂ inches in diameter. Remove towel; roll in finely chopped pecans. Rewrap in towel to prevent drying. Yield: 20 servings.

Suzanne Willingham, Xi Beta Mu
Montgomery, Alabama

EASY DATE-NUT ROLL

2 cups vanilla wafer
    crumbs
2 cups finely chopped
    pecans
1 8-ounce package
    chopped dates

²/₃ cup sweetened
    condensed milk
1 tablespoon water

Combine vanilla wafer crumbs with remaining ingredients in large bowl; mix well. Divide mixture into halves. Shape each into 8-inch roll. Chill, wrapped in waxed paper, overnight. Cut into slices at serving time. Yield: 24 servings.

Jeanette Young
St. Simons Island, Georgia

TEXAS MILLIONAIRE CANDY

1 cup sugar
1 cup packed light
    brown sugar
1 cup dark corn syrup
1 cup margarine
2 cups evaporated milk

1 tablespoon vanilla
    extract
1 pound pecans, shelled
2 9-ounce chocolate
    candy bars
4 ounces paraffin

Combine sugar, brown sugar, corn syrup, margarine and 1 cup evaporated milk in saucepan. Bring to a rolling boil, stirring constantly. Stir in remaining evaporated milk gradually. Cook to 240 to 248 degrees on candy thermometer, firm-ball stage. Remove from heat. Stir in vanilla and pecans. Pour into buttered 8-by-12-inch dish. Chill overnight. Cut into small squares. Melt chocolate candy with paraffin in double boiler over hot water. Dip squares into chocolate; place on waxed paper. Yield: 30 servings.

Beth Leatherwood, Preceptor Lambda Xi
Lamesa, Texas

MICROWAVE PRALINES

1 1-pound package
    light brown sugar
1 cup whipping cream

¹/₄ cup margarine
1 cup pecans

Combine brown sugar and whipping cream in glass bowl. Microwave, covered with waxed paper, for 13 minutes. Stir in margarine and pecans. Stir until cooled and of desired consistency. Drop by tablespoonfuls onto waxed paper. Let stand until cool. Yield: 24 servings.

Laura Key, Preceptor Lambda Sigma
Beaumont, Texas

TOFFEE CRUNCH

2 cups sugar
2 cups butter or
    margarine
Salt to taste

2 cups semisweet
    chocolate chips
Crushed pecans

Combine sugar, butter and salt in saucepan. Cook over medium heat to 300 degrees on candy thermometer, hard-crack stage, stirring constantly with wooden spoon. Pour quickly onto foil-lined baking sheet, spreading evenly. Let stand until firm. Melt chocolate chips in top of double boiler over hot water. Spread half the chocolate over top of candy. Sprinkle with half the pecans. Turn candy over. Spread with remaining chocolate. Sprinkle with remaining pecans. Cool until set. Break into pieces. Store in airtight container. Yield: 16 servings.

Ester Sullivan, Xi Epsilon Eta
Centreville, Virginia

SUGARPLUM SHERRIED WALNUTS

1¹/₂ cups packed light
    brown sugar
¹/₄ cup sherry
2 tablespoons light corn
    syrup
¹/₄ teaspoon salt

1 teaspoon pumpkin pie
    spice
6 cups walnut pieces or
    halves
1 cup sugar

Combine brown sugar, sherry, corn syrup, salt and pumpkin pie spice in heavy saucepan. Cook until brown sugar dissolves and mixture bubbles. Place walnuts in large bowl. Pour hot mixture over top; mix well. Place 1 cup sugar in large plastic bag. Add walnuts, tossing until lightly coated. Spread on baking sheet. Let stand until dry. Store in tightly covered container. Yield: 24 servings.

Myra Wilding, Laureate Beta Beta
Cleveland, Ohio

BETTER-THAN-TWIX BARS

1/2 cup crushed club crackers	*1 cup crushed graham crackers*
1/2 cup packed light brown sugar	*1/2 cup crushed club crackers*
1/2 cup sugar	*1/2 cup peanut butter*
1/2 cup butter or margarine	*1 cup semisweet chocolate chips*
1/4 cup milk	*1/2 cup butterscotch chips*

Line a 9-by-13-inch dish with 1/2 cup club cracker crumbs. Combine brown sugar, sugar, butter and milk in saucepan. Simmer over low heat for 5 minutes. Remove from heat. Stir in graham cracker crumbs. Spread over prepared layer. Sprinkle with 1/2 cup club cracker crumbs. Melt peanut butter, chocolate chips and butterscotch chips in saucepan over low heat. Spread over club cracker layer. Cut into bars when cool. Yield: 3 dozen.

Teri Hartman, Delta Phi
North Platte, Nebraska

ITALIAN TOASTED SLICES OR BISCOTTI

This Italian recipe goes back to my great-grandmother. During her era these took the place of doughnuts with your coffee.

6 eggs	*1/2 teaspoon salt*
1 cup sugar	*1 1/2 teaspoons baking powder*
1 cup corn oil	
1 teaspoon anise extract	*1 cup chopped walnuts*
2 1/2 cups all-purpose flour	

Preheat oven to 350 degrees. Combine eggs and sugar in mixer bowl; mix well. Add oil and anise extract; mix until blended. Add mixture of flour, salt and baking powder; mix well. Fold in walnuts. Spread in 10-by-15-inch baking pan. Bake for 20 minutes. Cool in pan for 15 minutes. Invert onto hard surface. Cut baked layer into thirds horizontally. Cut thirds into 1-by-5-inch slices vertically. Place on nonstick baking sheet. Reduce oven temperature to 275 degrees. Bake until toasted, turning once. Yield: 2 1/2 dozen.

Marlene Pape, Preceptor Laureate Alpha Zeta
Battle Creek, Michigan

BROWNIES DIPPED IN CHOCOLATE

I have taken these brownies to City Council teas and Installations.

1 package fudge brownie mix	*8 ounces cream cheese, softened*
1/3 cup milk	*1/2 teaspoon vanilla extract*
1/3 cup vegetable oil	
1 egg	*1 egg*
1 cup semisweet chocolate chips	*12 ounces chocolate candy wafers, melted*
1/4 cup sugar	

Preheat oven to 350 degrees. Combine brownie mix, milk, oil and 1 egg in medium bowl; mix by hand. Spread in greased 9-by-13-inch baking pan. Sprinkle chocolate chips over top. Combine sugar, cream cheese, vanilla and 1 egg in mixer bowl, beating until smooth. Spread over chocolate chips. Bake for 30 to 35 minutes or until brownies test done. Cool overnight or chill in freezer. Cut into bars and dip in melted chocolate. Place on waxed paper to cool. Chill in freezer until firm. Yield: 3 dozen.

Roberta Balser, Preceptor Epsilon
Davison, Michigan

CANDY BAR BROWNIES

4 eggs, beaten	*1/2 teaspoon baking powder*
2 cups sugar	
3/4 cup butter or margarine, softened	*1/3 cup baking cocoa*
2 teaspoons vanilla extract	*4 2-ounce Snickers bars, coarsely chopped*
1 1/2 cups all-purpose flour	*3 1 1/2-ounce Hershey's milk chocolate bars, finely chopped*
1/4 teaspoon salt	

Preheat oven to 350 degrees. Combine eggs, sugar, butter and vanilla in large bowl; mix well. Stir in mixture of flour, salt, baking powder and baking cocoa. Fold in chopped Snickers bars. Spread in greased and floured 9-by-13-inch baking pan. Sprinkle with Hershey's bars pieces. Bake for 35 minutes. Cool on wire rack. Cut into bars. Yield: 3 dozen.

Jan Rorrer, Alpha
Springfield, Missouri

COCONUT BROWNIES

1 cup butter or margarine, softened	*1 cup all-purpose flour*
	1 cup chopped peanuts
1/4 cup baking cocoa	*1/2 teaspoon salt*
2 cups sugar	*1/2 cup flaked coconut*
3 eggs	*1/2 teaspoon cinnamon*
1 teaspoon vanilla extract	*2 tablespoons sugar*

Preheat oven to 350 degrees. Melt 1/2 cup butter with baking cocoa in saucepan, blending well. Beat remaining 1/2 cup butter and 2 cups sugar in mixer bowl until light and fluffy. Add eggs and vanilla; mix well. Stir in cooled cocoa mixture. Add mixture of flour, peanuts and salt; mix well. Spread in greased and floured 9-by-13-inch baking pan. Sprinkle with mixture of coconut, cinnamon and 2 tablespoons sugar. Bake for 45 minutes. Cool on wire rack. Cut into 1 1/2-inch bars. Yield: 1 1/2 dozen.

Ann Melton, Preceptor Mu
Las Vegas, Nevada

HONEY BROWNIES

1/4 cup margarine, softened	2 ounces unsweetened chocolate, melted
3/4 cup sugar	1/2 cup all-purpose flour
1/3 cup honey	1/2 teaspoon salt
2 teaspoons vanilla extract	1 cup chopped nuts (optional)
2 eggs	

Preheat oven to 350 degrees. Cream margarine and sugar in mixer bowl until light and fluffy. Stir in honey and vanilla. Add eggs; mix well. Add melted chocolate, stirring until blended. Add mixture of flour and salt gradually to creamed mixture; mix well. Spread in greased 9-by-9-inch baking pan. Bake for 25 to 30 minutes or until brownies test done. Cut into bars when cool. Yield: 16 bars.

Kim Palmer, Zeta Nu
Princeton, Missouri

MY GRANDMOTHER'S CANDY BAR COOKIES

3/4 cup butter or margarine, softened	1 cup sifted confectioners' sugar
3/4 cup sifted confectioners' sugar	1 cup chopped pecans
1 teaspoon vanilla extract	1 cup semisweet chocolate chips
2 tablespoons evaporated milk	1/3 cup evaporated milk
1/4 teaspoon salt	2 tablespoons butter or margarine
2 cups sifted all-purpose flour	1 teaspoon vanilla extract
8 ounces light caramels	1/2 cup sifted confectioners' sugar
1/4 cup evaporated milk	Whole pecan halves
1/4 cup butter or margarine	

Preheat oven to 325 degrees. Cream 3/4 cup butter and 3/4 cup confectioners' sugar in mixer bowl until light and fluffy. Stir in 1 teaspoon vanilla and next 2 ingredients. Add flour; mix well. Divide dough into two portions. Roll on floured surface. Cut into 1 1/2-by-3-inch rectangles or 2-inch squares. Place on ungreased baking sheets. Bake for 12 to 16 minutes or until light brown. Remove to wire rack to cool. Melt caramels with 1/4 cup evaporated milk in double boiler; mix well. Remove from heat. Stir in 1/4 cup butter, 1 cup confectioners' sugar and 1 cup chopped pecans. Set aside. Melt chocolate chips with 1/3 cup evaporated milk in double boiler over low heat; mix well. Remove from heat. Stir in 2 table-spoons butter and next 2 ingredients. Remove from heat. Layer caramel and chocolate mixtures over baked cookies. Top each cookie with whole pecan half. Yield: 3 to 4 dozen.

Melissa Baker, Gamma Omega
Kingman, Arizona

CARAMEL DREAM BARS

1 2-layer package yellow cake mix	1 egg
1/3 cup margarine, softened	1 teaspoon vanilla extract
1 egg	1 cup chopped pecans
1 14-ounce can sweetened condensed milk	1 cup butterscotch chips

Preheat oven to 350 degrees. Combine cake mix, margarine and 1 egg in mixer bowl. Beat at high speed until crumbly. Press into nonstick 9-by-13-inch baking pan. Mix condensed milk, 1 egg and vanilla in medium bowl, beating until blended. Stir in pecans and butterscotch chips. Spread over prepared layer. Bake for 25 to 30 minutes or until light brown. Cool completely before cutting into bars. Yield: 32 bars.

Louise Summar, Alpha Master
Nashville, Tennessee

CHOCOLATE-BUTTERMILK SQUARES

This recipe is a favorite of my whole family, especially my husband. I have made it for the cookie exchange in my home and for the office cookie exchange for 30 years.

1 cup butter or margarine	1/2 cup butter or margarine
1/4 cup baking cocoa	1/4 cup baking cocoa
1 cup water	1/4 cup buttermilk
2 cups sugar	1 1-pound package confectioners' sugar
2 cups all-purpose flour	1 teaspoon vanilla extract
1/2 teaspoon salt	Salt to taste
1 teaspoon baking soda	3/4 cup sliced almonds
1/2 cup buttermilk	
2 eggs, beaten	
1 teaspoon vanilla extract	

Preheat oven to 350 degrees. Bring 1 cup butter, 1/4 cup baking cocoa and water to a boil in saucepan over medium heat, stirring to mix well. Remove from heat; cool. Combine sugar, flour and salt in large bowl; mix well. Add baking cocoa mixture; mix well. Stir in mixture of baking soda and buttermilk. Add eggs and 1 teaspoon vanilla; mix well. Spread in greased 10-by-15-inch baking pan. Bake for 20 minutes. Cool on wire rack. Combine 1/2 cup butter, 1/4 cup baking cocoa, 1/4 cup buttermilk, confectioners' sugar, 1 teaspoon vanilla and salt in mixer bowl, beating until of spreading consistency. Fold in almonds. Spread over brownies. Cut into squares. Yield: 4 dozen.

Gerri M. Manke, Xi Delta Chi
Ritzville, Washington

CHOCOLATE-MERINGUE BARS

1/2 teaspoon salt
1 teaspoon baking soda
2 cups all-purpose flour
1 cup butter or
*   margarine, softened*
1/3 cup sugar
1/2 cup packed light
*   brown sugar*
2 egg yolks
1 tablespoon cold water
1 teaspoon vanilla
*   extract*
1 cup semisweet
*   chocolate chips*
1/2 cup chopped pecans
2 egg whites, at room
*   temperature*
1 cup packed light
*   brown sugar*

Preheat oven to 275 degrees. Sift salt, baking soda and flour together. Cream butter and next 2 ingredients in mixer bowl until light and fluffy. Beat egg yolks, water and vanilla into creamed mixture until blended. Add dry ingredients; mix well. Spread into greased 10-by-15-inch baking pan. Sprinkle with chocolate chips and pecans. Beat egg whites in mixer bowl until stiff. Add 1 cup brown sugar gradually, beating constantly. Spread over prepared layers. Bake for 30 minutes. Cool before cutting into bars. Yield: 3 dozen.

Nancy Marie Sanders, Zeta Eta
Goshen, Alabama

CHOCOLATE-CARAMEL SHORTBREAD

1 cup butter or
*   margarine, softened*
1/2 cup confectioners'
*   sugar*
1/4 teaspoon salt
11/4 cups all-purpose
*   flour*
1/2 cup butter or
*   margarine*
3 tablespoons light corn
*   syrup*
1 14-ounce can
*   sweetened condensed*
*   milk*
1 teaspoon vanilla
*   extract*
3 ounces semisweet
*   chocolate, melted*

Preheat oven to 350 degrees. Cream butter and next 2 ingredients in mixer bowl until light and fluffy. Add flour; mix well. Press into greased 9-by-9-inch baking pan. Bake 30 to 35 minutes or until light brown. Cool slightly. Microwave 1/2 cup butter in microwave-safe dish for 1 minute. Stir in corn syrup and condensed milk. Microwave on High for 8 minutes or until mixture turns a light caramel color, stirring at 1 minute intervals. Stir in vanilla. Spread over warm baked layer. Drizzle with melted chocolate. Chill until firm. Cut into bars. Store, covered, at room temperature. Yield: 2 dozen.

Barbara Horlock, Laureate Alpha Lambda
Kelowna, British Columbia, Canada

Fiona Semaniuk, Omega, Edmonton, Alberta, Canada, makes Shortbread Cookies by creaming 1 cup butter with 3 tablespoons berry sugar, adding 2 cups flour and kneading on surface sprinkled with 3 tablespoons rice flour. Cut as desired and bake in preheated 350-degree oven until light brown.

CHOCOLATE-PEANUT BUTTER DREAMS

This is my family's favorite dessert. I enjoy serving it to company because everyone loves it! It is quick, easy and delicious.

2 cups quick-cooking
*   oats*
13/4 cups packed light
*   brown sugar*
1 cup all-purpose flour
1/2 cup whole wheat
*   flour*
1 teaspoon baking soda
1 cup butter or
*   margarine, softened*
1/2 cup chopped peanuts
1 egg, beaten
1 14-ounce can
*   sweetened condensed*
*   milk*
1/3 cup creamy peanut
*   butter*
2 cups semisweet
*   chocolate chips*

Preheat oven to 350 degrees. Combine oats, brown sugar, all-purpose flour, whole wheat flour and baking soda in medium bowl; mix well. Cut in butter until crumbly. Stir in peanuts. Reserve 13/4 cups crumb mixture. Add egg to remaining mixture; mix well. Press into nonstick 9-by-13-inch baking pan. Bake for 15 minutes. Spread mixture of condensed milk and peanut butter over baked layer. Sprinkle with mixture of reserved crumb mixture and chocolate chips. Bake 12 to 15 minutes or until edges are golden. Remove to wire rack to cool completely. Cut into bars. Yield: 4 dozen.

Jolynn Peterson, Epsilon
Brigham City, Utah

❖ WHITE CHOCOLATE-RASPBERRY BARS

1/2 cup butter or
*   margarine*
1 cup white chocolate
*   chips*
2 eggs
1/2 cup sugar
1 cup all-purpose flour
1/2 teaspoon salt
1 teaspoon Amaretto or
*   almond extract*
1/2 cup raspberry jam
1 cup white chocolate
*   chips*
1/2 cup sliced almonds

Preheat oven to 350 degrees. Melt butter in saucepan over low heat. Add 1 cup white chocolate chips; do not stir. Beat eggs in mixer bowl until foamy. Add sugar gradually, beating until lemon-colored. Stir in white chocolate chip mixture. Add flour, salt and Amaretto. Mix at low speed just until moistened. Divide batter into 2 portions. Spread 1 portion in greased and floured 9-by-9-inch baking pan. Bake for 15 minutes or until light brown. Heat jam in saucepan over low heat. Spread over warm baked layer. Spoon mixture of remaining butter and 1 cup white chocolate chips over jam, allowing jam to peek through batter. Sprinkle with almonds. Bake for 25 to 30 minutes or until toothpick inserted in center comes out clean. Cut into bars when cool. Yield: 16 to 24 bars.

Jan Adair, Eta Zeta
Wheaton, Illinois

ROCKY ROAD FUDGE BARS

1/2 cup butter or margarine	1 egg
1 ounce unsweetened chocolate	1/2 teaspoon vanilla extract
1 cup sugar	1/4 cup chopped nuts
1 cup all-purpose flour	1 cup semisweet chocolate chips
1/2 to 1 cup chopped nuts	2 cups miniature marshmallows
1 teaspoon baking powder	1/4 cup butter or margarine
1 teaspoon vanilla extract	1 ounce unsweetened chocolate
2 eggs	2 ounces cream cheese
6 ounces cream cheese, softened	1/4 cup milk
1/2 cup sugar	3 cups confectioners' sugar
2 tablespoons all-purpose flour	1 teaspoon vanilla extract
1/4 cup butter or margarine, softened	

Preheat oven to 350 degrees. Melt 1/2 cup butter and 1 ounce chocolate in saucepan over medium heat, mixing well. Add 1 cup sugar and next 5 ingredients; mix well. Spread in greased and floured 9-by-13-inch baking pan. Combine 6 ounces cream cheese and next 5 ingredients in mixer bowl. Beat at medium speed until light and fluffy. Stir in 1/4 cup nuts. Spread over prepared layer. Sprinkle with chocolate chips. Bake for 25 to 35 minutes or until toothpick inserted in center comes out clean. Sprinkle with marshmallows. Bake an additional 2 minutes. Combine 1/4 cup butter, 1 ounce chocolate, 2 ounces cream cheese and milk in saucepan over low heat, mixing well. Stir in confectioners' sugar and vanilla until of spreading consistency. Spread over marshmallows, swirling to mix. Cut into bars when cool. Store in refrigerator. Yield: 3 to 4 dozen.

Connie Henderson, Delta Phi
North Platte, Nebraska
*Linda M. Roper
Dumfries, Virginia

SIMPLY DELICIOUS BROWNIES

2 ounces unsweetened chocolate	1/2 teaspoon salt
1/3 cup vegetable oil	1/2 teaspoon baking soda
3/4 cup water	1 teaspoon almond extract
1 cup sugar	1 cup semisweet chocolate chips
1 egg, beaten	1/3 cup sliced almonds
1 1/4 cups all-purpose flour	

Preheat oven to 350 degrees. Melt chocolate with oil in 8-inch square baking pan, mixing well. Add water and next 6 ingredients in order given, mixing until blended. Spread batter to edges of pan. Sprinkle with chocolate chips and almonds. Bake for 30 to 40 minutes or until brownies test done. Yield: 1 dozen.

Joan Tice, Xi Gamma Tau
Mission, British Columbia, Canada

CONFECTION COOKIES

1 cup butter or margarine	1/4 cup all-purpose flour
1/2 cup sugar	2 cups chopped nuts
2 cups all-purpose flour	8 ounces flaked coconut
1/2 cup cornstarch	1/2 cup butter or margarine, softened
4 eggs	1 1-pound package confectioners' sugar
1 1-pound package light brown sugar	8 ounces cream cheese, softened
1/2 teaspoon baking powder	1 tablespoon vanilla or lemon extract
2 teaspoons vanilla extract	

Preheat oven to 300 degrees. Cream 1 cup butter and next 3 ingredients in mixer bowl until light and fluffy. Press onto greased 11-by-17-inch baking sheet. Bake for 15 minutes. Combine eggs and brown sugar in medium bowl; mix well. Add baking powder and next 2 ingredients; mix well. Stir in nuts and coconut. Spread over baked layer. Bake for 15 minutes. Increase oven temperature to 350 degrees. Bake an additional 5 minutes. Remove to wire rack to cool. Blend 1/2 cup butter and remaining ingredients in medium bowl until of spreading consistency. Frost baked layer. Cut into bars. Yield: 4 dozen.

Irene Finney, Laureate Delta Kappa
Sacramento, California

DREAM BARS

This is a delightful dessert with coffee after church or for your bridge group.

1/2 cup margarine, softened	2 tablespoons all-purpose flour
1/2 cup packed light brown sugar	1 teaspoon vanilla extract
1 cup all-purpose flour	1/8 teaspoon salt
1/2 teaspoon salt	2 eggs, beaten
1 cup packed light brown sugar	1 1/2 cups flaked coconut
	1 cup chopped nuts

Preheat oven to 350 degrees. Combine 1/2 cup margarine, 1/2 cup brown sugar, 1 cup flour and salt in medium bowl; mix well. Pat into nonstick 9-by-13-inch baking pan. Bake for 15 minutes. Mix 1 cup brown sugar, 2 tablespoons flour, vanilla, salt and eggs in medium bowl; mix well. Stir in coconut and nuts. Spread over baked layer. Bake for 20 minutes. Cut into bars while warm. Yield: 2 dozen.

Zandee Nelson, Preceptor Xi
Aurora, Nebraska

ENGLISH TOFFEE BARS

24 unsalted crackers	1/2 teaspoon vanilla
1 cup margarine	extract
1 cup packed light	1 cup semisweet
brown sugar	chocolate chips

Preheat oven to 375 degrees. Line crackers in bottom of greased 9-by-13-inch baking pan. Combine margarine and brown sugar in saucepan; mix well. Boil for 3 minutes. Stir in vanilla. Pour over crackers. Bake for 10 minutes. Cool for 5 minutes. Sprinkle baked layer with chocolate chips; spread to cover. Cut into bars. Yield: 3 dozen.

Elizabeth V. Walters, Alpha Theta
Auburn, Alabama
*Charlotte L. Murphy, Xi Upsilon Epsilon
Hallettsville, Texas

FRUITCAKE BARS

1/2 cup sifted all-	1/2 cup sugar
purpose flour	2 eggs, beaten
1/2 teaspoon baking	1/3 cup melted butter or
powder	margarine
1/2 teaspoon salt	1 teaspoon vanilla
1/4 teaspoon cinnamon	extract
1/8 teaspoon nutmeg	2 cups diced mixed
1 8-ounce can crushed	candied fruit
pineapple	1 cup chopped nuts

Preheat oven to 300 degrees. Sift flour and next 4 ingredients together. Boil undrained pineapple and sugar in large saucepan until sugar dissolves. Simmer until mixture is reduced to 2/3 cup. Remove from heat; cool. Add eggs, butter, vanilla, pineapple mixture and dry ingredients; mix well. Stir in candied fruit and nuts. Spread in foil-lined 8-by-8-inch baking pan. Bake for 1 hour. Remove to wire rack to cool completely. Cut into bars. Yield: 2 dozen.

Thelma Kay, Xi Zeta Delta
La Mirada, California

HONEY COOKIES

A favorite at family reunions, made by a favorite aunt.

1 cup shortening	1 teaspoon ginger
1 cup honey	1 teaspoon baking soda
1 cup packed light	3 cups sifted all-
brown sugar	purpose flour
1/4 cup water	2 eggs, beaten

Preheat oven to 350 degrees. Combine shortening and remaining ingredients in medium bowl; mix well. Spread in greased 10-by-15-inch baking pan. Bake for 20 to 25 minutes or until cookies test done. Cool slightly. May sprinkle with confectioners' sugar or frost with confectioners' sugar icing. Cut into bars. Yield: 2 dozen.

Mary Kay Simms, Laureate Beta
Beach Park, Illinois

JUMBO COOKIE

1/2 cup margarine,	1 egg
softened	1 1/2 cups all-purpose
3/4 cup packed light	flour
brown sugar	1/2 teaspoon salt
3 tablespoons sugar	3/4 teaspoon baking soda
1 1/2 teaspoons vanilla	1 1/2 cups semisweet
extract	chocolate chips

Cream margarine and brown sugar in mixer bowl until light and fluffy. Add sugar; mix well. Add vanilla and egg; mix well. Blend in flour, salt and baking soda at low speed, mixing well. Stir in 1 cup chocolate chips. Chill dough in refrigerator for 1 1/2 hours or in the freezer for 45 minutes. Preheat oven to 325 degrees. Press dough within 1 1/2 inches of edge in greased 12-inch round baking pan. Sprinkle with 1/2 cup chocolate chips. Bake for 30 to 35 minutes or until cookie tests done. May add chopped nuts, coconut, "M & M" chocolate candies or any combination of ingredients. Yield: 1 large cookie.

Janice Roth, Xi Epsilon Xi
Dodge City, Kansas

LUSCIOUS LEMON BARS

1 cup margarine,	2 cups sugar
softened	4 eggs, beaten
2 cups all-purpose flour	6 tablespoons lemon
1/2 cup confectioners'	juice
sugar	Grated rind of 1 lemon
1/4 cup all-purpose flour	Confectioners' sugar
1 teaspoon baking	
powder	

Preheat oven to 350 degrees. Combine margarine and next 2 ingredients in medium bowl; mix well. Pat into nonstick 9-by-13-inch baking pan. Bake for 15 minutes. Combine 1/4 cup flour and next 2 ingredients in medium bowl; mix well. Stir in eggs. Add lemon juice and lemon rind; mix well. Spread over baked layer. Bake for 20 minutes. Sprinkle with confectioners' sugar. Cut into bars. Yield: 3 dozen.

Carol Eggemeyer, Alpha Gamma Omega
San Angelo, Texas
*Lynda MacDuffee, Preceptor Lambda Omega
Simi Valley, California

LONDON TEA CAKES

This was a recipe of my great-aunt Matilda. It was always a favorite of mine.

1/2 cup shortening	1 1/2 cups all-purpose flour
1 cup sugar	2 1/2 teaspoons baking
3 egg yolks, beaten	powder
1 egg white, beaten	2 egg whites
1 teaspoon vanilla	1 cup packed light
extract	brown sugar
Salt to taste	1 cup chopped nuts

Preheat oven to 350 degrees. Cream shortening and sugar in mixer bowl until light and fluffy. Add egg yolks, egg white and vanilla; mix well. Add salt, flour and baking powder; mix well. Spread in greased 8-by-10-inch baking pan. Beat egg whites in mixer bowl until soft peaks form. Add brown sugar gradually, beating constantly until stiff peaks form. Fold in nuts. Spread over prepared layer. Bake for 30 minutes. Yield: 1 to 2 dozen.

Carol J. Donahoo, Xi Kappa Mu
Keystone Heights, Florida

MARS BARS-RICE KRISPIE SQUARES

4 Mars Bars	*1 cup semisweet*
1/2 cup margarine	*chocolate chips*
3 cups Rice Krispies	*1/4 cup margarine*

Heat Mars Bars and 1/2 cup margarine in double boiler until melted. Add cereal; mix well. Spread in greased 9-by-13-inch glass dish. Melt chocolate chips and 1/4 cup margarine in saucepan; mix well. Spread over prepared layer. Cool until firm. Cut into squares. Yield: 3 dozen.

Carol J. Babin, Alpha Zeta
Calgary, Alberta, Canada

NUT-JELLY BARS

This is an old Hungarian recipe.

1/2 cup butter or	*1 cup jam*
margarine, softened	*2 egg whites*
1/2 cup confectioners'	*1/2 cup sugar*
sugar	*1/2 teaspoon cinnamon*
2 egg yolks	*1 cup chopped nuts*
1 cup all-purpose flour	

Preheat oven to 350 degrees. Cream butter and confectioners' sugar in mixer bowl until light and fluffy. Beat in egg yolks until blended. Add flour; mix well. Press into ungreased 8-by-8-inch baking pan. Bake for 10 minutes. Spread jam over baked layer. Beat egg whites in mixer bowl until soft peaks form. Add sugar and cinnamon gradually, beating until stiff peaks form. Fold in nuts. Spread over jam. Bake for 20 minutes. Cut into bars. Yield: 10 to 12 bars.

Joan Spellman, Epsilon Master
Pembroke Pines, Florida

PECAN-MARSHMALLOW BARS

1 teaspoon vanilla	*1 cup chopped pecans*
extract	*2 to 3 cups miniature*
1/2 cup butter or	*marshmallows*
margarine	*6 tablespoons butter or*
1 cup sugar	*margarine, browned*
2 eggs	*11/2 cups confectioners'*
3/4 cup all-purpose flour	*sugar*
1 teaspoon baking powder	*1 teaspoon vanilla extract*
1/2 teaspoon salt	*Hot coffee*

Preheat oven to 350 degrees. Combine 1 teaspoon vanilla and next 7 ingredients in order listed in medium bowl; mix well. Press into greased 9-by-13-inch baking pan. Bake for 20 minutes. Sprinkle with marshmallows. Bake until marshmallows are light brown. Remove to wire rack to cool. Combine browned butter and next 2 ingredients in medium bowl; mix well. Add enough coffee to make of spreading consistency. Frost baked layer. Cut into bars. Yield: 3 dozen bars.

Marjorie Hartin, Gamma Omicron
Lacey, Washington

PEANUT BRITTLE COOKIES

You think you are eating candy!

1 cup all-purpose flour	*3 tablespoons beaten egg*
1/4 teaspoon baking soda	*1 teaspoon vanilla*
1/2 teaspoon cinnamon	*extract*
1/2 cup butter or	*11/2 cups finely chopped*
margarine, softened	*salted peanuts*
1/2 cup packed light	
brown sugar	

Preheat oven to 325 degrees. Sift flour and next 2 ingredients together. Cream butter and brown sugar in mixer bowl until light and fluffy. Add 2 tablespoons beaten egg and vanilla; mix well. Stir in 1 cup peanuts and dry ingredients. Spread in greased 10-by-14-inch baking sheet. Brush with 1 tablespoon beaten egg. Sprinkle with remaining 1/2 cup peanuts. Bake for 20 to 25 minutes or until edges pull from sides of pan. Cut into bars. Yield: 2 dozen.

Terri Natali, Xi Alpha Pi
Fresno, California

ROCKY ROAD PIZZA

1 cup butter or	*13/4 cups all-purpose*
margarine, softened	*flour*
1/2 cup sugar	*1 cup chopped peanuts*
1/2 cup packed light	*(optional)*
brown sugar	*1 cup miniature*
1 egg	*marshmallows*
1 teaspoon vanilla	*1 cup semisweet*
extract	*chocolate chips*

Preheat oven to 375 degrees. Cream butter and next 2 ingredients in mixer bowl until light and fluffy. Add egg and vanilla; mix well. Blend in flour at low speed until mixed. Spread in ungreased 14-inch round baking pan. Bake for 12 minutes or until golden brown. Sprinkle baked layer with peanuts, marshmallows and chocolate chips. Bake for an additional 6 to 8 minutes, or until marshmallows are brown. Remove to wire rack to cool completely. Cut into wedges. Yield: 32 servings.

Cindy Bentlage, Mu Epsilon
Jefferson City, Missouri

PUMPKIN BARS

A friend of mine gave her wedding guests a book of her relatives' favorite recipes as a momento of this special day.

2 cups all-purpose flour	1 cup vegetable oil
2 teaspoons cinnamon	3 ounces cream cheese,
1 teaspoon baking soda	softened
2 teaspoons baking	1/2 cup margarine,
powder	softened
1 teaspoon salt	1 teaspoon vanilla
4 eggs	extract
1 2/3 cups sugar	2 cups confectioners'
1 16-ounce can	sugar
pumpkin	

Preheat oven to 350 degrees. Mix flour and next 4 ingredients together. Combine eggs and next 3 ingredients in medium bowl; mix well. Stir in dry ingredients. Spread in ungreased 10-by-15-inch baking pan. Bake for 25 to 30 minutes or until edges pull from sides of pan. Frost with mixture of cream cheese, margarine, vanilla and confectioners' sugar. Cut into bars. Yield: 3 to 4 dozen.

Linda S. Phillips, Laureate Beta Eta
Sheffield Lake, Ohio

PUMPKIN CHEESECAKE BARS

1 16-ounce package	1 14-ounce can
pound cake mix	sweetened condensed
1 egg	milk
2 tablespoons melted	1 16-ounce can
butter or margarine	pumpkin
2 teaspoons pumpkin	2 teaspoons pumpkin
pie spice	pie spice
8 ounces cream cheese,	1/2 teaspoon salt
softened	1 cup chopped nuts
2 eggs	

Preheat oven to 350 degrees. Combine cake mix, 1 egg, butter and 2 teaspoons pumpkin pie spice in mixer bowl. Blend on low speed until crumbly. Press into nonstick 10-by-15-inch baking pan. Beat cream cheese in mixer bowl until fluffy. Blend in next 5 ingredients; mix well. Pour over prepared layer. Sprinkle with nuts. Bake 30 to 35 minutes or until firm. Chill and cut into bars. Store in refrigerator. Yield: 4 dozen.

Marie M. Bray, Preceptor Epsilon Kappa
Orlando, Florida

Rosalyn Higgins, Delta Nu, Columbia, South Carolina, makes Amaretto Lace Cookies by bringing 1/2 cup Amaretto, 1/2 cup butter or margarine, 2/3 cup packed dark brown sugar to a boil, adding 1 cup pecans and 1 cup flour and dropping 4 inches apart on greased cookie sheet. Bake in preheated 375-degree oven for 6 to 8 minutes, cool for 1 minute and roll into cones.

RAINBOW COOKIES

I make these cookies 2 weeks before Christmas which allows the cookies time to mellow, leaving them moist and full of almond flavor.

1 8-ounce can almond	6 to 8 drops of red food
paste	coloring
1 cup butter or	6 to 8 drops of green
margarine, softened	food coloring
1 cup sugar	1/4 cup red jelly or jam
4 egg yolks	1/4 cup apple jelly or jam
2 cups all-purpose flour	1 cup semisweet
4 egg whites	chocolate chips, melted

Preheat oven to 350 degrees. Grease bottoms of three 9-by-13-inch baking pans. Line pans with waxed paper; grease the paper. Cream almond paste and next 3 ingredients in mixer bowl until light and fluffy. Stir in flour. Beat egg whites in mixer bowl until soft peaks form. Fold into almond mixture; mix well. Divide dough into three portions. Mix one portion with red food coloring and one portion with green food coloring, leaving the remaining portion plain. Spread in prepared pans. Bake for 10 to 12 minutes or until edges are light brown. Invert onto wire racks. Remove waxed paper. Invert onto another wire rack. Cool completely. Place green baked layer on large piece of plastic wrap. Spread with red jelly. Top with plain baked layer. Spread with apple jelly. Top with red baked layer. Bring plastic wrap over layers. Place on baking sheet; top with heavy pan or cutting board to compress layers. Chill overnight. Frost with melted chocolate chips. Let stand until firm. Trim edges; cut crosswise into 1/2-inch strips; cut each strip into 4 or 5 pieces. Store in airtight container. Yield: 8 dozen.

Karen Redekopp, Xi Beta Lambda
Kelowna, British Columbia, Canada

SWEET MARIE BARS

This was a favorite dessert of mine as a child.

1/2 cup peanut butter	2 cups crisp rice cereal
1/2 cup light corn syrup	4 ounces milk
1/2 cup packed light	chocolate, melted
brown sugar	2 tablespoons peanut
1/2 cup chopped salted	butter
peanuts	

Combine 1/2 cup peanut butter and next 2 ingredients in heavy skillet; mix well. Cook just until mixture comes to a simmer. Stir in peanuts and cereal. Spread in buttered glass dish. Cool completely. Frost with mixture of melted chocolate and 2 tablespoons peanut butter. Let stand until firm. Cut into bars. Yield: 2 dozen.

Lorraine Brown, Mu
Santa Monica, California

LAST-MINUTE MIRACLES

A cookie this simple should never come out right—but it always does! It is a favorite snack for unexpected guests at our home.

1 cup peanut butter	1 teaspoon vanilla
1 cup sugar	extract
1 egg	

Preheat oven to 350 degrees. Combine first 3 ingredients in medium bowl; mix well. Stir in vanilla. Shape into 1-inch balls. Place on ungreased cookie sheet. Flatten with knife or glass. Bake for 8 to 10 minutes or until brown. Remove to wire rack to cool. Yield: 1 1/2 dozen.

Lori Wright-Lear, Gamma Kappa
Gallatin, Missouri

LEMON COOKIES

My mother-in-law gave me this recipe when I needed a quick dessert for a birthday celebration at work. I have had many compliments and requests for these cookies.

1 2-layer package	2 cups whipped topping
lemon cake mix	1 cup chopped walnuts
1 egg or egg substitute	Confectioners' sugar

Preheat oven to 350 degrees. Combine cake mix and egg in medium bowl; mix well. Fold in whipped topping. Stir in walnuts. Shape into balls. Roll in confectioners' sugar. Place 2 inches apart on nonstick cookie sheet. Bake for 10 minutes. Remove to wire rack to cool completely. Yield: 3 1/2 to 4 dozen.

Kathryn J. Roberts, Theta Omega
Beloit, Kansas

COCONUT FLAKE MACAROONS

I made these cookies for a 4-H cooking project many years ago. They are very healthy—low in fat.

1/4 teaspoon salt	1/2 teaspoon vanilla
2 egg whites	extract
1 cup sugar	1 cup shredded coconut
1 tablespoon all-	2 cups cornflakes
purpose flour	

Preheat oven to 325 degrees. Beat salt and egg whites in mixer bowl until foamy. Add sugar 2 tablespoons at a time, beating until soft peaks form. Fold in flour, vanilla and coconut. Stir in cornflakes. Drop by rounded teaspoonfuls 2 inches apart onto greased cookie sheet. Bake for 18 to 20 minutes or until light brown. Yield: 2 to 3 dozen.

Louise E. Morrison, Xi Kappa
Wilmington, Ohio

HICKORY NUT MACAROONS

No oven temperature was given originally on this recipe because the macaroons were baked in a wood stove. They were watched until they turned brown.

2 cups packed light	1 teaspoon baking
brown sugar	powder
6 tablespoons water	1/2 teaspoon baking soda
1/4 cup butter or	2 cups chopped hickory
margarine, softened	nuts
2 eggs	
2 cups sifted all-	
purpose flour	

Preheat oven to 325 degrees. Cream brown sugar and next 2 ingredients in mixer bowl until light and fluffy. Add eggs; mix well. Stir in flour and next 2 ingredients. Fold in hickory nuts. Drop by teaspoonfuls onto greased cookie sheet. Bake for 12 to 15 minutes or until light brown. Yield: 2 dozen.

Myrian Long, Laureate Nu
Ashland, Ohio

MK'S THREE-IN-ONE COOKIES

My grown daughter and I bake these cookies each year at Christmas.

3 cups all-purpose flour	3 eggs
3/4 teaspoon salt	3 cups finely chopped
1 1/2 teaspoons baking	pecans
soda	1 1/2 teaspoons vanilla
1 cup butter-flavored	extract
shortening	1 cup flaked coconut
1 1/2 cups sugar	1 cup miniature
3/4 cup packed light	semisweet chocolate
brown sugar	chips

Preheat oven to 350 degrees. Sift flour and next 2 ingredients together. Combine shortening, sugar and brown sugar in mixer bowl; mix well. Add eggs, beating until light and fluffy. Stir in dry ingredients. Add pecans and vanilla, mixing well. Divide dough into 3 portions. Add coconut to 1 portion and chocolate chips to 1 portion, leaving third portion plain. Drop by teaspoonfuls onto nonstick cookie sheet. Bake for 10 minutes or until brown. Yield: 9 dozen.

Margaret M. Kallus, Xi Upsilon Epsilon
Hallettsville, Texas

Deanna Porter, Beta Zeta Alpha, Canyon, Texas, makes Double Delicious Bars by layering 1 cup melted margarine, 3 cups graham cracker crumbs, 2 cans sweetened condensed milk, 24 ounces chocolate chips and 2 cups peanut butter chips in baking dish. Bake in preheated 325 to 350-degree oven for 25 to 30 minutes.

POTATO CHIP COOKIES

My grandma used to make these cookies for "forenoon brunch" and "coffee." They are so simple, delicious and crunchy—and a great way to use up those potato chips that keep tempting you!

1 cup confectioners' sugar
1 cup butter or margarine, softened
1 egg yolk
1 teaspoon vanilla extract
1½ cups all-purpose flour
1 cup crushed potato chips
½ cup ground walnuts
Confectioners' sugar

Preheat oven to 350 degrees. Cream confectioners' sugar and butter in mixer bowl until light and fluffy. Add egg yolk and next two ingredients; mix well. Stir in potato chips and walnuts. Drop by teaspoonfuls onto ungreased cookie sheet. Bake for 15 minutes. Sprinkle with additional confectioners' sugar. Yield: 2 dozen.

Teri Farney, Zeta Eta
Derby, Kansas

MOCK SCOTCH CAKES

1 cup butter or margarine, softened
½ cup cornstarch
½ cup confectioners' sugar
1 teaspoon vanilla extract
1½ cups all-purpose flour

Preheat oven to 300 degrees. Cream butter and next two ingredients in mixer bowl until light and fluffy. Add vanilla; mix well. Stir in flour. Drop by teaspoonfuls onto nonstick cookie sheet. Bake for 25 minutes. May frost with your favorite icing. Yield: 2 dozen.

Kathryn Manderville, Xi Rho
Millerton, New Brunswick, Canada

SOFT ROCKS

3 cups all-purpose flour
1 teaspoon baking soda
1 teaspoon cinnamon
1 cup butter or margarine, softened
1½ cups sugar
3 eggs, beaten
1 teaspoon vanilla extract
16 ounces dates, chopped
8 ounces walnuts, chopped
8 ounces grapes, chopped

Preheat oven to 375 degrees. Mix flour and next 2 ingredients together. Cream butter and sugar in mixer bowl until light and fluffy. Add eggs and vanilla; mix well. Add dry ingredients; mix well. Stir in dates, walnuts and grapes. Drop by teaspoonfuls onto nonstick cookie sheet. Bake for 10 to 12 minutes or until brown. Yield: 3 dozen.

Elizabeth I. Morgans, Laureate Delta Iota
Tamaqua, Pennsylvania

CHOCOLATE-PEPPERMINT CREAMS

My grandmother always made these for the Christmas Eve family gathering.

3 cups sifted all-purpose flour
1¼ teaspoons baking soda
1 teaspoon salt
¾ cup butter or margarine
1½ cups packed light brown sugar
2 tablespoons water
2 cups semisweet chocolate chips
2 eggs
3 cups sifted confectioners' sugar
⅓ cup butter or margarine, softened
⅛ teaspoon peppermint extract
Salt to taste
¼ cup milk

Preheat oven to 350 degrees. Sift flour, baking soda and 1 teaspoon salt together. Melt ¾ cup butter with brown sugar and water in saucepan; mix well. Stir in chocolate chips until melted. Add eggs, beating until blended. Stir in dry ingredients. Drop by heaping teaspoonfuls onto cookie sheet lined with greased foil. Bake for 8 to 10 minutes or until cookies test done. Remove to wire rack to cool. Combine 1 cup confectioners' sugar, ⅓ cup butter, peppermint extract and salt to taste in mixer bowl, beating until blended. Add remaining confectioners' sugar alternately with milk, stirring until of spreading consistency. Spread frosting on half the cookies; top with remaining cookies. Yield: 4 dozen.

Dawn Alison Byrum, Alpha Omicron
Anthony, New Mexico

CREAM CHEESE PINWHEELS

1 cup butter or margarine, softened
8 ounces cream cheese, softened
2 cups all-purpose flour
Confectioners' sugar
Apricot preserves
Confectioners' sugar icing
Chopped nuts

Preheat oven to 375 degrees. Cream butter and cream cheese in mixer bowl until light and fluffy. Add flour, blending well. Chill dough. Roll ⅛-inch thick rectangle on surface sprinkled with confectioners' sugar. Cut into 3-inch squares. Make 2-inch cut from each corner toward center. Fold outside points alternately to center; press to secure. Place on nonstick cookie sheet. Bake for 12 minutes. Cool slightly. Fill centers with apricot preserves. Frost with confectioners' sugar icing; sprinkle with nuts. Yield: 2 dozen.

Nancy J. Klenke, Xi Zeta Eta
St. John, Kansas

FILLED ICEBOX COOKIES

1 pound raisins or dates, ground	1 cup shortening
1/2 cup sugar	3 eggs
1/2 cup chopped nuts	4 cups all-purpose flour
1/2 cup water	1 teaspoon baking soda
2 cups packed light brown sugar	1 teaspoon salt

Combine raisins and next 3 ingredients in double boiler; mix well. Cook over medium heat until of desired consistency; set aside. Cream brown sugar and shortening in mixer bowl until light and fluffy. Add eggs; mix well. Add mixture of flour, baking soda and salt, mixing well. Roll into rectangle on floured surface. Spread with cooled raisin mixture. Roll as for jelly roll, sealing edge and ends. Chill overnight. Preheat oven to 400 degrees. Cut dough into 1-inch thick slices. Place on nonstick cookie sheet. Bake for 7 to 8 minutes or until brown. Yield: 4 dozen.

Bettie Carson, Preceptor
Huntington, Oregon

HUNGARIAN KIFLIKS

My mother-in-law brought this recipe from Hungary in 1910.

2 1/2 cups all-purpose flour	3 egg whites
3 egg yolks	1/2 cup sugar
1/2 cup sour cream	1/2 teaspoon vanilla extract (optional)
3/4 cup butter or margarine, softened	1 teaspoon cinnamon
1/2 teaspoon vanilla extract (optional)	12 ounces walnuts, ground

Mix flour and next 4 ingredients in medium bowl until consistency of medium dough. Shape into 2-inch balls. Chill for 3 hours. Preheat oven to 350 degrees. Beat egg whites in mixer bowl until soft peaks form. Add sugar gradually, beating until stiff peaks form. Fold in 1/2 teaspoon vanilla, cinnamon and walnuts. Roll each dough ball into a circle on floured surface. Cut into wedges; spread with walnut mixture. Roll up from wide end. Shape into crescents on ungreased cookie sheet. Bake for 12 to 15 minutes or until brown. Yield: 5 dozen.

Thelma Hoffer, Delta Master
Mansfield, Ohio

MELTING MOMENTS COOKIES

1 cup butter or margarine, softened	1 cup confectioners' sugar
3/4 cup cornstarch	2 tablespoons butter or margarine
1/2 cup confectioners' sugar	1 drop of vanilla extract
1 cup all-purpose flour	Milk

Blend first 4 ingredients in mixer bowl until smooth. Chill for several hours. Preheat oven to 350 degrees. Shape dough into 1-inch balls. Place on nonstick cookie sheet. Make indentation in center of each with thumb. Bake 12 to 15 minutes or until firm. Remove to wire rack to cool. Combine 1 cup confectioners' sugar and next 2 ingredients in medium bowl; mix well. Add enough milk to make of spreading consistency. Spoon frosting into each thumbprint. May tint frosting with food coloring. Yield: 3 dozen.

Tommie May, Xi Rho Zeta
Houston, Texas

MELTING WAFERS

2 1/2 cups all-purpose flour	2 cups confectioners' sugar
1/2 teaspoon salt	1/4 cup margarine, softened
1 cup margarine, softened	2 to 4 tablespoons milk
1/3 cup whipping cream	2 teaspoons vanilla
Sugar	

Mix flour and salt in medium bowl. Cut in margarine until crumbly. Stir in cream. Divide into 3 portions. Chill for 2 hours. Preheat oven to 375 degrees. Roll dough 1/8 inch thick between waxed paper. Cut into 1 1/2-inch circles. Place on ungreased baking sheet. Sprinkle with sugar; prick with fork twice. Bake for 8 to 9 minutes or until brown. Remove to wire rack to cool. Combine confectioners' sugar and 1/4 cup margarine in mixer bowl; mix well. Add enough milk to make of spreading consistency. Stir in vanilla. Spread half the cookies with frosting; top with remaining cookies. Yield: 4 dozen.

Jane F. Uebelacker, Eta Rho
New Brighton, Pennsylvania

SOUR CREAM PASTRIES

1 cup butter or margarine, softened	1/2 cup apricot preserves
2 cups sifted all-purpose flour	1/2 cup flaked coconut
1 egg yolk, beaten	1/4 cup finely chopped pecans
1/2 cup sour cream	Sugar

Cut butter into flour in medium bowl until crumbly. Add mixture of egg yolk and sour cream; mix well. Chill for several hours to overnight. Preheat oven to 350 degrees. Divide dough into 4 portions. Roll each portion into a circle on lightly floured surface. Spread each with 2 tablespoons apricot preserves. Sprinkle with 2 tablespoons coconut and 1 tablespoon pecans. Cut into 12 wedges. Roll up from wide end. Shape into crescents on ungreased cookie sheet. Sprinkle with sugar. Bake for 20 minutes. Remove to wire rack to cool. Yield: 4 dozen.

Nancy Cooper, Phi Master
Arlington, Texas

GINGERBREAD MEN

3/4 cup packed light brown sugar	2 teaspoons ginger
1/2 cup butter or margarine, softened	1 1/2 teaspoons baking soda
2 eggs	1/2 teaspoon allspice
1/4 cup molasses	1/2 teaspoon cinnamon
3 1/4 cups all-purpose flour	1/2 teaspoon nutmeg
	1/2 teaspoon salt

Cream brown sugar and butter in mixer bowl until light and fluffy. Add eggs and molasses; mix well. Stir in flour and remaining ingredients. Chill, covered, for 1 hour. Preheat oven to 350 degrees. Roll dough 1/8 inch thick on floured surface. Cut into gingerbread men shapes. Place on greased cookie sheet. Bake for 10 minutes. Remove to wire rack to cool. Decorate as desired. Yield: 2 dozen.

Anne Humcke, Laureate Alpha Epsilon
Fort Wayne, Indiana

GRANDMA MCKIMMY'S CHRISTMAS COOKIES

This recipe has been handed down through the family for 50 years. These cookies take a lot of work, but they are worth it. The children say it would not be Christmas without them.

4 cups sifted all-purpose flour	1 egg
1 teaspoon salt	1 cup sour cream
1 teaspoon nutmeg	1 teaspoon vanilla extract
1 teaspoon baking soda	1 cup finely chopped nuts
1 1/4 cups sugar	
1 cup butter or margarine, softened	

Mix flour and next 3 ingredients together. Cream sugar and butter in mixer bowl until light and fluffy. Add egg; mix well. Stir in sour cream and vanilla. Add dry ingredients; mix well. Fold in nuts. Divide into 3 portions. Chill, wrapped in waxed paper, overnight. Preheat oven to 400 degrees. Roll dough on floured surface. Cut with cookie cutter. Place on nonstick cookie sheet. Bake for 8 minutes or until light brown. May decorate with icing or colored sugar. Yield: 4 dozen.

Donna J. DeLancey, Laureate Alpha Epsilon
Vail, Arizona

Donna S. Miller, Member-at-Large, Cape Girardeau, Missouri, makes Easy Butterscotch Squares by preparing and cooking a package of vanilla pudding mix. Stir in a package of yellow cake mix, spread in baking pan and sprinkle with butterscotch chips. Bake slightly longer than directions on the mix package and cut into squares.

GRANDMA TAYLOR'S FORM COOKIES

The fifth generation now enjoys these cookies for Christmas, Easter and Halloween. The grandchildren call them "dough cookies."

4 cups all-purpose flour	2 tablespoons milk
1/4 teaspoon salt	1 egg white
1/2 cup shortening	2 teaspoons water
1/2 cup margarine	3/4 cup confectioners' sugar
2 eggs	1/2 teaspoon vanilla extract
1 1/2 cups sugar	
1 teaspoon vanilla extract	Food coloring
1 teaspoon (scant) baking soda	

Preheat oven to 375 degrees. Combine flour and salt in medium bowl; mix well. Cut in shortening and margarine until crumbly. Beat eggs, sugar and 1 teaspoon vanilla in mixer bowl until blended. Add mixture of baking soda and milk; mix well. Add to flour mixture; mix well. Roll dough thin on floured surface. Cut into desired shapes. Place on greased cookie sheet. Bake until light brown. Beat egg white in mixer bowl until stiff. Add water and confectioners' sugar, beating until of spreading consistency. Stir in 1/2 teaspoon vanilla and food coloring. Frost cooled cookies. May sprinkle cookies with colored sugar before baking. Yield: 4 to 5 dozen.

Barbara Anderson, Iota Master
Columbus, Ohio

LITTLE FRUITCAKE COOKIES

This recipe was handed down from my great-grandmother. We always bake these cookies at Thanksgiving and eat them at Christmas. My grandmother called this the secret family recipe and only revealed it to her children.

2 1/2 cups chopped raisins	2 tablespoons cinnamon
1 cup chopped currants	1 tablespoon ginger
2 1/2 cups chopped nuts	1 teaspoon vanilla extract
3 cups sugar	
1 cup packed light brown sugar	1 teaspoon lemon juice
1 cup shortening	2 teaspoons baking powder
1 cup butter or margarine, softened	1 teaspoon baking soda
1 cup sorghum molasses	1/2 cup vinegar or sweet pickle juice
4 eggs	8 1/2 cups (about) all-purpose flour
2 tablespoons ground cloves	

Mix raisins and next 14 ingredients in order given in large bowl. Dissolve baking soda in vinegar. Add to mixture; mix well. Stir in flour. Chill overnight. Preheat oven to 375 degrees. Roll dough on floured surface. Cut into desired shapes. Place on nonstick cookie sheet. Bake for 10 to 12 minutes or until brown. Remove to wire rack to cool. Store in airtight container, separated by layers of waxed paper. May place a sliced apple in container to soften and flavor cookies. Yield: 5 dozen.

Dawn Porter, Theta Omega
Salisbury, Missouri

BASIC SUGAR COOKIES

This was my grandmother's recipe and she would bake them every Christmas. She lived to be 96.

1¹/2 cups sugar	1 teaspoon baking soda
1 cup margarine, softened	¹/2 teaspoon salt
3 eggs	1 teaspoon vanilla
4¹/2 cups all-purpose flour	extract

Preheat oven to 325 degrees. Cream sugar and margarine in mixer bowl until light and fluffy. Add eggs; mix well. Sift in flour, stirring to blend. Add baking soda and next 2 ingredients; mix well. Roll on floured surface. Cut into desired shapes. Place on nonstick cookie sheet. Bake for 6 to 8 minutes or until brown. Yield: 5 dozen.

Laurie Stein, Lambda Eta
Manning, Iowa

THE BEST SUGAR COOKIES

Every time I make these cookies, everyone wants the recipe. They melt in your mouth! I always double the recipe so I won't run out.

2¹/2 cups all-purpose flour	1 teaspoon vanilla extract
1 teaspoon baking soda	³/4 cup butter or margarine, softened
1 teaspoon cream of tartar	2 teaspoons vanilla extract
1 cup margarine, softened	3 to 4 cups confectioners' sugar
1¹/2 cups confectioners' sugar	2 to 3 tablespoons milk
1 egg	Food coloring

Preheat oven to 350 degrees. Mix flour and next 2 ingredients together. Cream margarine and 1¹/2 cups confectioners' sugar in mixer bowl until light and fluffy. Add egg and 1 teaspoon vanilla; mix well. Stir in dry ingredients. Roll ¹/4 inch thick on floured surface. Cut into desired shapes. Place on nonstick cookie sheet. Bake for 8 minutes or until light brown. Combine butter and remaining ingredients in mixer bowl. Beat until of spreading consistency. Frost cooled cookies. Store in airtight container. Yield: 3 dozen.

Lori A. Cardinal, Epsilon Alpha
Fond du Lac, Wisconsin

CONFECTIONERS' SUGAR COOKIES

2¹/2 cups all-purpose flour	1¹/2 cups confectioners' sugar
1 teaspoon baking soda	1 egg
1 teaspoon cream of tartar	1 teaspoon vanilla extract
1 cup butter or margarine, softened	¹/2 teaspoon almond extract

Mix flour, baking soda and cream of tartar. Cream butter and remaining ingredients in mixer bowl until light and fluffy. Stir in dry ingredients. Chill, covered, for 2 to 3 hours. Preheat oven to 375 degrees. Divide dough into several portions. Roll ¹/4 inch thick on floured surface. Cut into desired shapes. Place on foil-lined cookie sheet. Bake for 7 to 8 minutes or until light brown. May sprinkle with colored sugar before baking. Yield: 3 dozen.

Ellen Bricker, Preceptor Chi
Tallahassee, Florida

SUGAR COOKIES

My mother baked these cookies when I was a child. She developed this recipe over many years, but her recipe measurements were not in cups or tablespoons. She used "shortening the size of 2 eggs, 3 bowls of flour, dash of nutmeg, etc." I spent one summer converting the recipe to measurements I could use.

6 cups all-purpose flour	1 teaspoon salt
2 cups sugar	¹/2 teaspoon nutmeg
1¹/2 cups shortening	3 eggs, beaten
1 tablespoon (heaping) baking powder	²/3 cup (about) milk

Preheat oven to 350 degrees. Combine flour, sugar and shortening in mixer bowl; mix well. Add baking powder and remaining ingredients; mix well. Roll ¹/4 to ¹/2 inch thick on floured surface. Cut with cookie cutter. Place on nonstick cookie sheet. Bake for 10 to 15 minutes or until cookies test done. May sprinkle with mixture of cinnamon and sugar before baking or frost baked cookies with your favorite icing. Yield: 2 dozen.

Geneal Frazier, Preceptor Alpha
Tooele, Utah

Lynda M. Jones, Xi Zeta Rho, Wichita, Kansas, involves the whole family in glazing sugar cookies. They blend a 1-pound package of confectioners' sugar with about 3 ounces water, or enough to make of desired consistency and colors it with food coloring. They brush the glaze on and let stand until dry.

APRICOT-NUT SPIRALS

1/2 cup margarine, softened	1/2 teaspoon baking powder
1/4 cup shortening	6 ounces dried apricots, finely chopped
1 cup sugar	
3 tablespoons milk	1/2 cup finely chopped hazelnuts
1/2 teaspoon vanilla extract	1/2 cup sugar
2 cups all-purpose flour	1/2 cup water

Cream margarine and next 2 ingredients in mixer bowl until light and fluffy. Add milk and vanilla; mix well. Add mixture of flour and baking powder, mixing well. Chill for 1 hour. Combine apricots and next 3 ingredients in saucepan; mix well. Cook over low heat until water is absorbed, stirring constantly. Set aside. Divide dough into 2 portions. Roll each portion into 6-by-16-inch rectangle on floured surface. Top with 1/2 of apricot mixture. Roll as for jelly roll, sealing edge and ends. Chill, wrapped in waxed paper, for 1 hour. Preheat oven to 375 degrees. Cut roll into 1/4-inch slices. Place on greased cookie sheet. Bake for 10 minutes. Yield: 2 dozen slices.

Sherri Giger, Laureate Alpha Theta
Rifle, Colorado

APRICOT BALLS

This is one of my favorite cookies. They keep a long time in the refrigerator.

16 ounces dried apricots, ground	1 14-ounce can sweetened condensed milk
1 cup chopped nuts	
1 cup shredded coconut	Confectioners' sugar

Combine apricots and next 2 ingredients in medium bowl; mix well. Stir in condensed milk. Shape into 1-inch balls; roll in confectioners' sugar. Chill until serving time. Yield: 2 dozen.

Carol Julian, Preceptor Pi
Columbia, Missouri

WALNUT-BOURBON BALLS

21/2 cups finely crushed vanilla wafers	3 tablespoons light corn syrup
1 cup confectioners' sugar	1/4 cup bourbon, rum or wine
2 tablespoons baking cocoa	Confectioners' sugar
1 cup finely chopped walnuts	

Combine first four ingredients in medium bowl; mix well. Stir in corn syrup and bourbon. Shape into 1-inch balls; roll in additional confectioners' sugar. Yield: 2 dozen.

Betty J. Buckles, Laureate Phi
Phoenix, Arizona

BUTTERSCOTCH-ALMOND COOKIES

1 teaspoon baking soda	4 cups all-purpose flour
2 tablespoons vinegar	Salt to taste
1 cup packed light brown sugar	1 teaspoon almond extract
1 cup sugar	1 teaspoon vanilla extract
11/2 cups shortening	Sugar
2 eggs	
2 teaspoons baking powder	

Preheat oven to 350 degrees. Dissolve baking soda in vinegar in small bowl; set aside. Cream brown sugar and next 2 ingredients in mixer bowl until light and fluffy. Add eggs; mix well. Stir in vinegar mixture. Add baking powder and next 4 ingredients; mix well. Shape into 1-inch balls. Place on nonstick cookie sheet. Flatten with fork. Bake for 8 to 10 minutes or until set. Sprinkle warm cookies with additional sugar. Yield: 4 dozen.

Cheryl Waddingham, Zeta Theta
Rutherfordton, North Carolina

BUTTERSCOTCH ICEBOX COOKIES

3 cups all-purpose flour	2 eggs, beaten
1 teaspoon salt	1 teaspoon vanilla extract
1/2 teaspoon baking soda	
1 teaspoon cream of tartar	1 cup chopped nuts
1/2 cup shortening	1 cup coconut
2 cups packed light brown sugar	

Sift flour and next 3 ingredients together. Cream shortening and brown sugar in mixer bowl until light and fluffy. Add eggs; mix well. Stir in vanilla. Add dry ingredients; mix well. Stir in nuts and coconut. Shape into log 2 inches in diameter. Chill overnight. Preheat oven to 375 degrees. Cut dough into thin slices. Place on greased cookie sheet. Bake 10 to 12 minutes or until set. Yield: 8 dozen.

Kathleen Cunningham, Xi Epsilon
Aberdeen, Washington

CAKE BOX COOKIES FROM GRANDMA JEWEL

This is the first family recipe I received as a new bride.

1 2-layer package any flavor cake mix	8 ounces whipped topping
1 egg	Confectioners' sugar

Mix first 3 ingredients in medium bowl. Chill overnight. Preheat oven to 350 degrees. Shape dough into 1-inch balls. Roll in confectioners' sugar. Place on greased and floured cookie sheet. Bake for 10 minutes. Yield: 3 to 4 dozen.

Lesa Ritchie, Xi Zeta Pi
Pryor, Oklahoma

CHERRY WINKS

2¹/4 cups all-purpose flour	1 teaspoon vanilla extract
1 teaspoon baking powder	1 cup chopped pecans
¹/2 teaspoon baking soda	¹/3 cup chopped maraschino cherries
³/4 cup shortening	1 cup chopped dates
1 cup sugar	2¹/2 cups crushed cornflakes
2 eggs	15 maraschino cherries, cut into quarters
2 tablespoons milk	

Preheat oven to 375 degrees. Sift flour and next 2 ingredients together. Cream shortening and sugar in mixer bowl until light and fluffy. Add eggs and next 2 ingredients; mix well. Stir in dry ingredients gradually. Fold in pecans and next 2 ingredients. Drop by rounded teaspoonfuls into cornflakes; toss lightly. Shape into balls. Place on greased cookie sheet. Top with maraschino quarter. Bake for 12 to 15 minutes or until brown. Yield: 5 dozen.

Cindy Layton, Xi Epsilon Nu
Cape Girardeau, Missouri

CHOCOLATE-MACADAMIA NUT COOKIES

¹/2 cup butter or margarine, softened	3 ounces unsweetened chocolate, melted
¹/2 cup shortening	2¹/2 cups all-purpose flour
¹/2 cup packed light brown sugar	¹/4 teaspoon salt
2 egg yolks	1 cup chopped macadamia nuts
¹/2 teaspoon vanilla extract	

Preheat oven to 375 degrees. Cream butter and shortening in mixer bowl until light and fluffy. Beat in brown sugar and next 3 ingredients. Stir in flour and salt. Fold in macadamia nuts. Shape into 1-inch balls. Place on nonstick cookie sheet. Bake for 10 to 12 minutes or until firm. Yield: 5 dozen.

Patricia A. Sugg, Laureate Alpha Nu
The Dalles, Oregon

CHOCOLATE SNOWBALLS

¹/4 cup butter or margarine	2 cups flaked coconut
¹/2 cup milk	2 cups quick-cooking oats
2 cups sugar	1 teaspoon vanilla extract
2 tablespoons baking cocoa	Flaked coconut

Combine butter and next 3 ingredients in saucepan; mix well. Boil for 3 to 4 minutes. Remove from heat; cool slightly. Add 2 cups coconut and next 2 ingredients; mix well. Shape into balls. Roll in flaked coconut. Store in refrigerator. Yield: 4 dozen.

Bonnie Nuttall, Beta Delta
Prince Rupert, British Columbia, Canada

DUNBAR'S DUNKERS

1 cup butter or margarine, softened	¹/2 cup chopped walnuts or pecans
1 cup packed light brown sugar	1 cup semisweet chocolate chips
1 cup sugar	3¹/2 cups all-purpose flour
1 egg	1 teaspoon baking soda
1 cup vegetable oil	1 teaspoon salt
1 cup oats	1 teaspoon vanilla extract
1 cup crushed cornflakes	
¹/2 cup shredded coconut	

Preheat oven to 325 degrees. Cream butter, brown sugar and sugar in mixer bowl until light and fluffy. Add egg; mix well. Blend in oil until smooth. Stir in oats, cornflakes, coconut, walnuts and chocolate chips. Add flour, baking soda, salt and vanilla, mixing well. Shape into 1-inch balls. Place on ungreased cookie sheet; flatten with fork dipped in water. Bake for 12 minutes. Cool on cookie sheet. Yield: 8 dozen.

Genevieve Garcia, Xi Mu Delta
Merced, California

❖ FUDGE PUDDLES

1¹/4 cups all-purpose flour	¹/2 teaspoon vanilla extract
³/4 teaspoon baking soda	1 cup milk chocolate chips
¹/2 teaspoon salt	1 cup semisweet chocolate chips
¹/2 cup butter or margarine, softened	1 14-ounce can sweetened condensed milk
¹/2 cup creamy peanut butter	1 teaspoon vanilla extract
¹/2 cup sugar	Chopped peanuts
¹/2 cup packed light brown sugar	
1 egg	

Mix flour, baking soda and salt together. Cream butter, peanut butter, sugar and brown sugar in mixer bowl until light and fluffy. Add egg and vanilla; mix well. Add dry ingredients; mix well. Chill for 1 hour. Preheat oven to 325 degrees. Shape dough into 1-inch balls. Place in lightly greased miniature muffin cups. Bake for 14 to 16 minutes or until light brown. Make depression in center of each. Melt chocolate chips with condensed milk in saucepan. Stir in vanilla. Spoon into depressions. Top with peanuts. May serve leftover warm fudge filling over ice cream. Yield: 4 dozen.

Riki Mazurkiewicz, Beta Delta
Havre, Montana

LYDIA'S KRINGLES

3 cups all-purpose flour	2 tablespoons butter or
1/2 teaspoon salt	margarine, softened
1 teaspoon baking soda	1 egg yolk
1 teaspoon baking	1 cup sour cream
powder	1/2 cup buttermilk
1 cup sugar	

Mix flour, salt, baking soda and baking powder together. Cream sugar and butter in mixer bowl until light and fluffy. Add mixture of egg yolk, sour cream and buttermilk to creamed mixture; mix well. Stir in dry ingredients. Chill overnight. Preheat oven to 375 degrees. Roll small portion of dough to length and thickness of pencil on floured surface. Connect ends; twist to form figure 8. Place on nonstick cookie sheet. Bake for 10 minutes. Yield: 3 dozen.

Marilyn Vogt, Epsilon Beta
Truman, Minnesota

MELTING MOMENTS

1 cup sifted all-purpose	1 cup butter or
flour	margarine, softened
1/2 cup confectioners'	1 can flaked coconut
sugar	
1/2 cup cornstarch	

Preheat oven to 300 degrees. Sift flour, confectioners' sugar and cornstarch in medium bowl; mix well. Blend in butter until soft dough forms. Shape into balls; roll in coconut. Place 1 1/2 inches apart on ungreased cookie sheet. Bake for 20 to 25 minutes or until light brown. Yield: 3 to 3 1/2 dozen.

Doris S. Bame, Beta Gamma
Carolina Beach, North Carolina

MEXICAN WEDDING CAKES

1 cup butter or	1/2 teaspoon salt
margarine, softened	2 cups all-purpose flour
1/2 cup confectioners'	1 cup finely chopped
sugar	pecans
2 teaspoons vanilla	Confectioners' sugar
extract	

Cream butter and 1/2 cup confectioners' sugar in mixer bowl until light and fluffy. Add vanilla, salt, flour and pecans; mix well. Chill until firm. Preheat oven to 350 degrees. Shape dough into 1-inch balls. Place on ungreased cookie sheet; flatten with glass dipped in flour. Bake for 20 minutes or until light brown. Remove from oven; roll in additional confectioners' sugar. Yield: 4 to 5 dozen.

Jean S. Kyle, Xi Phi
Montgomery, Alabama
*Marlene McKay, Zeta Mu
Abbotsford, British Columbia, Canada

GRANDMA'S MOLASSES COOKIES

This is a family favorite passed down from my grandmother.

6 cups all-purpose flour	1 1/2 teaspoons salt
6 teaspoons baking soda	2 1/4 cups shortening
1 1/2 teaspoons ground	3 cups sugar
cloves	3/4 cup molasses
1 1/2 teaspoons ginger	3 eggs
1 tablespoon cinnamon	Sugar

Sift flour and next 5 ingredients together. Melt shortening in saucepan. Let stand until cool. Add 3 cups sugar and next 2 ingredients; mix well. Stir in dry ingredients. Chill dough. Preheat oven to 350 degrees. Shape into 1 1/2-inch balls; roll in additional sugar. Place on greased cookie sheet. Bake for 12 minutes or until cracked on top. Yield: 6 1/2 dozen.

Pat Van Dootingh, Alpha Pi
Sandusky, Ohio

NORWEGIAN TOASTED COOKIES

I now bake these cookies for my grandchildren and soon will for my great-grandchildren.

4 1/2 cups all-purpose	2 cups sugar
flour	3 eggs
2 teaspoons baking	1/2 teaspoon vanilla
powder	extract
2 teaspoons cardamon	1/2 teaspoon almond
1 cup butter or	extract
margarine, softened	2 ounces ground nuts

Preheat oven to 350 degrees. Sift flour and next 2 ingredients together. Cream butter and sugar in mixer bowl until light and fluffy. Add eggs; mix well. Stir in dry ingredients. Add vanilla and next 2 ingredients, mixing well. Shape into 2 logs 2 inches in diameter. Place on nonstick cookie sheet. Bake for 25 minutes or until firm. Remove to wire rack to cool. Cut into 1/4-inch slices. Place on nonstick cookie sheet. Bake until golden brown. Yield: 6 dozen.

Kaye Schramm, Laureate Beta Epsilon
Sequim, Washington

OATMEAL COOKIES

2 cups margarine,	2 cups raisins
softened	1 1/2 cups shredded
3 cups packed light	coconut
brown sugar	1 cup semisweet
6 cups oats	chocolate chips
4 cups all-purpose flour	1 cup chopped pecans
2 teaspoons cinnamon	1 egg, beaten
2 teaspoons baking	2 tablespoons milk
powder	2 teaspoons vanilla
1 teaspoon baking soda	extract
1 1/2 teaspoons salt	Sugar

Preheat oven to 350 degrees. Combine margarine, brown sugar, oats, flour, cinnamon, baking powder, baking soda, salt, raisins, coconut, chocolate chips and pecans in large bowl; mix well. Reserve 4 cups mixture. Store remaining mixture, covered, in refrigerator for future use. Add egg, milk and vanilla to reserved mixture, stirring to form soft dough. Shape into 1¹/₂-inch balls. Place on greased cookie sheet; flatten with fork dipped in additional sugar. Bake for 15 to 20 minutes or until brown. Yield: 2 dozen.

Vicky Guindon, Alpha
Whitehorse, Yukon Territory, Canada

ORANGE CANDY COOKIES

2 cups sifted all-	¹/₂ cup sifted all-
purpose flour	purpose flour
¹/₂ teaspoon salt	12 ounces orange slice
1 teaspoon baking soda	candy, cut up
¹/₂ cup margarine,	¹/₂ cup flaked coconut
softened	¹/₂ cup chopped walnuts
1¹/₂ cups packed light	or pecans
brown sugar	¹/₂ cup oats
2 eggs	

Preheat oven to 325 degrees. Sift flour and next 2 ingredients together. Cream margarine and brown sugar in mixer bowl until light and fluffy. Add eggs; mix well. Stir in dry ingredients. Add mixture of ¹/₂ cup flour and orange candy; mix well.Stir in coconut, walnuts and oats. Shape into 1-inch balls. Place on nonstick cookie sheet. Flatten with fork. Bake for 10 to 12 minutes or until brown. May frost with mixture of confectioners' sugar, grated orange rind and orange juice. Yield: 3 dozen.

Dee St. John, Preceptor Beta Omega
Emporia, Kansas

SARAH'S PECAN SANDIES

1 cup butter or	2 cups sifted all-
margarine, softened	purpose flour
6 tablespoons	1 cup chopped pecans or
confectioners' sugar	pecan meal
2 teaspoons vanilla	Confectioners' sugar
extract	

Preheat oven to 325 degrees. Cream butter and confectioners' sugar in mixer bowl until light and fluffy. Add vanilla; mix well. Blend in flour until smooth. Stir in pecans. Shape into balls with floured hands. Place on greased cookie sheet. Bake for 25 minutes. Roll hot cookies in additional confectioners' sugar. Yield: 2 dozen.

Sarah Byerly, Preceptor Psi
Salisbury, North Carolina

AUNT KATHIE'S SAND TARTS

1 cup butter or	1 egg yolk
margarine, softened	3¹/₂ cups (about) all-
3 cups sugar	purpose flour
1 teaspoon vanilla	1 egg white, beaten
extract	Sugar and cinnamon
1 egg	Pecan or walnut halves

Cream butter and next 2 ingredients in mixer bowl until light and fluffy. Add egg and egg yolk; mix well. Add flour 1 cup at a time, stirring until of right consistency. Shape into log 3 inches in diameter. Chill until firm. Preheat oven to 325 degrees. Cut dough into thin slices. Place on nonstick cookie sheet. Brush with egg white. Sprinkle with sugar and cinnamon; top with pecan halves. Bake for 12 minutes. Yield: 12 dozen.

Vivian M. Byrd, Preceptor Eta Lambda
St. Augustine, Florida

PENNSYLVANIA DUTCH SAND TARTS

1 cup butter or	2 egg whites, stiffly
margarine, softened	beaten
1 cup sugar	¹/₂ cup chopped nuts
2 egg yolks	Cinnamon or colored
2 cups all-purpose flour	sugar

Cream butter and sugar in mixer bowl until light and fluffy. Add egg yolks; mix well. Add flour, mixing until blended. Shape into 2 logs 2 inches in diameter and 8 inches long. Chill overnight. Preheat oven to 350 degrees. Cut dough into ¹/₈-inch slices. Place on ungreased cookie sheet. Brush with egg whites. Sprinkle with nuts and cinnamon. Bake for 8 to 10 minutes or until golden brown. Yield: 3 dozen.

Susan M. Fritz, Lambda Mu
Hughesville, Pennsylvania

SCOTCH SHORTBREAD

2 cups butter	4 cups sifted all-
1 teaspoon vanilla	purpose flour
extract	1 tablespoon cornstarch
1 cup sugar	

Let butter stand in warm place overnight. Cream butter and vanilla in medium bowl with hands until mixture drips from fingertips. Add sugar 1 tablespoon at a time, mixing well after each addition. Blend in mixture of flour and cornstarch 2 tablespoons at a time; mix well. Shape into 6 loaves. Chill for 1 hour. Preheat oven to 350 degrees. Cut into ¹/₄ to ¹/₂-inch slices. Place on nonstick cookie sheet. Prick each cookie with fork. Bake for 10 to 20 minutes or until golden brown. Do not substitute margarine for butter in this recipe. Yield: 2¹/₂ dozen.

Theda Mills, Preceptor Beta Lambda
Springfield, Oregon

STRAWBERRY KRISPIES

I have made these cookies for 30 years, and now my 35-year old daughter makes them with her 12-year old daughter.

5 tablespoons butter
  or margarine, softened
1 cup sugar
2 eggs, slightly beaten
1¹/2 cups chopped dates
1 cup chopped nuts
1 teaspoon vanilla
  extract

¹/2 teaspoon salt
2¹/2 cups crisp rice cereal
1 3-ounce package red
  gelatin or red sugar
  crystals
Green confectioners'
  sugar frosting

Combine first 3 ingredients in medium skillet; mix well. Add dates. Cook until transparent, stirring constantly. Remove from heat. Stir in nuts and next 3 ingredients. Let stand to cool. Shape into balls; roll in gelatin. Top each with frosting. Yield: 2 dozen.

Martha L. Holcomb, Preceptor Beta Epsilon
Cedar Rapids, Iowa

ANGEL SUGAR COOKIES

1 cup shortening
1 cup margarine,
  softened
2 cups sugar
2 eggs
2 teaspoons vanilla
  extract

4 cups all-purpose flour
2 teaspoons (scant)
  baking soda
2 teaspoons cream of
  tartar
1 teaspoon salt
Sugar

Preheat oven to 350 degrees. Cream shortening and next 2 ingredients in mixer bowl until light and fluffy. Add eggs and vanilla; mix well. Stir in flour and next 3 ingredients. Shape into balls. Dip top half into cold water; dip in additional sugar. Place sugared side up on lightly greased cookie sheet. Bake for 10 minutes or until brown. Yield: 10 to 12 dozen.

Grace M. Baylor, Preceptor Alpha
Waynesboro, Pennsylvania

SUGAR COOKIES

2 cups all-purpose flour
1 teaspoon baking soda
¹/2 teaspoon salt
¹/2 teaspoon cream of
  tartar
¹/2 cup margarine,
  softened

¹/2 cup butter, softened
1 cup sugar
1 egg
1 teaspoon vanilla
  extract
Sugar

Preheat oven to 350 degrees. Mix flour and next 3 ingredients together. Cream margarine and next 2 ingredients in mixer bowl until light and fluffy. Add egg and vanilla; mix well. Stir in dry ingredients. Shape into balls. Place on nonstick cookie sheet; flatten with glass dipped in additional sugar. Bake for 10 minutes or until light brown. Yield: 4¹/2 dozen.

Cindy Fetcenko, Xi Beta Omega
Elyria, Ohio

CONFECTIONERS' SUGAR COOKIES

2 cups all-purpose flour
¹/2 teaspoon cream of
  tartar
¹/2 teaspoon baking soda
¹/2 cup butter or
  margarine, softened
¹/2 cup shortening

1 cup confectioners'
  sugar
1 egg, beaten
Salt to taste
2 teaspoons vanilla
  extract
Sugar

Preheat oven to 350 degrees. Combine flour and next 2 ingredients. Cream butter and next 2 ingredients in mixer bowl until light and fluffy. Add egg, salt and vanilla; mix well. Stir in dry ingredients. Shape into balls. Place on nonstick cookie sheet. Flatten with fork; sprinkle with sugar. Bake for 10 minutes. Yield: 3 dozen.

Gloria LeDosquet, Master Alpha
Williston, North Dakota

WORLD'S BEST SUGAR COOKIES

5 cups all-purpose flour
1 teaspoon baking soda
1 teaspoon cream of
  tartar
¹/4 teaspoon salt
1 cup confectioners'
  sugar
1 cup sugar

1 cup butter or
  margarine, softened
1 cup vegetable oil
2 eggs
2 teaspoons vanilla
  extract
Sugar

Preheat oven to 350 degrees. Combine flour and next 3 ingredients. Do not sift. Cream confectioners' sugar and next 3 ingredients in mixer bowl until light and fluffy. Add eggs and vanilla; mix well. Stir in dry ingredients. Shape into balls; roll in additional sugar. Place on ungreased cookie sheet. Flatten with glass dipped in sugar. Bake for 10 to 12 minutes or until brown. Yield: 6 dozen.

Gail A. Wages, Alpha Eta
Green River, Wyoming

WHIRLIGIG COOKIES

1¹/4 cups all-purpose
  flour
¹/2 teaspoon baking soda
¹/2 teaspoon salt
  (optional)
¹/2 cup shortening
¹/2 cup sugar

¹/2 cup packed light
  brown sugar
¹/2 cup creamy or
  crunchy peanut butter
1 egg
1 cup semisweet
  chocolate chips, melted

Preheat oven to 350 degrees. Sift flour, baking soda and salt together. Cream next 4 ingredients in mixer bowl until light and fluffy. Add egg; mix well. Stir in dry ingredients. Roll ¹/4-inch thick rectangle on lightly floured surface. Spread with cooled melted chocolate. Roll as for jelly roll, sealing edge and ends. Cut into ¹/4-inch slices. Place on ungreased cookie sheet. Bake for 12 minutes. Yield: 3 dozen.

Janeene Spangler, Laureate Beta Epsilon
Arkansas City, Kansas

WHITE CHOCOLATE-PECAN COOKIES

2²/3 cups all-purpose flour	2 eggs
1/2 teaspoon salt	2¹/2 teaspoons vanilla extract
1¹/2 teaspoons baking powder	10 ounces white chocolate chips
2 cups sugar	1 cup chopped pecans
1 cup margarine, softened	

Preheat oven to 350 degrees. Mix flour and next 3 ingredients together. Combine margarine and next 2 ingredients in medium bowl; mix well. Stir in flour mixture just until moistened. Fold in white chocolate chips and pecans. Shape into balls with a small ice cream scoop. Place 2 inches apart on nonstick cookie sheet. Flatten into 3/4-inch circles. Bake for 9 to 10 minutes or until brown. Yield: 3 dozen.

June Gallion, Delta
Indianapolis, Indiana

CRUNCHY CARAMEL 'N APPLE PIE

6 cups sliced unpeeled apples	1/3 cup packed light brown sugar
1 unbaked 9-inch pie shell	1/2 teaspoon cinnamon
3 caramel sheets	1/2 cup chopped pecans
1/2 cup all-purpose flour	1/3 cup margarine

Preheat oven to 375 degrees. Place half the apples in pie shell. Top with 2 caramel sheets. Add remaining apples; top with remaining caramel sheet, stretching to cover completely. Mix flour, brown sugar, cinnamon and pecans in bowl. Cut in margarine until crumbly. Sprinkle over top. Bake for 40 to 45 minutes or until apples are tender. Yield: 8 servings.

Rosemary Schoenfeld, Xi Eta Nu
College Station, Texas

VERONIKA'S GERMAN APPLE PIE

Veronika served this at a dinner party when I moved here from out of state and made me feel right at home.

6 to 7 large apples, peeled, sliced	1 egg
1¹/2 cups butter or margarine, softened	Salt to taste
	1¹/2 to 2 cups all-purpose flour
1¹/4 cups sugar	Confectioners' sugar
Cinnamon to taste	

Preheat oven to 350 degrees. Place apples in 8-inch pie plate. Cream butter, sugar and cinnamon in mixer bowl until well mixed. Dot 1/4 cup mixture over apples. Add egg, salt and enough flour to remaining butter mixture to form dough. Roll dough on floured surface. Place over apples. Cover with foil. Bake for 45 minutes. Bake, uncovered, for 15 to 20 minutes longer or until light brown. Cool for 10 minutes. Invert onto serving plate; sprinkle with confectioners' sugar. Serve warm or cool as desired. Yield: 8 servings.

Kim Dreyfuss, Alpha Kappa
Hot Springs, South Dakota

PEANUT CRUNCH-APPLE PIE

I entered this in a contest for different ways to prepare apples and won first prize.

1 cup sugar	3 tablespoons melted butter or margarine
2 tablespoons all-purpose flour	3 tablespoons crunchy peanut butter, chilled
1/2 teaspoon vanilla extract	1/4 cup sugar
2 teaspoons lemon juice	1/2 cup coarsely crushed cornflakes
1/4 teaspoon salt	1/8 teaspoon salt
5¹/2 cups thinly sliced tart apples	
1 unbaked 10-inch pie shell	

Preheat oven to 350 degrees. Combine 1 cup sugar, flour, vanilla, lemon juice and 1/4 teaspoon salt in bowl. Add apples; toss to mix well. Spoon into pie shell; drizzle with butter. Combine peanut butter, 1/4 cup sugar, cornflakes and 1/8 teaspoon salt in bowl; mix with pastry blender. Sprinkle over pie. Bake for 50 to 60 minutes or until golden brown. Yield: 8 servings.

Christine LaRue A. Kump, Zeta Master
Winchester, Virginia

FRESH VANILLA-APPLE PIE

I grew up with my grandmother's version of apple pie with vanilla instead of cinnamon. Everyone who tries it likes it.

2¹/2 cups shredded peeled apples	2 teaspoons vanilla extract
3/4 cup sugar	1 recipe 2-crust pie pastry
3/4 cup milk	2 tablespoons butter or margarine
3 tablespoons (scant) all-purpose flour	

Preheat oven to 350 degrees. Mix apples, sugar, milk, flour and vanilla in bowl. Spoon into pastry-lined 9-inch pie plate; dot with butter. Cut remaining pastry into strips. Weave into lattice on top of pie. Bake for 50 to 60 minutes or until crust is brown and apples are tender. Yield: 6 to 8 servings.

Cindy L. Mann, Pi Phi
Kansas City, Missouri

Marilyn Rasmussen, Xi Gamma Alpha, Norfolk, Nebraska, makes Frozen Cherry Pies with 1 can cherry pie filling, 1 can sweetened condensed milk, 1 large can crushed pineapple and a large container whipped topping. Freeze in 2 pie shells.

SOUR CREAM-APRICOT PIE

I won the grand prize with this recipe in a contest in our local newspaper.

1 cup finely chopped dried apricots	1 cup sour cream
1/4 cup water	1 1/2 teaspoons vanilla extract
3 eggs	1 unbaked deep-dish 9-inch pie shell
1 1/4 cups sugar	

Preheat oven to 400 degrees Combine apricots and water in small bowl; let stand until water is absorbed. Beat eggs in bowl. Add sugar gradually, beating until thick. Beat in sour cream and vanilla. Stir in apricots. Spoon into pie shell with high rim. Bake for 15 minutes. Reduce oven temperature to 350 degrees. Bake for 25 to 30 minutes longer or until set. Yield: 8 servings.

La Verne Bellumori, Laureate Gamma Alpha
Sarasota, Florida

GRAHAM-CHOCOLATE-BANANA PIE

You may use a prepared graham cracker crust with this filling, but the homemade one is much better.

2 cups fine graham cracker crumbs	2 cups milk
1/4 cup sugar	3 egg yolks, slightly beaten
1/2 cup melted butter or margarine	2 tablespoons butter or margarine
1 cup sugar	1 teaspoon vanilla extract
1/3 cup all-purpose flour	2 bananas, sliced
1/4 teaspoon salt	Whipped topping
2 1-ounce squares unsweetened chocolate, grated	

Mix graham cracker crumbs, 1/4 cup sugar and 1/2 cup melted butter in bowl. Press lightly into 9 to 10-inch pie plate. Mix 1 cup sugar, flour and salt in saucepan. Add mixture of chocolate and milk. Cook over medium heat until thickened, whisking constantly. Cook for 2 minutes longer. Stir a small amount of hot mixture into egg yolks; stir egg yolks into hot mixture. Cook for 2 minutes, stirring constantly; remove from heat. Stir in butter and vanilla. Place plastic wrap directly on surface; cool to room temperature. Spoon half the filling into crust. Stir bananas into remaining filling. Spoon over top. Spread with whipped topping. Yield: 6 to 8 servings.

Betty Jo Southers, Laureate Lambda
Ashland, Kentucky

Treva M. Scott, Preceptor Beta Beta, Neodesha, Kansas, makes Sure-Fire Pie Crusts of 1 cup flour, 1/2 cup shortening, 1/4 teaspoon salt and 1/4 cup water. Divide into 2 portions and freeze overnight.

JAMOCHA CRUNCH-BANANA PIE

Expect accolades for this pie! You always will be asked for the recipe.

2 1-ounce squares semisweet chocolate	1 package whipped topping mix
1 tablespoon butter or margarine	1 teaspoon instant coffee granules
1 3/4 cups granola or natural cereal	2 tablespoons hot chocolate mix
1 large banana, sliced	Chocolate curls
Jamocha almond fudge ice cream, softened	Sliced almonds

Melt chocolate and butter in small saucepan, stirring to mix well. Combine with cereal in small greased bowl; toss lightly to mix well. Spread in deep 9-inch pie plate. Chill in refrigerator. Arrange banana slices in prepared plate. Spoon ice cream over bananas, pressing down with back of spoon. Prepare whipped topping mix using package directions. Beat in coffee granules and hot chocolate mix. Swirl over ice cream. Freeze for 3 hours or until firm. Garnish with chocolate curls and almonds. Let stand at room temperature for 15 minutes before serving. Yield: 8 servings.

Wendy Lee Roney, Xi Delta Zeta
Mississauga, Ontario, Canada

BLACKBERRY-SOUR CREAM PIE

4 cups (or more) fresh blackberries	1/4 teaspoon salt
1 unbaked 9-inch pie shell	1 cup fine dry bread crumbs
1 cup sugar	2 tablespoons sugar
1 cup sour cream	1 tablespoon melted butter or margarine
6 tablespoons all-purpose flour	

Preheat oven to 375 degrees. Place blackberries in pie shell. Combine 1 cup sugar, sour cream, flour and salt in bowl; mix well. Spread over blackberries. Combine bread crumbs, 2 tablespoons sugar and butter in bowl; mix well. Sprinkle over pie. Bake for 40 to 45 minutes or until golden brown. May substitute 2 cans blackberries for fresh blackberries. Yield: 8 servings.

Lori Brockus, Xi Omicron Exemplar
Princeton, Kansas

BUTTERSCOTCH-CARAMEL PRALINE PIES

1/2 cup butter	16 ounces whipped topping
1 7-ounce can coconut	1 jar butterscotch-caramel ice cream topping
1 cup chopped pecans	
8 ounces cream cheese, softened	2 baked pie shells
1 14-ounce can sweetened condensed milk	

Melt butter in heavy saucepan over low heat. Stir in coconut and pecans. Cook until coconut is light brown, stirring constantly. Cool to room temperature. Beat cream cheese and condensed milk in mixer bowl until smooth. Fold in whipped topping. Layer whipped topping mixture, coconut mixture and ice cream topping 1/2 at a time in pie shells. Chill until serving time. Do not substitute margarine for butter. Yield: 16 servings.

Betty Nash, Preceptor
Elkhorn, West Virginia
*Delores Castleberry, Preceptor Nu
Oklahoma City, Oklahoma

HONEY-OATMEAL PIE

My Aunt Anne has always been known in the family for this pie.

1 all-ready refrigerator pie pastry	1/2 cup packed light brown sugar
2 eggs	1/2 cup sweetened shredded coconut
1 1/4 cups quick-cooking oats	
3/4 cup honey	1/2 cup melted butter or margarine
1/2 cup unsalted sunflower seed kernels	1/4 cup chopped dried apricots
1/2 cup raisins	1 teaspoon cinnamon

Preheat oven to 350 degrees. Line 9-inch pie plate with pastry; flute edge. Combine remaining ingredients in bowl; mix well. Spoon into pastry. Bake for 40 to 45 minutes or until set. Cool on wire rack for 1 hour. Yield: 8 servings.

Melissa McNew, Pi Omega
Henderson, Texas

BLUE RIBBON CHERRY PIE

This pie is always a sell-out at the annual church bazaar and a must for special occasions.

2 16-ounce cans tart cherries	1 cup lard or shortening
7 tablespoons all-purpose flour	3 cups all-purpose flour
1 1/2 cups sugar	1 teaspoon salt
1 teaspoon cinnamon	1 egg, beaten
2 tablespoons berry wine	1 teaspoon lemon juice or vinegar
1/2 teaspoon red food coloring	5 tablespoons cold water
	Cream or melted butter
	Sugar

Preheat oven to 400 degrees. Drain cherries, reserving 1 cup juice. Mix 7 tablespoons flour, 1 1/2 cups sugar and cinnamon in saucepan. Add reserved cherry juice, wine and food coloring; mix well. Cook over low heat until thickened, stirring constantly. Pour over cherries in bowl; mix gently. Cut lard into 3 cups flour and salt in bowl. Add egg, lemon juice and water; mix to form dough. Divide into 2 portions.

Roll into circles on floured surface. Fit 1 circle into 10-inch pie plate. Fill with cherry mixture. Top with remaining pastry. Brush with cream or melted butter; cut vents. Sprinkle with additional sugar. Bake for 20 to 25 minutes or until golden brown. May bake in 2 small pie plates if preferred. Yield: 8 servings.

Maribeth McLay, Preceptor Gamma
Boulder City, Nevada

CHERRY-NUT PIES

I take this pie to family reunions to carry on my mother's tradition. You can color it red for most occasions or green for St. Patrick's Day.

Juice of 2 lemons	1/3 cup sugar
1 14-ounce can sweetened condensed milk	1 cup chopped pecans
	1/2 pint whipping cream, whipped
1 16-ounce can tart pitted cherries, drained	Food coloring (optional)
	2 baked pie shells

Mix lemon juice into condensed milk in bowl. Add cherries, sugar and pecans; mix well. Fold in whipped cream. Color as desired. Spoon into pie shells. Chill for 3 hours to overnight. Yield: 12 to 16 servings.

Donna Langley, Preceptor Beta Chi
Guthrie, Oklahoma

BLACK FOREST PIE

4 1-ounce squares unsweetened chocolate	1 1/2 cups whipping cream
1 14-ounce can sweetened condensed milk	1 baked 9- or 10-inch pie shell
	1 21-ounce can cherry pie filling
1 teaspoon almond extract	Almonds

Melt chocolate with condensed milk in heavy saucepan over medium-low heat; remove from heat. Stir in almond extract. Spoon into large bowl; cool to room temperature. Whip cream in mixer bowl until soft peaks form. Beat chocolate mixture until smooth. Fold in whipped cream. Spoon into pie shell. Chill for 4 hours or until set. Spread pie filling over top. Garnish with almonds. Yield: 8 servings.

Jeanna Spilker, Chi
Shreveport, Louisiana

Ardie Koppelman, Preceptor, Spearfish, South Dakota, makes Hershey Bar Pie by melting 16 large marshmallows with 1/2 cup milk. Stir in 8-ounce Hershey bar with almonds and cool. Fold in whipped cream, spoon into graham cracker pie shell and chill.

❖ CHOCOLATE-AMARETTO MOUSSE PIE

This pie is so rich that we could hardly eat a whole piece. Somehow, however, it was always gone by morning and Dad had gained five pounds!

2 cups semisweet chocolate chips	1/4 cup butter or margarine
2 tablespoons butter or margarine	1/4 cup water
	1/2 cup Amaretto
1 14-ounce can sweetened condensed milk	2 cups whipping cream, whipped
1/4 teaspoon salt	Almonds

Line 9-inch pie plate smoothly with foil. Melt 1 cup chocolate chips with 2 tablespoons butter in saucepan over very low heat. Spread quickly in even layer in prepared pie plate. Freeze for 30 minutes. Combine remaining 1 cup chocolate chips, condensed milk, salt and 1/4 cup butter in saucepan. Cook over low heat until smooth, stirring to mix well. Stir in water gradually. Cook over medium heat for 5 minutes. Add liqueur. Cook for 5 minutes or until thickened, stirring constantly. Cool to room temperature. Reserve some of the whipped cream for garnish. Fold remaining whipped cream into chocolate mixture. Lift chocolate pie shell gently from plate and remove foil; return to pie plate. Spoon filling into shell. Garnish with reserved whipped cream and almonds. Chill for 3 hours or until set. Yield: 8 servings.

Jami Page, Alpha Beta Rho
Warrensburg, Missouri

HEAVENLY CHOCOLATE ANGEL PIE

1 cup sugar	1 tablespoon confectioners' sugar
1/4 teaspoon cream of tartar	2 egg whites, stiffly beaten
4 egg whites	
1/4 cup chopped pecans	8 ounces whipped topping
1 bar German's sweet chocolate	1/2 cup chopped pecans
2 1/2 teaspoons water	Chocolate curls
2 egg yolks	Whipped topping

Preheat oven to 275 degrees. Sift sugar with cream of tartar. Beat 4 egg whites in mixer bowl until stiff but not dry. Add sugar mixture gradually, beating until glossy peaks form. Fold in pecans. Spread 1/4 inch thick over bottom of greased 9-inch pie plate; spread side of pie plate 1 inch thick. Bake for 1 hour or until light brown and crisp to touch. Cool away from drafts; meringue may fall and crack in center. Microwave chocolate in glass bowl on High for 2 minutes or until melted, stirring after 1 minute. Blend in water. Beat in egg yolks 1 at a time. Add confectioners' sugar; mix well. Fold in 2 beaten egg whites and 8 ounces whipped topping. Spoon into meringue shell. Sprinkle with chopped pecans.

Freeze until firm. Let stand at room temperature during meal. Garnish with chocolate curls and additional whipped topping. Yield: 8 to 10 servings.

Barbara Tillman, Laureate Omicron
Crestview, Florida

CHOCOLATE CUSTARD PIE

2 1-ounce squares semisweet chocolate	2 teaspoons vanilla extract
1 14-ounce can sweetened condensed milk	1 unbaked 9-inch pie shell
	4 ounces whipped topping
3 eggs, beaten	
1 1/2 cups hot water	

Preheat oven to 425 degrees. Melt chocolate with condensed milk in heavy saucepan over low heat; remove from heat. Stir in eggs gradually. Add hot water and vanilla; mix well. Spoon into pie shell. Bake for 10 minutes. Reduce oven temperature to 300 degrees. Bake for 25 to 30 minutes or until knife inserted near center comes out clean. Cool to room temperature. Chill in refrigerator. Spread with whipped topping. Yield: 8 servings.

Lynda Klasel, Xi Omega Nu
Rosenberg, Texas

EASY CHOCOLATE PIE

2 4-ounce packages German's sweet chocolate	2 tablespoons sugar (optional)
	8 ounces whipped topping
1/2 cup milk	
8 ounces cream cheese, softened	1 9-inch chocolate wafer pie shell

Break or cut chocolate along scores into 8 pieces. Combine 5 pieces chocolate with 1/4 cup milk in glass bowl. Microwave on High for 1 1/2 to 2 minutes or until melted; stir until smooth. Beat in remaining 1/4 cup milk, cream cheese and sugar. Fold in whipped topping. Spoon into pie shell. Freeze until firm. Let stand for 30 minutes. Melt remaining 3 pieces chocolate in microwave or heavy saucepan. Drizzle over pie. Yield: 8 servings.

Gretchen Florence, Preceptor Beta Omega
Emporia, Kansas

CHOCOLATE MERINGUE PIE

3/4 cup sugar	3 tablespoons hot water
1/4 teaspoon cream of tartar	1 teaspoon vanilla extract
3 egg whites	1 cup whipping cream, whipped
1/2 cup chopped walnuts	
3/4 cup semisweet chocolate	

Preheat oven to 275 degrees. Sift sugar and cream of tartar together. Beat egg whites in mixer bowl until stiff but not dry. Add sugar mixture gradually, beating constantly. Spread in buttered 9-inch pie plate. Sprinkle with walnuts. Bake for 1 hour or until crisp. Cool completely. Melt chocolate chips in double boiler. Stir in hot water. Cook until thickened, stirring constantly. Add vanilla. Cool to room temperature. Fold in whipped cream. Spoon into meringue shell. Chill for 3 hours or longer. May serve with additional whipped cream. Yield: 8 servings.

Joyce Garlow, Laureate Alpha Phi
Loveland, Colorado

CHOCOLATE-RASPBERRY CREAM PIE

1 tablespoon cornstarch	1/2 teaspoon vanilla
3 tablespoons sugar	extract
1 package frozen	1/2 cup whipping cream,
unsweetened	whipped
raspberries, thawed	2 1-ounce squares
1 baked 9-inch pie shell	semisweet chocolate
8 ounces cream cheese,	3 tablespoons butter or
softened	margarine
1/3 cup sugar	

Mix cornstarch and 3 tablespoons sugar in medium saucepan. Stir in raspberries. Cook over medium heat for 6 to 8 minutes or until thickened, stirring constantly. Cool to room temperature. Spread in pie shell. Beat cream cheese with 1/3 cup sugar and vanilla in medium mixer bowl until fluffy. Fold in whipped cream. Spread over raspberry layer. Chill for 1 hour or until firm. Melt chocolate with butter in saucepan, stirring until smooth. Cool for 10 minutes. Spread evenly over cream cheese layer. Chill for several hours to overnight. Let stand at room temperature for 15 minutes before serving. May top servings with additional whipped cream, raspberries or chocolate leaves. Yield: 6 to 8 servings.

Linda Stoltz, Epsilon Delta
Cambridge, Ontario, Canada

CHOCOLATE-TOFFEE PIE

1 1/4 cups finely crushed	1/4 cup almond brickle
graham crackers	chips
1/4 cup sugar	1 tablespoon margarine
6 tablespoons melted	2 egg yolks
margarine	1 teaspoon vanilla
1/2 cup miniature	extract
semisweet chocolate	1 cup whipping cream
chips	1/4 cup sifted
1/4 cup all-purpose	confectioners' sugar
flour	1 teaspoon vanilla
1/8 teaspoon salt	extract
1/3 cup sugar	1/4 cup almond brickle
1 1/2 cups milk	chips
1/2 cup miniature	Additional chocolate
semisweet chocolate	chips and almond
chips	brickle chips

Preheat oven to 375 degrees. Mix graham cracker crumbs and 1/4 cup sugar in bowl. Stir in 6 tablespoons melted margarine and 1/2 cup chocolate chips. Press over bottom and side of 9-inch pie plate. Bake for 6 to 9 minutes or until light brown. Cool to room temperature. Mix flour, salt and 1/3 cup sugar in saucepan. Stir in milk gradually. Add 1/2 cup chocolate chips, 1/4 cup almond brickle chips and 1 tablespoon margarine. Cook until thickened, stirring constantly; reduce heat. Cook for 2 minutes longer. Stir a small amount of hot mixture into egg yolks; stir egg yolks into hot mixture. Cook for 2 minutes, stirring constantly. Stir in 1 teaspoon vanilla. Spoon into pie shell. Chill until serving time. Beat whipping cream with confectioners' sugar and remaining 1 teaspoon vanilla in mixer bowl until soft peaks form. Fold in 1/4 cup almond brickle chips. Spread over pie; sprinkle with additional chocolate chips and almond brickle chips. Yield: 8 servings.

Ruth Fuller Lature, Preceptor Chi
Hopkinsville, Kentucky

EASY FUDGE-PECAN PIE

1/2 cup margarine	1 teaspoon vanilla
3 tablespoons baking	extract
cocoa	3/4 cup evaporated milk
3/4 cup hot water	1 cup pecan halves
2 cups sugar	1 unbaked 9-inch pie shell
1/2 cup all-purpose flour	Whipped topping or ice
1/8 teaspoon salt	cream

Preheat oven to 350 degrees. Melt margarine in small saucepan over low heat. Blend in baking cocoa and water. Add mixture of sugar, flour and salt; mix well. Stir in vanilla, evaporated milk and pecans. Spoon into pie shell. Bake for 50 minutes. Serve warm with whipped topping or ice cream. Yield: 8 servings.

Karolyn M. Cook, Xi Theta Beta
Larned, Kansas

FUDGE PIE

1/2 cup margarine	2 eggs
1 1/2 squares baking	1 teaspoon vanilla
chocolate	extract
1 cup sugar	1/2 cup nuts (optional)
1/2 cup all-purpose flour	

Preheat oven to 325 degrees. Melt margarine and chocolate in small saucepan over low heat, stirring to mix well. Stir in sugar and flour. Add eggs; beat just until smooth. Stir in vanilla and nuts. Spoon into greased 8-inch foil baking pan. Bake for 22 to 25 minutes or until pie has a brownie-like gloss and fudgy texture. Serve with whipped topping, whipped cream or ice cream. Yield: 6 to 8 servings.

G'Nell Betts, Preceptor Gamma Xi
Weslaco, Texas

HOT FUDGE MUD PIE

Warning: this pie has been labeled an aphrodisiac.

1 8¹/₂-ounce package
  Oreo cookies, finely
  crushed
¹/₂ cup melted butter or
  margarine
1¹/₂ pints coffee ice
  cream, softened
2 1-ounce squares
  unsweetened chocolate
1¹/₂ cups sugar
¹/₂ cup butter or
  margarine
³/₄ cup evaporated milk
¹/₂ teaspoon vanilla
  extract
¹/₂ teaspoon salt
Almonds
Whipped cream and
  shaved chocolate

Preheat oven to 375 degrees. Mix cookie crumbs and melted butter in 9-inch pie plate; press evenly over bottom and side of plate. Bake for 10 minutes. Cool to room temperature. Spread with ice cream. Freeze for 1¹/₂ hours or until firm. Combine next 6 ingredients in medium saucepan. Bring to a boil, stirring to mix well. Cool slightly; sauce will be thin. Pour over servings; sprinkle with almonds. Garnish with whipped cream and shaved chocolate.
Yield: 8 servings.

Linda Lea Rowse, Xi Beta Sigma
150 Mile House, British Columbia, Canada

TASTY COCONUT PIES

I am always asked to bake these for church socials and bake sales.

2 12-ounce cans
  evaporated milk
1 cup sugar
5 egg yolks
¹/₂ cup butter or
  margarine
¹/₄ cup cornstarch
1 cup coconut
2 baked pie shells
5 egg whites
¹/₄ cup sugar
Coconut

Preheat oven to 350 degrees. Combine evaporated milk, 1 cup sugar, egg yolks and butter in medium saucepan; mix well. Cook until butter melts, stirring constantly. Stir in cornstarch dissolved in a small amount of water. Cook until thickened, stirring constantly. Fold in 1 cup coconut. Spoon into pie shells. Beat egg whites with ¹/₄ cup sugar in mixer bowl until stiff peaks form. Spread on pies. Sprinkle with additional coconut. Bake until golden brown.
Yield: 12 to 16 servings.

Mazie Bradshaw, Xi Nu Delta
Dunnellon, Florida

Donna McGregor, Beta Iota, Owen Sound, Ontario, Canada, makes Butter Tarts of 1¹/₄ cups packed brown sugar, ¹/₃ cup corn syrup, 1 teaspoon vinegar, 3 tablespoons butter or margarine, 1 teaspoon vanilla extract, 2 eggs and 1 cup raisins. Spoon into unbaked tart shells and bake in preheated 425-degree oven for 10 minutes. Reduce temperature to 350 degrees and bake for 15 minutes longer.

KAHLUA-CAPPUCINO PIE

1 9-inch chocolate
  cookie or graham
  cracker pie shell
2 cups vanilla ice
  cream, softened
1 teaspoon instant
  coffee granules
2 tablespoons coffee
  liqueur
2 cups chocolate-
  almond-fudge ice
  cream, softened
1 tablespoon coffee
  liqueur
1 cup whipping cream
1 tablespoon coffee
  liqueur
¹/₄ cup toasted sliced
  almonds (optional)

Freeze pie shell until firm. Combine vanilla ice cream with mixture of instant coffee granules and 2 tablespoons liqueur in bowl; mix well. Spoon into pie shell. Freeze until firm. Combine chocolate-almond-fudge ice cream with 1 tablespoon liqueur in bowl; mix well. Spread over frozen layer. Freeze until firm. Whip cream with 1 tablespoon liqueur in mixer bowl. Spread over pie. Freeze until firm. Top with sliced almonds. Yield: 8 servings.

Dianna Haley, Preceptor Alpha Zeta
Nevada, Iowa

CANDY BAR PIE

1 unbaked pie shell
5 Snickers candy bars
¹/₂ cup sugar
12 ounces cream cheese,
  softened
2 eggs
1 cup sour cream
1 cup peanut butter
²/₃ cup semisweet
  chocolate chips
3 tablespoons whipping
  cream

Preheat oven to 450 degrees. Bake pie shell for 5 minutes; reduce oven temperature to 325 degrees. Slice candy bars ¹/₄ inch thick. Arrange over crust. Beat sugar with cream cheese in mixer bowl until light. Add eggs, sour cream and peanut butter; mix well. Spoon into prepared pie shell. Bake for 35 minutes. Melt chocolate chips with cream in small saucepan. Spoon over pie. Chill until serving time.
Yield: 6 to 8 servings.

Jeanne M. Crane, Lambda Iota
Medina, New York

MOM'S LEMON MERINGUE PIE

3 egg yolks
1¹/₂ cups milk, scalded
1 cup sugar
2 tablespoons all-
  purpose flour
¹/₄ teaspoon salt
1 tablespoon butter or
  margarine
Juice and grated rind of
  1 lemon
1 baked 9-inch pie shell
1 recipe meringue

Preheat oven to 325 degrees. Beat egg yolks with ¹/₄ cup scalded milk in medium saucepan. Add mixture of sugar, flour and salt; mix well. Stir in remaining 1¹/₄ cups milk. Bring to a boil; remove from heat. Stir in butter, lemon juice and lemon rind. Spoon into pie shell. Top with meringue. Bake for 20 minutes or until golden brown. Yield: 6 to 8 servings.

Patricia Holz, Iota Chi
Le Mars, Iowa

LIGHT LEMON MOUSSE PIE

1 envelope unflavored gelatin	1 cup confectioners' sugar
2/3 cup lemon juice	16 ounces light whipped topping
1/4 cup cold water	
2 teaspoons grated lemon rind	1 chocolate graham cracker pie shell
8 drops of yellow food coloring	Lemon peel, shaved chocolate or whipped topping
8 ounces light cream cheese, softened	

Mix gelatin, lemon juice and water in small saucepan; let stand for 2 minutes. Cook over low heat until gelatin dissolves. Stir in lemon rind and food coloring. Beat cream cheese with confectioners' sugar in small bowl until smooth. Add gelatin mixture gradually, mixing until smooth. Chill for 20 minutes or until slightly thickened. Fold in 16 ounces whipped topping. Spoon into pie shell. Chill until firm. Garnish with strips of lemon peel, shaved chocolate or additional whipped topping. Yield: 8 servings.

Kathleen Nelson, Xi Epsilon Beta
Strasburg, Virginia

LIQUEUR PIE

This pie is a real winner and looks spectacular on a buffet table. I have served it to hundreds of people on special occasions.

2 cups finely crushed chocolate wafers	1/4 cup cold water
1/2 cup melted butter or margarine	1/4 cup boiling water
Grated orange rind to taste	1/3 cup orange liqueur
6 egg yolks	2 cups whipping cream, whipped
1 cup sugar	2 squares semisweet chocolate
1 1/2 tablespoons unflavored gelatin	

Mix wafer crumbs, melted butter and orange rind in greased 10-inch springform pan. Spread evenly in pan. Beat egg yolks and sugar in mixer bowl for 3 minutes. Soften gelatin in cold water in bowl. Stir in boiling water until gelatin dissolves. Add to egg yolk mixture with liqueur; beat at high speed until smooth. Fold in whipped cream. Spoon into pie shell. Grate chocolate over top. Chill for 5 hours or longer. Place on serving plate; remove side of pan. May omit orange rind and use other flavor liqueur. May substitute vanilla wafer crumbs for chocolate

wafer crumbs, almonds for grated chocolate and use almond liqueur. Yield: 8 to 10 servings.

Evelyn Wiltshire, Preceptor Alpha Phi
Gloucester, Ontario, Canada

PEACH CREAM PIE

1 cup all-purpose flour	3/4 cup sugar
1/2 teaspoon salt	2 tablespoons all-purpose flour
1/3 cup plus 1 tablespoon shortening	1 cup whipping cream
2 1/2 tablespoons ice water	Salt to taste
1 3/4 cups drained sliced peaches	Cinnamon to taste

Preheat oven to 350 degrees. Mix 1 cup flour and 1/2 teaspoon salt with shortening with pastry blender in medium bowl until crumbly. Add ice water; mix with fork to form dough. Chill in refrigerator. Roll on floured surface; fit into pie plate. Spread peaches in prepared pie plate. Combine sugar, 2 tablespoons flour, cream and salt in medium bowl; mix well. Spoon over peaches; sprinkle with cinnamon. Bake for 30 to 35 minutes or until set. Yield: 8 servings.

Betty L. Stone, Xi Delta Delta
Portland, Indiana

PEACHES 'N CREAM PIE

My friends and family request this pie every fall at "peach season."

1/2 cup butter or margarine, softened	8 ounces cream cheese, softened
2/3 cup sugar	1/3 cup sugar
2 eggs	1/4 cup sour cream
1 cup all-purpose flour	1 egg
1 teaspoon baking powder	1/4 teaspoon salt
1 teaspoon vanilla extract	Sliced fresh peaches
1 tablespoon peach juice	1 cup sour cream
1 unbaked 10-inch pie shell	2 tablespoons brown sugar

Preheat oven to 325 degrees. Cream butter with 2/3 cup sugar in large mixer bowl until fluffy. Beat in 2 eggs. Add mixture of flour and baking powder; mix well. Stir in vanilla and peach juice. Spread over pie shell. Blend cream cheese and 1/3 cup sugar in medium mixer bowl until light. Beat in 1/4 cup sour cream, 1 egg and salt. Spread over cream cheese mixture. Arrange peach slices over top. Bake for 30 to 35 minutes. Blend 1 cup sour cream and brown sugar in small bowl. Spoon over pie. Bake for 5 minutes longer. Chill until serving time. May omit pie shell if preferred. Yield: 8 servings.

Merrilee George, Preceptor Alpha Eta
Bellevue, Washington

PEACH PARFAIT PIE

1 3-ounce package orange gelatin	2 cups sliced peaches
1 cup boiling water	1 graham cracker pie shell
1 pint vanilla ice cream, softened	Graham cracker crumbs

Dissolve gelatin in boiling water in bowl. Add ice cream, stirring until smooth. Fold in peaches. Spoon into pie shell. Sprinkle with graham cracker crumbs. Chill until set. May sweeten peaches if desired. Yield: 8 servings.

Mary Agnes Iback, Laureate Alpha Beta
Ft. Myers, Florida

PEANUT BUTTER PIE

1 4-ounce package vanilla pudding mix	1 cup confectioners' sugar
1³/4 cups milk	1 baked pie shell
¹/2 cup chunky peanut butter	12 ounces whipped topping

Prepare pudding mix with milk using package directions. Mix peanut butter and confectioners' sugar in small bowl until crumbly. Layer half the crumbs mixture, pudding and remaining crumb mixture in pie shell. Top with whipped topping. Chill until serving time. Yield: 8 servings.

Kelly A. Smith, Delta Eta
Muncie, Indiana

PEANUT BUTTER-CREAM CHEESE PIES

¹/2 cup peanut butter	32 ounces whipped topping
1 1-pound package confectioners' sugar	2 chocolate cookie pie shells or 2 baked 9-inch pie shells
16 ounces cream cheese, softened	
¹/2 14-ounce can sweetened condensed milk	

Combine peanut butter, confectioners' sugar, cream cheese and condensed milk in food processor container; process until smooth. Combine with half the whipped topping in bowl; mix gently. Spoon into pie shells; top with remaining whipped topping. Freeze until serving time. May drizzle with melted chocolate if desired. Yield: 16 servings.

Gwen Kirchner, Epsilon Tau
Louisville, Kentucky

Melina Moraine, Laureate Alpha Beta, Ft. Myers, Florida, makes Cottage Cheese Pie by mixing 1¹/2 cups strained cottage cheese, 1 egg, 2 tablespoons cornstarch, ¹/2 cup sugar, 1 cup milk, 2 tablespoons butter or margarine and 1 teaspoon vanilla extract and pouring into pie shell. Bake in preheated 350-degree oven until set.

FRESH PEAR CRUMB PIE

6 cups thinly sliced firm pears	¹/2 cup all-purpose flour
3 tablespoons lemon juice	¹/2 cup sugar
¹/2 cup sugar	¹/2 teaspoon ginger
2 tablespoons all-purpose flour	1 teaspoon cinnamon
1 unbaked 10-inch pie shell	¹/4 cup butter or margarine

Preheat oven to 375 degrees. Drizzle pears with lemon juice; toss with mixture of ¹/2 cup sugar and 2 tablespoons flour in bowl. Spread in pie shell. Combine ¹/2 cup flour, ¹/2 cup sugar, ginger and cinnamon in medium bowl. Cut in butter until crumbly. Sprinkle over pears. Bake for 50 to 55 minutes or until pears are tender and top is brown. Yield: 8 servings.

Pam J. Siminske
Omaha, Nebraska

PEANUT-CREAM PIE SUPREME

¹/2 cup margarine or butter, softened	8 ounces cream cheese, softened
¹/2 cup sugar	¹/2 cup creamy peanut butter
1 egg	1 cup confectioners' sugar
³/4 cup semisweet chocolate chips, melted	1 egg
³/4 teaspoon vanilla extract	1¹/2 cups whipped topping
1 baked 9-inch pie shell	¹/4 cup finely chopped peanuts
¹/2 cup finely chopped peanuts	Chocolate curls

Cream margarine and sugar in mixer bowl until light. Beat in 1 egg at medium speed for 2 to 3 minutes. Blend in chocolate and vanilla. Spread 1 cup mixture evenly in pie shell; sprinkle with ¹/2 cup peanuts. Combine cream cheese, peanut butter, confectioners' sugar, 1 egg and whipped topping in bowl; mix until smooth. Spread in prepared pie shell. Top with remaining chocolate mixture; sprinkle with ¹/4 cup peanuts. Garnish with chocolate curls. Yield: 8 to 10 servings.

Pat Morehart, Xi Alpha Iota
Eyota, Minnesota

PECAN CHEESECAKE PIE

8 ounces cream cheese, softened	1¹/4 cups chopped pecans
¹/3 cup sugar	1 cup light corn syrup
1 teaspoon vanilla extract	¹/2 cup sugar
1 egg	3 eggs
1 unbaked 10-inch pie shell	1 teaspoon vanilla extract

Preheat oven to 350 degrees. Combine cream cheese, 1/3 cup sugar, 1 teaspoon vanilla and 1 egg in medium mixer bowl; beat until smooth. Spoon into pie shell; sprinkle with pecans. Blend corn syrup, 1/2 cup sugar, 3 eggs and 1 teaspoon vanilla in medium bowl until smooth. Spoon evenly over pecans. Bake on center oven rack for 50 to 60 minutes or until center is set and pastry is golden brown. Cool on wire rack. Yield: 8 servings.

Barbara Humphrey, Xi Lambda Sigma
Royalton, Illinois
*Alisa Woods, Psi Eta
Camden, Missouri
*Valarie Phillips, Beta Theta
Oak Hill, West Virginia

PINEAPPLE PIE

4 eggs	*3 tablespoons lemon*
1 16-ounce can crushed	*juice*
pineapple	*1/2 teaspoon vanilla*
1 3/4 cups sugar	*extract*
3 tablespoons all-	*Salt to taste*
purpose flour	*1 unbaked 10-inch pie*
3 tablespoons melted	*shell*
margarine	

Preheat oven to 375 degrees. Beat eggs slightly in medium bowl with fork. Add pineapple, sugar, flour, margarine, lemon juice, vanilla and salt; mix gently. Spoon into pie shell. Bake for 1 hour. Yield: 8 servings.

Virginia L. Singleton, Preceptor Iota Sigma
Dallas, Texas

RASPBERRY BAVARIAN PIE

1/3 cup butter or	*2 egg whites*
margarine, softened	*1 cup sugar*
2 1/2 tablespoons sugar	*1 tablespoon lemon juice*
1 egg yolk	*1/8 teaspoon salt*
1/3 teaspoon salt	*1/4 teaspoon each*
1 cup all-purpose flour	*vanilla and almond*
1/3 cup finely chopped	*extract*
almonds	*1 cup whipping cream,*
1 10-ounce package	*whipped*
frozen raspberries,	
partially thawed,	
drained	

Preheat oven to 400 degrees. Cream butter and 2 1/2 tablespoons sugar in medium mixer bowl until light and fluffy. Add egg yolk and 1/3 teaspoon salt; mix well. Add flour and almonds; mix well. Press into pie plate. Bake for 12 minutes. Cool to room temperature. Combine raspberries, egg whites, 1 cup sugar, lemon juice, 1/8 teaspoon salt, 1/4 teaspoon vanilla and almond extract in large mixer bowl. Beat at high speed for 12 to 15 minutes. Fold in whipped cream. Spoon into pie shell. Freeze until serving time. Yield: 8 servings.

Kristine Clark, Xi Delta Lambda
Gig Harbor, Washington

RASPBERRY-PORT PIE

1 cup Port	*1 baked 9- or 10-inch*
1 cup water	*pie shell*
1 6-ounce package	*1 cup whipping cream*
raspberry gelatin	*2 tablespoons sugar*
1 10-ounce package	*Salt to taste*
frozen raspberries	*1/4 cup ground nuts*
1 pint ice cream,	*Whole raspberries*
softened	

Bring wine and water to a boil in medium saucepan. Stir in gelatin until dissolved. Stir in frozen raspberries and ice cream. Chill until partially set. Reserve 1 cup raspberry mixture. Chill remaining raspberry mixture until thick. Spoon into pie shell. Chill until set. Beat whipping cream in medium mixer bowl until soft peaks form. Beat in sugar and salt. Fold in reserved raspberry mixture. Spoon over congealed layer. Chill for 5 hours. Garnish with nuts and whole raspberries. Yield: 8 servings.

Jean Martin, Beta Delta
Ossian, Iowa

RHUBARB CRUNCH PIE

This is my great-grandma's recipe, inspired by the first rhubarb in the spring.

2 cups chopped	*1 9-inch pie shell*
rhubarb	*1/2 cup packed light*
1 egg, slightly beaten	*brown sugar*
2 tablespoons all-	*1/3 cup butter or*
purpose flour	*margarine*
1 cup sugar	*3/4 cup all-purpose flour*
1 teaspoon vanilla	
extract	

Preheat oven to 425 degrees. Combine rhubarb, egg, 2 tablespoons flour, sugar and vanilla in bowl; mix well. Spoon into pie shell. Mix brown sugar, butter and 3/4 cup flour until crumbly. Sprinkle over pie. Bake for 15 minutes. Reduce oven temperature to 350 degrees. Bake for 30 minutes longer. May microwave on High for 7 minutes, turning every minute and then bake at 400 degrees for 10 minutes. May replace all-purpose flour with blended oats or Vita-Mix or add a few cornflakes. Yield: 6 to 8 servings.

Portia L. Speck, Laureate Nu
Ashland, Ohio

GRANDMA'S SOUR CREAM-RAISIN PIE

1 unbaked 9-inch pie shell	1/4 teaspoon salt
1 1/2 cups dark raisins	2 cups milk
3/4 cup sugar	3 egg yolks, beaten
1/4 cup cornstarch	1 cup sour cream
1/2 teaspoon cinnamon	1 tablespoon lemon juice
1/4 teaspoon nutmeg	1 cup whipping cream, whipped (optional)

Preheat oven to 450 degrees. Bake pie shell for 10 minutes or until light brown. Cool to room temperature. Combine next 6 ingredients in 2-quart saucepan. Stir in milk. Bring to a boil over medium heat, stirring constantly. Boil for 1 minute; remove from heat. Stir a small amount of hot mixture into egg yolks; stir egg yolks into hot mixture. Stir in sour cream. Cook just until mixture begins to bubble; remove from heat. Add lemon juice. Cool for 10 minutes. Spoon into pie shell. Chill for 2 hours or until set. Top with whipped cream. Yield: 8 servings.

Melodie Huffman, Theta
Vincennes, Indiana

SPY PIES

1 10-ounce package frozen blueberries, strawberries or raspberries	1 tablespoon lemon juice
	1 cup sugar
	1 package whipped topping mix, prepared
2 egg whites	2 baked 9-inch pie shells

Mix first 4 ingredients in large mixer bowl. Beat for 15 minutes. Fold in whipped topping. Spoon into pie shells. Freeze until serving time. Yield: 12 servings.

Helen Neumann, Psi Iota
Theodosia, Missouri

SWEET POTATO PIE SUPREME

4 eggs	1 teaspoon vanilla extract
1 1/2 cups mashed cooked sweet potatoes	1 unbaked 10-inch pie shell
1/3 cup sugar	1 tablespoon grated orange rind
2 tablespoons honey	
2/3 cup milk	1/2 teaspoon nutmeg
1/2 cup crushed black walnuts	1 cup whipping cream, whipped
1/3 cup orange juice	
Salt to taste	

Preheat oven to 450 degrees. Beat first 3 ingredients in mixer bowl until smooth. Add honey and milk; mix well. Add walnuts, orange juice, salt and vanilla; mix well. Spoon into pie shell. Bake for 10 minutes. Reduce oven temperature to 300 to 350 degrees. Bake pie for 30 minutes longer or until set. Cool to room temperature. Sprinkle with orange rind and nutmeg. Serve with whipped cream. Yield: 8 servings.

Nena L. Taylor, Xi Lambda Iota
Vandenberg AFB, California

WHITE CHRISTMAS PIE

1 envelope unflavored gelatin	1 cup whipped cream or whipped topping
1/4 cup cold water	3 egg whites
1/4 cup all-purpose flour	1/4 to 1/2 cup sugar
1/4 cup sugar	1/4 teaspoon cream of tartar
1/2 teaspoon salt	
1 1/2 cups milk	1 cup coconut
3/4 teaspoon vanilla extract	1 baked 9-inch pie shell
1/4 teaspoon almond extract	

Soften gelatin in water in cup. Mix flour, 1/4 cup sugar and salt in saucepan. Stir in milk gradually. Cook over low heat until thickened and bubbly, stirring constantly. Cook for 1 minute longer. Stir in gelatin until dissolved. Beat until smooth. Add flavorings. Fold in whipped cream. Beat egg whites with 1/4 cup sugar and cream of tartar in mixer bowl until stiff peaks form. Fold into filling with coconut. Spoon into pie shell. Chill for 2 hours or longer. Let stand at room temperature for several minutes before serving. Yield: 8 servings.

Carmaleta M. DeLozier, Alpha Beta Upsilon
Deepwater, Missouri

TRULY YUMMY BUTTER TARTS

My sister and I remove the pastry and eat a plateful of these, telling ourselves that we can eat twice as many without the pastry.

1 1/2 cups packed light brown sugar	3/4 teaspoon salt
	1 cup melted butter or margarine
1 1/2 cups light corn syrup	
3 eggs	60 unbaked miniature tart shells
1 1/2 cups raisins	

Preheat oven to 325 degrees. Add first 5 ingredients to melted butter in bowl; mix well. Fill tart shells 2/3 full. Bake for 20 to 25 minutes or until puffed and light brown. Yield: 60 tarts.

Sonja Susut, Preceptor Beta
Moose Jaw, Saskatchewan, Canada

FRUIT-TOPPED LEMON TARTS

1 21-ounce can lemon pie filling	Fruit such as grapes, berries, sliced bananas or kiwifruit and mandarin oranges or pineapple, cut into chunks
1 8-ounce can crushed pineapple, drained	
6 individual graham cracker tart shells	

Combine pie filling and crushed pineapple in bowl; mix well. Spoon 1/2 cup into each tart shell. Arrange drained fruit as desired on top of tarts. Chill until serving time. Yield: 6 tarts.

Celeste Fulk, Zeta Omega
Weston, Missouri

NORWAY TART

1/2 cup butter or margarine, softened	1/2 cup butter or margarine, softened
1/2 cup sugar	1/2 teaspoon almond extract
1 egg	2 eggs
1 1/2 cups all-purpose flour	1 tablespoon all-purpose flour
1 teaspoon baking powder	2 ounces almonds, finely chopped
1/2 cup raspberry jam	
2/3 cup sugar	

Preheat oven to 325 degrees. Combine 1/2 cup butter, 1/2 cup sugar and 1 egg in medium mixer bowl, beating until light. Add 1 1/2 cups flour and baking powder; mix well. Pat over bottom and 1 inch up side of round 9-inch tart pan or springform pan. Spread with jam. Cream 2/3 cup sugar, 1/2 cup butter and almond extract in mixer bowl until fluffy. Beat in 2 eggs 1 at a time. Add 1 tablespoon flour; mix well. Stir in almonds. Spoon into prepared tart pan. Bake for 40 to 45 minutes or until set. Yield: 12 servings.

Ali Laan, Laureate Delta
Caldwell, Idaho

PECAN TARTS

1 cup chopped pecans	1/4 cup melted butter or margarine
16 unbaked tart shells	1 teaspoon vanilla extract
1 cup sugar	
4 eggs	
1 cup light corn syrup	

Preheat oven to 350 degrees. Sprinkle pecans into tart shells. Mix sugar and eggs in medium bowl. Stir in next 3 ingredients. Spoon into tart shells; place on baking sheet. Bake for 30 to 40 minutes or until set. Yield: 16 servings.

Karen Richardson
Wingate, North Carolina

PLUM TART

1/2 cup butter or margarine	1/2 cup sugar
1 1/2 cups all-purpose flour	2 tablespoons all-purpose flour
1/3 cup sugar	1/4 teaspoon almond extract
1/4 teaspoon cinnamon	Slivered almonds
1 1/2 cups chopped purple plums	Whipped cream

Preheat oven to 375 degrees. Cut butter into mixture of 1 1/2 cups flour, 1/3 cup sugar and cinnamon in bowl. Press into tart pan. Combine plums with 1/2 cup sugar, 2 tablespoons flour, almond extract and almonds in bowl; mix gently. Spoon into prepared pan. Bake for 45 minutes. Garnish with whipped cream. Yield: 8 servings.

Joan Girbav, Beta Delta
Prince Rupert, British Columbia, Canada

CHERRY PASTRY SQUARES

1 cup sugar	2 teaspoons baking powder
1 cup shortening	1 teaspoon baking soda
2 eggs	3 21-ounce cans cherry pie filling
Milk	Sugar
1 teaspoon vanilla extract	
4 cups all-purpose flour	

Preheat oven to 350 degrees. Cream 1 cup sugar and shortening in mixer bowl until light and fluffy. Combine eggs with enough milk to measure 1 cup. Add to creamed mixture with vanilla; mix well. Add flour, baking powder and baking soda; mix to form pastry. Divide into 2 portions. Pat 1 portion into 10-by-15-inch baking pan. Spread pie filling evenly over pastry. Roll remaining pastry on floured surface; cut into strips. Arrange strips in lattice-fashion over cherry filling; sprinkle with additional sugar. Bake for 35 to 40 minutes or until golden brown. Cut into servings. Yield: 14 servings.

Carol Baker, Xi Eta Xi
Edinboro, Pennsylvania

ITALIAN PLUM PASTRY

1 1/2 cups sifted all-purpose flour	3/4 cup sugar
1 teaspoon sugar	2 tablespoons all-purpose flour
1/2 teaspoon salt	1/4 teaspoon salt
1/2 cup corn oil	2 tablespoons margarine
2 tablespoons milk	
1 1/2 pounds Italian plums, cut into halves, pitted	

Preheat oven to 400 degrees. Sift 1 1/2 cups flour, 1 teaspoon sugar and 1/2 teaspoon salt into medium bowl. Combine oil and milk in small bowl; whisk until smooth. Add all at once to flour mixture; mix well with fork. Press over bottom and side of 9-inch pie plate. Arrange plums in prepared plate. Combine 3/4 cup sugar, 2 tablespoons flour and 1/4 teaspoon salt in small bowl. Mix in margarine with fork until crumbly. Sprinkle over plums. Bake for 40 to 45 minutes or until edge of pastry is brown. Yield: 6 to 8 servings.

Dawn M. Moore, Xi Delta Psi
Bourbonnais, Illinois

Lorna M. Webber, Laureate Beta, Dartmouth, Nova Scotia, Canada, makes a Green Tomato Pie. Mix 3 cups sliced green tomatoes, 1 1/3 cups sugar, 3 tablespoons all-purpose flour, 6 tablespoons lemon juice, 1 tablespoon grated lemon rind and 1/4 teaspoon salt. Spoon into pastry-lined pie plate, dot with 3 tablespoons butter or margarine, top with pastry and bake in preheated 450-degree oven for 10 minutes. Reduce temperature. Bake at 350 degrees for 30 minutes longer.

BAKLAVA

24 sheets phyllo pastry	8 ounces almonds,
8 ounces unsalted	chopped
butter or unsalted	1 cup sugar
margarine, melted	1 tablespoon lemon juice
Cinnamon to taste	1/2 cup water

Preheat oven to 350 degrees. Cut phyllo sheets into halves; keep unused sheets covered with damp cloth. Layer half the sheets in buttered 9-by-13-inch baking dish, brushing each sheet with butter. Sprinkle with cinnamon and almonds. Layer remaining phyllo sheets over top, brushing each sheet with butter. Cut into diamond shapes with sharp knife. Bake for 20 to 25 minutes or until golden brown. Heat sugar, lemon juice and water in small saucepan until sugar dissolves. Simmer for 10 minutes. Pour over hot baked layer. Let stand until cool. Yield: 12 servings.

Alison Malati, Xi Beta Omega
Okmulgee, Oklahoma

CHERRY CREAM PUFF RING

1 cup water	1 4-ounce package
1/2 cup butter or	vanilla instant
margarine	pudding mix
1 cup all-purpose flour	1/4 teaspoon almond
4 eggs	extract
1 cup milk	1 21-ounce can cherry
3/4 cup sour cream	pie filling

Preheat oven to 400 degrees. Bring water and butter to a boil in 1-quart saucepan. Add flour, stirring for 1 minute or until mixture forms ball; remove from heat. Beat in eggs at low speed for 2 minutes. Drop by tablespoonfuls into 8-inch ring on greased baking sheet; smooth with spatula. Bake for 50 to 60 minutes or until puffed and golden brown. Cut off top of ring with sharp knife; discard pastry filaments. Combine milk, sour cream, pudding mix and almond extract in medium mixer bowl; beat at low speed for 1 minute or until smooth. Spoon into pastry ring. Spoon 1/2 cup pie filling over pudding; replace top of ring. Spoon remaining pie filling over top. Chill until serving time. Yield: 10 to 12 servings.

Joyce Gibson, Eta Chi
Woodstock, Virginia

RUSSIAN PASTRY

1/2 cup margarine	1 cup all-purpose flour
1 cup all-purpose flour	3 eggs
1/4 cup water	2 cups prepared vanilla
1/2 cup margarine	frosting
1 cup water	1/4 cup sliced almonds
1 teaspoon almond	
extract	

Preheat oven to 350 degrees. Cut 1/2 cup margarine into 1 cup flour in bowl. Add 1/4 cup water; mix to form pastry. Roll into thin square on floured surface. Cut into 4 strips; place on baking sheet. Bring 1/2 cup margarine, 1 cup water and almond extract to a boil in medium saucepan. Add 1 cup flour, stirring until mixture forms ball. Beat in eggs 1 at a time. Spread over pastry strips. Bake for 1 hour or until golden brown. Cool to room temperature. Spread with frosting; sprinkle with almonds. Slice diagonally. Yield: 8 to 10 servings.

Jill Crosina, Alpha Psi
Williams Lake, British Columbia, Canada

COCONUT-PECAN PIE

3 eggs	1 teaspoon vinegar
1/2 cup packed light	1 teaspoon vanilla
brown sugar	extract
1 cup cream of coconut	1 unbaked 9-inch pie
1 cup pecan pieces or	shell
halves	Whipped cream
2 tablespoons melted	Chopped pecans
butter or margarine	

Preheat oven to 350 degrees. Beat eggs in medium bowl. Add brown sugar; stir until brown sugar dissolves. Add next 5 ingredients; mix well. Spoon into pie shell. Bake for 30 to 35 minutes or until center is puffed. Cool on wire rack. Chill until serving time. Spoon whipped cream onto servings; sprinkle with chopped pecans. Add 1/2 cup coconut for Double Coconut-Pecan Pie. Yield: 8 servings.

Photograph for this recipe is on the Cover.

FLUFFY GRASSHOPPER PIE

2 cups finely crushed	3 tablespoons bottled
chocolate sandwich	lemon juice
cookies	1/4 cup green Crème de
1/4 cup melted margarine	Menthe
8 ounces cream cheese,	1/4 cup white Crème de
softened	Menthe
1 14-ounce can	4 ounces whipped
sweetened condensed	topping
milk	

Mix cookie crumbs and margarine in bowl. Press mixture over bottom and side of buttered 9-inch pie plate. Chill in refrigerator. Beat cream cheese in mixer bowl until light. Add condensed milk gradually, beating constantly until smooth. Stir in lemon juice and liqueurs. Fold in whipped topping. Chill for 20 minutes. Spoon into prepared pie shell. Chill or freeze for 4 hours or longer. Garnish as desired. Yield: 8 servings.

Photograph for this recipe of on the Cover.

CHERRY AND ALMOND MOUSSE PIE

1 1-ounce square unsweetened chocolate	3/4 teaspoon almond extract
1 14-ounce can sweetened condensed milk	1 cup whipping cream, whipped
1/4 teaspoon almond extract	1 10-ounce jar red maraschino cherries, drained
1 baked 9-inch pie shell	1/2 cup chopped toasted almonds
8 ounces cream cheese	Chocolate curls
1 cup cold water	Toasted almonds
1 4-ounce package vanilla instant pudding mix	

Melt unsweetened chocolate with 1/2 cup condensed milk in heavy saucepan; mix well. Stir in 1/4 teaspoon almond extract. Spread in pie shell. Beat cream cheese in mixer bowl until light. Beat in remaining condensed milk, water, pudding mix and 3/4 teaspoon almond extract gradually. Fold in whipped cream. Reserve 5 or 6 cherries for garnish. Chop remaining cherries. Fold chopped cherries and 1/2 cup almonds into pie filling. Spoon into prepared pie shell. Chill for 4 hours or until set. Garnish with reserved cherries, chocolate curls and additional almonds. Yield: 8 servings.

Photograph for this recipe is on the Cover.

PEPPERED BEEF TENDERLOIN ROAST

1 tablespoon green peppercorns in brine, drained, finely chopped	1 teaspoon salt
5 cloves of garlic, finely chopped	1 teaspoon freshly ground pepper
2 tablespoons finely chopped fresh rosemary	1 3-to 4-pound beef tenderloin, trimmed
	2 tablespoons olive oil or vegetable oil
	1 1/4 cups beef stock

Combine peppercorns, garlic, rosemary, salt and pepper in small bowl. Rub mixture over roast. Wrap tightly in plastic wrap. Marinate in refrigerator for 4 to 48 hours. Preheat oven to 425 degrees. Let roast stand until room temperature. Brown in olive oil in large Dutch oven for 4 minutes on each side. Place rack in Dutch oven; place roast on rack. Roast, uncovered, for 10 to 12 minutes per pound or to 135 degrees on meat thermometer for rare or 155 degrees for medium. Allow for internal temperature of roast to increase by about 5 degrees after removal from oven. Let stand for 15 minutes. Stir beef stock into drippings in Dutch oven. Simmer until reduced to 3/4 cup. Strain into serving bowl. Serve with roast. Yield: 10 to 12 servings.

Photograph for this recipe is on page 1.

MINI PUMPKINS WITH PEAS AND ONIONS

10 to 12 miniature pumpkins	6 cups frozen peas with pearl onions, cooked

Preheat oven to 425 degrees. Cut two 1-inch slits in sides of each pumpkin; place in baking pan. Bake for 30 to 40 minutes or until tender. Cut slice from top of each pumpkin; scoop out seed. Spoon mixture of peas and onions into pumpkins; arrange on serving plate. Yield: 10 to 12 servings.

Photograph for this recipe is on page 1.

WILD RICE-MUSHROOM CASSEROLE

3 6-ounce packages long grain and wild rice mix	1 green bell pepper, chopped
3 or 4 stalks celery, chopped	12 fresh mushrooms, sliced
4 green onions, chopped	3/4 cup whipping cream

Preheat oven to 350 degrees. Cook rice using package directions. Combine rice with celery, onions, green pepper and mushrooms in bowl; mix well. Spoon into 2-quart baking dish. Pour whipping cream over top. Bake for 10 minutes or until bubbly, stirring several times. Yield: 10 to 12 servings.

Photograph for this recipe is on page 1.

LIGHT ROTINI LUNCHEON SALAD

8 ounces uncooked rotini	2 cups thinly sliced green bell pepper
2 cups chopped cooked chicken	1 8-ounce bottle of reduced-calorie zesty Italian salad dressing
2 cups cherry tomato halves	Salt and pepper to taste
2 cups broccoli flowerets	

Cook rotini using package directions; drain. Rinse with cold water and drain. Combine with remaining ingredients in serving bowl; mix lightly. Chill until serving time. Yield: 6 servings.

Photograph for this recipe is on page 2.

LIGHT TUNA AND SHELLS

8 ounces uncooked shell macaroni	1/4 cup finely chopped onion
1 7-ounce can water-pack tuna, drained, flaked	1 8-ounce bottle of reduced-calorie creamy cucumber salad dressing
1 cup thinly sliced celery	Salt and pepper to taste
1/2 cup sliced carrots	
1/2 cup sliced sweet pickles	

Cook macaroni using package directions; drain. Rinse with cold water and drain. Combine with remaining ingredients in serving bowl; mix lightly. Chill until serving time. Yield: 4 to 6 servings.

Photograph for this recipe is on page 2.

Metric Equivalents

A *lthough the United States has opted to postpone converting to metric measurements, most other countries, including England and Canada, use the metric system. The following chart provides convenient approximate equivalents for allowing use of regular kitchen measures when cooking from foreign recipes.*

Volume

These metric measures are approximate benchmarks for purposes of home food preparation.
1 milliliter = 1 cubic centimeter = 1 gram

Liquid	Dry
1 teaspoon = 5 milliliters	1 quart = 1 liter
1 tablespoon = 15 milliliters	1 ounce = 30 grams
1 fluid ounce = 30 milliliters	1 pound = 450 grams
1 cup = 250 milliliters	2.2 pounds = 1 kilogram
1 pint = 500 milliliters	

Weight

1 ounce = 28 grams
1 pound = 450 grams

Length

1 inch = 2½ centimeters
1/16 inch = 1 millimeter

Formulas Using Conversion Factors

When approximate conversions are not accurate enough, use these formulas to convert measures from one system to another.

Measurements	Formulas
ounces to grams:	# ounces x 28.3 = # grams
grams to ounces:	# grams x 0.035 = # ounces
pounds to grams:	# pounds x 453.6 = # grams
pounds to kilograms:	# pounds x 0.45 = # kilograms
ounces to milliliters:	# ounces x 30 = # milliliters
cups to liters:	# cups x 0.24 = # liters
inches to centimeters:	# inches x 2.54 = # centimeters
centimeters to inches:	# centimeters x 0.39 = # inches

Approximate Weight to Volume

Some ingredients which we commonly measure by volume are measured by weight in foreign recipes. Here are a few examples for easy reference.

flour, all-purpose, unsifted	1 pound = 450 grams = 3 1/2 cups
flour, all-purpose, sifted	1 pound = 450 grams = 4 cups
sugar, granulated	1 pound = 450 grams = 2 cups
sugar, brown, packed	1 pound = 450 grams = 2 1/4 cups
sugar, confectioners'	1 pound = 450 grams = 4 cups
sugar, confectioners', sifted	1 pound = 450 grams = 4 1/2 cups
butter	1 pound = 450 grams = 2 cups

Temperature

Remember that foreign recipes frequently express temperatures in Centigrade rather than Fahrenheit.

Temperatures	Fahrenheit	Centigrade
room temperature	68°	20°
water boils	212°	100°
baking temperature	350°	177°
baking temperature	375°	190.5°
baking temperature	400°	204.4°
baking temperature	425°	218.3°
baking temperature	450°	232°

Use the following formulas when temperature conversions are necessary.

Centigrade degrees x $9/5$ + 32 = Fahrenheit degrees
Fahrenheit degrees - 32 x $5/9$ = Centigrade degrees

American Measurement Equivalents

1 tablespoon = 3 teaspoons	12 tablespoons = 3/4 cup
2 tablespoons = 1 ounce	16 tablespoons = 1 cup
4 tablespoons = 1/4 cup	1 cup = 8 ounces
5 tablespoons + 1 teaspoon = 1/3 cup	2 cups = 1 pint
	4 cups = 1 quart
8 tablespoons = 1/2 cup	4 quarts = 1 gallon

Merit Winners

Index

Beta Sigma Phi Cookbooks

available from *Favorite Recipes® Press* are chock-full of home-tested recipes from Beta Sigma Phi members that earn you the best compliment of all... "More Please!"

Every cookbook includes:

- ☆ color photos or black-and-white photos
- ☆ delicious, family-pleasing recipes
- ☆ lay-flat binding
- ☆ wipe-clean color covers
- ☆ easy-to-read format
- ☆ comprehensive index

To place your order, call our **toll free** number

1-800-251-1520

or clip and mail the convenient form below.

BETA SIGMA PHI COOKBOOKS	Item #	Qty.	U.S. Retail Price	Canadian Retail Price	Total
The Best of Beta Sigma Phi Cookbook	88285		$9.95	$12.95	
Home Sweet Home Cooking: Company's Coming	01260		$9.95	$12.95	
Home Sweet Home Cooking: Family Favorites	01252		$9.95	$12.95	
Food In The Fast Lane	94323		$9.95	$12.95	
Shipping and Handling		1	$1.95	$2.95	
TOTAL AMOUNT					

☐ Payment Enclosed
☐ Please Charge My ☐ MasterCard ☐ Visa ☐ Discover

Signature_____

Account Number_____

Name _____

Address _____

City_____State ____ Zip_____

No COD orders please.
Call our toll free number for faster ordering.
Prices subject to change.
Books offered subject to availability.
Please allow 30 days for delivery.

Mail completed order form to:

Favorite Recipes® Press
P.O. Box 305141
Nashville, TN 37230